THE USBORNE INTERNET-LINKED ENCYCLOPEDIA OF WORLD HISTORY

THE USBORNE INTERNET-LINKED ENCYCLOPEDIA OF WORLD HISTORY

Jane Bingham, Fiona Chandler and Sam Taplin

Designed by Susie McCaffrey, Linda Penny, Melissa Alaverdy and Steve Page

Consultants: Dr. Anne Millard, Gary Mills and Dr. David Norman

Illustrated by Inklink Firenze, Giacinto Gaudenzi, Ian Jackson, Jeremy Gower, Nicholas Hewetson, Lorenzo Cecchi, Justine Torode, David Cuzik, Gary Bines and David Wright

Managing editor: Jane Chisholm

Managing designer: Mary Cartwright

Page 1: Part of a fan belonging to an Ancient Egyptian pharaoh

Opposite: A golden statue of the Buddha from a 14th-century temple in Thailand

Contents

Medieval World

The Last 500 Years

Internet Links

This book contains descriptions of more than 200 Web sites which have been specially chosen to build on the information in the book. If you have access to the Internet and would like to use it to discover more about world history, go to the Usborne Quicklinks site at **www.usborne-quicklinks.com** Here you will find direct links to all the Web sites listed in the book.

Usborne Quicklinks

To visit the Web sites described in this book, go to the Usborne Quicklinks Web site at **www.usborne-quicklinks.com** and enter the keyword "history". There, you will find:

- Links to all the Web sites described in this book.
- Free pictures from this book to download for your own personal use.

Suggested sites

Each of the four sections of the book begins with a list of exciting Web sites where you can find out more about a period of history. For example, the list of Internet links for the Ancient World (pages 106 to 107) includes huge interactive sites on the Ancient Egyptians, the Greeks and the Romans.

There are also links to relevant Web sites all the way through the book. Look at the top corner of a page to find a special Web site for that page. At these sites, you can play a history game, tour a building, watch a video clip, or find pictures and information about the topics on the page.

Site availability

The links in Usborne Quicklinks are regularly reviewed and updated, but occasionally you may get a message that a site is unavailable. This might only be temporary, so try again later, or even the next day.

If any of the sites close down, we will, if possible, find suitable alternatives, so you will always find an up-to-date list of sites at Usborne Quicklinks.

Downloadable pictures

All the maps and some of the pictures from this book can be downloaded and printed out, free of charge, for your own personal use, such as illustrating project work.

Downloadable pictures have a ★ symbol beside them. They may not be used for any commercial or profit-related purpose. To print out these pictures go to **www.usborne-quicklinks.com** Then, follow the instructions for downloadable pictures.

What you need

Most of the Web sites listed in this book can be accessed with a standard home computer and a Web browser (the software that enables you to display information from the Internet). We recommend:

- a PC with Microsoft® Windows® 98 or later version, or a Macintosh computer with System 9.0 or later, and 64Mb RAM
- a browser such as Microsoft® Internet Explorer 5, or Netscape® 6 or later versions
- connection to the Internet via a modem (preferably 56Kbps) or a faster digital or cable line
- an account with an Internet Service Provider (ISP)
- a sound card to hear sound files

Internet help

To find out more about how to use the Internet, open your Web browser and then click on "Help" at the top of the screen.

You'll find lots of advice on how to explore the Web, including information on how to print out Web pages, and help on making bookmarks for sites that you would like to visit again.

Extras

Some Web sites need additional programs, called plug-ins, to play sound files or show videos, animations or 3-D images. If you go to a site but do not have the necessary plug-in, a message should come up on the screen.

There is usually a button on the site that you can click on to download a plug-in. Alternatively, go to **www.usborne-quicklinks.com** and click on "Net Help" to download plug-in programs. Here is a list of plug-ins that you might need:

QuickTime – lets you view videos.
Shockwave® – enables you to play animations and interactive programs.
RealPlayer® – lets you play videos and hear sound files.
iPIX® – allows you to view panoramic videos.

Internet safety

When using the Internet, please make sure you follow these guidelines:

- Ask your parent's or guardian's permission before you connect to the Internet.
- If you write a message in a Web site guest book or on a message board, do not include any personal information, such as your full name, address or telephone number, and ask an adult before you give your e-mail address.
- If a Web site asks you to log in or register by typing your name or e-mail address, ask permission from an adult first.
- Never arrange to meet anyone you have talked to on the Internet.

Note for parents and guardians

The Web sites described in this book are reviewed regularly, but the content of a Web site may change at any time and Usborne Publishing is not responsible for the content on any Web site other than its own. We recommend that children are supervised while on the Internet, that they do not use Internet Chat Rooms, and that you use Internet filtering software to block unsuitable material. Please ensure that your children follow the safety guidelines printed above. For more information, see the "Net Help" area on the Usborne Quicklinks Web site.

Prehistoric hand paintings on a cave wall in South America

PREHISTORIC WORLD

Prehistoric World Internet Links

Here is a list of some of the most exciting and interesting Web sites on prehistoric life. To visit the sites, go to **www.usborne-quicklinks.com** and enter the keyword "history".

WEB SITE 1 Read about the birth of the universe, then click on "Universe in One Year" to see the entire history of the universe squeezed into one year.

WEB SITE 2 An amazing site packed with fascinating facts and beautiful pictures. Click on "Dinosaur Worlds" for a series of interactive adventures in which you travel back in time to meet the dinosaurs.

WEB SITE 3 Take a journey through time with this illustrated history of prehistoric life. Click on the underlined words and pictures to view even more photographs, reconstructions and information.

WEB SITE 4 An excellent selection of online exhibits from the Field Museum of Natural History in Chicago. Click on "Sue" to meet the biggest *Tyrannosaurus rex* ever discovered, or go to the "Life over Time" section for an interactive journey through prehistoric time.

WEB SITE 5 A fantastic children's site from the American Museum of Natural History in New York. You can find out about different dinosaurs by using a pack of interactive information cards, learn to draw dinosaurs, and even read an interview with a dinosaur!

WEB SITE 6 Tour the prehistoric exhibits at the National Museum of Natural History in Washington, DC, and see early mammals, birds and sea reptiles as well as dinosaurs.

WEB SITE 7 Explore this exciting Web site filled with 3-D images, sounds and video clips, and take a closer look through prehistoric time to find out if dinosaurs were doomed, or whether they adapted as their surroundings changed.

WEB SITE 8 The online exhibits of the Natural History Museum in Maastricht have stunning pictures and good information about dinosaurs and other prehistoric creatures. Explore the temporary exhibits or take a virtual tour of the museum. In each gallery, click on the white words to find out more.

WEB SITE 9 Browse through an online exhibition about some amazing dinosaur fossils found in the Gobi Desert in Mongolia. Click on "Exhibition Highlights" to find out about the fossils and see lifelike models of the dinosaurs.

WEB SITE 10 A fascinating site about scientists hunting for fossils in South America. Click on "What does a paleontologist see?" to examine rocks for hidden fossils.

WEB SITE 11 An enormous site covering everything you could ever want to know about dinosaurs. There are fact files on different dinosaurs, plus sections on fossils and plants, as well as puzzles, games and quizzes.

WEB SITE 12 Examine exciting 3-D models and reconstructions, and read fascinating articles about dinosaurs. Find out about *Tyrannosaurus rex*'s powerful sense of smell, why fossilized dinosaur skulls are very rare, and how birds and dinosaurs are linked.

WEB SITE 13 Make your own dinosaurs! At this fun site you can print out drawings of *Triceratops*, *Stegosaurus* and others, then cut, fold and paste them to make models.

WEB SITE 14 A great site from the Natural History Museum in London. Click on "Quest" to investigate a set of mysterious rocks, bones and other objects and see how old they are. Or try the dinosaur data files, which have plenty of information as well as pictures showing how big each dinosaur was compared to a person.

WEB SITE 15 Join an online hunt for dinosaur eggs around the world, find out how experts try to "hatch" the eggs, and look at 3-D models of baby dinosaurs inside their eggs.

WEB SITE 16 Find out about the different types of early humans, and click on "Interactive Adventure" to travel back in time and experience life as a prehistoric hunter.

WEB SITE 17 A site where you can examine the skulls of early humans and other primates in 3-D. As you turn each skull, you can read about how humans evolved.

WEB SITE 18 An excellent site on early humans. Experience life as a Neanderthal in "A Neanderthal's Day", learn about famous fossils and click on "Follow your Roots" to discover how modern humans evolved.

WEB SITE 19 At this beautiful site you can explore the mysterious cave of Lascaux in France, which is decorated with stunning prehistoric paintings. You can also find out how the paintings were created.

WEB SITE 20 Here you can see lots of pictures of the places where early humans lived, including amazing huts made from mammoth bones.

WEB SITE 21 Dinosaurs like the one on the opposite page died out around 66 million years ago. Find out how experts think this happened.

Prehistoric Time

Scientists believe that the Earth was formed about 4,550 million years ago. This is such a vast length of time that it is almost impossible for anyone to imagine.

People have been around for only a tiny fraction of the time that the Earth has existed. If you think of all of prehistoric time as just one year, then the Earth would have been formed on January 1, but humans would not have appeared until one minute to midnight on December 31!

Experts divide prehistoric time into several periods, each lasting many millions of years. The diagram on these two pages shows the main prehistoric periods. You can also see when different plants and animals appeared on the Earth.

4,550 MILLION YEARS AGO
The Earth is formed.

The Earth's surface is covered with volcanoes.

The first living cells appear.

PRECAMBRIAN PERIOD
(say "pree-cam-bree-un")

The first soft-bodied creatures

550 MILLION YEARS AGO

CAMBRIAN PERIOD
(say "cam-bree-un")

The first creatures with skeletons

510 MILLION YEARS AGO

ORDOVICIAN PERIOD
(say "or-doh-vishy-un")

The first fish

The first land plants

440 MILLION YEARS AGO

SILURIAN PERIOD
(say "sy-loor-ee-un")

The first creatures on land

408 MILLION YEARS AGO

DEVONIAN PERIOD
(say "div-ohn-ee-un")

The first amphibians

362 MILLION YEARS AGO

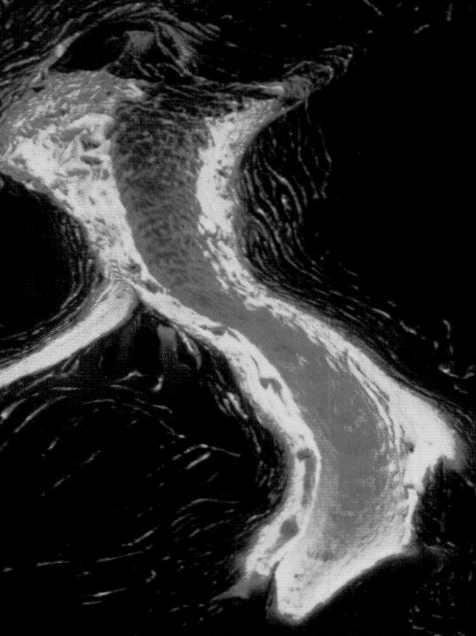

Hot, liquid rock pouring from a volcano

Internet link: For a link to a Web site with a clickable timeline of the prehistoric periods, go to **www.usborne-quicklinks.com**

What Are Fossils?

Fossils are the remains of creatures and plants that lived millions of years ago. They provide a fascinating picture of life on Earth before any history was written down.

Fossils in the rock

Many fossils are made from animal bones or shells that have been preserved in rock. It takes millions of years for a fossil to form, but the process begins when a creature is buried under layers of sand and mud, called sediment. This usually happens under water, at the bottom of lakes, rivers or seas.

Gradually, the layers of sediment covering the creature are pressed down hard until they turn into rock. This layered rock is called sedimentary rock. Water trickles through the rock and soaks into the creature's skeleton. The water has minerals dissolved in it, which slowly harden (or crystallize), turning the skeleton into a fossil.

★ Fossil of an ammonite, a sea creature with a pearly shell

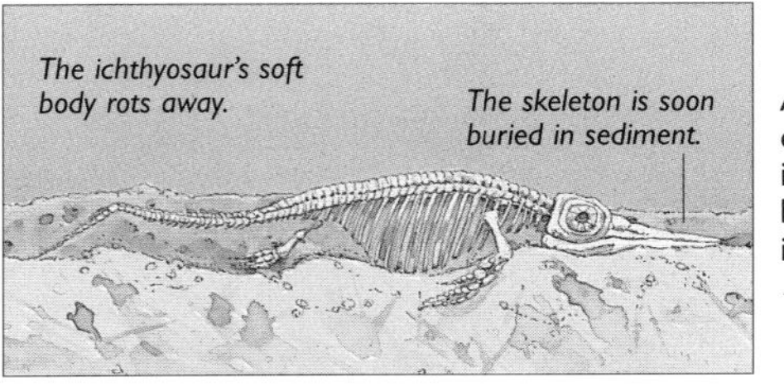

A sea reptile, called an ichthyosaur, being buried in the seabed ★

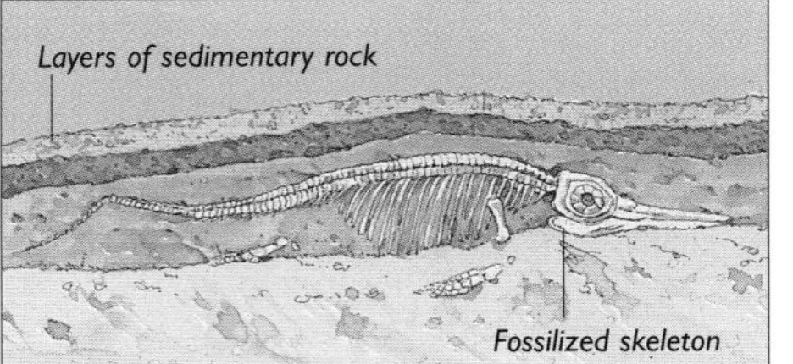

Fossil of an ichthyosaur inside layers of rock ★

Making shapes

Some skeletons that were buried in sediment have dissolved away, leaving their shapes in the rock. Some of the shapes have stayed empty, but others have been filled with hardened minerals, creating a fossil called a cast.

This shape was left by the skeleton of a starfish. ★

Coming to the surface

Fossils can now be found in sedimentary rocks on land, even though most fossils were originally formed under water. This is because, over millions of years, rocks that were once under water were gradually pushed up out of the water to become dry land (see page 23).

Buried bones

Experts have discovered many bones belonging to early humans and animals. Some of these bones were preserved in rock, but others were buried in very dry sand or in underground caves where no air could reach them.

The skull of an apelike ancestor of the first humans

Carbon fossils

Many plants and insects from prehistoric swamps were buried deep underground. Gradually, they heated up and turned into a sooty, black substance, called carbon. Most of the plants and creatures were squeezed together to make solid coal, but some formed delicate carbon fossils.

Soft-bodied survivors

It is very unusual to find fossils of creatures with soft bodies, but some have been discovered in the Burgess Shale, in Canada. These fossils were probably formed after a group of sea creatures was buried by a sudden mud slide. The mud then hardened into rock, creating very detailed fossils.

Fossil of a soft-bodied creature ★ called *Hallucigenia*

Trapped in amber

The bodies of some insects have survived for millions of years. These insects were stuck in sticky sap that oozed from trees. When the sap hardened, it turned into a yellow stone called amber, and any creatures trapped inside were perfectly preserved.

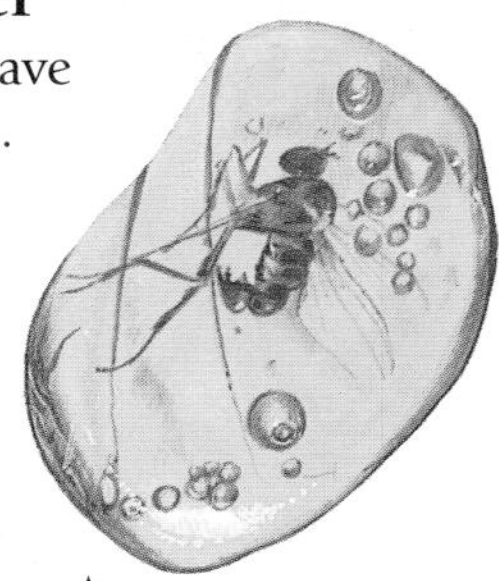

★ A prehistoric insect trapped in amber

Leaving traces

Some prehistoric creatures have left clear evidence of their way of life. Footprints made by animals and humans and trails made by creatures like worms have been preserved in hardened mud.

Some eggs and droppings left behind by animals have also turned into fossils.

All these kinds of evidence are known as trace fossils.

A dinosaur leaving its footprints in soft mud

Clues from Fossils

Experts who study fossils are called palaeontologists. By piecing together information from fossils, they can build up a surprisingly detailed picture of life on Earth millions of years ago.

Beginning with bones

Most fossils found by palaeontologists show the bones, teeth or shells of prehistoric creatures. When they discover a set of bones, palaeontologists take notes, photographs and sketches before anything is moved. This helps them to understand how the skeleton fits together.

Flesh on the bones

Experts can get a good idea of what a creature looked like from the shape of its skeleton. Markings on bones show where muscles were attached, and the size of the bones suggests how heavy an animal was. Sometimes, other evidence can help to build up a picture. For example, fossil prints of dinosaurs' skin show that it was scaly.

Moving around

As well as studying skeletons to see how creatures moved, palaeontologists also examine fossil footprints and trails. Footprints show whether an animal walked with its legs close together or far apart, and whether it lived alone or in a group.

Chewing and eating

The shape of an animal's teeth shows what kind of food it could chew. Experts also examine fossilized droppings to see what creatures ate, and occasionally they find an animal's last meal perfectly preserved in its stomach!

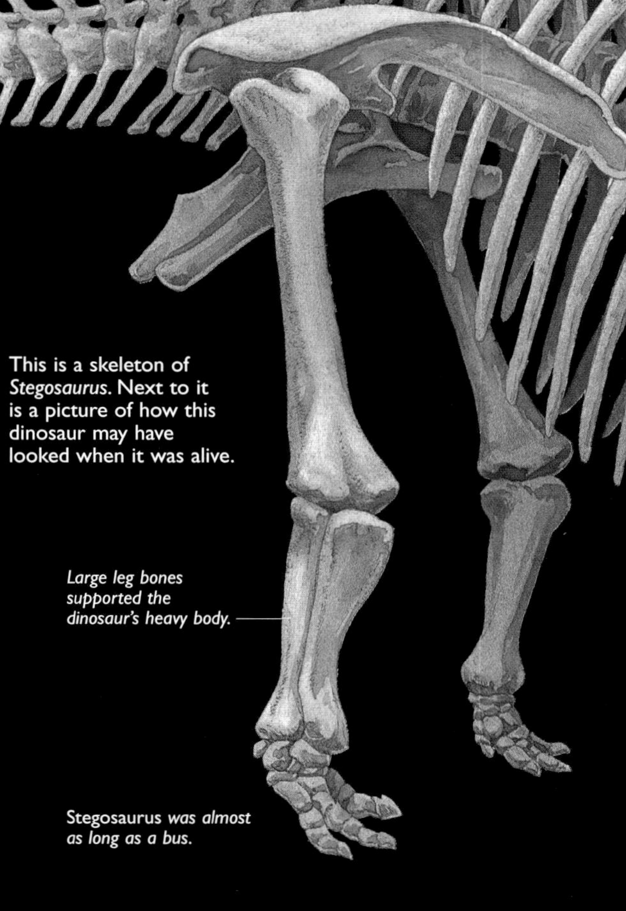

This is a skeleton of *Stegosaurus*. Next to it is a picture of how this dinosaur may have looked when it was alive.

Large leg bones supported the dinosaur's heavy body.

Stegosaurus *was almost as long as a bus.*

Internet link: For a link to a Web site where you can have fun solving some online fossil puzzles, go to ***www.usborne-quicklinks.com***

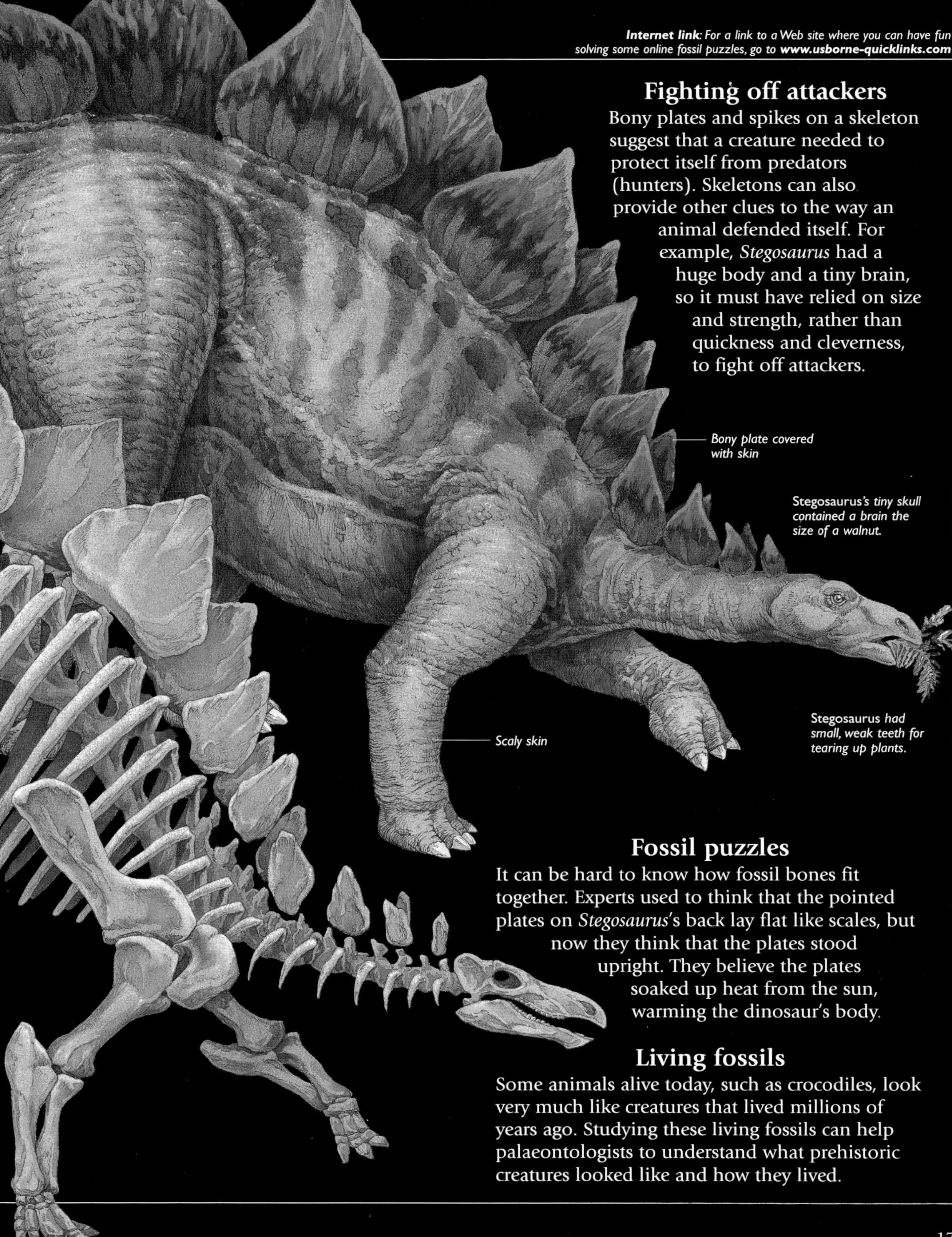

Fighting off attackers

Bony plates and spikes on a skeleton suggest that a creature needed to protect itself from predators (hunters). Skeletons can also provide other clues to the way an animal defended itself. For example, *Stegosaurus* had a huge body and a tiny brain, so it must have relied on size and strength, rather than quickness and cleverness, to fight off attackers.

Fossil puzzles

It can be hard to know how fossil bones fit together. Experts used to think that the pointed plates on *Stegosaurus*'s back lay flat like scales, but now they think that the plates stood upright. They believe the plates soaked up heat from the sun, warming the dinosaur's body.

Living fossils

Some animals alive today, such as crocodiles, look very much like creatures that lived millions of years ago. Studying these living fossils can help palaeontologists to understand what prehistoric creatures looked like and how they lived.

The Story of Life

Many of the plants and animals that lived in prehistoric times were very different from those that are around today. This is partly because lots of prehistoric forms of life have died out, and partly because all living things gradually change with time.

The first creatures on Earth were very simple animals. Over millions of years, these creatures changed, or evolved, into new kinds of animals. This process of change is called evolution.

How evolution works

The first person to explain how evolution works was a scientist named Charles Darwin, who lived from 1809 to 1882. His general explanation is still accepted by scientists today.

Charles Darwin

Darwin realized that no two animals are exactly the same. For example, one deer may have slightly longer legs than another. Long legs are useful for escaping from attackers, so this deer will be more likely to survive and have young. The young may also have longer legs, like their parent. Over time, a new kind of longer-legged deer could evolve.

4 Today's birds have hollow bones and no teeth, so their bodies are very light. Their strong wings are ideally suited for flying.

3 Feathered arms grew into wings. This early bird had teeth, like a dinosaur, and a heavy body.

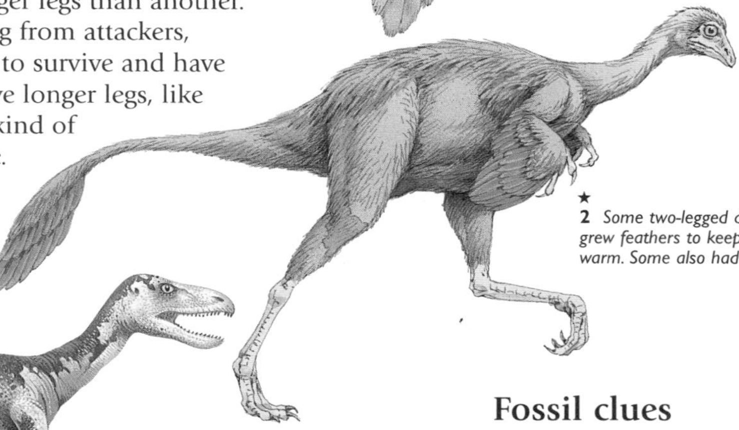

2 Some two-legged dinosaurs grew feathers to keep themselves warm. Some also had beaks.

These pictures show how, with a series of small changes, one kind of animal can gradually evolve into a completely new creature.

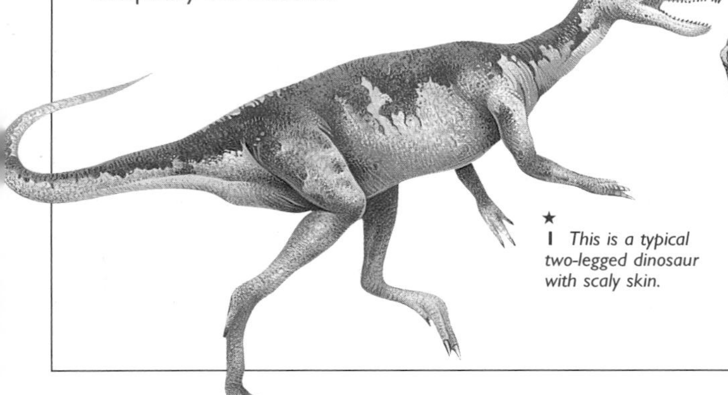

1 This is a typical two-legged dinosaur with scaly skin.

Fossil clues

The oldest fossils that have been found all show extremely simple forms of life. Fossils of complex creatures, such as reptiles and birds, are only found in much newer rocks. This suggests that living things did not appear on the Earth all at once, so they must have evolved gradually.

Animal families

To understand how one kind of animal could have evolved from another, scientists need to find out which animals are closely related. They do this by dividing them into groups.

All the members of a group have something in common with each other. The more things two animals have in common, the more closely they are related.

The biggest groups are called kingdoms. For example, all animals belong to the animal kingdom. Inside this group, there are smaller groups, with even smaller ones inside them.

The smallest group of all is known as a species. Animals that belong to the same species look very similar and can breed together.

Lions and leopards belong to different species, but both of them are big cats and members of the cat family.

Here you can see how big cats fit into different groups within the animal kingdom. As you read down the page, notice how the creatures in each new group have more and more in common with each other.

The animal kingdom
(all animals)

Vertebrates
(all animals with a backbone)

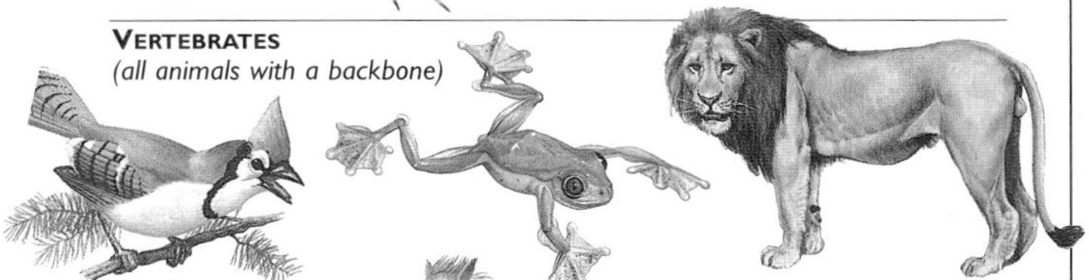

Mammals
(all animals with hair that feed their young with milk)

Carnivores
(all meat-eating mammals)

The cat family

Big cats

Lions belong to a species called Panthera leo.

Leopards belong to a species called Panthera pardus.

Naming species

Scientists have given each species of plant and animal a special name. The name is written in Latin and is often a good description of the species. For example, the first humans that walked completely upright are known as *Homo erectus*, which means "upright man".

The Birth of the Earth

The Earth is a tiny planet in a vast universe. The universe is made up of billions of stars and planets and enormous clouds of gas, all separated by huge empty spaces. The stars are grouped in galaxies, each one containing millions of stars.

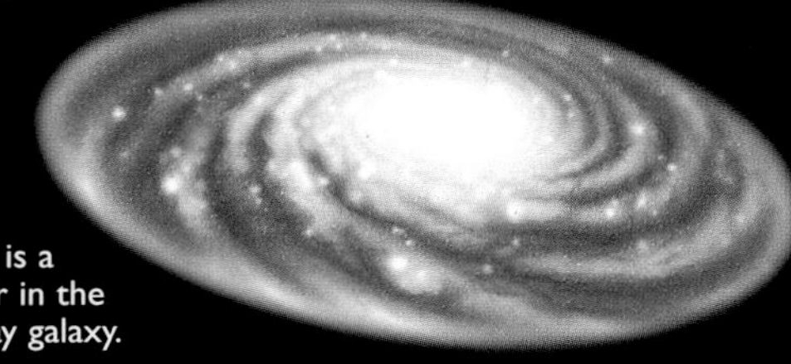

Our Sun is a small star in the Milky Way galaxy.

The Big Bang

Scientists think that the universe began over 15,000 million years ago with an unimaginably violent explosion, called the Big Bang. The Big Bang created a huge fireball, which cooled and formed tiny particles. Everything in the universe is made of these tiny particles, called matter.

These pictures show what may have happened after the Big Bang.

1 The fireball spread out and the universe began to expand. (It is still expanding today.)

2 As the fireball cooled, tiny particles collected into thick, swirling clouds of gas and dust.

3 The clouds pulled in more and more dust and gas. The gases became hotter until they began to burn, and stars formed.

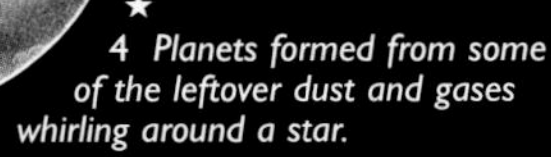

4 Planets formed from some of the leftover dust and gases whirling around a star.

Planet Earth

The Earth was formed about 4,550 million years ago from a cloud of dust and gas spinning around the Sun. Gradually, the Earth grew hotter and hotter, until it turned into a ball of liquid rock and metal. Lighter materials floated to the surface, where they cooled into a hard, rocky crust. The rocks underneath stayed hot and liquid.

This cutaway picture shows inside the Earth, as it is today.

The Earth's crust is a thin layer of rock up to 65km (40 miles) deep.

The crust rests on a layer of hot, partly melted rock, called the mantle.

The outer core is made of hot, liquid metal.

The solid inner core is made mostly of iron. It is extremely hot.

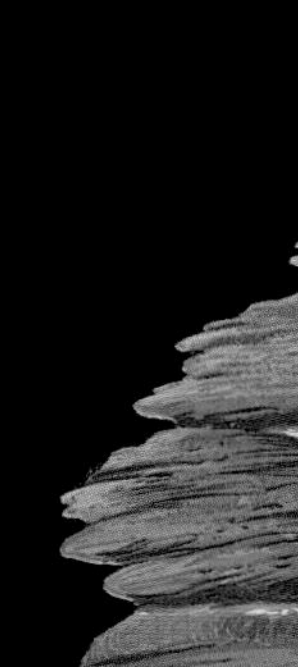

A lifeless planet

For millions of years after the Earth was formed, nothing could live there. There was no water, no breathable air, and no protection from the harmful rays of the Sun. Volcanoes poured out red-hot liquid rock, and the Earth's surface was battered by giant rocks, called meteorites, that fell from space.

The first oceans

Volcanoes on the Earth's surface sent out great clouds of steam and gas that collected in a thick layer around the Earth. As the clouds thickened and cooled, the steam turned into water, and it started to rain. It rained for thousands of years, flooding the Earth and creating the oceans.

This scene shows how the Earth might have looked 4,000 million years ago.

There are no living creatures, because there is no oxygen for them to breathe.

Falling meteorites

Volcanoes pour out liquid rock from deep inside the Earth.

Liquid rock inside the Earth is called magma. When it reaches the surface, it is called lava.

The lava cools and hardens to form new rocks.

Volcanoes belch out clouds of gas and steam.

The surface of the Earth is dry and rocky. There are no plants.

This huge hole, called a crater, was made by a meteorite smashing into the ground.

Liquid rock bubbles up through cracks in the Earth's crust.

Boiling seas

Huge meteorites continued to batter the Earth until around 3,800 million years ago. As the meteorites hit the Earth's surface, they gave off heat. Scientists think that there may have been enough heat to make the oceans boil. This would have destroyed any very early forms of life.

The Changing World

The Earth has not always looked the way it does today. Ever since our planet was formed, its surface has been changing. New rocks are being created all the time, and the land is constantly changing shape.

A giant jigsaw puzzle

The Earth's crust is divided into several huge pieces, called plates, which fit together like a gigantic jigsaw puzzle. Most plates are made up partly of dry land (known as continental crust) and partly of ocean floor (known as oceanic crust).

This picture shows some of the Earth's plates, with one of them lifted up.

Moving plates

The ground beneath your feet may seem solid, but it is actually moving. The plates that make up the crust are floating on hot, toffee-like rock just beneath the Earth's surface. This hot rock (or magma) moves around constantly, carrying the plates with it. Some plates are pushed together, while others are pulled apart.

This picture shows how the plates move around on the surface of the Earth.

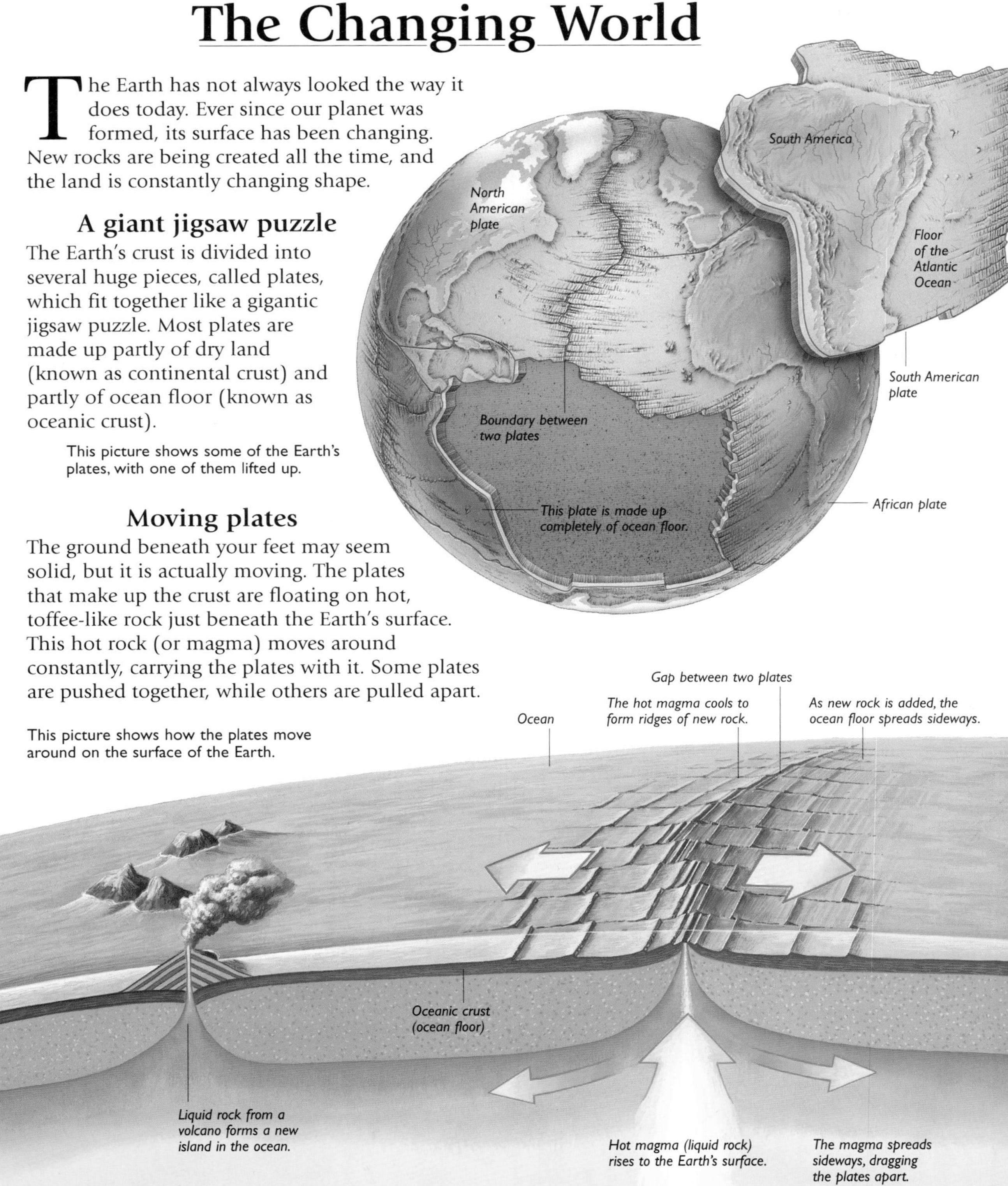

Making mountains

This is Mount Everest, which is part of a group of mountains called the Himalayas. The Himalayas were formed when the plate carrying India crashed into the continent of Asia.

When two plates are pushed together, the land crumples up at the edges to form great ranges of mountains. Mountains formed like this are called fold mountains. They include some of the highest mountains in the world.

Drifting continents

The Earth's plates move at about the same speed that your fingernails grow. Over millions of years, this movement can make the continents drift huge distances. About 250 million years ago, all the continents joined to form a giant supercontinent called Pangaea, which then slowly split apart.

These maps show how Pangaea split up to form the continents we know today.

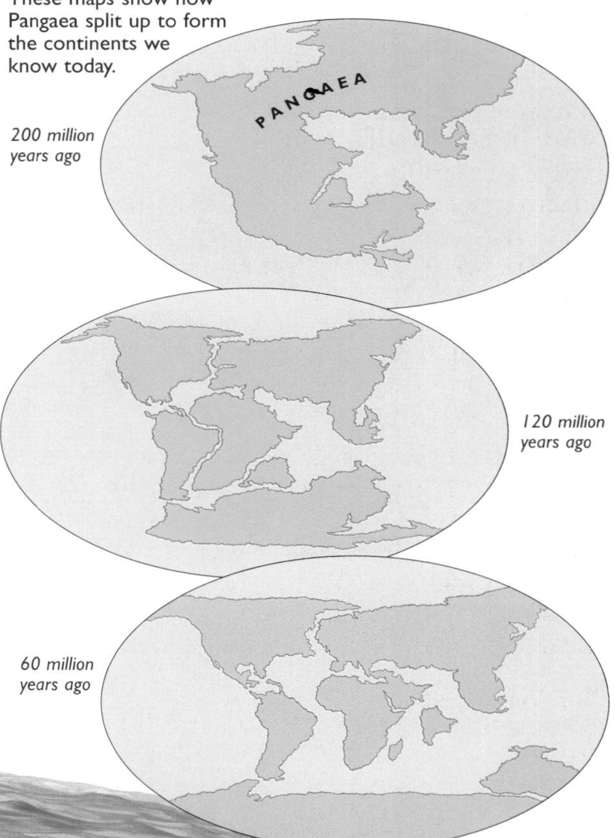

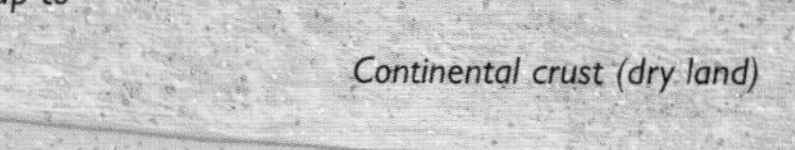

The Beginning of Life

All living things are made up of tiny units, called cells. Cells are made mostly of chemicals called proteins, but where did these chemicals first come from?

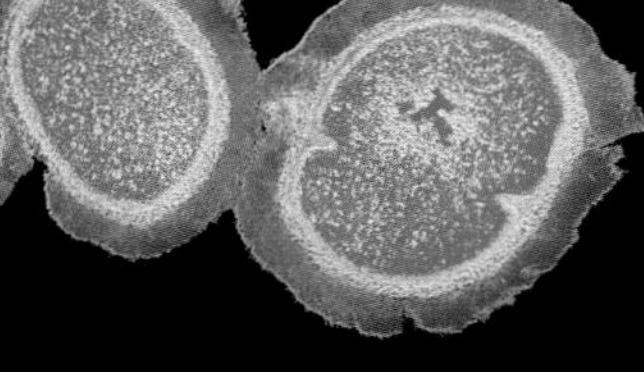

Simple cells shown 33,000 times bigger than their real size

Chemical soup

About 3,800 million years ago, the Earth's surface was covered in volcanoes which poured out poisonous gases. The gases dissolved in the warm water of the oceans, producing a kind of chemical "soup". Scientists think that these chemicals reacted with each other to form more complex chemicals, like the ones that make up proteins.

Electricity from lightning like this may have helped the chemicals to react.

From proteins to cells

Although scientists understand how the first proteins may have formed, they are not sure how these proteins came together to form something as complicated as a living cell.

The first cells may have formed in the seas. A film of proteins floating on the surface of the water may have broken up to form tiny spheres (balls) with chemicals trapped inside.

Cells could also have formed around hot water springs. The proteins may have melted together and then formed tiny, cell-like spheres as they cooled.

Another idea is that the clay at the bottom of shallow seas helped tiny blobs of protein to stick together and form some of the chemicals found in cells.

Blue bacteria

The first living things were made of just one cell each. They were rather like bacteria (germs). Millions of years later, some bacteria, known as blue-green algae, began to use sunlight and water to make their food. This process is called photosynthesis and it is how all plants live.

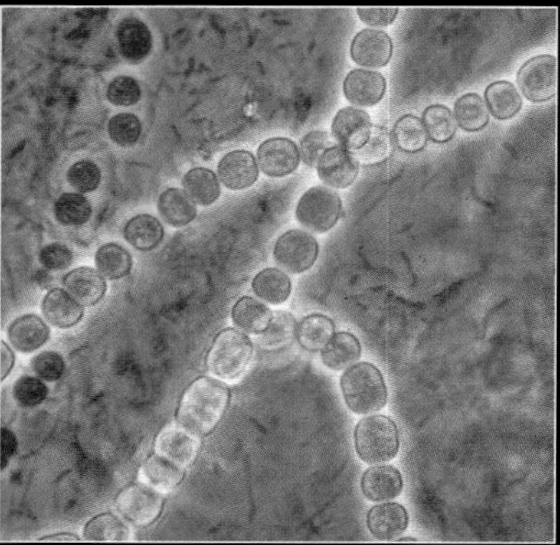

These blue-green algae have been magnified over 1,000 times.

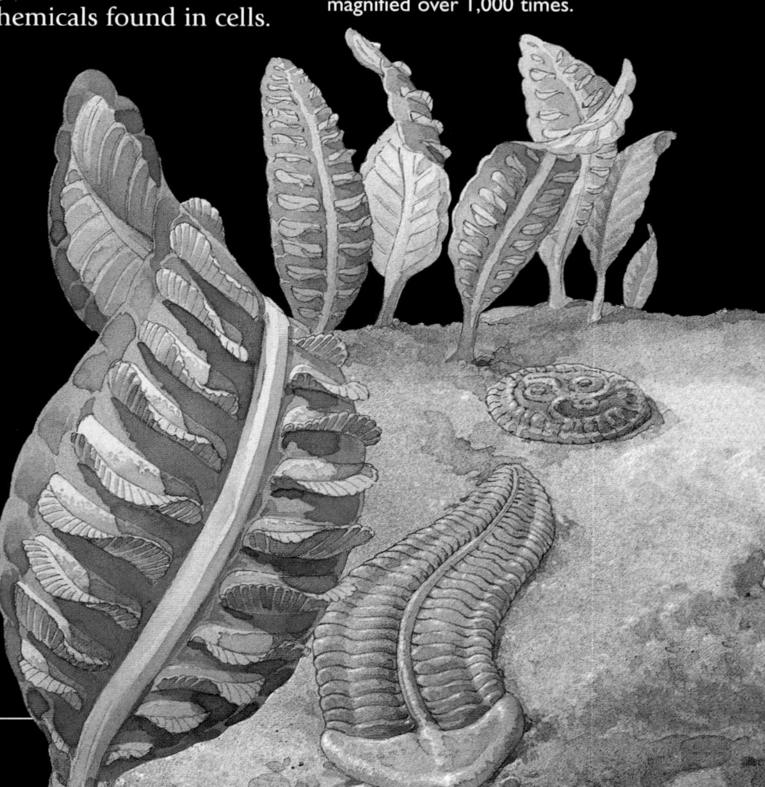

The first fossils

Stromatolites

The earliest evidence of life on Earth comes from fossils known as stromatolites, which contain the remains of large groups of blue-green algae. Some of them are 3,500 million years old.

Some algae in the early seas became trapped in a kind of chemical paste. The paste hardened into a glassy substance, preserving the algae as microscopic fossils.

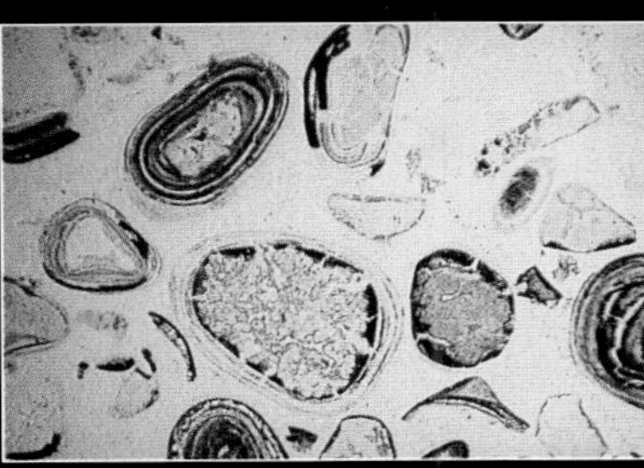

These fossilized algae were photographed under a powerful microscope.

A change of atmosphere

The Earth is surrounded by a thick layer of gases, called the atmosphere. For millions of years, the Earth's atmosphere contained no oxygen (the gas that animals need to breathe).

When plants make their food by photosynthesis, they produce oxygen. As the number of blue-green algae increased, oxygen began to build up in the atmosphere. This allowed many new forms of life to develop.

The first animals?

The earliest traces of animals are tracks left on the seabed by worms. The first animals had soft bodies, which do not fossilize easily, so it is very rare to find fossils of the animals themselves.

By 600 million years ago, a variety of weird and wonderful creatures had evolved. Some of them seem so strange that scientists are not sure if they are really animals at all.

The creatures in this scene lived in the sea from 600 to 550 million years ago.

The fossils of all these soft-bodied creatures were found in the Ediacara Hills of southern Australia.

Strange, disc-shaped creatures drift through the water.

These sea pens look like plants, but each one is actually a group of tiny animals.

This creature, called Spriggina, *is a mystery. It may have been a type of flat, crawling worm.*

Some scientists think Spriggina *may have been attached to the sea floor by its "head".*

Dickinsonia *(a flat, worm-like animal) crawls over the seabed.*

Creatures feed on the blue-green algae that covers the seabed.

Sea pens are attached to the seabed.

Tribrachidium, *a mysterious jellyfish-shaped creature, creeps along the sea floor.*

Shells and Skeletons

At first, life on Earth evolved very slowly. It took over 3,000 million years for simple cells to evolve into the first soft-bodied animals (see page 25). Then, around 550 million years ago, at the start of the Cambrian Period*, an amazing variety of new creatures began to appear in the seas.

Many of these new creatures had hard shells or outer skeletons to support and protect their soft bodies. Some of them also had legs with joints. Creatures with jointed legs and an outer skeleton are called arthropods.

A trilobite, a common Cambrian arthropod

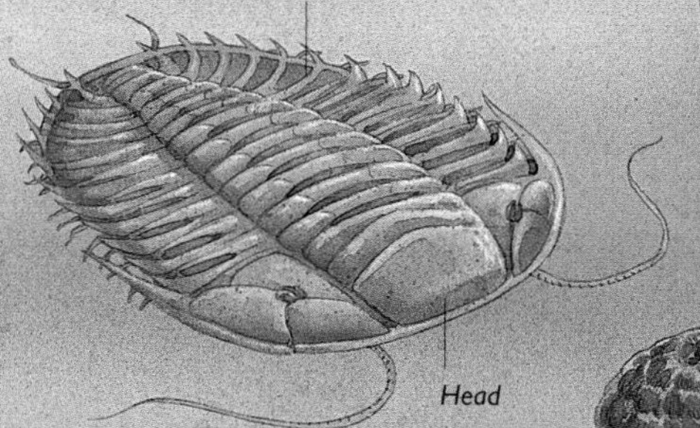

The body is divided into segments.

Head

Each segment has a hard outer casing. This is the animal's skeleton.

Curious creatures

The fossils of some bizarre Cambrian creatures have been found in rocks known as the Burgess Shale, in Canada. These fossils are unusual because they show even soft-bodied creatures in fantastic detail. In some fossils, the animal's last meal can still be seen inside its body.

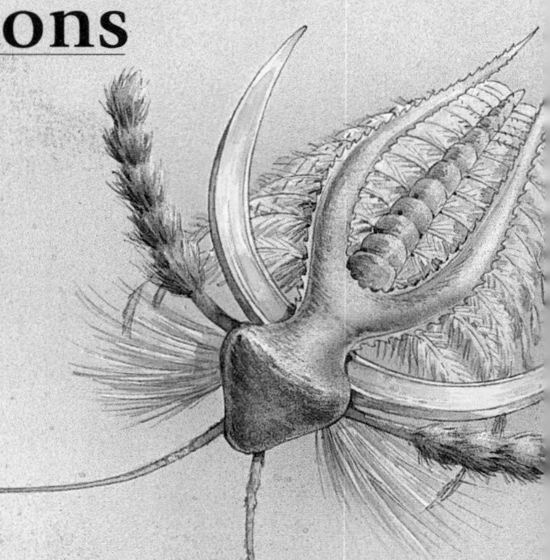

This scene shows some of the strange creatures of the Burgess Shale.

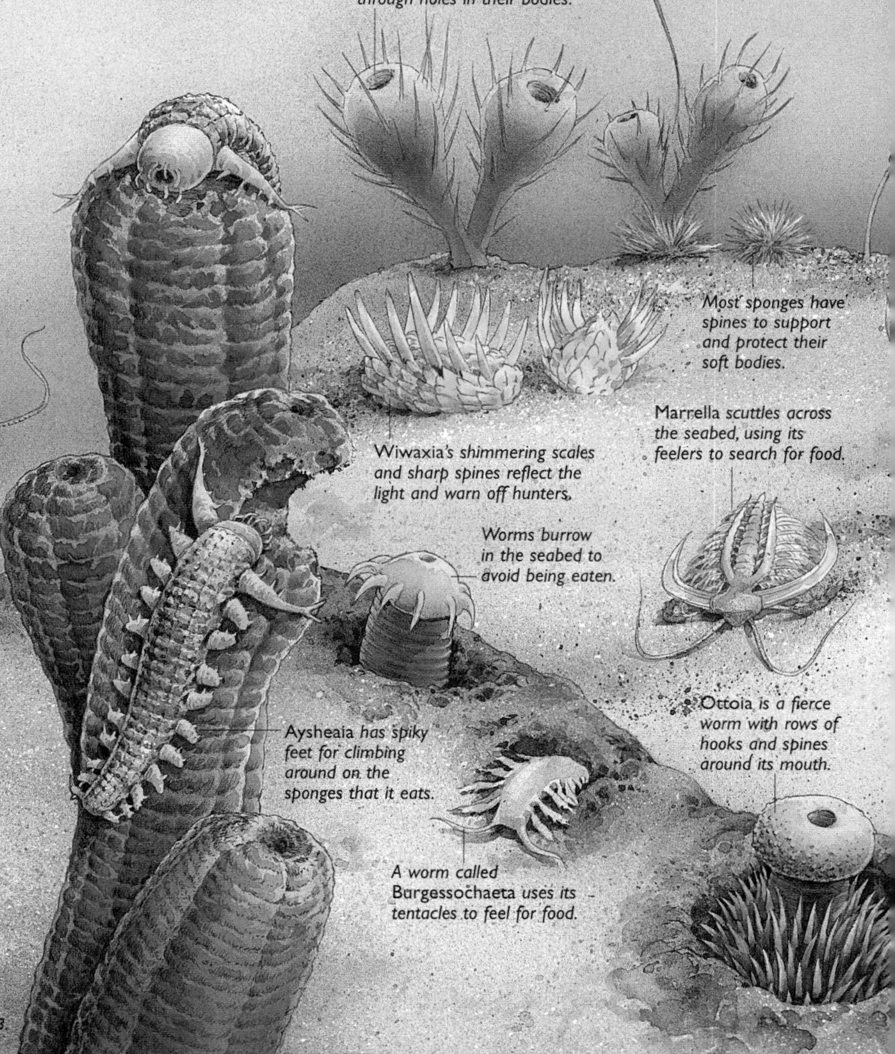

Sponges feed on tiny food particles which they suck in through holes in their bodies.

Marrella has long spines to protect itself from hunters.

Most sponges have spines to support and protect their soft bodies.

Marrella scuttles across the seabed, using its feelers to search for food.

Wiwaxia's shimmering scales and sharp spines reflect the light and warn off hunters.

Worms burrow in the seabed to avoid being eaten.

Ottoia is a fierce worm with rows of hooks and spines around its mouth.

Aysheaia has spiky feet for climbing around on the sponges that it eats.

A worm called Burgessochaeta uses its tentacles to feel for food.

The first hunters

At the start of the Cambrian Period, some animals began to hunt and eat other animals. Soft-bodied creatures may have grown shells and skeletons around this time, as a way of defending themselves.

EARLY LIFE

* Find out about prehistoric time periods on pages 12 and 13.

Internet link: *For a link to a Web site where you can watch a video about the discovery of Anomalocaris, go to* **www.usborne-quicklinks.com**

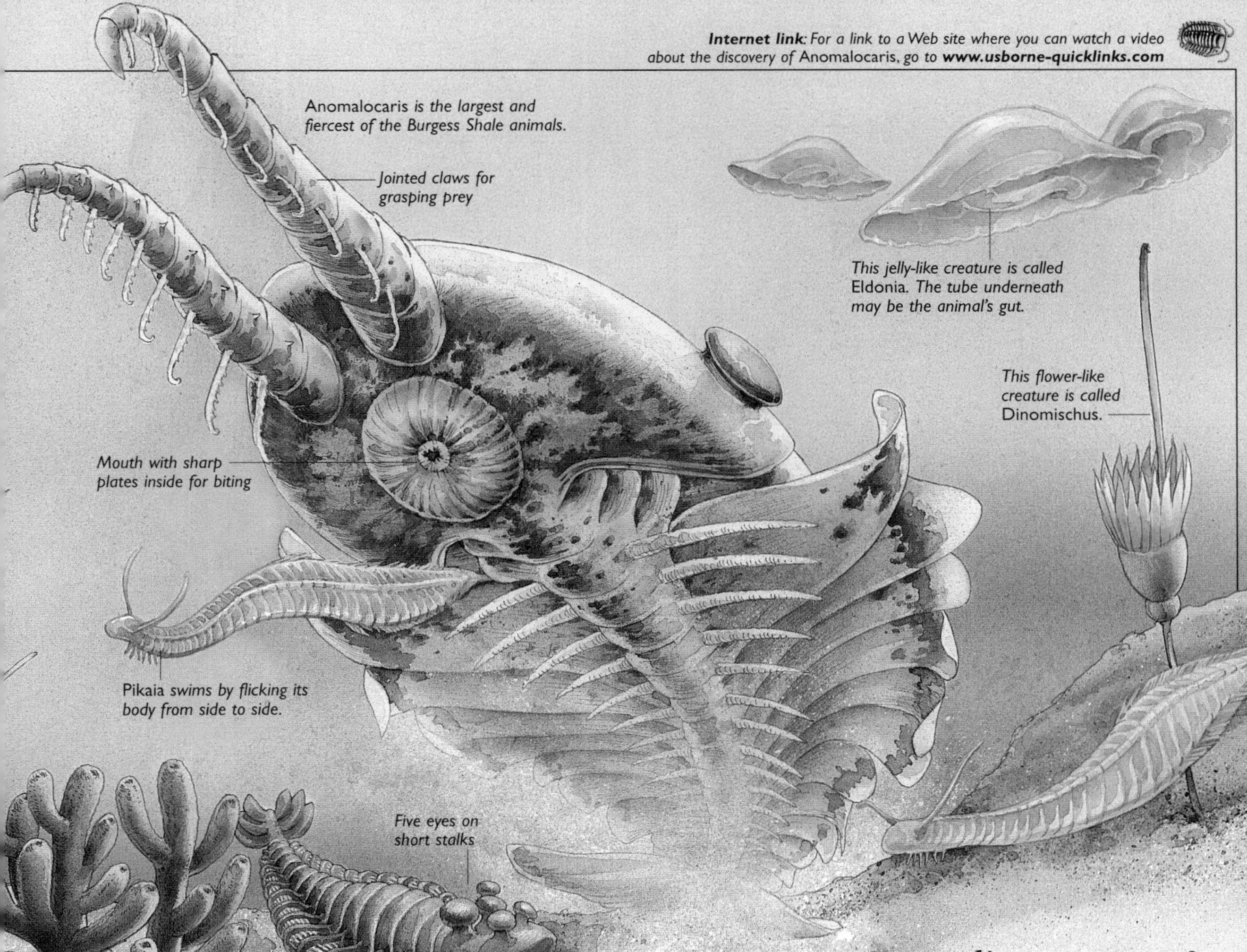

Anomalocaris *is the largest and fiercest of the Burgess Shale animals.*

Jointed claws for grasping prey

Mouth with sharp plates inside for biting

This jelly-like creature is called Eldonia. *The tube underneath may be the animal's gut.*

This flower-like creature is called Dinomischus.

Pikaia *swims by flicking its body from side to side.*

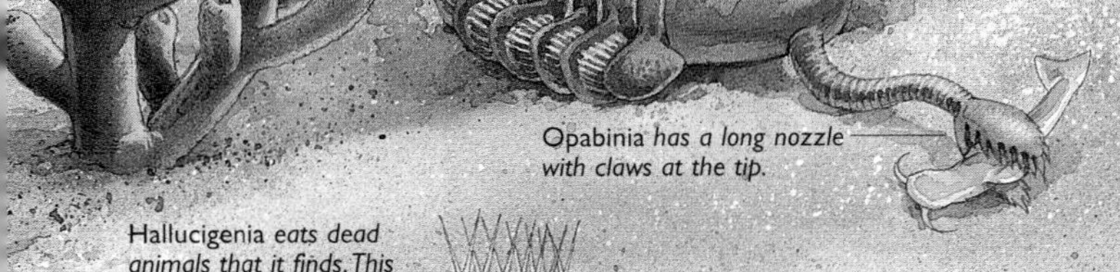

Five eyes on short stalks

Opabinia *has a long nozzle with claws at the tip.*

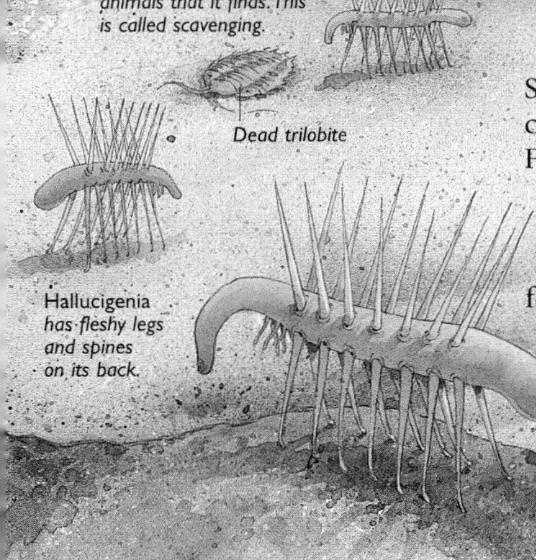

Hallucigenia *eats dead animals that it finds. This is called scavenging.*

Dead trilobite

Hallucigenia *has fleshy legs and spines on its back.*

Stilts or spines?

Some of the Burgess Shale creatures are extremely puzzling. For many years, scientists thought that *Hallucigenia* walked on stilt-like legs and had tentacles on its back. Fossils found recently in China show that the "stilts" are actually spines on the creature's back. Scientists had been looking at the animal upside down!

Our earliest ancestors?

One of the most important creatures of the Burgess Shale is a small, eel-like animal called *Pikaia*. It belongs to a group of animals called chordates, which have a stiff rod running down their spine. Humans are also chordates, so *Pikaia* could be one of our earliest ancestors.

Scientists in China have recently discovered a chordate called *Cathaymyrus*, which is even older than *Pikaia*. Perhaps this is where the human story begins?

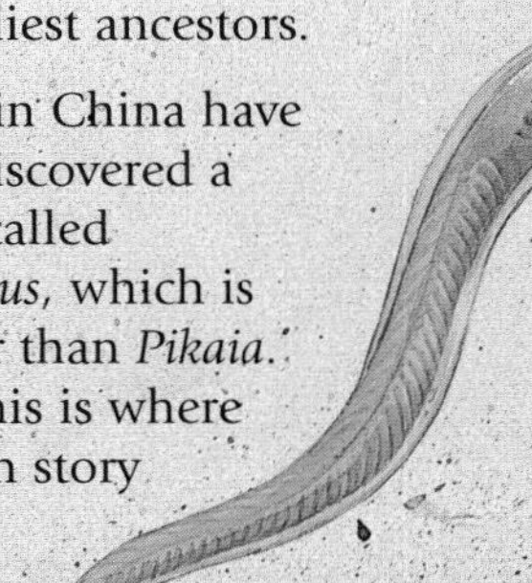

Cathaymyrus

The Crowded Seas

Around 510 million years ago, many of the strange Cambrian creatures died out. They were replaced by an enormous variety of new creatures which thrived in the warm, shallow seas of the Ordovician and Silurian Periods. Some of these creatures, such as starfish, sea lilies and corals, are still around today.

Starfish on stalks

Starfish belong to a group of animals called echinoderms, which means "spiny-skinned". Their cousins, the sea lilies, are rather like starfish on stalks. Sea lilies have lots of waving arms covered in sticky suckers, which trap tiny particles of food.

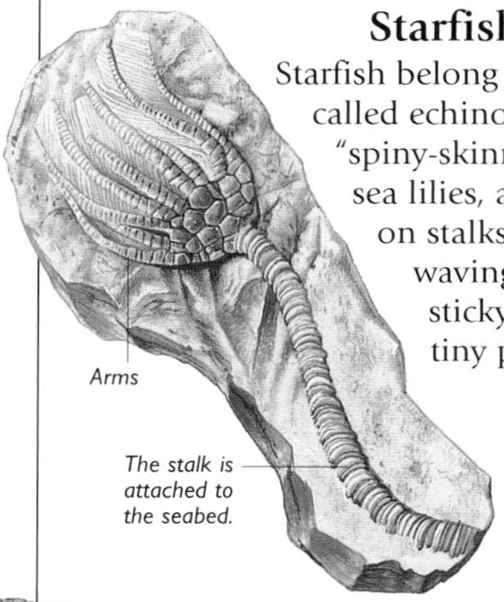

Fossil of a prehistoric sea lily ★

Colonies of corals

Corals are tiny, bag-like creatures that live together in large groups, or colonies. They use their tentacles to sweep food into their mouths.

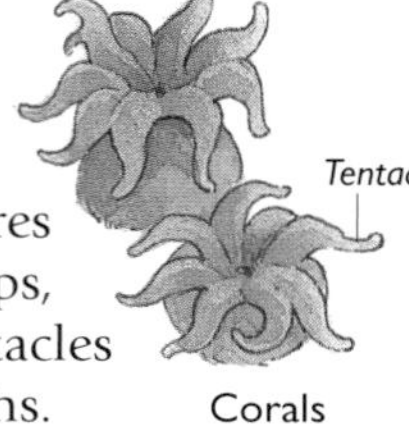

Corals

Corals have hard, chalky skeletons that support their soft bodies. Over time, the skeletons build up to form rocky mounds called reefs. The first coral reefs appeared 450 million years ago, during the Ordovician Period.

This scene shows an Ordovician coral reef.

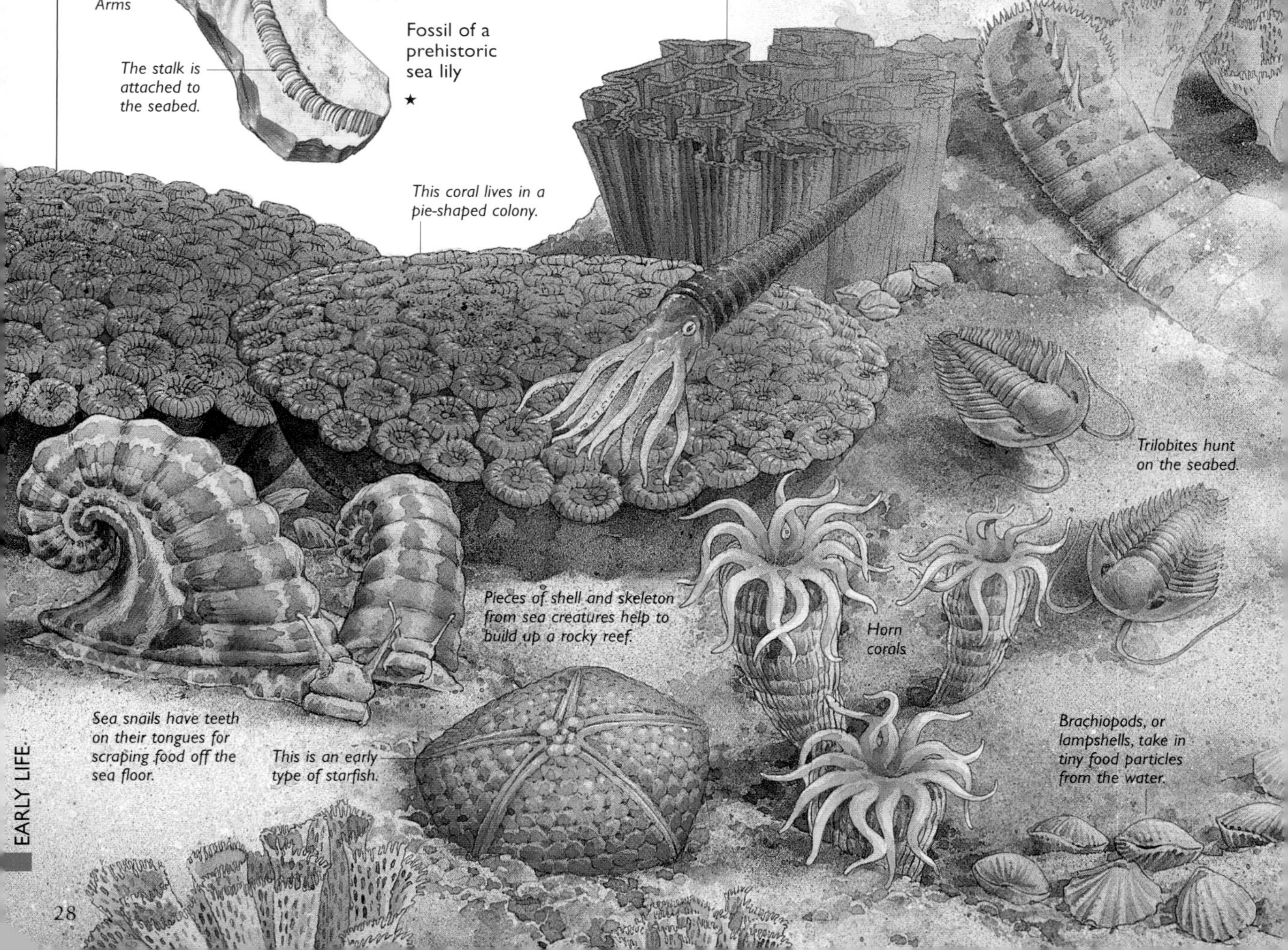

Creatures in cups

Tiny creatures called graptolites also lived in colonies. A colony of graptolites was made up of lots of hard, horny cups all linked together. Each cup contained a single animal. Colonies may have lived on the seabed or floated in the water.

Powerful predators

Animals that hunt and eat other animals are called predators. During the Ordovician and Silurian Periods, predators became experts at chasing and catching their prey.

One group of predators were the nautiloids. They had excellent eyesight and long, grasping tentacles for catching food. Nautiloids were fast swimmers and moved around by shooting water in and out of their shells.

The most ferocious predators were the eurypterids, or sea scorpions. The largest of these was the giant *Pterygotus*, which grew up to 2m (6ft 6in) long. It had sharp pincers in front of its mouth, and used its tail as a paddle for moving quickly through the water.

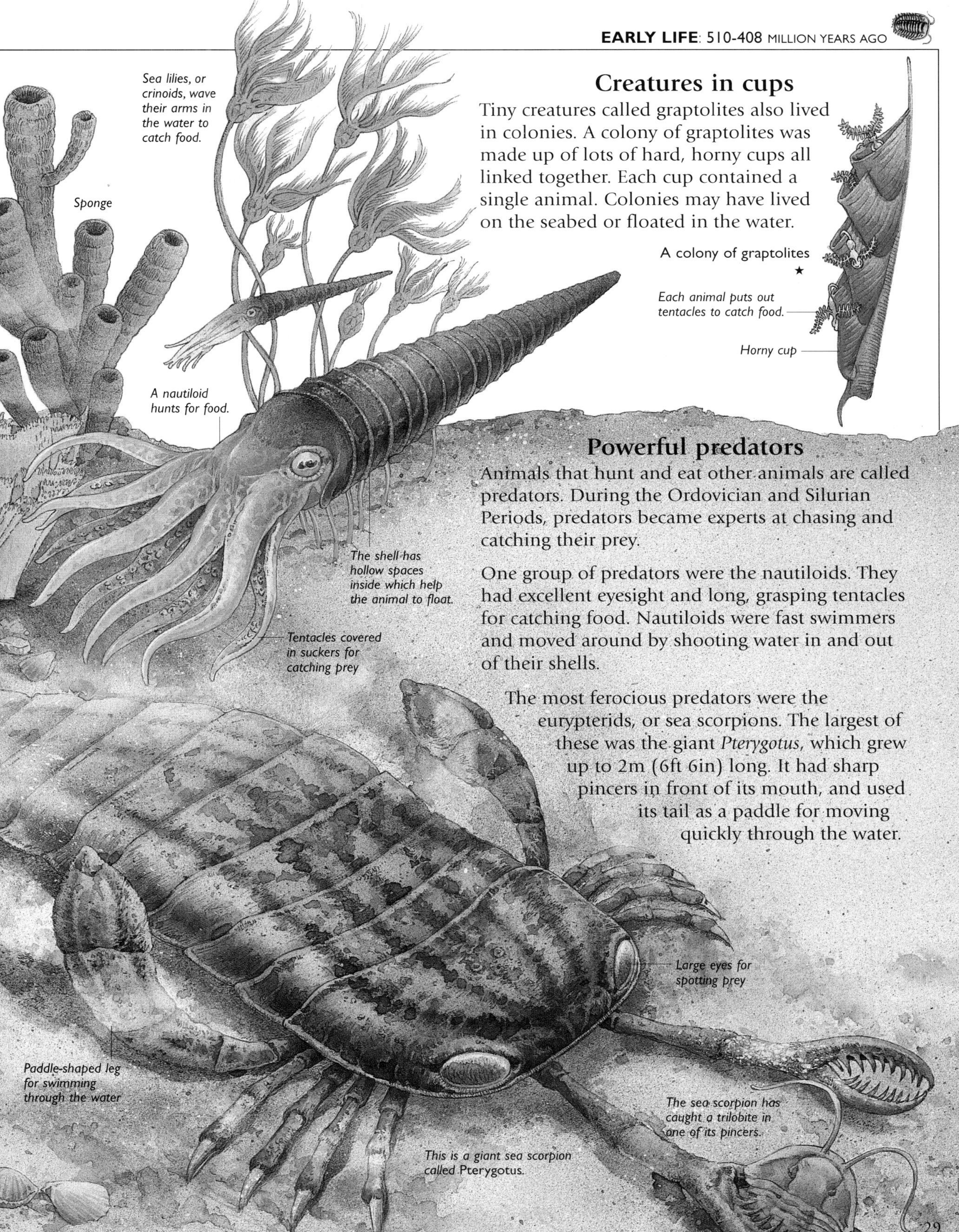

The First Fish

Fish first appeared around 510 million years ago, at the beginning of the Ordovician Period. They were the first creatures that had a backbone to support their bodies. Animals with a backbone are called vertebrates.

Jawless fish

The first fish had no jaws for opening and closing their mouths. They lived at the bottom of the sea, where they could suck up small particles of food from the seabed.

★ *Sacabambaspis*, an early jawless fish

Hard, bony plating around the head and body

Fish with jaws

The first fish with jaws appeared during the Silurian Period. They are known as acanthodians, or "spiny sharks", although they were not actually sharks at all.

Fish that had jaws could use their mouths for grasping and biting, so they could eat a much greater variety of food. Many of them became hunters.

This picture shows some fish that lived during the Devonian Period from 408 to 362 million years ago.

These small fish are acanthodians.

These are the fish's gills. They take in oxygen from the water, so the fish can breathe.

Sharp, pointed teeth for grasping prey

Ferocious fish

A group of fish called placoderms, or "plated skins", were particularly fierce hunters. Some placoderms were gigantic, and had powerful jaws lined with sharp, jagged plates of bone.

The first sharks

Sharks first appeared during the Devonian Period. A shark's skeleton is not made of bone, but of cartilage (the same stuff that makes up the hard part of your nose). Cartilage is lighter than bone, and this helped the sharks to float.

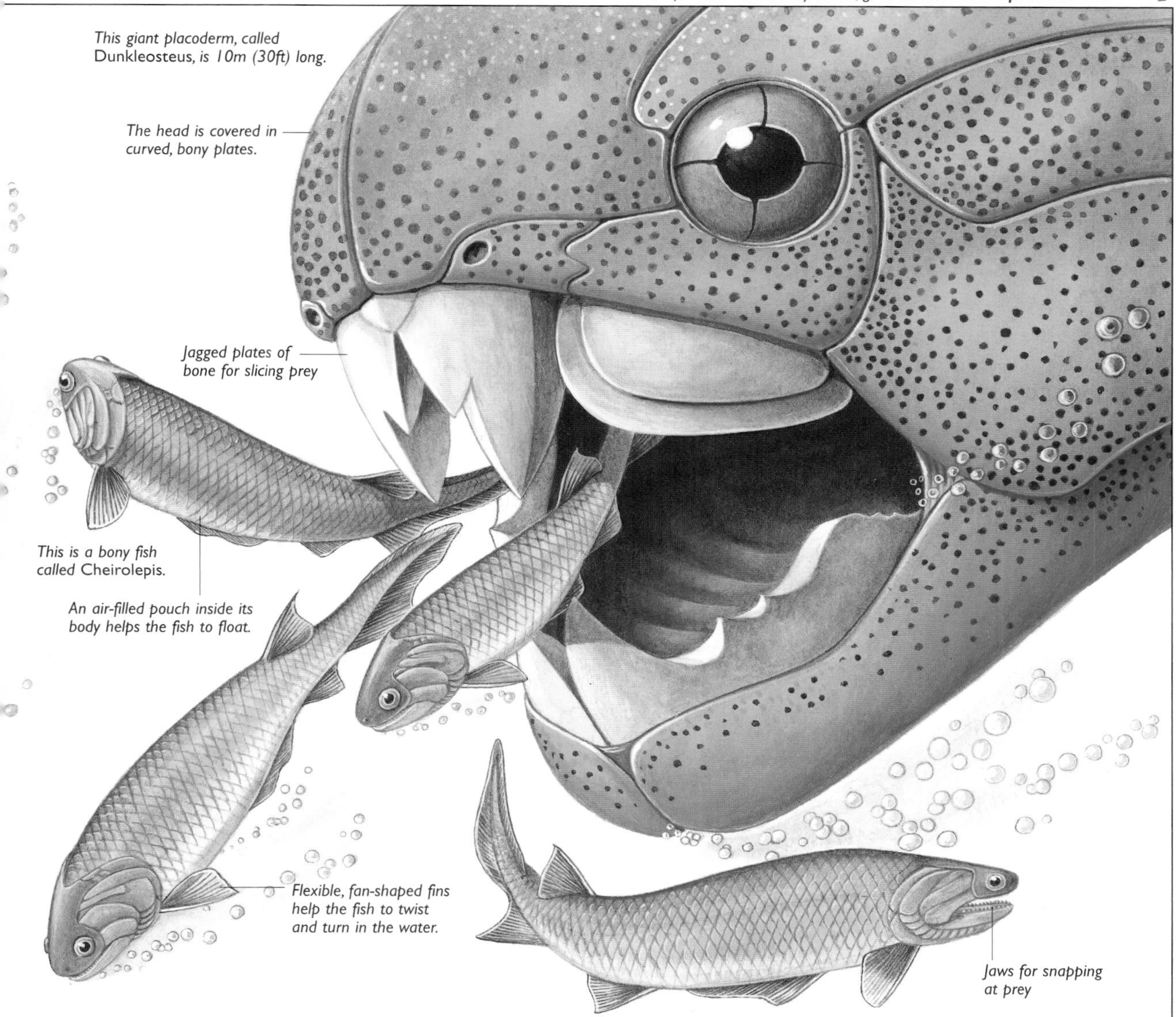

Internet link: *For a link to a Web site where you can see video clips, pictures and information about early sharks, go to* **www.usborne-quicklinks.com**

This giant placoderm, called Dunkleosteus, *is 10m (30ft) long.*

The head is covered in curved, bony plates.

Jagged plates of bone for slicing prey

This is a bony fish called Cheirolepis.

An air-filled pouch inside its body helps the fish to float.

Flexible, fan-shaped fins help the fish to twist and turn in the water.

Jaws for snapping at prey

Bony fish

Most fish that are alive today have bony skeletons. Almost all bony fish belong to a group known as "ray fins". They have delicate, fan-shaped fins supported by fine, bony rods (or rays).

A few bony fish belong to a group known as "fleshy fins". Their thick fins are mainly bone and muscle, with a fringe of fine rays around the edges. It was from these fish that the first land-living vertebrates evolved (see pages 34 and 35).

This is a coelacanth, a fleshy-finned fish which has hardly changed since Devonian times.

Life on Land

Life on Earth began in the seas. For millions of years, the Earth's surface was scorched by harmful ultraviolet light from the sun, and there was almost no life on land. Simple plants, called algae, grew at the edges of the sea, but the rest of the land was rocky and completely bare.

Gradually, a layer of gas called ozone built up around the Earth. The ozone blocked out some of the sun's rays and made it possible for plants and animals to survive on land.

Plants on land

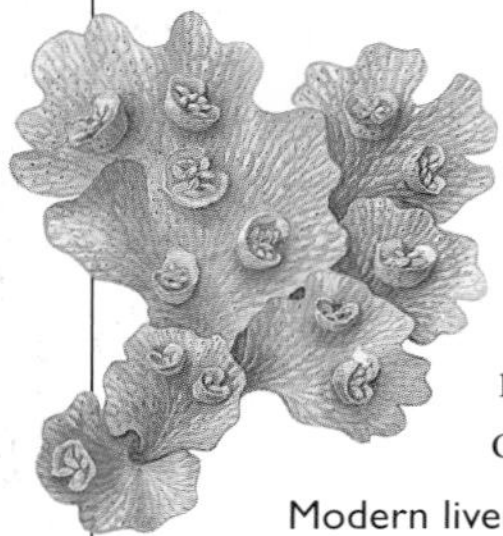

The first known land plants appeared about 440 million years ago, near the end of the Ordovician Period. They were probably relatives of modern mosses and liverworts, and they only grew in very damp places.

Modern liverwort

Problems for plants

To survive on dry land, plants need roots to take in water from the ground and a network of tubes to carry the water from the roots to the stem. The outside of the plant has to be waterproof, so it doesn't dry out, and the stem must be strong enough to keep the plant upright.

The first known plant to have all these features was *Cooksonia*, which appeared about 420 million years ago.

★ *Cooksonia*

Animals on land

Once there were plants on land, there was food for animals to eat. The first creatures to move from water onto land were arthropods, such as spiders, millipedes and insects.

This picture shows some of the plants and animals that lived on land around 400 million years ago.

This leafless plant is called Aglaophyton.

Inside here are tiny cells, called spores, which blow away in the wind and grow into new plants.

Rhyniella *is a tiny, wingless insect.*

Centipedes have poisonous fangs for catching their prey.

Spores and seeds

The earliest plants produced tiny cells, called spores, which grew into new plants. During the Devonian Period, some plants, such as seed-ferns, began to produce seeds instead of spores. Seeds are tougher than spores and can grow in drier soil. This helped plants to spread into areas where there was less water.

★ Fossil of a seed-fern

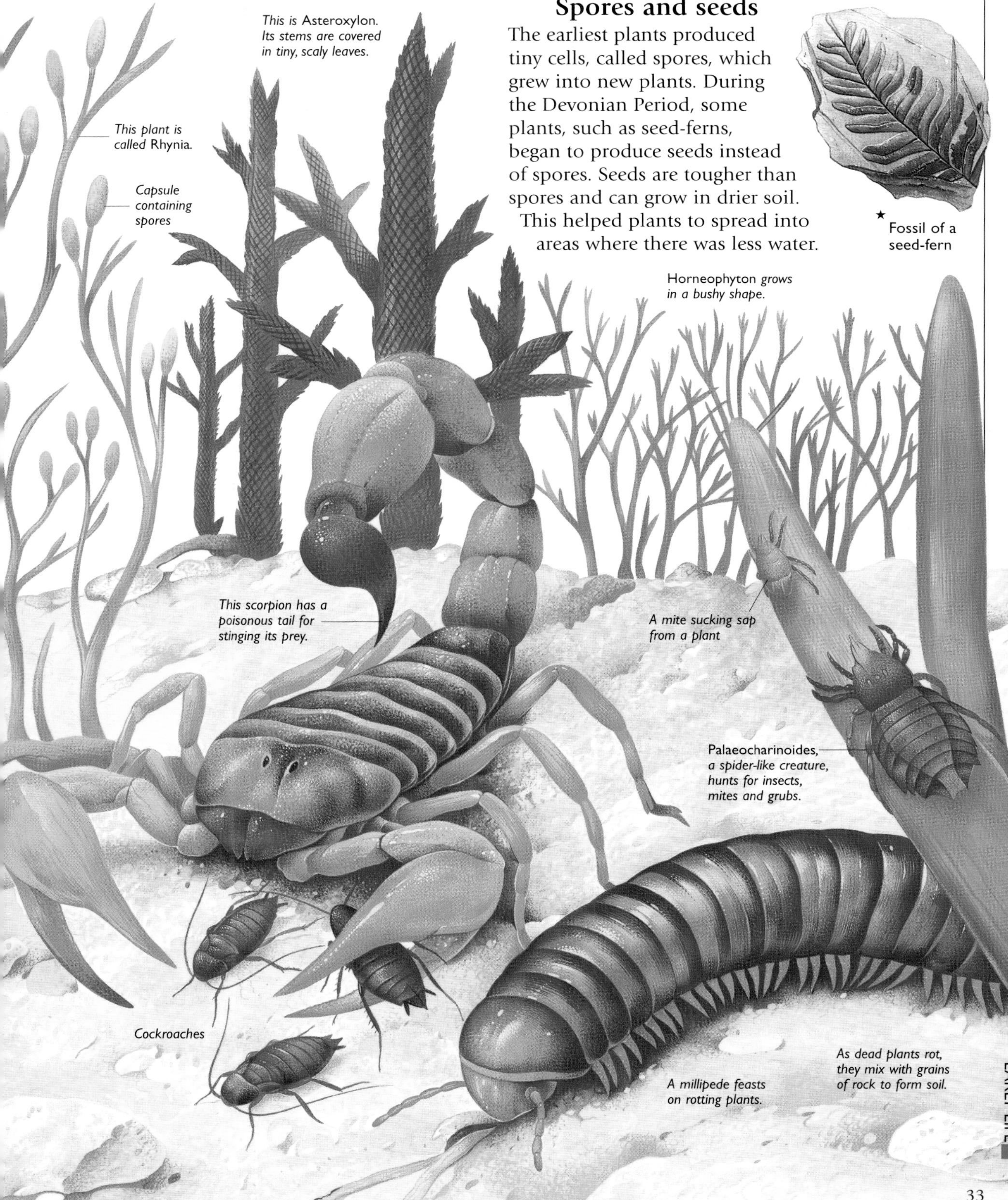

This is Asteroxylon. *Its stems are covered in tiny, scaly leaves.*

This plant is called Rhynia.

Capsule containing spores

Horneophyton *grows in a bushy shape.*

This scorpion has a poisonous tail for stinging its prey.

A mite sucking sap from a plant

Palaeocharinoides, *a spider-like creature, hunts for insects, mites and grubs.*

Cockroaches

A millipede feasts on rotting plants.

As dead plants rot, they mix with grains of rock to form soil.

Fish out of Water

During the Devonian Period, the Earth's climate grew warmer, and there were long periods of dry weather. Lakes and rivers became shallower and contained less oxygen, so the fish that lived in them had to adapt in order to survive.

Lungs and legs

One group of fish, the "fleshy fins", had lungs as well as gills. This meant that they could breathe air if there wasn't enough oxygen in the water. They may have used their strong, muscular fins to push their heads above the water.

Scientists believe that the muscular fins of these fish gradually evolved into four legs. The bones that supported their fins are very similar to the leg bones of land animals.

Why did fish grow legs?

Experts used to think that fish evolved legs so that they could walk to new ponds, if the pond where they were living dried up. Now, scientists believe that fish evolved legs and lungs to help them live in shallow water, rather than to help them get onto land.

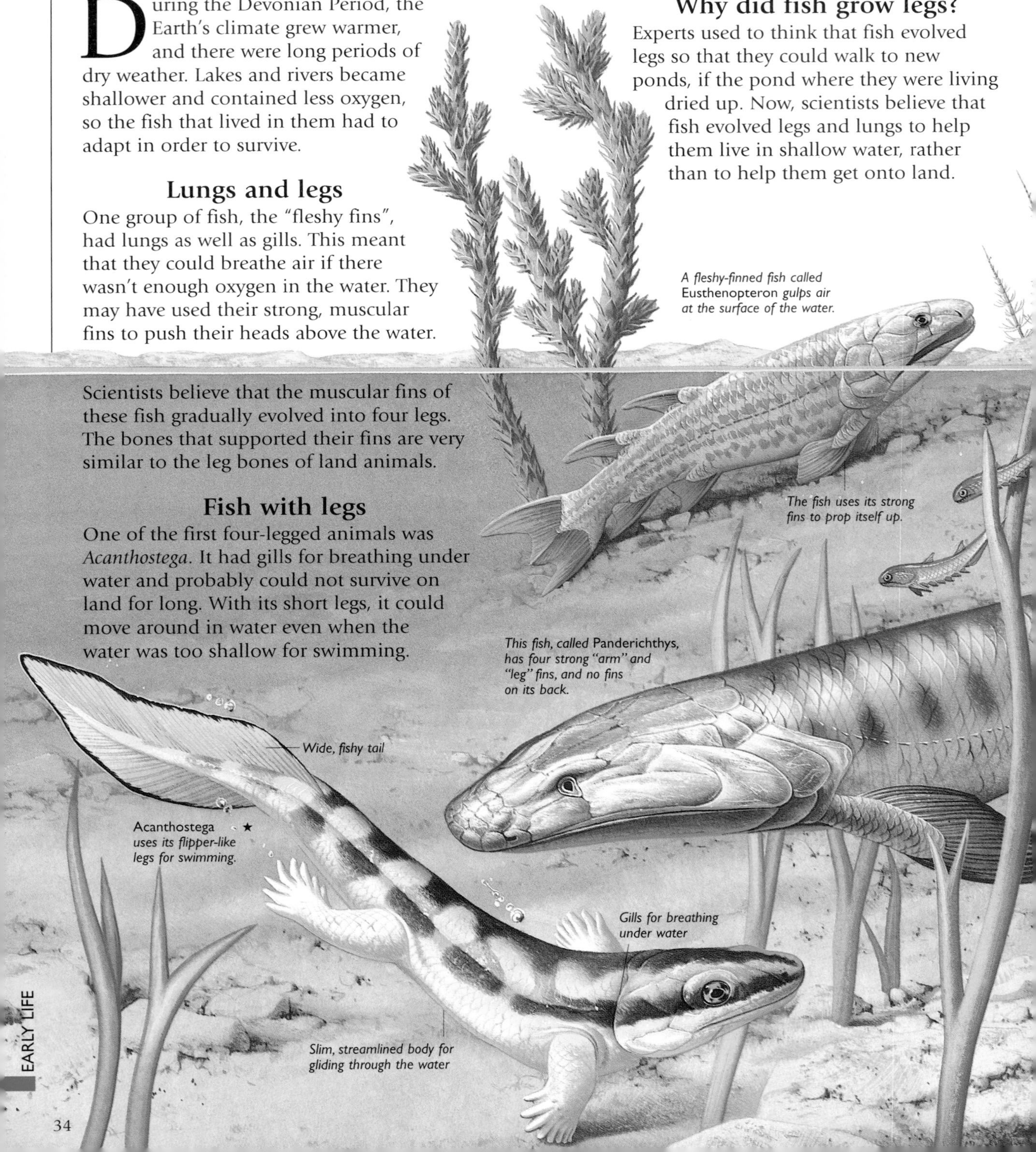

A fleshy-finned fish called Eusthenopteron *gulps air at the surface of the water.*

The fish uses its strong fins to prop itself up.

Fish with legs

One of the first four-legged animals was *Acanthostega*. It had gills for breathing under water and probably could not survive on land for long. With its short legs, it could move around in water even when the water was too shallow for swimming.

This fish, called Panderichthys, *has four strong "arm" and "leg" fins, and no fins on its back.*

Wide, fishy tail

Acanthostega ★ *uses its flipper-like legs for swimming.*

Gills for breathing under water

Slim, streamlined body for gliding through the water

Onto the land

About 375 million years ago, an animal called *Ichthyostega* appeared. It lived mainly in the water, but it could also breathe air and crawl onto land. It probably returned to the water to lay its eggs. Animals that live on land, but lay their eggs in the water, are called amphibians.

This scene shows some creatures that would have lived in a shallow Devonian lake.

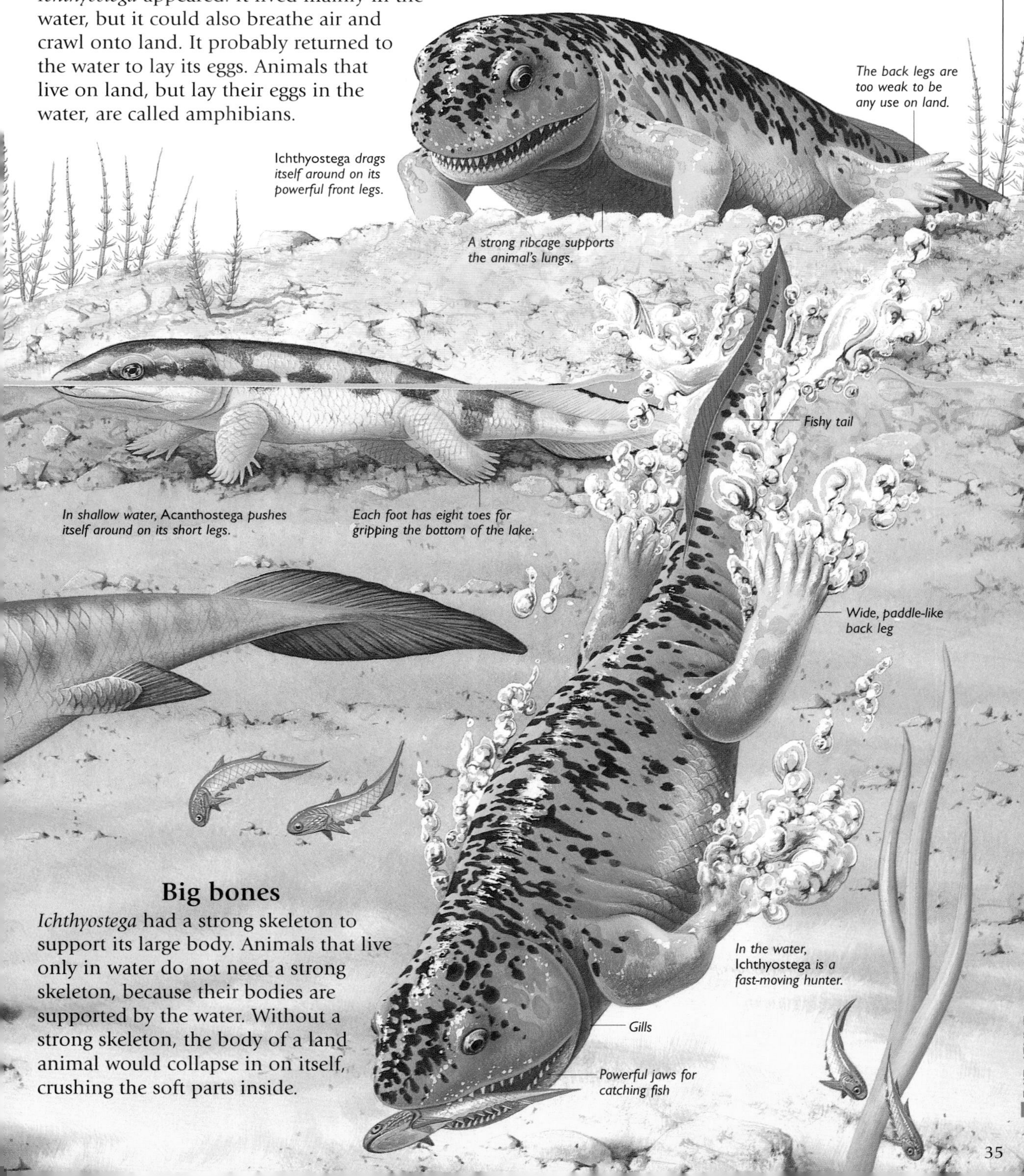

Ichthyostega *drags itself around on its powerful front legs.*

The back legs are too weak to be any use on land.

A strong ribcage supports the animal's lungs.

Fishy tail

In shallow water, Acanthostega *pushes itself around on its short legs.*

Each foot has eight toes for gripping the bottom of the lake.

Wide, paddle-like back leg

In the water, Ichthyostega *is a fast-moving hunter.*

Gills

Powerful jaws for catching fish

Big bones

Ichthyostega had a strong skeleton to support its large body. Animals that live only in water do not need a strong skeleton, because their bodies are supported by the water. Without a strong skeleton, the body of a land animal would collapse in on itself, crushing the soft parts inside.

Swamps and Forests

At the start of the Carboniferous Period, 362 million years ago, large areas of the world were covered in swamps. The weather was warm and wet, and these vast, steamy swamps were ideal places for plants and trees to grow. Thick forests of gigantic trees spread out across whole continents.

The trees in a Carboniferous forest were very different from those that are around today. The tallest trees were the giant clubmosses (moss-like plants with upright stems). They had green, scaly bark and reached heights of 50m (150ft).

This scene shows some of the plants and creatures that lived in a Carboniferous coal swamp about 350 million years ago.

Lepidodendron *is the tallest of the giant clubmosses.*

Meganeura, *a giant dragonfly, has wings that measure 60cm (2ft) across.*

A microsaur, a lizard-like amphibian, lounges on a fallen tree trunk.

Diplocaulus *has strange fins on its head to help it swim.*

A giant millipede feeds on rotting leaves.

Keraterpeton *uses its long tail for swimming.*

Gephyrostegus *has spiky teeth for eating insects.*

Creating coal

Dead plants and fallen trees piled up on the forest floor, and were gradually buried under layers of mud. Over millions of years, the plants and trees were squeezed until they hardened and turned into coal. This coal is still being mined in some parts of the world today.

Big bugs

The Carboniferous swamps swarmed with huge insects, spiders and bugs. Giant dragonflies, the first creatures with wings, fluttered through the trees. Millipedes up to 2m (6ft 6in) long crept around in the dead leaves, and enormous spiders spun simple webs to catch their prey.

The age of amphibians

During the Carboniferous Period, a great variety of amphibians evolved. Some were small, lizard-like creatures that scampered around on the forest floor in search of insects to eat. Some hunted in the water like crocodiles. Others gradually lost their legs and could no longer live on land at all.

Like amphibians today, the early amphibians laid their soft, jelly-covered eggs in ponds or streams. This meant that they had to stay close to water. If animals were going to live successfully on land, they had to find a way around this problem.

What Are Reptiles?

Around 300 million years ago, a new group of creatures, called reptiles, evolved from amphibians. Reptiles were the first vertebrates (animals with a backbone) that were able to live on land all the time. Present-day reptiles, such as lizards, crocodiles and tortoises, show us how the early reptiles may have lived.

Keeping warm

Reptiles are ectothermic, or cold-blooded. This means that they cannot produce their own heat. Instead, they rely on heat from the sun to keep their bodies warm.

A crocodile warming itself in the sun

At night, reptiles get cold and have to rest. In the morning, they lie in the sun until their bodies warm up. Then, they can start to move around in search of food.

Land legs

Animals that live on land need strong legs to lift their bodies off the ground, so they can move around easily. A typical reptile has legs that stick out on either side of its body. As the animal runs, its whole body twists from side to side, so its skeleton needs to be very strong and flexible.

Scaly skin

On land, animals lose water all the time through their skin. If they lose too much water, they dry up and die. Reptiles have scaly, waterproof skin to stop their bodies from drying out.

This picture shows *Hylonomus*, one of the earliest known reptiles.

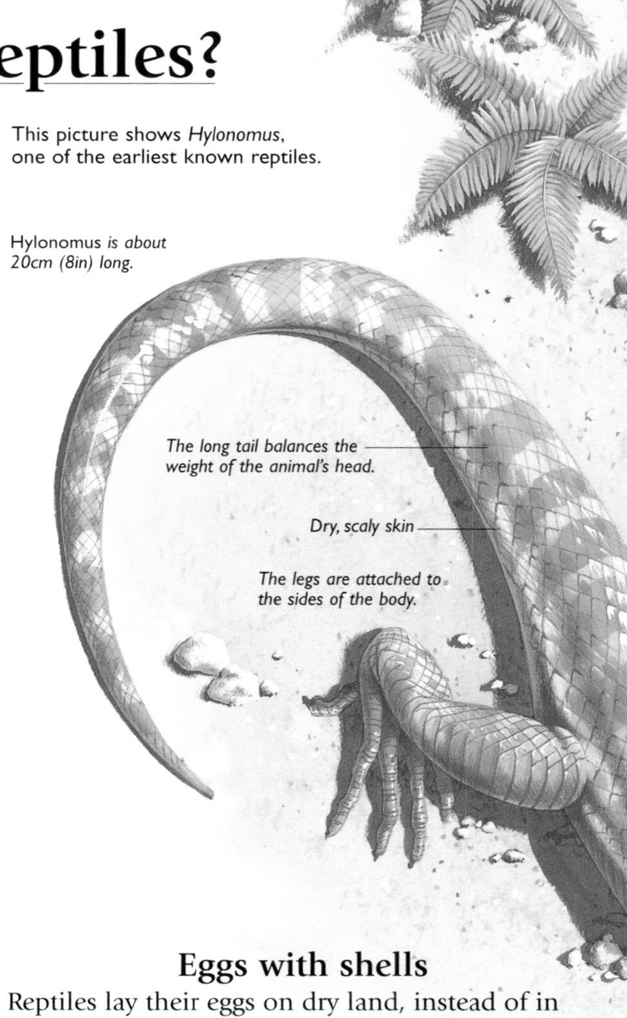

Eggs with shells

Reptiles lay their eggs on dry land, instead of in the water as amphibians do. Reptile eggs have a leathery, waterproof shell which protects the baby inside and stops it from drying out. The baby grows inside the egg and only hatches out when it is big enough to survive on its own.

★ Inside a reptile egg

The yolk provides food for the baby reptile.

Baby reptile

A bag of liquid protects the baby from knocks.

Shell

Recognizing reptiles

Scientists identify early reptiles by the shape of their skulls and jaws. The first reptiles had a more powerful bite than their amphibian ancestors. This made them better hunters and also allowed them to eat plants for the first time.

Hylonomus eats insects, such as these cockroaches.

The first reptiles

The earliest known reptiles, such as *Hylonomus*, were small, lizard-like creatures. They were well suited to life on land and did not need to live close to water. This meant that they could spread out into drier areas. These small creatures were the ancestors of every type of land animal alive today.

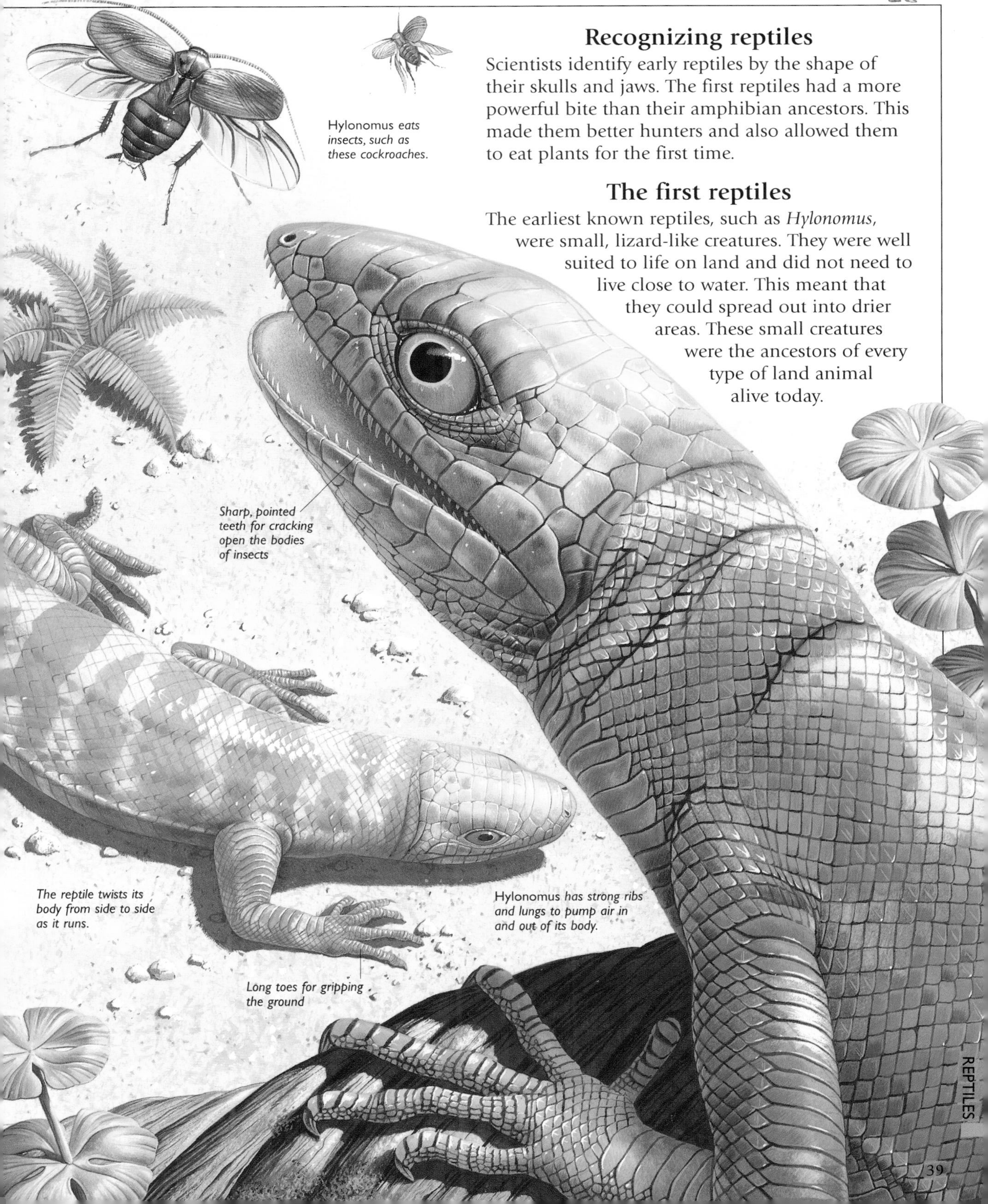

Sharp, pointed teeth for cracking open the bodies of insects

The reptile twists its body from side to side as it runs.

Hylonomus has strong ribs and lungs to pump air in and out of its body.

Long toes for gripping the ground

Early Reptiles

Once reptiles had evolved, they spread out very quickly on land. By 290 million years ago, at the start of the Permian Period, several new types of reptiles had appeared. Some of these new reptiles were large meat-eaters, or carnivores, that hunted other reptiles. Others were plant-eaters, or herbivores.

Early plant-eaters

A pareiasaur, an early plant-eating reptile

One group of small, plant-eating reptiles had chisel-shaped teeth which they may have used for digging up roots. Other plant-eaters, called pareiasaurs, were as big as a hippo. Pareiasaurs had strong, blunt teeth for grinding up plants. Their backs and heads were covered in hard, bony plates.

Sails of skin

During the Permian Period, the largest and most successful animals were a group of reptiles known as synapsids. Some early synapsids had a tall sail of skin on their backs, which they probably used to control their body temperature.

This picture shows some sail-backed synapsids.

The sail soaks up heat from the sun, warming the reptile's body.

Bony spine

The reptiles cool down by turning their bodies around, so the thin edge of the sail faces the sun.

Edaphosaurus *is a plant-eater. Its jaws are lined with blunt, chisel-shaped teeth.*

Dimetrodon *is a meat-eater. It has two types of teeth for stabbing and slashing its prey.*

When the reptile walks, its long body twists from side to side.

Longer legs

About 270 million years ago, the synapsid reptiles began to change. Instead of having short, sprawling legs, they developed longer legs that grew directly under their bodies. This allowed them to take bigger strides and move around faster. These new, improved reptiles are known as therapsids.

This scene shows *Moschops*, a plant-eating therapsid, being attacked by a group of smaller meat-eaters, called *Lycaenops*.

Moschops *may have used its thick, bony skull in head-butting contests to compete for a mate.*

Moschops *is 5m (16ft) long and has a huge, barrel-shaped body.*

The front legs stick out at the sides.

The back legs are directly under the body.

Lycaenops *is a fast-moving hunter. It has huge fangs for stabbing its prey.*

Long legs for extra speed

Land and sea

During the Permian Period, all the Earth's continents joined together to form one giant supercontinent (see page 23). This meant that reptiles could spread out to all parts of the world. At the same time, vast numbers of sea creatures died out, because the shallow seas around the continents disappeared.

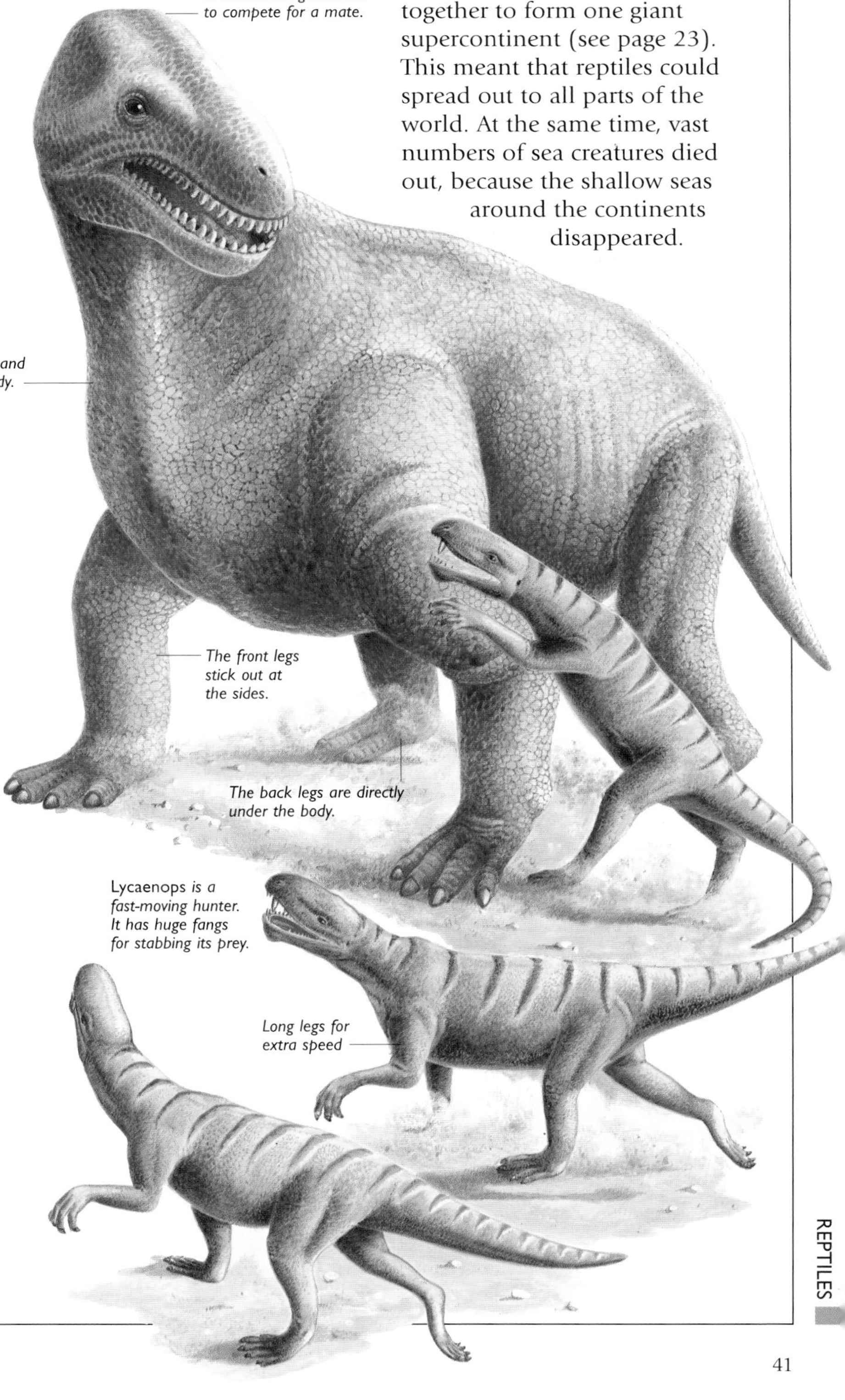

Back to the water

Although reptiles had evolved to cope with life on dry land, some reptiles went back to living in the water. One of the earliest to do this was *Mesosaurus*.

Mesosaurus, an early sea reptile ★

Mesosaurus had long, spiky teeth which it used to trap small, shrimp-like creatures in its mouth. It may have had a fin on its tail and webbed feet to help it swim.

The Rise of the Reptiles

At the start of the Triassic Period, about 245 million years ago, the most common creatures on Earth were animals known as cynodonts (say "sigh-no-donts") and dicynodonts (say "die-sigh-no-donts"). These were both new types of therapsid reptiles (see page 41).

Tusks and beaks

Dicynodonts were plant-eaters. They had two tusks at the sides of their jaws for digging up roots, and a tough beak for slicing through plant stems. They ground up their food using sharp, horny plates on the roof of their mouths.

Reptiles with fur

Cynodonts had slim, dog-like bodies and long legs. They also had powerful jaws lined with different types of teeth for cutting, stabbing and chewing. Some cynodonts probably grew fur to help keep their bodies warm. Unlike other reptiles, they may even have been able to produce their own body heat.

Near the end of the Triassic Period, furry cynodonts evolved into a completely new group of animals, called mammals (see pages 60 and 61).

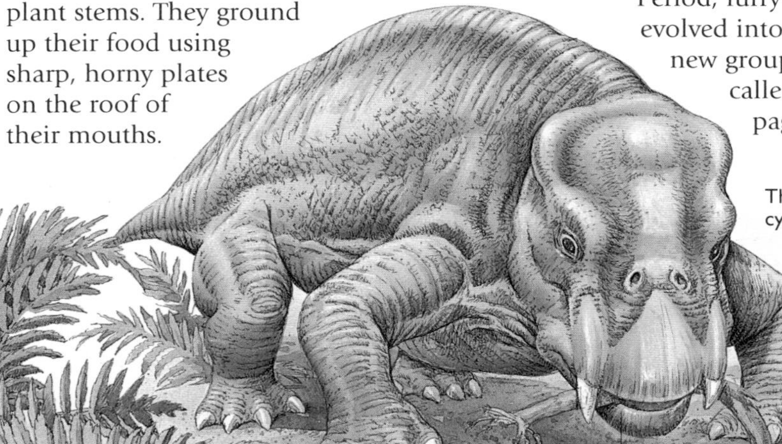

This scene shows some cynodonts and dicynodonts.

Lystrosaurus, a typical dicynodont, pulls up plants with its tusks.

Lystrosaurus *has a barrel-shaped body and short, stout legs.*

A cynodont called Thrinaxodon *with its pups*

Fur helps to keep heat inside the body.

Ruling reptiles

Another group of reptiles that lived in the Triassic Period were the archosaurs, or "ruling reptiles". Early archosaurs had rows of bony plates along their backs. While they were resting, their legs sprawled out to the sides. However, they could also tuck their legs under their bodies to help them run faster.

★ *Lagosuchus*, a two-legged archosaur, was a fast runner.

★ *Eoraptor*, one of the first dinosaurs, was a fast-moving hunter.

Later in the Triassic Period, some archosaurs began to walk on their back legs, rather than on all fours. They had a short body and a long tail to help them keep their balance.

★ *Euparkeria*, an early archosaur, ran on all fours.

★ *Stagonolepis* was a crocodile-like archosaur with bony plates on its back.

The first dinosaurs

About 225 million years ago, the first dinosaurs evolved from small, two-legged archosaurs, such as *Lagosuchus*. Dinosaurs were different from other reptiles because they had longer, more upright legs that swung from front to back, instead of sticking out at the sides.

Once dinosaurs had evolved, many new types appeared. Their upright legs could carry a lot of weight and helped them to run fast. For the next 160 million years, they were the largest, strongest and fastest land animals in the world.

Meat-eating Monsters

The first dinosaurs on Earth were meat-eaters. Meat-eating dinosaurs are known as theropods, which means "beast foot". All theropods walked on their two back legs and had viciously sharp claws on their feet.

The earliest theropods were fairly small, less than 1.5m (5ft) from nose to tail. They had long, powerful legs for running fast and used their clawed hands for grasping prey.

A wide variety of theropods evolved from these early dinosaurs. Many of them stayed small and agile, but others grew monstrously large.

Beaks and brains

One group of theropods, known as "ostrich dinosaurs", had beaks instead of teeth. They had larger brains than most reptiles and were probably fairly intelligent.

Gallimimus, an ostrich-like theropod ★

Ostrich dinosaurs were very fast runners, and may have reached speeds of over 55km (35 miles) an hour.

Small and speedy

One of the smallest dinosaurs was *Compsognathus*, which was no bigger than a cat. It hunted lizards and other tiny animals, and used its long tail to help it balance as it ran.

★ *Compsognathus* chasing a lizard

Clawed hands for holding onto prey

★ *Coelophysis*

Fast and fierce

Coelophysis was a ferocious and fast-moving hunter. It had a slim body with hollow bones, which made it very light and agile. It used its sharp, saw-like teeth to slice up its prey, and may even have eaten its own young.

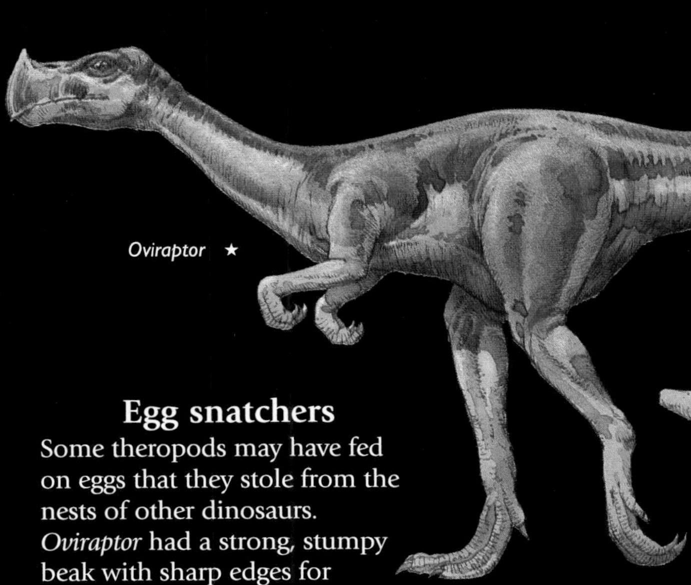

Oviraptor ★

Egg snatchers

Some theropods may have fed on eggs that they stole from the nests of other dinosaurs. *Oviraptor* had a strong, stumpy beak with sharp edges for cracking open thick-shelled eggs.

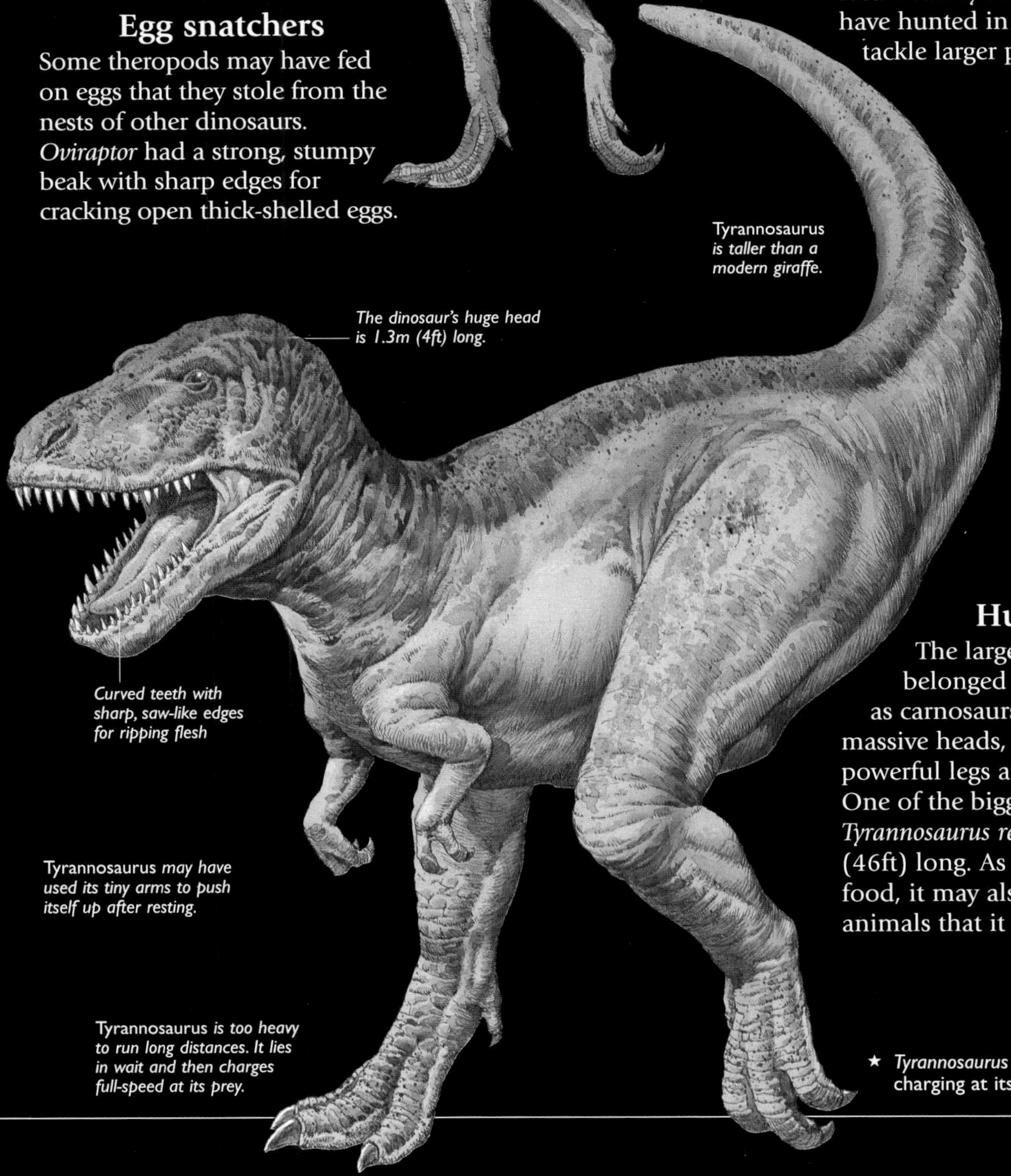

Killer claws

Deinonychus was only about 2m (6ft 6in) long, but it was a fierce hunter. It leaped on its prey and held on with its hands. At the same time, it kicked with the huge claws on its back feet. *Deinonychus* may have hunted in groups to tackle larger prey.

Tyrannosaurus *is taller than a modern giraffe.*

The dinosaur's huge head is 1.3m (4ft) long.

Deinonychus

Curved teeth with sharp, saw-like edges for ripping flesh

Huge hunters

The largest theropods belonged to a group known as carnosaurs. They had massive heads, strong necks, powerful legs and short arms. One of the biggest carnosaurs was *Tyrannosaurus rex*, which was 14m (46ft) long. As well as hunting for food, it may also have eaten dead animals that it found.

Tyrannosaurus *may have used its tiny arms to push itself up after resting.*

Tyrannosaurus *is too heavy to run long distances. It lies in wait and then charges full-speed at its prey.*

★ *Tyrannosaurus rex* charging at its prey

Gentle Giants

The biggest land animals that ever lived were a group of dinosaurs called sauropods. They were plant-eaters with large bodies, small heads, and extremely long necks and tails.

Early sauropods

The early sauropods were much smaller than their later relatives, measuring only 4-6m (13-20ft) from nose to tail. Unlike meat-eating dinosaurs, they walked mainly on all fours. However, some early sauropods could stand up on their back legs to eat leaves from trees.

An early sauropod

Huge and heavy

The really gigantic sauropods appeared about 160 million years ago, during the Jurassic Period. An animal named *Seismosaurus* is thought to have been the biggest. It was probably 40-50m (130-165ft) long and may have weighed as much as 20 African elephants!

This scene shows some giant sauropods from the Jurassic Period.

Sauropods usually walk on all fours.

Diplodocus *has a strong, arched back to carry the weight of its massive stomach.*

The long neck is balanced by the weight of the tail.

Tiny head

Whip-like tail for lashing out at attackers

Strong, pillar-like legs

Diplodocus *is longer than two buses placed end to end.*

Like all sauropods, Seismosaurus *spends most of its time feeding.*

Weight lifting

Sauropods needed massive leg bones to support their great weight. Their backbones were also very strong, but they were sometimes cut away at the sides, instead of being solid. This made the animals lighter, so they had less weight to carry.

Hard to swallow

Sauropods had gappy, peg-like teeth which only grew at the front of their mouths. Teeth like this were ideal for stripping the leaves off trees, but were hopeless for chewing, so sauropods had to swallow their food whole.

Stomach stones

Plants and leaves are tough and very hard to digest, especially if they haven't been chewed properly. To help break down their food, sauropods swallowed large pebbles. These stones tumbled around in the animal's huge stomach, grinding the plants into a thick soup.

On its back legs, Apatosaurus can reach leaves high up in the trees.

Some sauropods have nostrils on top of their heads.

The dinosaur props itself up with its tail.

A group of sauropods can completely wreck a forest.

★

Brachiosaurus *has long front legs, so it doesn't need to stand up on its back legs to reach the treetops.*

Big bodyguards

Sauropods lived in large groups, or herds. When the herd was on the move, the larger adults walked on the outside of the group, with the baby dinosaurs in the middle. This made it harder for predators (hunters) to attack the babies.

Beaks and Crests

Some plant-eating dinosaurs, called ornithopods, were fast-moving and agile. They had bird-like feet and a horny beak for nipping off leaves and shoots to eat. All ornithopods could run on their two back legs to escape from predators (hunters).

Biting and chewing

One early ornithopod, called *Heterodontosaurus*, had large tusks behind its beak. It may have used these to defend itself against predators or rival males. *Heterodontosaurus* was one of the first dinosaurs to have cheeks. These stopped any food from falling out of the animal's mouth while it was chewing.

Heterodontosaurus ★

Small and swift

A small ornithopod called *Hypsilophodon* was a particularly fast runner, probably reaching speeds of 45km (30 miles) an hour. It had long legs and used its stiff tail to help it balance while running.

★ *Hypsilophodon*

Spikes and hoofs

Iguanodon was a large, heavy ornithopod, measuring up to 10m (33ft) long. It had a vicious spike on each thumb, which it used to fight off attackers. Its three middle fingers had hoofs, so it must have walked on all fours some of the time.

Iguanodon ★

Duck-billed dinosaurs

By about 80 million years ago, the most common plant-eating dinosaurs on Earth were a group of ornithopods known as hadrosaurs, or duck-billed dinosaurs. They had broad beaks, powerful jaws and thousands of small, sharp teeth for grinding up tough plants.

Broad, horny beak for slicing through plants

★ *Adult hadrosaurs feed on pine needles and flowering plants, such as magnolia.*

Incredible crests

Many hadrosaurs had strange spikes or crests on their heads. Some of these crests had hollow tubes inside. By blowing air through its crest, a hadrosaur may have been able to make booming noises to warn others of danger, or to attract a mate.

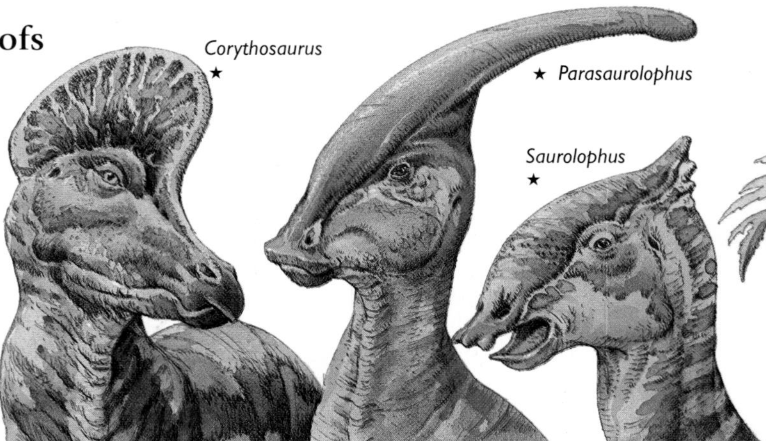

Corythosaurus ★

★ *Parasaurolophus*

Saurolophus ★

Mothers and babies

Hadrosaurs lived together in large herds. At the same time each year, the herd returned to the same place, so the females could lay their eggs. Unlike most reptiles, hadrosaurs guarded their eggs carefully, and looked after their babies until they could survive on their own.

This picture shows a group of hadrosaurs with their babies.

Horns, Clubs and Spikes

Some plant-eating dinosaurs were too big and heavy to escape from the fierce, meat-eating dinosaurs that hunted them. Instead, they developed a range of horns, clubs and spikes to protect themselves from predators.

Bone heads

The pachycephalosaurs, or bone-headed dinosaurs, had a thick dome of solid bone on the top of their heads. They charged headfirst at their opponents, using their enormous skulls as battering rams.

Head-banging contests

As well as fighting off hunters, bone-headed dinosaur males probably fought each other to prove which was the strongest. They may have banged their skulls together until the weakest gave up.

Spikes and clubs

Ankylosaurs were covered from head to tail with bony plates. Vicious-looking spikes grew from these plates, and some ankylosaurs had a bony lump at the end of their tails, which they swung around like a club.

Two bone-headed dinosaurs charging at each other ★

The dinosaurs' thick skulls are surrounded by a fringe of bony lumps.

Euoplocephalus, a very well-protected ankylosaur ★

Euoplocephalus *can swing its tail with great force.*

Plates, knobs and spikes protect this dinosaur.

Pointed plates

Stegosaurs had two rows of upright plates running along their backs. The plates protected the stegosaurs from attack. They were probably also used to soak up heat from the sun, like the sails of the sail-backed reptiles (see page 40).

Bony plates covered with skin

Stegosaurus, the largest known stegosaur ★

Horns and frills

One of the last groups of dinosaurs to appear on Earth were the ceratopians. They had curved horns on their heads and a huge frill of bone around their necks and shoulders. Male ceratopians probably fought each other, as well as charging at attackers.

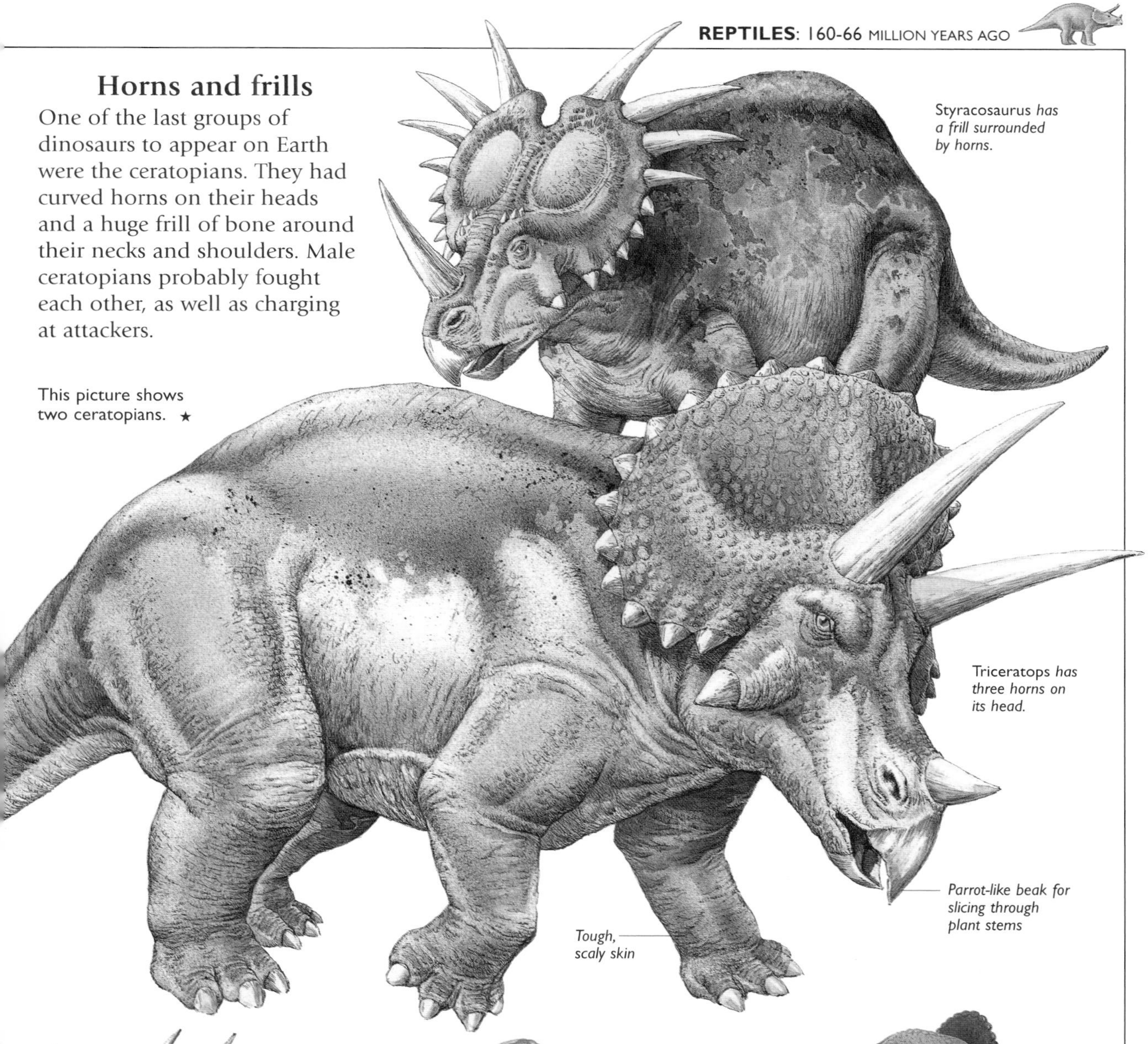

This picture shows two ceratopians. ★

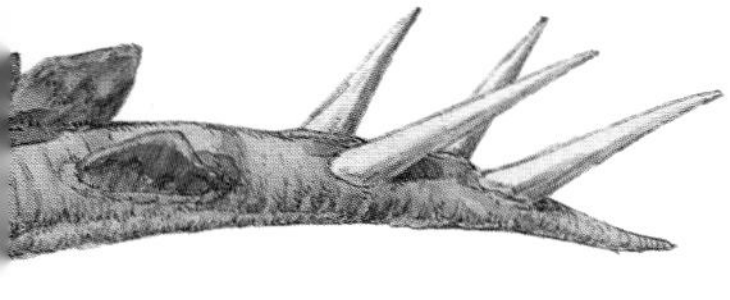

Styracosaurus has a frill surrounded by horns.

Triceratops has three horns on its head.

Parrot-like beak for slicing through plant stems

Tough, scaly skin

Scary circle

Experts think that adult ceratopians defended their babies from attack by forming a circle around them. The adults probably shook their huge heads to scare predators away.

Ceratopians ★ defending their young

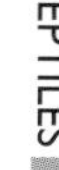

Reptiles of the Seas

While the dinosaurs were living on the land, other reptiles were swimming in the seas. Reptiles probably entered the oceans about 290 million years ago (see page 41). Gradually, their bodies changed to help them live under water.

Early sea reptiles

By the start of the Triassic Period, about 245 million years ago, there were two kinds of reptiles living in the sea. Placodonts were turtle-shaped creatures. Some of them were good swimmers, but others spent most of their time on dry land.

A placodont called *Henodus*

A nothosaur called *Nothosaurus*

Nothosaurs had long, thin bodies that could glide smoothly through the water, and they may have had webbed feet as well. They used their big, sharp teeth for catching fish.

Swimming with flippers

At the start of the Jurassic Period, around 200 million years ago, a group of long-necked reptiles called plesiosaurs evolved. Instead of legs, plesiosaurs had big, paddle-shaped flippers which they flapped like wings as they moved through the water.

Sea monsters

Some plesiosaurs became ferocious hunters. One group, called the pliosaurs, had massive jaws full of sharp teeth for stabbing their prey. Pliosaurs hunted in the depths of the oceans, searching for sharks, big squids and other swimming reptiles. Some pliosaurs were enormous, reaching lengths of over 12m (40ft).

This picture shows some reptiles that lived in the Jurassic seas.

This squid-like creature is called a belemnite.

Peloneustes *is a fast-moving pliosaur.*

Internet link: *For a link to a Web site where you can enter the world of the sea reptiles, go to* **www.usborne-quicklinks.com**

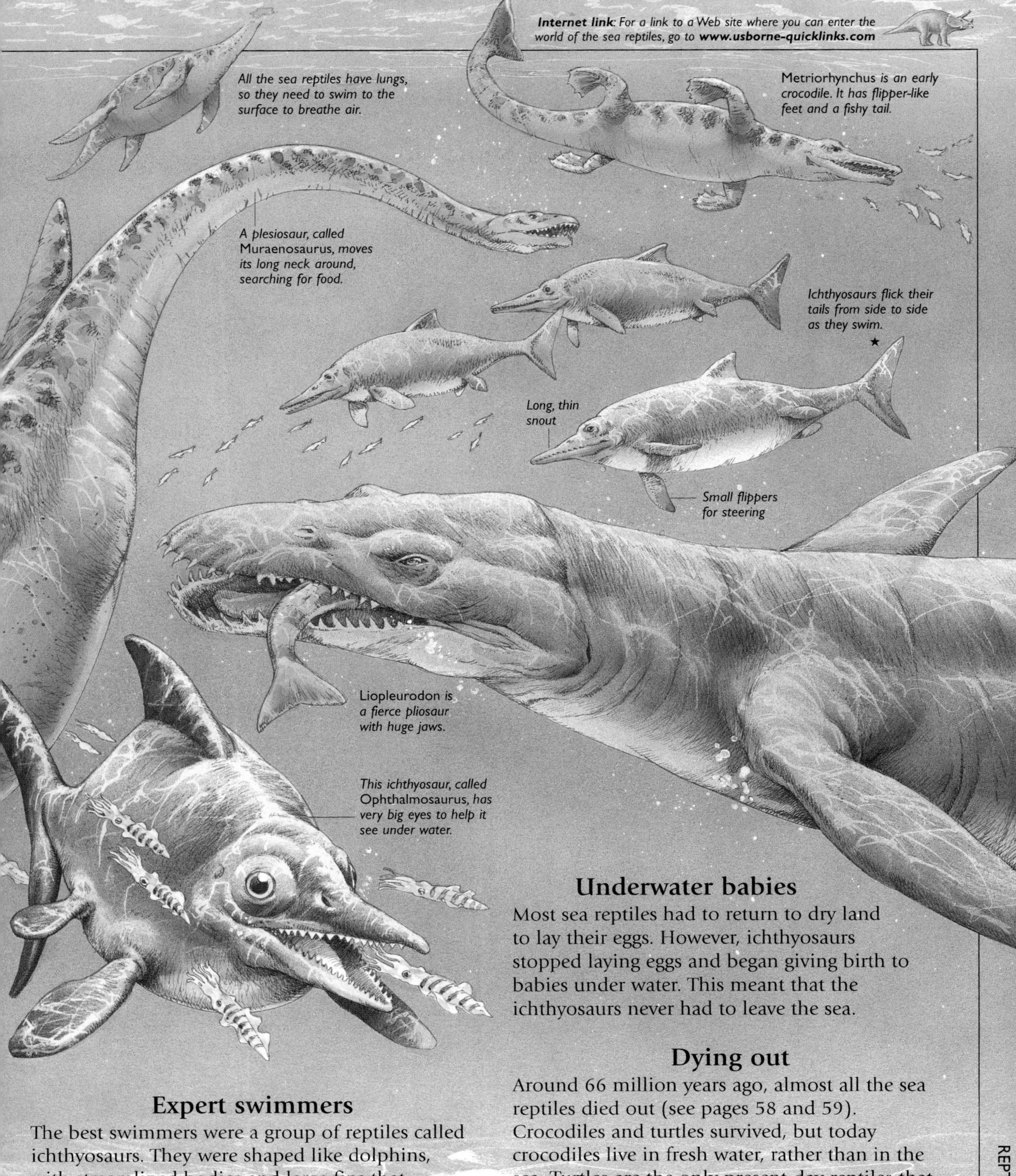

Underwater babies

Most sea reptiles had to return to dry land to lay their eggs. However, ichthyosaurs stopped laying eggs and began giving birth to babies under water. This meant that the ichthyosaurs never had to leave the sea.

Dying out

Around 66 million years ago, almost all the sea reptiles died out (see pages 58 and 59). Crocodiles and turtles survived, but today crocodiles live in fresh water, rather than in the sea. Turtles are the only present-day reptiles that spend their lives in the ocean.

Expert swimmers

The best swimmers were a group of reptiles called ichthyosaurs. They were shaped like dolphins, with streamlined bodies and large fins that helped them to glide swiftly through the ocean.

Flying Reptiles

Around 225 million years ago, during the Triassic Period, some reptiles evolved wings. These flying reptiles are known as pterosaurs. Pterosaurs may have evolved from tree-climbing reptiles which gradually grew wings to help them glide from branch to branch.

★ *Sharovipteryx*, an early gliding reptile, may have been an ancestor of the pterosaurs.

Flap of skin

Another idea is that pterosaurs were descended from reptiles called archosaurs (see page 43). Archosaurs ran along the ground on two legs, and some may have developed wings to help them catch flying insects.

Short-tailed insect-eaters

Near the end of the Jurassic Period, some new, short-tailed pterosaurs appeared. These pterosaurs could twist and turn in the air far more easily than their long-tailed ancestors. They probably caught fast-moving insects.

Pterodactylus slept hanging upside down.

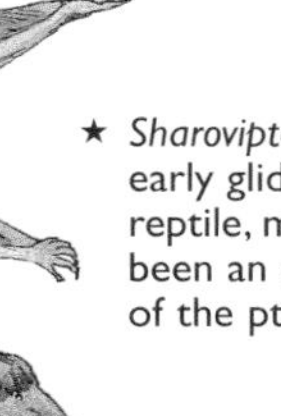

Pterodactylus hunted insects. ★

Like all pterosaurs, Pterodactylus *had excellent eyesight for spotting its prey.*

Each wing was supported by a very long finger.

Leathery wing

Early flyers

By the start of the Jurassic Period, about 200 million years ago, several types of pterosaurs had appeared. They all had big, leathery wings, short necks and long, bony tails. Some of them flew over the ocean, catching fish in their pointed jaws.

Rhamphorhynchus was an early pterosaur that caught fish.

Bony tail

Internet link: *For a link to a Web site where you can fly with the pterosaurs, go to* **www.usborne-quicklinks.com**

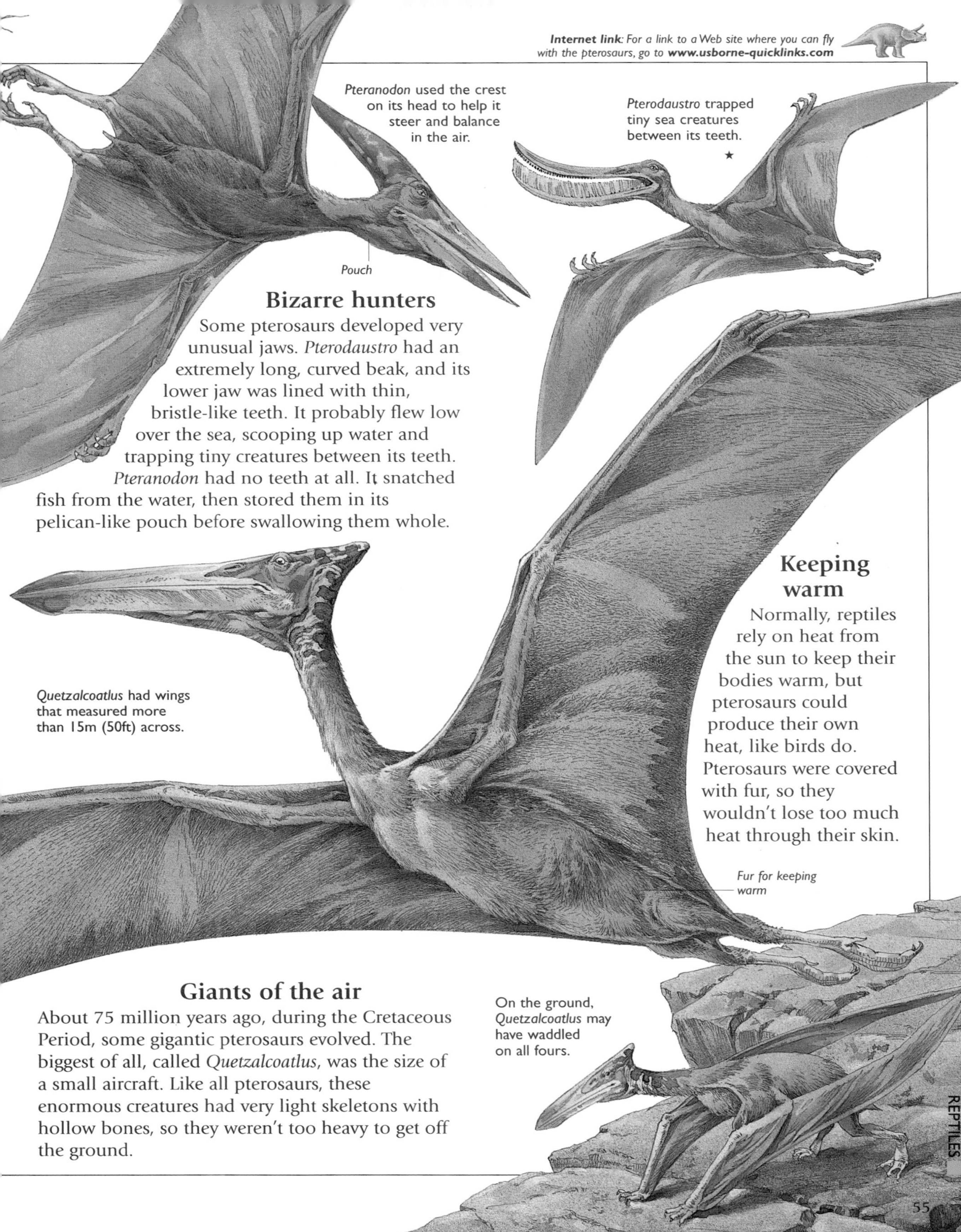

Pteranodon used the crest on its head to help it steer and balance in the air.

Pterodaustro trapped tiny sea creatures between its teeth. ★

Pouch

Bizarre hunters

Some pterosaurs developed very unusual jaws. *Pterodaustro* had an extremely long, curved beak, and its lower jaw was lined with thin, bristle-like teeth. It probably flew low over the sea, scooping up water and trapping tiny creatures between its teeth. *Pteranodon* had no teeth at all. It snatched fish from the water, then stored them in its pelican-like pouch before swallowing them whole.

Keeping warm

Normally, reptiles rely on heat from the sun to keep their bodies warm, but pterosaurs could produce their own heat, like birds do. Pterosaurs were covered with fur, so they wouldn't lose too much heat through their skin.

Quetzalcoatlus had wings that measured more than 15m (50ft) across.

Fur for keeping warm

Giants of the air

About 75 million years ago, during the Cretaceous Period, some gigantic pterosaurs evolved. The biggest of all, called *Quetzalcoatlus*, was the size of a small aircraft. Like all pterosaurs, these enormous creatures had very light skeletons with hollow bones, so they weren't too heavy to get off the ground.

On the ground, *Quetzalcoatlus* may have waddled on all fours.

The First Bird

For many years, experts were not sure how birds evolved. However, they now think that birds are descended from small, meat-eating dinosaurs that ran along the ground on their back legs.

Dinosaurs and birds

Dinosaurs and birds are surprisingly similar. Dinosaurs laid eggs with hard shells, like birds do. Some even made nests, and cared for their young until they were old enough to survive on their own. Many dinosaurs had bird-like skeletons, and some had beaks.

Dinosaurs with feathers

In 1996, scientists discovered a fossil of a dinosaur called *Sinosauropteryx*. This fossil showed that *Sinosauropteryx* had a fluffy covering all over its body.

★ *Sinosauropteryx*

Other fossils have recently been found showing dinosaurs with short feathers on their bodies, tails and arms. Dinosaurs may have evolved feathers to keep themselves warm, or to attract a mate.

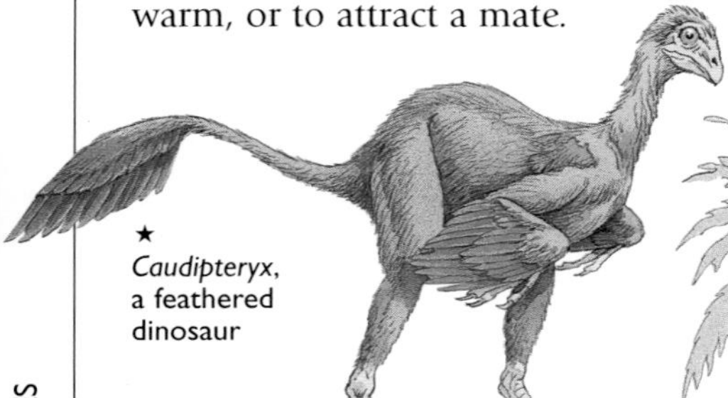

★ *Caudipteryx*, a feathered dinosaur

Flapping and leaping

Experts are not sure how feathered dinosaurs began to fly. They may have started flapping their arms while chasing insects, and accidentally learned to fly. Another explanation is that some dinosaurs learned to climb trees, and then began flying as they leaped between branches.

Early bird

The first true bird we know of appeared about 150 million years ago, during the Jurassic Period. It is called *Archaeopteryx*, which means "ancient feather". Although it had feathers and wings, like birds today, *Archaeopteryx* had teeth and a long, bony tail, like a dinosaur. It also had claws on its wings.

This picture shows *Archaeopteryx* in a forest.

A long tail helps to keep the bird steady in the air.

Into the air

Archaeopteryx was probably too heavy to take off from the ground. Instead, it scampered up trees, then launched itself into the air, hunting for insects. Once in the air, it could flap its wings quite powerfully. However, it may not have been able to change direction very quickly while it was flying.

Pieces of a puzzle

Experts have known about *Archaeopteryx* since 1860, when the first fossil of this creature was found. The recent discovery that some dinosaurs had feathers has finally helped to prove the link between dinosaurs and birds.

★ Fossil of *Archaeopteryx*

The Death of the Dinosaurs

Around 66 million years ago, at the end of the Cretaceous Period, lots of creatures died out completely. All the dinosaurs became extinct, except for some feathered ones that had evolved into birds. Flying reptiles and most sea reptiles also died out. No one is certain why this happened, but scientists have given several different explanations.

Deadly rock?

Near the end of the Cretaceous Period, the Earth was struck by an enormous rock, or meteorite, measuring up to 10km (6 miles) across. As it hit the Earth, the meteorite would have smashed into tiny pieces, surrounding the planet in clouds of dust.

The dust clouds would have made the Earth cold and dark for months, killing off any creatures that needed warmth to survive. Without light, many plants must have died as well, leaving the animals with nothing to eat. The meteorite could also have caused massive earthquakes and giant tidal waves.

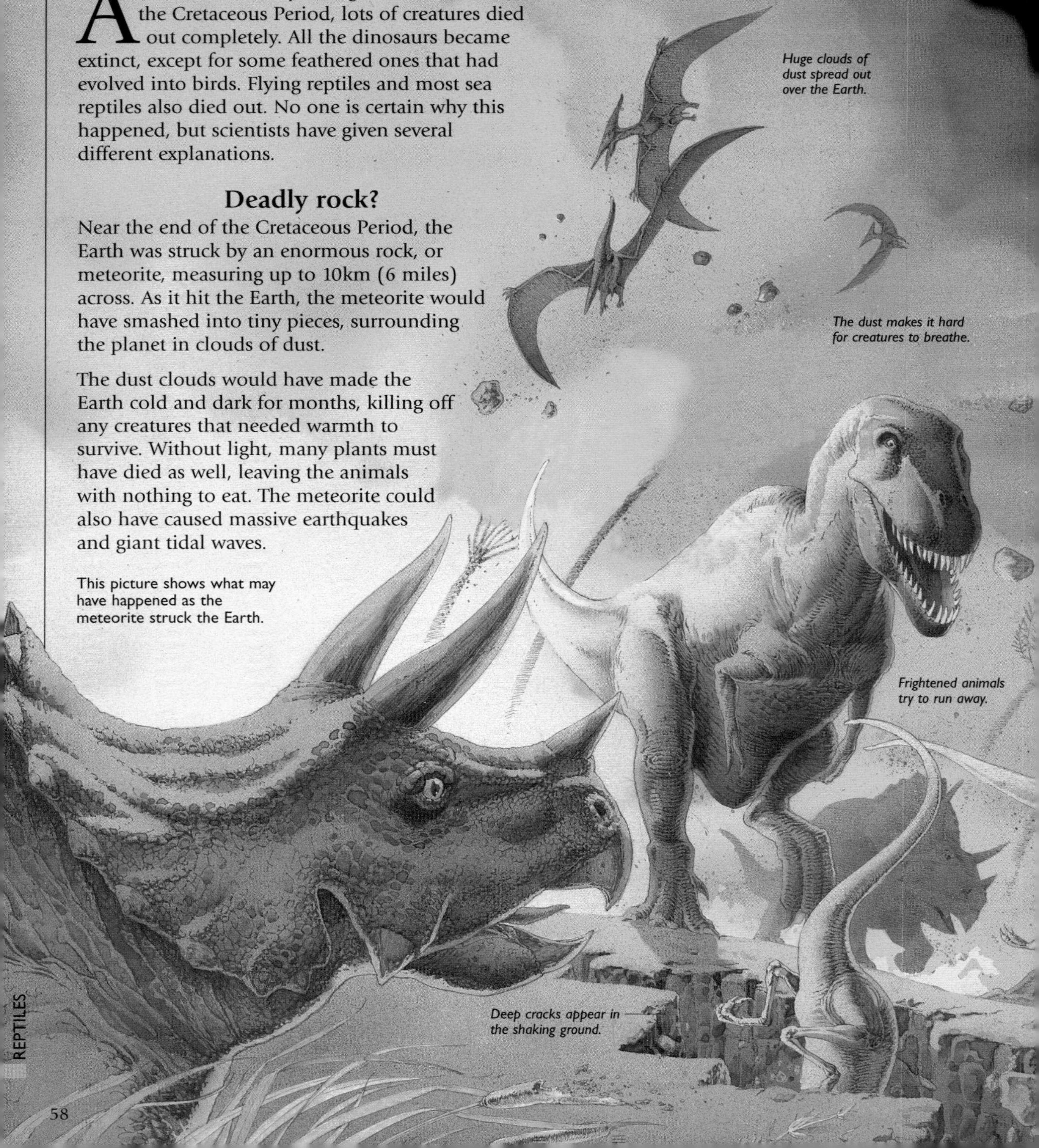

This picture shows what may have happened as the meteorite struck the Earth.

Huge clouds of dust spread out over the Earth.

The dust makes it hard for creatures to breathe.

Frightened animals try to run away.

Deep cracks appear in the shaking ground.

Lava shower?

Another explanation is that many volcanoes all over the world may have erupted at around the same time. The erupting volcanoes would have poured out vast amounts of hot lava (liquid rock) onto the Earth's surface, and sent clouds of dust and poisonous gases high into the air. These gases could also have caused harmful acid rain to fall.

Red-hot lava pouring from a volcano

Climate change?

By 66 million years ago, the weather all over the world had become cooler and more changeable. Dinosaurs relied on heat from the sun to keep themselves warm, and they may not have been able to cope with a changing climate.

Several causes

There is probably no single reason why so many animals died out. The meteorite must have killed off many creatures, but animals may also have been affected by a change in the weather.

The survivors

Mysteriously, some creatures did not die out. Some reptiles, such as lizards and snakes, survived, as well as most birds, insects and amphibians. Other survivors were a group of animals called mammals (see page 60).

Dragonfly (insect)

Some creatures that survived

Gull (bird)

Lizard (reptile)

Rat (mammal)

Many creatures are killed or injured by pieces of flying rock.

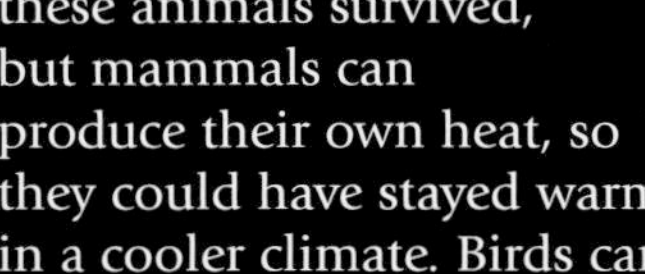

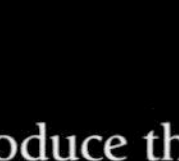

Frog (amphibian)

No one is sure why these animals survived, but mammals can produce their own heat, so they could have stayed warm in a cooler climate. Birds can also produce their own heat, and small reptiles, such as lizards, could have burrowed underground to keep warm.

The First Mammals

Around 200 million years ago, a new group of creatures, called mammals, began to appear on the Earth. The first mammals were tiny, insect-eating animals that looked like mice or shrews.

Megazostrodon, ★ one of the first mammals

What is a mammal?

Mammals have hair or bristles on their skin, and feed their babies with milk. Their bodies are endothermic, or warm-blooded. This means that they can produce their own heat and stay warm, even when the weather gets cold. Mammals also have several different kinds of teeth, which they use for cutting and chewing a variety of foods.

Reptile ancestors

Around 90 million years before the first mammals appeared, a group of reptiles evolved that had large heads, short legs and barrel-shaped bodies. They are known as synapsids (see pages 40 and 41).

By the start of the Triassic Period, some synapsids had become furry and had developed varied teeth. Some of them may even have been able to stay warm all the time, like mammals. Experts believe that the first mammals evolved from small, furry synapsids.

Thrinaxodon, a furry synapsid the size of a small dog ★

Living with the dinosaurs

The first mammals appeared around the same time as the first dinosaurs, but unlike the dinosaurs they did not change or develop fast. For more than 100 million years, until the dinosaurs died out, mammals stayed very small. They scurried around quietly, and usually only came out at night, when most other creatures were asleep.

This picture shows some early mammals in a forest at evening time.

The mammals try to keep out of the dinosaurs' way.

Some plant-eating mammals look like voles.

Mammals have large eyes so they can see at night.

Shrew-like mammal

Egg-laying mammals

The first mammals probably all laid eggs, like their reptile ancestors did. However, unlike reptiles, the mammals fed their young with milk. Egg-laying mammals are called monotremes. Two types of monotremes still survive in Australia and Papua New Guinea. They are the spiny anteaters and the duck-billed platypus.

Duck-billed platypus
★

Mammals with Pouches

The first mammals probably all laid eggs (see page 61), but around 100 million years ago some mammals started giving birth to very tiny babies. The babies crawled up into a pouch on their mother's stomach and continued to grow there.

Mammals with pouches are called marsupials. Today, marsupials are found mainly in Australia, but a few species live in North and South America.

Marsupial babies

Newborn marsupials are no bigger than a bee. The baby stays in its mother's pouch and drinks milk from her nipples until it is fully developed and ready to explore the outside world.

Baby

Pouch

Diagram of a kangaroo, a present-day marsupial ★

Placentals

A few million years after the first marsupials appeared, a different kind of mammal, called a placental, evolved. Placental mothers keep their babies inside their bodies until the babies are large enough to survive on their own. Most mammals alive today are placentals.

Placental babies

Before they are born, placental babies get their food from a part of their mother's body called the placenta. After the babies are born, the mother looks after them and feeds them with milk from her nipples.

Diagram of an elephant, ★ a present-day placental

Mammals spread out

At the time of the early mammals, the Earth's surface looked very different from the way it does today. All the continents were linked to each other, so marsupials and placentals could spread out across the world.

However, at the same time as the mammals were spreading out, the continents were very slowly drifting apart. This meant that some mammals became stranded in different parts of the world.

The marsupial Procoptodon is an ancestor of today's kangaroos.

Marsupials in Australia

Around 85,000 years ago, Australia became an island. By that time, no placentals had reached Australia, but a wide range of marsupials developed there.

This scene shows some of the marsupials that lived in Australia 10,000 years ago.

The rise of the placentals

In many parts of the world, the marsupials died out completely. This happened because placentals are generally better at surviving than marsupials. Tiny babies are safer inside their mother's body than they are in a pouch, and placentals are better at training their young to survive.

Marsupials survive

In a few parts of the world, marsupials have thrived. They have coped especially well in Australia because they are able to stop giving birth when the weather becomes too hot and dry for their young to survive. When the weather gets cooler, they start having babies again.

The Rise of the Mammals

After the dinosaurs died out, around 66 million years ago, life became less dangerous for the mammals. They started to eat a wide range of foods and began to explore new places to live.

By 30 million years ago, a great variety of mammals had evolved. They spread out all over the world, and soon became the fastest, strongest and most intelligent group of creatures on Earth.

Plant-eaters

Many early mammals ate soft plants and leaves. Most of these plant-eaters were slow-moving and clumsy, and some of them grew to be much bigger than any land mammals today.

Rodents

Mammals with very strong teeth gnawed and nibbled at roots, bushes and tree trunks. These gnawing animals are known as rodents. Some of the early rodents looked like rats, rabbits and hares.

Palaeolagus, an early rabbit

Birbalomys, an ancestor of the guinea pig

Stylinodon, a badger-sized rodent ★

Uintatherium, a rhino-sized plant-eater ★

Didolodus, a pig-sized plant-eater

Tree-climbers

One group of mammals, called primates, learned to climb trees. Over millions of years, primates evolved into apes, and then into human beings. Most of the early primates looked like squirrels, monkeys and lemurs.

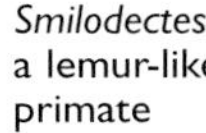

Smilodectes, a lemur-like primate

Branisella, an early monkey ★

Into the air

Some tree-climbing mammals grew flaps of skin between their legs so that they could glide from tree to tree. Around the same time, a group of insect-eaters gradually evolved into bats, with wings of thin skin supported by very long "fingers".

Icaronycteris, an early bat ★

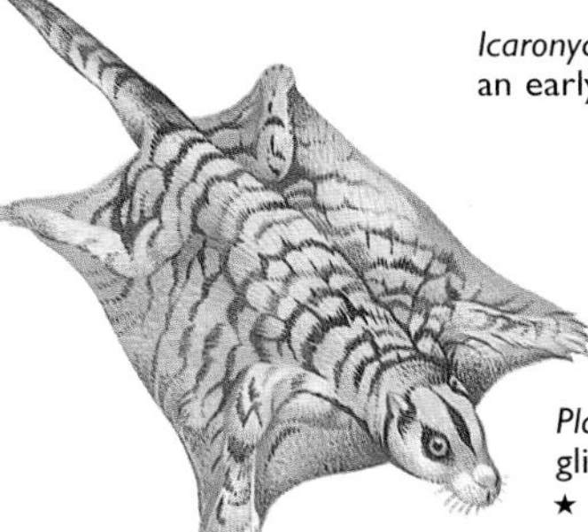

Planetetherium, a gliding mammal ★

Meat-eaters

Some mammals ate meat, instead of plants or insects. Some of these early hunters looked like weasels and otters, and others looked like lions, wolves and bears.

★ *Patriofelis*, an early big cat

Cladosictis, an otter-like meat-eater

Into the oceans

A few land mammals managed to move into the oceans. They developed smooth, streamlined bodies which were suited to life in the water. Slowly, the early sea mammals evolved into whales, dolphins and seals.

Pakicetus, the earliest known whale

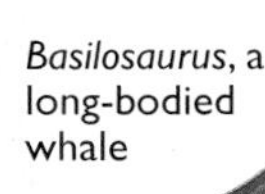

Basilosaurus, a long-bodied whale ★

Hunters and Scavengers

Around 60 million years ago, some mammals began to hunt and eat other animals. At first, these meat-eating mammals were not very fast or clever, but gradually they evolved into expert hunters.

Early meat-eaters

The first meat-eating mammals were called creodonts. They had small brains, short legs and flat feet. This did not matter much, because the plant-eating mammals that they hunted were as unintelligent and slow-moving as they were.

This picture shows the creodont *Sarkastodon* chasing a plant-eater called *Hyrachyus*.

Like most creodonts, Sarkastodon *cannot run very fast.*

Sarkastodon's *teeth are not very good at tearing up meat.*

Scavengers

Some of the early meat-eaters ate dead animals that they found, instead of going hunting. Animals that do this are called scavengers. Scavengers developed special teeth for crushing bones, so that they could eat the soft bone marrow inside.

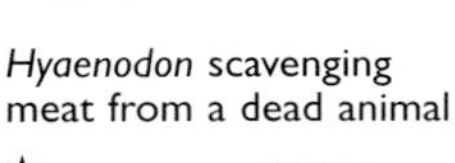

Hyaenodon scavenging meat from a dead animal

★

Better hunters

Gradually, some plant-eating mammals became very good at running and started to live in herds (see pages 68 and 69). This meant that the animals that hunted them had to change too.

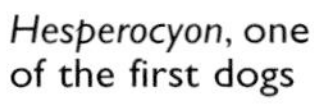

Hesperocyon, one of the first dogs

Cerdocyon, an ancestor of the fox

A new group of meat-eating mammals evolved that were fast-moving, powerful and cunning. These mammals, known as carnivores, had excellent hearing and eyesight, and a strong sense of smell. Today's dogs and cats are descended from these early carnivores.

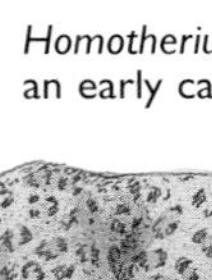

Homotherium, an early cat

Dinofelis, a panther-like cat

Hunting in teams

Around six million years ago, early dogs and wolves began to hunt in teams, or packs. This meant that they could hunt animals much larger than themselves. Some big cats, such as lions, also hunted in teams.

Today, wolves still hunt together in packs. These wolves are howling to other members of their pack to show that they are ready to start hunting.

Chasing and stalking

Dogs chased after their prey until the hunted animals were exhausted, but cats hunted in a different way. First, they stalked their prey (followed it very quietly), and then they pounced on it swiftly and suddenly.

Teeth and claws

Carnivores developed sharp claws for holding their prey, and long, pointed teeth for tearing up meat. Some big cats, known as sabre-toothed cats, had incredibly long, blade-like teeth, or fangs.

In this scene, a sabre-toothed cat, called *Smilodon*, is stalking its prey. ★

Powerful neck and shoulders

Smilodon *uses its curved fangs for stabbing its prey and tearing up meat.*

Another cat prowls through the long grass.

Smilodon *pads very quietly on its soft paws.*

Sharp claws for grasping prey

Plant-eaters' Problems

The first plant-eating mammals (or herbivores) were slow-moving creatures with small brains. Most of them were the size of today's pigs or badgers, but a few were incredibly tall and heavy.

This is *Indricotherium*, the largest mammal that ever lived on land. ★

Indricotherium *munches leaves from the tops of trees.*

Indricotherium *is 8m (26ft) tall and weighs as much as four elephants.*

The growth of the grasslands

Around 40 million years ago, the weather all over the world began to get cooler. Gradually, most of the tropical forests were replaced by grassy plains. The herbivores were forced to eat grass, which is tough to chew and hard to digest, and many animals died out because they couldn't cope with their new food.

Horns and tusks

The early herbivores wandered through forests nibbling leaves and plants. They were hunted by meat-eating mammals, and some of them developed strange-looking horns and tusks to defend themselves against predators (hunters).

Brontotherium had two huge horns on its nose. ★

Eating grass

Slowly, new kinds of herbivores evolved that were able to eat grass. Animals that eat grass are known as grazers. They have flat teeth with ridges that are very good at grinding. Grazers chew and swallow their food several times, bringing partly digested food back up into their mouths, so that they can chew it again. This repeated chewing of food is known as "chewing the cud".

Roaming the plains

The grasslands provided plenty of food and the number of grazers increased rapidly. By 25 million years ago, the first deer, cattle, sheep and antelope had all appeared on the plains. They lived in large groups, or herds, that roamed over the grasslands.

This picture shows a herd of *Illingoceros* (early antelope) being chased by wolves.

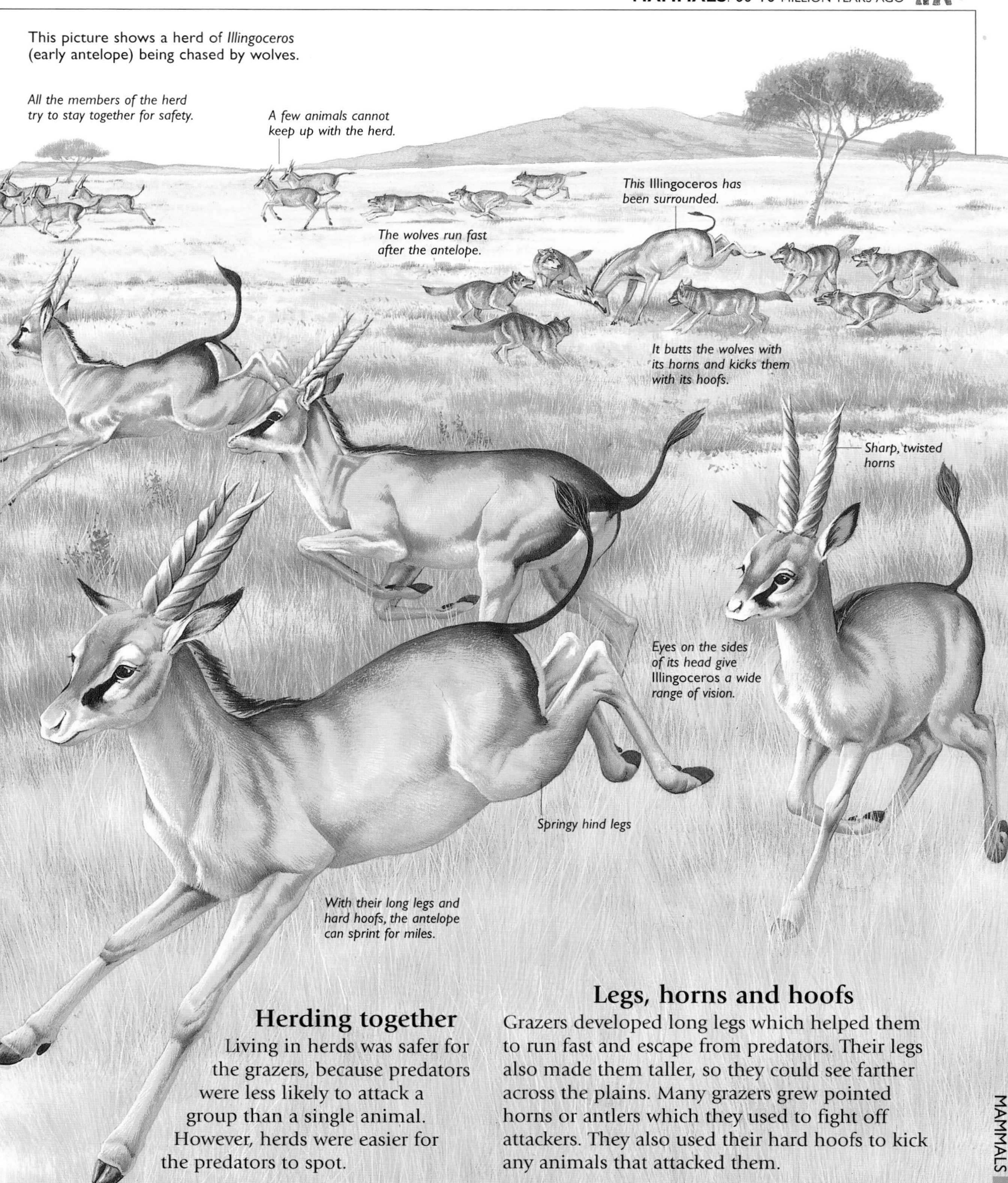

Herding together

Living in herds was safer for the grazers, because predators were less likely to attack a group than a single animal. However, herds were easier for the predators to spot.

Legs, horns and hoofs

Grazers developed long legs which helped them to run fast and escape from predators. Their legs also made them taller, so they could see farther across the plains. Many grazers grew pointed horns or antlers which they used to fight off attackers. They also used their hard hoofs to kick any animals that attacked them.

The Horse's Tale

The first horses lived around 50 million years ago, when the Earth was covered with forests. They were much smaller than horses today (about the size of a small dog) and they wandered through the forests, nibbling soft leaves. Sometimes, the horses were attacked by vicious giant birds.

This picture shows a giant bird, called *Diatryma*, chasing *Hyracotherium*, the earliest known species of horse.

★

Diatryma is a powerful runner, but it can't fly.

Disappearing forests

Gradually, the forests where the early horses lived were replaced by vast, grassy plains (see page 68). This meant that the horses had to change in order to survive.

Bigger and faster

By 35 million years ago, horses had grown longer legs for running on the plains, and had developed stronger teeth for chewing tough grass. They also lost a toe from each of their front feet and began to run on their strong middle toes. This new way of running made them lighter on their feet.

Diatryma is 2m (6ft) tall.

Hyracotherium is only 40cm (15in) tall.

Short neck

Small, blunt teeth

Hyracotherium has four toes on its front feet and three toes on its hind feet.

The horse's toes spread out to stop it from sinking into soft ground.

Living on the plains

By around 10 million years ago, horses had grown to the size of small ponies. They lived in herds on the open plains and were very good at chewing and digesting grass. The horses had to run very fast to escape from wild cats and dogs, but they could also use their hoofs to fight off attackers.

A group of *Merychippus* (early horses) on the plains

The pattern on the horses' coats makes them hard to spot in long grass.

Sometimes, two males fight each other to see which one is stronger.

Long, powerful neck

Very small side toes

Strong middle toe capped with a tough hoof

Long, slender legs for running fast

These horses have sharp front teeth for cutting grass, and strong back teeth for chewing it.

A new kind of horse

About five million years ago, a new kind of horse, called *Equus,* appeared in North America. These horses were larger than *Merychippus* and each of their feet had a single, hoof-covered toe. They spread from America to Asia and Europe, and eventually to Africa and India. *Equus* is the only kind of horse living in the world today.

These pictures show how horses evolved over 45 million years. ★

Hyracotherium *(50 million years ago)*

Mesohippus *(35 million years ago)*

Merychippus *(10 million years ago)*

Equus *(5 million years ago)*

Animals of South America

Around 50 million years after the first mammals appeared, the area of land that is now South America became cut off from North America.

Even though the mammals of South America developed completely separately from any other animals, many of them looked like mammals from other parts of the world. This is because creatures evolve to suit their surroundings, so animals living in the same kind of surroundings tend to evolve in a similar way.

Mammals with pouches

A wide range of marsupials (mammals with pouches) evolved in South America, although almost no marsupials live there today. Most of these creatures were hunters and many of them looked like meat-eating mammals from other parts of the world.

Thomashuxleya looked like a warthog.

Macrauchenia had a camel-like body and a short trunk.

Diadiaphorus looked like a horse.

Theosodon was an ancestor of the llama.

Toxodon looked like a hippo.

Argyrolagus was a marsupial that looked like a kangaroo rat.

Thylacosmilus was a marsupial that looked like a big cat.

Plant-eaters and gnawers

As well as the marsupials, many kinds of placental mammals (see page 62) developed in South America. These animals ate soft plants and grasses or gnawed at roots and branches. Most of them looked like plant-eaters or rodents (gnawers) from other parts of the world, but a few, like *Macrauchenia*, were very unusual.

Protypotherium looked like a rabbit.

Strange creatures

Two kinds of South American mammals were completely different from any other animals in the world. These were the sloths and the glyptodonts. Sloths had long, thick hair and moved extremely slowly, and glyptodonts had a bony dome on their backs to protect them.

Changing places

Around five million years ago, North and South America became joined by a bridge of land. Some South American mammals, such as sloths, glyptodonts and porcupines, began to move north, while northern mammals, such as rabbits, horses and big cats, began spreading south.

The North American porcupine originally came from South America.

★ *Megatherium* was a giant sloth that lived on the ground.

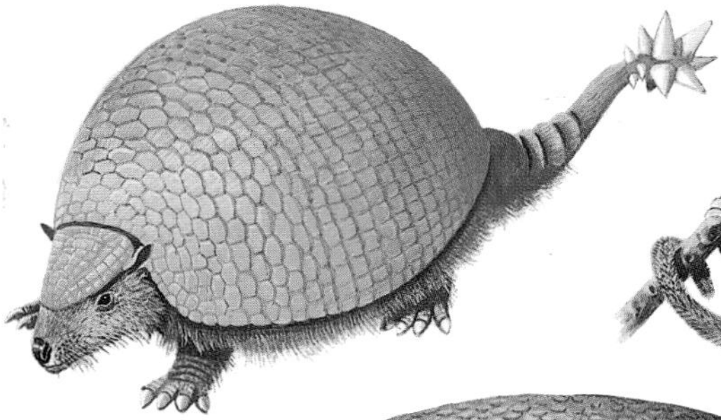

Daedicurus was a glyptodont with a viciously spiked tail.

Hapalops was a tree-climbing sloth.

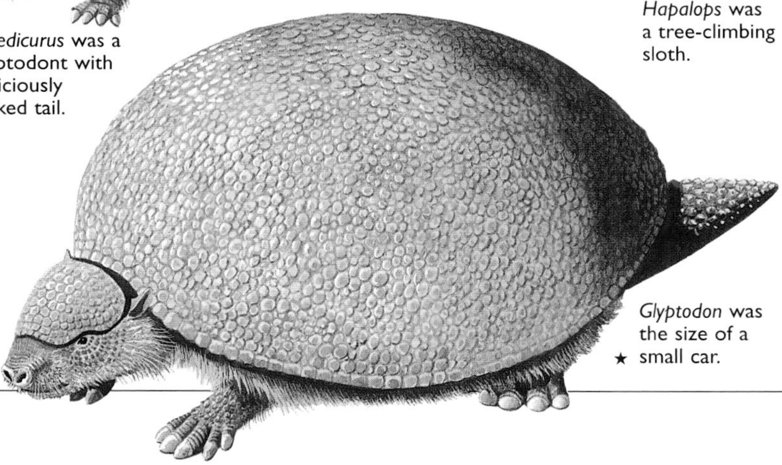

★ *Glyptodon* was the size of a small car.

Dying out

Not long after North and South America became joined, many species of South American mammals died out. Experts used to think that this happened because the mammals of the south could not compete with the northern mammals. However, many southern species were already disappearing by the time the northern mammals arrived in the south.

Changes in the weather

No one knows why so many South American mammals became extinct. However, around the time that North and South America joined together, the weather all over the world became very changeable. Some southern mammals may have died out because, unlike the mammals of the north, they were not used to changes in their climate.

The Elephant's Story

The earliest ancestors of today's elephants were long-bodied, pig-like creatures that lived in the swamps of Africa around 40 million years ago. They wallowed around in the water, feeding on soft-leaved plants.

The early elephant *Moeritherium* spent most of its life in the water.

Trunks and tusks

Over millions of years, the early elephants became taller. This made it hard for them to reach down to the plants that they ate. Gradually, their upper lips and noses grew longer and developed into a short trunk.

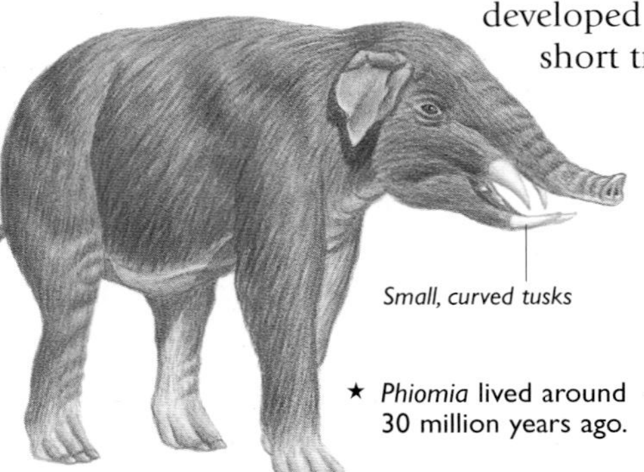

★ *Phiomia* lived around 30 million years ago.

The elephants used their trunks to suck up water and shovel plants into their mouths. They also grew curved tusks which helped them to scoop up their food.

Extraordinary elephants

Many different kinds of elephants evolved in Africa, Asia, Europe and America, and some of them had teeth, tusks and trunks that grew in strange shapes. However, around five million years ago, an elephant called *Stegodon* evolved which looked very similar to elephants today.

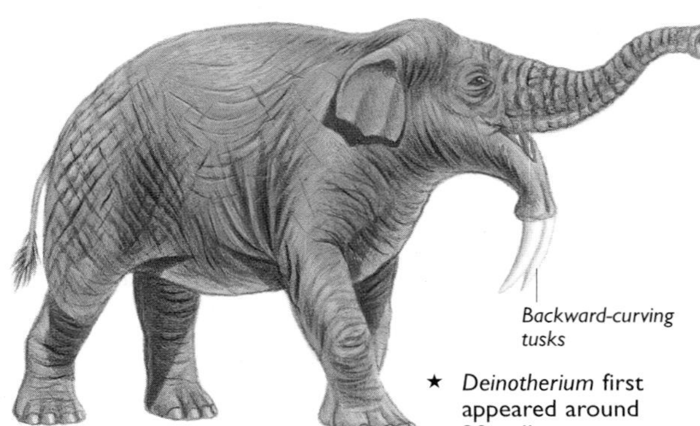

★ *Deinotherium* first appeared around 20 million years ago.

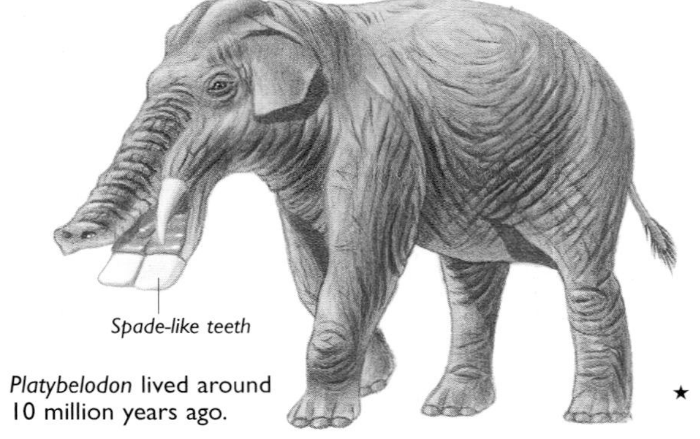

Platybelodon lived around 10 million years ago. ★

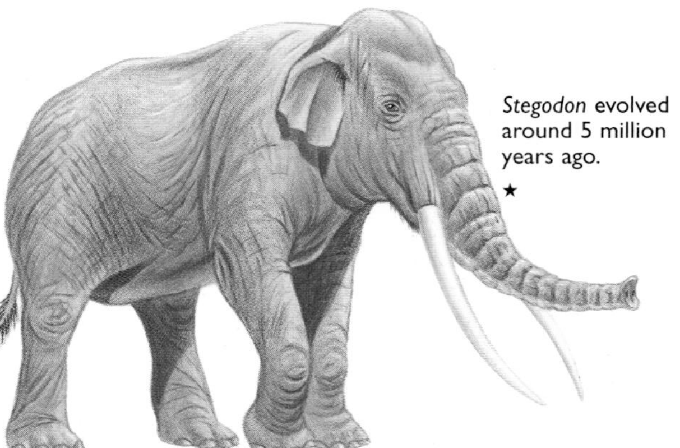

Stegodon evolved around 5 million years ago. ★

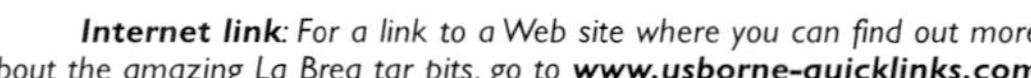

Mammoths drowned in tar

Around two million years ago, a group of enormous elephants, called mammoths, appeared. Mammoths measured up to 4.5m (15ft) tall, and had very long, curved tusks.

Fossils of mammoths and other animals have been found at La Brea, near Los Angeles in the USA. Around 15,000 years ago, there were several pits filled with tar in this area. The tar became covered with rainwater, and many animals thought the pits were drinking pools. Hundreds of creatures became stuck in the tar and drowned.

Vulture

Mammoths come to the pool to drink.

Wolves and wild cats feed on any animals that have drowned.

This picture shows a tar pit at La Brea.

Elephant ancestors

Around 10,000 years ago, the mammoths died out. This may have happened because the weather became too warm for them or because they were hunted by humans. Two groups of elephants survived in Africa and Asia. They were the ancestors of today's elephants.

African elephants like these are descended from elephants that lived in Africa about four million years ago.

Animals of the Ice Age

Several times in the history of the Earth, large parts of the world have been buried under thick sheets of ice. Each time, the ice has stayed frozen for thousands of years, and these long, freezing periods are known as ice ages.

The last ice age

The last ice age began around 100,000 years ago and ended around 10,000 years ago. During this time, large areas of land in the northern half of the world were covered in ice.

This map shows the world during the last ice age.

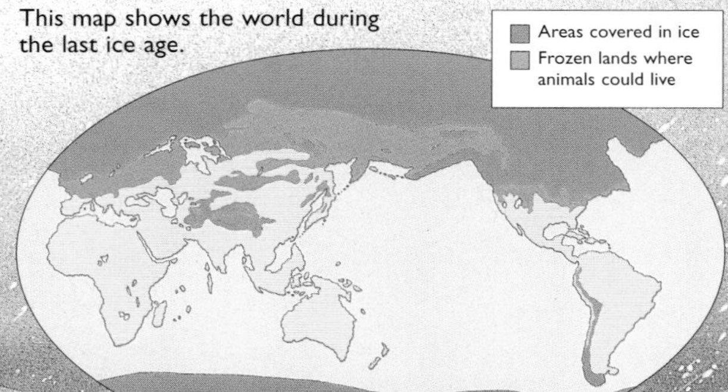

Frozen mammoths

This baby mammoth was discovered in the ice of Siberia in 1977.

Sometimes, animals fell into ponds which later froze solid. The animals' bodies were trapped in ice and could not rot away, so they were preserved for thousands of years. Several woolly mammoths have been found in the ice of Siberia, in northern Russia. Some of these mammoths were covered with hair, and some still had their last meal preserved in their stomachs.

Woolly mammoths

Living on the edge

At the start of the last ice age, many animals moved to warmer areas, but some stayed in the frozen lands near the edge of the ice sheets. Very cold places where the ground is always frozen are known as tundra. The animals of the tundra grew thick coats to keep themselves warm. Most of them ate mosses, lichens and small bushes, but some were hunters.

This scene shows some of the animals that lived in the tundra.

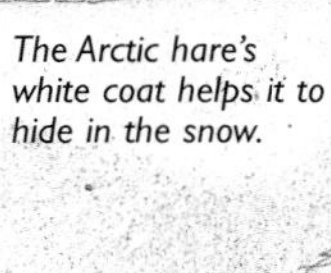
The Arctic hare's white coat helps it to hide in the snow.

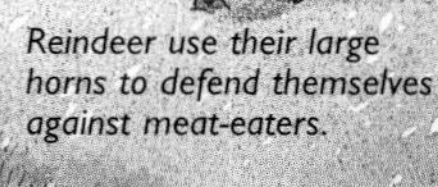
Reindeer use their large horns to defend themselves against meat-eaters.

The Arctic fox is a cunning hunter.

Between the ice ages

The last ice age was one of a series of ice ages that began two million years ago. In between these freezing periods, the weather became very warm. Thick forests grew where the ice sheets had been, and animals that were used to the cold were forced to travel to cooler areas. Meanwhile, heat-loving animals, such as hippos and lions, were able to live in places as far north as Europe and North America.

Disappearing animals

At the end of the last ice age, around 10,000 years ago, many animals died out. No one knows exactly why this happened, but one reason must have been the change in the weather. Some animals, such as mammoths, were hunted by early humans, and this could be another reason why they disappeared.

Icy winds whistle across the tundra.

The woolly rhinoceros is covered with thick hair.

Lichens and mosses grow on rocks.

Bears shelter in caves when the weather becomes very cold.

Musk oxen roam the tundra, searching for plants to eat.

Small plants and bushes poke up through the snow.

Apes and Monkeys

Apes, monkeys and humans all belong to a group of mammals known as primates. The first primates appeared on the Earth about 66 million years ago. They were small, squirrel-like creatures that scurried around in the trees.

Plesiadapis, an early primate ★

Sharp claws

This picture shows monkeys and apes in a forest around 14 million years ago.

Mesopithecus *monkeys live in the treetops.*

This monkey is teaching its young to climb.

Gigantopithecus *is an enormous ape. It is around 2.5m (8ft) tall.*

Gigantopithecus *lives on the forest floor. It is too heavy to climb trees.*

Fingers and toes

Gradually, some early primates began to change. Instead of claws, they grew fingers and toes with sensitive tips. Fingers and toes were useful for judging the thickness of branches and for holding onto them tightly.

Seeing in 3-D

Primates developed much better eyesight than most other mammals. Each of their eyes saw a different picture, and their brains put the pictures together to make a three-dimensional image. Seeing in 3-D helped primates to judge distances when they leaped from one branch to another.

Early monkeys and apes

By around 30 million years ago, some primates had evolved into the first monkeys and apes. Even the earliest monkeys were expert tree-climbers, and some monkeys developed long, curling tails for grasping branches. Apes were bigger and stronger than monkeys. They had broad chests, flexible shoulders and strong arms, which helped them to swing from tree to tree.

Learning to survive

Climbing and balancing are difficult things to do, and apes and monkeys evolved big brains to help them cope with life in the trees. They began to live in large groups, and to look after each other. They also spent a long time bringing up their babies and teaching them how to survive.

Climbing and walking

Over millions of years, different apes and monkeys learned to live in different parts of the trees, so that they could all find enough food to eat. Some even left the trees and started living on the ground.

When they were on the ground, some apes sometimes walked on two feet instead of crawling on all fours. This left their hands free for carrying food. However, they couldn't stand up straight, which made it hard to walk very far on two feet.

This monkey is cleaning another monkey's fur. This is called grooming.

Monkeys and apes use their fingers and thumbs to make a tight grip.

This Dryopithecus *ape is using its strong arms to swing between branches.*

This ape, called Ramapithecus, *may have been able to walk for short distances on two feet.*

Ramapithecus *uses its hands to carry food.*

On the ground, Dryopithecus *walks on all fours.*

Changing faces

Most early primates had long noses, or snouts, for sniffing out their food, and long, pointed teeth for nibbling fruit and insects. However, some later apes relied on their eyes instead of their noses to find food, so their snouts gradually became shorter. Their teeth also became shorter and flatter, so they could grind up the tough plants and grasses that grew on the ground.

Southern Apes

Over five million years ago, some apes in Africa started learning to walk upright. Apes that walk upright are called hominids. We are hominids too, but the earliest ones were very different from us. They were much shorter than us, and had small brains and apelike faces.

The earliest known hominid is called *Australopithecus*, which means "southern ape". It lived from around five million to a million years ago.

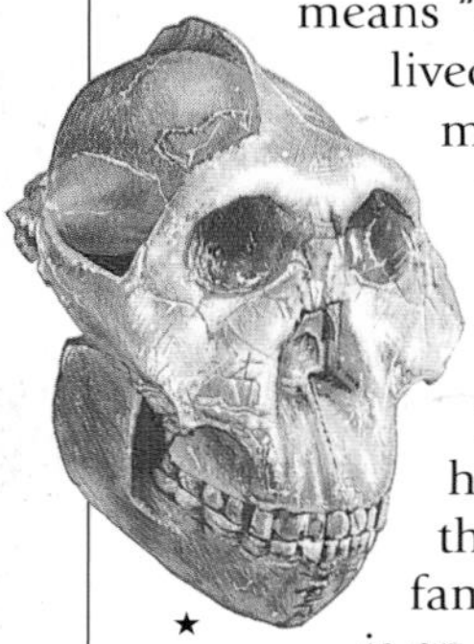

Australopithecus skull

Experts dig up new hominid bones all the time. The most famous set of bones is an *Australopithecus* skeleton from Hadar, in Ethiopia. The skeleton has been named "Lucy".

Finding footprints

At Laetoli, in Tanzania, experts have found a trail of *Australopithecus* footprints preserved in volcanic ash. This proves that Lucy and her friends had started walking upright.

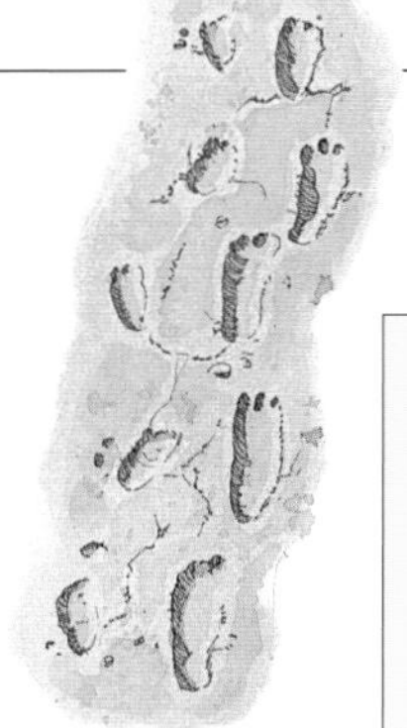

The footprints at Laetoli

Swinging through trees

At first, *Australopithecus* spent a lot of time in the trees. It had long, curved fingers and toes, and long arms, which helped it to grip branches and swing between them. However, its knees were like ours, which shows that it could also walk upright.

This picture shows a group of early *Australopithecus*.

Most Australopithecus *are less than 1.5m (5ft) tall.*

The group lives at the edge of a thick forest.

Walking on two feet leaves the hands free for carrying things.

Stones are useful for cracking open tough-skinned fruit.

Australopithecus *has a hairy body and an apelike face.*

Why did apes stand up?

Nobody is sure why some apes began walking upright, but one explanation is the weather.

Between seven and four million years ago, the Earth's climate got much cooler. In East Africa, the forests where *Australopithecus* lived began to disappear. It was harder to find fruit and leaves to eat, so *Australopithecus* had to travel farther to find food. Using two legs was less tiring than using four.

Standing upright also made it easier for *Australopithecus* to spot dangerous animals in the tall grass at the edge of the forest.

Different types

Eventually, *Australopithecus* seems to have evolved into several different types. Some are known as "gracile" (slender), while others are known as "robust" (large and strong). The "robust" *Australopithecus* had very powerful jaws, which allowed it to eat tough grasses and roots.

Some of the group are eating leaves and fruit from the trees.

Beyond the forest are large areas of grassland, called savannah.

Long, powerful arms

Long, curved toes and fingers for grasping branches

Standing upright, Australopithecus *can see a wild cat lying in wait.*

This group of Australopithecus *has walked across the grassland to find food.*

Some of the group use sticks to break open a termites' nest, so they can eat the insects.

The Tool-makers

Around two and a half million years ago, a new species of hominid, called *Homo habilis,* evolved in Africa. For more than a million years, it lived alongside *Australopithecus* (see pages 80 and 81).

Homo habilis had a bigger brain than *Australopithecus*, and was more skilled. (Its name means "skilled man" in Latin.) It is sometimes known as "handy man" and is often thought of as the first human.

New skills

Australopithecus picked up sticks and stones and used them as tools, but *Homo habilis* could make its own tools. It made thin stone tools (called flakes) for cutting, and larger ones (called choppers) for smashing hard objects, such as nuts. These tools were made from flint, which is easy to shape.

Shaping stones

Homo habilis made its tools by striking two rocks together. A long thin stone, called a hammerstone, was used to chip sharp flakes from a larger stone. This is known as stone knapping.

A group of *Homo habilis* making and using tools ★

Sharpening sticks

Homo habilis probably made a wooden tool, called a digging stick, by sharpening one end of a branch with a stone flake. It may have used the sharpened sticks to dig up roots to eat.

Stealing meat

Although *Homo habilis* probably did no hunting, it did eat meat. Groups of *Homo habilis* used sharp stone tools to remove meat from the bodies of dead animals that they found. Their tools helped them to work fast, so they could get away before any wild animals attacked them.

This picture shows a group of *Homo habilis* stripping meat from a dead elephant.

Starting to wander

Eating meat allowed *Homo habilis* to travel farther than *Australopithecus*. Because it no longer had to live so close to plants and fruit, it could explore wider areas. Its new diet also gave it more energy and helped its brain grow bigger.

The Coming of Fire

A million years after *Homo habilis* appeared (see page 82), a new hominid with an even bigger brain evolved in Africa. This species walked completely upright and is known as *Homo erectus*, which means "upright man" in Latin. *Homo erectus* people learned how to use fire, which gave them much more control over their lives.

Finding fire

Homo erectus people probably could not light fires themselves. Instead, they may have found fires that had started when lightning struck dry grass. They probably carried a burning branch away to a cave or a camp, then kept the same fire burning for days, or even weeks.

This picture shows *Homo erectus* people using fire in their cave.

Safe and warm

Fire kept *Homo erectus* people warm at night. It could also be used as a weapon against dangerous animals, which were scared away by the blaze.

Cooking food

Homo erectus people discovered that meat and plants were tastier when they were heated, and they began to cook their food. Cooked food is easier to chew, so their teeth and jaws gradually became smaller. As they ate more meat, their bodies grew stronger and taller, and their brains became bigger.

Lighting the darkness

By keeping a fire burning, *Homo erectus* people could see clearly after it got dark. This meant that, unlike earlier hominids, they did not have to go to sleep when the sun went down, but could continue working at night.

Better tools

Homo erectus people used fire to make better tools. They hardened the ends of wooden spears by holding them in the flames, and heated stones to make them easier to shape. They made the heated stones into tools called hand axes, which had very sharp edges.

Hand axe ★

People can work at night using the light of the fire.

People keep warm by the fire.

This woman is cooking meat.

This man is keeping the fire going with branches.

These plants have been cooked in the fire.

People use hand axes for cutting up meat.

Wooden spears hardening in the fire

This woman is pushing a rock into the fire. Heated rocks are easier to shape.

Making homes

A fire provided a place where *Homo erectus* people could gather. They could make a safe home around a fire anywhere, and so they began to settle in lots of different places. Gradually, they spread out farther and farther from Africa (see page 86).

The First Explorers

For over three million years, hominids lived only in eastern and southern Africa. This changed around 1.8 million years ago, when *Homo erectus* people began to move into new areas.

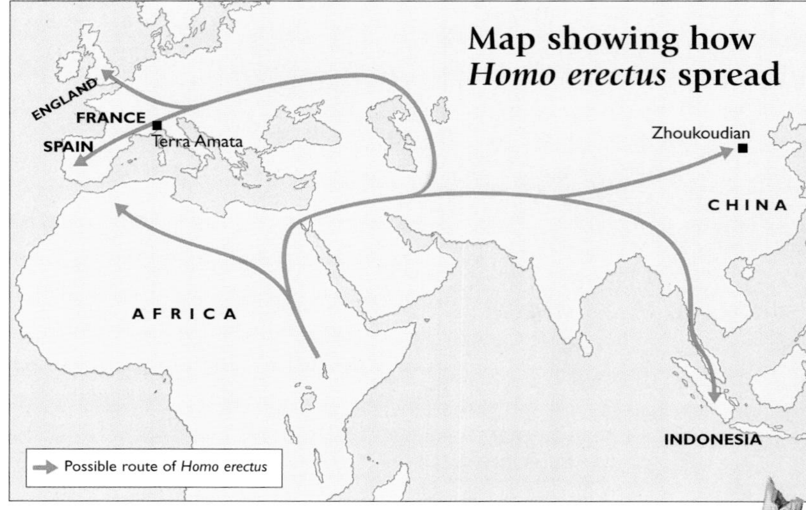

Out of Africa

Gradually, *Homo erectus* people spread out, until they had explored most of Africa. Some groups moved slowly east and eventually reached Indonesia and China.

Life in a Chinese cave

One group settled in a large cave near Zhoukoudian, in China. *Homo erectus* people lived there for 250,000 years.

Skulls and antlers

The people at Zhoukoudian ate meat from deer and horses, which they may have hunted. They made stone tools by hammering rocks with deer antlers, and also made drinking bowls from deer skulls.

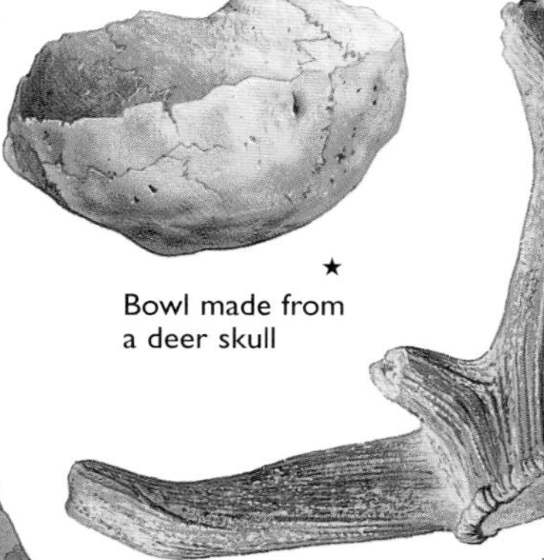

Bowl made from a deer skull

Part of a deer antler used as a hammer

This scene shows *Homo erectus* people in the Zhoukoudian cave.

Discovering Europe

Homo erectus people probably arrived in Europe about 500,000 years ago. They moved around from place to place, hunting, fishing and gathering plants to eat. Eventually, they reached as far west as Spain and as far north as England.

Life on the coast

Some groups of *Homo erectus* people returned each year to stay in the same place. One group stayed every spring at a place called Terra Amata, on the south coast of France, where they may have built shelters from branches. They used wooden spears to hunt animals and catch fish.

Using fire

Homo erectus people could use fire to keep themselves warm. This meant they could move out of Africa, and into cooler areas. Their fires also kept wild animals away, so fewer people were killed, and their numbers started to grow.

Why did they travel?

Experts think that *Homo erectus* people had to travel to find enough food, because there were more people to feed. They hunted wandering animals, and the animals may have led them to new places.

This picture shows *Homo erectus* people hunting deer at Terra Amata.

Hunters of the Ice Age

Around 200,000 years ago, a new kind of people started to evolve from *Homo erectus*. These new people had bigger brains than earlier people, and are known as *Homo sapiens*, which means "wise man" in Latin.

The Neanderthal people were an early type of *Homo sapiens*. They are named after the Neander Valley in Germany, where their bones were first found. Neanderthals appeared in Europe and western Asia during an ice age, when a large part of the Earth was covered in ice and snow (see page 76).

Big and clever

For a long time, people thought Neanderthals were unintelligent, apelike creatures, but experts now think differently. Neanderthals had strong, muscular bodies and a ridge of bone above their eyes, but otherwise they were very like us. Some of them had brains that were bigger than ours.

Finding food

In the long, frozen winters of the ice age, it was hard to find plants to eat, so Neanderthals ate a lot of meat. They stripped meat from dead animals that they found, and they also hunted animals, such as horses and reindeer.

Hunting with fire

Mammoths and rhinos were too dangerous to approach but, like all animals, they were scared of fire. Sometimes, Neanderthal hunters chased these huge animals with burning branches and forced them over the edge of a cliff. The animals were killed, and the hunters could then remove the meat from the dead bodies.

This scene shows Neanderthal hunters chasing mammoths over a cliff.

The mammoths are terrified by the fire and the men's shouts.

Keeping warm

During the freezing winters, Neanderthals needed warm clothes to keep out the cold. They probably made simple tunics by knotting animal skins together. Neanderthals often sheltered in caves, but out in the open they may have made shelters from branches and animal skins.

New tools

Neanderthals made better tools than earlier people. They had different tools for hunting, cutting food, and shaping wood. They also used their powerful jaws as extra tools, for tearing meat from animal bones and for cleaning animal skins.

Early Families

Neanderthals were more intelligent than earlier people, and they developed a more organized way of life. This helped them to survive in the freezing cold of the ice age. They worked together in family groups and cared for anyone in their family who was sick or injured.

Helping the injured

Hunting wild animals was very dangerous, and injuries were common. Some men were so badly hurt that they could never hunt again. These men were probably looked after by their families for the rest of their lives.

Gifts for the dead?

Some experts think that the Neanderthals believed in life after death. Animal horns, stone tools and pollen from flowers have all been found in Neanderthal graves. These objects may have been placed in the graves as gifts to help dead people in the afterlife.

In this picture, a dead Neanderthal is being buried by his family and friends.

Burying the dead

Neanderthals were the first people to bury their dead, instead of just leaving the bodies to decay. They dug a hole with sharpened sticks and stones, then laid the body carefully inside it.

Starting to talk

No one really knows when people started speaking, but some experts think that Neanderthals were the first people who learned how to talk. They probably only used simple words, with lots of hand signals as well. Being able to communicate helped the Neanderthals to work together and to organize hunts. They were also able to warn each other of danger.

This scene shows Neanderthals running to warn their family that wolves are approaching.

Lots of people gather to bury the man.

The end of the Neanderthals

Around 40,000 years ago, the Neanderthals began to die out. A new type of people, who were very good at hunting, had appeared in Europe and Asia (see pages 92 to 95).

The new hunters gradually drove the Neanderthals away from the best hunting areas. Many Neanderthals starved to death, and others became weak and died of illnesses. By 30,000 years ago, they had died out completely.

The First Modern People

Around 150,000 years ago, a new type of *Homo sapiens* evolved. This species, known as *Homo sapiens sapiens*, is the one that all human beings belong to today. All modern people have a large, rounded skull, a straight forehead and a small jaw.

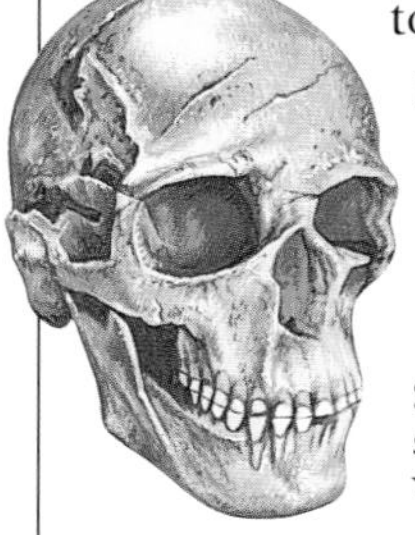

Skull of *Homo sapiens sapiens* ★

Hunting and gathering

The first modern people lived by hunting animals and gathering plants to eat. They kept moving from one place to another to find food. People who live like this are called hunter-gatherers. Some hunter-gatherers returned to the same place at the same time each year, and stayed there until the food ran out, before moving on.

Working together

These early people could talk just as well as people can today. Talking helped them to work together in big groups, or tribes. Each tribe probably had a leader who organized hunts.

This scene shows how a tribe of people may have lived 40,000 years ago.

These people are using slings to kill sea birds.

Seal hunters

These people are collecting mussels and crabs to eat.

This boy is cleaning an animal skin with a stone scraper.

This man is telling some children about his hunting adventures.

This woman is sewing animal-skin clothes with a bone needle.

Tools with handles

By 40,000 years ago, people were making tools with handles. They made spears by fitting sharp stone blades into long sticks. They also carved pieces of bone into jagged blades and tied them to sticks, to make harpoons. Bone was used to make fish-hooks as well.

These men are from a different tribe. They have come to trade stone blades for seashells.

Sewing clothes

People began to sew animal skins together to make clothes. They made needles from bone, and used thin strips of leather as thread.

Trading and talking

As they wandered from place to place, tribes of people traded tools and valuable objects with each other. People from different tribes told each other about their experiences and passed on information about new places.

The spirit world

People seem to have believed that the world was controlled by powerful spirits, or gods. They probably tried to contact these gods by holding religious ceremonies. Perhaps they asked the gods to help them with their hunting, or to protect dead people in the afterlife?

New Worlds

Modern people evolved from an earlier type of people known as *Homo erectus* (see pages 84 to 87). Some experts believe that these new people evolved in several places at roughly the same time. But many other experts think that modern people first appeared in Africa, then spread out slowly across the rest of the world.

Spreading out

Modern people probably began to travel beyond Africa to Europe and Asia around 100,000 years ago. Gradually, they replaced the earlier people that lived in these places, and by about 30,000 years ago, they were the only humans left on Earth.

Across the sea

Around 50,000 years ago, during the last ice age, groups of people set off in boats from Southeast Asia. Nobody knows why they did this. They may have been searching for food, or for more land, or perhaps they were just exploring.

Following herds

Some tribes of people in Europe and Asia hunted wandering herds of animals, such as reindeer or bison. They followed the herds all through the year, and the animals led them to new places.

Bison

The first Americans

At times, the sea level was so low that Asia and North America were connected by a stretch of dry land, called Beringia. Herds of animals wandered across Beringia, to and from Asia and North America.

Some time between 30,000 and 12,000 years ago, tribes of people followed the herds from Asia into North America. These hunters gradually moved south until they had occupied all of North and South America.

This picture shows people from Southeast Asia on a voyage to find new land.

Finding Australia

During the ice age, the sea level was much lower than it is today. This meant that there were lots of little islands where voyagers could stop and rest. However, they still had to cross miles of water between islands, and many people must have been lost at sea. Eventually, some voyagers reached the shores of Australia. They were the first people who ever lived there.

Wooden paddle

Some of the boats are made from bamboo stems tied together with thin strips of bamboo.

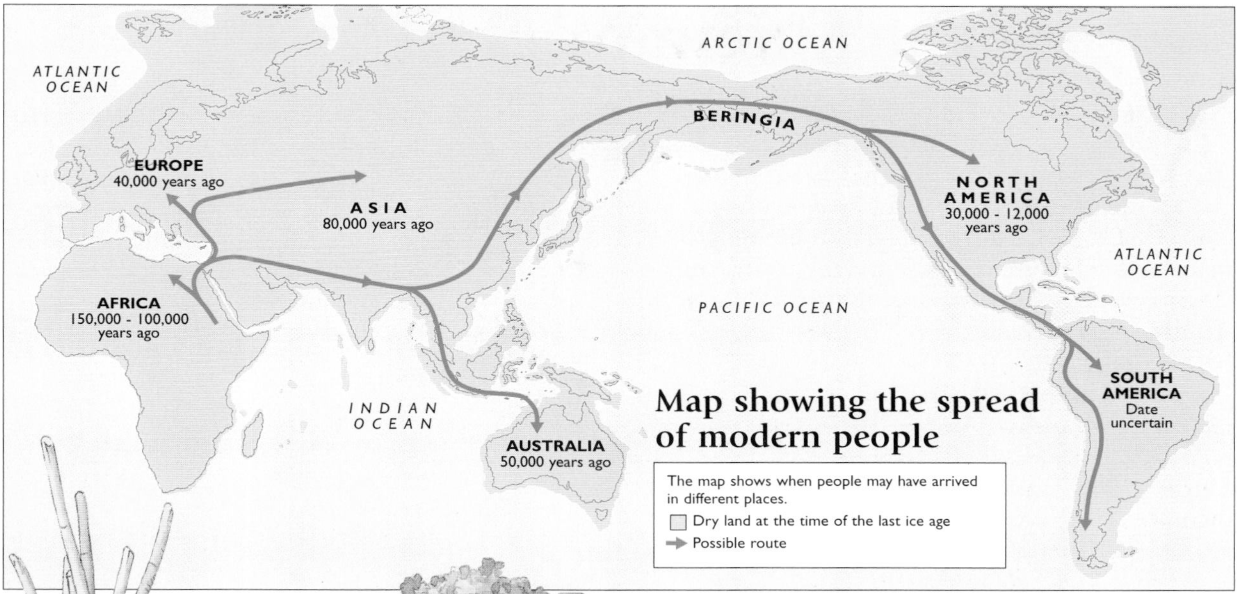

Map showing the spread of modern people

The map shows when people may have arrived in different places.

Dry land at the time of the last ice age

Possible route

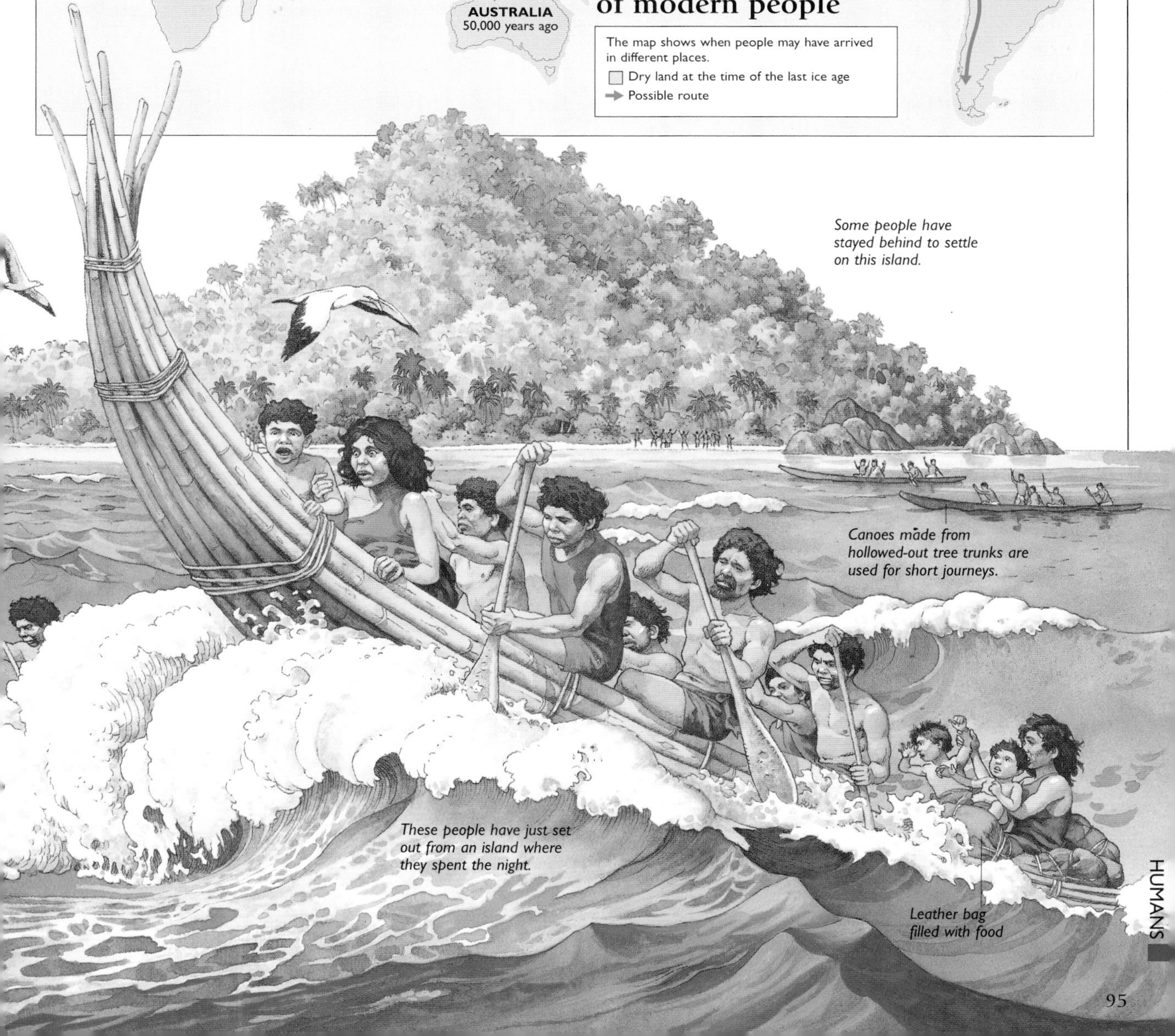

Some people have stayed behind to settle on this island.

Canoes made from hollowed-out tree trunks are used for short journeys.

These people have just set out from an island where they spent the night.

Leather bag filled with food

The Mammoth-hunters

Around 30,000 years ago, during the last ice age, tribes of people arrived on the freezing plains of eastern Europe. These people quickly adapted to living in such a cold and empty place. They became experts at hunting the mammoths that wandered across the plains, and they made almost everything they needed from the mammoths' bodies.

Hunting mammoths

Like other people at this time, the mammoth-hunters used a weapon called a spearthrower, which allowed them to throw their spears much farther than before. This made it possible to attack dangerous animals, such as mammoths, from a safe distance.

Mammoth-bone huts

There were few hills or caves on the plains, so the mammoth-hunters had nowhere to shelter from the snow and wind. Because hardly any trees grew there either, people had no wood to build huts. Instead, the mammoth-hunters made their homes from mammoth bones and skins.

This picture shows some mammoth-hunters and their huts.

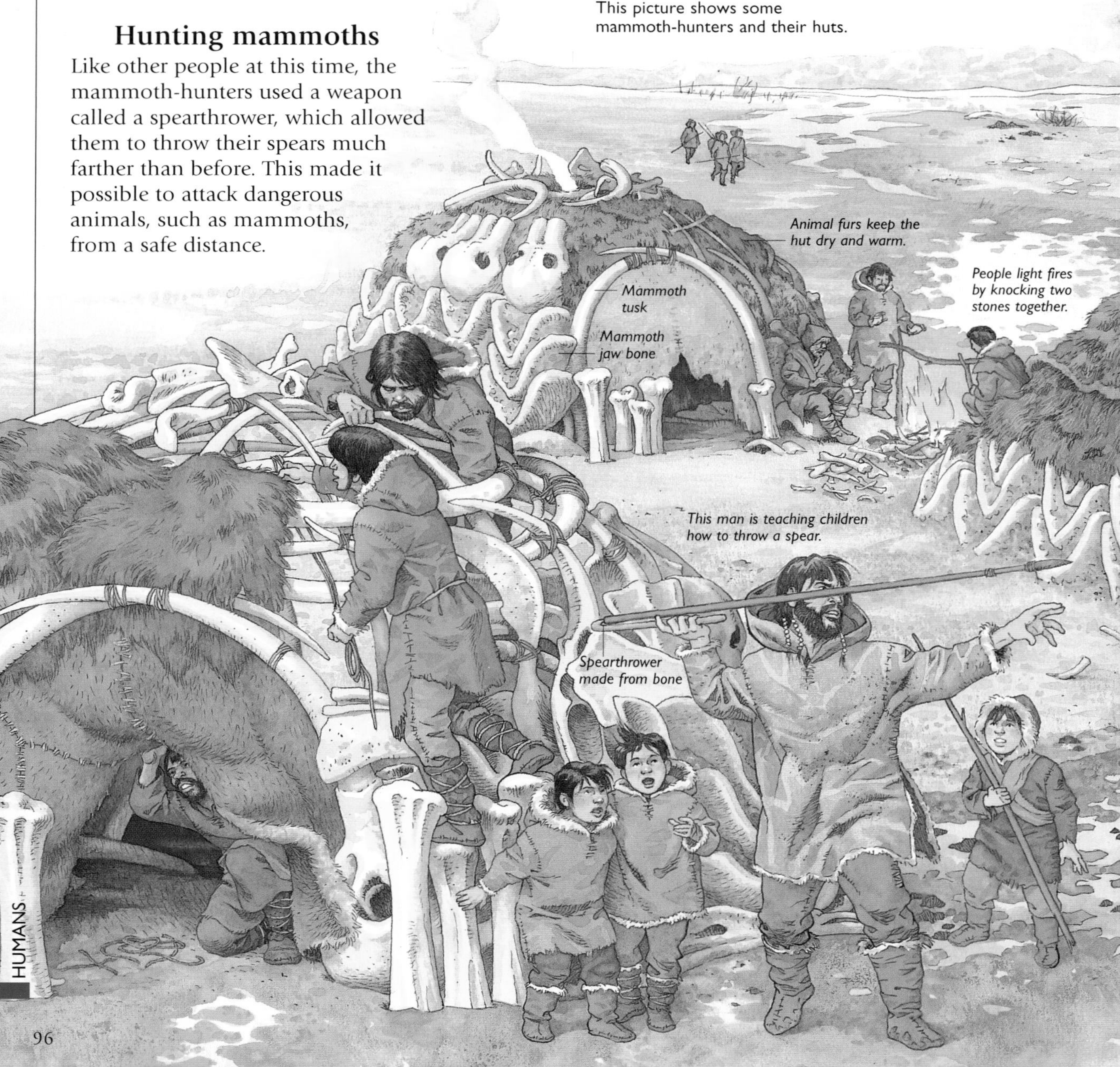

Music and dancing

The mammoth-hunters made some of the first musical instruments that we know about. They used mammoth skulls and shoulder bones as drums, and hollowed out small bones to make flutes.

People probably danced to the music. Dancing may have been a way of bringing everyone in the tribe closer together. It may also have been part of a religious ceremony.

Mammoth-hunters playing music and dancing ★

This man is making a stone knife.

These women are making necklaces from shells and animal teeth.

Warm clothes

In the winter, the mammoth-hunters wore warm leather clothes made from mammoth skins sewn tightly together. They also wore leather boots and fur mittens.

Shells and beads

Sometimes, people sewed seashells or feathers onto their clothes. They also made strings of beads from shells and animal teeth, and used ivory from mammoth tusks to make bracelets. These decorated clothes and ornaments may have been worn at religious ceremonies, and tribe leaders may have had their own special decorations.

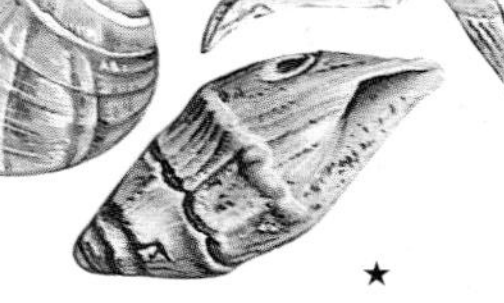
★ Beads made from shells and animal teeth

The First Artists

Around 35,000 years ago, people began to paint pictures on the walls of caves. Cave paintings have been found in many parts of the world, but the most famous ones are in France and Spain. Nobody knows why these pictures were created, but tribes may have used the painted caves for meetings and ceremonies.

Painting caves

The first paints were made by grinding soft rocks into a paste. Artists used their fingers to draw the outline of a painting. Then, they shaded in the picture by dipping a piece of animal fur in paint and pressing it onto the cave wall.

The first priests?

Sometimes, artists painted strange creatures that seem to be part human and part animal. These paintings may be portraits of early priests dressed as animals. Tribes may have held religious ceremonies in the caves where these figures were painted.

This picture shows the kind of ceremony that may have taken place in a painted cave.

Painted animals

Most of the cave paintings show animals, such as bison, deer, horses and mammoths. People may have thought that the painted animals were magical and would bring them luck with their hunting.

Baking clay

Around this time, artists also discovered how to harden clay by baking it. Clay models of people and animals have been found in eastern Europe.

The first calendars?

Experts have found pieces of bone and antler with lots of tiny shapes carved on them. The shapes were carved by early people, and they seem to show the changing shape of the moon at different times of the month. Perhaps these carvings were the first calendars?

Making models

Early artists carved small statues from ivory or bone. Many of the statues show women, who may represent goddesses, and others show animals.

Ivory model of a person with a lion's head

Body painting

As well as painting on cave walls, people used bright red soil to decorate dead bodies before they were buried. They may also have painted themselves with sacred symbols before taking part in religious ceremonies.

From Hunting to Farming

Around 12,000 years ago, the last ice age began to come to an end. All over the world, the weather became warmer, and the ice melted away in many areas. Huge forests began to grow where the ice had been.

After the ice age ended, some big animals, such as mammoths, died out. People had to rely on hunting deer, wild pigs and other small animals.

Most people moved around to find food, staying in a different place each season. However, some tribes of people found places where they could hunt animals, catch fish and gather plants throughout the year. This meant that these tribes could settle down and live in the same place all the time.

Taming animals

People may have started to tame horses during the last ice age. Later, hunters took baby wolves back to their camp and looked after them. The wolves began to see people as their friends, and they became tame. The wolves' babies grew up to be tame as well, and eventually these animals became working dogs. Hunters used the dogs to help them find and kill wild animals.

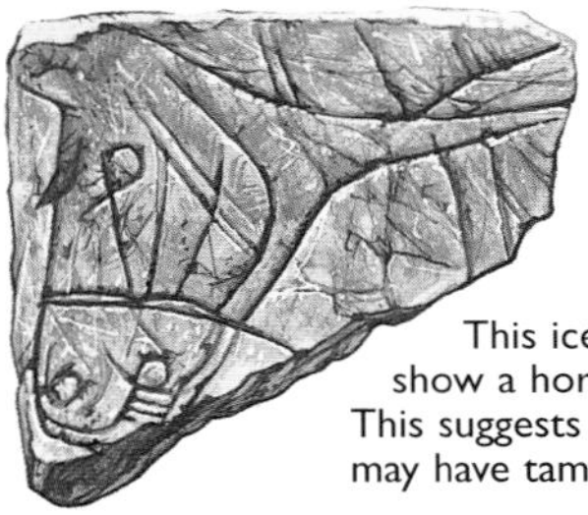

This ice age carving seems to show a horse wearing a harness. This suggests that early people may have tamed horses.

This picture shows a tribe of hunters living in a forest.

These people are using sticks to knock down nuts from a tree.

This girl has taken some honey from a bees' nest.

These women are gathering fruit and berries.

Wooden bowl

People use stone axes to chop up wood.

Canoe made from a tree trunk

Fishing net made from vines

Keeping herds

Some people began to tame lots of different animals, and eventually tribes started keeping herds of sheep, goats and cattle. This meant that people always had meat to eat and milk to drink, as well as fur and skins to make clothes.

Growing crops

Around 10,000 years ago, some tribes in the Middle East began to plant seeds and grow crops, such as wheat and barley. Once they had discovered farming, people could grow their own food, as well as going hunting and fishing.

Starting to settle

Groups of early farmers settled near the fields where their crops grew. They built huts for themselves and shelters for their animals. This was the beginning of village life.

Detail from the golden throne of the Egyptian pharaoh Tutankhamun

ANCIENT WORLD

Looking at the Ancient World

This section of the book covers a period of about 10,000 years, starting with the very first farmers and ending with the collapse of the Roman Empire.

From villages to empires

The discovery of farming in the Middle East, about 12,000 years ago, led to dramatic changes in the way people lived. Over the next 7,000 years, villages, towns and cities were built, writing was invented, and the first great civilizations appeared. This pattern was soon repeated in China, India and Europe, and later in Central and South America.

A gold statue of a king from the ancient Hittite Empire

The ancient world was the age of warriors and empires. Across the globe a series of great empires rose and fell, and some of these produced leaders, buildings and writings that are still famous today. This period also saw the birth of most of the world's main religions.

Where did it happen?

To check which area of the world you are reading about, look at the bottom corner of each page. The different areas of the world are shown on the map below.

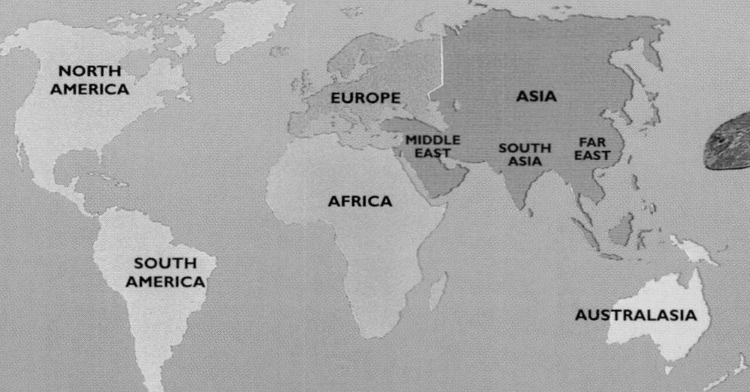

How do we know?

Amazingly, after so many thousands of years, some ancient buildings are still standing today, although most lie buried underground. Experts, called archaeologists, uncover the ruins and study the objects they find there.

Stonehenge, in southern England, still survives 5,000 years after it was built.

When did it happen?

Dates are usually counted from before or after the birth of Christ. Dates before Christ's birth are shown by the letters "BC" (before Christ). For example, 50BC means 50 years before Christ was born. BC dates are counted back from 1BC, so 100BC is earlier than 50BC. There is a timeline across the bottom of each double page to help you see when events took place.

The letters "AD" show that an event happened after the birth of Christ. AD stands for *anno Domini*, which is Latin for "in the year of the Lord".

If a date has a letter "c." in front of it, this means that experts aren't sure exactly when the event took place. The "c." stands for *circa*, which means "about" in Latin.

Internet link: *For a link to a Web site where you can try your hand as an archaeologist, go to* ***www.usborne-quicklinks.com***

This model boat from an Egyptian tomb shows how ancient Egyptian boats were sailed and steered.

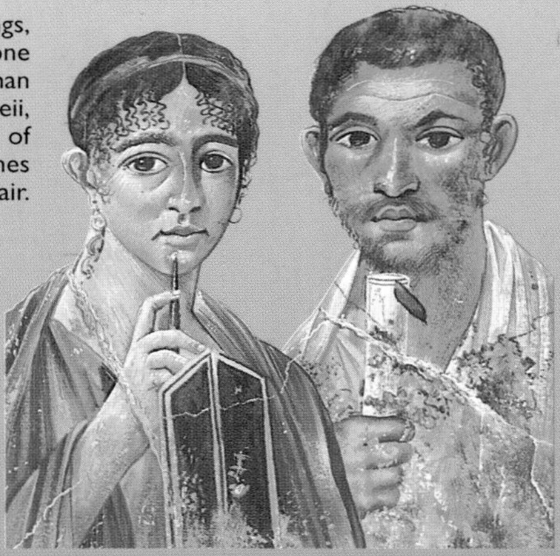

Wall paintings, like this one from the Roman town of Pompeii, show details of people's clothes and hair.

Objects from houses and tombs, such as weapons, tools, pots, furniture and fragments of cloth, give us valuable clues about how people lived in ancient times. Tombs and buildings may also contain statues, wall paintings and mosaics that show important people, or scenes from daily life.

Archaeologists also study the waste that ancient people threw away. Animal bones and seeds tell us what food people ate and what the climate and landscape were like at the time.

Ancient writing has been found on pieces of clay, on the walls of buildings and on scrolls of papyrus (a type of paper). These writings tell us about ancient rulers, laws and religious beliefs.

Ancient World Internet Links

This list includes general Web sites on the ancient world, as well as sites on Egypt, Greece and Rome. To visit the sites, go to **www.usborne-quicklinks.com** and enter the keyword "history".

WEB SITE 1 An online, interactive children's museum of the ancient world with lots of information, photos, puzzles and games. Covers Egypt, Greece, Rome, Africa and the Near East.

WEB SITE 2 A great site from the Metropolitan Museum of Art in New York. Enter and then click on "Explore and Learn" for interactive exhibits on Egypt, Assyria and the Greeks. Or click on "The Collection" to see highlights of the museum's collections from Egypt, Greece, Rome and the Near East.

WEB SITE 3 View highlights from the Oriental Institute in Chicago, or go on a virtual tour of the museum. Includes objects from Egypt, Assyria, Mesopotamia and Persia (Iran).

WEB SITE 4 Click on "Collections" to see highlights from the Oriental (Near Eastern), Egyptian, Greek and Roman collections in the Louvre Museum in Paris. Includes stunning photographs of each object, with a description.

WEB SITE 5 A good selection of online exhibits from the University of Pennsylvania Museum. Explore the Greek world, read the story of the Olympic Games or go to the "Egypt" section to write your name in hieroglyphics.

WEB SITE 6 A vast online library from Tufts University, USA, with over 33,000 pictures of ancient Greece and Rome. Search the site, or click on "Classics", then "Art & Arch. Catalogs", for photos and information about buildings, coins, sculpture and vases.

WEB SITE 7 On this intriguing site, click on "Exhibitions" to see incredible 3-D reconstructions of Greek ruins that bring to life some of the finest architecture in the ancient world.

WEB SITE 8 Take an unforgettable virtual tour of the seven wonders of the ancient world, with masses of information, photos, computer reconstructions and cutaway pictures.

WEB SITE 9 Ancient people around the world often linked their gods and goddesses with the Sun, Moon, stars and planets, and with different kinds of weather. Click on the underlined words to read myths and stories from many different cultures.

WEB SITE 10 A superb interactive site on ancient Egypt from the British Museum in London, which explores Egyptian life, religion, mummies, pharaohs, pyramids and temples, using photos, clickable pictures and games.

WEB SITE 11 Tour the temples and tombs of Egypt and see the pyramids close up. This exciting site has a selection of stunning panoramic movies with detailed descriptions of each building.

WEB SITE 12 Read about some of the latest archaeological discoveries in Egypt and find out how these ancient sites are being conserved for the future.

WEB SITE 13 See the sights of ancient Egypt using an interactive map. Click on each place for photos and a description.

WEB SITE 14 Explore the Valley of the Kings in Egypt and find out about the pharaohs who were buried there. This excellent site has details of all the tombs with photos, diagrams and panoramic movies.

WEB SITE 15 An interactive site with video clips, clickable maps, 3-D reconstructions, profiles of famous Greeks and a special feature on the Acropolis in Athens. You can even learn to speak like an ancient Greek.

WEB SITE 16 A fun site about Greek myths, with masses of information and pictures of gods, heroes and monsters. The "Homework Help" section is ideal for school projects.

WEB SITE 17 Explore the Sphinx and the Great Pyramid in Egypt.

This is the Sphinx at Giza, in Egypt. Behind it is the Great Pyramid, the largest stone building ever built.

WEB SITE 18 An excellent children's site on the Romans, which covers Roman history, religion, family life, pastimes, travel and the army. Each topic features fun facts, activities and a quiz.

WEB SITE 19 Lots of information on the Romans, with a brief history of the Empire and a look at famous Romans, great builders and Roman achievements. Includes interactive maps and a useful timeline of all the emperors.

WEB SITE 20 This detailed site looks at the daily life, history and religion of Rome, and includes profiles of famous Romans. You can also explore a clickable picture of the Roman Forum, or marketplace.

WEB SITE 21 Watch as Roman ruins are restored to the way they looked 2,000 years ago on this fascinating site. Select a photograph, then click on the enlarged image to see the reconstruction of a Roman ruin appear before your eyes.

The First Farmers

The very first people hunted wild animals, caught fish and gathered nuts, plants and berries to eat. It was thousands of years before people learned how to farm.

Farming began in the Middle East, in an area we call the Fertile Crescent. Around 10,000BC, the weather there became wetter and warmer, so plants could grow more easily.

Cutting wheat with a tool called a sickle

People noticed that seeds which had fallen on the ground grew into plants. They began to collect the seeds and plant them on purpose. The first crops grown like this were wild wheat and barley.

Around the same time, people learned how to tame animals. This meant that they always had plenty of meat, milk and wool. They could also use cattle for working in the fields.

These pots were made by early farmers.

Once people knew how to farm, they no longer needed to move around to hunt for food. They began to settle down in villages and had time to learn new skills, such as spinning, weaving and making pots.

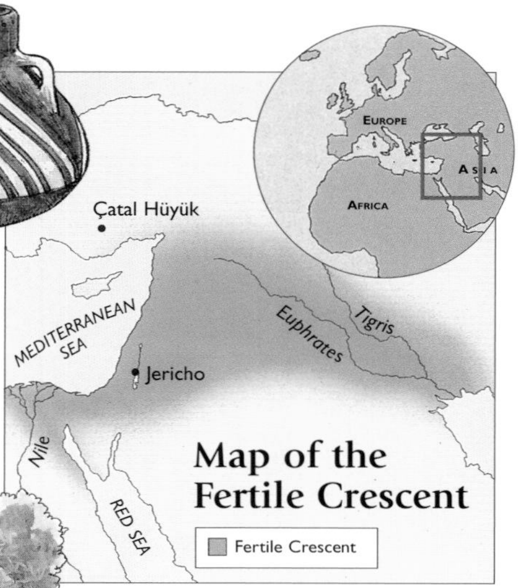

Map of the Fertile Crescent

Fertile Crescent

Çatal Hüyük

MEDITERRANEAN SEA

Jericho

Euphrates

Tigris

Nile

RED SEA

EUROPE

ASIA

AFRICA

In this picture of an early village, one house has been cut away to let you see inside.

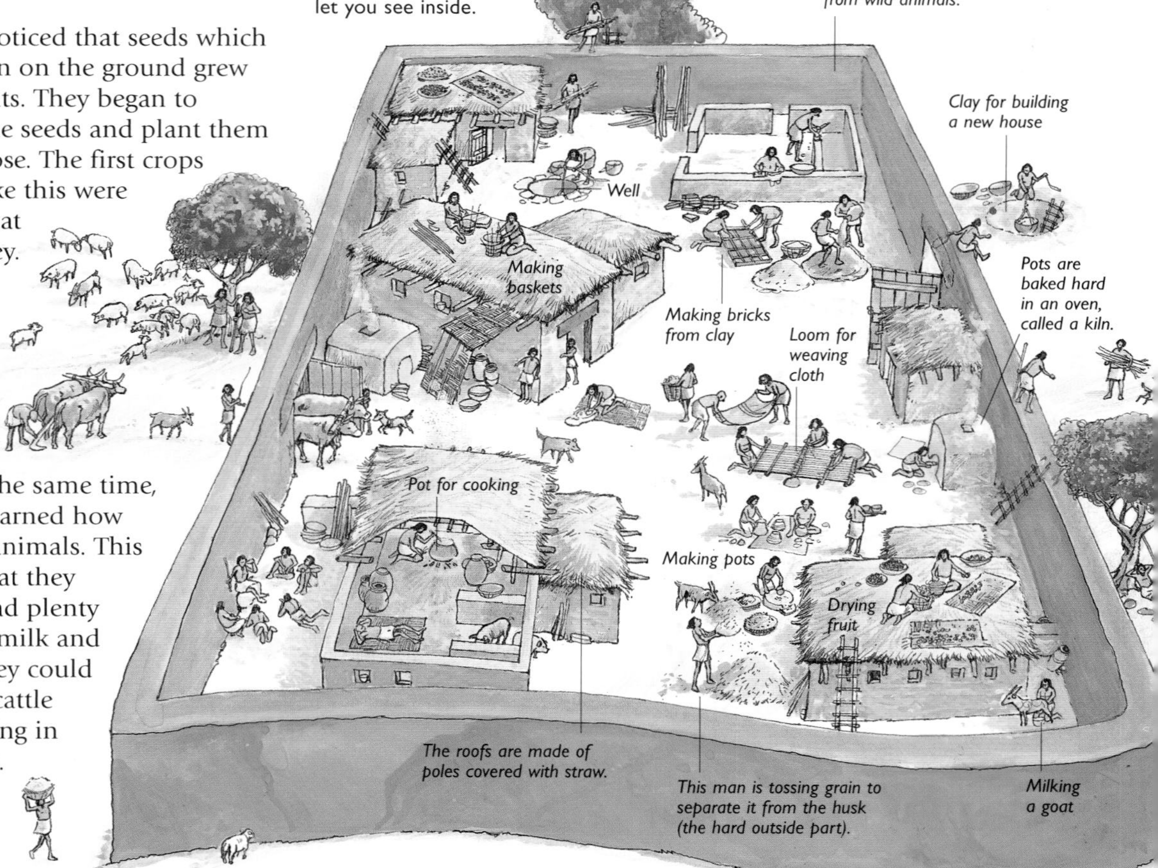

A wall protects the village from wild animals.

Clay for building a new house

Well

Making baskets

Making bricks from clay

Loom for weaving cloth

Pots are baked hard in an oven, called a kiln.

Pot for cooking

Making pots

Drying fruit

The roofs are made of poles covered with straw.

This man is tossing grain to separate it from the husk (the hard outside part).

Milking a goat

10,000BC | 5000BC | 4000BC | 3000BC

The First Towns

Slowly, small farming villages grew into towns. The oldest town that has been found so far is at Jericho.

Jericho

The people of Jericho lived in small, round houses made of mud bricks.

A cutaway picture of a house in Jericho ★

Dead people were buried underneath the houses. Their skulls may have been put on display, as a way of showing respect.

Skull found at Jericho ★

Cowrie shells in place of eyes

Plaster filling

Jericho grew rich by trading with other communities, and people in the nearby villages became jealous. To protect themselves, the people of Jericho built a massive stone wall around the town.

Building the walls of Jericho

Çatal Hüyük

Çatal Hüyük (pronounced "chatal hoo-yook") was the largest of the early towns. Around 6,000 people lived there.

This cutaway picture shows part of Çatal Hüyük. ★

Apple trees

People climb into the houses through a hole in the roof.

If enemies attack, the ladders are pulled up.

All the houses are joined together.

Clay bench covered with reeds

The houses have one main room.

Fireplace

The walls are made of mud bricks.

Cattle and goats are kept for meat and milk.

When someone in Çatal Hüyük died, the body was left outside to rot. The skeleton was buried under a bench in the house or in a shrine room, where the people prayed to their gods.

This picture shows a shrine room at Çatal Hüyük.

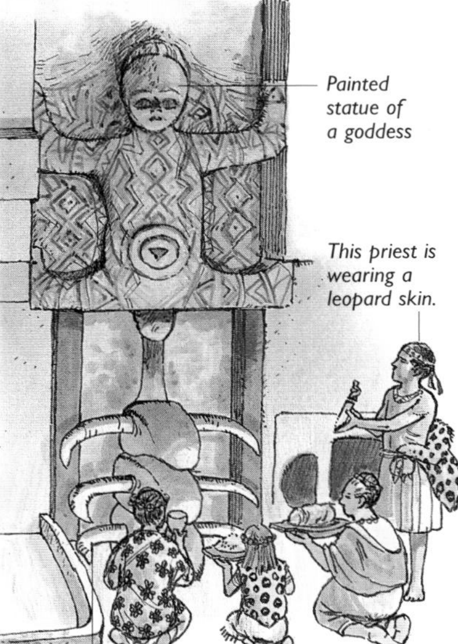

Painted statue of a goddess

This priest is wearing a leopard skin.

Model of a bull's head with real horns

These priestesses have brought offerings of food and drink for the goddess.

The Çatal Hüyük people made clay sculptures of very large women. Some experts think that these are models of a great Mother Goddess.

Clay figure from Çatal Hüyük

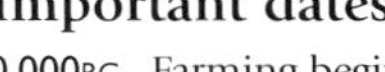

Important dates

c.10,000BC	Farming begins in the Fertile Crescent.
c.8000BC	Jericho grows into a wealthy town.
c.6250-5650BC	Çatal Hüyük is at its largest.

The First Civilization

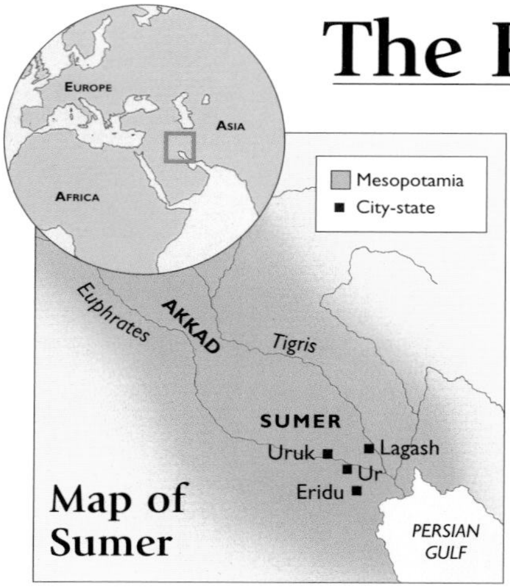
Europe
Asia
Africa
Mesopotamia
City-state
Euphrates
AKKAD
Tigris
SUMER
Uruk
Lagash
Ur
Eridu
PERSIAN GULF

Map of Sumer

From around 5000BC, farmers settled in the wide valley between the Tigris and Euphrates rivers. This area became known as Mesopotamia, which means "the land between two rivers". The first civilization grew up in Sumer, in the southern part of Mesopotamia.

The flat land of Sumer was good for farming, but there was very little rain. Once a year, the two rivers flooded, soaking the dry ground. The Sumerians built ditches and canals, to store the water and carry it to the fields.

Farmers mending a canal

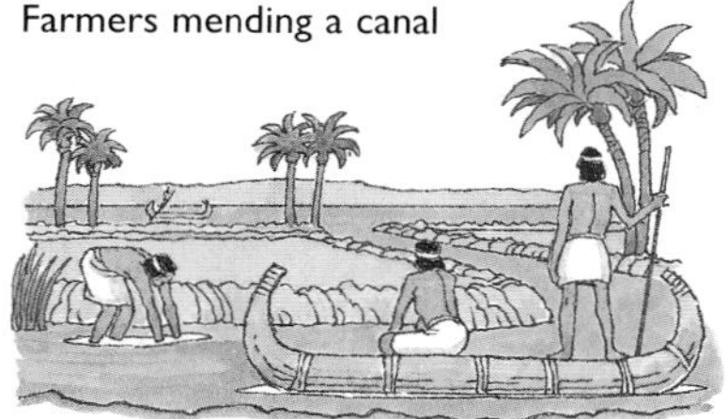

Farmers were soon able to grow more crops than they could eat. There was no need for everyone to farm, so some people had time to learn specialist skills, such as pottery and weaving.

The finished bricks are left to dry in the sun.
Bricks are shaped in a wooden frame.

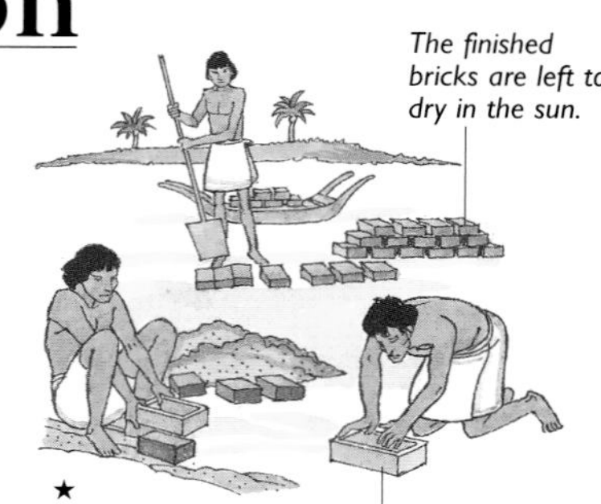

★ These people are making mud bricks.

At first, the Sumerians lived in houses made of reeds. Later, they learned how to make bricks from mud and straw.

Small farming villages gradually grew into huge walled cities, each with its own temple. Each city had a ruler who also had control of the farmland around the city. Cities organized like this are called city-states.

This picture shows part of the Sumerian city of Ur.

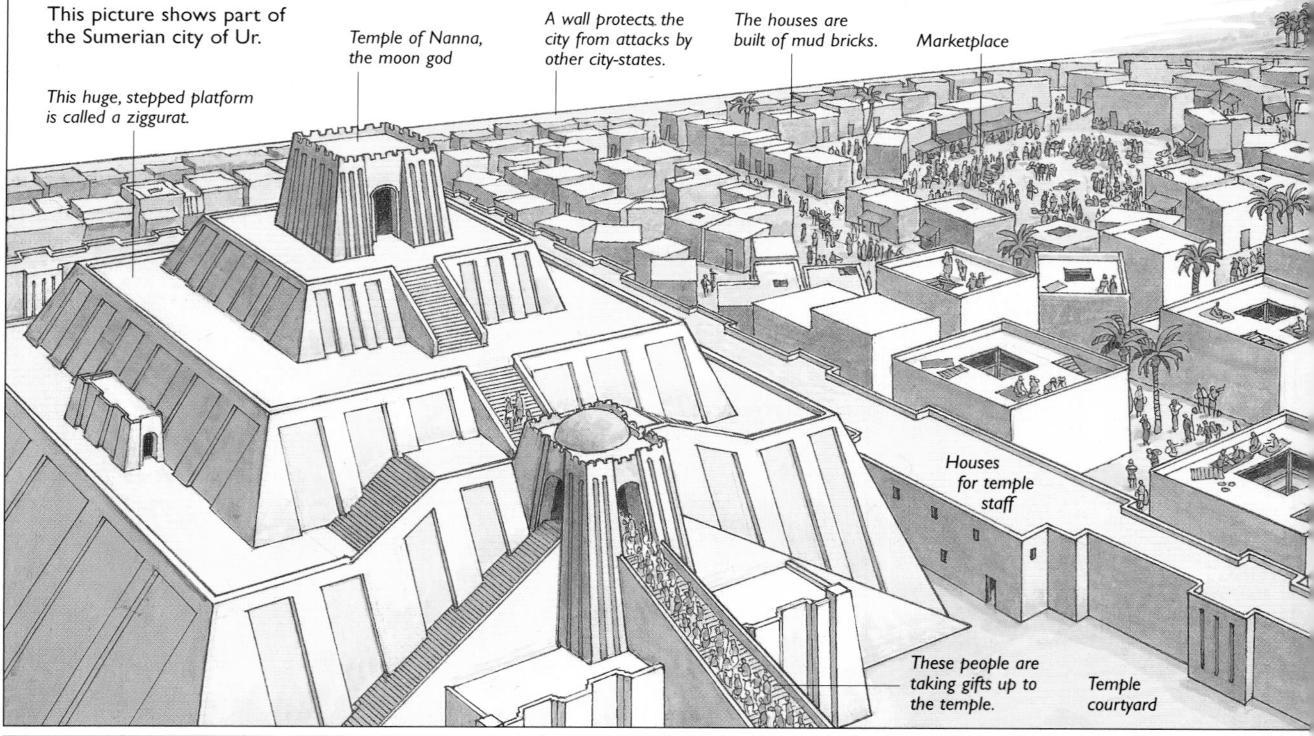
Temple of Nanna, the moon god
A wall protects the city from attacks by other city-states.
The houses are built of mud bricks.
Marketplace
This huge, stepped platform is called a ziggurat.
Houses for temple staff
These people are taking gifts up to the temple.
Temple courtyard

10,000BC 5000BC 4000BC 3000BC

The invention of writing

Farmers had to give part of their crop to the temple, and temple officials needed to know if a farmer had paid his share. Writing probably developed as a way of recording this information.

Farmers bringing grain to the temple

1 At first, people drew simple pictures of the objects they wanted to record. These pictures are called pictograms.

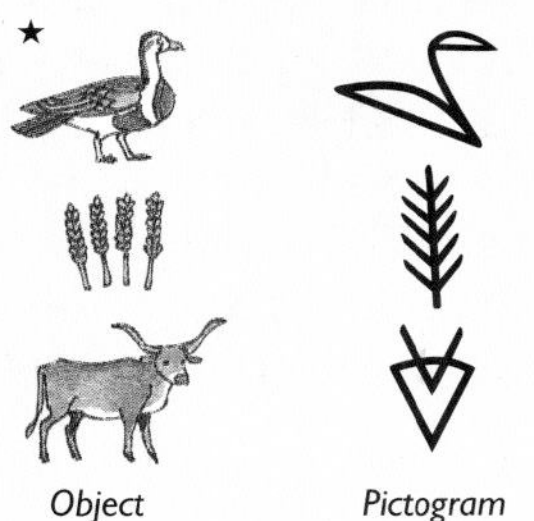

2 The pictures were drawn one below the other on a piece of wet clay.

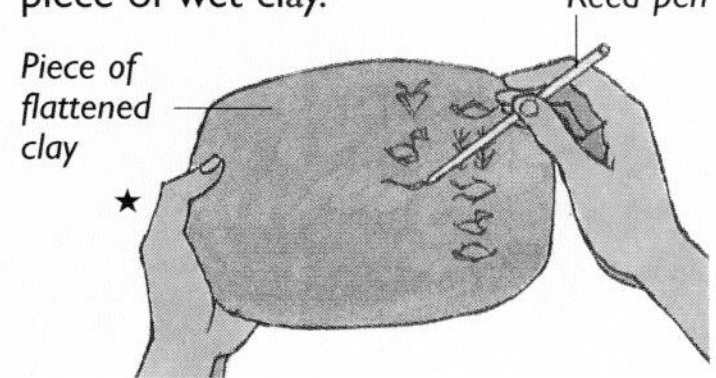

3 Later, people turned the clay around and wrote from side to side. This stopped them from smudging the pictures they had already drawn.

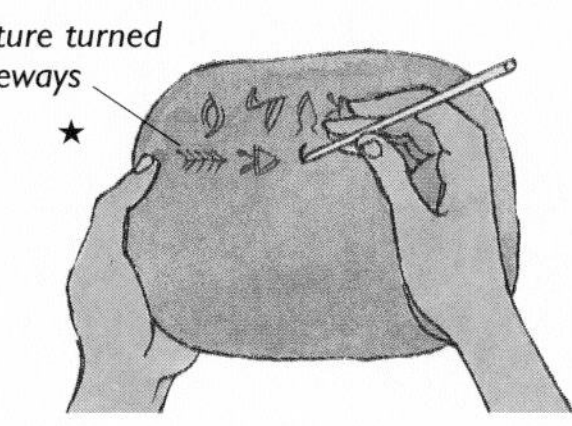

4 Because of the shape of the reed pen, the pictures gradually changed into wedge-shaped symbols, which we call cuneiform writing. Cuneiform means "wedge-shaped".

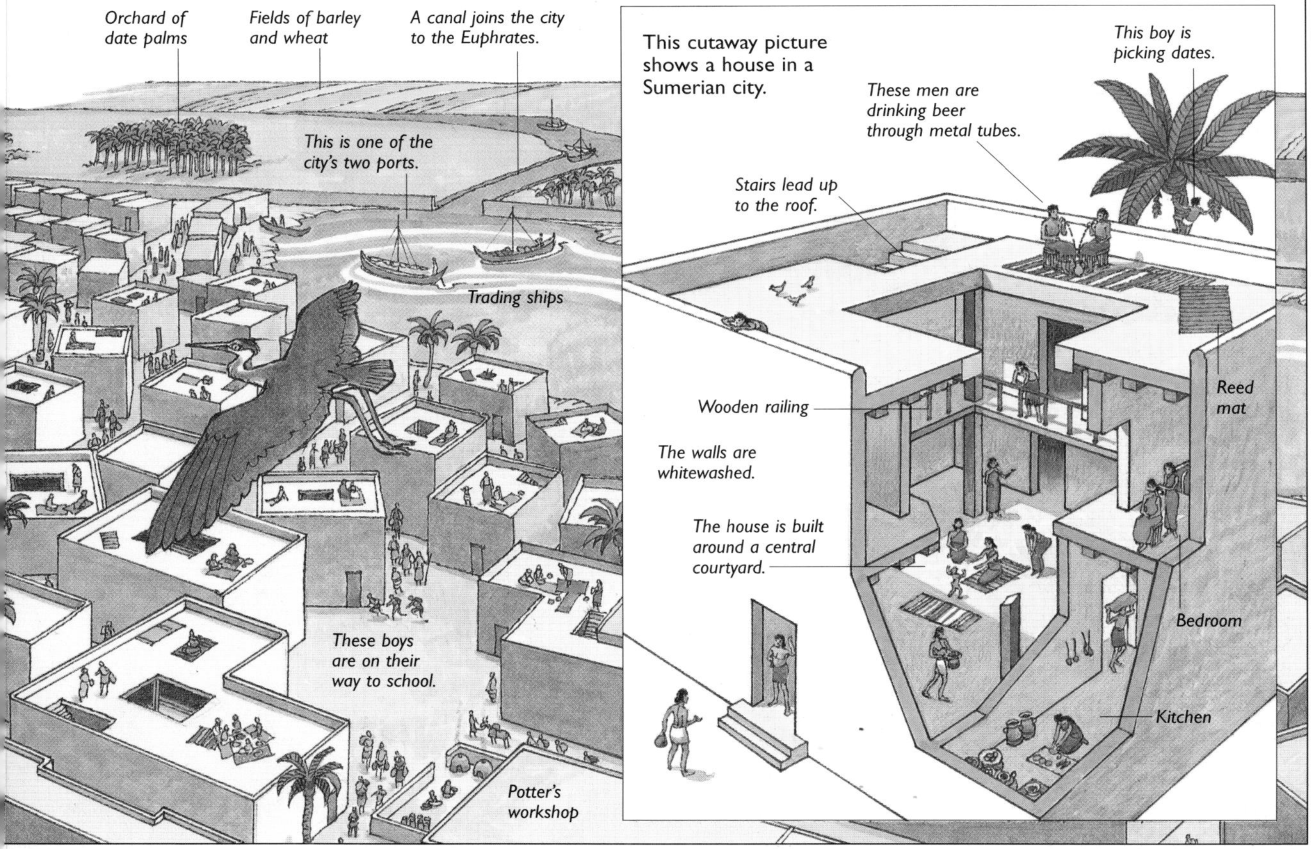

Orchard of date palms

Fields of barley and wheat

A canal joins the city to the Euphrates.

This is one of the city's two ports.

Trading ships

These boys are on their way to school.

Potter's workshop

This cutaway picture shows a house in a Sumerian city.

This boy is picking dates.

These men are drinking beer through metal tubes.

Stairs lead up to the roof.

Wooden railing

Reed mat

The walls are whitewashed.

The house is built around a central courtyard.

Bedroom

Kitchen

2000BC | 1000BC | 500BC | AD1 | AD500

Crafts and Trade

There was no stone, metal or strong wood in Sumer, so all these things had to be brought in from other lands. In exchange, the Sumerians sold grain and wool, as well as the pots and metal objects they made in their workshops.

Sumerian traders sailed along canals and rivers into the Persian Gulf and beyond. They traded with merchants from as far away as the Mediterranean Coast in the west and the Indus Valley in the east.

Metalwork

The Sumerians were skilled metalworkers, and made beautiful objects from gold, silver and copper.

Gold dagger and sheath

In this picture, merchants are trading at a busy Sumerian market.

Stone is floated down the river on wooden rafts.

Wood from the mountains in the north

This trading ship has just come back from the Persian Gulf.

Wine jars

This trader has brought back a cargo of gold, copper, ivory and semi-precious stones.

This man is selling vegetables.

A man called a scribe lists the goods as they are unloaded.

Jar of oil

Basket of grain

Rolls of cloth

This trader has come from Syria.

These merchants are setting off on a trading expedition.

This man is selling fish.

Pots and wheels

Sumer had plenty of clay for making pottery. Pots were shaped by hand until around 3500BC, when the potter's wheel was invented.

Potters at work ★

Pots are shaped on a wheel.

Pots are baked hard in an oven called a kiln.

Boys mix the clay with their feet.

People soon realized that wheels could be attached to carts or chariots, and used for getting around. A donkey pulling a cart could carry three times as much as it could on its back.

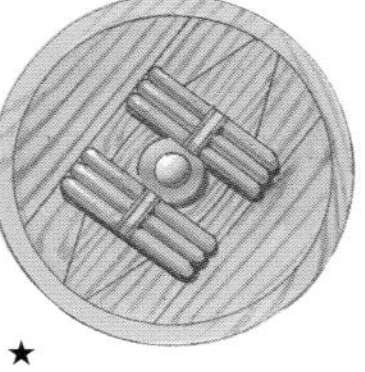

Wheel from a Sumerian chariot ★

Stone carving

Sculptors carved small stone statues of people praying. People believed that if they placed a statue in the temple, the statue would pray for them.

★ Stone statue of a temple official

Kings and War

Each city in Sumer was run by a group of noblemen. In times of war, they chose a leader who ruled until the war was over. As wars became more frequent, the war-leaders ruled for longer periods of time. In the end, they became kings who ruled for life, and handed power down to their sons.

Sargon of Akkad ★

Sargon of Akkad

Sargon came from Akkad, the land just north of Sumer. He was a skilled soldier and had control of a huge army. He conquered the whole of Sumer and Akkad, creating the world's first empire.

This mosaic shows Sumerian soldiers in battle. ★

Sumerian soldier wearing a cloak and helmet

This is one of the enemy prisoners. He will be killed or sold as a slave.

Chariot

Donkeys

This soldier is about to throw his spear.

This is the charioteer. He drives the chariot.

Body of an enemy soldier

Gutian tribesmen

The Akkadian Empire lasted nearly 200 years until it was destroyed by a tribe called the Gutians.

The end of Sumer

The King of Ur won back the Sumerians' land and, for a short time, he ruled all of Sumer and Akkad. Around 2000BC, Sumer was invaded by a tribe known as the Amorites. The land split up into many small states, and later became part of the Babylonian Empire (see page 132).

Royal tombs

The early kings and queens of the city of Ur were buried in large pits filled with amazing treasures. The tombs also contained the bodies of dozens of guards and servants, who had taken poison and died to be with their rulers.

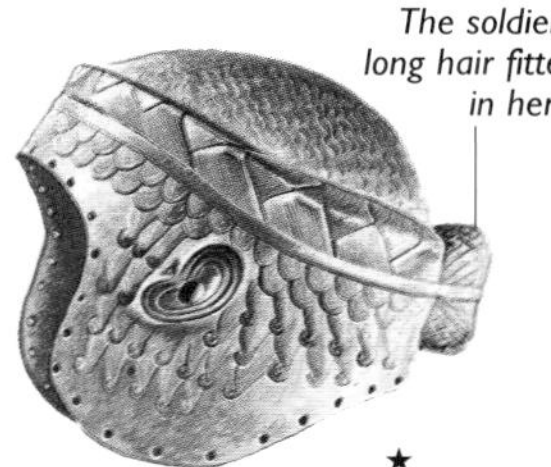

The soldier's long hair fitted in here.

Golden helmet from one of the tombs at Ur ★

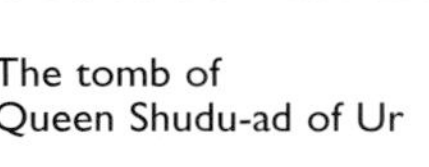

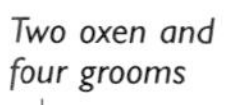

The tomb of Queen Shudu-ad of Ur

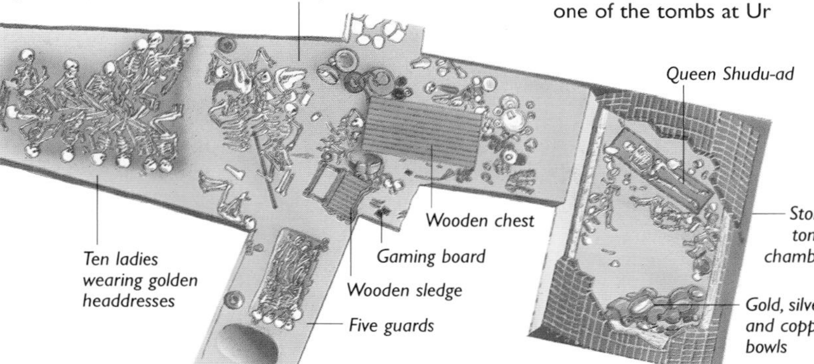

Two oxen and four grooms

Queen Shudu-ad

Wooden chest

Stone tomb chamber

Ten ladies wearing golden headdresses

Gaming board

Wooden sledge

Five guards

Gold, silver and copper bowls

Important dates

c.5000BC	Farmers settle in Sumer.
c.3500BC	The wheel is invented. The first cities are built.
c.3300BC	Picture writing is invented.
c.3100BC	Cuneiform writing is used.
c.2500BC	The royal tombs are built at Ur.
c.2350-2150BC	Sumer is part of the Akkadian Empire.
c.2100BC	The King of Ur rules Sumer and Akkad. The ziggurat at Ur is built.
c.2000BC	The Amorites invade.

Farmers of the Nile Valley

Europe
Asia
Africa
Map of Egypt
MEDITERRANEAN SEA
Nile Delta
LOWER EGYPT
Giza
Memphis
Nile
Western Desert
RED SEA
Eastern Desert
UPPER EGYPT
Valley of the Kings
Thebes
Nile Valley
Border between Lower and Upper Egypt

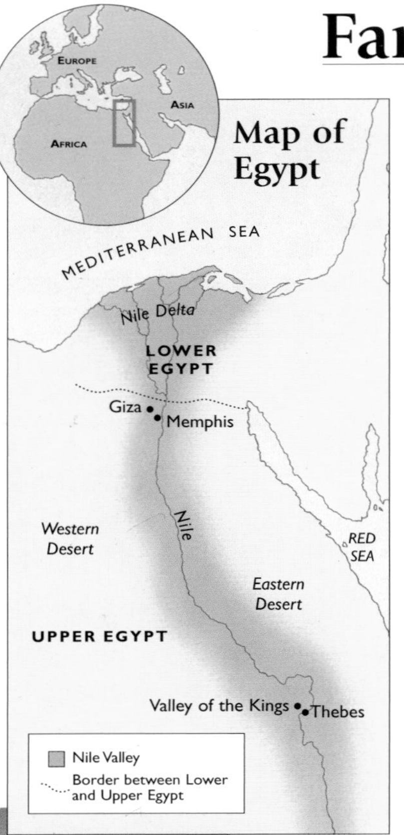

Ancient Egypt was a long, narrow country which stretched along the Nile Valley. It was surrounded on both sides by desert.

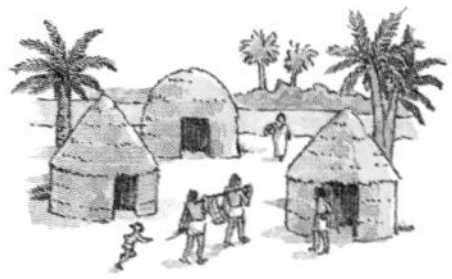

Villages grew up along the Nile, because the land on either side of the river was good to farm. Every spring, melted snow from the mountains south of Egypt flowed into the Nile, and in July the river flooded. After several months, the water level fell, leaving behind rich, fertile soil.

Gradually, the farming villages of the Nile Valley joined together to form larger communities. By around 3100BC, there were two separate kingdoms, called Lower Egypt and Upper Egypt.

The two kingdoms fought a battle, which was won by King Menes of Upper Egypt. Lower and Upper Egypt became one country, and Menes built a capital city at Memphis for the new, united land.

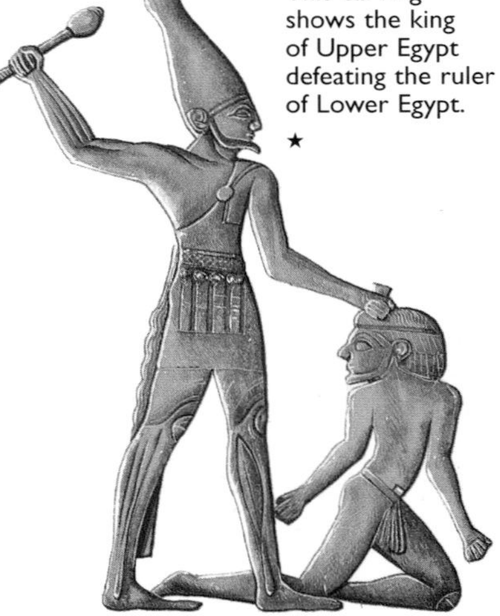

This carving shows the king of Upper Egypt defeating the ruler of Lower Egypt. ★

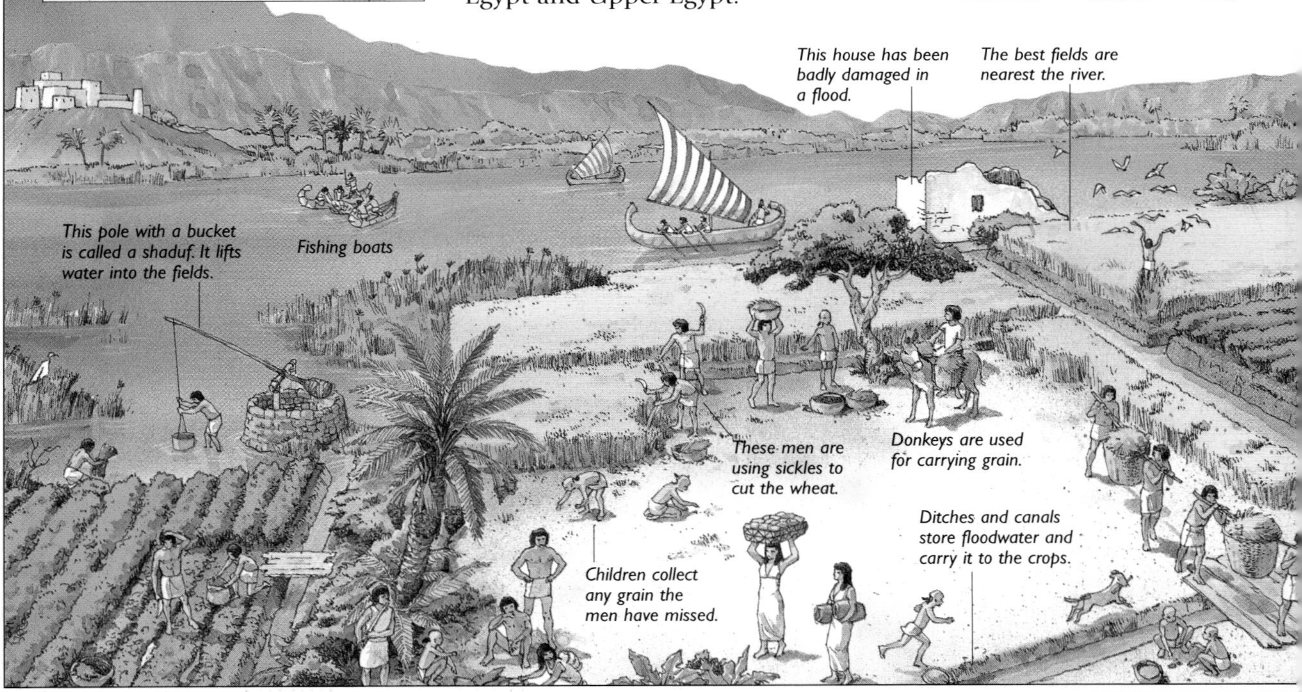

This house has been badly damaged in a flood.
The best fields are nearest the river.
This pole with a bucket is called a shaduf. It lifts water into the fields.
Fishing boats
These men are using sickles to cut the wheat.
Donkeys are used for carrying grain.
Ditches and canals store floodwater and carry it to the crops.
Children collect any grain the men have missed.

10,000BC | 5000BC | 4000BC | 3000BC

AFRICA

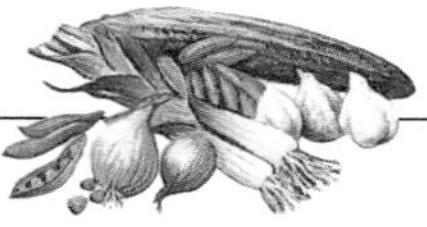

Crops

The Egyptians grew peas, beans, onions, garlic, leeks, cucumbers, grapes, melons, pomegranates, figs and dates. Grapes and pomegranates were made into wine.

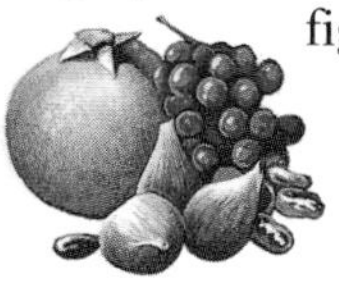

Wine was made by stamping on the grapes to squeeze out the juice. ★

The main crops were wheat and barley, which were used to make bread and beer. People sometimes added honey or garlic to their bread to make it more tasty.

Animals

Wooden model of a cow stall

Egyptian farmers kept cattle, sheep, goats, pigs, geese, ducks and pigeons. Cattle were used to work in the fields, as well as for meat. Egypt had very little grassland, so cows were often kept in stalls.

The farmer's year

While the land was flooded, no work could be done in the fields. In November, after the floodwater had gone down, the farmer prepared his fields and planted his crops. In the spring, the whole family helped with the harvest. Then, the farmer mended the ditches that carried water to the fields, ready for the next year's flood.

This tomb painting shows an Egyptian farmer working in the fields. His wife is scattering seeds on the ground.

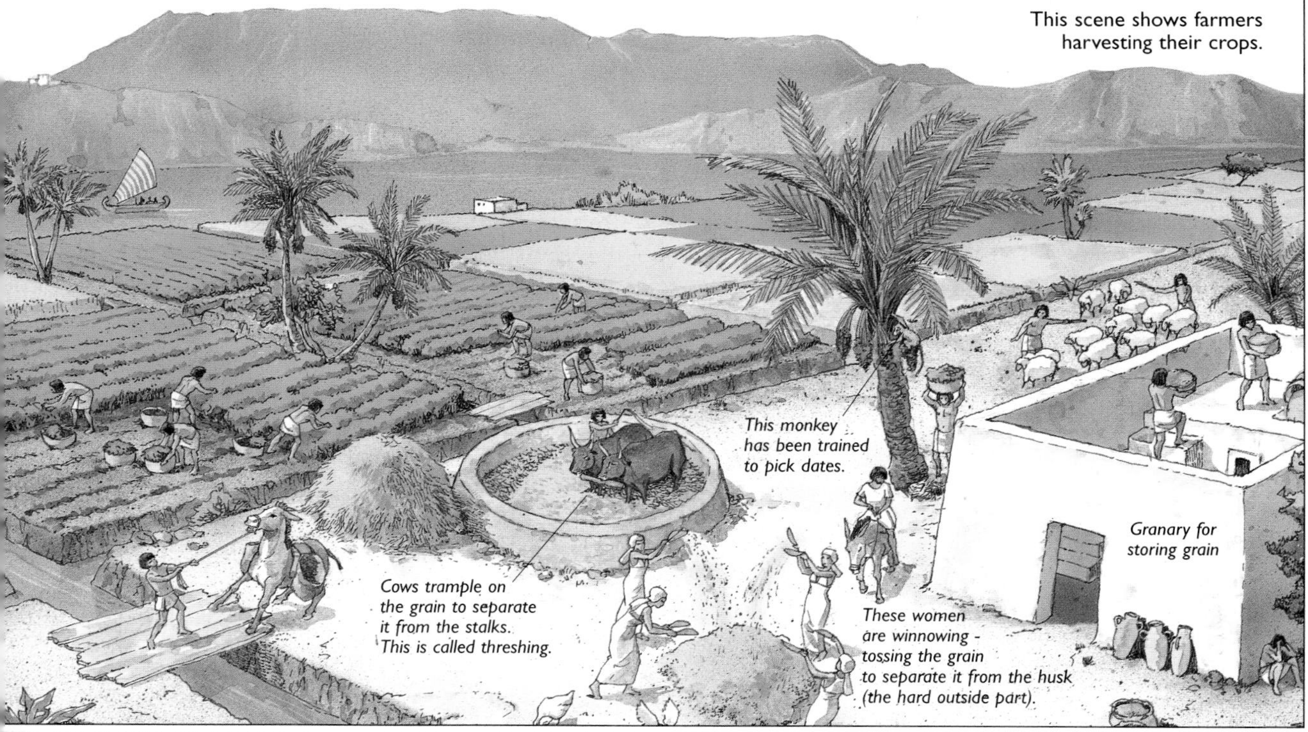

This scene shows farmers harvesting their crops.

This monkey has been trained to pick dates.

Granary for storing grain

Cows trample on the grain to separate it from the stalks. This is called threshing.

These women are winnowing - tossing the grain to separate it from the husk (the hard outside part).

Mummies and Pyramids

Experts divide Egyptian history into three main periods of time, called the Old Kingdom, the Middle Kingdom and the New Kingdom. The information on these two pages comes from all three periods.

Mummies

The Egyptians tried to stop dead bodies from decaying, because they thought this would allow the dead person to go on living in the Next World. These specially preserved bodies are called mummies.

These pictures show how a mummy was made.

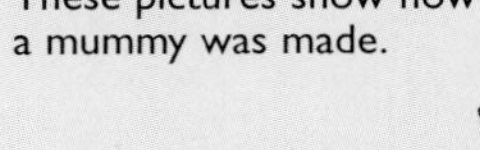

1 The brain and internal organs were taken out and put in jars called canopic jars.

2 The body was covered with a salt, called natron, to dry it out. Then, the insides were stuffed with linen, natron, sawdust and sweet-smelling spices.

3 The body was wrapped in bandages. Lucky charms, called amulets, were placed between the layers.

4 A mask was put over the mummy's face. A priest dressed as Anubis, god of the dead, prayed over the body.

Coffins

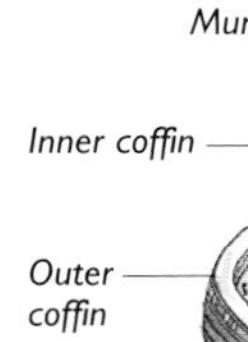

A mummy inside a nest of coffins

The first coffins were simple wooden boxes. Later, in the New Kingdom, mummies were put in a nest of two or three human-shaped coffins, one inside the other. These coffins were often brightly painted.

Tomb treasure

The tombs of rich Egyptians were filled with everything the dead person might need in the Next World. Kings were buried with amazing treasures, but robbers soon broke into the tombs and stole the treasure, so very little has been found.

This golden funeral mask belonged to the boy-king, Tutankhamun.

Internet link: *For a link to a Web site where you can explore inside the Great Pyramid, go to* **www.usborne-quicklinks.com**

The pyramids

During the Old and Middle Kingdoms, the Egyptians built huge pyramids as tombs for their kings, or pharaohs. There are over 30 pyramids in Egypt, but the most famous ones are at Giza, where three pharaohs and their chief wives are buried.

This picture shows the two largest pyramids at Giza, just after the death of the pharaoh Khafre.

Khafre will be buried in this pyramid.

This is the mortuary temple. A priest will come here every day to bring food and drink for the spirit of the dead pharaoh.

This is the Great Pyramid. Khafre's father, Khufu, is buried here.

The smooth sides are meant to look like the rays of the sun.

These tombs, called mastabas, are for important noblemen.

A huge statue of the Sphinx guards the pyramids. It has a human head and a lion's body.

These small pyramids are for the queen and the pharaoh's other wives.

A passageway links the valley temple to the mortuary temple.

In the valley temple, priests will prepare the pharaoh's body for burial.

A funeral boat brings Khafre's body from his palace at Memphis.

The Great Pyramid

The Great Pyramid is the largest stone building ever built. It is 147m (482ft) high and contains over two million stone blocks.

This picture shows the inside of the Great Pyramid. ★

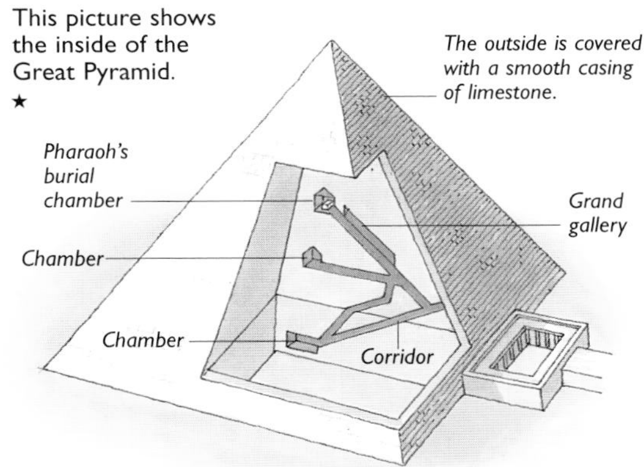

Later tombs

In the New Kingdom, the pharaohs were buried in tombs cut deep into the rock in a hidden valley, called the Valley of the Kings. Although the tombs were hard to find, almost all of them were robbed. The tomb of Tutankhamun was the only one that escaped.

A funeral procession to the Valley of the Kings

Important dates

c.5000BC	Farming begins in the Nile Valley.
c.3100BC	King Menes unites Upper and Lower Egypt.
c.2686BC	The Old Kingdom begins.
c.2180BC	The Old Kingdom ends in famine and civil war.
c.2040BC	Egypt is reunited. The Middle Kingdom begins.
c.1720BC	Egypt is invaded by people called the Hyksos. The Middle Kingdom ends.

Cities of the Indus Valley

The land in the Indus Valley was good for farming, and the river flooded every year, just like the rivers in Sumer and Egypt. Farmers used the floodwater to help them grow more food.

Soon, there was no need for everyone to farm, so some people could do other jobs. People built towns, learned new crafts and started to trade.

By around 2500BC, there were over a hundred towns and cities in the Indus Valley. The two largest were Mohenjo-daro and Harappa.

Map of the Indus Valley

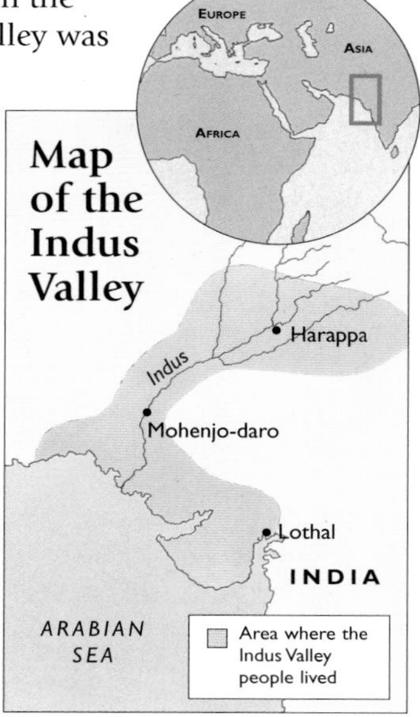

The Great Bath

The Great Bath at Mohenjo-daro

Inside the fortress at Mohenjo-daro was a large bathhouse. Priests or rulers may have bathed here before religious ceremonies.

This statue probably shows an Indus Valley priest or ruler. ★

The city of Mohenjo-daro

Like other Indus Valley cities, Mohenjo-daro was carefully planned. In the middle was a walled fortress, which was built on a huge, man-made hill. Another wall surrounded the city.

This picture shows a typical street in Mohenjo-daro. Part of one house has been cut away to let you see inside.

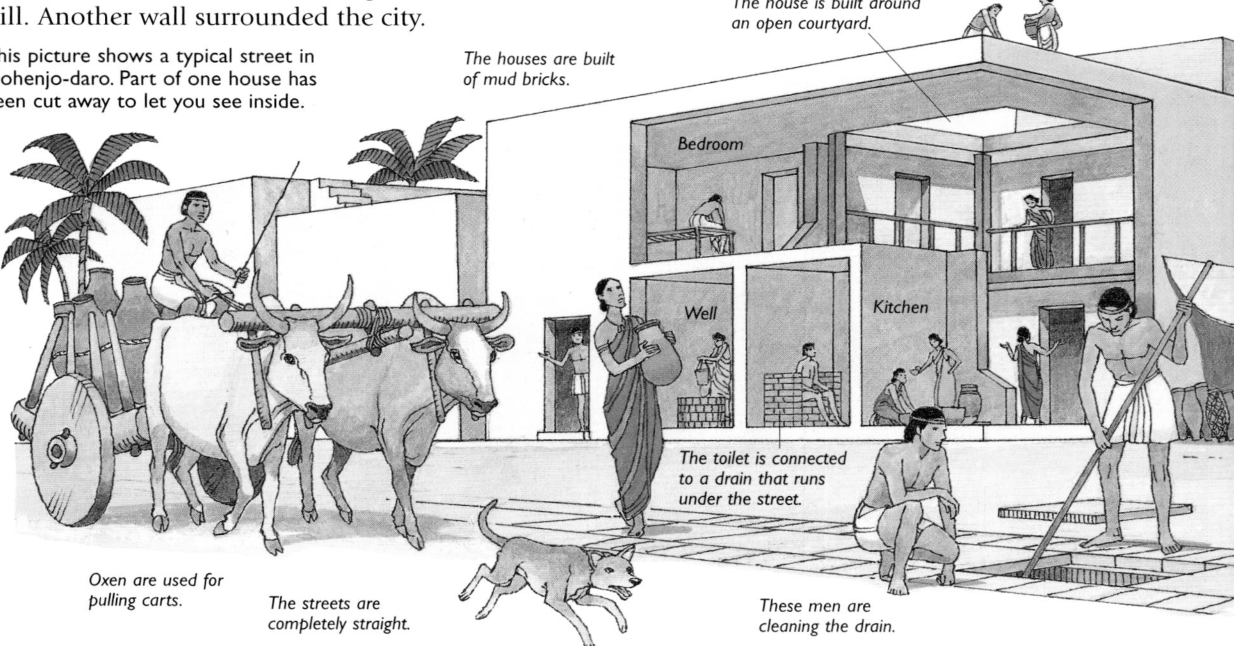

SOUTH ASIA

10,000BC 5000BC 4000BC 3000BC

The Great Granary

Farmers in Mohenjo-daro had to give part of their crop to the city. The grain was stored in a huge granary inside the fortress, so it could be used if there was a bad harvest and food was short.

The Great Granary at Mohenjo-daro

Crafts

Potters made cooking pots, storage jars, drinking cups and objects such as children's toys.

Indus Valley pot

The head moves when this wire is pulled.

Toy pig

Toy ox

Beads for necklaces and bracelets were made from gold, clay and semi-precious stones.

Bead necklace

The farmers of the Indus Valley were the first people to grow cotton and weave it into cloth.

Picking cotton

Stoneworkers made carved seals with writing and pictures of animals on them. Traders may have had their own personal seal, which they used to stamp their name onto pieces of clay.

Carved stone seal of a humped bull

So far, no one has been able to read the Indus Valley writing.

Trade

We know that the Indus people traded with Sumer because their pottery and beads have been found there. They also sold wood, cotton and spices.

A trading ship sets sail from the port at Lothal.

The end of a civilization

From around 1800BC, the Indus Valley civilization began to collapse, but no one is really sure why this happened.

The people may have ruined their farmland by growing too many crops and cutting down too many trees. There may have been quarrels between cities, or a disaster, such as a flood.

Finally, the area was invaded by people known as the Aryans, who brought with them a new way of life (see page 174).

Important dates

c.3500BC	Farmers settle in the Indus Valley.
c.2500-1800BC	The Indus Valley civilization is at its most successful.
c.1500BC	The Aryans invade.

Europe's First Villages

Red deer

Thousands of years ago, Europe was much colder than it is today, and in the north the land was covered in ice. When the weather warmed up, plants and trees were able to grow again, and wild animals roamed the forests.

Wild boar

People relied on hunting animals and collecting wild plants to eat. They set up camps where they could find food, and moved on when the seasons changed and the food ran out.

Early Europeans

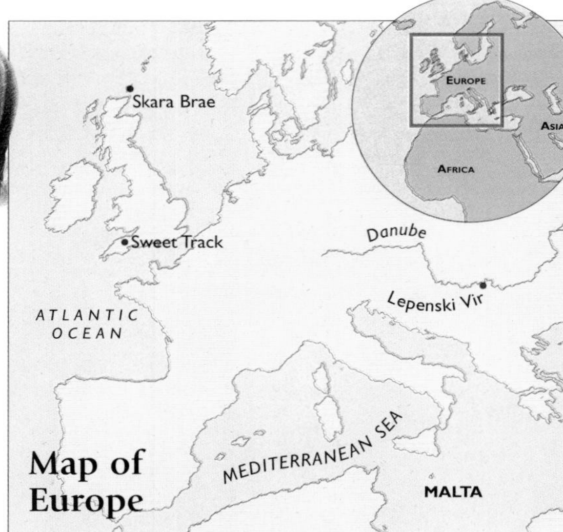

Map of Europe

Sculpture of a fish's head from Lepenski Vir

In some places, there was so much food all year that people could settle down. At Lepenski Vir, people built a village on the banks of the Danube, where there was always plenty of fish to catch.

Farmers of the forests

Around 6000BC, life in Europe began to change, as farming spread from the Middle East. In the thick forests that covered most of Europe, farmers cut down trees to make space for fields, and used the wood to build houses.

This picture shows an early European farming village. One house has been cut away to let you see inside.

10,000BC 5000BC 4000BC 3000BC

Stone shelters

Inside a house at Skara Brae ★

The early Europeans built their houses from whatever they could find nearby. At Skara Brae in the Orkney Islands there were hardly any trees, so people built houses of stone. They even had stone furniture.

Home and dry

In marshy areas, people built long wooden walkways so they could move around easily from one village to another. The Sweet Track in southwestern England stretched for 1.8km (just over a mile).

Farmers on the Sweet Track

Temples and tombs

Stone temples at Tarxien

Some early farmers worked together to create buildings from massive blocks of stone. At Tarxien on the island of Malta, people built temples where they sacrificed animals to their great Mother Goddess.

In western Europe, stone tombs were built and covered with huge mounds of earth. Each tomb had several chambers and had room for up to 40 bodies.

Inside a stone tomb

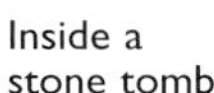

Important dates

c.6000-5000BC	Fishing people live at Lepenski Vir.
c.6000-4000BC	Farming spreads across most of Europe.
c.4500BC	People begin building stone tombs.
c.3800BC	The Sweet Track is built.
c.3500BC	The first temple is built at Tarxien.
c.3100BC	Skara Brae is built.

The Monument Builders

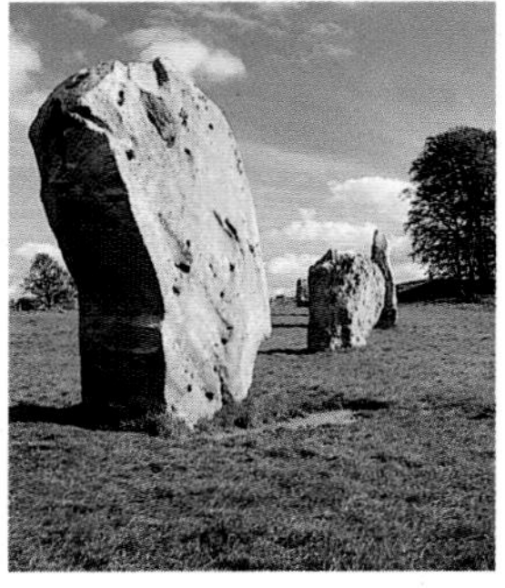

Standing stones at Avebury in southern England

Around 3200BC, people in northwestern Europe began building great circles and lines of standing stones. They also stuck wooden poles in the ground to make circles called wood henges, but most of these have rotted away.

Map of Europe
SCANDINAVIA
NORTH SEA
BALTIC SEA
ATLANTIC OCEAN
Avebury
Stonehenge
Amber
Europe
Asia
Africa
Stone circle
Tin mine
Areas where amber was found

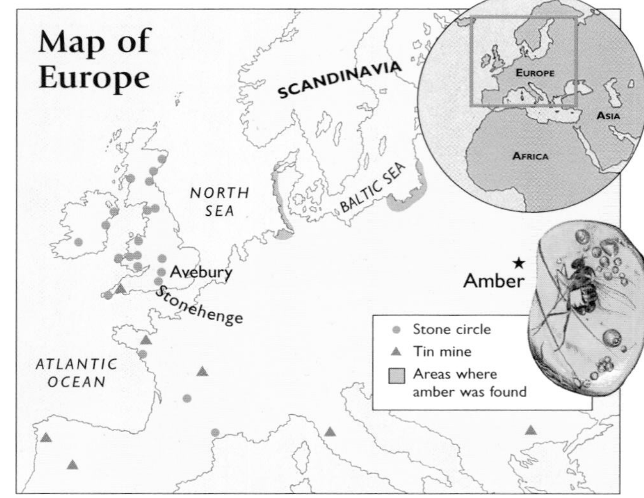

All of these massive monuments were used in religious ceremonies. Some experts think that the mysterious stone circles were also used as giant outdoor calendars.

Building Stonehenge

Stonehenge in southern England is the most spectacular of all the stone circles. It was built in stages over a period of more than a thousand years, and was finally finished around 1500BC.

This picture shows Stonehenge being built.

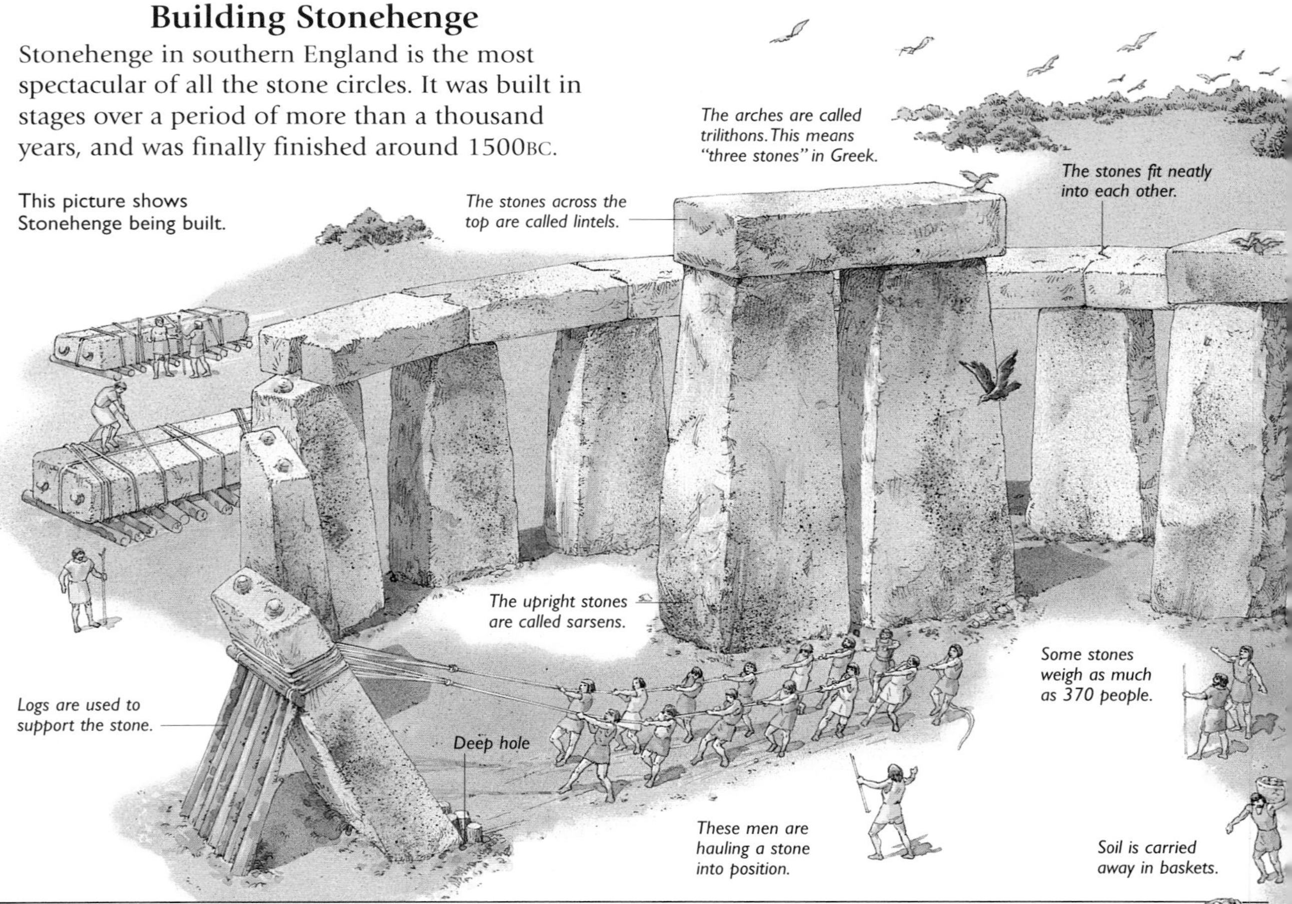

The arches are called trilithons. This means "three stones" in Greek.
The stones fit neatly into each other.
The stones across the top are called lintels.
The upright stones are called sarsens.
Some stones weigh as much as 370 people.
Logs are used to support the stone.
Deep hole
These men are hauling a stone into position.
Soil is carried away in baskets.

10,000BC 5000BC 4000BC 3000BC

Mastering metal

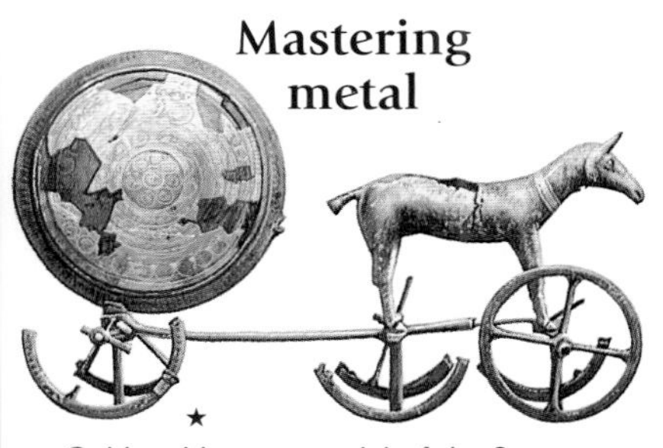

Gold and bronze model of the Sun on a horse-drawn chariot ★

Some people in Europe were using copper over 6000 years ago. Later, people learned how to make bronze by mixing copper with tin. Bronze weapons and tools were much harder than copper ones, and were very valuable.

Trading for tin

The tin needed to make bronze was only found in a few places in Europe (see map), so most people had to trade for it. The people of Scandinavia traded amber from the shores of the Baltic Sea for the metals they needed.

Bronze figure from Scandinavia ★

Tombs and treasure

Golden cup ★

The monument builders believed in life after death, and buried people with the weapons and tools they would need in the Next World. The tombs of wealthy people were filled with bronze swords and daggers, as well as beautiful golden objects.

A tomb called a round barrow

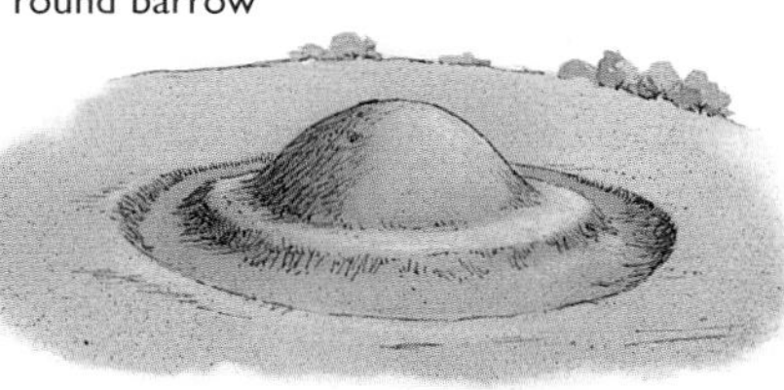

Important people were buried in round stone tombs covered with a great mound of earth. Each tomb held just one body. These tombs, called round barrows, are often found near stone circles.

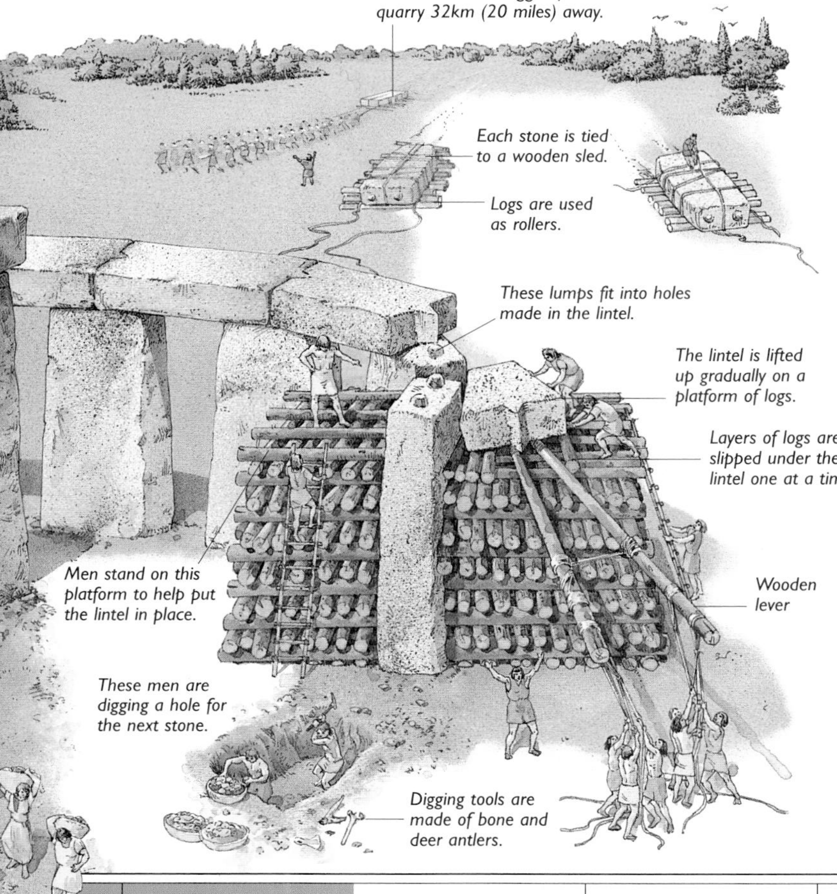

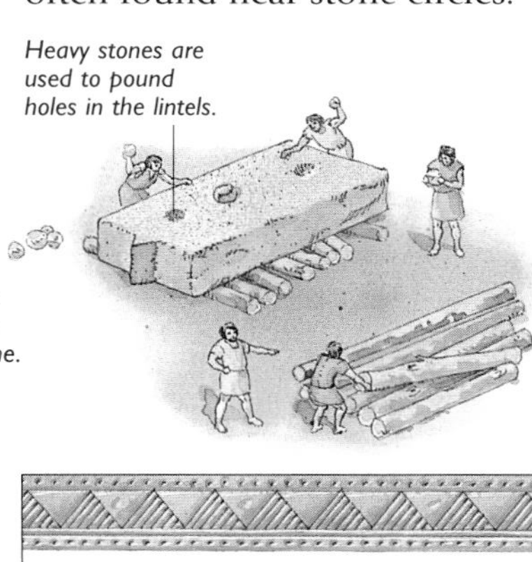

Important dates

c.3200BC	People in northwestern Europe begin building stone circles.
c.3000-1500BC	Stonehenge is built.
c.2500BC	Metalworkers in Europe make bronze.

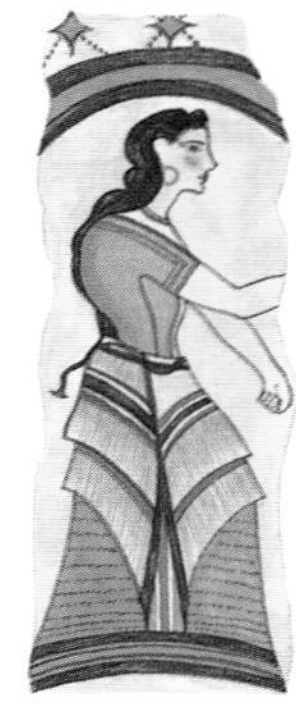

Wall painting of a Minoan woman ★

Palaces and Legends

The Minoans lived on the island of Crete in the Mediterranean Sea. Their way of life slowly grew into the first great civilization in Europe. The Minoans take their name from King Minos, who is said to have ruled the island.

Palace
GREECE
EUROPE
ASIA
AFRICA
Thera
MEDITERRANEAN SEA
Knossos
Mallia
Phaestos
Zakro
CRETE

Map of Crete

The legend of King Minos

According to a Greek legend, the god Zeus fell in love with a beautiful princess called Europa. He turned himself into a bull and swam to Crete with the princess on his back. King Minos of Crete was one of Princess Europa's sons.

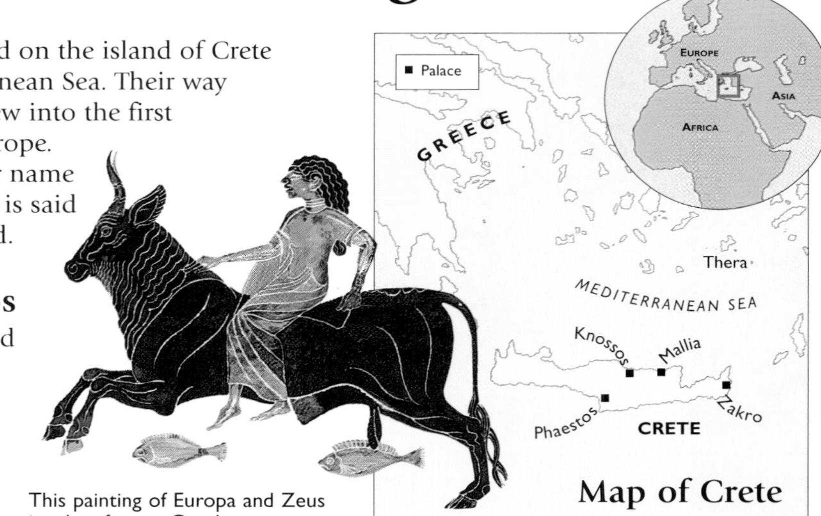

This painting of Europa and Zeus is taken from a Greek vase.

The palace at Knossos

Each of the main towns on Crete was built around a huge palace, but the one at Knossos was the largest. It had over a thousand rooms, which were linked by corridors, staircases and courtyards.

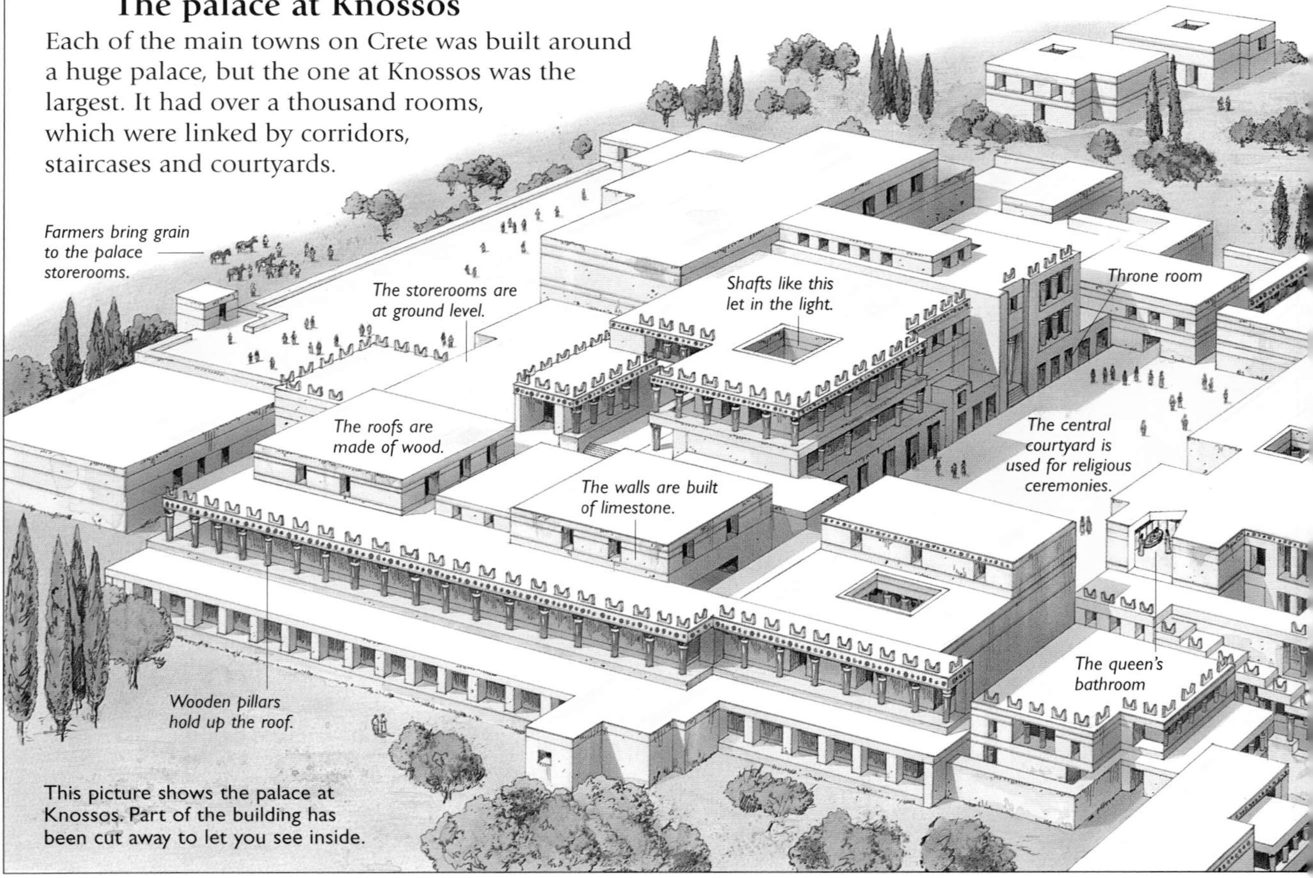

Farmers bring grain to the palace storerooms.
The storerooms are at ground level.
Shafts like this let in the light.
Throne room
The roofs are made of wood.
The walls are built of limestone.
The central courtyard is used for religious ceremonies.
Wooden pillars hold up the roof.
The queen's bathroom

This picture shows the palace at Knossos. Part of the building has been cut away to let you see inside.

EUROPE

10,000BC | 5000BC | 4000BC | 3000BC

Storerooms

Farmers had to give some of their produce to the palace, where it was kept in the storerooms. Some of it was used to feed court officials and to pay the palace craftworkers. The rest was traded abroad.

Grain, oil and wine were stored in huge earthenware jars.

Painted walls

The palace walls were decorated with bright paintings called frescoes. A fresco is a picture which is painted on a wall while the plaster is still damp. The Minoans painted vivid scenes of palace life, plants and animals.

Fresco of a group of dolphins

★

The throne room

The king carried out ceremonies in the throne room. The throne in Knossos is made of stone and is the oldest throne in Europe still standing in its proper place. The walls are painted with frescoes of plants and mythical creatures, called griffins.

This is the brightly painted throne room at Knossos.

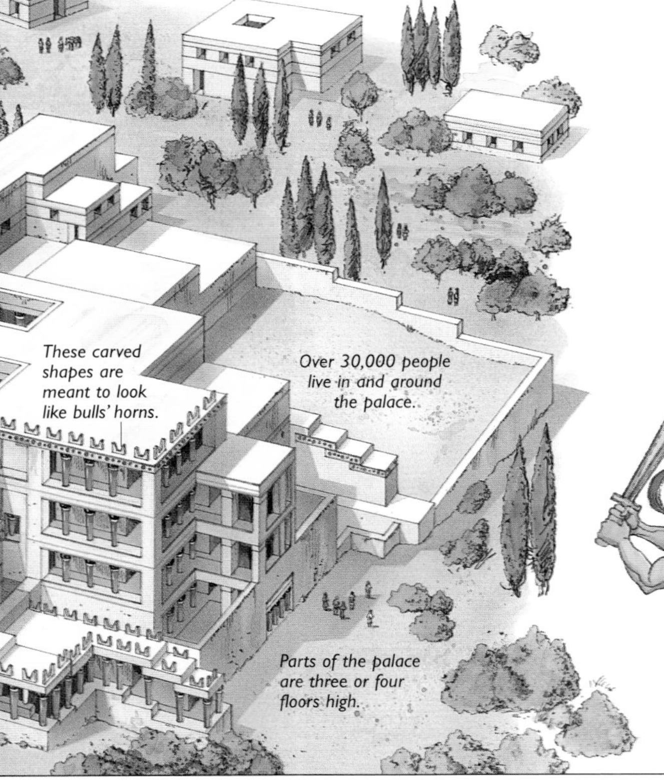

The legend of the Minotaur

According to legend, the Minotaur was half-bull and half-man, and lived in a huge maze under the palace at Knossos. A young Greek prince called Theseus set out to kill it. The daughter of King Minos gave Theseus a magic sword and a ball of thread. As he went deeper into the maze, Theseus unwound the thread, leaving a trail behind him. He used the sword to kill the monster and then followed the thread back to the outside world.

★

★ Theseus prepares to kill the Minotaur.

Life on Crete

Most people on Crete were farmers. They kept animals, such as cattle, sheep, goats and pigs, and grew wheat, barley, vegetables, plums, grapes and olives. People also ate a lot of fish, which they caught in the sea around the island.

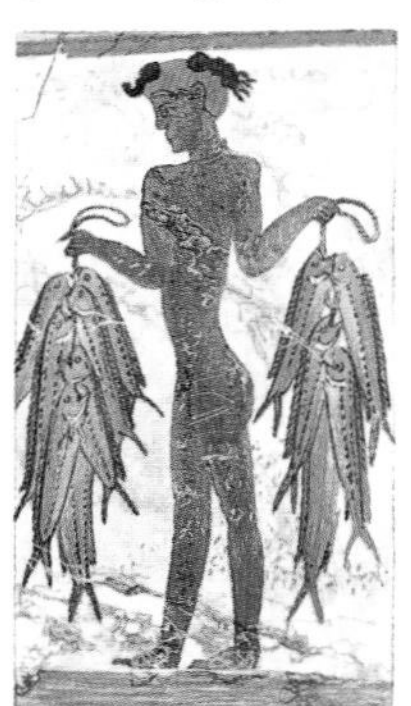

Wall painting of a fisherman holding his catch of mackerel

Travel and trade

The Minoans were skilled sailors. They had a large fleet of ships and sailed all around the eastern Mediterranean. Minoan merchants sold pottery, grain, wine and olive oil, and brought back gold, silver, jewels, ivory and linen. They were successful traders and became very rich.

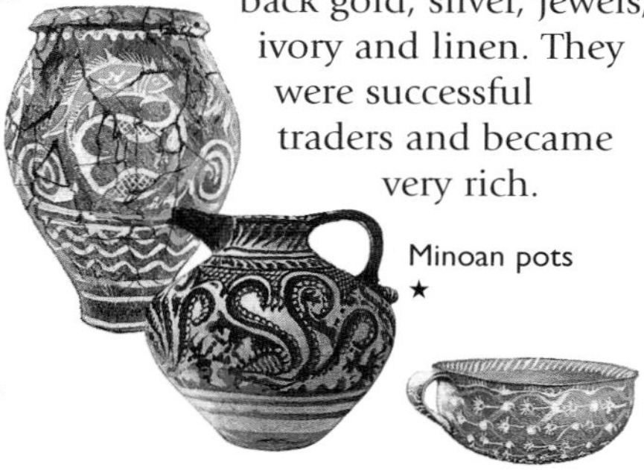

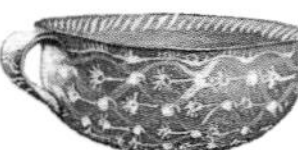

Minoan pots ★

Writing

Once the Minoans began to store goods and trade with other lands, they needed to keep a record of who owned what. At first they used pictograms (picture writing), but later they invented a form of writing which experts call Linear A. So far, no one has been able to understand what it says.

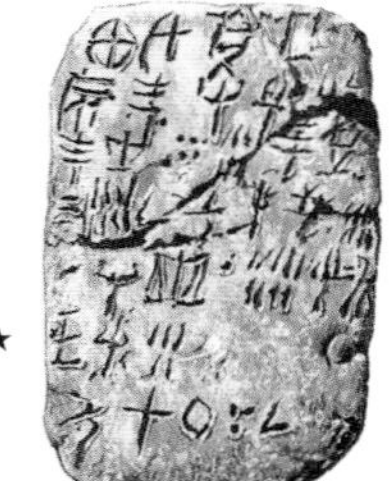

★ Stone tablet carved with Linear A writing

This picture of a busy Minoan town gives an idea of what life on Crete was like.

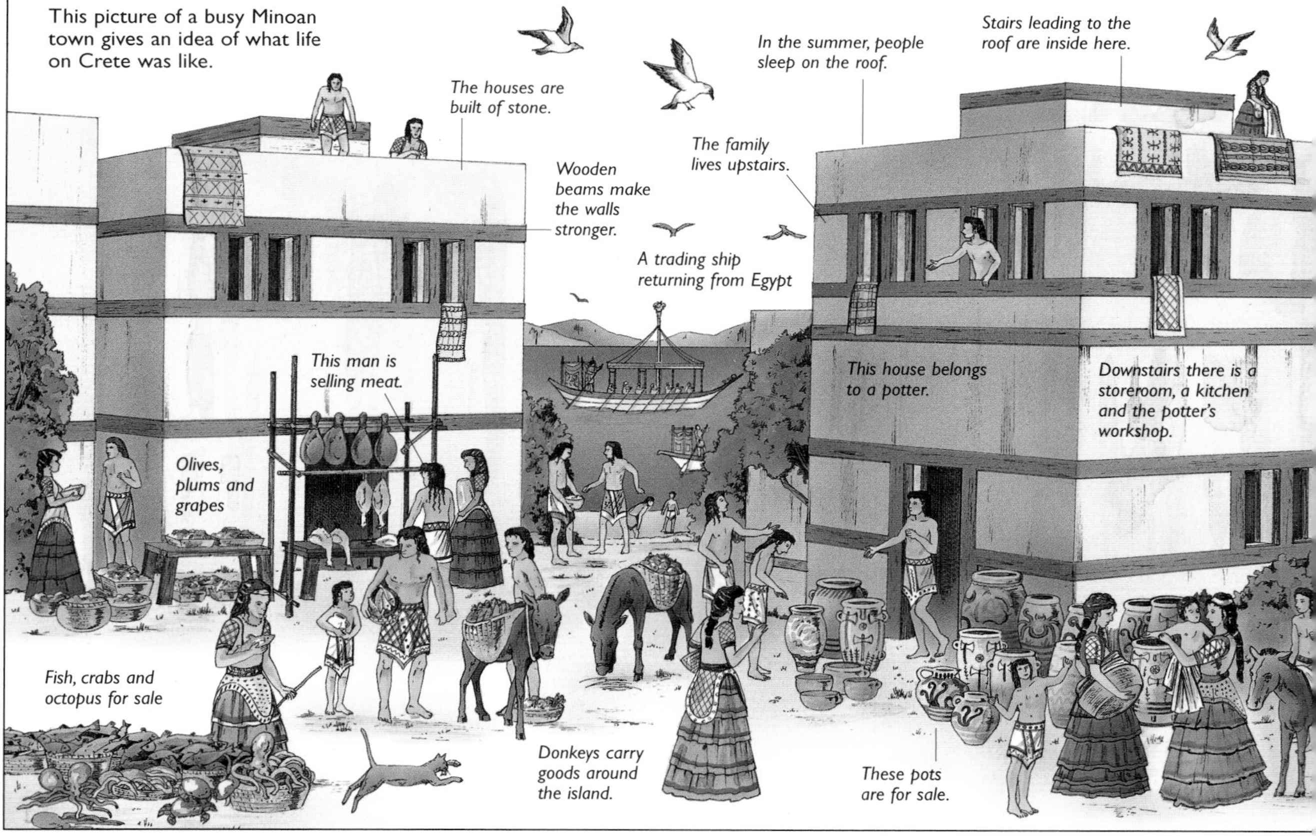
The houses are built of stone.
In the summer, people sleep on the roof.
Stairs leading to the roof are inside here.
The family lives upstairs.
Wooden beams make the walls stronger.
A trading ship returning from Egypt
This man is selling meat.
This house belongs to a potter.
Downstairs there is a storeroom, a kitchen and the potter's workshop.
Olives, plums and grapes
Fish, crabs and octopus for sale
Donkeys carry goods around the island.
These pots are for sale.

EUROPE

10,000BC | 5000BC | 4000BC | 3000BC

Bull-leaping

The Minoans enjoyed an extremely dangerous sport known as bull-leaping. Highly trained acrobats grasped the horns of a charging bull and somersaulted over its back. The bull was sacred to the sea god, so bull-leaping may have been part of a religious ceremony.

This wall painting shows a team ★ of bull-leapers.

Religion

The Minoans did not build huge temples. Instead, they prayed and made offerings to their gods and goddesses in special rooms inside the palaces, or at small outdoor shrines.

A disaster like the one shown here may have helped bring the Minoan civilization to an end.

The end of the Minoans

Around 1450BC, there was a major disaster on Crete. The palaces were badly damaged, but no one is sure exactly how this happened. Around this time, a volcano on the nearby island of Thera erupted. This may have caused an earthquake or a giant tidal wave, which wrecked the Minoans' towns. Falling ash from the volcano may have ruined their farmland.

At around the same time, Crete was invaded by people known as the Mycenaeans, who came from Greece (see pages 128 to 131). The Minoans never really recovered and their civilization gradually died out.

Important dates

c.6000BC	Farmers settle on Crete.
c.2500BC	Towns begin to grow up.
c.1900BC	The first palaces are built. Picture writing is used.
c.1700BC	The palaces are destroyed by an earthquake.
c.1700-1450BC	The palaces are rebuilt. Crete is at its most powerful.
c.1650BC	Linear A writing is used.
c.1450BC	The palaces are destroyed. The Mycenaeans invade. The Minoan civilization gradually dies out.

Palaces and Tombs

EUROPE
ASIA
AFRICA
GREECE
AEGEAN SEA
MEDITERRANEAN SEA
Troy
Athens
Mycenae
Pylos
Sparta
Knossos
CRETE

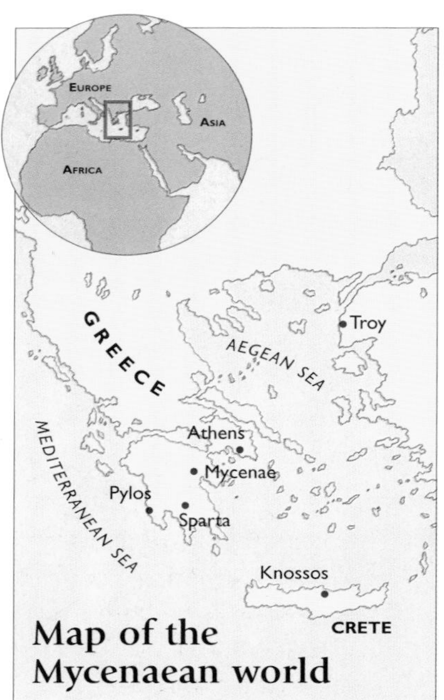

Map of the Mycenaean world

Around 1600BC, the country now called Greece was divided into small kingdoms. Each kingdom was made up of a walled city and the land around it. The people who lived in Greece at this time became known as Mycenaeans, because Mycenae was the most important kingdom.

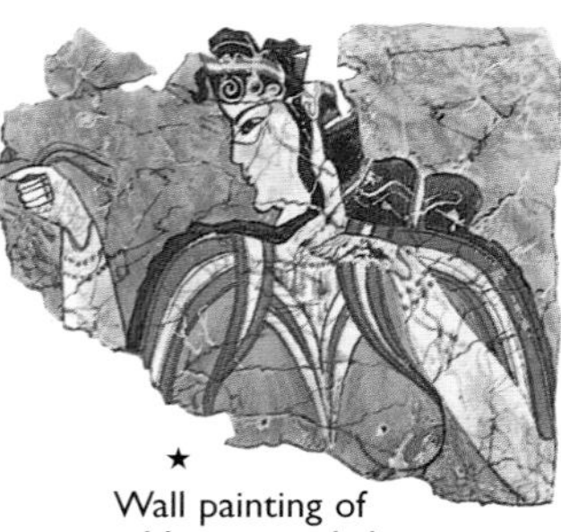

★ Wall painting of a Mycenaean lady

Mycenaean kings lived in magnificent palaces which contained offices, workshops and storerooms, as well as the king's private rooms. The most important room was the great hall, called the megaron.

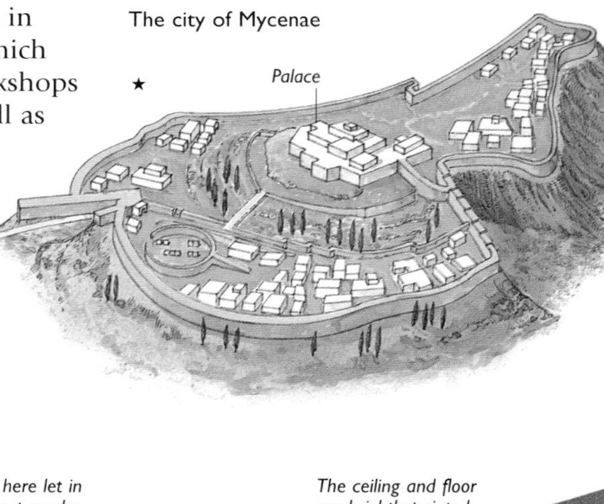

The city of Mycenae

Palace

★

This picture shows a feast in the megaron (great hall) of a Mycenaean palace.

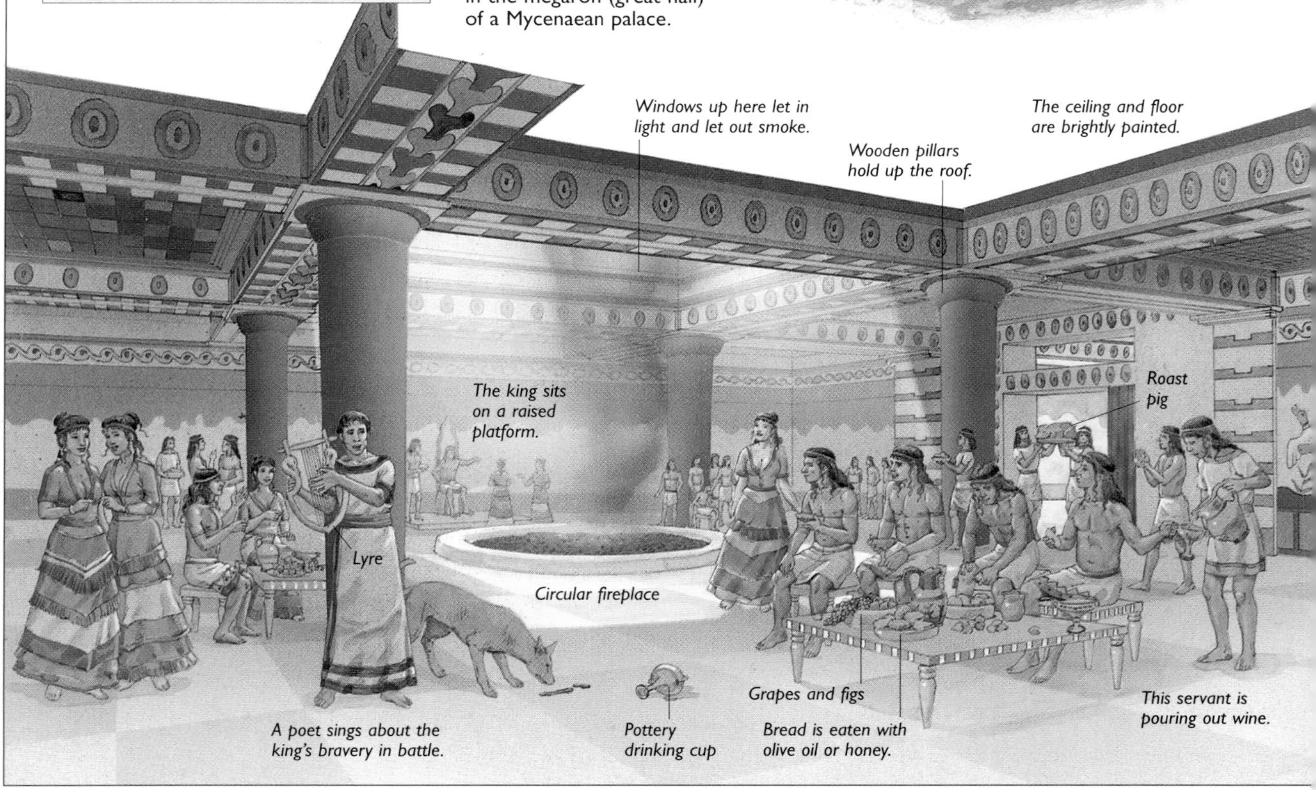

Windows up here let in light and let out smoke.
The ceiling and floor are brightly painted.
Wooden pillars hold up the roof.
Roast pig
The king sits on a raised platform.
Lyre
Circular fireplace
Grapes and figs
This servant is pouring out wine.
A poet sings about the king's bravery in battle.
Pottery drinking cup
Bread is eaten with olive oil or honey.

10,000BC 5000BC 4000BC 3000BC

Workshops

Mycenaean pots

Metalworkers, potters and weavers worked for the king and had their workshops in the palace. Some of the things they made were traded abroad.

Offices

Scribes kept a record of all the goods stored in the palace. They wrote on clay tablets and used a form of writing which we call Linear B.

Mycenaean scribes at work

Clay tablet ★

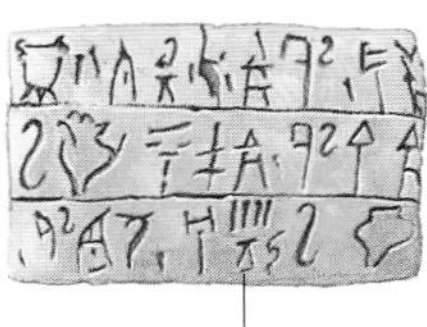

Linear B writing

Bathrooms

One palace had a room with a built-in bathtub. The bathtub had no drain, so the water had to be scooped out with a jug and poured away.

★ The bathroom in the palace at Pylos

Early tombs

The early kings of Mycenae and their families were buried in deep pits, called shaft graves. The graves were protected by a circular stone wall.

A circle of graves at Mycenae

Each grave is marked by a stone slab.

A cutaway picture of a shaft grave

Tomb treasure

Mycenaean tombs were filled with gold and silver ornaments, goblets, swords and daggers. Shaft graves were difficult for robbers to break into, so a lot of this treasure has survived.

★ This golden funeral mask was found in a shaft grave at Mycenae.

Beehive tombs

The later Mycenaean kings were buried in huge, beehive-shaped tombs, called tholos tombs. These tombs were built under great mounds of earth.

This cutaway picture of a tholos tomb shows a king's funeral.

Priests and priestesses bring offerings of food and wine.

These sheep will be sacrificed.

The inside is covered with gold rosettes.

Musicians

The doorway is decorated with carved green and red stones.

The king's body is surrounded by treasure.

EUROPE

2000BC 1000BC 500BC AD1 AD500

Warriors and Traders

War was an important part of Mycenaean life. Kings and nobles trained as warriors, skilled metalworkers made weapons from bronze, and poets told about the bravery of soldiers in battle.

Vase showing Mycenaean warriors

Hunting

When nobles were not at war, they used their chariots for hunting. They killed wild boar and used the tusks to decorate the helmets they wore in battle.

★ Hunting wild boar

When a city went to war, the king led his army into battle. He and his nobles rode in fast chariots, while the ordinary soldiers marched on foot.

In this picture, the king of the city of Mycenae is leading his army to war. ★

People cheer as the soldiers pass by.

The city walls are built of huge blocks of stone.

This is the Lion Gate. It is the main entrance to Mycenae.

Helmet covered with boars' tusks

Some warriors wear a bronze suit to protect them.

This huge rectangular shield is called a tower shield.

Some shields are shaped like a figure eight.

The chariots are made of wood and oxhide.

The king wears a helmet decorated with a horn.

Foot soldier

The shields are made of oxhide stretched over a wooden frame.

The invasion of Crete

Around 1450BC, Mycenaean warriors sailed to Crete and took control of the palace at Knossos. They also took over the Minoans' sea trade and became the leading traders in the eastern Mediterranean.

Mycenaean warships

Trade

Mycenaean traders sailed to places as far apart as Egypt and Italy. They bought ivory and precious metals in exchange for wine, olive oil, and objects such as weapons, pots and bowls.

This scene shows part of a busy Mycenaean trading port.

The siege of Troy

Around 1250BC, the city of Troy (in modern Turkey) was destroyed. A famous tale is told about this real event.

According to the legend, Paris, prince of Troy, fell in love with Helen, the beautiful wife of a Mycenaean king. Paris took Helen off to Troy, so the angry Mycenaeans attacked the city and kept it surrounded for ten years.

One day, they left a huge wooden horse outside the walls of Troy and pretended to sail away. The Trojans thought the horse would bring them luck and dragged it into the city.

Mycenaean soldiers climbing out of the wooden horse ★

That night, Mycenaean soldiers, who were hiding inside the horse, climbed out. They opened the city gates and let in the rest of their army. Troy was destroyed and Helen was reunited with her husband.

The end of the Mycenaeans

From around 1250BC, there were many bad harvests. Some of the Mycenaeans attacked each other's cities, and stole cattle and crops. Some may even have left Greece to search for new homes, and their cities were gradually abandoned.

Important dates

c.2000BC	The Mycenaeans settle in Greece.
c.1600-1200BC	The Mycenaeans are rich and powerful.
c.1450BC	Knossos is taken over.
c.1250BC	Troy is destroyed.
c.1200BC	The cities are gradually abandoned.

The Empire of Hammurabi

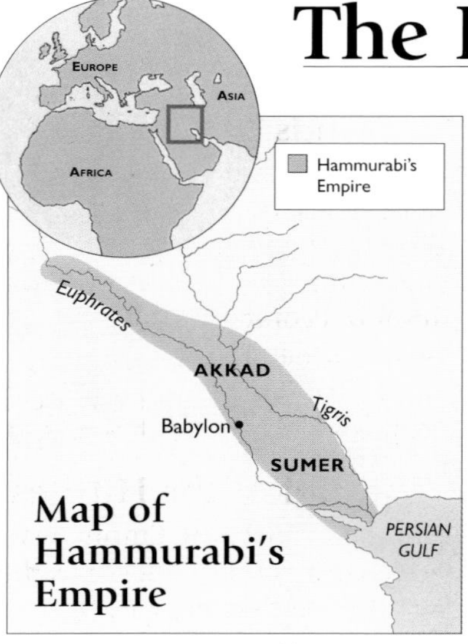

Map of Hammurabi's Empire

Around 2000BC, the lands of Sumer and Akkad were invaded by desert tribes known as Amorites. They took control of several cities, including Babylon. Each city was then ruled by a different Amorite family.

Amorite invaders

Around 1792BC, a young man called Hammurabi became King of Babylon. He fought the other Amorite kings and conquered the whole of Sumer and Akkad, creating a powerful empire.

★ This picture of King Hammurabi is based on a stone carving.

Hammurabi's laws

Hammurabi put together one set of laws and punishments for all the people in his Empire. These laws were carved on a stone pillar for everyone to see.

These pictures show some of Hammurabi's laws.

If a surgeon carried out an operation that killed a patient, he had his hand cut off.

If an architect built a house that collapsed and killed someone, he was put to death.

A man who owed money to someone could lend him his wife as a slave.

Gods and legends

★

Priests told how the god Marduk saved the world from a terrifying sea monster.

The Babylonians had many different gods, but Marduk was the most important one. Some people believed that Marduk created the world by building a huge raft on the ocean and pouring dust on top of it.

The end of the Empire

After Hammurabi died, his Empire grew weaker. Around 1595BC, the city of Babylon was raided by the Hittites, and the Empire collapsed. (To find out what happened in Babylon later on, see pages 150 and 151.)

Important dates

c.2000BC	The Amorites invade.
c.1792-1750BC	King Hammurabi rules Babylon and creates the Babylonian Empire.
c.1595BC	The Hittites raid Babylon, and the Empire collapses.

The Hittite Empire

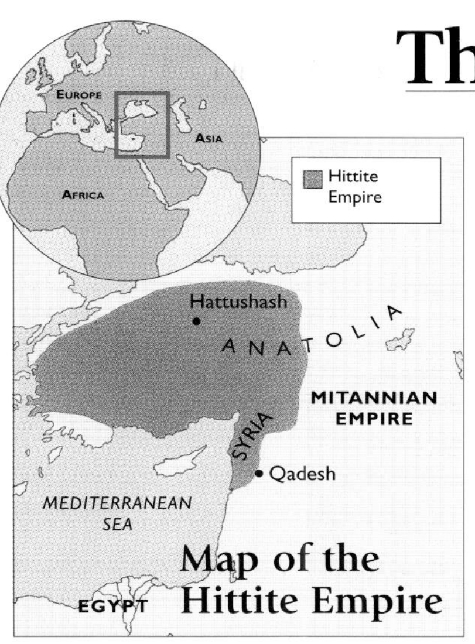

Map of the Hittite Empire

In around 2000BC, the Hittite people settled in Anatolia (in modern Turkey). By around 1650BC, they had all joined together to form one kingdom, with a capital city at Hattushash.

Warriors

The Hittites were tough warriors. They rode into battle in war chariots and carried iron weapons, which were stronger than the bronze weapons used by their enemies.

Kings and wars

The greatest Hittite king was Shuppiluliuma. He invaded Syria, destroyed the nearby Mitannian Empire and built up a powerful empire of his own.

The Hittites and the Egyptians were bitter enemies. They fought a fierce battle at Qadesh, which neither side won. The two countries later made peace.

★ Gold statue of a Hittite king

Gods

The Hittites had many gods, but their chief god was called Teshub. People believed that he controlled the weather.

Teshub holding a flash of lightning

The end of the Hittites

Around 1195BC, the Empire was attacked by raiders known as the Sea Peoples (see page 141). Some Hittites survived in Syria, but the Empire collapsed.

In this scene, Hittite warriors are leaving the city of Hattushash to go to war.
★

Important dates

c.2000BC	The Hittites settle in Anatolia.
c.1650BC	Hattushash is the capital of the Hittite kingdom.
c.1380-1340BC	King Shuppiluliuma rules.
c.1285BC	The Battle of Qadesh
c.1195BC	The Hittites are defeated by the Sea Peoples.

BABYLONIANS
HITTITES
2000BC | 1000BC | 500BC | AD1 | AD500

The Egyptian Empire

Around 1720BC, Egypt was invaded by people called the Hyksos. They had horses and chariots, and easily defeated the Egyptian soldiers who fought on foot. The Egyptians gradually learned how to use chariots and drove the Hyksos out of Egypt. Then, they began to invade nearby lands and quickly built up a large empire.

Egyptian painting showing a horse and chariot

Warrior pharaohs

The Egyptians were led into battle by their pharaohs (kings), who were skilled soldiers. The greatest warrior pharaoh was Tuthmosis III, who led his army to war 17 times. During his rule, the Egyptian Empire was at its largest.

The most dangerous of Egypt's enemies were the Hittites. Pharaoh Ramesses II fought against them for over 30 years. The two countries finally made peace, and Ramesses married a Hittite princess.

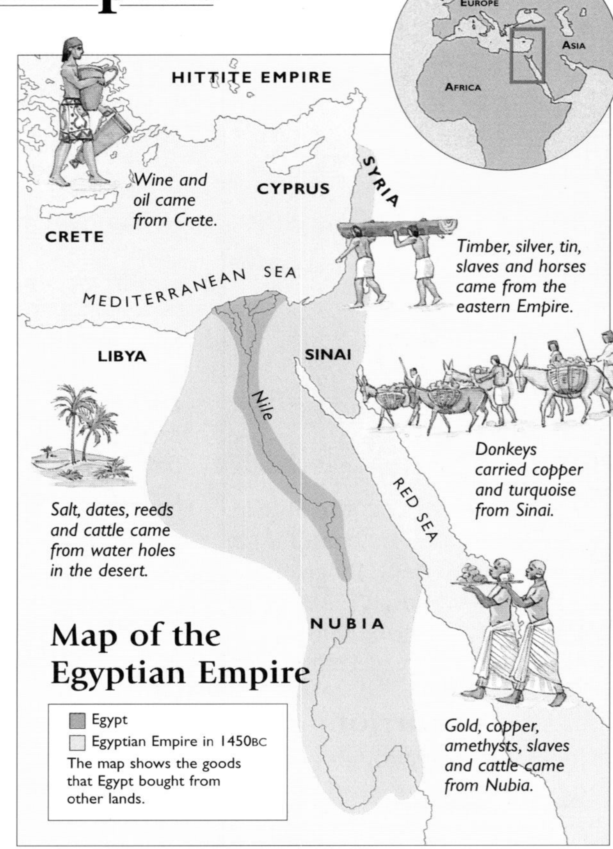

Map of the Egyptian Empire

Statue of Tuthmosis III ★

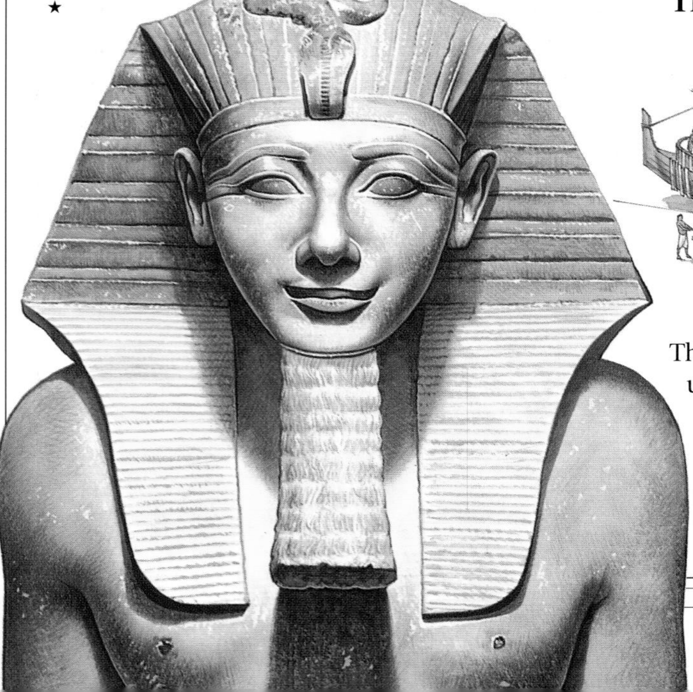

Trading trips

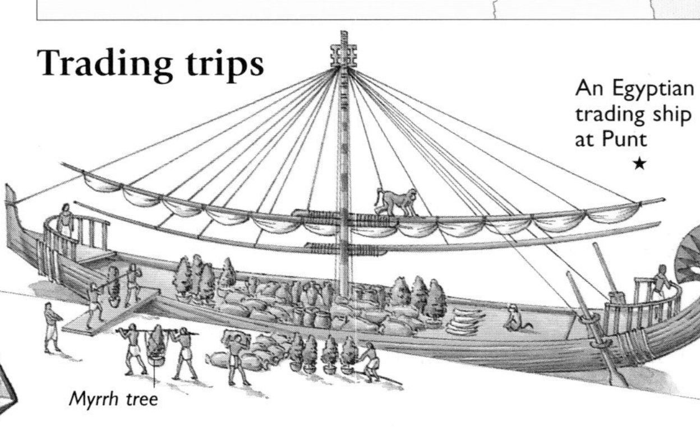

An Egyptian trading ship at Punt ★

The Egyptians had their own gold mines and could use the gold to buy the things they needed. They traded with other lands in their Empire and beyond (see map above). Some traders even went as far as Punt, a place on the east coast of Africa. There, they bought valuable myrrh trees, which were used to make sweet-smelling incense.

★ In this scene, visitors are bringing gifts to the pharaoh's court. Some pillars have been taken out to show more of the throne room.

The pharaoh's court

People came from all over the Empire to the pharaoh's court. They brought goods to trade and rich gifts for the pharaoh. The gifts were a kind of tax, called tribute, that all conquered people had to pay. Some foreign rulers even sent their daughters to marry the pharaoh, who had many wives.

Travel

There were few roads in Egypt, as they would have been washed away by floods each year. The easiest way to travel was by boat along the Nile. Trading ships also sailed to ports on the Red Sea and in the eastern Mediterranean.

Tomb painting of a nobleman's boat

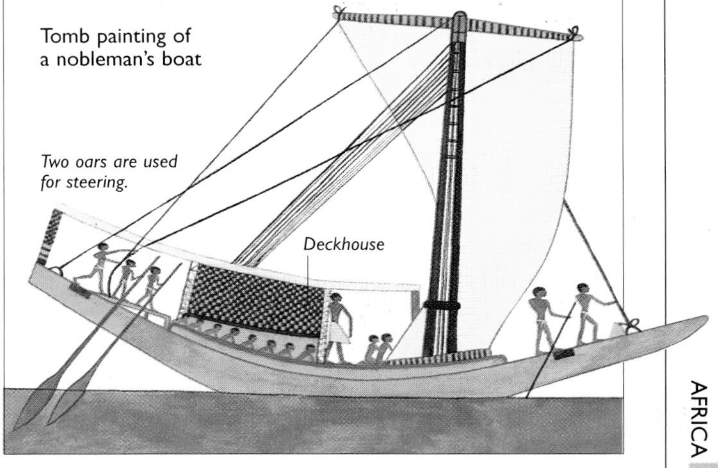

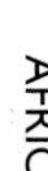

Temples and Gods

The Egyptians had many different gods and goddesses. Most of them were linked with a special animal or bird, and they were often shown in paintings and carvings with the head of that animal or bird. This made them easy to recognize.

Here you can see some Egyptian gods and goddesses.

★ *Ma'at, goddess of truth and justice*

★ *Re, the sun god, was sometimes shown with a hawk's head.*

Thoth, god of wisdom and writing, had the head of an ibis (a kind of bird). ★

★ *Anubis, god of the dead, had a jackal's head.*

Amun was king of the gods during the New Kingdom. ★

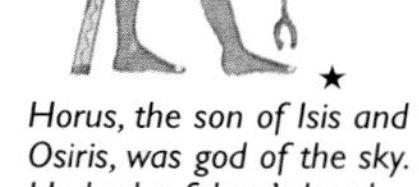

★ *Horus, the son of Isis and Osiris, was god of the sky. He had a falcon's head.*

Osiris, ruler of the dead ★

★ *Isis, the sister and wife of Osiris, was goddess of crafts.*

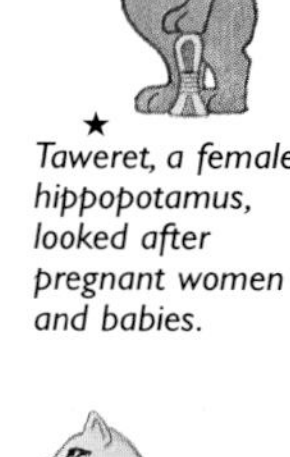

★ *Taweret, a female hippopotamus, looked after pregnant women and babies.*

★ *Bast, the cat goddess*

This temple at Abu Simbel in Nubia was carved out of solid rock.

The Egyptians built many huge, stone temples along the banks of the Nile. They believed that their gods and goddesses lived in these temples.

Inside each temple was a statue of the god who lived there. Every morning, priests woke the god, washed the statue, dressed it, gave it food and prayed to it.

Ordinary people did not normally go inside the temple. They only saw the statue of the god on festival days, when it was taken out and carried around the town.

This is the festival of Bast, the cat goddess. The procession is just leaving the temple.

10,000BC | 5000BC | 4000BC | 3000BC

Attached to the temple were craft workshops, a library and a school, and many different people worked there.

Some people who worked in the temple

A temple school

A few boys from rich families went to the temple school to learn how to read and write. Older boys could study history, geography, religion, languages, mathematics and medicine. Girls did not go to school. They were taught at home by their mothers.

Writing

The Egyptians wrote in pictures or signs, which we call hieroglyphs. Scribes wrote on special paper, called papyrus, which was made from reeds. Ink was made in solid blocks and had to be mixed with water.

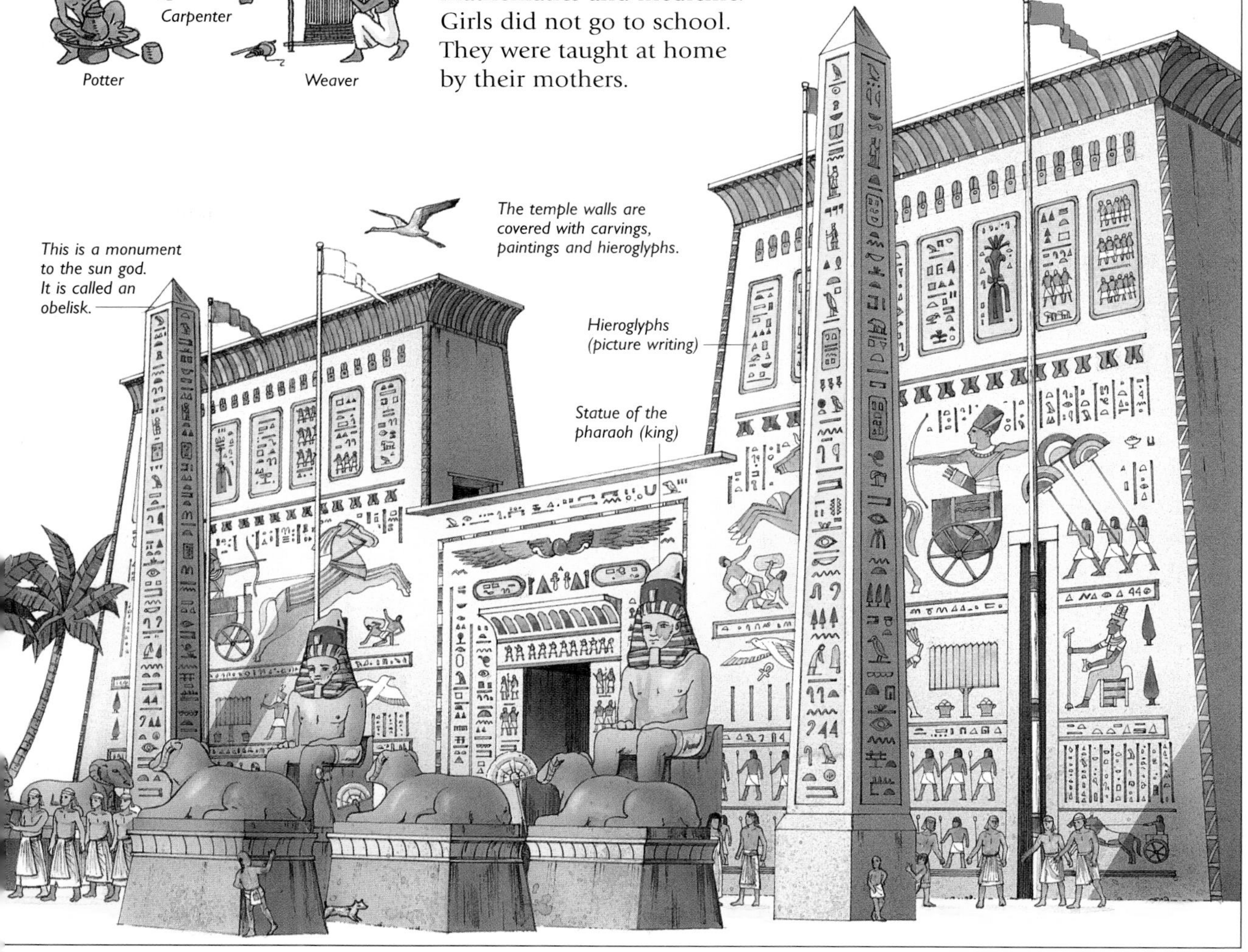

This is a monument to the sun god. It is called an obelisk.

The temple walls are covered with carvings, paintings and hieroglyphs.

Hieroglyphs (picture writing)

Statue of the pharaoh (king)

2000BC | 1000BC | 500BC | AD1 | AD500

Life at Home

Egyptian houses were built of bricks made from a mixture of mud and straw. The bricks were shaped in a wooden frame and were then left to dry in the sun. Most houses only had one or two rooms, but rich people lived in large, luxurious villas.

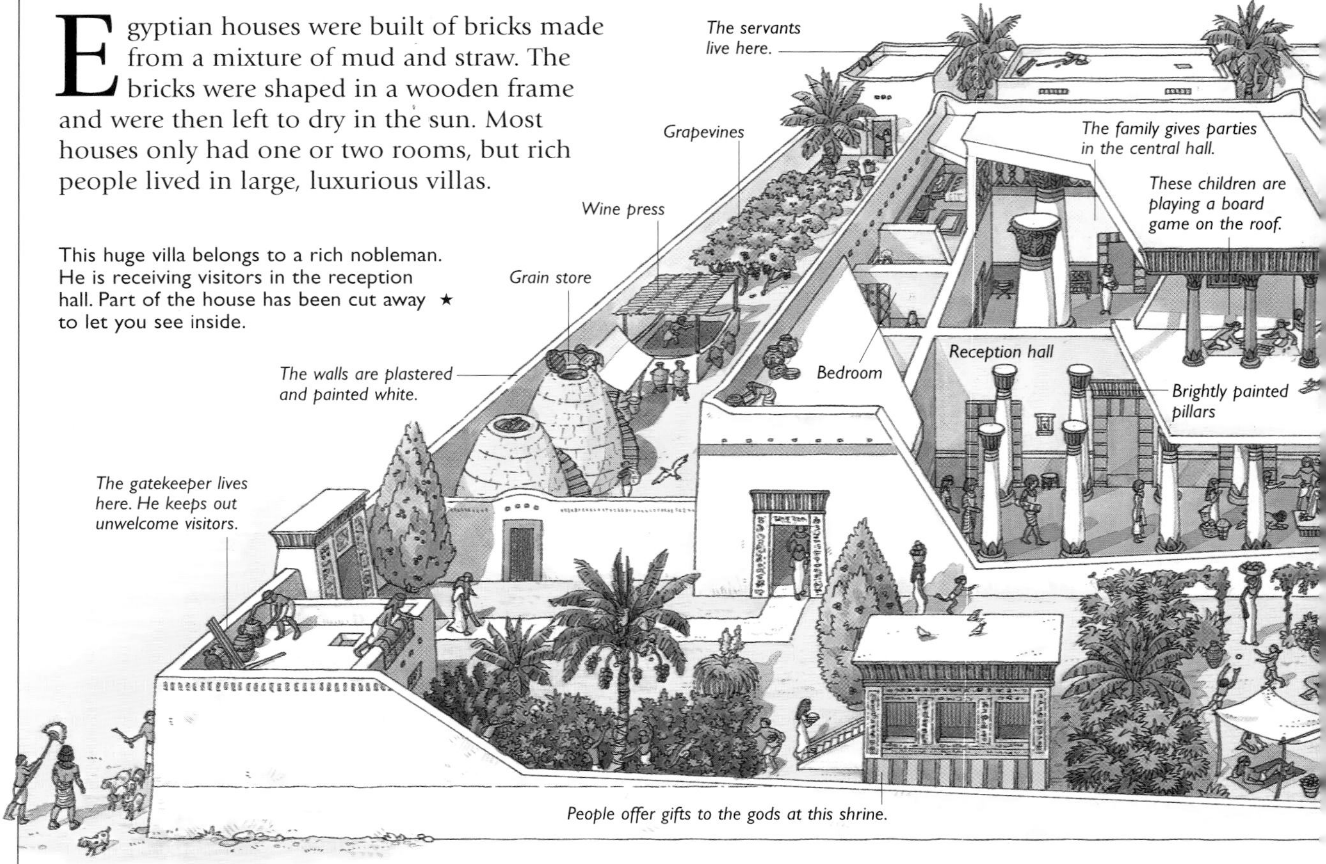

This huge villa belongs to a rich nobleman. He is receiving visitors in the reception hall. Part of the house has been cut away ★ to let you see inside.

The servants live here.

Grapevines

Wine press

Grain store

The family gives parties in the central hall.

These children are playing a board game on the roof.

Reception hall

Bedroom

The walls are plastered and painted white.

Brightly painted pillars

The gatekeeper lives here. He keeps out unwelcome visitors.

People offer gifts to the gods at this shrine.

Parties

Rich Egyptians often gave large parties with lots of food and drink. Guests were entertained by musicians, singers, dancers, jugglers and acrobats. Servants put cones of perfumed fat on the guests' heads. As the fat melted and ran down their faces, it cooled them down and made them smell nice.

This Egyptian painting shows guests, dancers and musicians at a party.

Games

The Egyptians had several types of board games, such as the two shown on the right, but no one is sure how they were played. Children played with balls, spinning tops, dolls and animals made from wood or pottery.

★ Hounds and jackals

Senet ★

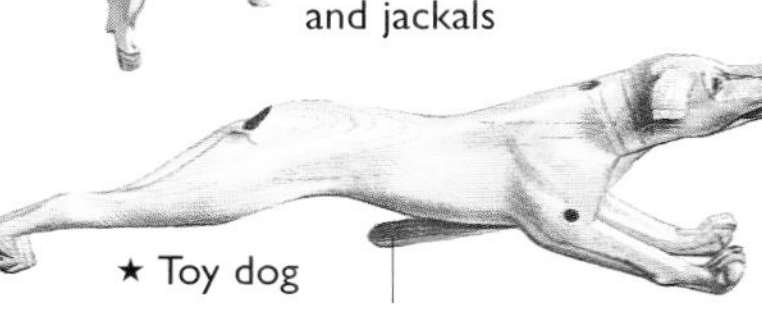

★ Toy dog

This handle opens the dog's mouth.

★ Hippo made of painted pottery

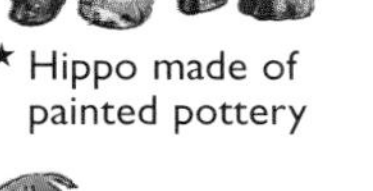

★ Clay balls

Cattle pens

Well

Fish pond

Walled garden

Shade to keep off the sun

The end of the Egyptian Empire

The last great warrior pharaoh was Ramesses III. He defended Egypt against raiders known as the Sea Peoples (see page 141).

After Ramesses died, the Empire grew weaker. Civil war broke out and Egypt was invaded by the Assyrians, then by the Nubians and later by the Persians.

In 332BC, Egypt was conquered by Alexander the Great (see pages 160 and 161). After Alexander's death, the country was ruled by the Ptolemy family, who were descended from one of his generals.

In 32BC, Rome went to war with Egypt. The Egyptians were defeated and Queen Cleopatra, the last Ptolemy ruler, killed herself. Egypt then became part of the Roman Empire.

Cleopatra

Sports

The most popular sports were hunting and fishing. Noblemen hunted water birds and river animals, such as hippos and crocodiles. People also enjoyed wrestling, fencing and energetic games, such as tug-of-war.

This picture of a tug-of-war comes from an Egyptian wall painting.

Hunting a hippo from a reed boat

Important dates

c.1720BC	The Hyksos invade Egypt. The Middle Kingdom ends.
c.1570BC	The Hyksos are driven out. The New Kingdom begins.
c.1450BC	The Egyptian Empire is at its largest.
c.1280BC	Ramesses II makes peace with the Hittites.
c.1190BC	The Sea Peoples attack.
c.1070BC	The New Kingdom ends in civil war.
671BC	The Assyrians invade.
525BC	The Persians invade.
332BC	Alexander the Great conquers Egypt.
30BC	Egypt becomes part of the Roman Empire.

The People of Canaan

Map of Canaan

Trade

Canaanite merchants set sail from ports such as Byblos and Ugarit. They traded all around the eastern Mediterranean.

In this picture, a Canaanite merchant is getting ready to set off for Egypt. ★

A scribe lists all the goods that are to be loaded onto the ship.

These slaves will be sold to an Egyptian nobleman.

Merchant

This cedarwood will be used to build boats in Egypt.

Jar of olives

Ivory box

Brightly dyed cloth

Golden cups and vases

Jar of oil

Wine jars

The land of Canaan lay at the eastern end of the Mediterranean Sea. The people of Canaan were farmers and traders, who lived in many small kingdoms. Each kingdom had a walled city with villages and farmland around it.

The walled city of Ebla

The huge cedar trees which grew in the north were very valuable, and Canaan became rich. It was fought over constantly by empire builders, such as the Egyptians and the Hittites. From around 1550BC, most of Canaan was ruled by Egypt.

Cedar tree

Gods

The Canaanites had many gods, but the most powerful one was Baal, the god of rain, storms and war. His wife, Astarte, was the goddess of love.

Statue of Baal ★

Priests sacrificed animals at hilltop shrines.

Writing

The Canaanites invented an alphabet with just 27 letters. It was much easier to use than Egyptian or Sumerian writing, which had hundreds of signs.

★
Clay tablet carved with Canaanite writing

Invasions

Between 1195BC and 1190BC, Canaan was invaded by the Sea Peoples (see opposite page). Some Sea Peoples settled in the south, but the Canaanites kept control in the north.

Raiders of the Mediterranean

The Sea Peoples probably came from Greece, the Greek islands and southwestern Turkey. Around 1195BC, troubles at home forced them to look for somewhere else to live, and they invaded the eastern Mediterranean.

An army of Sea Peoples destroyed the Hittite Empire, then some of them sailed south, attacking towns on the coast of Canaan. Others made their way on foot, killing and destroying as they went.

Sea Peoples on the move

Women and children travel in carts.

Around 1190BC, the Sea Peoples attacked Egypt. They fought on land and sea, and were defeated in a fierce battle off the coast of Egypt.

The Philistines

After their defeat, the Sea Peoples scattered around the Mediterranean. One tribe, called the Peleset, settled in southern Canaan which was later named Palestine after them. In the Bible, they are known as Philistines.

The Philistines had strong iron weapons which helped them to conquer nearby tribes, such as the Hebrews (see pages 142 and 143).

★ Philistine coffins were made of pottery.

This picture shows the sea battle between the Sea Peoples and the Egyptians.

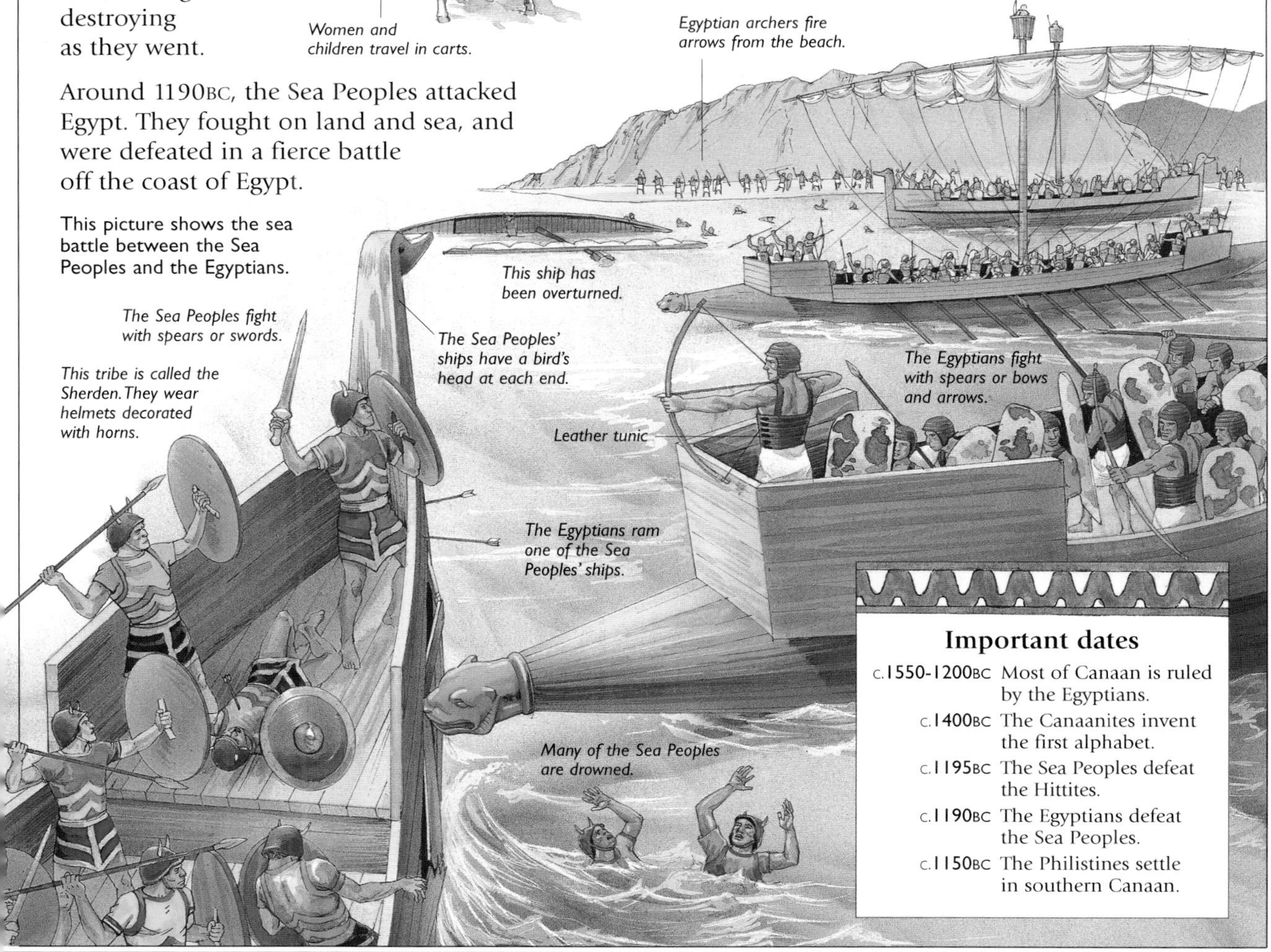

Egyptian archers fire arrows from the beach.

This ship has been overturned.

The Sea Peoples fight with spears or swords.

The Sea Peoples' ships have a bird's head at each end.

This tribe is called the Sherden. They wear helmets decorated with horns.

The Egyptians fight with spears or bows and arrows.

Leather tunic

The Egyptians ram one of the Sea Peoples' ships.

Many of the Sea Peoples are drowned.

Important dates

c.1550-1200BC	Most of Canaan is ruled by the Egyptians.
c.1400BC	The Canaanites invent the first alphabet.
c.1195BC	The Sea Peoples defeat the Hittites.
c.1190BC	The Egyptians defeat the Sea Peoples.
c.1150BC	The Philistines settle in southern Canaan.

CANAANITES

SEA PEOPLES

2000BC 1000BC 500BC AD1 AD500

The Hebrew Kingdoms

The early Hebrews lived in tents.

The early Hebrew tribes wandered along the edges of the desert near the land of Canaan. Unlike most people in ancient times, they believed in only one god. They thought he would look after them if they obeyed him.

The great escape

You can read about the Hebrews in the Old Testament of the Bible. One famous story tells how they were forced to work for the kings of Egypt. Led by a man called Moses, they escaped across the desert into Canaan.

The Hebrews' escape from Egypt is known as the Exodus.

Conquering Canaan

The Hebrews probably arrived in Canaan around 1250BC. After many battles, they won some land and settled down to farm.

This cutaway picture shows the house of a Hebrew farmer. ★

Fighting the Philistines

The Hebrews had to fight to defend their land against the Philistines who had settled on the coast. The Hebrews chose a man called Saul to be their king and lead them into battle, but the hero of the war was a boy called David. The Bible tells how he killed the Philistines' strongest warrior with a stone hurled from a sling.

David kills the Philistine warrior Goliath. ★

King David

David became king when Saul died. He defeated the Philistines and united the Hebrews into one kingdom, called Israel. He captured Jerusalem and made it his capital city.

Internet link: *For a link to a Web site about the Israelites and Canaanites, with lots of information, maps and photos, go to* **www.usborne-quicklinks.com**

King Solomon

David's son, Solomon, set up trade links with other lands, such as Phoenicia, and made Israel rich and powerful. He used part of his wealth to build a great temple in Jerusalem for his people's god.

Outside Solomon's temple was a bronze basin filled with holy water.

This cutaway picture shows Solomon's temple in Jerusalem.

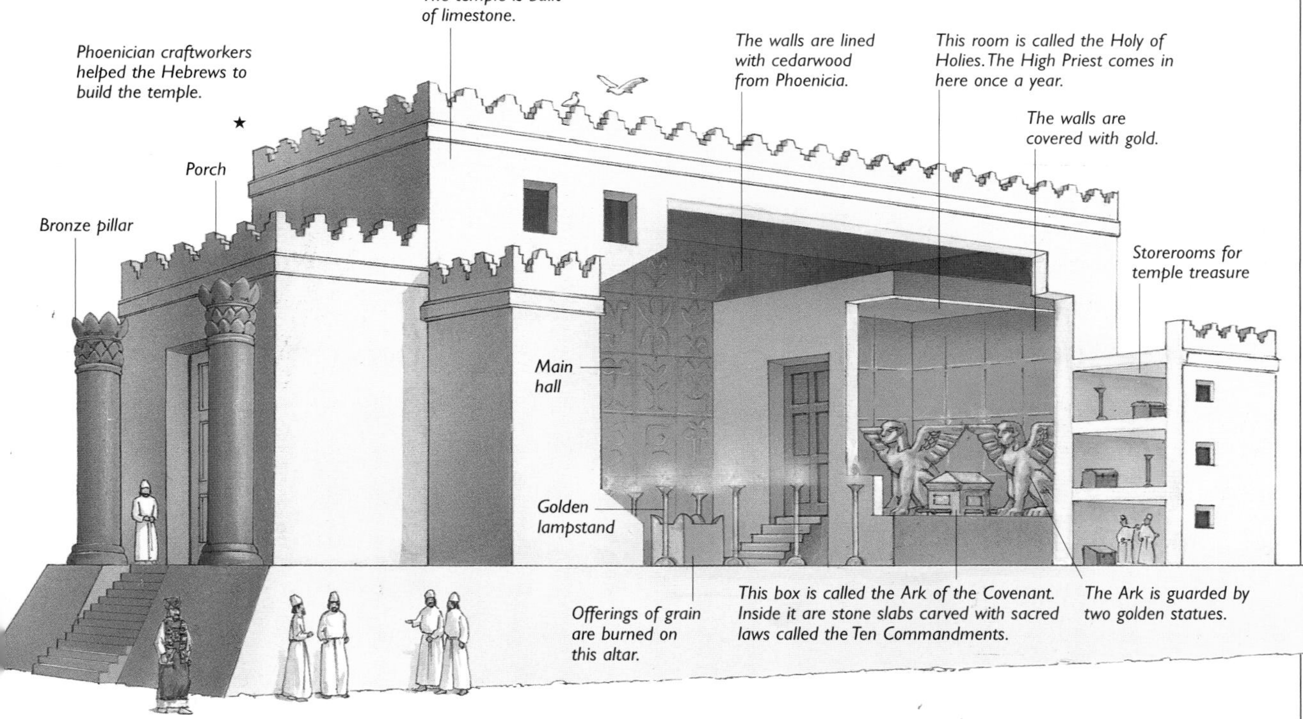

The temple is built of limestone.

Phoenician craftworkers helped the Hebrews to build the temple.

The walls are lined with cedarwood from Phoenicia.

This room is called the Holy of Holies. The High Priest comes in here once a year.

The walls are covered with gold.

Porch

Bronze pillar

Storerooms for temple treasure

Main hall

Golden lampstand

Offerings of grain are burned on this altar.

This box is called the Ark of the Covenant. Inside it are stone slabs carved with sacred laws called the Ten Commandments.

The Ark is guarded by two golden statues.

Two kingdoms

After Solomon's death, quarrels broke out between the north and the south. The country split into two kingdoms, Israel in the north and Judah in the south.

The end of the Hebrew kingdoms

In 722BC, the Assyrians invaded Israel and took control. The Israelites later rebelled and many were taken to Assyria as slaves. Judah was conquered by the Babylonians, who destroyed Jerusalem and took the Judeans prisoner. The Judeans, who became known as Jews, were allowed to return home after the Babylonian Empire collapsed.

The people of Judah were taken to Babylon as slaves.

Important dates

c.1250BC	The Hebrews arrive in Canaan.
c.1020BC	Saul becomes king.
c.1000-965BC	King David rules. The Philistines are defeated.
c.965-928BC	King Solomon rules. The temple is built.
c.926BC	The kingdom splits in two, Israel and Judah.
722BC	The Assyrians invade Israel.
587BC	The Babylonians destroy Jerusalem. The people of Judah are taken prisoner.

Traders from Phoenicia

The Phoenicians were descended from the Canaanites, who lived at the eastern end of the Mediterranean Sea (see page 140). From around 1200BC, they became the most successful traders in the ancient world.

Cities by the sea

The main Phoenician trading ports were the cities of Tyre, Sidon and Byblos. The cities were protected by strong walls and each one had its own king, who lived in a luxurious palace.

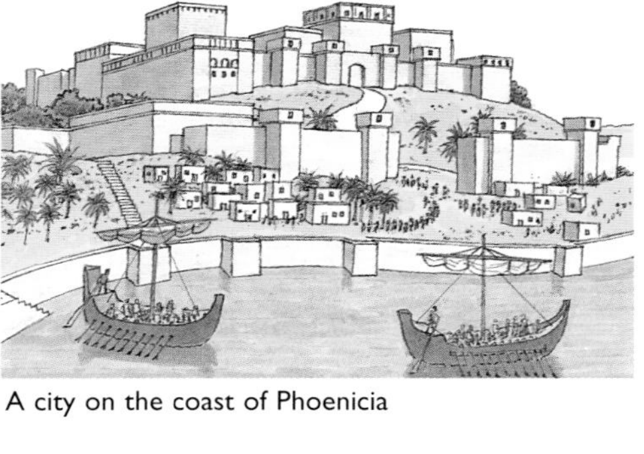

A city on the coast of Phoenicia

Crafts

★ Glass bead

★ Ivory carving

Skilled craftworkers made objects for traders to sell abroad. The Phoenicians were known for their fine ivory carvings and their beautiful glass bottles and beads.

Purple people

The Phoenicians used a shellfish, called a murex, to make an expensive purple dye. The name "Phoenician" comes from a Greek word meaning "purple men".

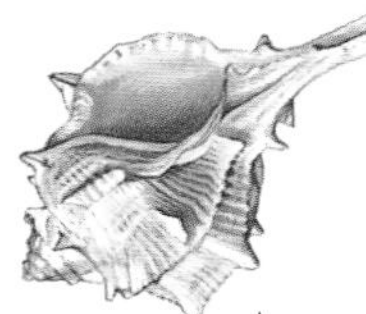

★ Murex shell

Ships and sailing

The Phoenicians were expert sailors. Their sturdy trading ships sailed all over the Mediterranean and beyond, probably even reaching the British Isles. One expedition sailed all the way around Africa.

This picture shows a ship being loaded with cargo at a busy Phoenician trading port.

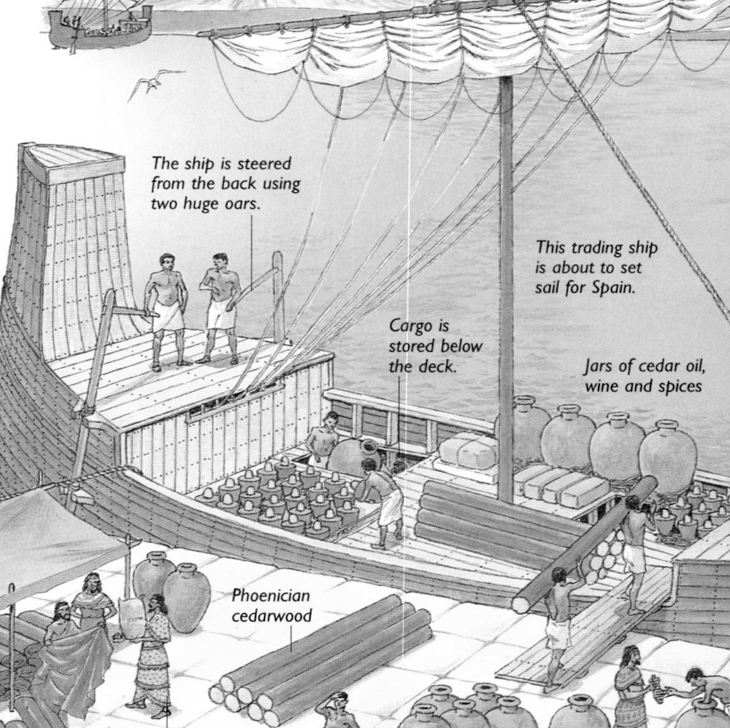

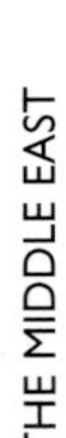

10,000BC 5000BC 4000BC 3000BC

Map of the Phoenician world

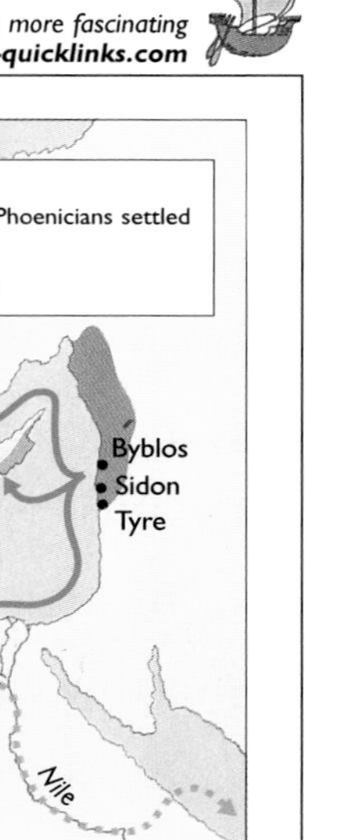

A warship sails ahead to protect trading ships from pirates.

A warship with two rows of oars is called a bireme.

The ship is made of cedarwood and pine.

This is the merchant who owns the ship.

The city of Carthage

Merchants set up trading posts and colonies around the Mediterranean. The most famous one was Carthage on the north coast of Africa. It was set up by a Phoenician princess called Dido, who tricked the local African ruler into giving her enough land to build a city.

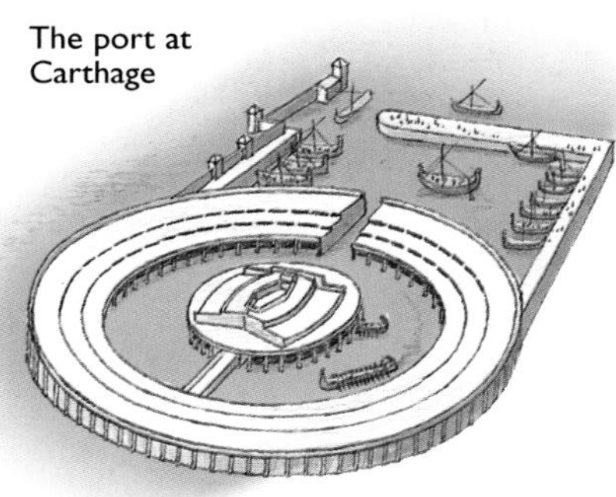

The port at Carthage

Writing

The Phoenicians invented a simple alphabet with just 22 letters. It gradually developed into the alphabet we use today.

Part of the Phoenician alphabet

Phoenician letters	𐤇	𐤊	𐤋	𐤌	𐤍	𐤒
Modern letters	H	K	L	M	N	Q

The end of the Phoenicians

Although the Phoenicians became part of the mighty empires of Assyria, Babylon and Persia, their way of life survived until they were conquered by Alexander the Great in 332BC. The city of Carthage remained powerful for another 200 years, but was totally destroyed by the Romans in 146BC.

Roman soldiers destroying Carthage

Important dates

c.1200-1000BC	The Phoenicians become rich and powerful.
c.814BC	Carthage is built.
c.701BC	Phoenicia is conquered by the Assyrians.
332BC	Phoenicia is conquered by Alexander the Great.
146BC	Carthage is destroyed by the Romans.

2000BC 1000BC 500BC AD1 AD500

The Assyrians at War

In early times, the Assyrians lived in a small area of farmland by a river called the Tigris. Around 2000BC, they were taken over by invaders who made Assyria into a kingdom.

The Assyrians were warlike people. They often attacked the surrounding lands, but were always beaten back. Finally, led by a series of strong kings, they conquered the nearby kingdoms and built up a huge empire.

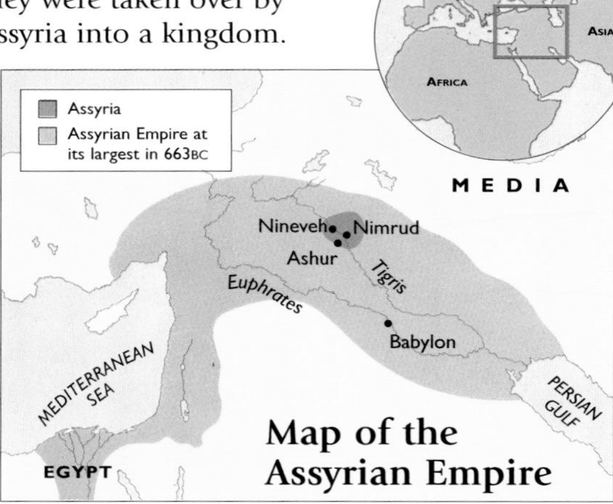

Map of the Assyrian Empire

Cruel conquerors

Conquered people had to pay heavy taxes to the Assyrian king, and anyone who refused to pay was brutally punished. Cities that rebelled were attacked.

The man in this carving is paying his taxes by giving a camel.

Going to war

Every year, the mighty Assyrian army set out to conquer new lands. Soldiers had to travel great distances before going into battle.

This picture shows the Assyrian army crossing a river.

Attacking a city

The Assyrians were experts at attacking cities. They kept the city surrounded, so no one could escape. Then, they battered down the walls and captured the city.

In this scene, the Assyrians are attacking a rebel city.

Punishing rebels

Often, a captured city was destroyed and its people were taken prisoner or killed. Many were tortured to death. The Assyrians hoped this would teach other cities not to rebel, but instead it made them even more unpopular.

This picture shows Assyrian soldiers destroying a captured city. ★

The Assyrians at Home

Most people in Assyria were farmers. They dug ditches to carry water to their fields and grew barley, sesame, grapes and vegetables. Farmers also kept sheep, goats and cattle.

An Assyrian farmer at work

Gods and spirits

The Assyrians believed that their land belonged to Ashur, their chief god. They had many other gods and goddesses, and also believed in evil spirits.

Mighty kings

Assyrian kings thought that they were chosen by the gods to rule Assyria and conquer new lands. They gave themselves grand titles, such as "King of the Universe". The king also served the gods by building temples and leading religious festivals.

Statue of King Ashurnasirpal II ★

Cities and palaces

The Assyrians built magnificent cities with beautiful palaces and temples. Their first capital city at Ashur was named after their god. Later, King Ashurnasirpal II built a new capital city at Nimrud.

The throne room in Ashurnasirpal's palace at Nimrud ★

By the time of Ashurbanipal, the last great Assyrian king, the capital had been moved to another new city at Nineveh.

This picture shows King Ashurbanipal and his queen in the palace garden at Nineveh.

Double flute

Harp

The king's dogs

Lotus flowers grow in the pool.

Musicians

THE MIDDLE EAST

4000BC 3000BC

Internet link: *For a link to a Web site where you can find out more about Nimrud and see a virtual reality picture of Ashurnasirpal's palace, go to* **www.usborne-quicklinks.com**

Libraries

An Assyrian library

Each clay tablet is covered in writing.

The palace at Nineveh had a library filled with hundreds of clay tablets, which King Ashurbanipal collected from around the Empire. There were tablets on history, religion, mathematics and medicine.

Lion hunting

When Assyrian kings were not at war, they hunted lions to show off their skill and bravery. The lions were kept in special parks so that the king could hunt whenever he wanted.

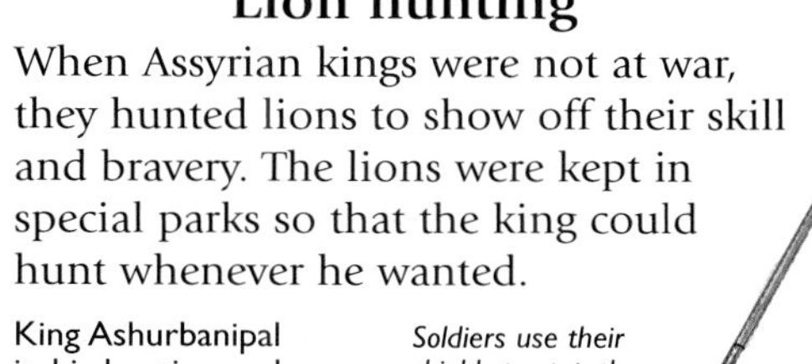

King Ashurbanipal in his hunting park ★

Soldiers use their shields to stop the lions from escaping.

The king is about to kill a lion with his spear.

The lions are kept in cages.

Grapevines keep off the sun.

Servants fan the king and queen to keep them cool and chase away flies.

Cakes made of honey and figs

The king lies on a couch.

Burning incense perfumes the air.

The furniture is decorated with gold and ivory.

The end of the Empire

In the end, the Assyrian Empire became too big to control. People rebelled and the Empire began to break up. In 612BC, the people of Babylon and nearby Media joined together to attack Assyria. The cities of Ashur and Nineveh were completely destroyed and the Empire collapsed.

Median soldier

Important dates

c.2000BC	Assyria becomes a kingdom.
c.1000-663BC	The Assyrians build up a powerful empire.
883-859BC	King Ashurnasirpal II rules. Nimrud is built.
704-681BC	King Sennacherib builds the city of Nineveh.
668-627BC	King Ashurbanipal rules.
612-609BC	The Babylonians and the Medes attack Assyria. The Empire collapses.

2000BC 1000BC 500BC AD1 AD500

The City of Babylon

Babylon first became powerful under its great king Hammurabi (see page 132). When his Empire collapsed, the city was taken over by a tribe called the Kassites, who ruled peacefully for over 400 years.

After around 730BC, Babylon became part of the Assyrian Empire. The people of Babylon often rebelled against the Assyrians, who eventually attacked and destroyed the city.

In 625BC, a Babylonian general called Nabopolassar made himself King of Babylon. He joined with the people of nearby Media to defeat the Assyrians. He and his son, King Nebuchadnezzar II, rebuilt Babylon and made it one of the richest cities in the world.

Pottery head of a Kassite priestess

This picture shows the city of Babylon during the New Year Festival.

10,000BC 5000BC 4000BC 3000BC

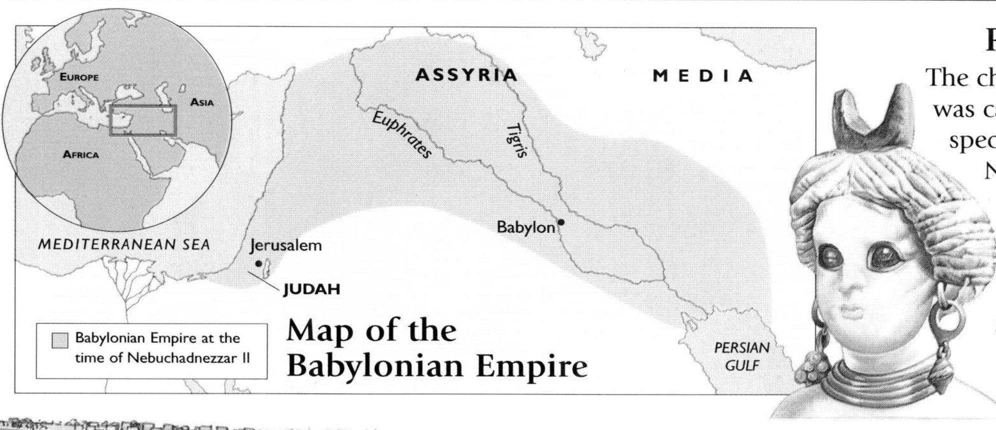

Map of the Babylonian Empire

Religion

The chief god of Babylon was called Marduk. His special festival was the New Year Festival which lasted 11 days. The chief goddess was Ishtar, the goddess of love and war.

★ Statue of the goddess Ishtar

Building an empire

King Nebuchadnezzar II fought many wars and built up a large empire. One of his most famous wars was against the people of Judah. When they rebelled, he destroyed Jerusalem, their capital city, and took thousands of them to Babylon as slaves.

Machinery carries water to the top of the Hanging Gardens.

Water runs down the terraces and keeps the soil wet.

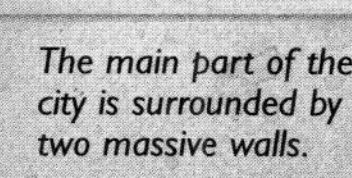

The main part of the city is surrounded by two massive walls.

Telling the future

The Babylonians believed that they could tell the future by looking at the insides of dead animals. Priests had clay models which showed them what to look for.

Clay model of a sheep's liver ★

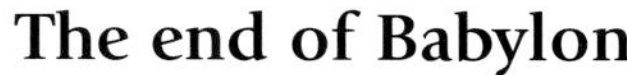

The end of Babylon

In 539BC, Babylon was captured by an army from Persia (modern Iran) and became part of the powerful Persian Empire (see pages 152 and 153).

Important dates

c.1595-1155BC	The Kassites rule Babylon.
c.730BC	Babylon becomes part of the Assyrian Empire.
689BC	Babylon is destroyed.
625-605BC	King Nabopolassar rules. The Assyrians are defeated.
605-562BC	King Nebuchadnezzar II rules. Babylon is rebuilt.
539BC	Babylon becomes part of the Persian Empire.

The Power of Persia

Persia is the old name for the country we now call Iran. Around 1300BC, the area was invaded by two tribes known as the Medes and the Persians. They set up two kingdoms, Media in the north and Persia in the south.

Frieze showing Persian soldiers ★

In 550BC, King Cyrus II of Persia defeated the Medes, took over their lands and built up a huge empire. Later, under King Darius I, the Persian Empire grew to become the largest the world had ever seen.

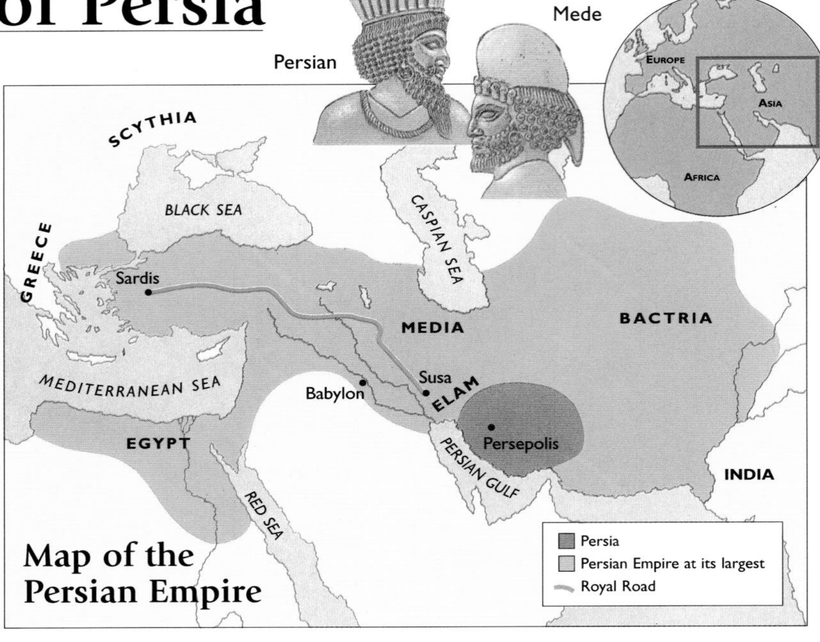

Map of the Persian Empire

★ Persian armlet made of solid gold

Running the Empire

King Darius collected taxes from conquered people all over the Empire and became fabulously rich. He allowed people to keep their religion and way of life, as long as they paid their taxes.

Darius divided his vast Empire into regions, each one run by a local ruler called a satrap. Officials kept an eye on the satraps and made sure they stayed loyal to the king.

The Royal Road

Darius built good roads across the Empire, so that messengers could travel more quickly. The Royal Road stretched 2700km (1680 miles) from Sardis in the west to the capital city at Susa.

A messenger arrives at an inn along the Royal Road.

This picture shows King Darius receiving visitors in his throne room.

Internet link: *For a link to a Web site where you can see some stunning photos of Persepolis as it is today, go to* **www.usborne-quicklinks.com**

Persepolis

Darius used some of his wealth to build a magnificent palace at Persepolis. During the New Year Festival, officials from every part of the Empire came to the palace with gifts for the king.

This picture shows people arriving at Persepolis for the New Year Festival. ★

This is the Great Hall, where the king receives his visitors. It can hold 10,000 people.

The tops of the pillars are carved in the shape of bulls.

Inside, the Great Hall is decorated with gold, silver, ivory and ebony (a dark wood).

Staircase covered with carvings

This man has brought a camel from Bactria.

An African carrying ivory

Visitors wait outside in the courtyard.

Persian officials

A Scythian brings cloth and a golden armlet.

This Indian is carrying pots of gold dust.

A Babylonian with gifts of gold and silver bowls

A Mede shows people where to wait.

This man is from Elam. He has brought a lion cub for the king.

Guards

Religion

The Persians followed the teachings of a prophet called Zarathustra (or Zoroaster), who taught that there was only one god. Fire was holy, and priests (called Magi) kept a sacred fire burning.

Priests carried twigs to feed the sacred fire.

The end of the Persian Empire

For many years, Persia was at war with Greece. The Persians won some battles, but were eventually beaten back. (You can find out more about these wars on page 155.)

After the death of Darius's son, King Xerxes I, the Empire grew weaker. In 331BC, Persia was conquered by Alexander the Great (see pages 160 and 161).

Important dates

c.1300BC	The Medes and the Persians settle down.
c.700-600BC	The kingdoms of Persia and Media are set up.
559-530BC	Cyrus II rules Persia.
550BC	Cyrus defeats the Medes.
522-486BC	Darius I rules Persia. The Empire is at its largest.
490-479BC	The Persians are at war with Greece.
486-465BC	Xerxes I rules Persia.
331-330BC	Persia is conquered by Alexander the Great. Persepolis is burned.

The Greeks at War

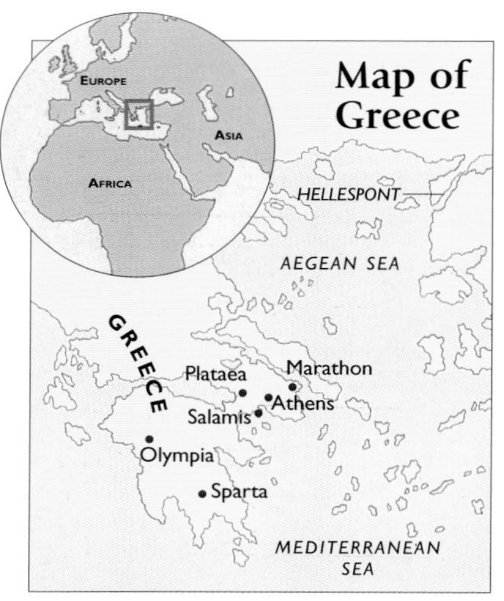

Soldiers and armies

All the city-states had their own army, and they were often at war with each other. Heavily armed foot soldiers, called hoplites, were the most important part of an army.

Spear

Horsehair crest

Bronze helmet

Shield of bronze, wood and leather

Bronze and leather breastplate

Sword

Bronze leg guard (called a greave)

A Greek hoplite ★

This picture shows a group of hoplites (foot soldiers) charging at the enemy. ★

Hoplites fight in closely packed rows. A block of soldiers is called a phalanx.

Flute music helps the men keep in step with each other.

Soldiers at the front lower their spears.

If this soldier is killed, the man behind him will take his place.

The soldiers are protected by a wall of overlapping shields.

After the Mycenaean civilization collapsed (see page 131), life in Greece was hard. People had to spend all their time growing food and forgot many of the skills they had learned, such as writing. This period of time is called the Greek Dark Ages.

Greek trading ship ★

From around 800BC, the Greeks began to trade with other lands and became richer. They lived in small city-states with their own rulers and customs. Each city-state was made up of a city and the farmland around it. The two most important states were Athens and Sparta.

Sparta

The fiercest warriors in Greece came from Sparta. All Spartan men were full-time soldiers who spent their lives training and fighting.

Boys were taken from their mothers at the age of seven to begin their training. Girls had to keep fit, too, so that they would have strong, healthy babies.

★ Bronze statue of a Spartan warrior

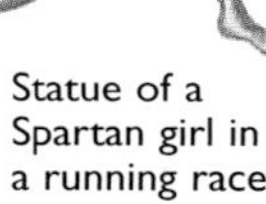

Statue of a Spartan girl in a running race

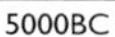

10,000BC 5000BC 3000BC

Internet link: *For a link to a Web site where you can see photos of a full-size replica of a Greek trireme, go to* **www.usborne-quicklinks.com**

The first marathon

In 490BC, the Persians invaded Greece. The Greeks fought back and defeated them in a fierce battle at Marathon. A runner carried the good news over 32km (20 miles) to Athens, and then died of exhaustion. The modern marathon race is named after this famous event.

The first marathon runner

The Persians fight back

In 480BC, the Persians attacked again. They built a bridge of boats tied together with ropes, and crossed the stretch of water known as the Hellespont. Then, they marched into Greece and destroyed the city of Athens.

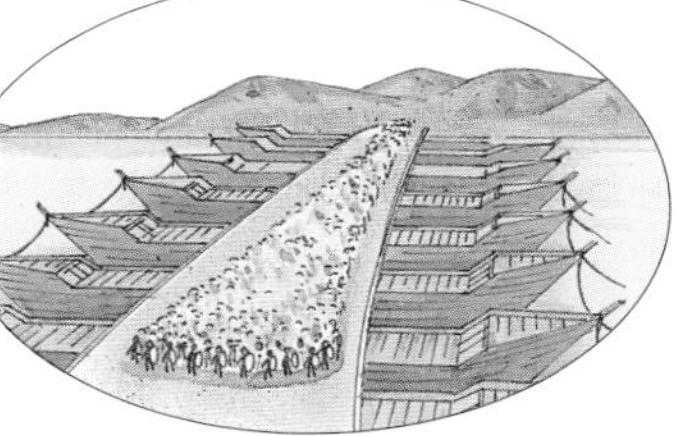

The Persian army crossing the Hellespont

Victory for Greece

The Greeks won a great sea battle near the island of Salamis. They trapped the Persian fleet in a narrow channel of water and wrecked over 200 Persian ships. The Greek army finally defeated the Persians in a huge land battle at Plataea.

This picture shows the sea battle between the Greeks and the Persians at Salamis.

A ship with three rows of oars is called a trireme. All the ships in this picture are triremes.

Each ship is rowed by 170 oarsmen.

This ship has been rammed and is sinking.

The Persian ships are decorated with a dragon's head.

The ships are steered using two oars at the back.

Archers hide behind a row of shields.

Greek archer

Greek hoplites throw spears at the Persians.

A bronze ram smashes into the side of the Persian ship.

The painted eyes are meant to scare the enemy and help the ship see where it is going.

The Greek oarsmen row at full speed.

Life in Ancient Greece

Although the Greeks were almost always at war, they managed to create one of the greatest civilizations in history. The time from 500BC to 350BC is known as the Classical Period.

Life at home

While Greek men went out to work, shop and meet their friends, women stayed at home. They ran the household, looked after the children and supervised the slaves.

This picture shows a dinner party in the andron (dining room). ★

The house in this cutaway picture belongs to a rich Greek family. ★

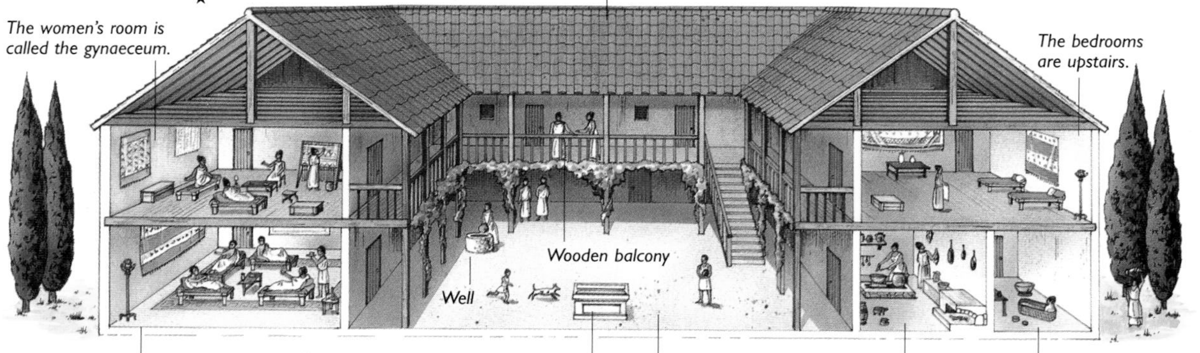

This picture shows women in the gynaeceum, where they spend most of their time. ★

School

Boys from rich families started school when they were seven years old. They learned reading, writing, mathematics, music, poetry, athletics and dancing. Girls stayed at home and were taught by their mothers.

Vase painting of a boy learning to read

The Olympic Games

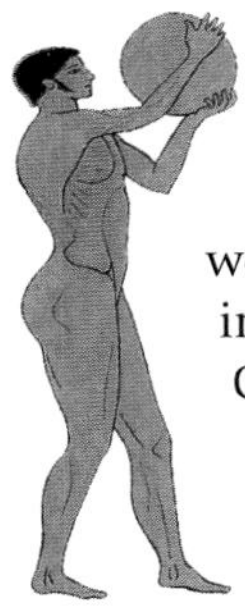

Athletics was a popular pastime for men in ancient Greece, and competitions were held all over the country. The most important was the Olympic Games. The Games were held every four years at Olympia, as part of a festival for Zeus, the king of the gods.

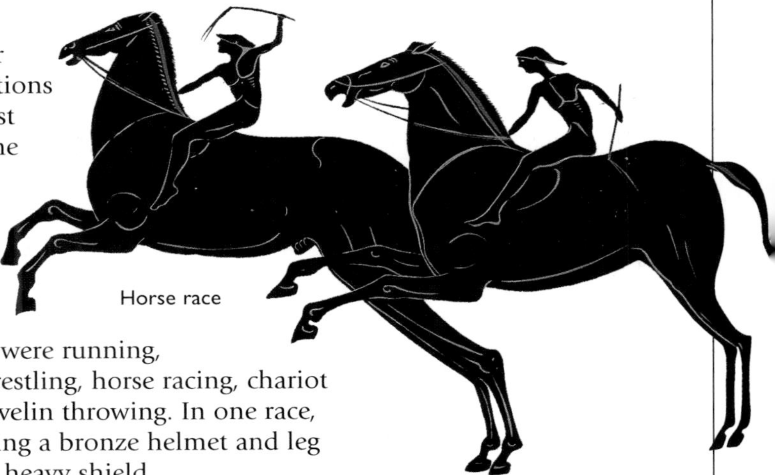

Discus thrower

Horse race

The main events at the Olympic Games were running, jumping, boxing, wrestling, horse racing, chariot racing, discus and javelin throwing. In one race, men had to run wearing a bronze helmet and leg guards and carrying a heavy shield.

Athlete with helmet, shield and leg guards

Drama

The first great plays in the world were written by the ancient Greeks. The plays were performed as part of religious festivals to please the gods. These festivals lasted several days and there was a prize for the best play.

★ Greek actors wore painted masks to show what sort of character they were playing.

This picture shows a play being performed.

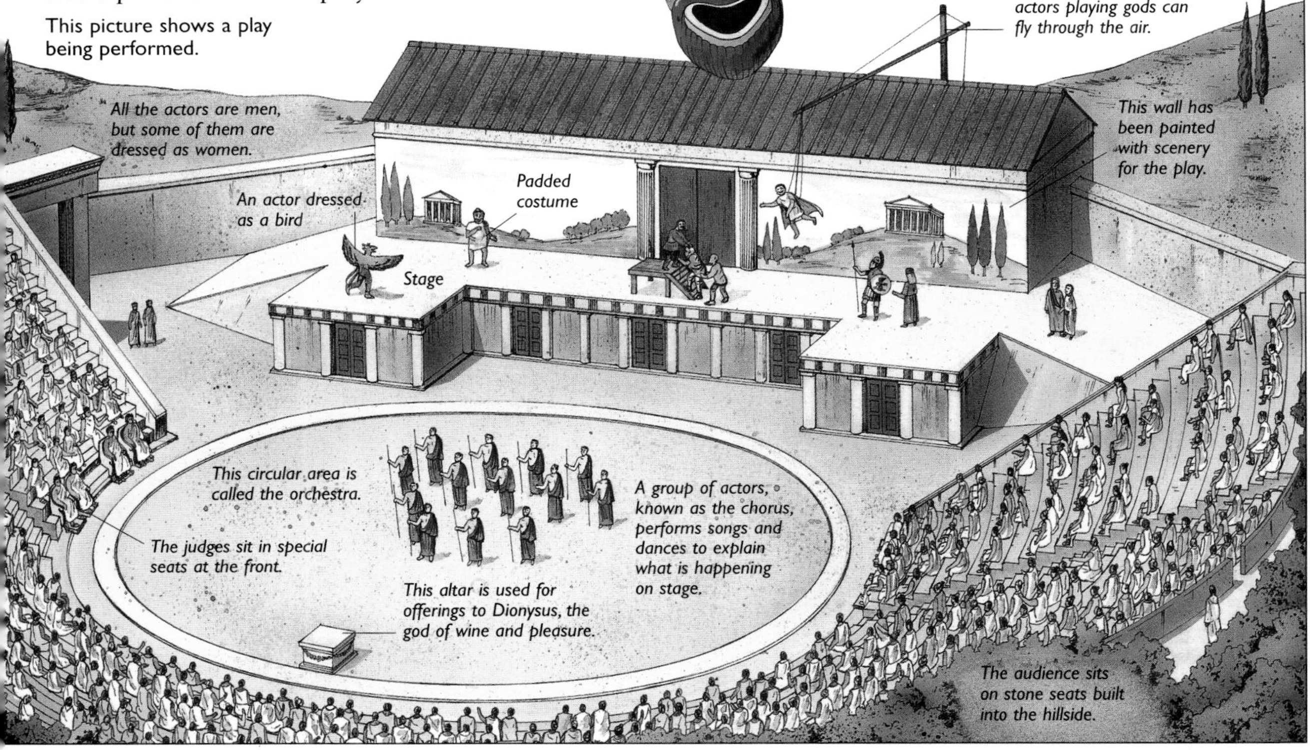

A crane is used so that actors playing gods can fly through the air.

All the actors are men, but some of them are dressed as women.

This wall has been painted with scenery for the play.

Padded costume

An actor dressed as a bird

Stage

This circular area is called the orchestra.

A group of actors, known as the chorus, performs songs and dances to explain what is happening on stage.

The judges sit in special seats at the front.

This altar is used for offerings to Dionysus, the god of wine and pleasure.

The audience sits on stone seats built into the hillside.

2000BC | 1000BC | 500BC | AD1 | AD500

The City of Athens

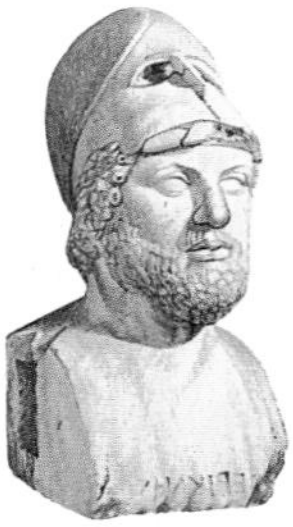

★ Perikles

After the wars with Persia, the Greeks were afraid that the Persians might attack again. Led by the city of Athens, many of the Greek city-states joined forces to defend themselves, and Athens built up a strong navy.

Trade in Athens increased, and the city became rich and powerful. Perikles, Athens' greatest leader, used this new wealth to rebuild the city.

This picture shows the marketplace (or agora) in the middle of Athens.
★

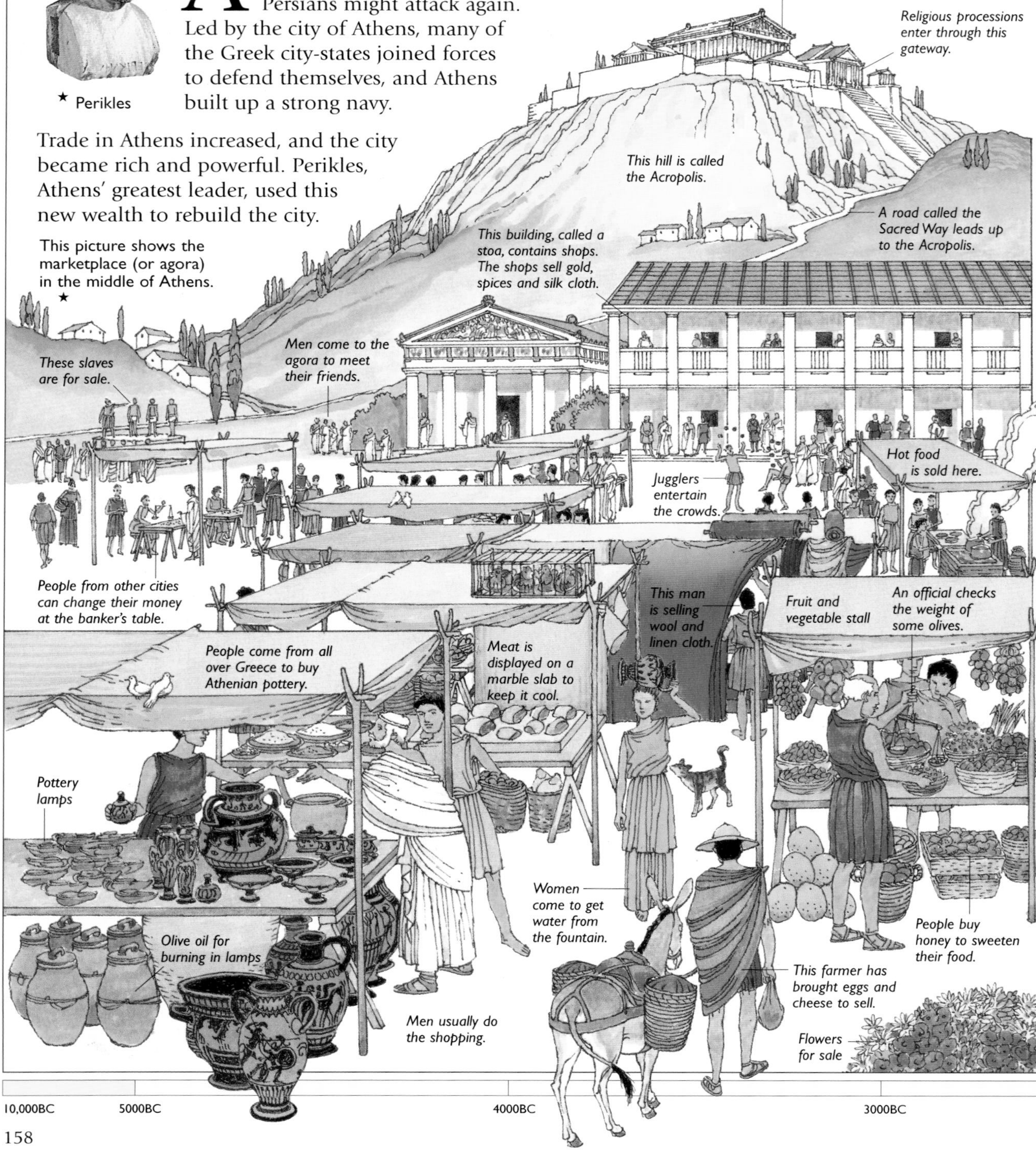

This is the temple of Athene, the goddess of wisdom and war. It is called the Parthenon.

Religious processions enter through this gateway.

This hill is called the Acropolis.

A road called the Sacred Way leads up to the Acropolis.

This building, called a stoa, contains shops. The shops sell gold, spices and silk cloth.

These slaves are for sale.

Men come to the agora to meet their friends.

Hot food is sold here.

Jugglers entertain the crowds.

People from other cities can change their money at the banker's table.

This man is selling wool and linen cloth.

Fruit and vegetable stall

An official checks the weight of some olives.

People come from all over Greece to buy Athenian pottery.

Meat is displayed on a marble slab to keep it cool.

Pottery lamps

Women come to get water from the fountain.

People buy honey to sweeten their food.

Olive oil for burning in lamps

This farmer has brought eggs and cheese to sell.

Men usually do the shopping.

Flowers for sale

Power to the people

In Athens, all free men had a say in how the city was run. They met once every ten days to discuss new laws, and took decisions by voting. This type of government is called democracy, which means "rule by the people". Women, foreigners and slaves were not allowed to vote.

A politician making a speech to the men of Athens

Beautiful buildings

The Greeks built magnificent temples from gleaming white marble. Most temples had a triangular-shaped roof held up by rows of columns (pillars). All over the world, people have copied the style of Greek buildings.

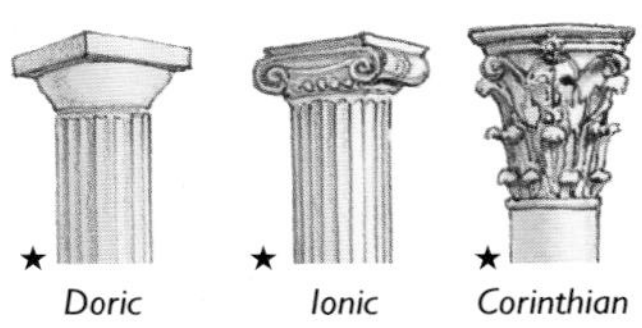

Greek columns were built in three different styles.

This is the Parthenon in Athens, a Greek temple which was built in the Doric style.

Science and learning

Greek thinkers asked themselves questions about how people should behave. Two of the most famous, Socrates and Plato, lived in Athens.

★ Plato

Socrates ★

Scientists tried to explain how the world worked. They studied plants, animals, the human body, the Sun and the stars.

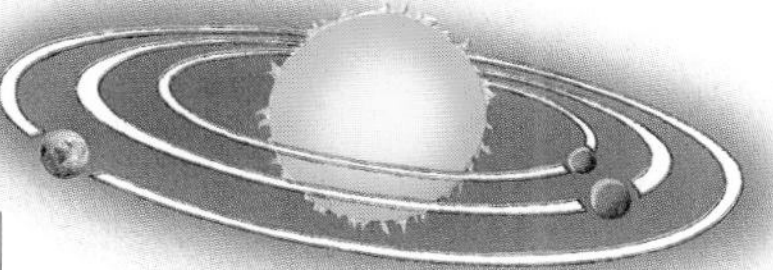

One astronomer found out that the Earth moves around the Sun.

Scholars, such as Pythagoras, discovered rules that are still used in mathematics today.

Manuscript showing Pythagoras' ideas about triangles

A Greek called Herodotus wrote the first proper history book in the world. It was about the Persian Wars.

Herodotus interviewed survivors of the Persian Wars.

War with Sparta

Some of the Greek city-states grew worried that Athens had become too powerful and, in 431BC, war broke out between Athens and Sparta. The other city-states joined in, and the war (called the Peloponnesian War) lasted 27 years. Athens was finally defeated, but all the city-states were left weak and exhausted.

Vase painting of Greek soldiers

Alexander the Great

The Greek city-states kept on fighting each other even after the Peloponnesian War was over. They were too busy to see what was happening in the kingdom of Macedonia to the north.

King Philip II of Macedonia

The Macedonian king, Philip II, had built up a strong army of well-trained soldiers. He began to conquer the Greek city-states and, by 338BC, he controlled all of Greece. Soon after this, Philip was murdered and his 20-year-old son, Alexander, became king.

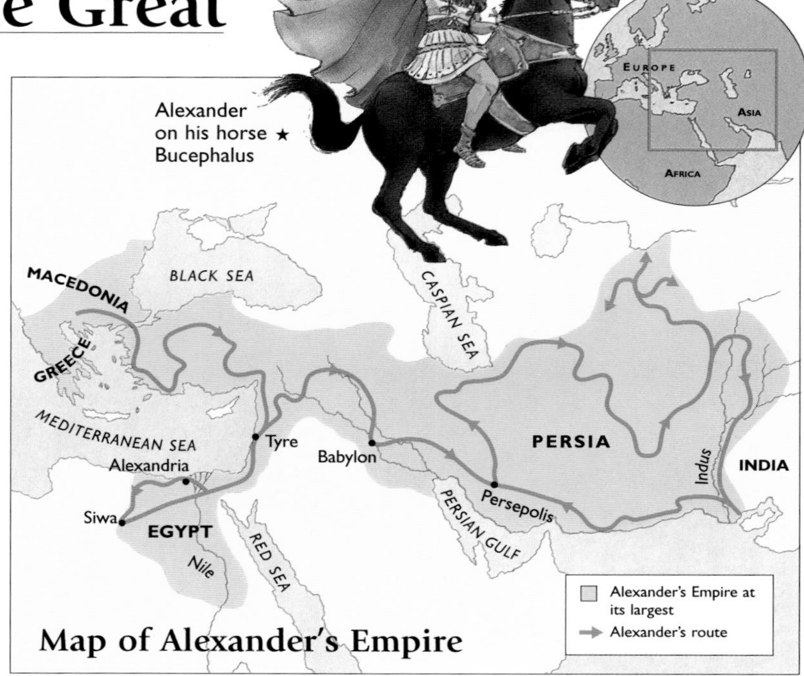

Map of Alexander's Empire

Alexander's conquests

Alexander was a brave soldier and a brilliant commander. He led his army on a journey of over 32,000km (almost 20,000 miles), creating the largest empire in the ancient world. Today, he is known as Alexander the Great.

Part of a mosaic showing Alexander in battle

1 Alexander attacked the port of Tyre, using rocks fired from catapults on boats. It took months to capture the city.

2 The Egyptians welcomed Alexander. At Siwa, a desert oasis, he was greeted as the son of the Egyptian god Amun.

3 The Persians were defeated by Alexander in 331BC. His army later captured the palace of Persepolis and set it on fire.

4 In India, Alexander defeated a king called Porus, whose army rode on hundreds of war elephants.

Alexandria

Alexander built new Greek-style cities all over his Empire and named many of them after himself. The most famous is Alexandria in Egypt. Scholars came to Alexandria from all over the Greek world to study and discuss new ideas. Many things were invented there, including the first lighthouse in the world.

This picture shows the lighthouse at Alexandria.

Statue of Zeus, king of the gods

The lighthouse, known as the Pharos, was one of the seven wonders of the ancient world.

Bronze mirrors reflect the light. It can be seen 50km (30 miles) away.

A fire is kept burning at the top.

Carts filled with wood for the fire are pulled up a ramp inside the lighthouse.

The second level has eight sides.

The first level has four sides.

Inside are rooms for the lighthouse workers and guards.

A causeway links the lighthouse to the mainland.

The base is built of massive stone blocks. The rest is made of marble.

A trading ship returning from the Black Sea

Alexander's death

Alexander had to return from India because his exhausted troops refused to go any farther. Soon after reaching Babylon, he caught a fever and died. He was just 33 years old.

Statue of Alexander wearing a lion skin

After Alexander

After Alexander's death, his generals fought each other for control of the Empire. Antigonas took Greece and Macedonia. Ptolemy won Egypt, where his family ruled for the next 300 years. The rest was taken by Seleucus and became known as the Seleucid Empire. In the end, all three kingdoms were conquered by the Romans.

Egyptian carving of Ptolemy

Important dates

c.1100-800BC	The Greek Dark Ages
c.776BC	The first Olympic Games
c.508BC	Democracy begins in Athens.
490-479BC	The Persian Wars
461-429BC	Perikles leads Athens.
447-438BC	The Parthenon is built.
431-404BC	The Peloponnesian War
338BC	Philip II of Macedonia takes control of Greece.
336-323BC	Alexander rules Greece and builds up his Empire.
323-281BC	Alexander's generals fight. The Empire splits up.
146BC	Greece becomes part of the Roman Empire.

2000BC 1000BC 500BC AD1 AD500

Riders of the Plains

Among the many tribes who roamed across the plains of central Asia was a tribe of horsemen known as the Scythians. By around 700BC, they had moved into the land north of the Black Sea, conquering the people who lived there.

Scythian horseman

Map of the Scythian world

EUROPE
ASIA
AFRICA
BLACK SEA
PERSIAN EMPIRE
GREECE
MEDITERRANEAN SEA
Scythian lands
Areas where the Greeks settled

Scythians in battle

Bloody battles

Scythian warriors were skilled at fighting on horseback. They were excellent archers, but also fought with spears and battle-axes. After a battle, they used the skulls of their dead enemies to make drinking cups.

Life on the move

The Scythians bred horses and kept herds of cattle and sheep. They were nomads (wandering people) who were always on the move, looking for grass where their animals could graze. They lived in tents which they could pack up and carry with them.

In this picture of a Scythian camp, one tent has been cut away to let you see inside.

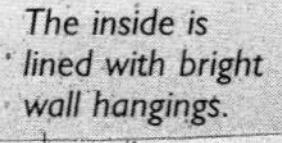

The tents are made of felt.

The larger tents have two or three rooms inside.

This slave is an Assyrian soldier who was captured in battle.

This woman is cooking a beef stew.

This girl is doing embroidery.

Carved wooden table

The inside is lined with bright wall hangings.

Carpets and cushions make the tent comfortable.

Copper cooking pot

This boy is drinking horse's milk.

Bowls are made of leather, clay or wood.

This woman is sewing felt shapes onto cloth to make a wall hanging.

Dead and buried

When a Scythian chief died, he was buried with his most precious possessions under a huge mound (called a kurgan). A year later, 50 men and horses were killed and placed around the mound.

This scene shows the funeral procession of a Scythian chief.

★

★ Golden comb from a Scythian tomb

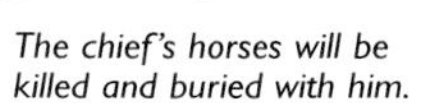

These servants will be sacrificed so they can serve the chief in the Next World.

The chief's horses will be killed and buried with him.

The chief's body is covered with golden rings, bracelets and necklaces.

The chief's wife

People shave their heads and cut themselves to show their grief.

This man is about to cut off his ear.

Wealth and weakness

The Scythians sold wheat grown by farmers whose lands they had conquered. They traded with the Greeks and bought precious metals from merchants in central Asia. They also taxed traders passing through their lands and became very rich.

Around 300BC, the Scythians' power began to weaken, and they were eventually conquered by King Mithridates who ruled the land south of the Black Sea.

Important dates

c.700-600BC	Scythian warriors raid nearby lands.
514BC	The Scythians fight off an attack by the Persians.
c.400-300BC	The Scythians are rich and successful.
110-106BC	The Scythians are defeated.

The People of Early China

Asia

Area ruled by the Shang kings

Yellow

Yangtze

YELLOW SEA

Early Chinese pot

Map of China

China is surrounded by mountains, deserts and seas, and for thousands of years it was cut off from the rest of the world. The way of life that grew up there was quite different from life anywhere else in the ancient world.

The first farmers

Around 5000BC, people began farming along the banks of the Yellow River. They grew millet (a type of grain), fruit, nuts and vegetables, and kept pigs, dogs and chickens. Along the Yangtze River, where it was warmer and wetter, people grew rice.

A farmer planting rice shoots

The first Chinese farmers built villages, used stone tools for working in the fields and made beautiful painted pots.

This picture shows an early Chinese farming village. Part of one house has been cut away to let you see inside. ★

Silk and silkworms

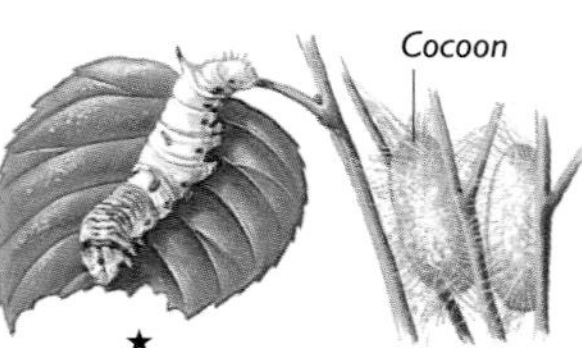

★ A silkworm feeding on a mulberry leaf

The cocoons are rinsed in hot water to loosen the threads.

A woman blows on the fire to keep it hot.

★ Unwinding thread from silk cocoons

Silk thread is made by silkworms (a type of caterpillar), who spin it into cocoons to protect themselves while they turn into moths. The Chinese were the first to learn how to unwind the thread from the cocoons and spin it into fine silk cloth.

10,000BC 5000BC 4000BC 3000BC

The Shang kings

By around 1765BC, a large part of China was ruled by a family (or dynasty) of kings called the Shang. When a king died, he was buried in a huge pit filled with precious objects. People and animals were sacrificed and placed in the pit with him.

This scene shows the funeral ceremony of a Shang king. ★

Horses are led down a ramp into the burial pit.

These servants have been sacrificed so they can serve the king in the Next World.

The king's body

The king's chariot and horses are buried beside him.

Bronze pots and carved jade ornaments

After the ceremony, slaves will fill the pit with soil.

Kings and nobles

Around 1027BC, the Shang kings were conquered by people called the Zhou. The new Zhou kings allowed noble families to own land in return for their loyalty and help in times of war.

A Zhou noble in his war chariot

As the nobles became more powerful, the Zhou kings began to lose control. Nobles set up their own small kingdoms and fought each other constantly to try to win more land.

Mastering metal

Craftworkers in Shang China learned how to make weapons and containers from bronze. People used elaborate bronze cauldrons to prepare food and wine for their dead ancestors, who they thought were gods.

Bronze cauldron

Writing on bones

Writing in China began around 1400BC. To help them tell the future, priests carved questions on bones called oracle bones. They heated the bones until they cracked, and then "read" the pattern made by the cracks to find the answers to their questions.

Early Chinese writing

Oracle bone ★

Confucius

A thinker called K'ung Fu-tzu (or Confucius) lived during this troubled time. He taught that war would only end when people knew the right way to behave. People should obey their rulers, and rulers should be kind to their people.

Confucius

THE FAR EAST

2000BC 1000BC 500BC AD1 AD500

China's First Emperor

Qin Shi Huangdi

By around 480BC, China was made up of seven kingdoms which were constantly at war with each other. By 221BC, the kingdom of Qin (pronounced "chin") had conquered all the others, and the King of Qin controlled a huge empire. He called himself Qin Shi Huangdi, which means "First Emperor of China".

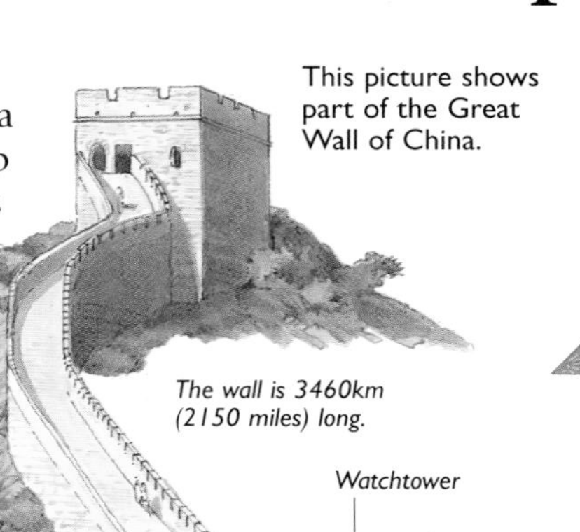
This picture shows part of the Great Wall of China.

The wall is 3460km (2150 miles) long.

Watchtower

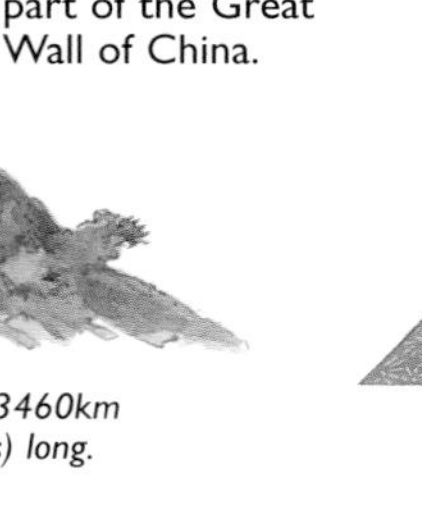

A Chinese noble

Controlling the nobles

To prevent powerful nobles from rebelling against him, Shi Huangdi forced them to move to the capital city, Xianyang, where he could keep an eye on them. Weapons belonging to the nobles' armies were taken away and melted down.

The Great Wall of China

Shi Huangdi had a massive wall built to protect his Empire from attacks by northern tribes (later called the Huns). The Great Wall was made by joining together a series of smaller walls put up by earlier rulers. It is still the biggest man-made structure in the world.

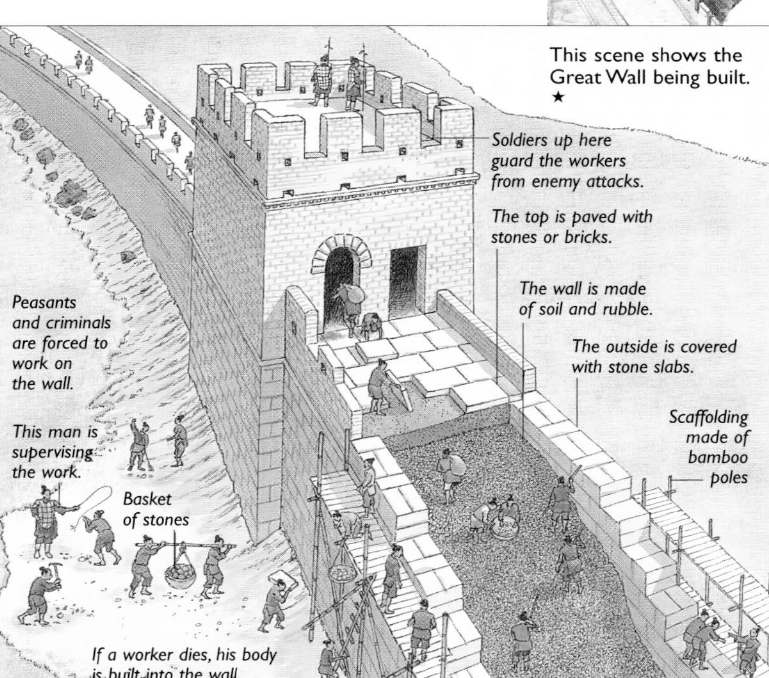

This scene shows the Great Wall being built. ★

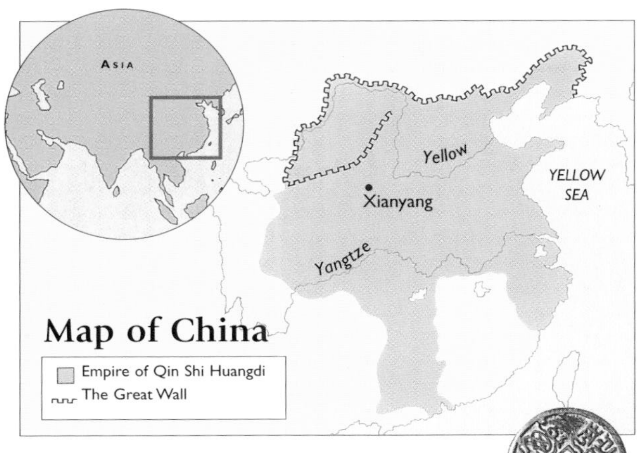

Uniting the Empire

Shi Huangdi built new roads and canals to link the different parts of his Empire. He also made everyone use the same type of coins and the same weights and measures. This made it much easier for people to trade with each other.

Chinese coins

To make sure that his orders could be understood by everyone, Shi Huangdi introduced a standard form of writing throughout the Empire.

This Chinese symbol means "by order of the emperor".

Punishing protestors

Shi Huangdi believed that people were evil and had to be forced to obey the law. Anyone who disobeyed was brutally punished. He ordered the burning of any books that did not agree with his ideas, and scholars who protested were thrown into a pit and buried alive.

This picture shows the burning of the books.

The terracotta army

When Shi Huangdi died in 210BC, he was buried in a huge tomb guarded by an army of over 7,500 life-size model warriors. The warriors were made of terracotta (a type of pottery) and carried real weapons. It is said that crossbows were set to fire automatically at anyone who tried to break into the tomb.

Terracotta warriors standing guard around the emperor's tomb

The face of each warrior is different.

The Han Dynasty

Wooden model of a Han noble

Soon after the first emperor died, rebellions broke out and the Empire collapsed. In 202BC, a soldier called Liu Bang took control of the country and made himself emperor. He was the first of a dynasty (family) of emperors called the Han, who ruled China for the next 400 years.

Official business

An official with his attendants

The Han emperors had lots of officials to help them run their Empire. The officials collected taxes, looked after roads and canals, and made sure that everyone obeyed the law.

Tough tests

Anyone who wanted to be an official had to take exams. People were asked questions on ancient poetry and the teachings of the thinker Confucius.

Officials taking an exam

This scene shows part of Ch'ang-an, the capital city of the early Han emperors. ★

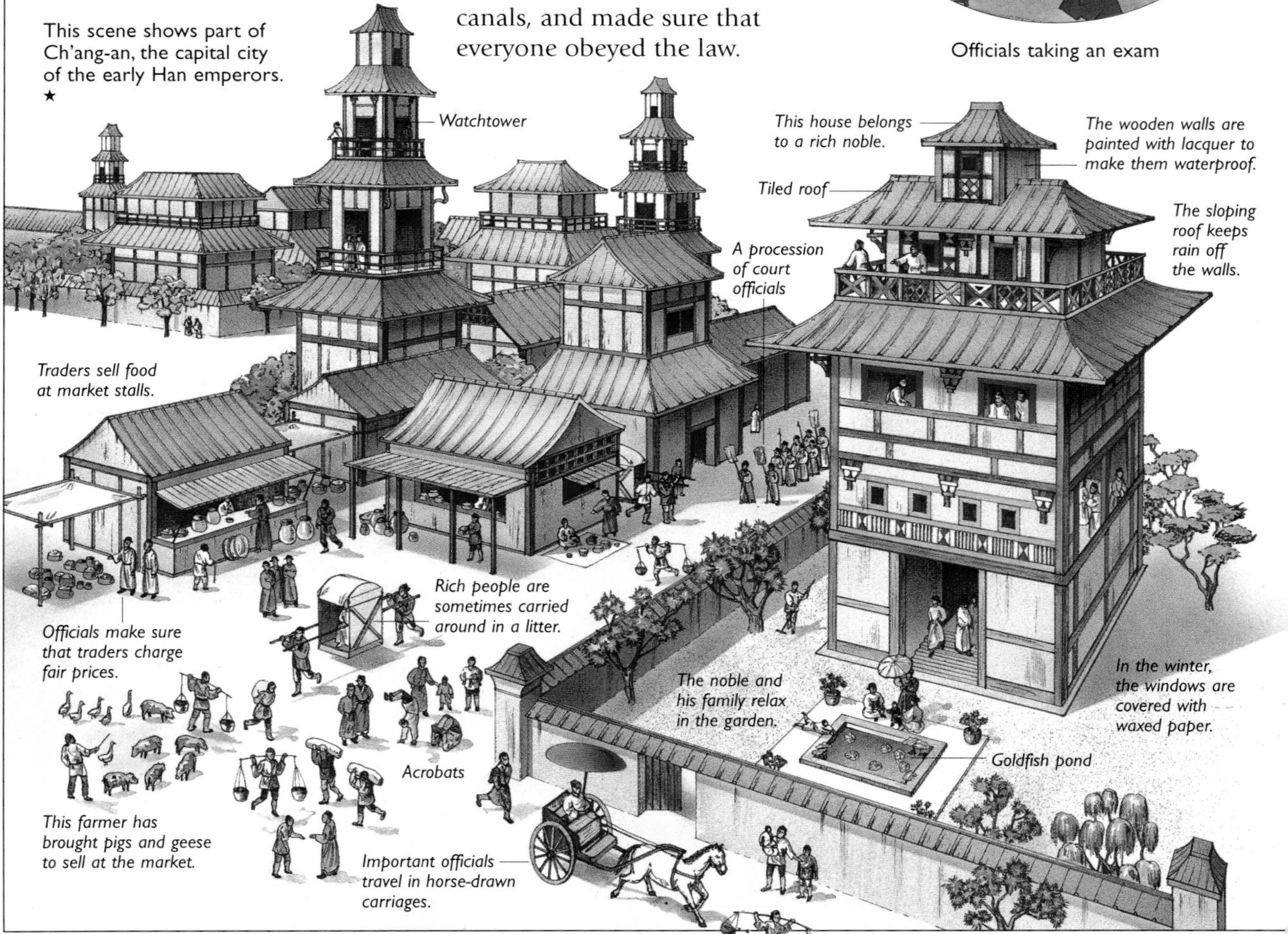

Watchtower

This house belongs to a rich noble.

The wooden walls are painted with lacquer to make them waterproof.

Tiled roof

The sloping roof keeps rain off the walls.

A procession of court officials

Traders sell food at market stalls.

Rich people are sometimes carried around in a litter.

Officials make sure that traders charge fair prices.

The noble and his family relax in the garden.

In the winter, the windows are covered with waxed paper.

Goldfish pond

Acrobats

This farmer has brought pigs and geese to sell at the market.

Important officials travel in horse-drawn carriages.

10,000BC 5000BC 4000BC 3000BC

The Silk Road

Around 105BC, Chinese merchants began to travel across Asia to trade with merchants in the West. Camels carried Chinese silk, spices and precious stones along a route known as the Silk Road, which stretched all the way from China to the Mediterranean Sea.

★ Chinese silk banner

Map of China

TO THE WEST
Ch'ang-an
Yellow
Luoyang
Yangtze
YELLOW SEA
SOUTH CHINA SEA
ASIA
Han Empire
Silk Road

★ Wooden bowl covered with shiny lacquer

Tombs and treasure

Han tombs were filled with everything the dead person might need in the Next World, such as clothes, food, medicines, cups and bowls. One prince and his wife were buried in suits made of jade (a hard, green stone). People thought this would stop the bodies from rotting away.

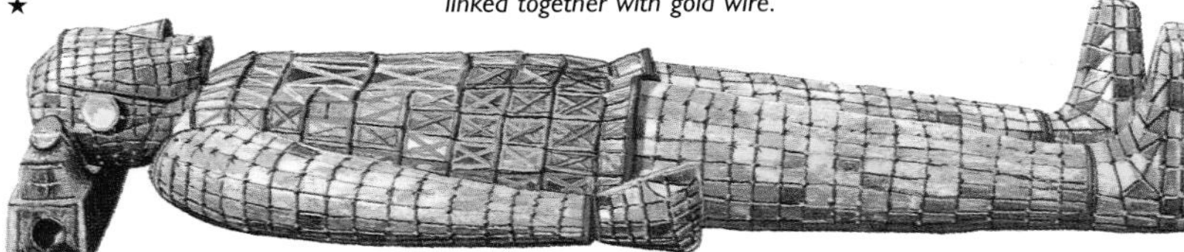

The jade burial suit of Princess Tou Wan ★

The suit is made from over 2,000 pieces of polished jade linked together with gold wire.

Wars and quarrels

The Han emperors fought to defend the Empire against tribes of Huns from the north, and eventually defeated them. The Huns gave up attacking China and moved away to the west.

However, quarrels between the royal family and their courtiers weakened the power of the emperor. In AD220, the last Han emperor gave up his throne, and the Empire fell apart.

Inventions

The Chinese were the first people to make paper. They dipped a bamboo screen into a mixture of pulped tree bark, plants and rags. A thin layer of pulp was left to dry on the screen.

Making paper ★

Chinese scientists invented many other things that are still used today, such as the compass, the wheelbarrow, and the ship's rudder (used for steering).

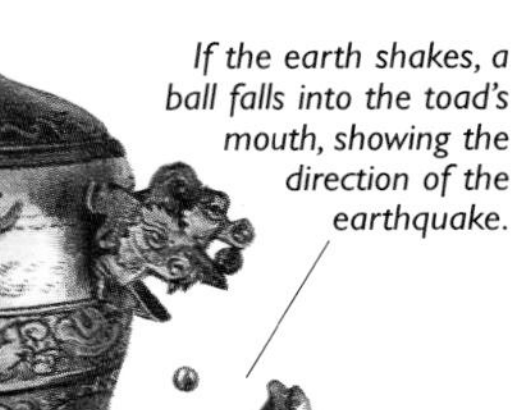

If the earth shakes, a ball falls into the toad's mouth, showing the direction of the earthquake.

Chinese machine for detecting earthquakes ★

Important dates

c.5000BC	Farming begins in China.
c.4000BC	Rice farming begins.
c.2700BC	Silk making begins.
1766-1027BC	The Shang dynasty
c.1400BC	Writing on oracle bones
1027-221BC	The Zhou dynasty
c.722-481BC	The Zhou kings lose power. The nobles fight each other.
551BC	Confucius is born.
481-221BC	Seven kingdoms are at war (the Warring States Period).
221-210BC	Qin Shi Huangdi rules as China's first emperor.
202BC-AD220	The Han dynasty
c.AD1-100	Buddhism spreads from India (see page 174).
c.AD100	Paper is invented.

The People of Ancient Japan

★ Jomon vase

From around 9000BC to 500BC, the people of Japan lived by hunting, fishing and collecting nuts and berries to eat. There was so much food around that they did not think of farming. This long period of time is called the Jomon Period.

SEA OF JAPAN

JAPAN

ASIA

PACIFIC OCEAN

Map of Japan

Area where the Yamato tribe lived

Tombs and warriors

The early Yamato emperors were buried in stone tombs under enormous keyhole-shaped mounds of earth. Small clay models of warriors were placed around the mound to guard it.

This picture shows the tomb of a Yamato emperor.

This picture shows a typical Jomon village. ★

The thatched walls of the houses are held up by branches.

These hunters have caught a wild boar.

This man is trying to catch a tuna fish.

This girl is collecting shellfish.

This woman is coiling strips of clay to make a pot.

People wear animal skins.

This woman is cooking dinner.

Fishbones and old shells are thrown in a heap.

The keyhole-shaped burial mound is 485m (1590ft) long.

Gateway

The mound is surrounded by water.

Tomb model (or haniwa) of a Yamato warrior ★

Bronze bell

New skills

Around 500BC, settlers moved to Japan from the mainland of Asia. They brought new skills with them, such as rice farming and metalworking, and lived in tribes ruled by a chieftain.

The first emperors

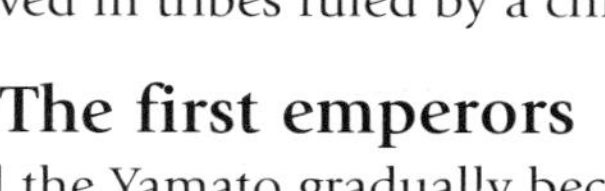

A tribe called the Yamato gradually became more powerful than the others. The Yamato chieftains were the first emperors of Japan. During their rule, many new ideas, such as writing, were brought over from China.

The Japanese believed their emperors were descended from the Sun Goddess.

Important dates

c.9000-500BC	People hunt and fish for food (the Jomon Period).
c.500BC-AD300	Rice farming and metalworking begin (the Yayoi Period).
c.AD300-500	Yamato rulers take control of central Japan.
c.AD450	Writing is introduced from China.

JAPANESE

10,000BC 5000BC 4000BC 3000BC

The Riches of Arabia

The deserts of Arabia are among the hottest and driest places on earth. Only a few nomads (wandering people) lived there, roaming around from one water hole to another.

Arab nomads lived in tents.

Around 1000BC, Arabs learned how to tame camels, which meant they could travel farther across the desert.

Camels can travel for up to eight days without water.

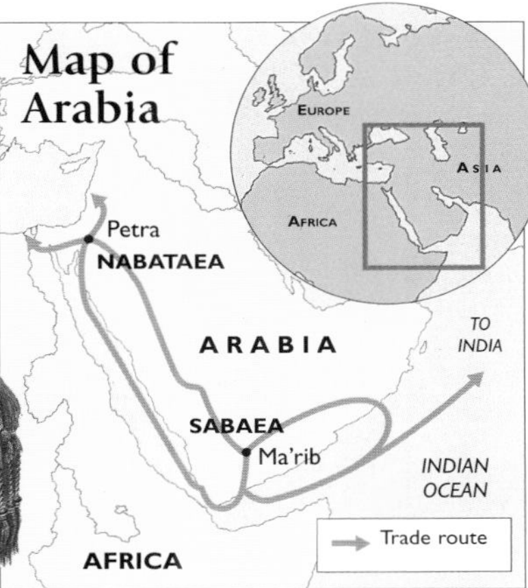

Kingdoms of the south

Along the south coast of Arabia, where there was more rain, rich kingdoms grew up. The most famous is Sabaea. Its capital city, Ma'rib, had a huge dam to control the water supply.

The Bible tells how the Queen of Sabaea (or Sheba) visited King Solomon of Israel.

Sweet smells

In the southern kingdoms, two special types of bushes grew. Their sap was used to make frankincense and myrrh (types of sweet-smelling incense).

Collecting sap to make incense

Incense was burned in religious ceremonies all over the ancient world as an offering to the gods. It was also used to make perfumes and medicines.

An Egyptian priest burning incense

Arab traders with their camels

Routes to riches

Merchants from India brought spices and jewels to ports on the south coast of Arabia. Arab traders carried these goods to Egypt or the Mediterranean, and sold them at a great price.

The city of Petra

At the northern end of the trade routes was the kingdom of Nabataea. Its capital city, Petra, was built in a narrow valley surrounded by rocky cliffs.

Rich people of Petra had spectacular tombs carved out of solid rock.

Important dates

c.1000BC	The Arabs tame camels.
c.500BC-AD100	Sabaea is at its most powerful.
c.100BC-AD150	Nabataea is rich and powerful.

Life in Ancient Africa

Kushite pots

Thousands of years ago, the Sahara Desert was an area of grassland and lakes. The people who lived there hunted wild cattle, giraffes, rhinos and hippos. Then, around 6000BC, the Saharan people learned how to tame animals and began to herd cattle rather than hunt them.

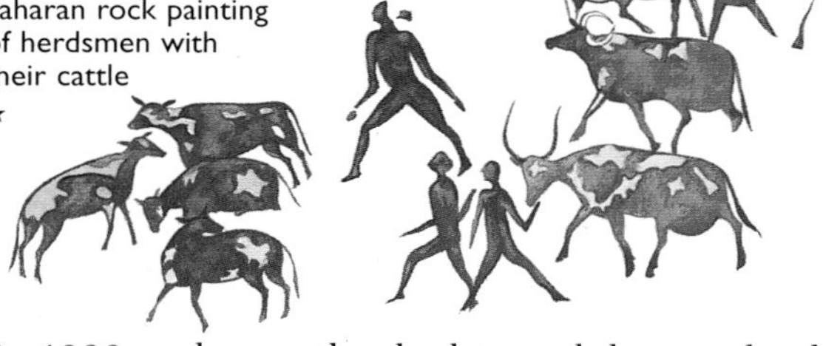

Saharan rock painting of herdsmen with their cattle ★

By 4000BC, dry weather had turned the grassland into desert. The Sahara Desert split Africa in two, and life north of the Sahara developed very differently from life in the south.

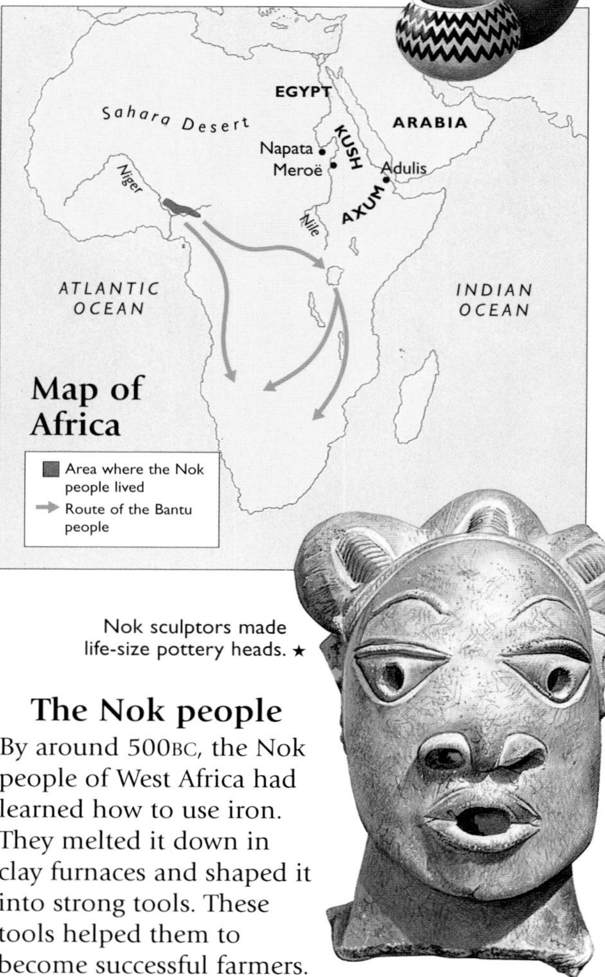

The kingdom of Kush

For hundreds of years, the kingdom of Kush in the Nile Valley was ruled by the Egyptians. Around 1000BC, the Kushites broke free and later went on to conquer Egypt themselves.

Egyptian picture of a Kushite prisoner of war

Until around 590BC, the capital city of Kush was at Napata. Then, a new capital was built at Meroë where there was better farmland. The people of Meroë mined iron, which they used to make weapons and tools. They grew rich by trading with India and the lands around the Mediterranean.

The kings and queens of Meroë were buried under steep-sided pyramids. ★

Nok sculptors made life-size pottery heads. ★

The Nok people

By around 500BC, the Nok people of West Africa had learned how to use iron. They melted it down in clay furnaces and shaped it into strong tools. These tools helped them to become successful farmers.

This picture shows Nok people using a furnace. ★

10,000BC 5000BC 4000BC 3000BC

Internet link: *For a link to a Web site about Kush and Meroë, go to* **www.usborne-quicklinks.com**

The spread of farming

Most Africans south of the Sahara hunted wild animals and gathered plants to eat, but the Bantu tribes of West Africa were farmers. Around 500BC, they began to move south and east looking for new land. By AD500, they had reached the southern tip of Africa, and farming had spread to most of the continent.

A cutaway picture of a Bantu house ★

Framework of wooden poles

Layers of clay and thatched grass

The inside is plastered with clay.

This man is making farming tools from iron.

The floor is raised on wooden logs.

Doorway

The riches of Axum

Around AD100, the kingdom of Axum grew up on the Red Sea coast. Axum became rich by trading with Arabia, India and parts of the Roman Empire. Merchants from other lands stopped at the port of Adulis on their way to and from India.

This scene shows merchants at the port of Adulis.

Standing stones

The kings of Axum used some of their wealth to build magnificent palaces and tall stone towers. Each tower marked the tomb of a king.

The huge tower shown here was carved from a single block of stone.

A Christian king

Around AD320, missionaries brought the Christian religion to Axum, and King Ezana of Axum became the first Christian king in Africa. (See pages 192 and 193 for more about Christianity.)

Axumite ★ gold coin

Important dates

c.6000BC	People in the Sahara tame cattle.
c.4000BC	The Sahara grasslands have turned to desert.
c.1600-1000BC	The kingdom of Kush is ruled by Egypt.
c.750-664BC	Kushite kings conquer and rule Egypt.
c.590BC	Meroë becomes the capital city of Kush.
c.500BC-AD200	The Nok people are at their most successful.
c.500BC-AD500	The Bantu people move through Africa.
c.AD100-700	The kingdom of Axum is rich and powerful.
c.AD330-350	King Ezana rules Axum.

The Ideas of India

Around 1500BC, tribes of people known as Aryans began to arrive in the Indus Valley (in modern Pakistan). Gradually, they spread out across northern India and settled down.

From hymns to Hinduism

Aryan priests sang hymns to their many gods. The Aryans did not write, so the hymns were passed on by word of mouth. Many years later, they were written down in holy books called the Vedas. These writings became very important in the Hindu religion, which is the main religion in India today.

Shiva the destroyer, one of the many Hindu gods ★

A class of their own

The early Aryans divided people into different classes according to their jobs. Later, children always belonged to the same class as their parents. This way of grouping people was known as the caste system.

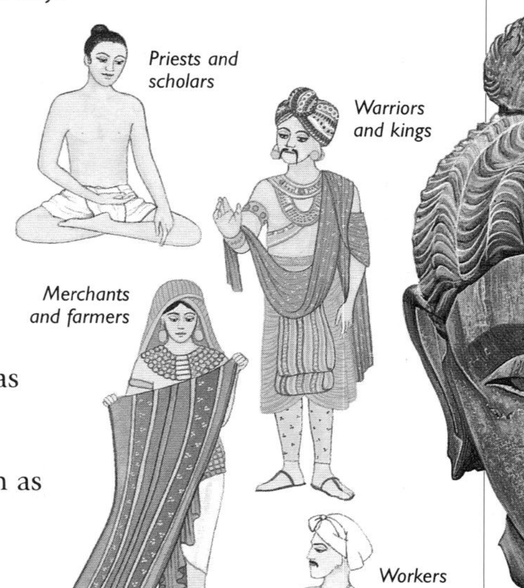

The four main groups in the caste system ★

The beginning of Buddhism

Siddhartha in his chariot

The Buddhist religion was started by an Indian prince called Siddhartha Gautama. One day, when he was out riding in his chariot, Siddhartha came across sickness, old age and death for the first time.

Siddhartha was very upset by what he saw and decided to find a way to escape suffering and live in peace. He left his palace and became a wandering holy man.

Siddhartha as a holy man

After many years, Siddhartha realized that people suffer because they want things and only care about themselves. Because of this understanding, he became known as the Buddha, which means the "enlightened one". People listened to the Buddha teaching, and his ideas spread.

★ Statue of the Buddha's head

SOUTH ASIA

10,000BC 5000BC 4000BC 3000BC

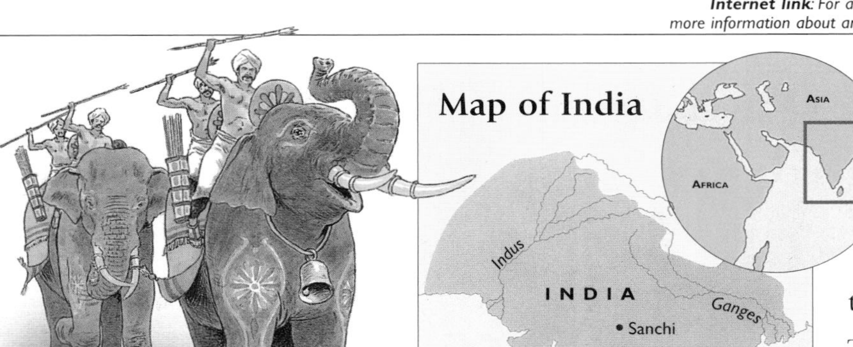

Indian war elephants

The Mauryan Empire

By 500BC, northern India was made up of many small kingdoms. In 321BC, a warrior named Chandragupta Maurya seized one of these kingdoms and went on to conquer most of India, creating the Mauryan Empire. The Empire was at its largest under Chandragupta's grandson, Asoka.

A Buddhist emperor

For 11 years, Asoka fought to make his Empire bigger. Then, in one battle, so many people were killed that he decided to become a Buddhist and give up fighting. Asoka promised to rule his people with kindness, and had his promises carved on stone pillars all over his Empire.

These lions decorated the top of one of Asoka's pillars. ★

During Asoka's rule, many Buddhist monasteries and monuments were built. Huge stone domes, called stupas, were built at places connected with the Buddha's life.

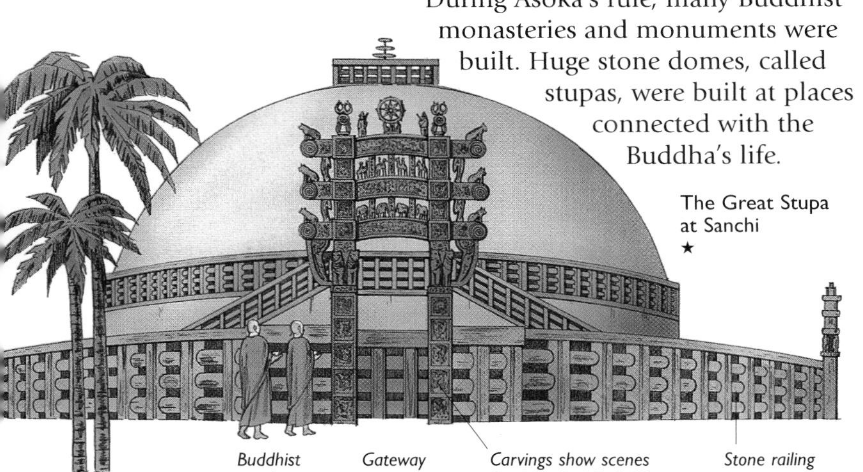

The Great Stupa at Sanchi ★

Painting and poetry

After Asoka's death, the Empire grew weaker, and in the end it split up. India was not united again until AD320, when a new family of emperors called the Guptas took over.

The Gupta Empire is famous for its beautiful painting and sculpture. Classical Indian music and dance developed during this time, and the poet Kalidasa wrote about nature and love.

Part of a wall painting from the Buddhist cave temples at Ajanta

Important dates

c.1500BC	The Aryans arrive.
c.560-480BC	Siddhartha Gautama (the Buddha) lives.
327-325BC	Alexander the Great tries to conquer north India (see pages 160 and 161).
321BC	Chandragupta Maurya sets up the Mauryan Empire.
272-231BC	Asoka is emperor.
185BC	The Mauryan Empire collapses.
AD320-535	The Gupta Empire

The First North Americans

People first arrived in North America at least 15,000 years ago, and probably much earlier. At that time, a large part of the Earth was covered in ice and snow. America and Asia were joined by a bridge of land and ice, and the first North Americans walked across from Asia.

Hunting a mammoth

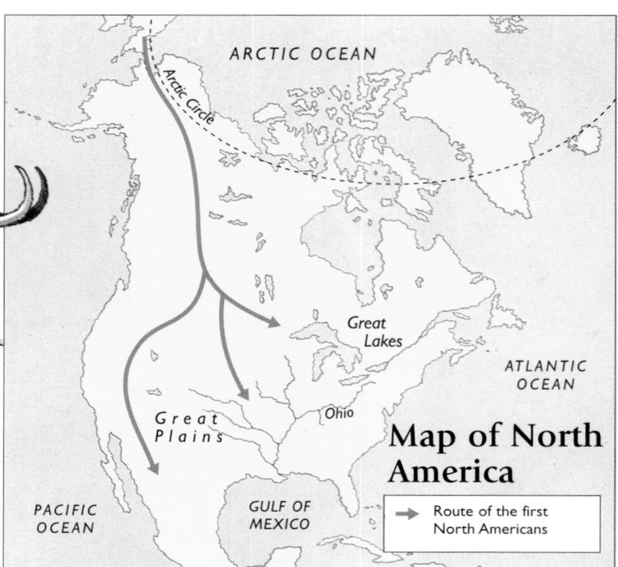

Map of North America

At first, people roamed around hunting large animals, such as mammoths, horses and buffalo, but by 8000BC most of these animals had died out. Hunters had to find smaller animals, and relied more on picking wild plants to eat.

Wild plants

Plums

Rosehips

A prickly pear

A gourd

People spread out across the plains, woodlands, mountains, deserts and icy wastes of North America. They began to settle down, and a different way of life grew up in each of these areas.

These men are cutting up a dead buffalo.

★ This picture shows people of the Great Plains hunting buffalo.

This man has just thrown his spear.

Some buffalo are killed with spears.

The hunters are disguised as wolves.

The buffalo are being chased over the edge of a cliff.

Hunters of the Plains

Buffalo were one of the few large animals that did not die out, and the people of the Great Plains hunted them for their meat and skins. The skins were scraped clean and made into clothes and tents.

Scraping a buffalo skin

Ivory knife used for cutting ice

Hunters of the Arctic

The people who settled in the far north had to survive in the freezing lands of the Arctic. They caught fish, and hunted walrus and seals. In winter, they used blocks of ice to build shelters called igloos.

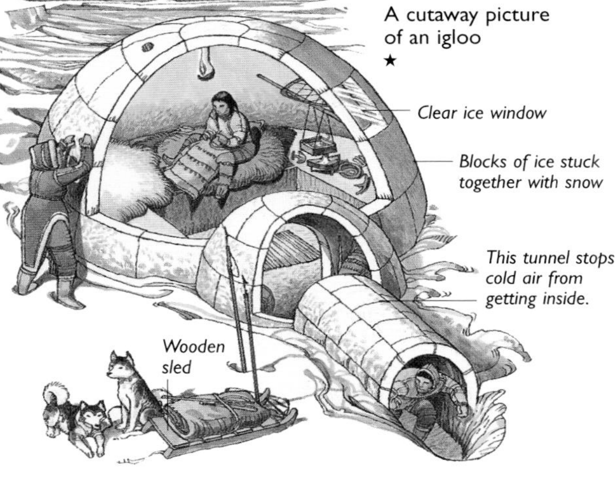

A cutaway picture of an igloo ★

Woodland tribes

The Adena people lived in the eastern woodlands along the Ohio River. They hunted deer, caught fish and collected berries. They also grew plants, such as beans, gourds and sunflowers.

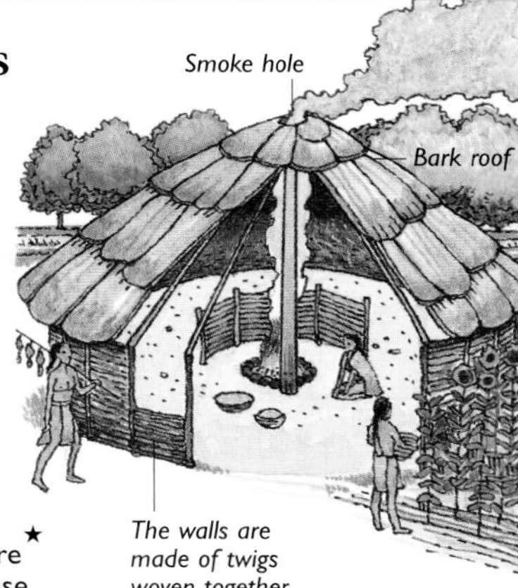

A cutaway picture of an Adena house ★

The Adena, and the Hopewell people who came after them, are famous for the huge earth mounds they built. Some of the mounds were pyramid-shaped, but others were shaped like animals.

The Great Serpent Mound is 217m (712ft) long.

Desert tribes

In the deserts of the southwest, people lived by hunting small animals and collecting nuts, seeds and wild fruits. Later, some tribes learned to grow corn, beans and squashes.

This scene shows a group of desert people known as Basketmakers. ★

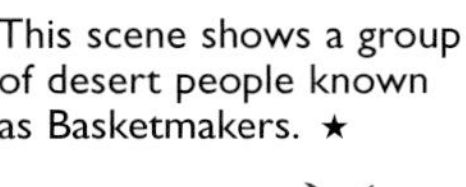

The Hopewell traded with other tribes from the Great Lakes to the Gulf of Mexico. They brought back copper, shells and alligator teeth, which they used to make necklaces and ornaments.

Carved copper bird

Important dates

c.10,000-8000BC	Early North Americans hunt large animals.
c.8000-1000BC	People spread out and learn new ways of life.
c.2000BC	People settle in the Arctic.
c.1000-300BC	The Adena people
c.300BC-AD550	The Hopewell people
c.AD1-500	Early Basketmakers

2000BC 1000BC 500BC AD1 AD500

The People of Ancient Peru

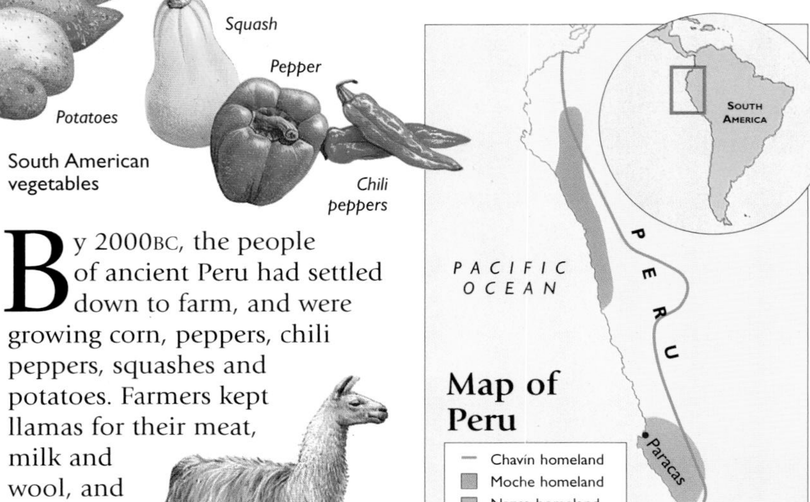

South American vegetables

By 2000BC, the people of ancient Peru had settled down to farm, and were growing corn, peppers, chili peppers, squashes and potatoes. Farmers kept llamas for their meat, milk and wool, and also used them for carrying loads.

Llama

Gods and gold

Around 1200BC, the Chavín people created the first civilization in South America. They were skilled stoneworkers and built huge temples filled with sculptures and carvings of their snarling, animal-like gods. The Chavín were also the first people in the Americas to make things from gold.

This gold ornament may have been made for a Chavín priest. ★

Cloth pictures

Paracas embroidery ★

The Paracas people of southern Peru were skilled at weaving and embroidery. When someone died, the body was placed in a basket and was wrapped in layers of beautifully embroidered cloth.

Drawings in the desert

The Nazca people are famous for the giant outlines of animals and shapes that they made in the desert. Experts think that these drawings may have been done to persuade the gods to send rain.

The giant spider shown in this picture is 45m (148ft) long.

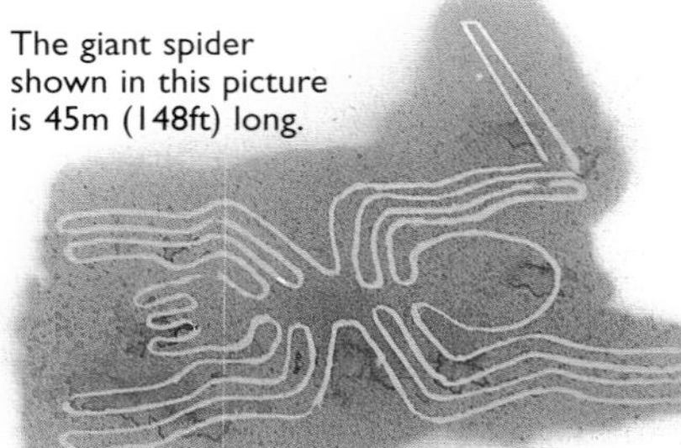

Priests and pottery

In the north, the Moche people were ruled by powerful warrior-priests. They conquered nearby tribes, and often sacrificed prisoners of war to their gods. The Moche are famous for making pots in human shapes.

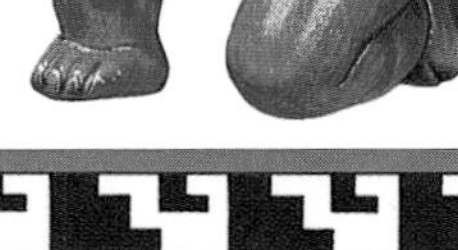

A pot in the shape of a Moche warrior ★

Important dates

c.2000BC	The people of Peru first grow corn.
c.1200-300BC	The Chavín people
c.500BC-AD200	The Paracas people
c.200BC-AD600	The Nazca people
c.AD1-700	The Moche people

The Olmecs

Corn plant

The Olmecs lived on a swampy plain beside the Gulf of Mexico. They had no farm animals to provide them with meat, so growing crops was very important. Corn was the main crop, but farmers also grew beans, squashes, chili peppers and avocados.

Map of Olmec lands

NORTH AMERICA
SOUTH AMERICA
GULF OF MEXICO
La Venta
San Lorenzo
PACIFIC OCEAN
Area where the Olmecs lived

Gods and games

By around 1200BC, the Olmecs had begun building a series of temples to their gods at a place called San Lorenzo. Later, San Lorenzo was destroyed and a new place of worship was built at La Venta.

★ Carving of the Olmecs' jaguar god

This picture shows a religious ceremony at La Venta. ★

Priest

Some experts think this mosaic shows the face of the jaguar god.

The mosaic has just been finished.

Blocks of green stone

Blue clay

The mosaic is buried immediately, because it is too holy to look at.

As part of their religion, the Olmecs played a sacred ball game. Players used a hard rubber ball and wore helmets to protect their heads. Some of the players may have been sacrificed at the end of the game.

Olmec ball-players ★

Huge heads

The Olmecs are best known for the massive stone heads that they carved. Some of these are almost 3m (10ft) high. Experts think that the heads may show different Olmec rulers.

This huge stone head was carved from a single block of stone.

The end of the Olmecs

Around 400BC, the temples at La Venta were abandoned. The Olmecs died out, but their way of life influenced many of the people who came after them (see pages 180 and 181).

Important dates

c.1200BC	San Lorenzo is built.
c.900BC	San Lorenzo is destroyed.
c.400BC	La Venta is abandoned.

Ancient Cities of the Americas

The city of Teotihuacán (in modern Mexico) was the biggest ancient city in the Americas. People began building it around 100BC, and by AD500 it was the sixth largest city in the world.

In the middle of Teotihuacán was the Citadel, where the rulers of the city lived in splendid palaces. Most other people lived in large apartment buildings, which had room for several families.

The rain god of Teotihuacán

Crafts

Craftworkers in Teotihuacán shaped pots and figures from clay, carved ornaments from polished stones and shells, and made tools and weapons from obsidian (a hard glassy rock).

Clay figure from Teotihuacán ★

Trade

Teotihuacán was an important trading city. In the marketplace, merchants traded pottery and obsidian tools for seashells, sweet-smelling incense and the beautiful tail feathers of the quetzal bird. The feathers were used to decorate the clothes of rich people.

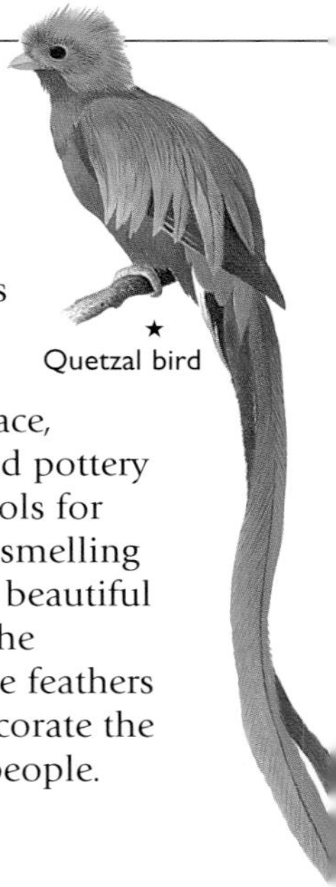

★ Quetzal bird

This picture shows part of the city of Teotihuacán.

People from all over Central America come to worship at the city's temples.

People climb the steps to the temple at the top.

This is the Pyramid of the Sun. It is 70m (230ft) high.

Corn, beans and pumpkins are grown in fields around the city.

Underneath this pyramid is a cave where people believe the Sun and the Moon were born.

The pyramid is made of soil and rubble.

The outside is plastered and painted.

★ *Apartment building*

This is the Avenue of the Dead. It leads in a straight line to the Citadel and the marketplace.

This is the Pyramid of the Moon.

Each of these small pyramids has a temple on top.

THE AMERICAS

10,000BC | 5000BC | 4000BC | 3000BC

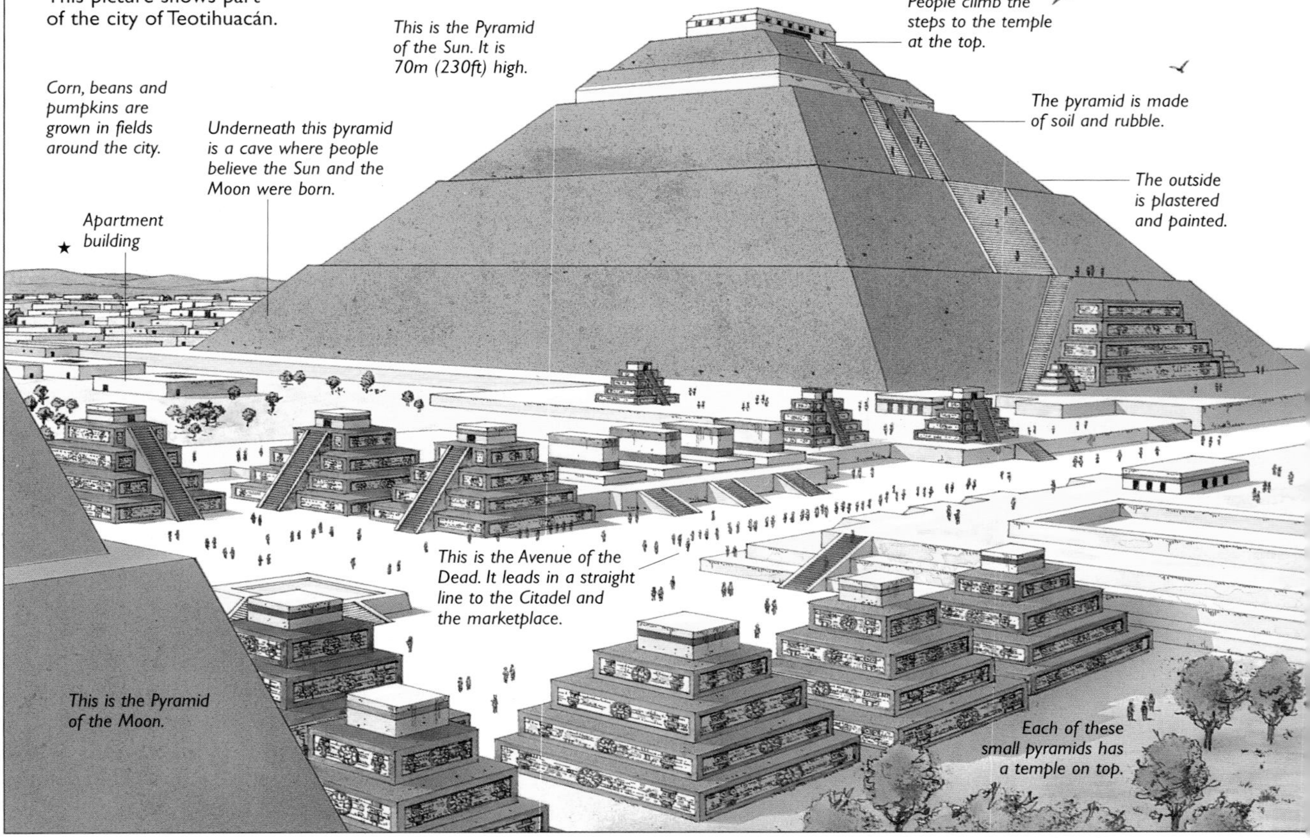

These men are carving a giant stone pillar.

Cities in the jungle

The spectacular stone cities of the Maya people lay deep in the Central American rainforest. Mayan cities were built around a complex of squares, temples, palaces and ball courts (where people played a sacred ball game). The buildings were covered in carvings of Mayan gods and kings.

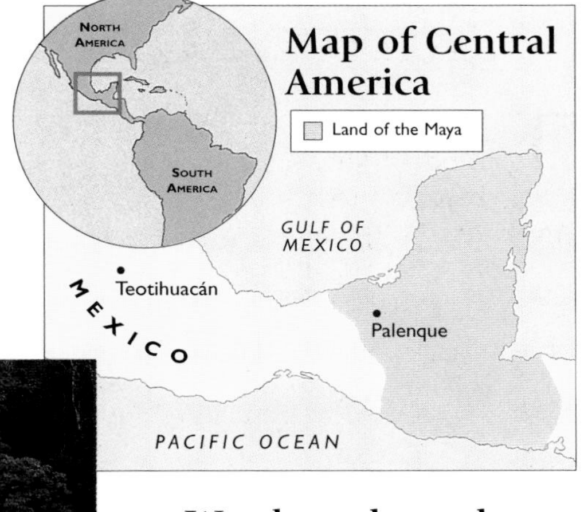

This is the Temple of Inscriptions in the Mayan city of Palenque.

Words and numbers

The Maya invented a writing system using picture signs (or glyphs) and wrote in books made of bark paper. Experts are just beginning to understand what this writing means.

Part of a Mayan book

Zero One Five

The Maya used three symbols to write all the numbers. They were using the number "zero" hundreds of years before anyone else thought of the idea.

Twelve

Blood, war and sacrifice

The Maya had many gods, and thought they could please them by making offerings of human blood. One way of doing this was to pull a string of thorns through a hole in the tongue.

Carving of a queen offering blood ★

Mayan warrior ★

The kings of the different Mayan cities were often at war with each other. They fought for power and riches, and took prisoners to sacrifice to their gods.

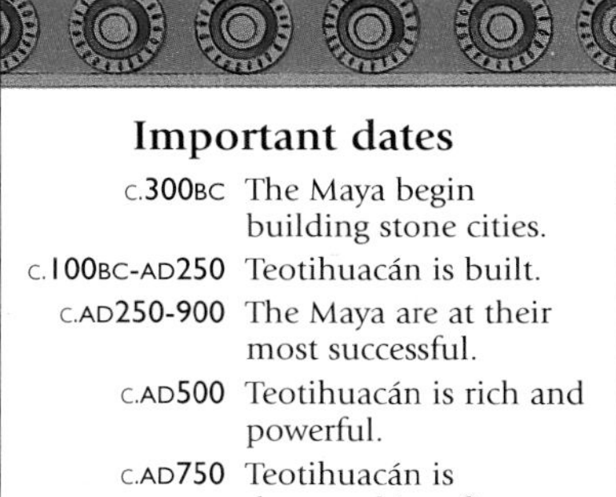

Important dates

c.300BC	The Maya begin building stone cities.
c.100BC-AD250	Teotihuacán is built.
c.AD250-900	The Maya are at their most successful.
c.AD500	Teotihuacán is rich and powerful.
c.AD750	Teotihuacán is destroyed in a fire.

2000BC 1000BC 500BC AD1 AD500

The Celtic Tribes

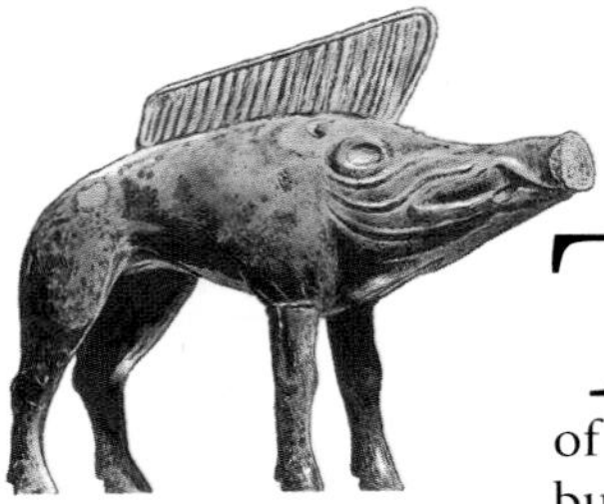

Celtic statue of a boar, a symbol of strength

The people known as Celts were made up of many different tribes, but they all had a similar language and way of life. This way of life had grown up near a place called Hallstatt (in modern Austria) by around 800BC.

The Celts gradually spread out across most of Europe, settling in the lands they conquered. One group even settled as far away as Asia Minor (modern Turkey).

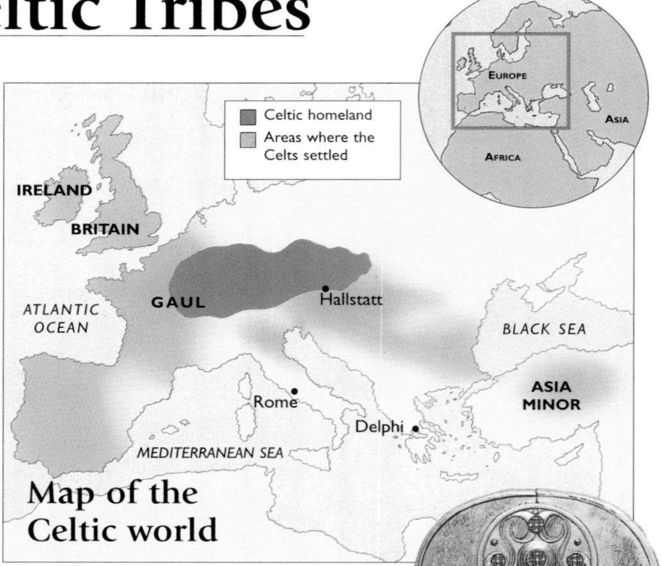

Celtic homeland
Areas where the Celts settled
IRELAND
BRITAIN
GAUL
Hallstatt
ATLANTIC OCEAN
BLACK SEA
ASIA MINOR
Rome
Delphi
MEDITERRANEAN SEA
EUROPE
ASIA
AFRICA

Map of the Celtic world

Life at home

Wherever the Celts settled, they set up farms and small villages. Their houses were built of wood or stone and had one big room inside, where the family cooked, ate and slept.

This cutaway picture shows a typical Celtic house. ★

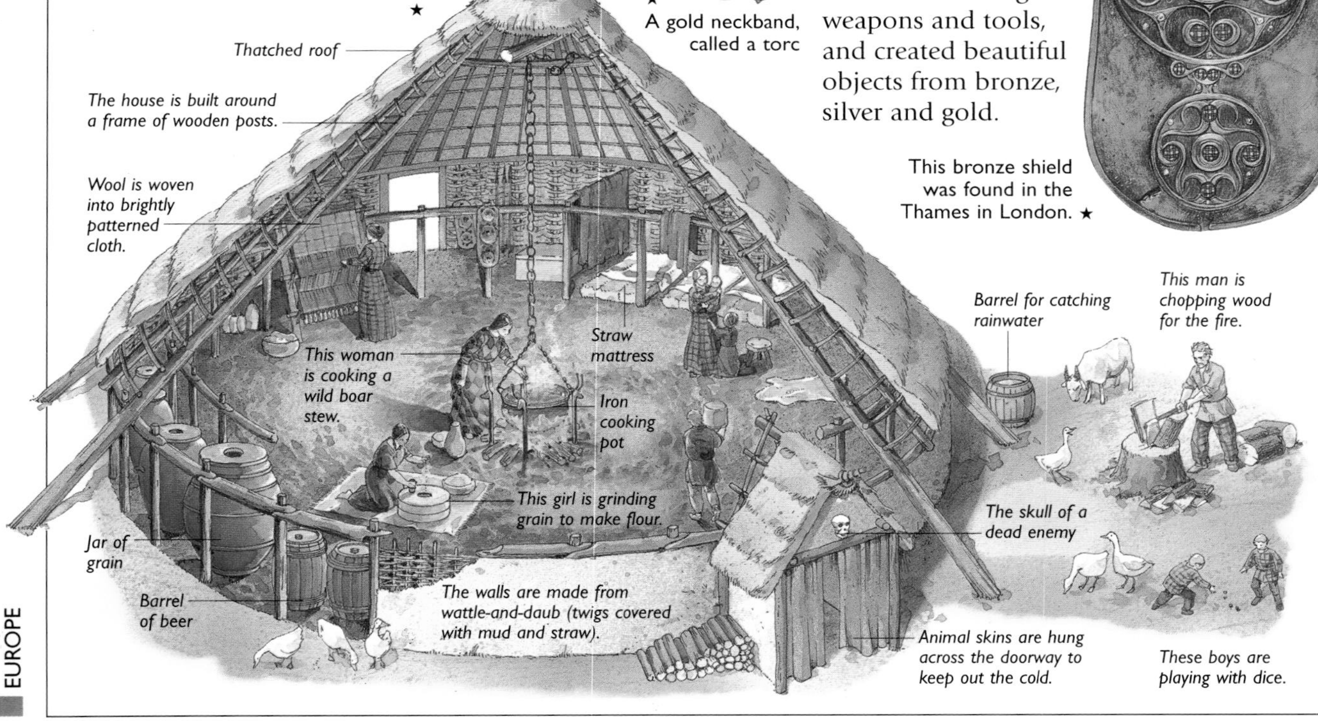

Thatched roof

The house is built around a frame of wooden posts.

Wool is woven into brightly patterned cloth.

This woman is cooking a wild boar stew.

Straw mattress

Iron cooking pot

This girl is grinding grain to make flour.

Jar of grain

Barrel of beer

The walls are made from wattle-and-daub (twigs covered with mud and straw).

Animal skins are hung across the doorway to keep out the cold.

The skull of a dead enemy

Barrel for catching rainwater

This man is chopping wood for the fire.

These boys are playing with dice.

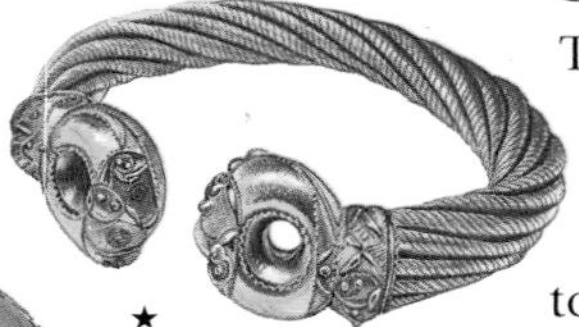

★ A gold neckband, called a torc

Celtic crafts

The Celts were highly skilled metalworkers. They used iron to make strong weapons and tools, and created beautiful objects from bronze, silver and gold.

This bronze shield was found in the Thames in London. ★

Forts and fighting

The Celts were fierce warriors and their tribes often fought each other. They built large hilltop forts to protect their women, children and animals from attacks by enemies.

This picture shows Celtic warriors charging at an enemy. ★

The hillfort is surrounded by huge mounds of earth with ditches in between.

Houses

Nobles ride chariots into battle and then fight on foot.

War trumpets make a terrifying noise.

Warriors comb lime through their hair to make it spiky.

Wooden shield covered with leather

Some warriors fight on horseback.

Chariot wheels have a strong iron rim.

Warriors run yelling at the enemy.

Some warriors paint blue patterns on their bodies to make themselves look scary.

Feasts

Warriors held great feasts to celebrate their victories in battle. They were entertained by poet-musicians, called bards, who recited poems about the brave deeds of Celtic heroes.

A Celtic feast

A bard chanting a poem

Harp

This is the chieftain (leader) of the tribe.

Flagon of wine

A pig roasting on a spit

Religion

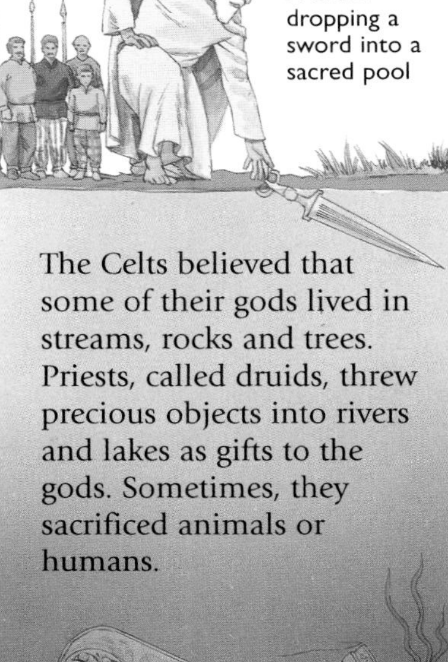

A druid dropping a sword into a sacred pool

The Celts believed that some of their gods lived in streams, rocks and trees. Priests, called druids, threw precious objects into rivers and lakes as gifts to the gods. Sometimes, they sacrificed animals or humans.

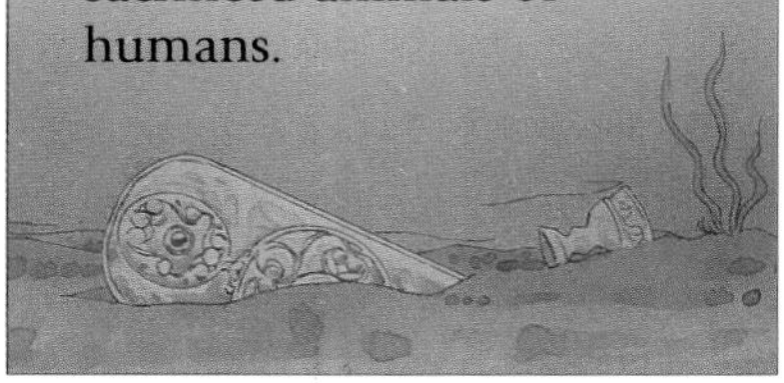

Roman conquerors

As the Roman Empire grew, the Celts fought hard to defend their lands. However, they were no match for the mighty Roman army, and in the end most of them were conquered. The Celtic way of life only survived in Ireland and in remote parts of Scotland and Wales.

Important dates

c.800BC	The Celtic way of life first appears.
c.390BC	The Celts destroy part of Rome.
c.279BC	The Celts attack and rob the Greek temple at Delphi.
c.278BC	The Celts reach Asia Minor.
58-51BC	The Roman general Julius Caesar conquers the Celts in Gaul (modern France).
AD43	The Romans invade Britain.

The Rise of Rome

The city of Rome began as a small farming village by a river called the Tiber. As time passed, more villages were built and eventually they joined together to form a city.

An early village in the Tiber Valley

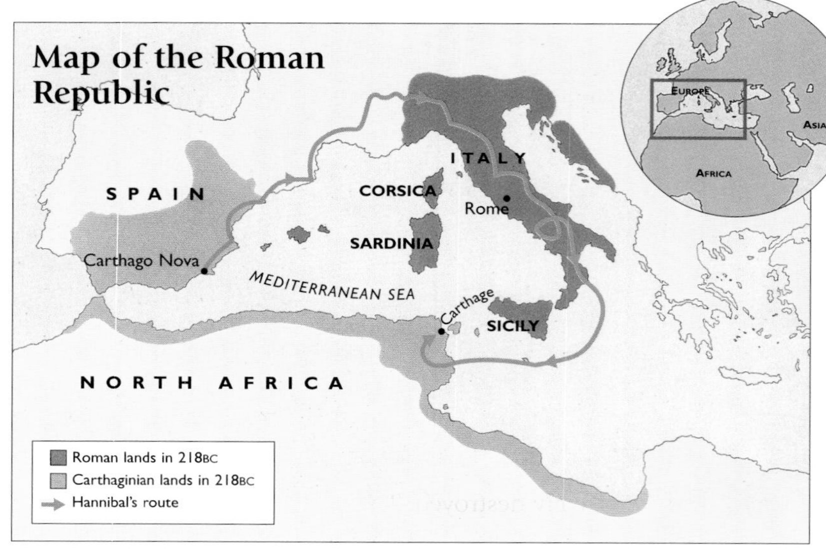

The story of Romulus

According to a Roman legend, the city was set up by a man named Romulus. As babies, he and his twin brother Remus had been left to die near the Tiber. They were found by a wolf, who fed them until they were rescued by a shepherd.

★ Statue of the wolf feeding Romulus and Remus

When the twins grew up, they decided to build a city on the banks of the Tiber, but they had a violent quarrel. Romulus killed his brother and named the city after himself. Tradition says this happened in 753BC.

The Roman Republic

Until around 509BC, Rome was ruled by kings. Then, the last king was driven out of the city and Rome became a republic. The Roman Republic was ruled by the Senate, a group of men (called senators) who came from the city's most important families. Led by the Senate, the Romans gradually conquered all of Italy.

Coin showing the Senate House

This picture shows a meeting of the Senate. Part of the seating has been cut away.

Conquering Carthage

In 264BC, a series of wars broke out between the Romans and the people of Carthage in North Africa. Both sides fought fiercely over who should control trade around the Mediterranean Sea.

The Carthaginians invaded Italy in 218BC. This picture shows them crossing the Alps.

The Carthaginian general, Hannibal, leading his troops

Only two of the 40 war elephants survived the journey.

10,000 soldiers died in the mountains.

The wars between Rome and Carthage are known as the Punic Wars. They ended in 146BC when Carthage was completely destroyed. The Romans took over the Carthaginian lands and went on to conquer all the kingdoms around the Mediterranean.

Blazing buildings and boats in the port at Carthage

Julius Caesar

As the Romans won more land, the senators argued over how things should be run. Rival groups of senators used the army to help them fight for power. In 49BC, a general called Julius Caesar marched with his army to Rome and seized power. Caesar brought peace, but some senators grew worried that he planned to make himself king, so they stabbed him to death.

Julius Caesar

The first emperor

After Julius Caesar died, there were more struggles for power. In 31BC, Caesar's great-nephew, Octavian, defeated his rival, Mark Antony, and won control of Rome. Octavian took the name Augustus, which means "respected one". He became Rome's first emperor.

Statue of the Emperor Augustus

Augustus is shown wearing the uniform of a Roman general.

The Roman Army

By the time Augustus became emperor, Rome controlled most of the land around the Mediterranean Sea. Over the next 150 years, the Romans conquered even more land, creating a vast empire that stretched from Britain to the Middle East. The Empire was at its largest in AD117 during the rule of the Emperor Trajan.

★ Emperor Augustus

★ Emperor Trajan

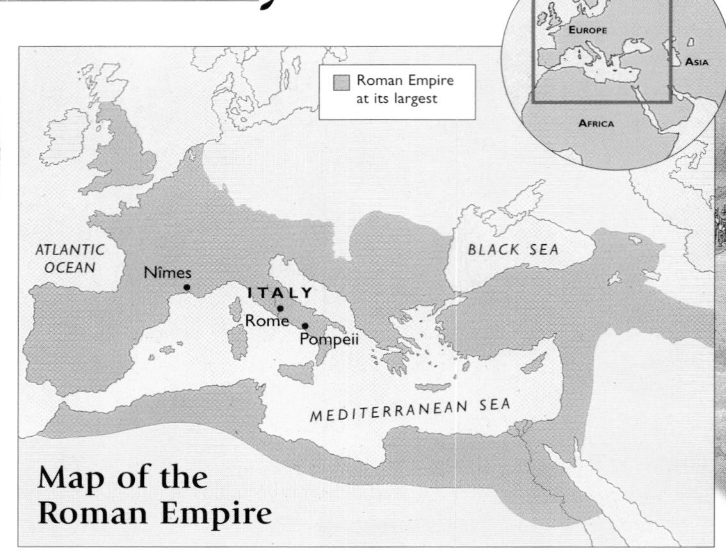

Map of the Roman Empire

The Romans won wars because they had a strong, well-organized army, and their soldiers fought in highly disciplined groups. A group of 80 soldiers was called a century, centuries were grouped into cohorts, and ten cohorts made up a legion.

A Roman legionary (foot soldier) ★

During the Republic, any man who owned land could be asked to fight for a while. By the time of the emperors, most soldiers were well-trained professionals, who made the army their career.

Attacking a city

The Romans were determined fighters and even conquered cities that were very well defended. They surrounded a city so no one could escape, and then used clever techniques to force their way in.

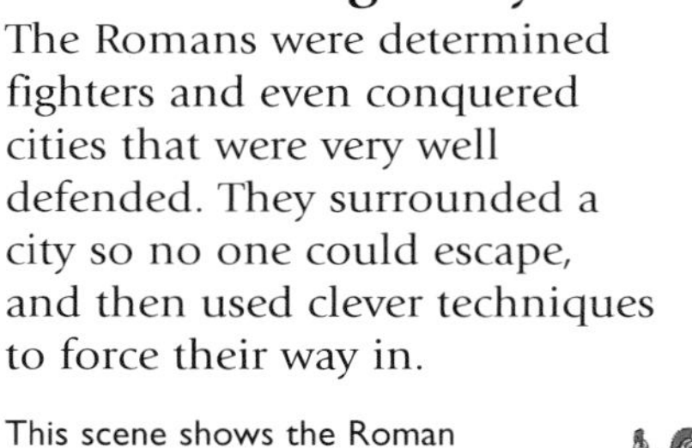

Soldiers move around under a roof of shields. This is called a tortoise.

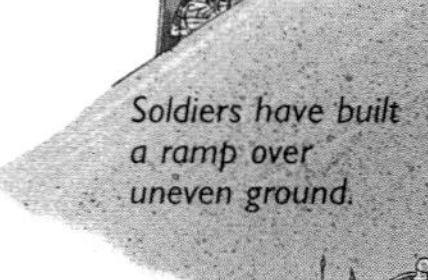

Soldiers have built a ramp over uneven ground.

This scene shows the Roman army attacking a walled city.

A wooden siege tower is wheeled into position.

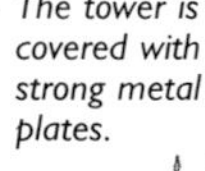

The tower is covered with strong metal plates.

On the road

To keep the Empire under control, soldiers had to be able to move quickly to wherever they were needed. A network of good roads was built linking every part of the Empire. On these roads, soldiers could march over 50km (30 miles) a day.

Soldiers on the move

Camps and forts

At the end of a long day's march, the soldiers had to build a camp for the night. The next morning, the camp was packed up and the army moved on. At the borders of the Empire, where soldiers were needed all the time, permanent stone forts were built.

Soldiers building a temporary camp

Life in a Roman Town

The Romans took their way of life to all the lands they conquered. Each area, or province, of the Empire was run by a governor who made sure that people paid their taxes, obeyed Roman laws and respected Roman gods.

Statue of Jupiter, king of the gods

Retired Roman soldiers settled down to farm the land they had conquered, settlements grew up near Roman camps and forts, and new towns were built all over the Empire.

Roman towns were very well planned. They had many fine public buildings, such as temples and baths, as well as houses, apartment blocks, shops and restaurants.

This scene shows a busy Roman town. Some of the walls have been cut away to let you see inside the buildings.

Internet link: *For a link to a Web site where you can explore the ancient town of Pompeii and see Mount Vesuvius erupt, go to* **www.usborne-quicklinks.com**

A life of luxury

While most townspeople lived in crowded apartment blocks, rich people had spacious houses with shady gardens. The houses were beautifully decorated inside. Some even had central heating under the floors and their own water supply.

This picture shows the reception hall (or atrium) of a Roman house. ★

Mosaic floor made of tiny pieces of stone

Rainwater collects in a pool.

This huge aqueduct, near the French town of Nîmes, is 49m (160ft) high.

Waterworks

Roman towns needed lots of fresh water to supply public baths, fountains and toilets. A system of pipes and channels (called aqueducts) took water to where it was needed. Engineers built tunnels and bridges to carry the water pipes across hills and valleys.

Buried treasure

Pompeii in southern Italy was a large, wealthy town. In August AD79, the nearby volcano Mount Vesuvius erupted. Pompeii was buried under clouds of ash and rivers of scorching lava (liquid rock). Experts have since dug through the lava to uncover the town, giving us an amazing picture of everyday life in Roman times.

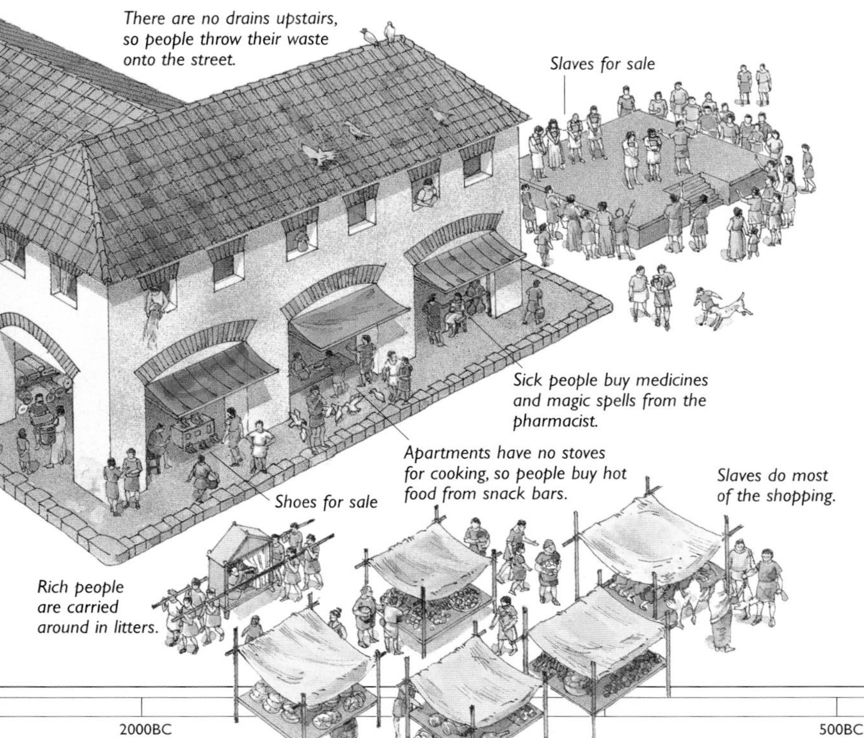

There are no drains upstairs, so people throw their waste onto the street.

Slaves for sale

Sick people buy medicines and magic spells from the pharmacist.

Apartments have no stoves for cooking, so people buy hot food from snack bars.

Slaves do most of the shopping.

Shoes for sale

Rich people are carried around in litters.

Wall painting from a house in Pompeii

Fun and Games

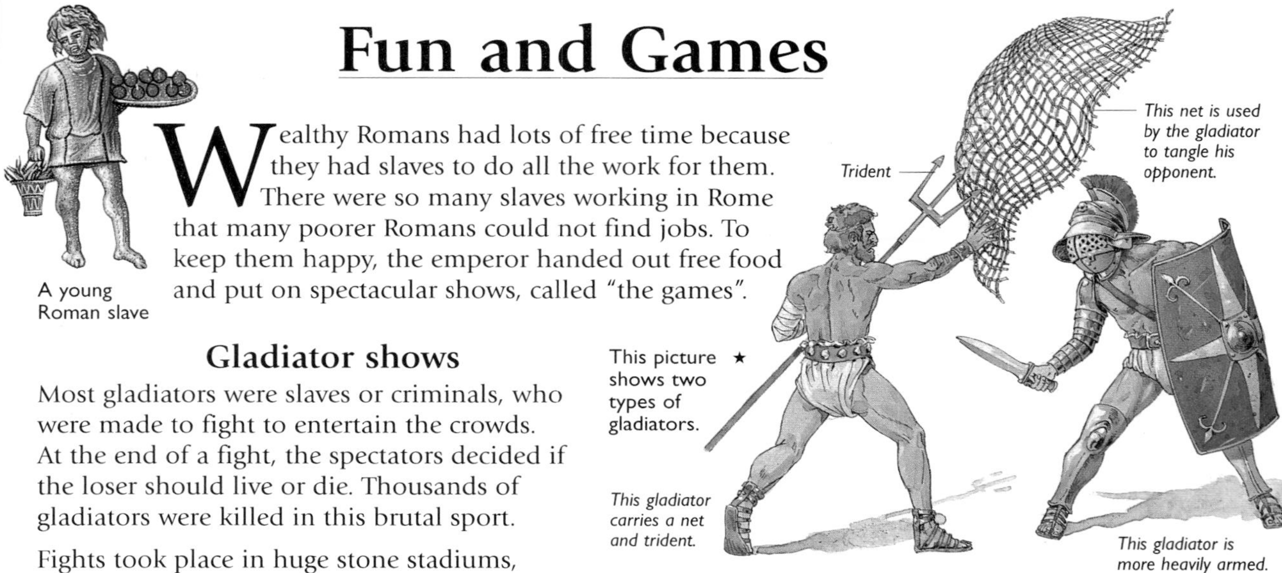

A young Roman slave

This picture ★ shows two types of gladiators.

This gladiator carries a net and trident.

This gladiator is more heavily armed.

Wealthy Romans had lots of free time because they had slaves to do all the work for them. There were so many slaves working in Rome that many poorer Romans could not find jobs. To keep them happy, the emperor handed out free food and put on spectacular shows, called "the games".

Gladiator shows

Most gladiators were slaves or criminals, who were made to fight to entertain the crowds. At the end of a fight, the spectators decided if the loser should live or die. Thousands of gladiators were killed in this brutal sport.

Fights took place in huge stone stadiums, called amphitheatres. The biggest of these was the Colosseum in Rome, which held 50,000 people. Sometimes, the arena was flooded, so that gladiators could take part in sea battles.

This cutaway picture shows a sea battle in the Colosseum. ★

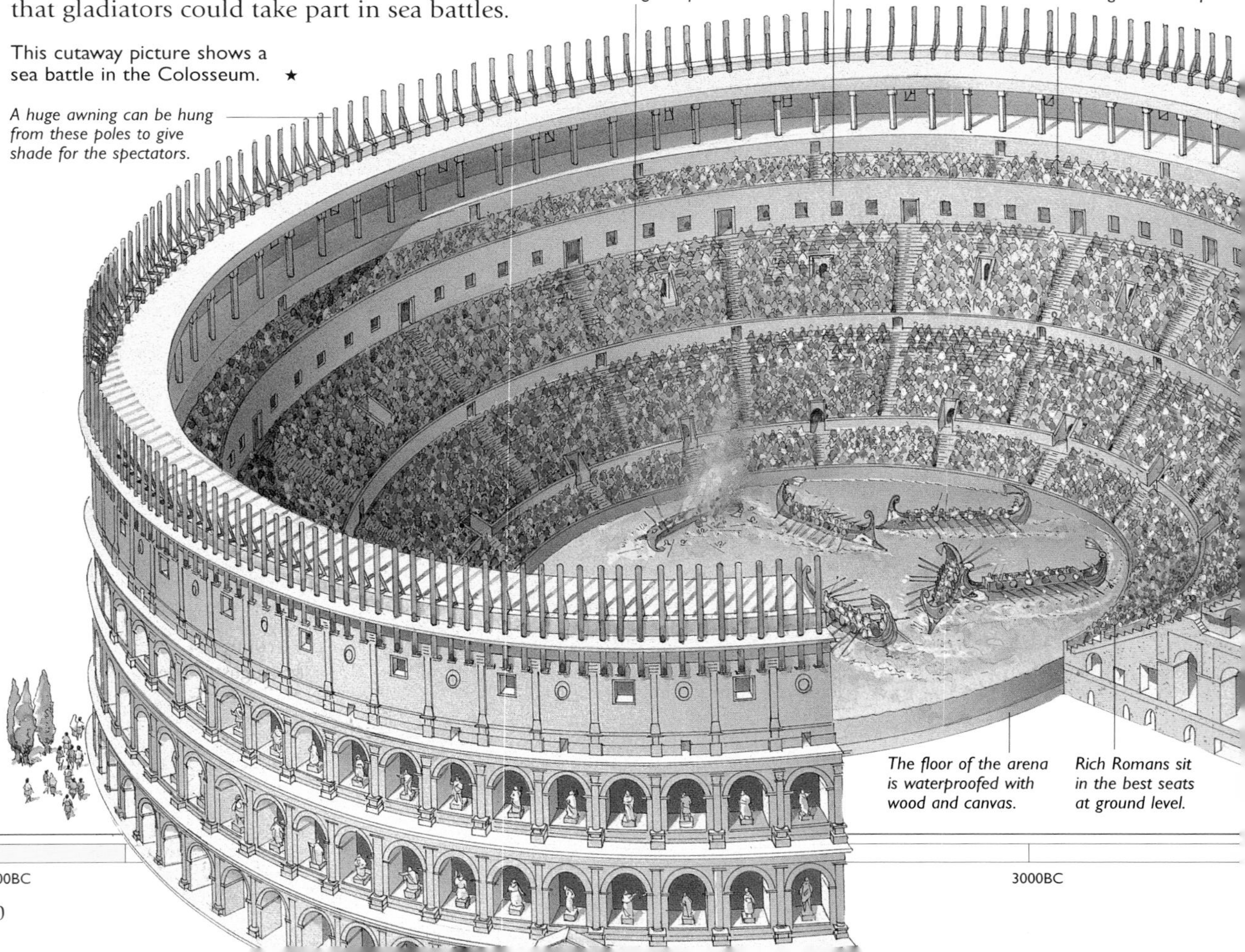

A huge awning can be hung from these poles to give shade for the spectators.

Poorer people sit higher up.

Women watch from behind this wall.

Slaves and foreigners stand right at the top.

The floor of the arena is waterproofed with wood and canvas.

Rich Romans sit in the best seats at ground level.

EUROPE

10,000BC 3000BC

Chariot races

A driver and horses in a chariot race ★

The reins are wound around the driver's body.

Racing chariots are very light for extra speed.

The most popular of the games were the chariot races, which were held at a racetrack called a circus. The races were exciting to watch but were very dangerous, as drivers were often thrown off and killed.

There are four teams. Drivers wear red, blue, green or white to show which team they belong to.

Pastimes

As well as going to the games, Romans enjoyed relaxing in the public parks and gardens. They played board games and also liked gambling games.

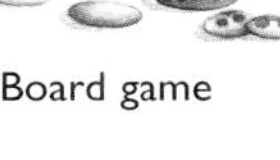

Board game

Coins and dice for gambling

Children had seesaws, swings, kites, hoops, marbles and dolls to play with.

Sometimes, they rode around in small carts pulled by geese.

Wooden dolls

Mosaic showing a child in a toy cart

Drama

The first Roman plays were copied from Greek ones and were quite serious. By the time of the emperors, people preferred watching comedies. The shows gradually became more and more spectacular, with lots of music, dancing and special effects. Some actors became so popular that they were mobbed by their fans.

Concrete (a Roman invention) makes the walls very strong.

The stone seats are supported by arches.

The outside is decorated with marble pillars and statues.

There are 80 entrances, so people can get in and out quickly.

Roman actors in their costumes ★

Important dates

753BC	The city of Rome is set up, according to legend.
c.509BC	Rome becomes a republic.
264BC	The Punic Wars start.
146BC	The Romans destroy Carthage.
49BC	Julius Caesar takes control of Rome.
27BC	Augustus becomes the first Emperor of Rome.
AD72-80	The Colosseum is built.
AD117	The Roman Empire is at its largest.

The Spread of Christianity

The Christian religion began with a Jew called Jesus, later known as Jesus Christ. You can read about his life and teachings in the New Testament of the Bible.

Mosaic showing Jesus as a shepherd

The life of Jesus

Jesus was born in Judea, a small province in the Roman Empire. At around the age of 30, he chose 12 men to be his disciples (followers) and began preaching. News spread that he could perform miracles, and crowds of people came to hear him.

This mosaic shows Jesus bringing a dead man back to life.

Jesus's teachings

Jesus taught that it was more important to love God and serve others than to obey the Jewish law. He said that people should stop doing wrong and make a fresh start, so that they could be part of God's kingdom.

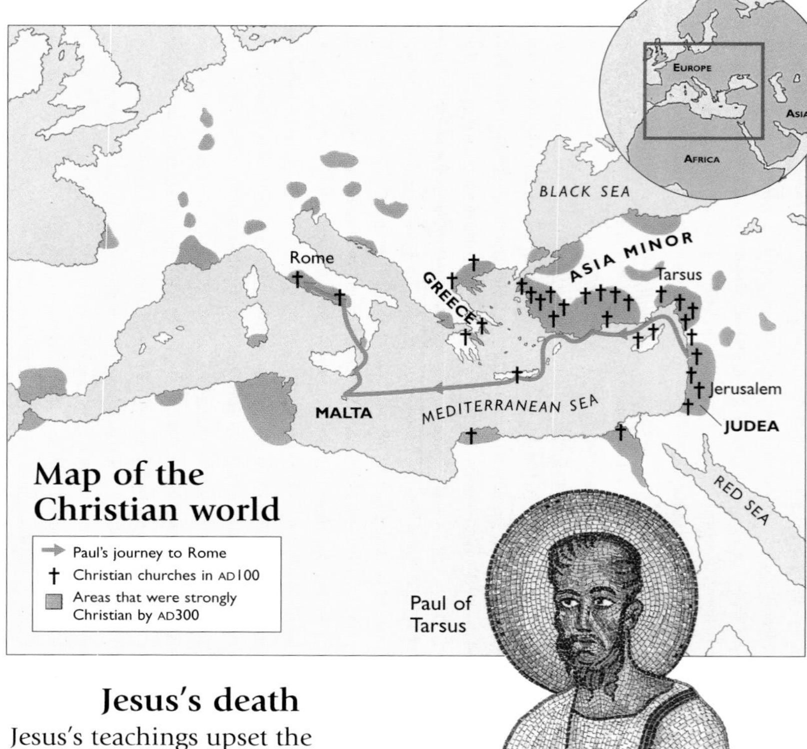

Map of the Christian world

Paul of Tarsus

Jesus's death

Jesus's teachings upset the Jewish religious leaders, and the Romans were afraid that his ideas might lead to a rebellion in Judea. He was arrested in Jerusalem and was crucified (nailed to a cross to die).

Ivory carving of Jesus on the cross

Spreading the word

After Jesus died, his teachings were spread by his followers, who said that he had risen from the dead. Paul of Tarsus took the Christian message to Asia Minor (modern Turkey), to Greece and even to Rome.

On his way to Rome, Paul was shipwrecked off the coast of Malta.

Hard times

Christianity spread quickly around the Roman Empire. Some emperors saw the Christians as rebels because they refused to worship Roman gods, and thousands were arrested, tortured and killed.

Many Christians were thrown to the lions for public entertainment.

To avoid being arrested, Christians often had to meet in secret. In Rome, they met in the catacombs, a series of tunnels under the city that were used as burial places.

Secret symbols

Christians used secret signs to show other Christians that they shared the same faith. One of these was the Chi-Ro sign ☧.

★ Portrait of a Christian family with the Chi-Ro sign

The Chi-Ro sign was made up of the first two letters of the word "Christ" in Greek. It has been found carved on tombs, statues and doorways, and on the walls of the catacombs.

This scene shows a group of Christians in the catacombs. ★

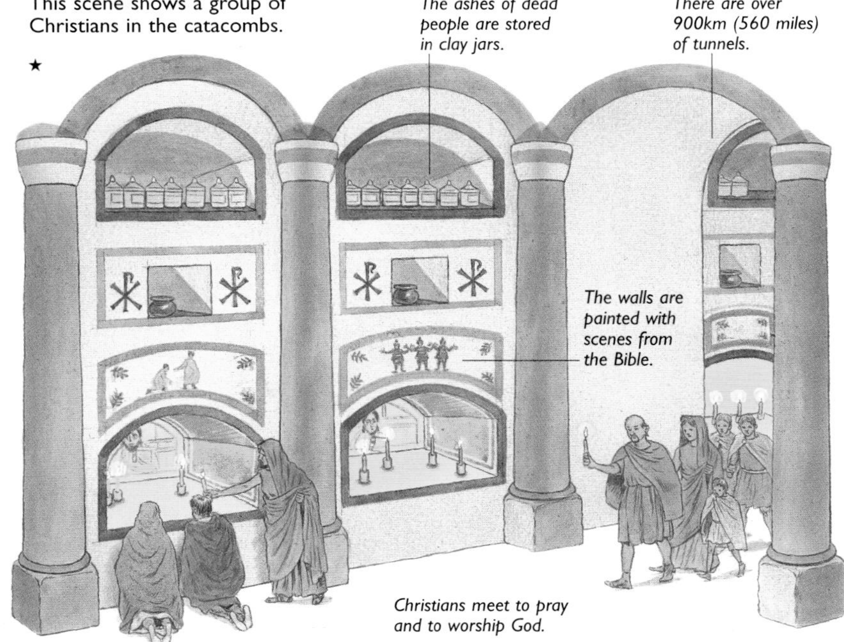

Christian emperors

The Emperor Constantine was the first Roman ruler to accept the Christian faith. After seeing a cross of light in the sky, he sent his army into battle with the Chi-Ro sign on their shields. Constantine won the battle and later became a Christian.

Constantine riding into battle

Constantine gave Christians the freedom to worship openly, and helped to spread Christianity across Europe. He built the first great Christian churches, and gave Christians special privileges. Finally, in AD391, the Emperor Theodosius made Christianity the official religion of the Roman Empire.

Important dates

c.5BC	Jesus Christ is born.
c.AD29	Jesus Christ is crucified.
AD45-58	Paul travels around Asia Minor and Greece.
AD58-60	Paul travels to Rome.
AD312	The Emperor Constantine makes Christianity legal.
AD391	Christianity becomes the official religion of the Roman Empire.

The Fall of Rome

Around AD200, the power of the Roman Empire began to weaken. The Roman armies started to choose their own emperors, and fighting broke out between different groups of soldiers. At the same time, the Empire was attacked by tribes from the northeast, known as Germani. The Romans called these people "barbarians".

A Germanic warrior

A throwing-axe, called a francisca

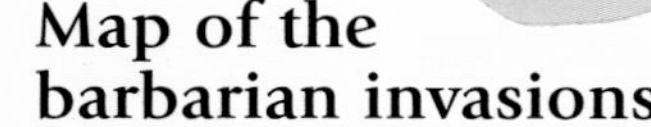

Map of the barbarian invasions

Defending the Empire

In AD284, a general called Diocletian became emperor. To defend the Empire against the barbarians, he reorganized the army and made it bigger. Diocletian realized that the Empire was too big for one person to control, so he split it in two. He ruled the eastern half himself, while the western half was ruled by a general called Maximian. Each emperor had a deputy to help him rule.

Statue of Diocletian and Maximian with their two deputies

The Emperor Constantine

When Diocletian retired, there were more struggles for power. In AD312, Constantine became Emperor of the West. Later, he took control of the East as well, reuniting the Empire.

Constantine moved the capital of the Roman Empire to the town of Byzantium on the Black Sea. He rebuilt Byzantium, filled it with treasures from around the Empire and renamed it Constantinople, after himself.

A later mosaic of Constantine holding a model of Constantinople

10,000BC 5000BC 3000BC

Asian invaders

Hun warriors in battle ★

Around AD370, eastern Europe was invaded by people from central Asia, known as the Huns. As the Huns moved across Europe, they pushed the Germanic tribes off their land and into the Roman Empire.

Peace at a price

The Romans allowed some Germanic tribes, such as the Visigoths, to settle inside the Empire, as long as they helped to fight off other barbarians.

Visigoth settlers

Rome in ruins

In AD395, the Roman Empire split permanently into East and West, and from then on waves of barbarians swept across the Western Empire (see map). The city of Rome was attacked by the Visigoths in AD410, and by the Vandals in AD455.

This scene shows Vandal warriors wrecking Rome.

The end of the Empire

In AD476, a Visigoth chief called Odoacer made himself King of Italy, and the Western Empire came to an end. The Eastern Empire, with its capital at Constantinople, lasted for another thousand years.

Many Romans are killed.

Buildings are set on fire.

Important dates

AD286 Diocletian splits the Roman Empire in two.

AD312 Constantine becomes Emperor of the West.

AD324 Constantine reunites the Empire.

c.AD370 The Huns arrive in Europe.

AD395 The Roman Empire splits permanently in two.

AD410 Rome is attacked by the Visigoths.

AD455 Rome is destroyed by the Vandals.

AD476 The Western Empire ends.

500BC AD1 AD500

Part of a 15th-century tapestry showing a scene from the Hundred Years' War

MEDIEVAL WORLD

Looking at the Medieval World

In this section of the book, you can find out what was happening all over the world from around 500 to around 1500. This time in history is known as the medieval period, or the Middle Ages.

A changing world

By the year 500, the Roman Empire had collapsed and tribes of people were roaming through Europe, looking for places to live. Over the next 500 years, these people settled down and created kingdoms of their own. Most of the kingdoms were led by strong Christian rulers, who encouraged art and learning, but also fought each other for land.

Meanwhile, in Arabia, the new religion of Islam was born, and great empires flourished in Africa, Asia and the Americas. For centuries, these empires were isolated from Europe, but by the end of the Middle Ages, European explorers were sailing to distant lands.

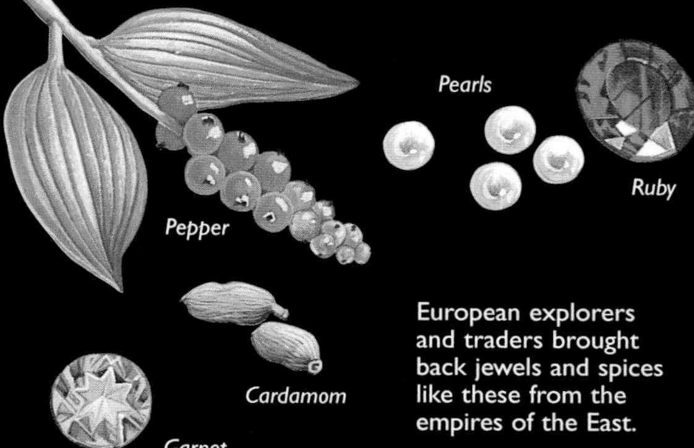

European explorers and traders brought back jewels and spices like these from the empires of the East.

This is a statue of Charlemagne, a great early Christian ruler.

When and where?

Important events and their dates are shown in boxes. If a date has a letter "c." in front of it, this means that experts aren't sure exactly when the event took place. (The "c." stands for *circa* which means "about" in Latin.)

To see which period of time you are reading about, take a look at the timeline at the bottom of each page. You can also check the bottom corner of the page to find out which area of the world you are in. The different areas of the world are marked on the map below.

Medieval works of art, such as paintings and carvings, often show important people and great events. These works of art can also reveal fascinating details about daily life.

Manuscripts like this show the skill of the monks who illustrated them.

In many parts of the medieval world, people wrote things down in handwritten books, called manuscripts. Scholars recorded events of the time, explorers described their travels, and inventors explained their ideas. Government officials kept records of taxes, laws and trials, while writers produced poems and stories based on real life.

How do we know?

Many buildings and objects have survived from medieval times, giving a vivid impression of life in the Middle Ages.

Other medieval buildings are now in ruins, or even buried underground. Experts, called archaeologists, uncover buried buildings and objects, and also use computer technology to help create a picture of how things used to look.

The carved head shown here is part of a ruined Mayan temple at Chichén Itzá, in Central America.

Medieval World Internet Links

These Web sites will help you to find out more about a range of medieval topics. To visit the sites, go to **www.usborne-quicklinks.com** and enter the keyword "history".

WEB SITE 1 A lively survey of the last 1,000 years, with video clips, maps, timelines and quizzes. Click on the first five episodes to learn about people and events all over the medieval world.

WEB SITE 2 A general introduction to life in medieval Europe, divided into topics such as religion, homes and clothing. The site includes fun interactive activities.

WEB SITE 3 Click on the people and buildings in a medieval street to learn about life in the Middle Ages. You can also take part in an archery contest and throw tomatoes at a thief in the stocks.

WEB SITE 4 A site on British castles. Click on "Castle Learning Center" for masses of facts about castle life, or select "Castle Links" where you'll find links to the Web sites of individual castles in Britain. There is also a section on castle ghosts!

WEB SITE 5 An attractive site on Welsh castles. The "Historical Essays" section has very good information and photos on castles and castle life. Click on "Castle Terminology" to find lists of castle words with their meanings.

WEB SITE 6 An interactive site on castle warfare. Click on "Medieval Arms Race" to learn about sieges and weapons.

WEB SITE 7 A fun site about cathedrals with interactive activities, a section on medieval stone carving, and links to individual cathedral Web sites.

WEB SITE 8 A large site on medieval architecture, with photos and plans of over a hundred buildings in France and Britain. The page on Chartres Cathedral in France is especially good. Click on "Glossary" for help with architectural terms.

WEB SITE 9 A great site from New York's Metropolitan Museum. Enter and click on "The Collection", then choose "The Cloisters" or "Medieval Art" to see highlights from the museum's medieval collections.

WEB SITE 10 A huge virtual gallery of European painting and sculpture dating from 1150 to 1750. The images are amazingly clear and can be enlarged to see details. Go on a guided tour, or click on the "Artist Index" to see the works of an individual artist. You can also use the search engine to find a specific group of pictures.

WEB SITE 11 A stunning selection of manuscript pages from the Getty Museum in Los Angeles. Click on "Manuscripts", then choose any of the four categories to see vivid images of manuscript pages and lots of detailed information.

WEB SITE 12 1,000 manuscript pages from the Bibliothèque Nationale in Paris. The collection is divided into themes such as history, science and technology, and sports and entertainment.

WEB SITE 13 An introduction to medieval and Renaissance musical instruments. Click on the name of an instrument to see a photo of it being played, hear how it sounds, and learn about its history.

WEB SITE 14 At this musical site, you can listen to over a hundred tunes and carols from the Middle Ages and the Renaissance.

WEB SITE 15 A simple introduction to the medieval legend of King Arthur with music and pictures.

WEB SITE 16 An exciting site on the Norman Conquest of England, which includes close-up pictures of the complete Bayeux Tapestry and lots of information about life in the early Middle Ages.

WEB SITE 17 A very attractive site on the art of the Maya people of Central America. Tour the city of Copán and view 140 images from Mayan vases.

WEB SITE 18 A spectacular photo tour of the Inca city of Machu Picchu. Includes close-up views inside temples, palaces and houses.

WEB SITE 19 Here, you can explore Pueblo towns and villages in the southwest of the USA. Click on places on the map to see photos and descriptions. Or take a virtual tour of two Pueblo towns and a rebuilt Pueblo room.

WEB SITE 20 Find out more about the Moors who ruled Spain during the Middle Ages. This detailed site includes photos, maps and timelines.

This is the Spanish city of Granada, which was ruled by Muslim Moors during the Middle Ages.

The Byzantine Empire

By the year 400, the Roman Empire had split into two parts. The Empire in the west was attacked by warlike tribes and collapsed in 476, but the Empire in the east survived for another thousand years. The eastern Empire was known as the Byzantine Empire because its capital city, Constantinople, was originally called Byzantium.

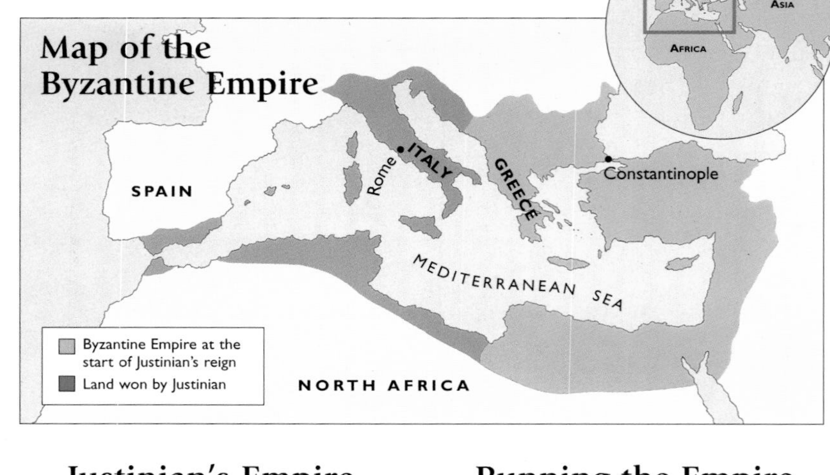

Mosaic of the Byzantine Emperor Justinian ★

Justinian's Empire

In the 6th century, the Byzantine Emperor Justinian won back many of the lands that had once been part of the Roman Empire. Under him, the Byzantine Empire was larger than it would ever be again.

Running the Empire

Justinian's dream was to create a great Christian empire. With the help of his wife, Theodora, he set up a new system of laws, and gave orders for many churches to be built. Priests, artists and merchants all visited his palace.

Justinian's palace in Constantinople

Merchants from North Africa visit Justinian's court.

Visitors grovel in front of the emperor.

500 600 700 800 900

Byzantine art

Byzantine artists were famous for their delicate embroidery and ivory carvings. They also created huge, glittering mosaics and painted dramatic religious portraits, called icons.

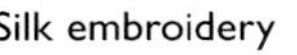

Silk embroidery

An icon of the Virgin Mary and Child

Defending the Empire

The Byzantines fought constant battles against Muslim Arabs and Turks. They were threatened by tribes from the north, and even had to fight against Crusaders from western Europe, who were supposed to be on their side (see page 241).

The end of the Empire

After Justinian's death, the Empire became smaller and smaller, and by 1400 only the land around Constantinople was left. In 1453, an army of Ottoman Turks attacked the city. After six weeks of fighting, the Byzantines surrendered and their Empire collapsed.

Religious split

Christians in the Byzantine Empire developed their own style of church building and held services in Greek, instead of Latin. The Byzantine Church was led by the Patriarch in Constantinople.

Justinian built the Cathedral of Saint Sophia in Constantinople. (It was later turned into a mosque.)

After many quarrels between the Patriarch and the Pope (the head of the Church in the west), the Byzantine Church split away from the Church in the west.

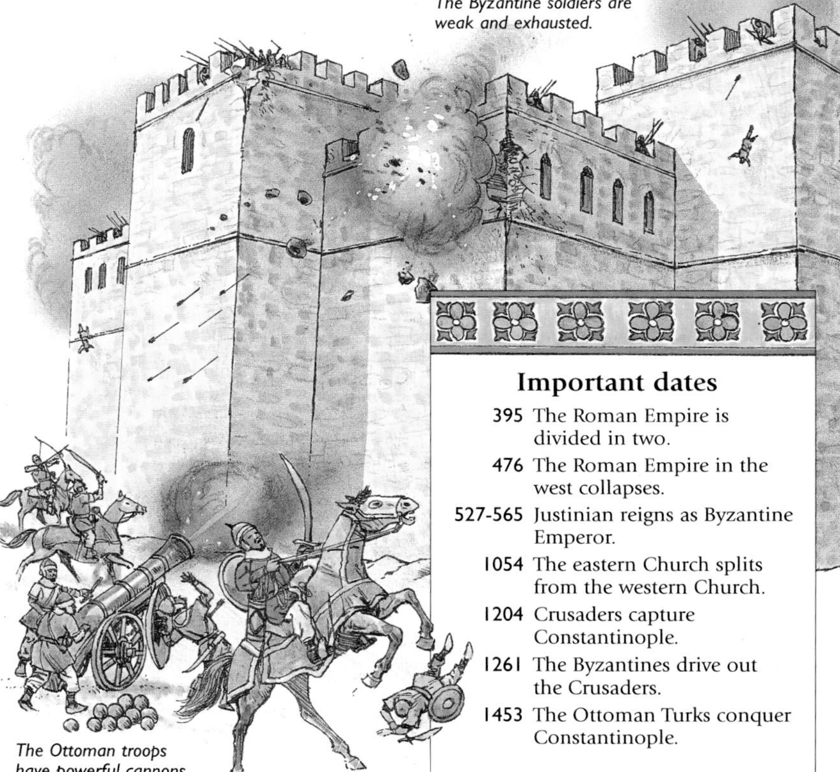

This picture shows the Ottomans' final attack on Constantinople.

The Byzantine soldiers are weak and exhausted.

The Ottoman troops have powerful cannons.

Important dates

- 395 The Roman Empire is divided in two.
- 476 The Roman Empire in the west collapses.
- 527-565 Justinian reigns as Byzantine Emperor.
- 1054 The eastern Church splits from the western Church.
- 1204 Crusaders capture Constantinople.
- 1261 The Byzantines drive out the Crusaders.
- 1453 The Ottoman Turks conquer Constantinople.

The Barbarian Kingdoms

The Romans first used the name "barbarian" to describe the tribes of warriors who invaded their Empire from the northeast. The barbarians swept across Europe destroying the Roman Empire, but, by around 500, they had begun to settle down in their own independent kingdoms.

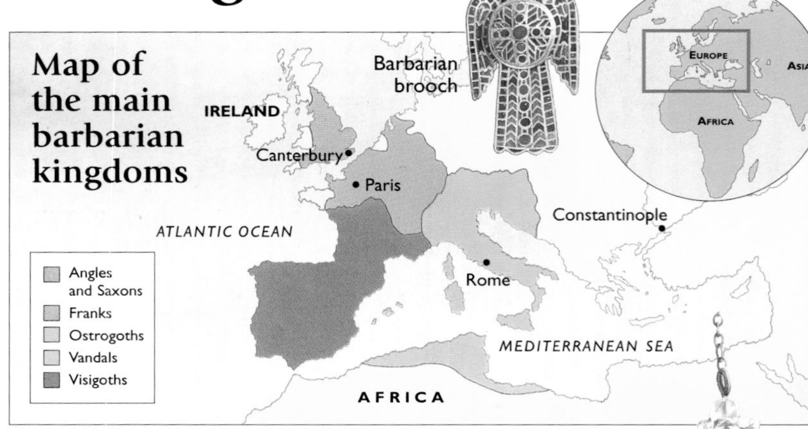

A barbarian warrior charging into battle

The kingdom of the Franks

The largest barbarian kingdom was created by Clovis, leader of the Franks. He made his capital in Paris and started a line of kings. The Frankish kingdom lasted for 300 years and was inherited by Charlemagne (see page 216).

Clovis and his queen Clothilda, painted by a later artist

Barbarian treasures

Some of the barbarians were very skilled at metalwork. They made elaborate swords and drinking cups, as well as beautiful crowns and brooches for their kings and chiefs.

Visigoth crown

Barbarian villages

The barbarians wanted to be rich like the Romans, but in fact they destroyed the Roman way of life. Most barbarians lived in small farming villages and let the Roman cities fall into ruins.

A barbarian village

Important dates

429-533	Vandal kingdom in North Africa
c.450-1066	Angles and Saxons rule parts of Britain.
456-711	Visigoth kingdom in Spain
481-511	Clovis rules over the Franks.
493-555	Ostrogoth kingdom in Italy
c.500-843	Frankish kingdom in France and Germany

500 600 700 800 900

Internet link: For a link to a Web site where you can see dragons, angels and birds from the Book of Kells, go to ***www.usborne-quicklinks.com***

Return to Christianity

A pagan god

Most barbarians were pagans who did not believe in Christ. Wherever they settled, churches were abandoned. By around 500, Christianity had almost disappeared in many parts of Europe.

Spreading the message

The leaders of the Church in Rome and Constantinople decided to send out monks to teach the Christian religion. Monks were also sent from Ireland, which had not been invaded by barbarians. Slowly, the barbarians became Christians, and churches and monasteries were built all over Europe.

Irish missionaries

Irish monks set up carved crosses near their monasteries.

Monks and manuscripts

Most barbarians could not read or write, but the monks made sure that learning did not die out. They kept holy books in their monasteries and made beautiful copies of them. These handwritten books, called manuscripts, were often beautifully illustrated.

★ Monks working on manuscripts

An illustration from a manuscript called the *Book of Kells*

Augustine and the Angles

A monk called Augustine was sent from Rome to preach to the Angles of southeast Britain. Thousands of Angles became Christians and their leader, King Ethelbert, made Augustine the first Archbishop of Canterbury.

Augustine preaching to the Angles

1200 1300 1400 1500

EUROPE

The Rise of Islam

In the year 610, a man called Mohammed started to teach a new religion in Arabia. The religion became known as Islam, and its followers were called Muslims.

Arabia in Mohammed's time

Mohammed's message

Mohammed said that people should obey Allah, the one true god. He taught Muslims to pray five times a day, to give money to the poor, and to go without food and drink during daylight hours in the month called Ramadan.

Muslims going on a pilgrimage

Mohammed also said that all Muslims should try to go on a pilgrimage (religious journey) to Mecca, the holy city of Islam.

Mosques

Muslims pray in beautiful buildings called mosques. They are called to prayer by a man called a muezzin who stands in a tower called a minaret. Pictures of animals and people are not allowed in mosques. Instead, mosques are decorated with patterned tiles.

This picture shows Muslims praying ★ in the courtyard of a mosque.

The Koran

Muslims believe that Mohammed received many messages from Allah. Mohammed's followers wrote down these messages in a holy book, called the Koran.

Decorated pages from the Koran

500 600 700 800 900

The spread of Islam

Mohammed began preaching in Mecca, but rich merchants drove him out of the city and in 622 he escaped to Medina. In 624, an army from Mecca attacked the Muslims in Medina. Mohammed and his followers fought bravely and won the Battle of al Badr. After this victory, many people in Arabia became Muslims.

A scene from the Battle of al Badr

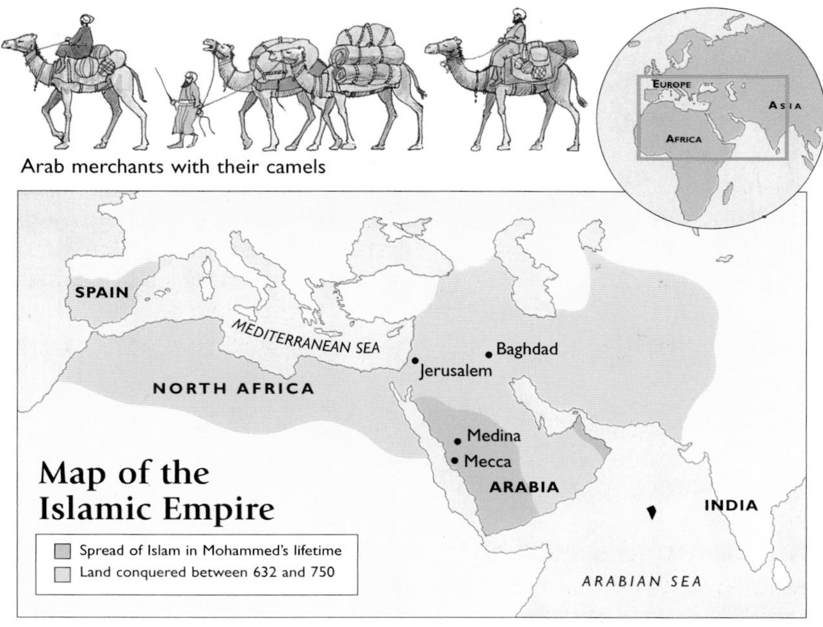

Arab merchants with their camels

Map of the Islamic Empire

Conquering caliphs

After Mohammed's death in 632, the Muslims were ruled by a series of leaders, called caliphs. The caliphs fought many battles to spread their religion. By 750, they had built up a vast Islamic Empire, stretching from northern India in the east to Spain in the west.

A caliph's army fighting a battle

Building mosques

Everywhere the caliphs conquered, they built mosques where people could pray. The Dome of the Rock in Jerusalem is part of a mosque that was built 50 years after the Arabs captured the city.

Traders and towns

The religion of Islam was spread by traders as well as soldiers. Arab merchants made journeys throughout the Empire and beyond, and, wherever the traders met, new Muslim towns grew up.

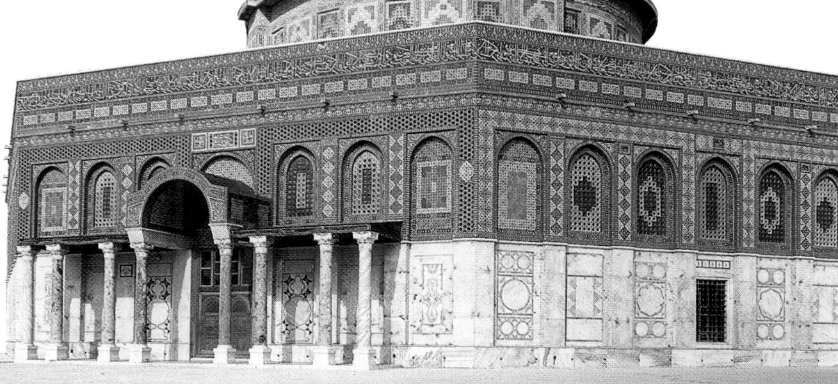
The Dome of the Rock in Jerusalem

The dome stands inside the Al-Aqsa mosque.

The Arab World

In 750, an Arab family called the Abbasids became the new caliphs (rulers) of the Islamic Empire (see map on page 207). The people of the Empire were united by the religion of Islam, and many of them spoke Arabic.

Arabian wealth

The Abbasid caliphs collected taxes from people all over the Empire. They became fabulously rich and lived a life of luxury in a beautiful palace in Baghdad (in modern Iraq).

A caliph having a massage

Learning

The Arabs were keen to learn from other people's ideas. They collected books from all over the world and kept them in libraries. Arab scholars studied works from ancient Greece, Persia, India and China, and translated them into Arabic. They also wrote many books of their own and taught students in universities.

A scholar teaching students

City life

Arabian cities were busy and crowded, but they were also well organized. People prayed and studied in mosques, and washed in public baths. Markets, called souks, were held in the cities' streets.

This picture shows an Arabian city street.

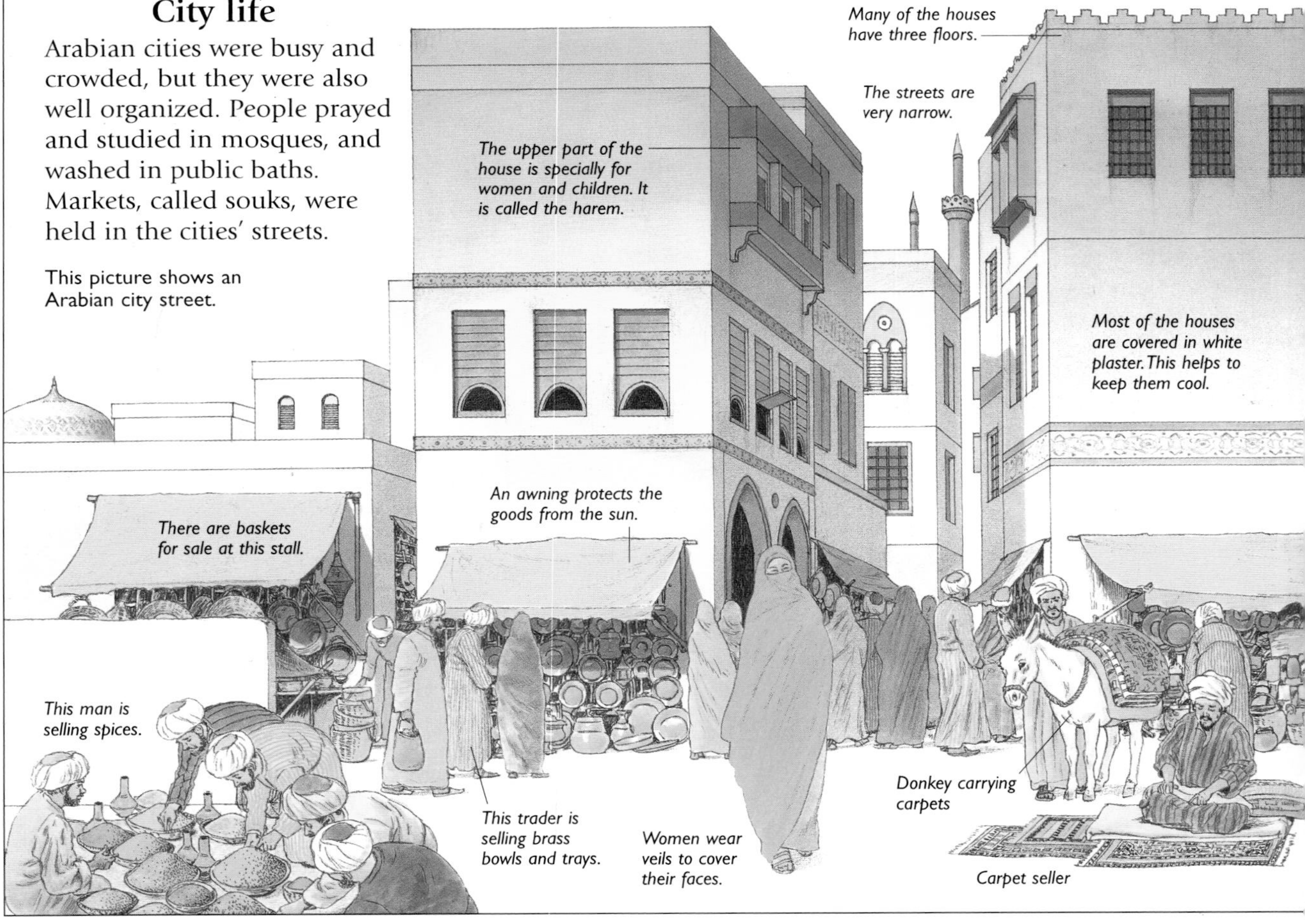

Many of the houses have three floors.

The streets are very narrow.

The upper part of the house is specially for women and children. It is called the harem.

Most of the houses are covered in white plaster. This helps to keep them cool.

There are baskets for sale at this stall.

An awning protects the goods from the sun.

This man is selling spices.

This trader is selling brass bowls and trays.

Women wear veils to cover their faces.

Donkey carrying carpets

Carpet seller

THE MIDDLE EAST

500 600 700 800 900

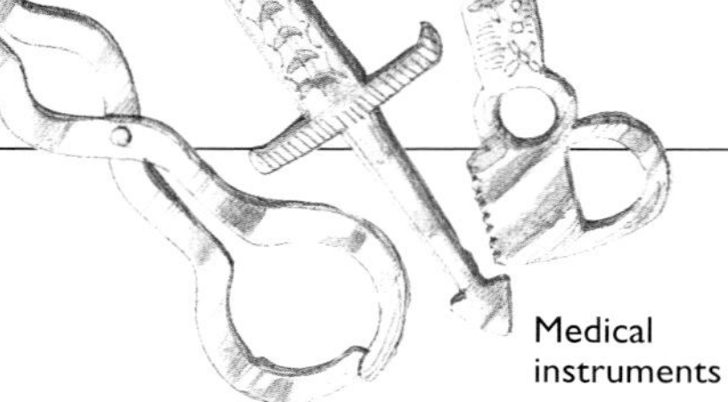

Medicine and science

Arab doctors learned about diseases and performed difficult operations. Scientists discovered how to make steel and how to make drugs from chemicals.

Inventors built amazing clocks, and engineers designed elaborate machines that were used to water fields.

Sailing and exploration

Arab merchants sailed to China, Africa and India, and explorers set off on long journeys to distant lands. Sailors and explorers used special instruments to help them find their way.

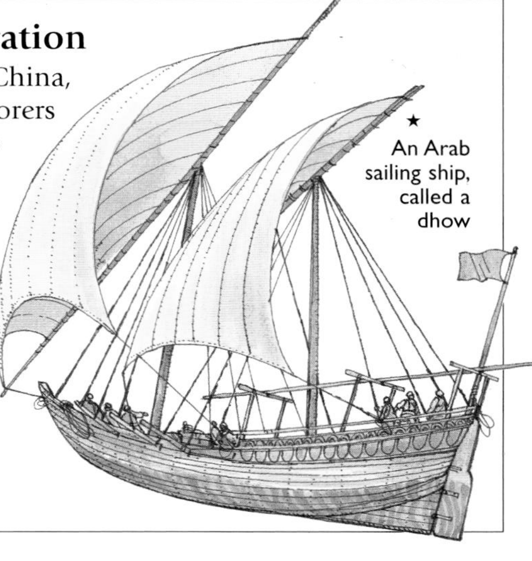

Astronomy

Astronomers studied the sky at night and made maps of the stars. These maps helped sailors and explorers to find their way across seas and deserts.

Arab astronomers at work

Arabic numbers

From India, the Arabs learned a simple way of writing numbers, including zero. Until then, most people had used Roman numbers, which were very complicated and had no zero. The numbers that we use today are based on Arabic numbers.

Arabic numbers from zero to nine

The end of the Islamic Empire

Although the Abbasid caliphs called themselves the rulers of the Islamic world, their Empire was divided by the end of the 8th century. Separate kingdoms grew up in Spain, Egypt and India, and religious quarrels split the people of the Empire.

In 1055, an army of Turks captured Baghdad. The Turks controlled the caliphs until 1258, when a Mongol army invaded Baghdad, and killed the last caliph.

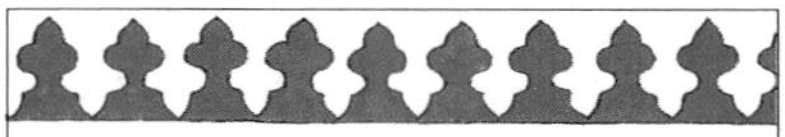

Important dates

c.570-632	Mohammed lives in Arabia. Most of Arabia is converted to Islam.
632-850	The first caliphs create a vast Islamic Empire.
750-1258	The Abbasid caliphs rule the Islamic Empire.
1055	The Turks take control of the caliphs.
1258	The Mongols conquer Baghdad. The Islamic Empire ends.

1100 1200 1300 1400 1500

Vikings at Home

A Viking farmer sowing seeds

The Vikings came from Sweden, Norway and Denmark (see map on page 212). Their name probably means "pirate" and they were fierce raiders and fighters. In their own lands, the Vikings were farmers, fishermen and craftworkers.

Farm life

Many of the Vikings were farmers. They grew crops and vegetables, and kept cows, pigs, chickens and goats. They also hunted wild animals.

Crafts

The Vikings were great metalworkers and carvers. They made elaborate weapons and necklaces, and beautiful carved objects.

★ Viking chesspiece

Viking homes

Thatched roof

Chest for storing clothes

The chief and his wife sleep in this bed.

Smoke hole

Wall hanging

This woman is weaving cloth at a loom.

Wooden frame

Carved door frame

This man is bringing wood for the fire.

In the winter, some animals are kept inside.

Toilet

Wall made from cane

This boy looks after the pigs.

★ This picture of a Viking longhouse has been cut away so you can see inside.

Most Vikings lived in large homes, called longhouses. Each longhouse belonged to a chief, and all the families who worked for the chief ate and slept in his house.

Internet link: *For a link to a Web site where you can find out how to play Viking games, go to* **www.usborne-quicklinks.com**

Death and burial

The Vikings buried people with food and treasure to take with them to the next life. Sometimes, a great warrior was buried on a ship. The ship was set on fire and people thought that it sailed to Valhalla, a kind of heaven where only warriors could go.

This picture shows a Viking ship burial.

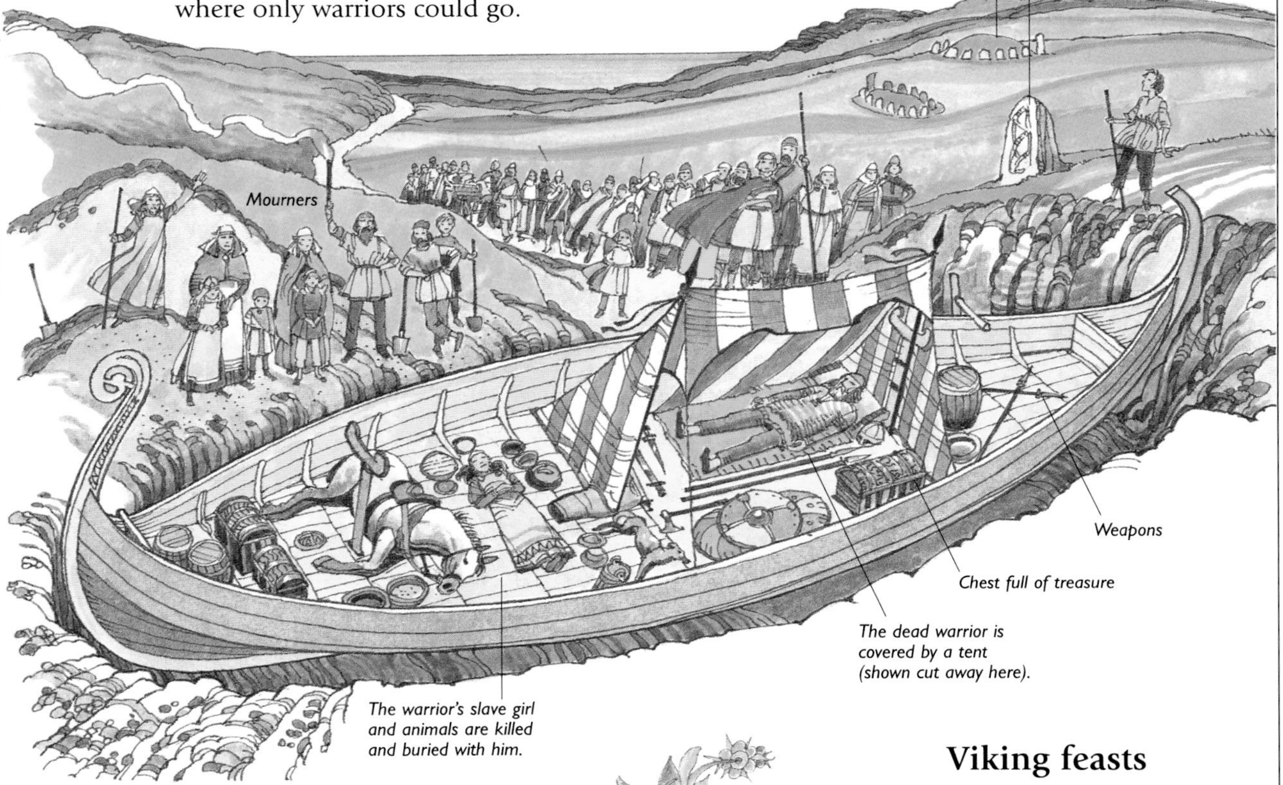

Grave marked by stones in the shape of a ship
Gravestone with carved letters, called runes
Mourners
Weapons
Chest full of treasure
The dead warrior is covered by a tent (shown cut away here).
The warrior's slave girl and animals are killed and buried with him.

Valhalla

People believed that dead warriors fought all day and feasted all night in Valhalla, the home of their chief god, Odin. Beautiful maidens, called valkyries, looked after the warriors.

Valkyrie
Dead warrior

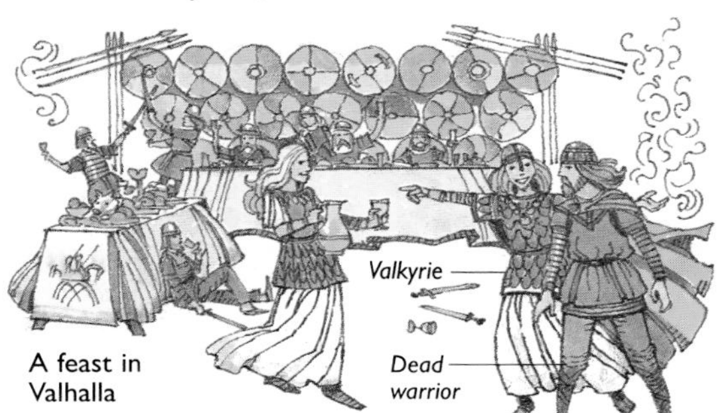

A feast in Valhalla

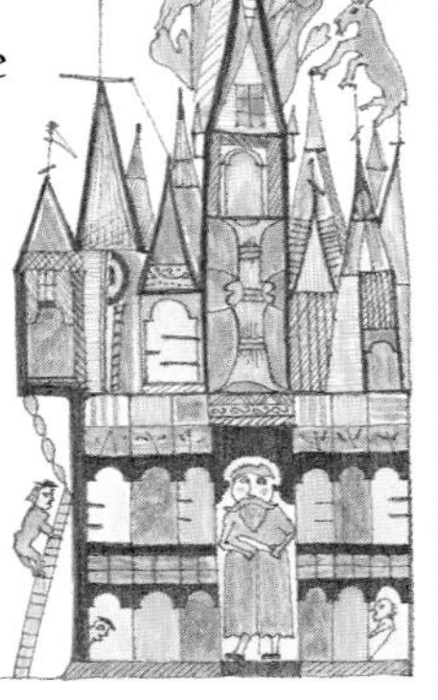

The chief god, Odin, outside Valhalla

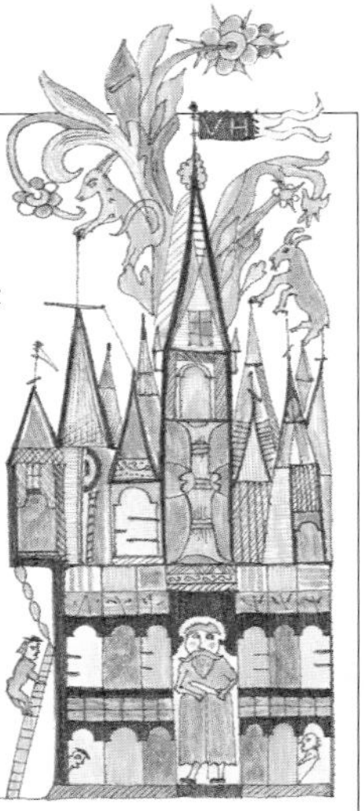

Viking feasts

The Vikings held rowdy feasts to celebrate their battles. Musicians played harps and pipes, and poets (called skalds) recited long poems about daring deeds.

A Viking feast

Skald (poet)

EUROPE

1100 1200 1300 1400 1500

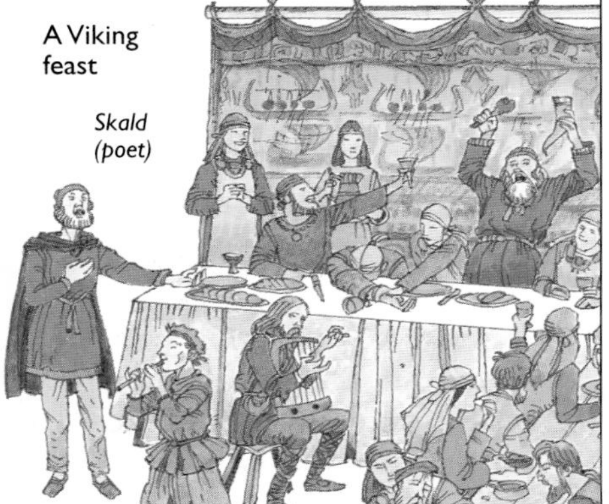

Vikings Abroad

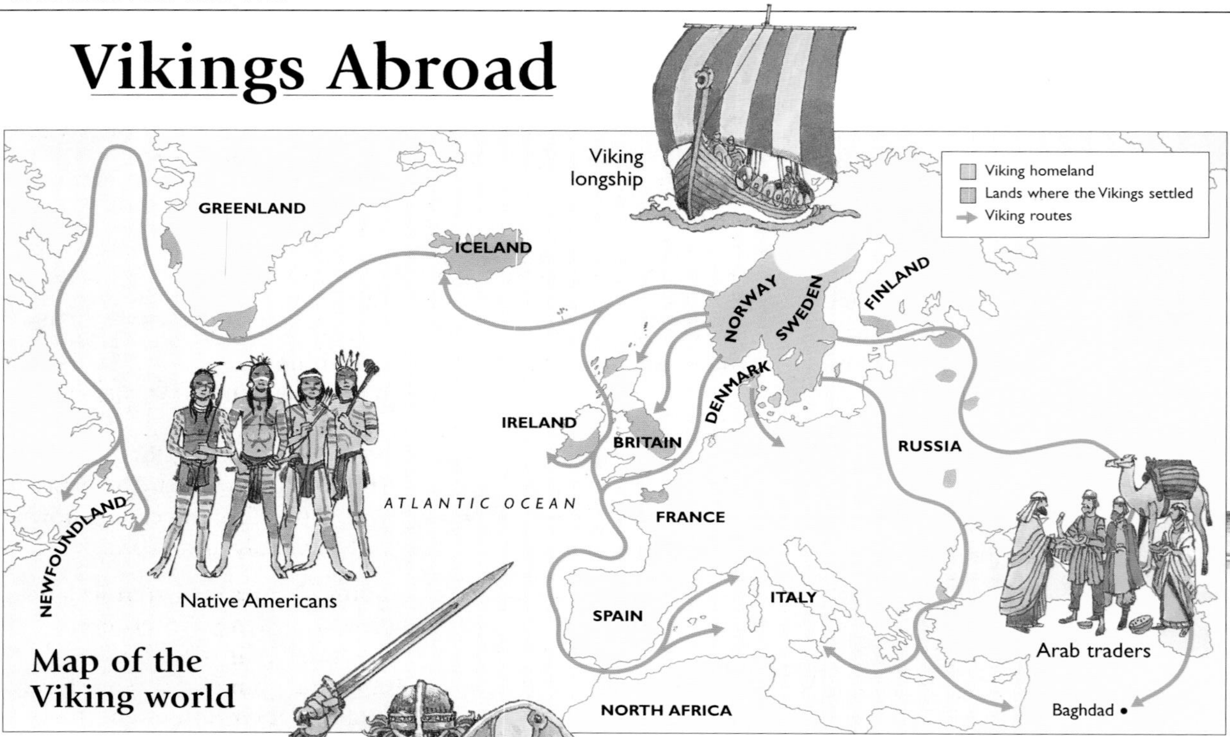

Map of the Viking world

The Vikings did not have enough land for everyone to farm, so around 790 some of them started to leave their homeland. Fierce raiders attacked the coast of Europe, explorers searched for new territory, and traders and settlers sailed to distant lands.

Viking raider ★

The raiders invaded large areas of Britain, Ireland, France and Italy. Later, some of them settled in these places.

Around 1100, the raids came to an end. By that time, many of the Vikings had become Christians and their people were much less violent.

Raiders

For over 300 years, Viking raiders terrorized the people of Europe. Ferocious warriors arrived in swift warships, called longships. Then, they fought their way inland, robbing towns and villages as they went.

Raiders steal treasure from churches and homes.

Many people are killed.

This picture shows a raid on a village. Part of the church has been cut away so you can see inside.

Explorers

Daring adventurers and traders sailed over seas and up rivers. When they could not sail any farther, the crew carried their boat, or dragged it on logs, to the next river.

Explorers dragging their boat overland

Eric the Red explored Greenland. His son, Leif Ericson, went farther west and reached America. The land he found, called Vinland, was probably modern Newfoundland.

Statue of Leif Ericson

Settlers

Boatloads of Viking settlers arrived in the newly discovered and conquered lands.

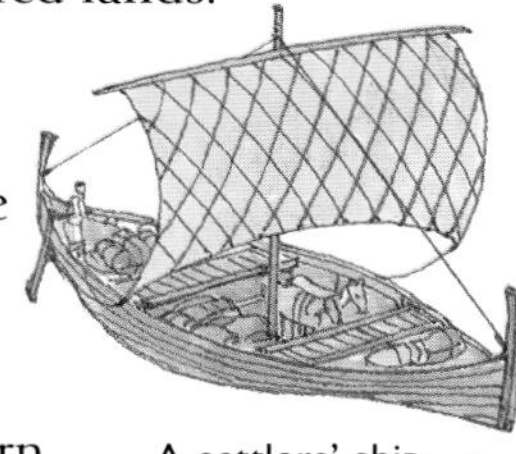

A settlers' ship, ★ called a knorr

In northern France, the Vikings were called Normans (northmen) and in eastern Europe they were known as the Rus (redheaded people). The areas where they lived became known as Normandy and Russia.

Some Vikings settled in Iceland and Greenland. Others even went to live in Vinland (in America), but Native Americans attacked their homes and they soon fled back to Greenland.

Native Americans attacking Vikings

Important dates

c.790	The Viking raids begin.
c.830-900	Frequent raids on the British Isles and France.
c.860	The Vikings settle in Russia.
c.900-911	The Vikings settle in Normandy.
c.983-986	The Vikings start a colony in Greenland.
c.1000	Leif Ericson reaches North America.
c.1100	The Viking raids end.

Traders

Viking merchants traded in Europe and beyond. Some adventurous traders even reached the Arab city of Baghdad. The Vikings sold swords, fur and ivory (from walrus tusks). In return, they bought silk, precious stones, carvings, and beautiful objects made from gold and silver.

This eastern statue was found in Viking lands.

Anglo-Saxon England

A Saxon ship arriving in Britain

Around the year 400, tribes of Angles, Saxons and Jutes began arriving in Britain from Denmark and northern Germany. These people were later known as Anglo-Saxons, and the land where they settled was called "Angle land", or England. By 600, England was divided into seven kingdoms, each ruled by a warrior king.

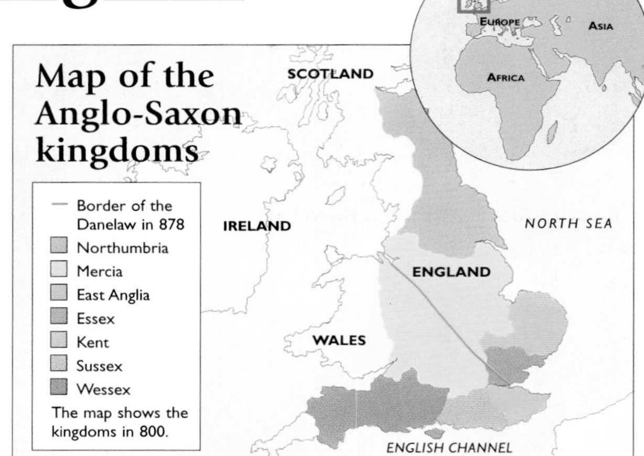

Thanes, churls and slaves

The Anglo-Saxon kings ruled over nobles (called thanes), farmers (called churls) and slaves. Thanes and churls were free, but they had to fight for their king. Slaves were owned by their masters.

A slave serving a thane at a feast

Village life

Most Anglo-Saxons lived in villages, although some of the villages grew into small towns. The men worked in the fields and went out hunting and fishing. The women cooked, made clothes and looked after the hens and pigs. Some villagers were potters, blacksmiths and carpenters.

This picture shows part of an Anglo-Saxon village. ★

Shepherd

Weaving shed

These women are weaving and spinning wool.

This man is using a pole lathe to help him make a wooden bowl.

He pushes a pedal to make the wood turn as he carves it.

Blacksmith

Buried treasure

Some Anglo-Saxon kings were buried in ships, surrounded by their treasures. Helmets, weapons and jewels have all been found in the ship graves of Anglo-Saxon kings.

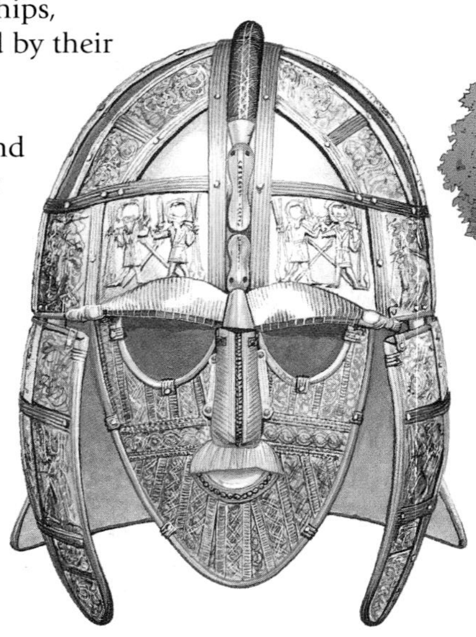

★ This helmet was found in a ship grave in East Anglia.

500 600 700 800 900

Fighting the Danes

Around 800, tribes of Danes (Vikings from Denmark) began to invade England. By 874, they had conquered all the kingdoms except Wessex. King Alfred of Wessex drove the Danes out of his kingdom and won back Sussex, Kent and Mercia, which all became part of Wessex.

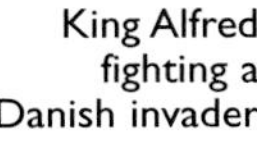

King Alfred fighting a Danish invader

Alfred the Great

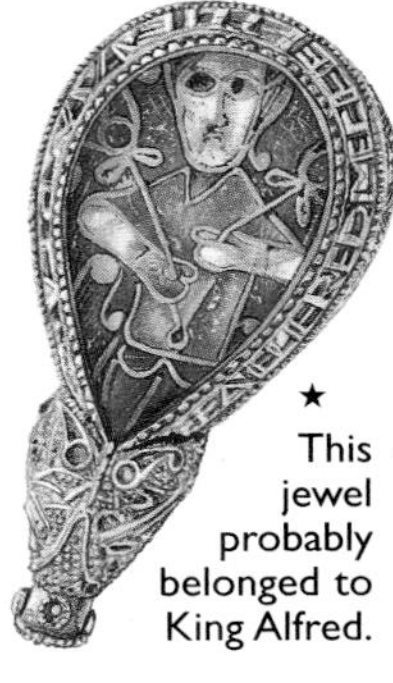

★ This jewel probably belonged to King Alfred.

King Alfred agreed that the Danes could settle in the eastern part of the country, called the Danelaw, while he ruled the rest of England (see map). Alfred built strong, walled towns and set up a navy. He made fair laws and encouraged art, religion and learning. Later, he became known as Alfred the Great.

Anglo-Saxons and Danes

In 924, Alfred's grandson, Athelstan, became king of all of England, but in 1013 the Danes invaded again. England was ruled by Danish kings for 30 years before the Anglo-Saxons regained control of their country.

Coin showing Cnut, King of England and Denmark

The end of the Anglo-Saxons

Edward the Confessor became King of England in 1042. He was a very religious man who rebuilt Westminster Abbey. When Edward died in 1066, Harold Earl of Wessex was crowned king, but he was soon defeated by the Normans, who conquered England (see page 218).

Edward the Confessor ★

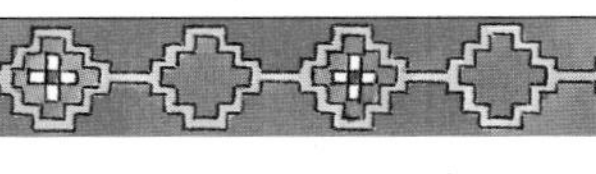

Important dates

c.410-520	Angles, Saxons and Jutes settle in England.
c.600	England is divided into seven kingdoms.
867-874	The Danes invade England.
871-899	Alfred is King of Wessex.
924-939	Athelstan rules England.
1013-1042	Danish kings rule England.
1042-1066	Edward the Confessor is King of England.
1066	The Normans conquer England.

Charlemagne's Empire

In 768, a young prince called Charles was crowned King of the Franks and inherited most of the land that is now France. (See page 204 for more about the Franks.) He was a brilliant soldier and a keen Christian, and he became known as Charlemagne, which means "Charles the Great".

Stained-glass portrait of Charlemagne ★

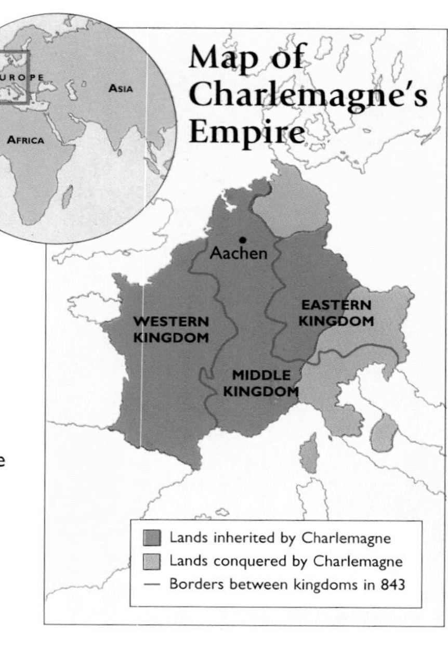

Building an empire

Charlemagne wanted to create a new Christian empire as large as the Roman Empire had been. For over 30 years, he fought for land, insisting that any non-Christians he conquered should join the Church. On Christmas Day 800, the Pope crowned him "Emperor of the Romans".

★ Pope Leo III crowning Charlemagne as Emperor of the Romans

Religion and learning

Charlemagne paid for churches and monasteries to be built all over his Empire. He encouraged scholars, artists and craftworkers to come and work in Aachen, where he had his palace.

Charlemagne's splendid palace at Aachen

After Charlemagne

Charlemagne's Empire did not last long after his death. By 843, the Empire had split into three kingdoms, and each kingdom was ruled by a member of Charlemagne's family. The three rulers fought against each other and their kingdoms became very weak.

Important dates

768	Charlemagne becomes King of the Franks.
773-804	Charlemagne builds up his Empire.
800-814	Charlemagne is emperor.
843	Charlemagne's Empire is split into three kingdoms.

The Holy Roman Empire

By 900, all three parts of Charlemagne's old Empire were in danger. Vikings had invaded the Western and Middle kingdoms, and tribes of Magyars (from present-day Hungary) were attacking the Eastern kingdom.

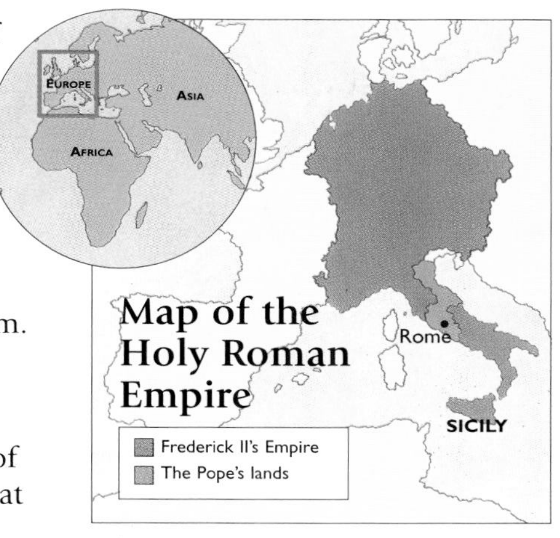

Map of the Holy Roman Empire

Otto the Great

In 955, Otto I, King of the Eastern kingdom (now part of Germany), beat the Magyars at the Battle of Lechfeld. The Magyars were pagans who did not believe in Christ, and the Pope was so pleased by Otto's victory that he crowned him "Holy Roman Emperor".

Emperor Otto's crown

The Battle of Lechfeld ★

Emperors and popes

After Otto, all the German kings had the title of "Holy Roman Emperor". They used their bishops to help them rule the Empire and had many quarrels with the popes over who had more power (see page 232).

The Wonder of the World

Emperor Frederick II inherited the kingdom of Sicily from his mother and ruled his Empire from there. Known as "the Wonder of the World", he kept wild animals, and welcomed astrologers and Muslim scholars to his court.

Emperor Frederick II ★

Important dates

955	The Battle of Lechfeld
962-973	Otto I is emperor.
1220-1250	Frederick II is emperor.
1250-1273	The Empire is weak.
1273-1291	Rudolf of Habsburg is emperor. He starts a new family of emperors.

1100 1200 1300 1400 1500

The Norman Conquests

The Normans were descendants of the Vikings who had settled in Normandy during the 900s. Like their Viking ancestors, the Normans were great sailors and warriors who were hungry for more land.

Norman ships

Map of the Norman conquests

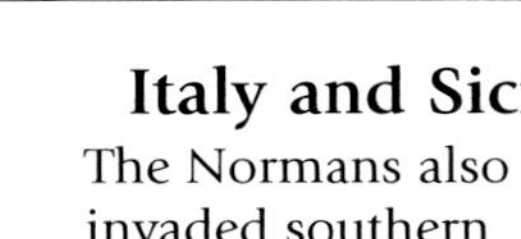

Invading England

Duke William of Normandy believed he should be King of England because of a promise made to him by the previous English king, Edward the Confessor. In 1066, William sailed to England and fought King Harold of England at Hastings. The Normans were victorious and Harold was killed in battle.

King Harold ★ of England

Norman horsemen fighting English foot soldiers at the Battle of Hastings ★

Italy and Sicily

The Normans also invaded southern Italy and the island of Sicily. In 1130, a Norman count became King of Sicily. For the next 60 years, the Normans ruled the island and the southern part of Italy.

Mosaic of Roger II, the first Norman King of Sicily

Ruling England

William was crowned the new King of England. He built castles all over the country and gave land to powerful nobles who promised to obey him.

Norman soldiers outside a castle

King William ★ the Conqueror

Important dates

1060-1130	The Normans gradually conquer Sicily and southern Italy.
1066	The Normans conquer England and Duke William becomes king.
1130-1204	The Normans are kings of Sicily.

500 600 700 800 900

The Hundred Years' War

After the Normans had conquered England, the French and English kings fought many wars over who owned land in France. The longest of these was the Hundred Years' War. It began when Edward III of England claimed that he should be King of France.

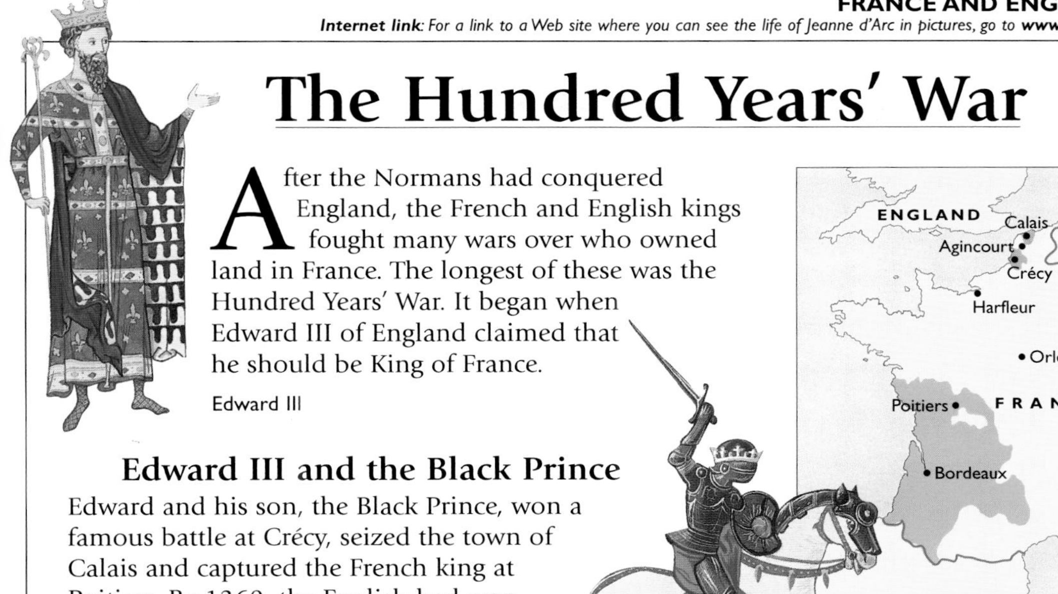

Edward III

Edward III and the Black Prince

Edward and his son, the Black Prince, won a famous battle at Crécy, seized the town of Calais and captured the French king at Poitiers. By 1360, the English had won a lot of land in France (see map), but over the next 40 years, they lost most of it.

The Black Prince

Henry V

In 1415, King Henry V of England captured Harfleur and won the Battle of Agincourt. Henry planned to be the next King of France, but the French king's son refused to accept this, and fighting broke out again.

This picture shows the start of the Battle of Agincourt.

★

The French knights lead the attack.

Many French knights and horses are killed or wounded.

English archers shoot at the French knights.

Wooden stakes protect the English.

Jeanne d'Arc

In 1429, the French made a comeback. Led by a peasant girl called Jeanne d'Arc, they drove the English out of Orléans. The English burned Jeanne as a witch, but the French continued to win back land. In 1453, a French army captured Bordeaux, and the war ended.

Jeanne d'Arc

Important dates

1337 The Hundred Years' War begins.
1346 The English win the Battle of Crécy.
1415 The English win the Battle of Agincourt.
1429 Jeanne d'Arc drives the English out of Orléans.
1453 The Hundred Years' War ends.

Kings, Nobles and Peasants

Life was very organized in medieval Europe. People were divided into four main groups and each group had different jobs to do. This way of life is now called the feudal system.

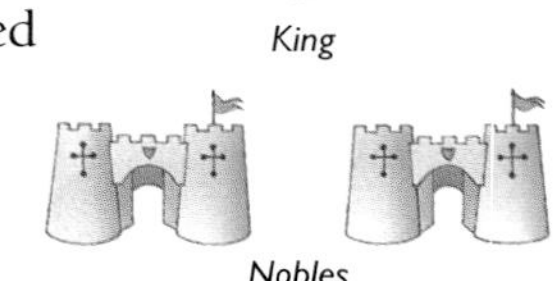

King

Nobles

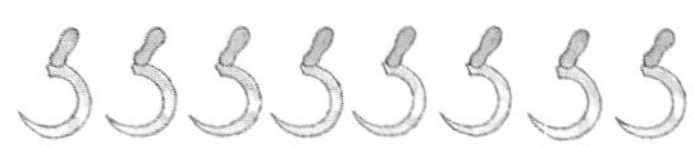

Knights

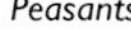

Peasants

This diagram shows the four main groups in the feudal system. ★

Knights

Nobles gave land to their knights as payment for their help in battle. Knights trained for war and fought for nobles and kings.

A knight training for war

Peasants

Peasants farmed the land of the knights, nobles and kings. In return, the landowners protected the peasants from enemy attacks. (To find out more about peasants, see pages 226 and 227.)

Kings

At the top of the feudal system was the king. He owned all the land in a country, made the laws and led the country's army.

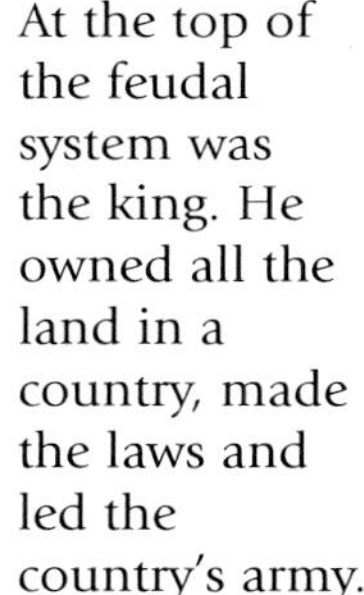

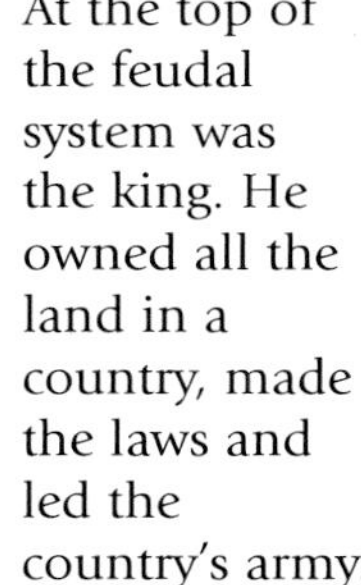

A king being crowned

Nobles

The king gave large areas of land to his nobles. In return for this land, the nobles promised to fight for the king and to provide him with knights for his army.

A noble promises to serve and obey his king. This promise is called "paying homage". ★

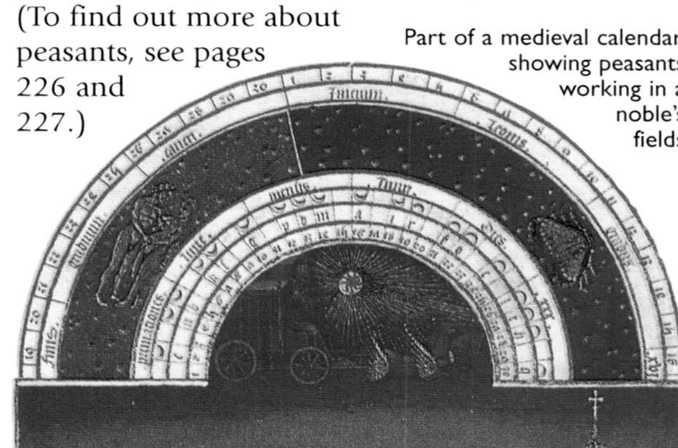

Part of a medieval calendar, showing peasants working in a noble's fields

EUROPE

500 600 700 800 900

The people rebel

In spite of their promises to serve and obey, nobles sometimes rebelled against their king, and peasants led revolts against their lords.

King John and his barons

King John of England was a strong king with a fierce temper. He kept his nobles (called barons) under tight control, but in 1215 they rebelled. The barons made John sign an agreement called Magna Carta. This said that the king had to talk to a council of barons and bishops before he made any big decisions.

King John

The birth of Parliament

In 1275, English knights and townsmen joined the barons and bishops in a new council, known as Parliament. Over the next hundred years, several councils like this were created to control the kings of Europe.

A meeting of the English Parliament

The Peasants' Revolt

In 1381, hundreds of English peasants tried to win more freedom by rebelling against the landowners. Led by Wat Tyler, the peasants marched to London and rioted in the streets. King Richard II met the rebels and promised to help them, but later he punished them.

This picture shows the peasants rioting in London.

★

Important dates

1215 King John signs Magna Carta.

1275 The English Parliament starts to meet regularly.

1381 The Peasants' Revolt

Knights, Soldiers and War

Foot soldiers defending a castle

During the Middle Ages, people had to be prepared for war at any time. Kings and nobles built castles to protect themselves from their enemies, knights and foot soldiers trained for war, and armies fought battles at home and abroad.

Defending a castle

A castle could be attacked by foreign invaders or by an enemy lord. Castles were designed to be extremely strong and easy to defend.

This picture shows an army attacking a castle.

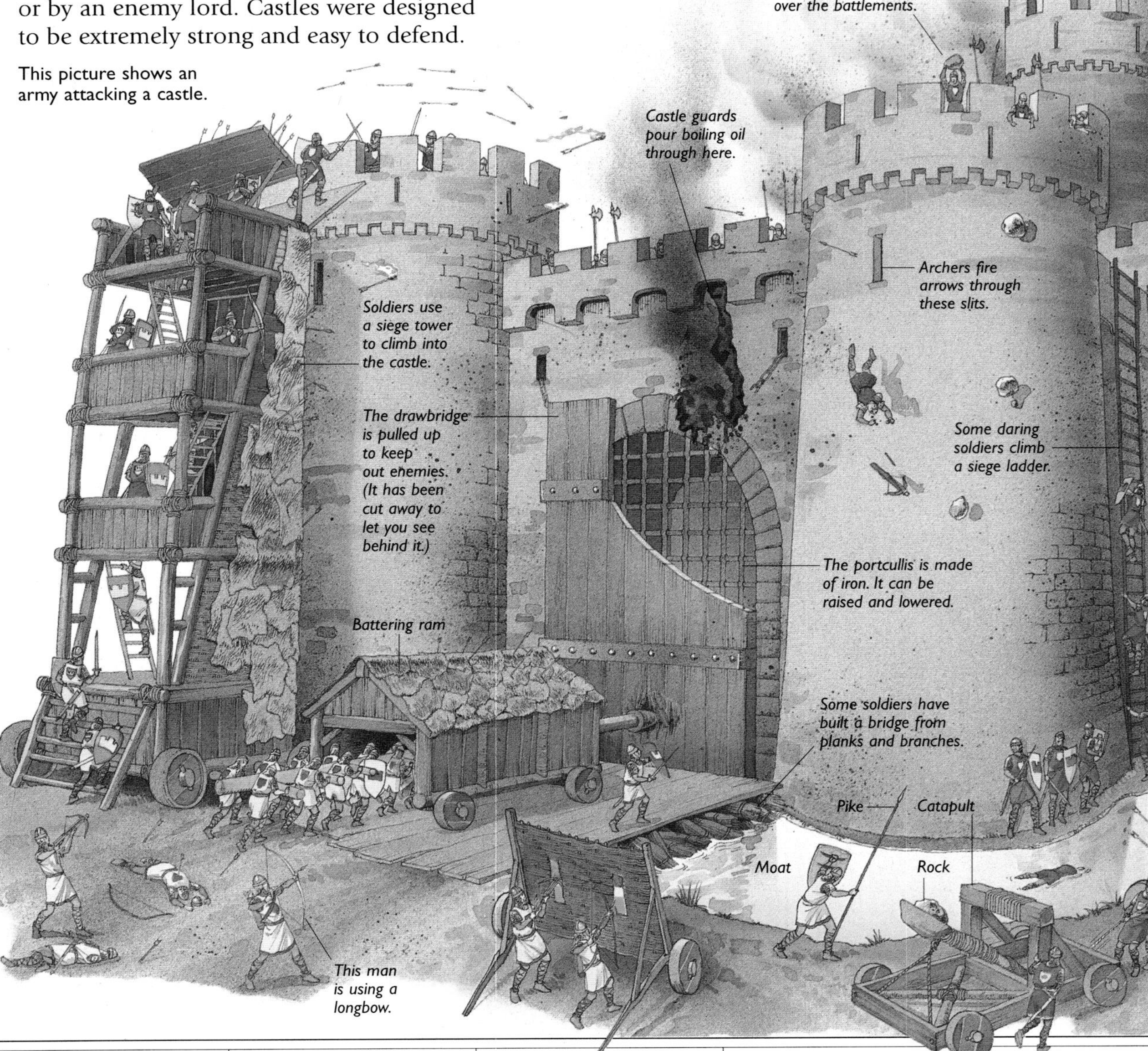

500 600 700 800 900

Becoming a knight

Only boys from noble families could become knights. First, a boy worked as a page in a castle, learning how to ride and fight. Then, he became a squire and looked after a knight. When the squire had proved that he was a brave warrior, he was knighted by a king or a noble.

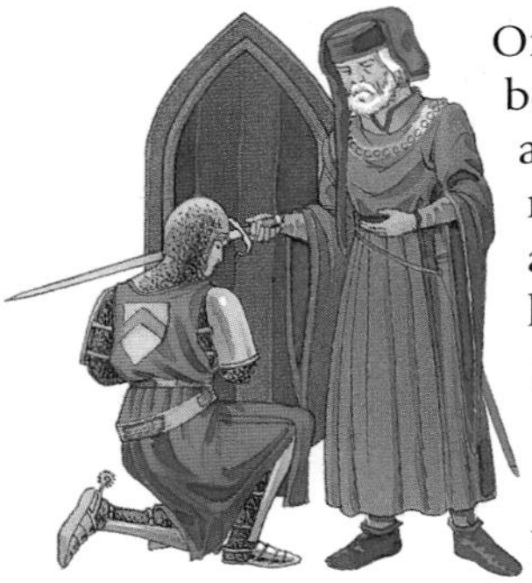

★ A noble knighting a squire

Knights in battle

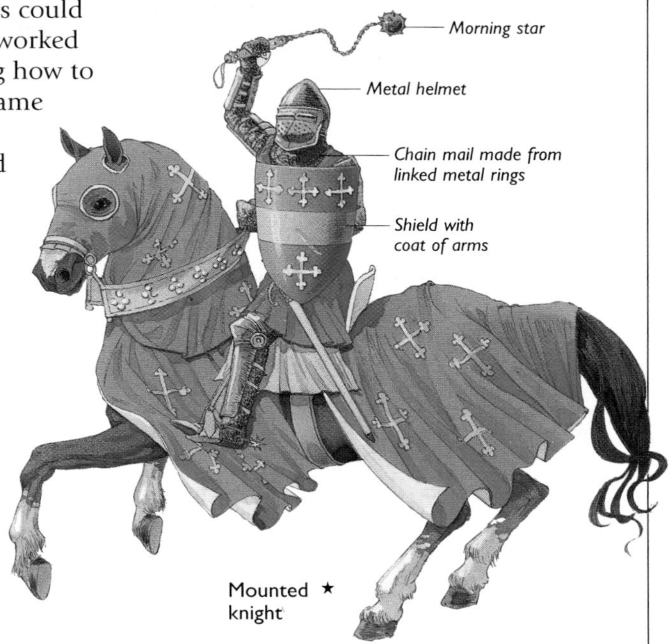

Mounted ★ knight

Knights fought on horseback, using swords, lances (long poles), axes, and vicious weapons called morning stars. Each knight wore a symbol, called a coat of arms, to show which family he belonged to.

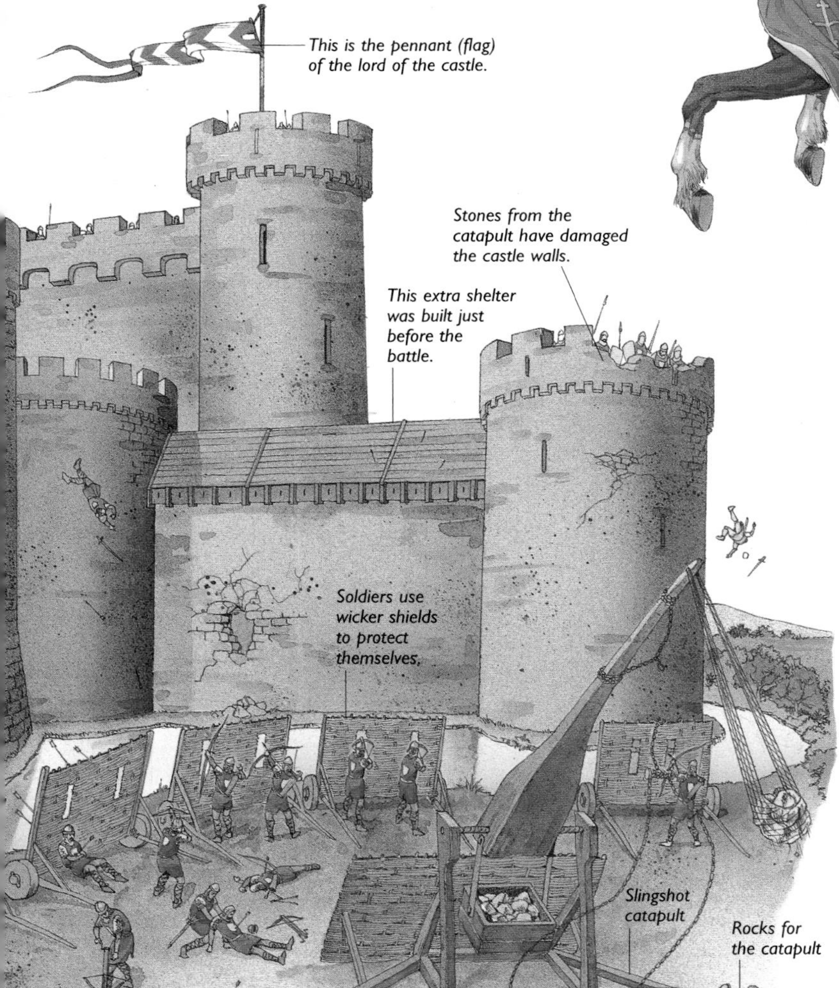

Foot soldiers

Foot soldiers served their lord by guarding his castle and fighting for him. They fought with daggers, pikes (long spears), crossbows and longbows.

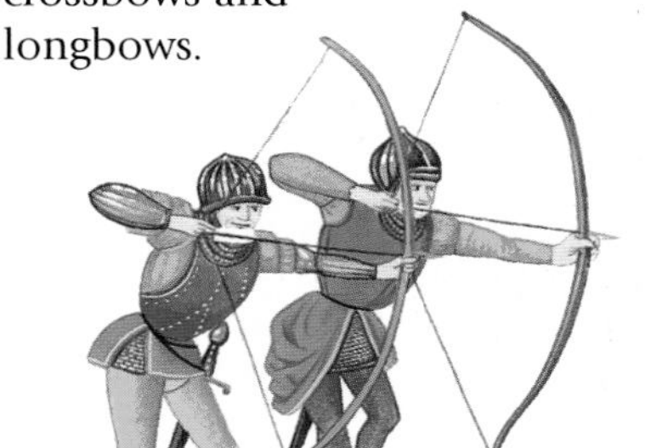

Medieval longbowmen

1100 1200 1300 1400 1500

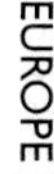

Living in a Castle

Kings and nobles lived in castles with their families, their servants and their soldiers. In times of peace, the lord of the castle managed his lands, kept law and order, and held feasts and tournaments.

This cutaway picture shows the central keep (tower) of a castle. ★

★ Plan of a castle

Hunting

Kings and nobles often went hunting in the countryside around their castles. They rode on horseback with packs of hounds, and hunted deer, wild boar, bears and wolves.

King John hunting deer in a forest

Falconry

Falconry was a popular sport in the Middle Ages. Lords and ladies had their own falcons and hawks, which were trained by falconers to catch small animals and birds.

Falconers

Pastimes

Nobles and their families enjoyed dancing, singing and playing musical instruments. They played games, such as chess, and ladies worked on fine embroidery.

A game of chess

Feasting

Lavish feasts were held in the great hall of a noble's castle. Pages served rich food and wine, jesters told jokes, and minstrels played their instruments and sang. Many different courses were served, and a feast could last for hours.

This picture shows a feast in a castle. ★

Tournaments

Tournaments, or mock battles, were often held in the castle grounds. The most popular sport at a tournament was jousting. In a joust, two knights charged at each other and each knight tried to knock his opponent to the ground.

★ Knights jousting at a tournament

Living in a Village

During the Middle Ages, most people lived in villages. A knight, known as the lord of the manor, owned all the land around a village and the peasants had to earn the right to farm some of his land. Some peasants were freemen, who paid money or food for their land, but others, called villeins, had to work part-time for their lord.

A peasant sowing seeds

This picture shows a medieval village.

This man is cutting wheat with a sickle.

These people are taking wool, eggs and cheese to sell in a nearby town.

Farming

Most villages had three large fields. One was planted with wheat and one with barley. The third field was left fallow (unplanted), so it would be fit for planting the next year. Each field was divided into strips for different families to farm. A family would have several strips in each of the three fields.

Other jobs

All the villagers worked on the land, but some, like the miller and the blacksmith, did other jobs as well. People gave them food in return for their work.

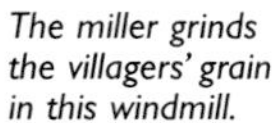

Village homes

Peasants lived in simple cottages with bare floors and no glass in the windows. They had to share their home with their animals.

This cottage has been cut away so you can see inside. ★

A medieval picture of a woman milking a cow

Food

People ate bread, porridge, fruit, vegetables and stew, washed down with watery beer. Eggs, meat and fish were luxuries. Some families kept a cow and made cheese, but they sold most of their cheese at the local market.

Fairs

At least once a year, a fair was held on the village green. Merchants came to buy and sell goods, people played games and held wrestling matches, and entertainers amused the crowds.

★ A village fair

Living in a Town

By the year 1100, small towns were starting to appear all over Europe. Many of these towns were built beside a castle. People living in a town paid rent to the lord of the castle, but they did not have to work for him and they could choose how to earn their living.

A medieval town

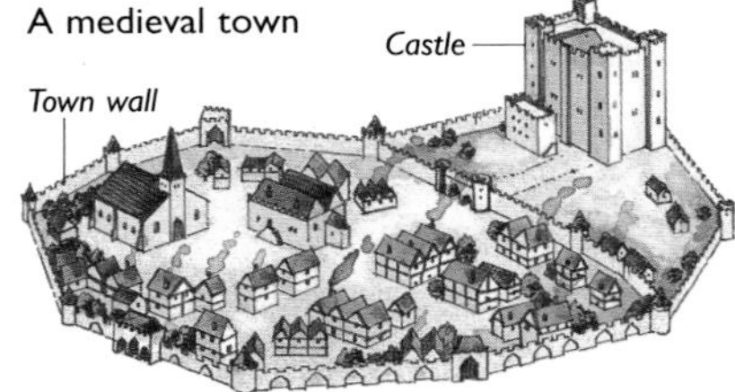

Craftworkers

Many craftworkers set up workshops in the towns. They made useful things, such as clothes, pots and pans, which they sold to the townspeople and to farmers who visited the towns.

Dyers dyeing cloth

Merchants

Merchants sold wool, wood and iron to the craftworkers. They also sold luxury goods from foreign lands, such as silk, jewels, wine and spices.

A wine merchant's boat

This picture shows part of a medieval town.

Wine merchant's house

Church

Cloth merchant's shop

Farmers bring food and wool to the market.

Marketplace

People throw waste into the streets.

Brewer

Drain

Beggar

Inn

The streets are very dirty.

This is the potter's workshop. His family lives upstairs.

Other jobs

Bakers, butchers and brewers provided food and drink for the townspeople. Innkeepers ran taverns, and priests and doctors came to work in the towns.

Town visitors

Farmers and traders came to the towns to buy and sell goods. Everyone who visited a town had to pay money, called a toll, before they were allowed in.

Guilds

Craftworkers who made the same things began to group together in special clubs, called guilds. The guilds made sure that everyone made high-quality goods and that prices and wages were fair. Merchants also had guilds to make sure that they traded fairly.

Blacksmiths' guild badge ★

Joining a guild

Most members of guilds were men. Before a man could join a guild, he had to work for seven years as an apprentice to a master craftsman. Then he made his "masterpiece". If it was good enough, he joined the guild as a journeyman. Only a few journeymen became masters.

A master testing his apprentices

Holy days and mystery plays

On special holy days, the guilds put on plays for the people of the town. Sometimes, they performed a long series of plays based on Bible stories. These plays became known as mystery plays, because they were produced by craftworkers, and the medieval word for craft was "maisterie".

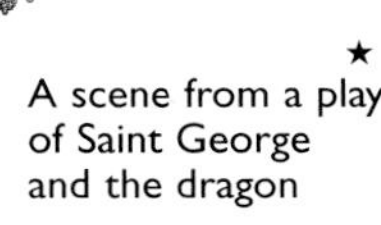

★ A scene from a play of Saint George and the dragon

A play of the Last Judgment

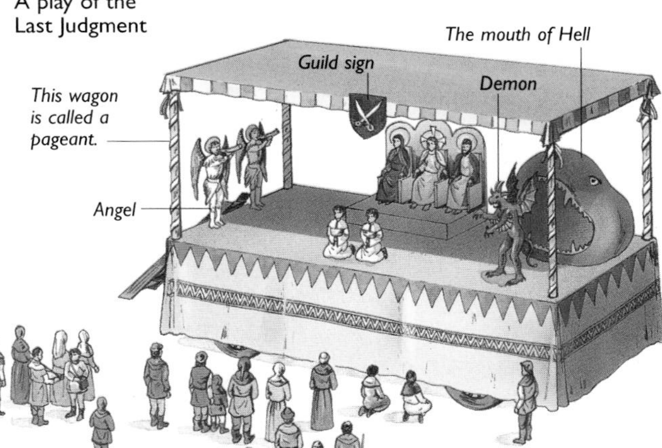

EUROPE

1100 1200 1300 1400 1500

Traders and Towns

By the 1300s, people in Europe could buy luxuries such as silk, jewels, sugar and spices. The merchants of Europe traded with Arab and Turkish merchants, who sold goods from places as far away as India, Africa and China.

Jewels, silk and spices from the East

Trade fairs

Several times a year, merchants from all over Europe met at trade fairs to buy and sell goods. The towns where the fairs were held became very rich.

A bishop blessing a trade fair

Mighty merchants

Medieval merchants employed workers to make goods, such as cloth, and paid for splendid buildings to be built in their towns. The leading merchants of a town met in a group, called a council, and made decisions about the way their town was run.

The cloth merchants of Bruges paid for this market hall.

Merchant bankers

As trade increased, many people needed to borrow money to buy goods. A group of merchants from Lombardy in northern Italy created the first bank, and other Italians soon set up banks all over Europe.

Merchant bankers counting money

Buying freedom

At first, townspeople paid rent to their local lord, but, as the towns grew richer, people wanted to be independent. In many towns, the people bought a document called a charter from their lord. The charter was stamped with the lord's seal to show that he had handed over his rights to the townspeople.

A seal on a town charter

★

City-states

Some great cities in Italy and Germany had their own rulers who lived in palaces and made laws for their cities. These independent cities were known as city-states.

Venice was one of the richest city-states.

EUROPE

500 600 700 800 900

The Hanseatic League

Some of the busiest trading towns in Europe were grouped around the North Sea and the Baltic Sea. These towns formed a club, or "hansa", later known as the Hanseatic League. By 1350, there were over 70 towns in the league. All the towns helped each other and followed strict trading rules.

This picture shows a busy port in a Hanseatic town.

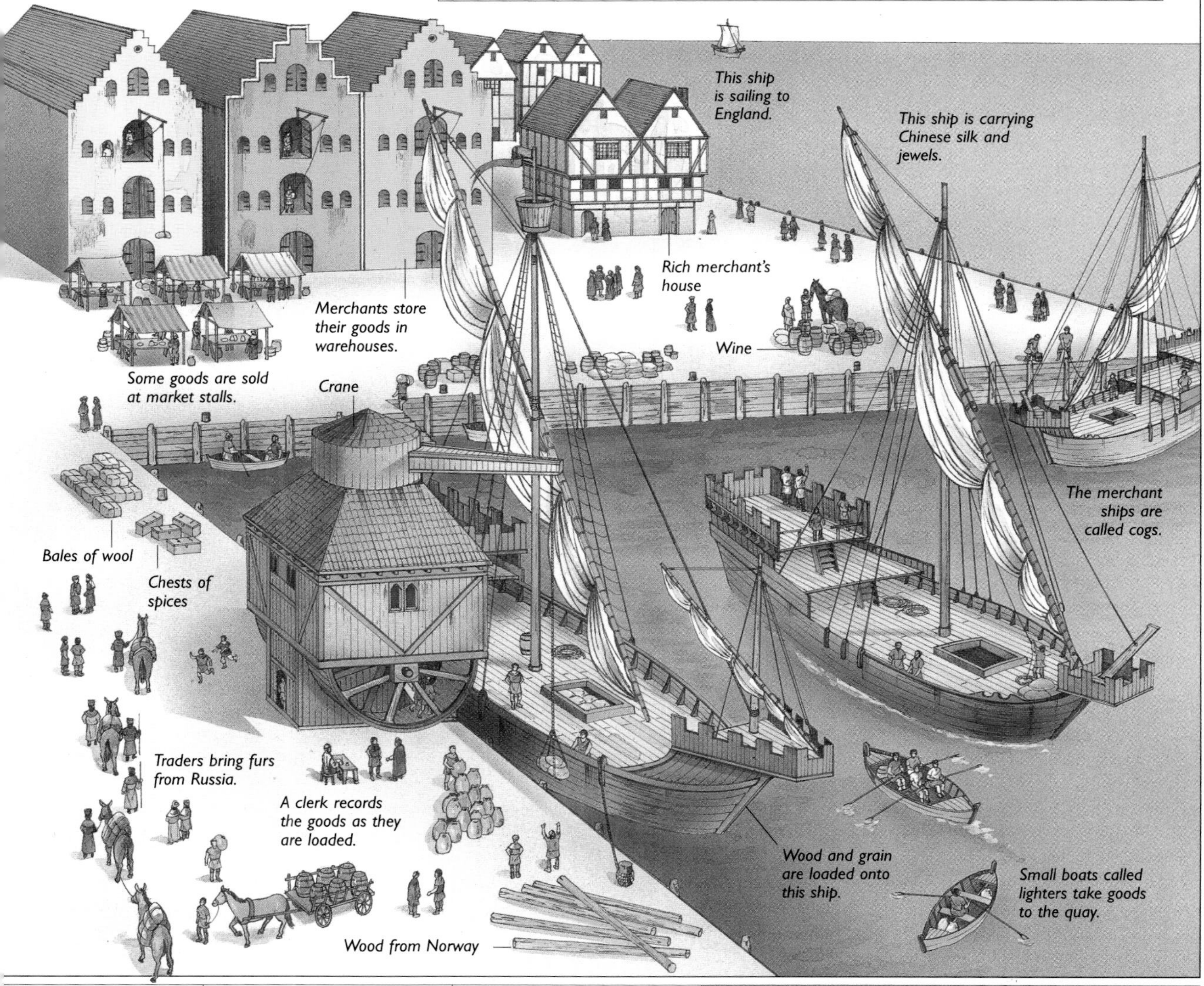

★

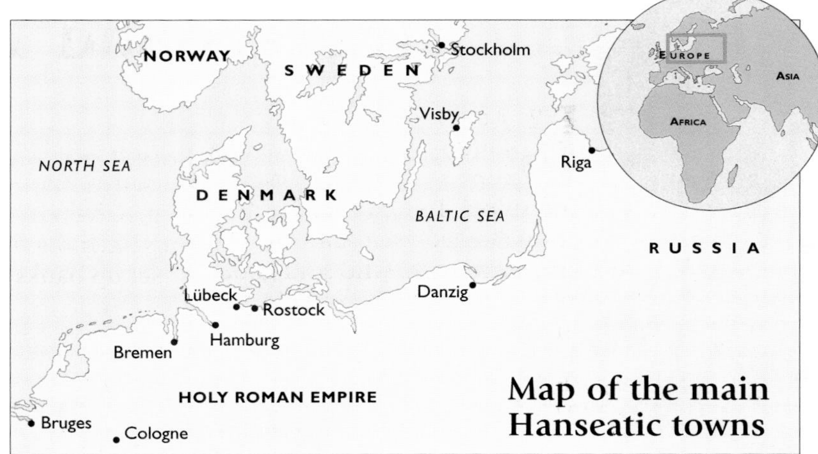

Map of the main Hanseatic towns

This ship is sailing to England.

This ship is carrying Chinese silk and jewels.

Rich merchant's house

Merchants store their goods in warehouses.

Wine

Some goods are sold at market stalls.

Crane

The merchant ships are called cogs.

Bales of wool

Chests of spices

Traders bring furs from Russia.

A clerk records the goods as they are loaded.

Wood and grain are loaded onto this ship.

Small boats called lighters take goods to the quay.

Wood from Norway

1100	1200	1300	1400	1500

The Power of the Popes

★ Mosaic of a medieval pope

The head of the Church in western Europe was the Pope, who lived in Rome. The popes wanted power over the rulers of Europe. They had bitter quarrels with the kings of France and the Holy Roman emperors. (See page 217 to find out more about the Holy Roman Empire.)

Pope and king

A French king, known as Philip the Fair, argued with Pope Boniface VIII over the king's right to collect taxes from lands owned by the Church. In 1303, Boniface announced that he had supreme power over all other rulers. This made Philip so angry that he took Boniface prisoner.

Pope Boniface

★ King Philip the Fair

Map of Europe

EUROPE
ASIA
AFRICA
ENGLAND
HOLY ROMAN EMPIRE
FRANCE
SPAIN
Avignon
Rome

- Followers of the Pope in Avignon
- Followers of the Pope in Rome
- Mostly followers of the Pope in Rome

Pope and emperor

The popes and the Holy Roman emperors both wanted to control all the bishops in the Holy Roman Empire. This led to fierce arguments. In 1077, Pope Gregory VII made Emperor Henry IV wait barefoot in the snow for three days, before he would forgive him.

Popes in France

In 1309, a French pope moved to Avignon in southern France. The popes stayed in France for a hundred years, and, for part of this time, rival popes ruled in Rome. Some countries followed the Avignon Pope and others supported the Pope in Rome (see map). This split in the Church was called the Great Schism.

★ This picture shows a procession in the city of Avignon.

500 600 700 800 900

EUROPE

Enemies of the Church

In the Middle Ages, it was very dangerous to behave differently from the way the leaders of the Church expected. Anyone who questioned the Church's teachings was punished severely, people who acted strangely were accused of witchcraft, and Jews were cruelly persecuted.

Persecuting Jews

Jews had to wear special clothes so they could be recognized. They were attacked and killed all over Europe, and were driven out of England, France and Spain.

A medieval Jew

A suspected witch

Trying witches

Suspected witches were given very unfair trials, such as trial by water. If they floated, they were guilty, and if they sank, they were innocent.

Hounding heretics

People who questioned the teachings of the Church were called heretics. The popes sent out monks, called inquisitors, to find heretics and persuade them to change their minds. If they refused, they were tortured or killed.

Heretics being burned to death

Crusaders and Cathars

Crusader knights attacking a Cathar city

The Cathars were heretics who believed that the world was evil. Their ideas spread rapidly through southern France and this frightened Pope Innocent III. Innocent started a war, called the Albigensian Crusade, which did not end until all the Cathars were wiped out.

The Crusaders built this cathedral at Albi after they had defeated the Cathars.

Preacher power

Jan Hus was a Czech preacher who attacked the power of the Pope and said that people should read the Bible for themselves. He was arrested and burned to death as a heretic. After his death, his supporters, called Hussites, rebelled against the Pope and the Holy Roman Emperor. The fighting lasted for 17 years and the Hussites won many towns in eastern Europe.

Jan Hus being led to his death

Important dates

1210-1229	The Albigensian Crusade
c.1230	Popes begin to use inquisitors.
1290	Jews are driven out of England.
1306	Jews are driven out of France.
1309-1417	Popes in Avignon
c.1372-1415	The life of Jan Hus
1378-1417	Popes in Avignon and Rome (the Great Schism)
1419-1436	The Hussite wars
1492	Jews are driven out of Spain.

Building a Cathedral

A bishop

Medieval bishops and archbishops gave orders that vast cathedrals should be built to show the glory of God. Most cathedrals took over a century to build. They were beautifully decorated with carvings, statues and stained-glass windows.

This picture shows a cathedral being built. ★

Spire

Wooden scaffolding

A machine called a winch lifts blocks of stone.

The roof is covered with sheets of lead.

Sometimes, workers fall and are killed.

Workshop

Carpenters make benches for priests to sit on.

These men are mixing mortar (cement).

The master mason tells the workmen what to do.

Stone cutters

Stone carver

Sculptors

The architect is showing the bishop a stained-glass window.

Stories in glass

Stained-glass windows in cathedrals and churches showed scenes from the Bible. Preachers used these pictures to teach people who could not read.

Window showing ★ a scene from the story of Noah's Ark

500 700 800 900

Going on a Pilgrimage

A pilgrim

During the Middle Ages, many Christians went on religious journeys called pilgrimages. They became pilgrims to show their love for God, and because they hoped that God would forgive their sins and cure their diseases.

Pilgrim routes

Pilgrims journeyed to holy places, called shrines, where saints were buried or sacred objects were kept. Many people made the journey to Jerusalem or Rome, and pilgrims flocked to Compostela in Spain, to visit the shrine of Saint James, the patron saint of pilgrims.

★ Saint James

Canterbury pilgrims

In England, pilgrims went to Canterbury to pray at the grave of Saint Thomas Becket, an archbishop who was murdered by the knights of King Henry II.

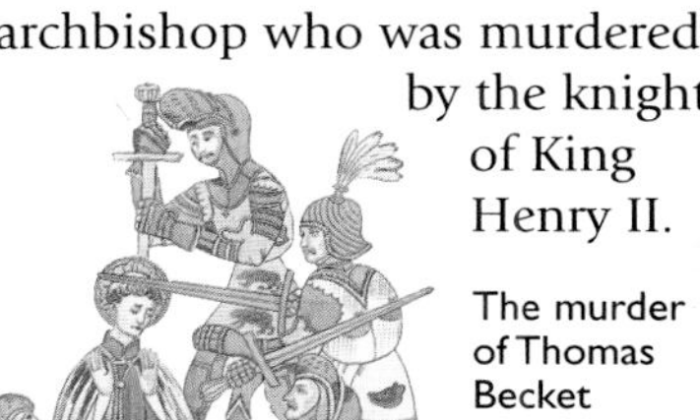
The murder of Thomas Becket

Pilgrims' tales

Although the pilgrims' journeys were difficult and dangerous, they could also be fun. In the medieval poem *The Canterbury Tales*, pilgrims tell each other stories as they travel along.

This picture shows pilgrims on their way to Canterbury.
★

Pilgrims stop at inns to eat and sleep.

Monks

Nuns

Sometimes, robbers attack the pilgrims.

This man is telling a story.

Sick child

Some people sing hymns.

This man is selling badges to pilgrims.

Rich people ride on horseback.

A priest preaches to the pilgrims.

This woman hopes that she will be cured.

This man is barefoot to show that he is sorry for his sins.

EUROPE

1100 1200 1300 1400 1500

Monks and Monasteries

A monk and a nun

Many Christians in the Middle Ages chose to serve God by becoming monks or nuns. They lived apart from the rest of the world in monasteries for men and convents for women. Monks and nuns prayed regularly, followed strict rules, and had special work to do each day.

This picture shows a monastery. Some of the walls have been cut away so you can see inside.

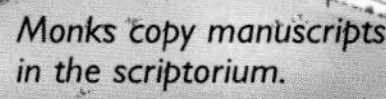

Monks praying together in their chapel

Becoming a monk

Monks had to promise to give up everything they owned, to obey their abbot (chief monk), and not to get married. Before a man made these promises, he joined the monastery as a novice, learning its rules and getting used to its way of life.

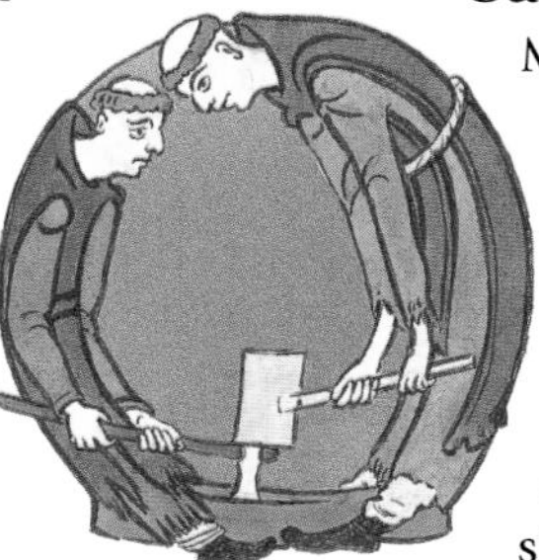

Monks splitting wood

Saint Benedict's rules

Medieval monks followed rules that were written by Saint Benedict in the 6th century. He said that monks should pray, study, and work hard in the fields. They should eat plain food, wear simple clothes (called habits) and look after the sick and the poor.

Monks sleep in the dormitory.

Some monks work in the fields.

The monastery is surrounded by a wall.

This walkway is called a cloister.

Chapel

Altar

These poor people are coming to ask for food.

Fishpond

Healing the sick

The monks grew herbs in their monastery gardens and used them to treat people who were sick. They kept careful records of which herbs worked, and became experts at making medicines.

Monks using herbs to make medicines ★

Making manuscripts

Unlike most people in the Middle Ages, many monks could read and write. They made handwritten books, called manuscripts, and decorated them with pictures and patterns.

★ A decorated letter in a medieval manuscript

Wealth and power

Rich people gave money and land to the monks, and many monasteries became very wealthy. Some monks stopped living a simple life, and instead of praying and working hard, they spent their time running their lands, and enjoying a life of luxury.

A monk greedily helps himself to a drink.

1100 | 1200 | 1300 | 1400 | 1500

Art in the Middle Ages

Most men and women in medieval Europe could not read, but they learned a lot by looking at pictures. People learned about Christianity from the paintings, carvings and stained-glass windows in their local church, and preachers used these images to illustrate their teachings.

Pictures in churches

Medieval churches were filled with images. Even the smallest churches had vivid paintings on their walls and simple carvings inside and out. Large churches and cathedrals were decorated with stunning stained-glass windows, delicate carvings and striking statues.

Painted statue of a German Christian princess ★

★ This window, which shows a coward running away from a rabbit, teaches people to be brave.

Curious carvings

Medieval carvers did not always show religious subjects. High up on church walls, they carved mischievous characters and monsters in stone. Some carvings on the outsides of churches had water spouts sticking out of their mouths. These carvings are known as gargoyles.

Carving of a monster ★

Art for the rich

Wealthy lords and ladies owned their own prayer books and Bibles, which were written by hand and beautifully illustrated. They also hung splendid tapestries on the walls of their castles. Many tapestries showed scenes of castle life.

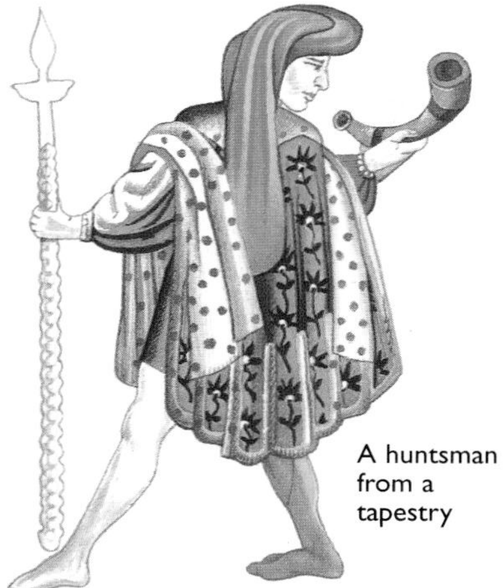

A huntsman from a tapestry

Golden treasures

Goldsmiths made elaborate objects, such as crowns, goblets, and crosses, and decorated them with precious jewels.

★ Decorated top of a bishop's staff (stick)

Inspiring images

This 14th-century painting shows the Virgin Mary and Jesus surrounded by angels in heaven. It was probably displayed on an altar (table) in a private chapel.

Skilled artists painted beautiful religious pictures on wooden panels. These paintings, known as altarpieces, stood on an altar (table) in a church or chapel, and inspired people to worship.

The artists did not try to make their pictures realistic. Instead, they aimed to create an impression of heaven, by painting glowing scenes with glittering golden backgrounds.

The Crusades

By the 1060s, Palestine, known as the Holy Land, was controlled by Muslim Turks. The Turks threatened Christian visitors to the Holy Land and attacked the Christian Byzantine Empire. When the Turks beat the Byzantines at the Battle of Manzikert (see page 252), Christians everywhere felt their religion was in danger.

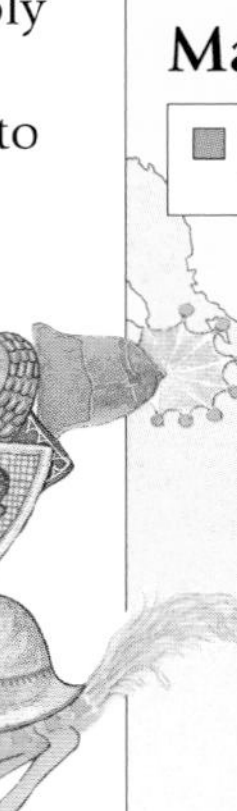

A Christian artist's view of a Muslim warrior

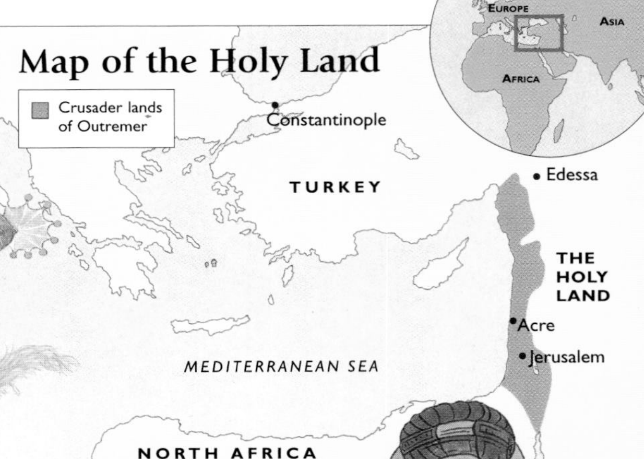

The call to battle

After the Turks' victory, the Byzantine Emperor asked the Christians of western Europe for help. In 1095, Pope Urban II preached a sermon in France. He urged Christians from all over Europe to go on a crusade, or holy war, to drive the Muslims out of the Holy Land.

Pope Urban preaching his famous sermon in France

The First Crusade

Nobles from France, Germany and Italy gathered their armies together and set off for the Holy Land. It took them three years to reach Jerusalem, but in 1099 they captured the city and the surrounding lands. The Crusaders called these lands Outremer, which means "the kingdom across the sea".

Saladin, a brave Muslim leader

The Muslims fight back

After the First Crusade, many Crusaders went home, leaving Outremer very weak. The Muslims seized the town of Edessa, and a Second Crusade failed to win it back. Under their brave leader, Saladin, the Muslims recaptured Jerusalem.

In this scene, an army of crusaders is trying to capture a walled city.

Muslim soldiers fighting fiercely

The Third Crusade

The Third Crusade was led by the rulers of England, France and Germany. They won many battles, and captured the city of Acre, but they did not win back Jerusalem.

Crusaders fighting Muslims ★ during the Third Crusade

Crusaders ride heavy horses that are good at charging.

Muslim warriors ride lightweight horses, so they can attack swiftly.

Richard the Lion Heart, King of England, leads his army.

Crusader knights

Groups of knights who were also monks were formed to fight the Muslims. The main groups were the Knights Templar, the Teutonic Knights and the Knights Hospitaller.

A Knight Templar

The end of the Crusades

Three more Crusades set out in the next hundred years. In 1229, the Muslims agreed that the Christians could take back Jerusalem, but this agreement did not last. The Muslims continued to win back land and in 1291 they conquered Acre, the last Crusader city.

The Fourth Crusade

The Fourth Crusade only went as far as Constantinople, the capital of the Byzantine Empire. Although the Crusaders were supposed to be on the same side as the Byzantines, they attacked their city and stole many of its treasures. The Crusaders ruled Constantinople for nearly 60 years.

This picture shows Saint Mark's Cathedral in Venice. The four bronze horses were stolen from Constantinople.

Important dates

1071	The Battle of Manzikert
1096-1099	The First Crusade
1099	The Crusaders capture Jerusalem.
1147-1149	The Second Crusade
1187	The Muslims recapture Jerusalem.
1189-1192	The Third Crusade
1191	The Crusaders capture Acre.
1202-1204	The Fourth Crusade
1204	The Crusaders capture Constantinople.
1229	The Crusaders control Jerusalem.
1244	The Muslims recapture Jerusalem.
1291	The Muslims recapture Acre. The Crusades end.

1100 1200 1300 1400 1500

The Black Death

In 1347, a ship returned to Italy from Asia, bringing with it a terrible plague (disease). The plague was called the Black Death because of the deadly black swellings it caused. In six years, it swept across Europe, killing roughly one in every three people.

A sick sailor being carried ashore

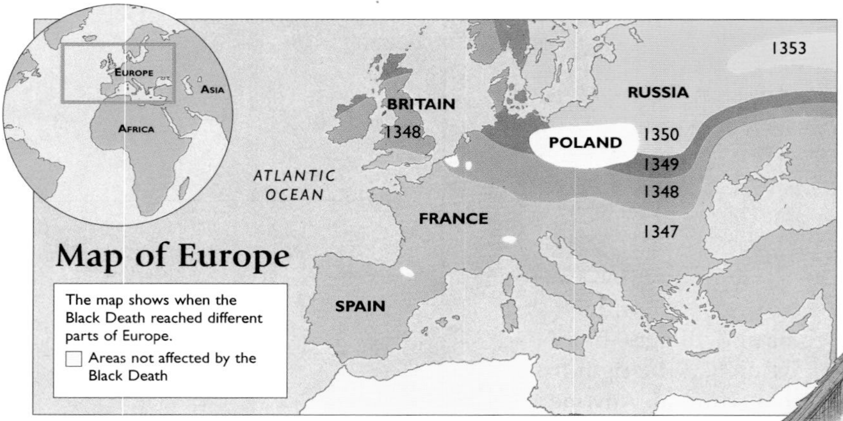

Map of Europe

The map shows when the Black Death reached different parts of Europe.

☐ Areas not affected by the Black Death

EUROPE
ASIA
AFRICA
ATLANTIC OCEAN
BRITAIN 1348
RUSSIA
POLAND
FRANCE
SPAIN
1353
1350
1349
1348
1347

Fatal fleas

The Black Death was spread by bloodsucking fleas that lived on black rats, but no one realized this. People tried many ways to stop the plague from spreading, but nothing worked.

People burning the clothes of the dead

Punishment from God

Many people thought that God had sent the Black Death as a punishment for their sins. A group of men, called the Flagellant Brothers, tried to stop the disease by whipping their bodies to punish themselves. They went from town to town and actually helped to spread the plague.

This picture shows a town infected with the Black Death. ★

The owners of these houses have escaped to the country.

Thieves steal food from empty houses.

The dead are taken away in carts.

Infected houses are marked with a cross.

Some Brothers whip themselves.

A group of Flagellant Brothers walks through the town.

Rats run through the streets.

This doctor is trying to protect himself by wearing a leather mask.

EUROPE

500 600 700 800 900

Criminals and Outlaws

Life in medieval Europe could be dangerous and violent. Thieves lurked in towns, robbers lay in wait on lonely roads, and quarrels sometimes led to deadly fights.

Catching criminals

Groups of men took turns being watchmen in their towns and villages, but everyone had the right to catch a criminal. Anyone who saw a crime take place could chase after the wrongdoer, calling out to others to join in. This noisy chase was called a "hue and cry".

This picture shows a hue and cry in a village.

Public punishments

Most punishments were carried out in public, to make people frightened of breaking the law. Wrongdoers could be locked in the stocks, or dragged through the streets and whipped, and people who committed serious crimes were put to death in front of large crowds.

A criminal being dragged through the streets

Harsh laws

There were many harsh laws in the Middle Ages, but some of the most hated were the forest laws. These laws allowed kings and nobles to hunt deer on their own lands, while any peasant who killed a deer was severely punished, and could even be put to death.

Outlaws

Sometimes, people ran away to escape punishment. These runaways became outlaws and lived in forests. They had no rights and it was not a crime to kill them. Many stories have been written about the famous English outlaw Robin Hood, but no one knows if he really existed.

Statue of Robin Hood ★

Kingdoms of the Celts

Celtic archer

By the year 500, barbarian tribes ruled most of Europe (see page 204), but some people, called the Celts, managed to stay independent. The Celts in Brittany remained separate from France until 1532, and the Welsh, Scots and Irish all fought to stay free of England.

Controlling Wales

The English kings wanted to control the princes who ruled Wales, so they gave land on the Welsh borders to powerful English nobles. These nobles, called marcher lords, kept the Welsh out of England, but also won Welsh lands for themselves.

Stained-glass portrait of a marcher lord

Welsh princes

Prince Llywelyn the Great united the Welsh princes and married the King of England's daughter. His son, Gruffydd, was taken prisoner by the English, but his grandson, Llywelyn ap Gruffydd, was accepted as the Prince of Wales by the English king.

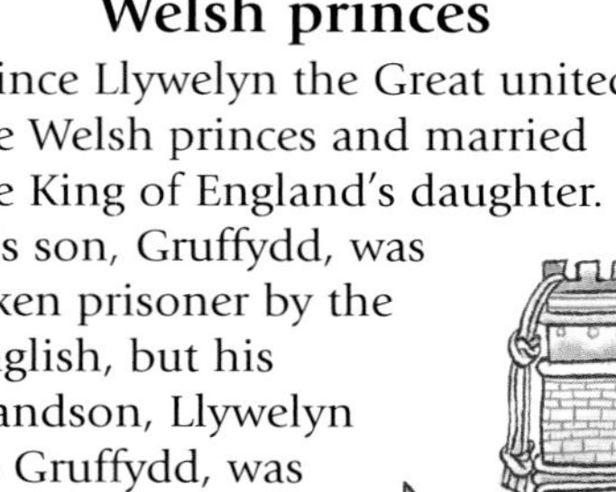

Gruffydd falling to his death from the Tower of London

Map of the Celtic kingdoms

Celtic kingdoms
Marcher lords' lands in 1280

EUROPE
ASIA
AFRICA
ATLANTIC OCEAN
SCOTLAND
Bannockburn
IRELAND
Dublin
ENGLAND
WALES
FRANCE
BRITTANY

The English triumph

Llywelyn ap Gruffydd gained control of most of Wales, but in 1276 King Edward I of England decided to fight the Welsh. Llywelyn was killed, Edward made his own son Prince of Wales, and the English built castles all over north Wales. After this, there were many Welsh rebellions, but none of them lasted for long.

Edward I naming his son Prince of Wales

This picture shows a Welsh army attacking an English castle.

500 600 700 800 900

Wallace of Scotland

Scotland had its own king, but in 1296 the Scots could not decide who should be their next king, so Edward I of England took over as ruler. This made the Scots furious, and a Scottish knight called William Wallace led them into battle against Edward. At first, Wallace was victorious, but later he was captured and killed.

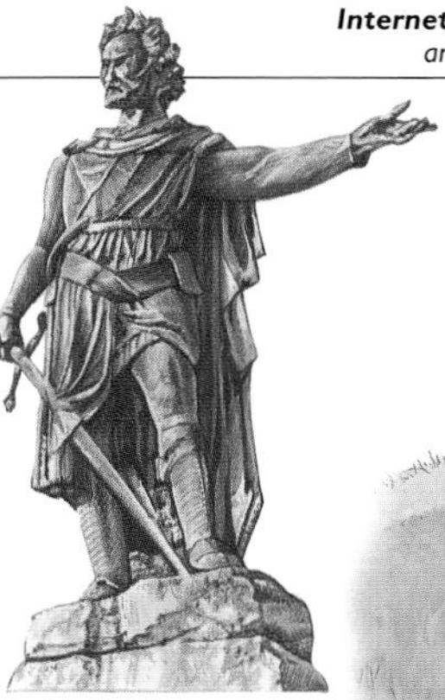

Statue of William Wallace ★

Bruce and Bannockburn

In 1306, Robert Bruce was secretly crowned King of Scotland. He defeated King Edward II of England at Bannockburn, and in 1328 Edward accepted that Scotland was an independent kingdom.

This picture shows the start of the Battle of Bannockburn. ★

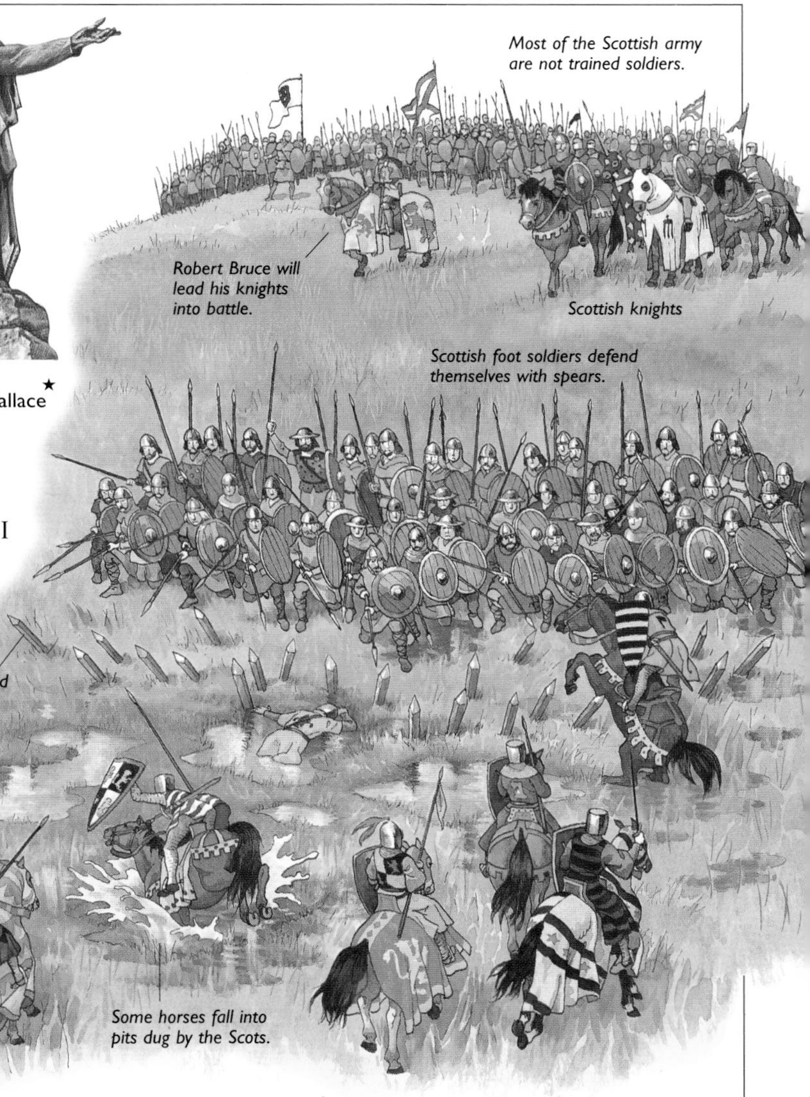

Most of the Scottish army are not trained soldiers.

Robert Bruce will lead his knights into battle.

Scottish knights

Scottish foot soldiers defend themselves with spears.

The Scots have planted stakes in the ground.

The English knights charge at the Scots.

The ground is wet and marshy.

Some horses fall into pits dug by the Scots.

The English in Ireland

In 1160, an English noble, nicknamed Strongbow, went to help an Irish king fight against his rivals. Strongbow married the king's daughter and seized Dublin. This alarmed the English king who started a campaign to win Irish land for himself. By 1400, the English controlled eastern Ireland, but the Irish won back most of their land over the next hundred years.

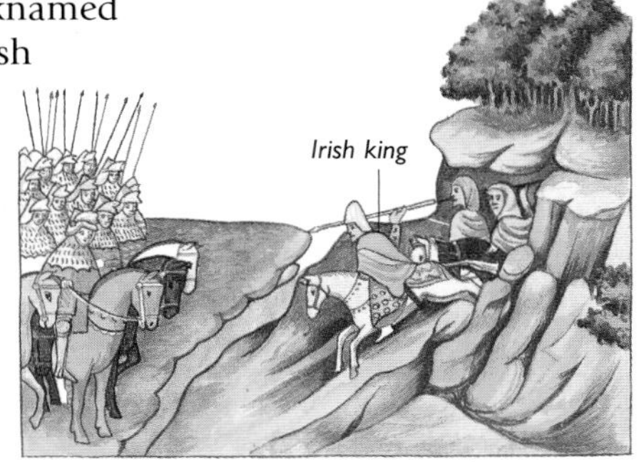

Irish warriors attacking an English army

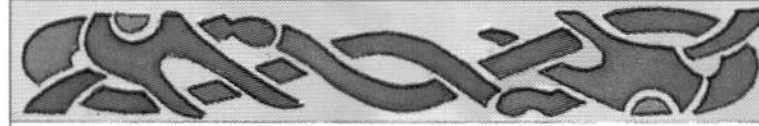

Important dates

1170	Strongbow seizes Dublin.
1258-1282	Llywelyn ap Gruffydd is Prince of Wales.
1301	Edward II becomes Prince of Wales.
1314	Battle of Bannockburn
1328	Edward II accepts Scotland's independence.
1532	Brittany becomes part of France.

The Rise of Burgundy

One of the most powerful nobles in medieval Europe was the Duke of Burgundy, who ruled over an area, called a duchy, in eastern France. When the Duke of Burgundy died in 1361, he left no son to inherit his land, so King Jean II of France made his youngest son, Philippe, the new Duke.

Duke Philippe and his descendants built up a huge duchy in France and Flanders (an area now made up of Holland, Belgium and northern France). The dukes collected taxes from cloth merchants, bankers and farmers, and became incredibly rich.

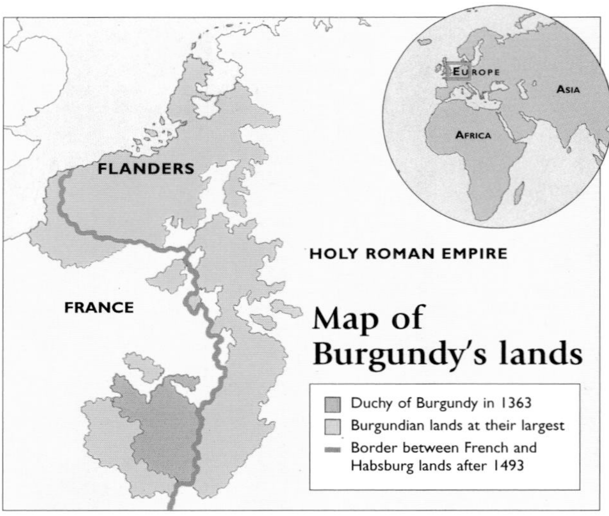

Supporters of the arts

The dukes of Burgundy paid artists and writers to produce works of art. The famous painter Jan van Eyck worked for the Burgundy family.

The Arnolfini Marriage, by Jan van Eyck, was painted to celebrate the wedding of an Italian merchant who had settled in Flanders.

Quarrels in France

The dukes of Burgundy fought against the Duke of Orléans and his supporters, the Armagnacs. They also argued with the kings of France. In 1419, Duke Jean of Burgundy was murdered, probably on the orders of the French king's son. After this, Burgundy supported England in the Hundred Years' War against France.

Marie and Maximilian

In 1476, Duke Charles the Bold of Burgundy arranged for his only child, Marie, to marry Prince Maximilian Habsburg of Austria. The following year, Charles died in battle, and the French king seized some of his lands. For the next 20 years, Maximilian fought the French over Burgundy.

Maximilian Habsburg

Burgundy divides

Maximilian was crowned Holy Roman Emperor in 1493. In the same year, he and the French king agreed to divide Burgundy between them. The French took all the Burgundian lands in France, except for a small part of the original duchy. The rest of Burgundy joined the Holy Roman Empire.

The court of Burgundy

Magnificent feasts and dances were held in the castles of Burgundy. The knights and ladies of the Burgundian court wore extravagant clothes and had beautiful manners.

A dance in a Burgundian castle

The musicians play from the gallery (balcony).

This poet is waiting to present his work to the duchess.

The duke's cup is held up high so no one can breathe on it.

This is the chancellor, who advises the duke.

Everyone at court wears fabulous clothes made from silk, satin, fur and velvet.

Important dates

1363-1404	Philippe the Good is Duke of Burgundy.
1410-1411	The Burgundians fight the Armagnacs.
1419	Jean the Fearless of Burgundy is murdered.
1477	Marie of Burgundy marries Maximilian Habsburg of Austria.
1477-1493	France and Austria fight over Burgundy.
1493	Maximilian Habsburg becomes Holy Roman Emperor. Burgundy is divided.

The Wars of the Roses

In 1455, a bitter struggle broke out between two branches of the English royal family. The opponents were the house (or family) of Lancaster and the house of York. Their struggle became known as the Wars of the Roses because both sides wore a rose emblem (or badge).

The white rose of York and the red ★ rose of Lancaster

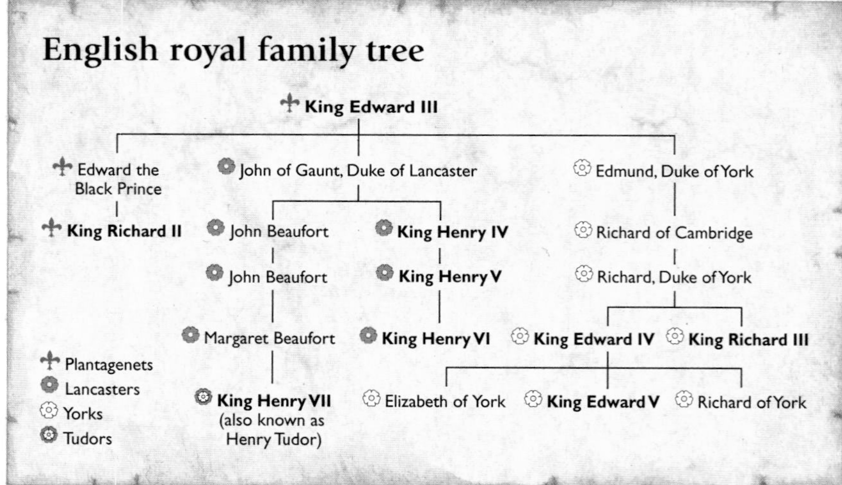

Lancaster weakens

King Henry VI came from the Lancaster family, but, unlike his father and grandfather, he was not a great warrior. He did nothing to stop the French from winning the Hundred Years' War and he could not control his nobles. He also suffered from periods of insanity.

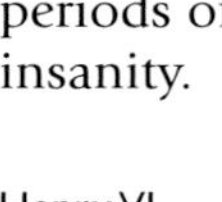

Henry VI

The struggle begins

In 1454, Parliament gave Richard, Duke of York, the right to rule on King Henry's behalf. The next year, a group of nobles, led by Henry's wife, refused to let Richard rule. The Yorkists and Lancastrians gathered their supporters and began to fight.

A Yorkist king

Edward IV's symbol was a white rose inside a sun.

After a series of battles, Henry VI escaped to Scotland, and Richard of York's son, Edward, was crowned King of England. Edward IV ruled for 22 years, but he struggled against the Lancastrians for the first 10 years of his reign.

Warwick the Kingmaker

The Earl of Warwick helped his cousin, Edward IV, become king, but later he supported Henry VI when he tried to be king again. Warwick became known as "the Kingmaker".

The Earl of Warwick plotting against King Edward IV ★

EUROPE

500 600 700 800 900

Richard III

Edward IV died when his oldest son, Edward, was 12 years old. Before Edward V could be crowned, his uncle, Richard of Gloucester, declared himself king. Few people dared to oppose Richard, and he was crowned Richard III.

Richard III

Princes in the Tower

Richard insisted that Edward and his brother should stay in the Tower of London. The boys were never seen again and many people thought that Richard had given orders for them to be killed.

The young princes, painted by a 19th-century artist

The end of Richard III

The Lancastrians were determined to get rid of King Richard. Their choice for a new king was Henry Tudor, a member of the Lancaster family. In 1484, Henry invaded England from France. He fought against King Richard at the Battle of Bosworth Field, and Richard was defeated and killed.

This picture shows Henry Tudor leading his troops to fight King Richard III.
★

There are about 4,000 men in Henry's army.

The Lancastrian nobles support Henry.

Henry Tudor

Many men join Henry's army.

Some Yorkist nobles have abandoned Richard and joined Henry's army.

The first of the Tudors

Henry Tudor was crowned King Henry VII of England. He united the families of Lancaster and York by marrying Elizabeth of York, daughter of Edward IV. The Wars of the Roses came to an end, and England was ruled by the Tudors until 1603.

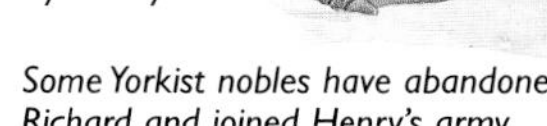

Important dates

1422-1461	Henry VI is king.
1455	The Wars of the Roses begin.
1461-1483	Edward IV is king.
1483	Edward V becomes king, but is never crowned.
1483-1485	Richard III is king.
1485	The Lancastrians win the Battle of Bosworth Field. The Wars of the Roses end.
1485-1509	Henry VII is king.

1100 1200 1300 1400 1500

Mongol Invaders

The Mongols were nomads (wandering people) who roamed the plains of central Asia. They lived in tents, called yurts, and were always on the move, searching for grasslands where their animals could feed. In battle, the Mongols were cruel and bloodthirsty.

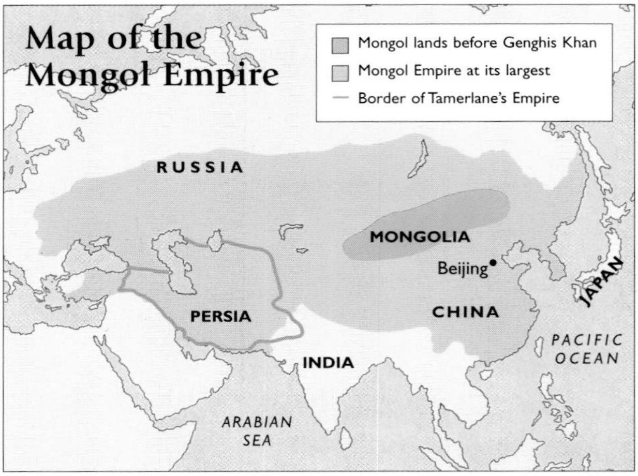

A Mongol yurt

Map of the Mongol Empire

Genghis Khan

Around 1180, a young Mongol warrior called Temujin began to lead daring raids on other Mongol tribes. He built up a powerful army and slowly brought all the tribes under his control. In 1206, the tribes named him Genghis Khan, which means "supreme ruler".

Genghis Khan

Building the Empire

Led by Genghis, the Mongols invaded northern China. Then, they swept eastward, killing thousands of people as they went. Genghis made laws for everyone in his Empire to obey, set up a messenger service, and encouraged trade.

After Genghis died, his sons and grandsons became khans (rulers). They won more land for their Empire in China, Europe and the Middle East.

This picture shows the Mongol army on the move.

Kublai Khan

Kublai Khan was a grandson of Genghis Khan. He conquered all of China and made Beijing his capital city.

★ Kublai Khan in Chinese dress

Kublai tried twice to invade Japan, but the Japanese resisted fiercely. He gave up trying to attack Japan when violent winds (called "kamikaze") wrecked his ships.

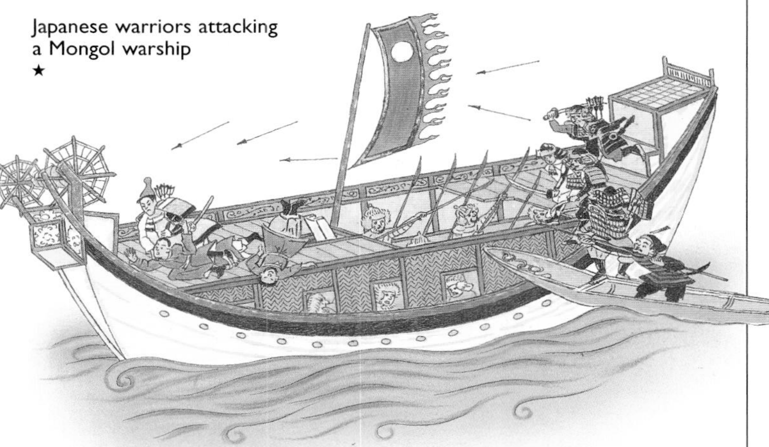

Japanese warriors attacking a Mongol warship ★

Tamerlane

After Kublai's rule, the Mongol Empire fell apart. Family quarrels made its rulers weak and many of the conquered people fought back. Then, in 1360, a Mongol leader called Tamerlane began to build a new empire. Tamerlane seized land in Persia, Russia and India, but the Empire did not last long after his death.

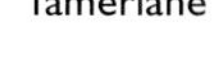

Tamerlane ★

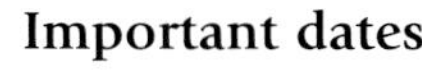

Important dates

1162	Temujin is born in Mongolia.
1206	Temujin is given the name Genghis Khan.
1206-1227	Genghis Khan builds the Mongol Empire.
1259-1294	Kublai Khan rules.
1279	The Mongol Empire is at its largest.
1360-1405	Tamerlane builds a new Mongol Empire.

Triumphs of the Turks

The Turks were wandering people who came from central Asia. Around 950, a tribe of Turks called the Seljuks began to sweep westward. They invaded the Islamic Empire which had become so weak that its ruler welcomed the Seljuks into his capital, Baghdad.

Map of Seljuk lands

EUROPE
ASIA
AFRICA
TURKEY
Manzikert
SYRIA
Baghdad
PERSIA
Jerusalem
PALESTINE
CENTRAL ASIA

Seljuk lands at their largest
Borders of the Islamic Empire
Borders of the Byzantine Empire

Seljuk warriors ★

The Crusaders fight back

Some Seljuks attacked Christian visitors to the Holy Land, and many Christians felt that they should fight for the land where their religion began. The Pope called for a crusade (holy war) against the Seljuks, and by 1100 the Crusaders had conquered most of Palestine (see page 240).

Seljuks attacking Christians

Winning land

In the 1050s, the Seljuks began invading the Byzantine Empire. They defeated the Byzantines at Manzikert and won Turkey. Later, they also captured Syria and Palestine (the Holy Land). Many Seljuks settled in their newly gained lands. They followed the Muslim religion and built elaborate mosques.

A Seljuk holy dancer, called a whirling dervish

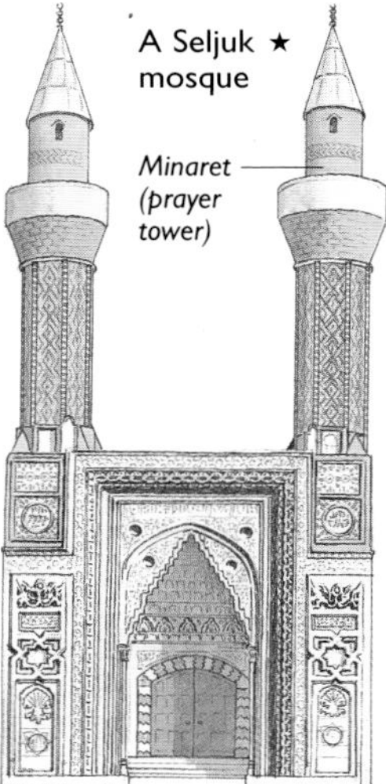

A Seljuk ★ mosque

The end of the Seljuks

By 1200, the Seljuks had split into small groups ruled by rival princes, and many Seljuk people rebelled against their leaders. When tribes of Mongols attacked them, the Seljuks were too weak to fight back. By 1300, the Mongols had conquered most of the Seljuk lands except Turkey.

Mongol soldiers

The rise of the Ottoman Empire

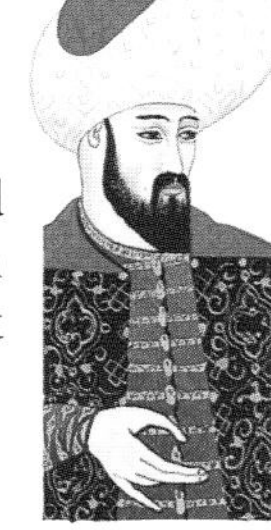

Osman I

In 1301, a Turkish prince called Osman declared himself Sultan (king) of all the Turks. He built up an army and began to win land. The land won by Osman and his descendants was called the Ottoman Empire.

Map of the Ottoman Empire

EUROPE
ASIA
AFRICA
BLACK SEA
Constantinople
TURKEY
Ottoman lands in 1301
Land won by Osman I
Ottoman Empire in 1500

Running the Empire

The Ottoman sultans were strong rulers as well as skilled soldiers. They made strict laws for their people, and built beautiful mosques, schools and baths in their cities.

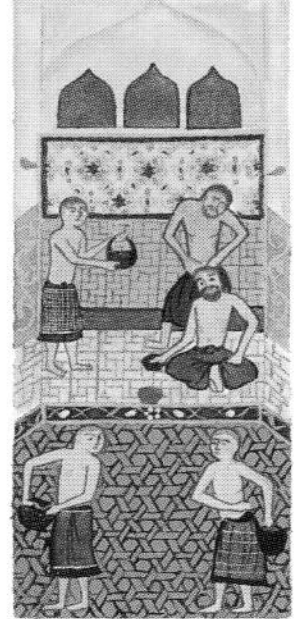

A public bath built for a sultan

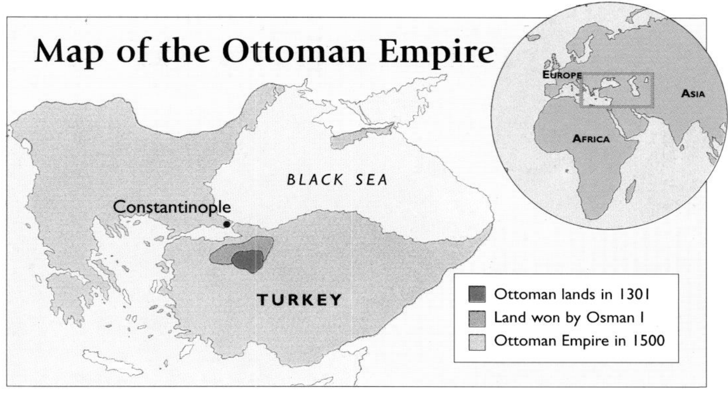

The fall of Constantinople

The Ottomans gradually won land from the Byzantine people, and in 1453 they captured Constantinople, the capital of the Byzantine Empire (see page 203). Sultan Mehmet II rebuilt Constantinople, which he renamed Istanbul, and made it the capital of the Ottoman Empire.

This picture shows the Ottomans marching through Constantinople after their victory.

★

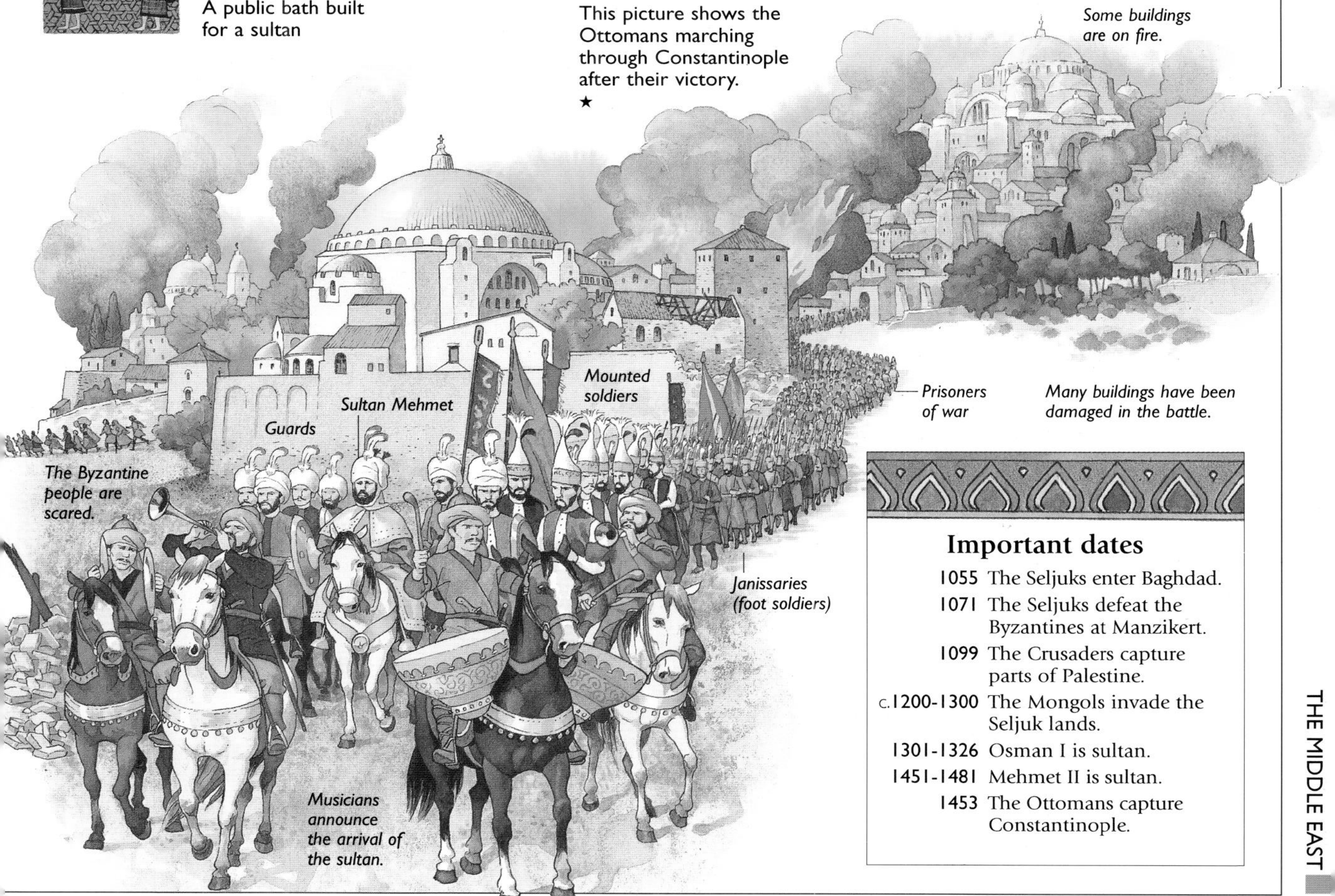

Some buildings are on fire.
Mounted soldiers
Sultan Mehmet
Guards
Prisoners of war
Many buildings have been damaged in the battle.
The Byzantine people are scared.
Janissaries (foot soldiers)
Musicians announce the arrival of the sultan.

Important dates

1055	The Seljuks enter Baghdad.
1071	The Seljuks defeat the Byzantines at Manzikert.
1099	The Crusaders capture parts of Palestine.
c.1200-1300	The Mongols invade the Seljuk lands.
1301-1326	Osman I is sultan.
1451-1481	Mehmet II is sultan.
1453	The Ottomans capture Constantinople.

1100 1200 1300 1400 1500

Kingdoms of Eastern Europe

During the 6th century, tribes of warriors from Asia began moving west into Europe. The warriors were pagans who did not believe in Christ, and the people of Europe were terrified of them.

The tribes created many warlike kingdoms in eastern Europe. Most of these kingdoms did not last long, but some of them later became powerful Christian countries.

Map of eastern Europe

EUROPE
ASIA
AFRICA
RUSSIA
BALTIC SEA
Tannenberg
LITHUANIA
HOLY ROMAN EMPIRE
Prague
Lechfeld

Poland
Hungary
Bohemia
Wallachia
Lands of the Teutonic Knights

Crown of Charles IV of Bohemia

Warriors from Asia

Magyars in Hungary

In the 800s, a tribe called the Magyars conquered the area now known as Hungary. The Magyars fought fiercely to win more land, but in 955 they were beaten by the Germans at the Battle of Lechfeld (see page 217).

The Holy Roman Empire

After the Germans' victory, the Pope set up the Holy Roman Empire and made the German king its emperor (see page 217). The Pope relied on the emperor to defend Christian Europe against invading pagan tribes.

The kingdom of Hungary

In 975, the Magyar leader, Géza, became a Christian, and in 1001 the Pope accepted Géza's son, Stephen, as the first King of Hungary. Stephen was a keen Christian who was later made a saint. He created a peaceful kingdom with strong laws, and most of the Magyars became Christians.

This picture shows King Stephen leading a religious procession.

★

Churches have been built all over Hungary.

Bishops and priests accompany their king.

500 600 800 900

Count Dracula of Transylvania

Transylvania was part of the mountainous kingdom of Wallachia. In the 15th century, it was ruled by a count called Vlad Tepes, who was famous for his cruelty. Vlad put thousands of people to death by impaling (spearing) them on wooden stakes. He was given the nickname Dracula, which means "dragon's son".

Count Dracula

The kingdom of Bohemia

The kingdom of Bohemia (now the Czech Republic) was created by a tribe of Slavs in the 800s. It grew into a rich and powerful country. In 1355, the Pope made Charles IV of Bohemia the Holy Roman Emperor, and Charles moved the capital of the Empire to Prague.

The Teutonic Knights

The Christian kingdom of Poland was threatened by pagan Prussians in the north, so the Poles asked the Teutonic Knights for help. The Teutonic Knights were soldier-monks from Germany who had fought in the Crusades.

The Knights conquered the Prussians and seized their lands. Then, they tried to win more land in Poland, Russia and Lithuania. Eventually, they were beaten by the Poles, the Lithuanians and their allies at the Battle of Tannenberg.

This picture shows Teutonic Knights attacking a Prussian village.

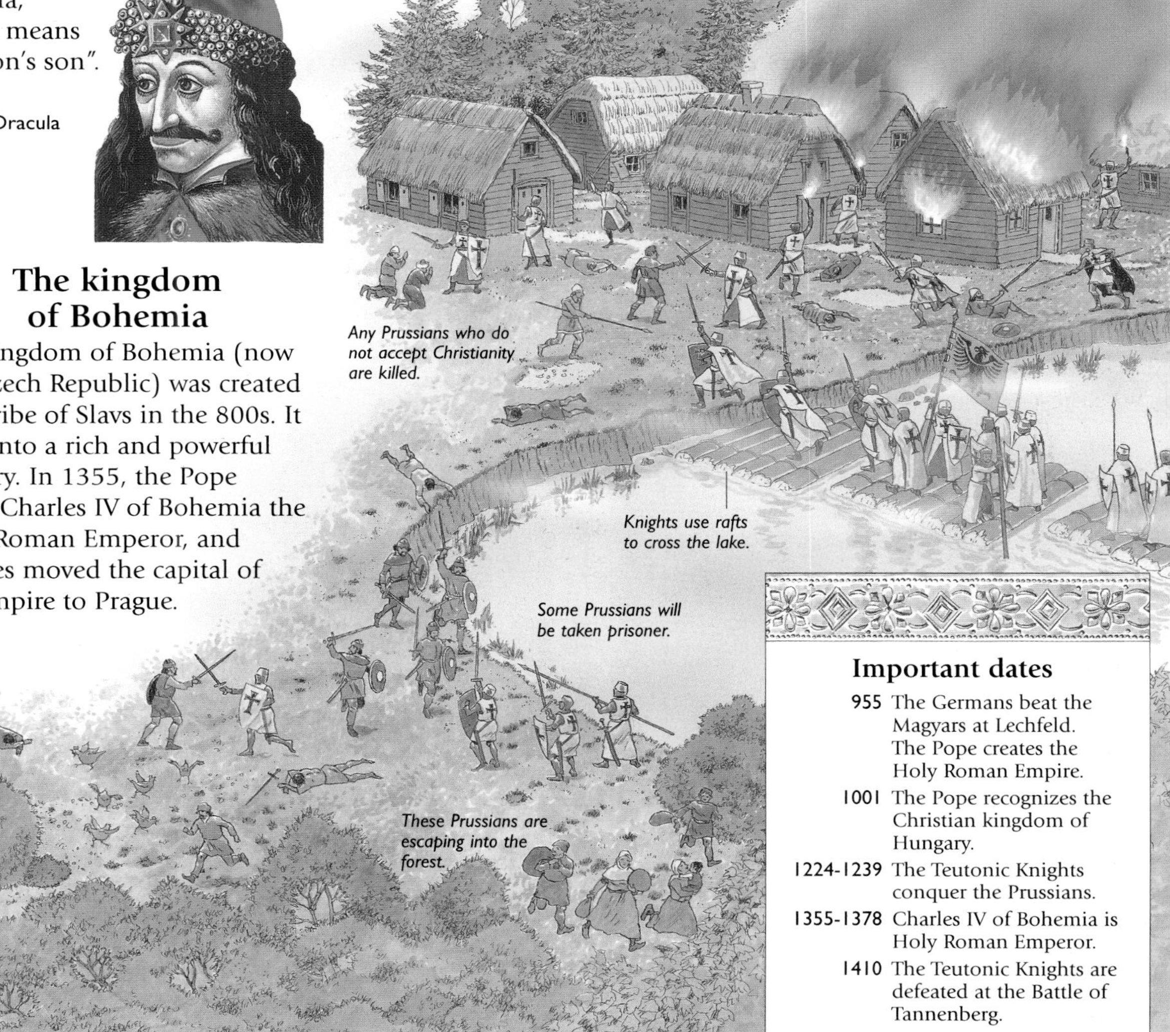

Important dates

- **955** The Germans beat the Magyars at Lechfeld. The Pope creates the Holy Roman Empire.
- **1001** The Pope recognizes the Christian kingdom of Hungary.
- **1224-1239** The Teutonic Knights conquer the Prussians.
- **1355-1378** Charles IV of Bohemia is Holy Roman Emperor.
- **1410** The Teutonic Knights are defeated at the Battle of Tannenberg.

The Rise of the Russians

Viking ship

Around the year 700, Vikings from Sweden began to travel down rivers into the area that is now western Russia. At first, the Vikings attacked the Slavs who were living there, but later they settled down and started to build towns.

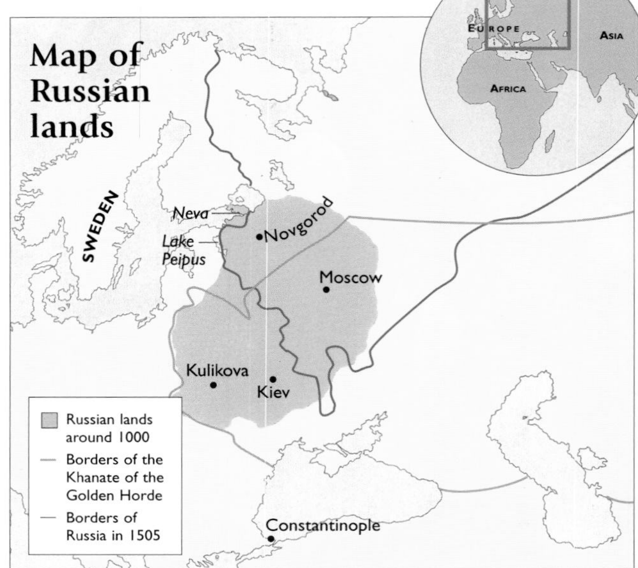

Rurik the Rus

Around 862, a Viking leader called Rurik captured the Slavic city of Novgorod and the lands around it. Rurik's followers were called the Rus, from which we get the name "Russian". The Russians won lots of land and, in 882, Kiev became their new capital city.

The city of Novgorod

Vladimir the Saint

Vladimir became Prince of Kiev in 978. He believed that he could turn people into Christians by forcing them to be baptized (washed in water as a sign of a new beginning). After his death, Vladimir was made a saint because so many of his people had become Christians.

Prince Vladimir

Yaroslav the Wise

Vladimir's son, Yaroslav, made Kiev into a rich and powerful city. He encouraged art and learning, created a strong government, and sent traders to Constantinople. Later, he became known as "Yaroslav the Wise".

Saint Sofia's cathedral in Kiev, built in Yaroslav's reign

This picture shows Russian people being baptized.

EUROPE

500 600 700 800 900

The Tartars arrive

The Russian rulers who came after Yaroslav were weak, and in 1240 Kiev was captured by tribes of Mongols, known in Russia as Tartars. The Tartars created a vast kingdom called the Khanate of the Golden Horde, and forced the Russian rulers to pay them large sums of money, called tribute.

A Tartar warrior ★

Nevsky's victories

While the Tartars were invading the south, the Russians in the north defeated a Swedish army on the banks of the Neva, and drove back German invaders at Lake Peipus. Their leader, Alexander, became a hero. He was called "Nevsky" because of his victory at the Neva.

Nevsky leading his troops into battle ★

The growth of Moscow

Nevsky's son, Daniel, was crowned Prince of Moscow in 1280. Over the next 200 years, the princes of Moscow built up a powerful kingdom called Muscovy. Moscow became the most important city in Russia and, in 1328, the head of the Russian Church settled there.

Artists from Muscovy painted beautiful religious pictures, called icons.

The Tartars weaken

By the 1350s, the Tartars were fighting amongst themselves. Their kingdom split up, and in 1380 they were defeated by the Muscovites at Kulikova, in southern Russia.

Ivan the Great

The Tartars' power was finally broken by Prince Ivan III of Moscow. Ivan conquered the city of Novgorod and went on to win more land. In 1480, he declared himself Tsar (emperor) of all the Russians and refused to pay the Tartars any more tribute. He built many beautiful buildings in his capital city of Moscow.

Ivan the Great, first Tsar of Russia

The Cathedral of the Annunciation in Moscow, built in Ivan's reign ★

Important dates

c.700	The Vikings arrive in Russia.
c.862	Rurik creates a Rus kingdom.
1240	The Battle of the Neva
c.1250-1480	The Tartars rule southern Russia.
1380	The Battle of Kulikova
1480-1505	Ivan the Great rules Russia.

1100 1200 1300 1400 1500

The Struggle for Spain

In 711, an army of African Muslims, known as Moors, crossed from North Africa into southern Spain. Spain had been ruled for 200 years by Visigoths (see page 204), but the Visigoths had become weak and were easily defeated by the new invaders.

Moorish warrior

Map of Spain

FRANCE

EUROPE

ASIA

AFRICA

Córdoba

Granada

NORTH AFRICA

- Border of al-Andalus in 1000
- Aragon
- Granada
- León and Castile
- Navarre
- Portugal
- Valencia

The map shows the main Spanish kingdoms in 1250.

The Moors move north

By 718, the Moors had conquered all of Spain except the mountainous kingdoms of the north. They also marched into France, but Charles Martel led an army of Franks against them. In 732, the Franks beat the Moors at the Battle of Poitiers, then they slowly drove them back into southern Spain.

Franks fighting Moors

Learning and leisure

The Moors of al-Andalus were famous for their civilized way of life. They studied science, mathematics and astronomy, composed music, and wrote poetry. They also enjoyed playing games, such as chess.

A medieval picture of Moors playing chess

The kingdom of al-Andalus

The Moors created a Muslim kingdom in southern Spain, called al-Andalus. The Moors were great traders and builders and their capital, Córdoba, became one of the richest cities in Europe.

The Great Mosque at Córdoba

The rise of the Christian kingdoms

Around 1000, al-Andalus became weaker and began to split into separate kingdoms. At the same time, the unconquered Christian kingdoms in the north were growing stronger. In 1037, León and Castile were united, and Aragon and Navarre gradually became more powerful. In 1139, the new kingdom of Portugal was created.

★ A king of León

500 600 700 800 900

The Christians fight back

For over 450 years, the rulers of the Christian kingdoms fought to drive the Moors out of Spain. The Christians gradually moved south, conquering cities as they went. This long struggle to win back land is known as the "Reconquista".

El Cid

The most famous soldier of the Reconquista was Rodrigo Diaz, known as El Cid, which means "the Lord". He led daring raids into Muslim lands and seized the kingdom of Valencia, which he ruled himself.

El Cid

The kingdom of Granada

By 1250, the Christians had won back all of Spain except the Muslim kingdom of Granada. One reason Granada survived so long was because its sultans (rulers) paid large sums of money, called tribute, to the kings of León and Castile. It was finally conquered in 1492.

★ A sultan of Granada

This picture shows a Christian army marching into battle.

Battle tent called a pavillion

Foot soldiers with crossbows and axes

Mounted knights

Noblemen ride beside the army.

The nobles and knights are very richly dressed.

Drummer

Standard-bearer

Heralds blow trumpets.

The Alhambra Palace in Granada

Important dates

- **711** The Moors invade Spain.
- **c.730** The Moors rule most of Spain.
- **732** Charles Martel defeats the Moors at Poitiers.
- **c.1000** The Moors' power in Spain starts to weaken.
- **1037-1492** The Christians win back Spain (the Reconquista).

1100 1200 1300 1400 1500

Conquerors of North Africa

The land along the north coast of Africa was one of the richest parts of the Roman Empire, but in 429 it was invaded by the Vandals (see page 204). The Vandals forced the people of North Africa to pay very high taxes, and let many Roman cities fall into ruins.

Map of North Africa

TURKEY
MEDITERRANEAN SEA
SYRIA
NORTH AFRICA
• Cairo
EGYPT
Sahara Desert
ARABIA
EUROPE
ASIA
AFRICA
Muslim land in 1500
— Border of Egypt

Mosaic of a Vandal

A Roman villa in North Africa

Byzantine rulers

In 533, the Byzantine Emperor Justinian drove the Vandals out of Africa. For the next 150 years, Byzantine rulers in North Africa tried to bring back the Roman way of life.

Coin showing the Emperor Justinian

Arab invaders

The Arabs invaded North Africa in 697, and by 750 it had become part of the Muslim Arab Empire. At first, North Africa was controlled by the Arab caliph (ruler), but slowly local rulers set up their own Muslim kingdoms.

Arab invaders

Fatimids in Egypt

In 969, a group of Muslims from Syria, called the Fatimids, seized control of Egypt. They set up an independent kingdom and their capital city, Cairo, became very rich. The Fatimids ruled for 200 years until they were conquered by the Arab leader, Saladin (see page 240).

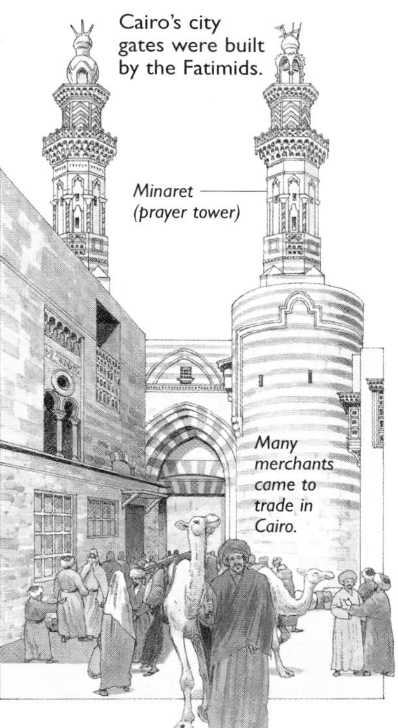

Cairo's city gates were built by the Fatimids.

Minaret (prayer tower)

Many merchants came to trade in Cairo.

Mamelukes in Egypt

Saladin's descendants stayed in power for 80 years, but in 1250 the Mamelukes took over. The Mamelukes were Muslim Turks who had once been slaves in Saladin's army. The most famous Mameluke leader was Sultan Baibars, who prevented tribes of Mongols from invading Africa.

A Mameluke warrior

Important dates

429-533	The Vandals rule North Africa.
533-697	The Byzantines rule North Africa.
697	The Arabs conquer North Africa.
750	North Africa is part of the Arab Empire.
969-1171	The Fatimids rule Egypt.
1250-1517	The Mamelukes rule Egypt.
1261	The Mamelukes defeat the Mongols.

NORTH AFRICA
EAST AFRICA
500 600 700 800 900

Internet link: For a link to a Web site where you can watch pilgrims visiting one of Lalibela's churches, go to **www.usborne-quicklinks.com**

Cities of East Africa

Around the year 1000, busy ports began to grow up on the coast of East Africa (see map). Merchants from Arabia, India and China sailed to these ports bringing tools, cloth, glass and china. In return, the Africans traded gold and ivory, iron and slaves, and even wild animals.

East Africans gave this giraffe to the Chinese emperor as a gift.

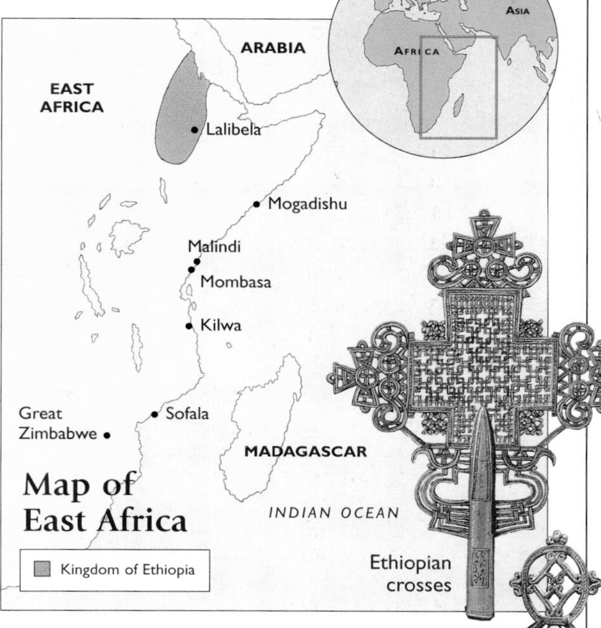

Map of East Africa

Ethiopian crosses

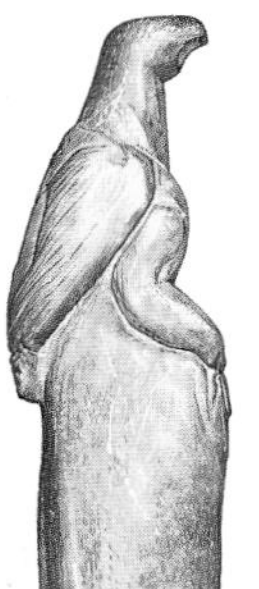

Stone bird from Great Zimbabwe

City of gold

People from all over southeast Africa brought gold to the city of Great Zimbabwe. The gold was collected in the city, then sent on to ports along the coast. The rulers of Great Zimbabwe became rich and powerful. They lived inside a walled fortress in the middle of the city.

The kingdom of Ethiopia

The Christian kingdom of Ethiopia was created around 1000. King Lalibela of Ethiopia believed that God had ordered him to carve churches out of rock. He built 11 churches which became very famous and the kingdom's main city was named after him.

One of King Lalibela's churches

This picture shows the fortress at Great Zimbabwe.

Important dates

c.1000	The kingdom of Ethiopia is created.
c.1000-1200	Trading ports grow up on the east coast of Africa.
1200-1230	King Lalibela's churches are built in Ethiopia.
c.1350	Great Zimbabwe is at its largest.

1100 1200 1300 1400 1500

Kingdoms of West Africa

Arab merchants

By the year 800, Arab merchants from North Africa were crossing the Sahara Desert to trade with the people of West Africa. The West Africans grew rich by trading gold, slaves, and ivory from elephants' tusks, and many powerful kingdoms grew up (see map).

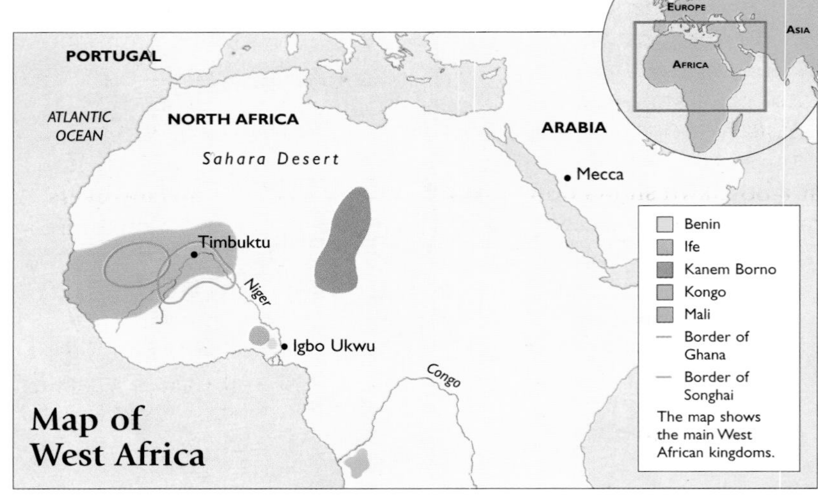

Map of West Africa

Kingdoms of gold

Between 300 and 1600, three great kingdoms rose and fell in the area south of the Sahara Desert. The kingdom of Ghana was followed by Mali and then by Songhai. Their people mined gold from rocks and their rulers became fabulously wealthy.

Rock with a crust of gold

Mansa Musa of Mali

The most famous West African ruler was King Mansa Musa of Mali. He was a Muslim and a strict, but fair, ruler. He went on a pilgrimage (religious journey) to Mecca in Arabia, giving away presents of gold as he went.

This map shows King Mansa Musa with an Arab merchant.

The city of Timbuktu

Timbuktu was one of Mali's most important cities. It had a large royal palace, a famous university, and many beautiful mosques. Muslim scholars from all over West Africa came to study at Timbuktu.

This picture shows part of the city of Timbuktu.

500 600 700 800 900

Rulers of the forest

By 800, there were several kingdoms in the forests around the mouth of the Niger. Most of the rulers of these kingdoms were priests, as well as kings. A burial chamber found at Igbo Ukwu shows how priest-kings were buried.

Cutaway picture of a ruler's burial chamber

The kingdom of Ife

The forest kingdom of Ife (pronounced "ee-feh") grew up around 1000. Its people were expert metalworkers who discovered a way of making figures from bronze. They made portraits of their past rulers and prayed to them.

★ Bronze head of a ruler from Ife

The kingdom of Benin

The richest forest kingdom was Benin. Its craftworkers made delicate ivory carvings and spectacular bronze statues, and its ruler (called an oba) lived in an enormous palace. Elaborate religious ceremonies were held at the palace.

★ A drummer at the oba's palace

The Portuguese arrive

In 1445, ships from Portugal reached the mouth of the Congo. Over the next 50 years, the Portuguese built trading towns along the West African coast. Some of the forest kingdoms, such as Benin, became very rich by trading with the Portuguese.

A Portuguese trading ship, called a caravel

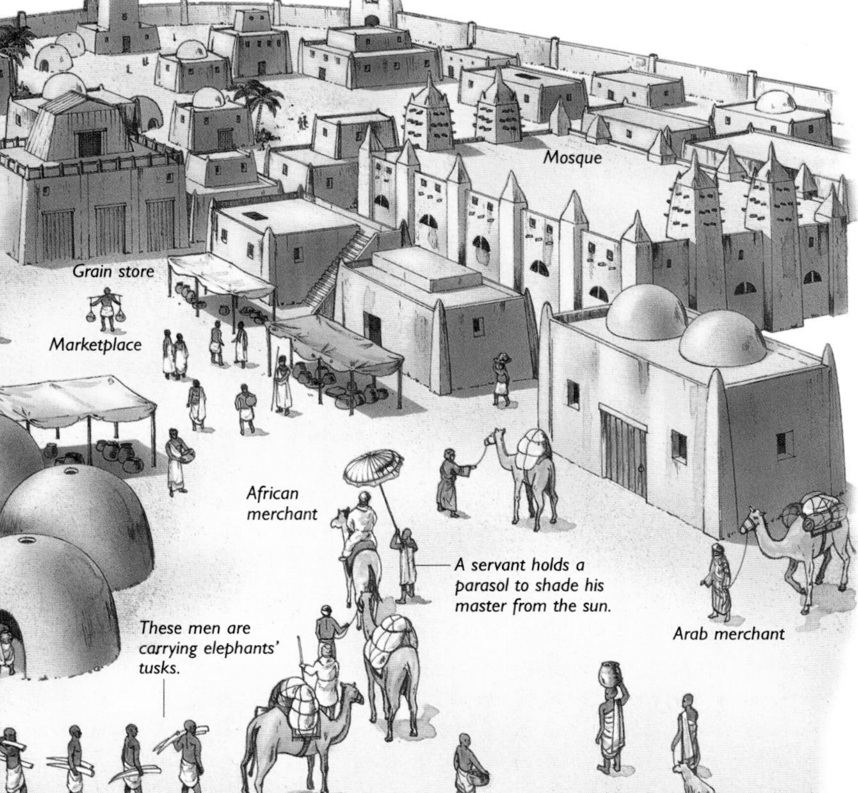

Important dates

c.300-1200	Kingdom of Ghana
c.800-1000	Kingdom of Igbo Ukwu
c.1000-1450	Kingdom of Ife
c.1000-1897	Kingdom of Benin
c.1200-1500	Kingdom of Mali
c.1312-1337	Mansa Musa rules Mali.
c.1350-1600	Kingdom of Songhai
c.1450	The Portuguese start trading in West Africa.

1100 1200 1300 1400 1500

Conquerors of Northern India

India split into small kingdoms around the year 550. These kingdoms were ruled by Hindu kings who prayed to many gods. The kingdoms of the south lasted for the next thousand years, but the kingdoms of the north were gradually conquered by Muslims.

An Indian king

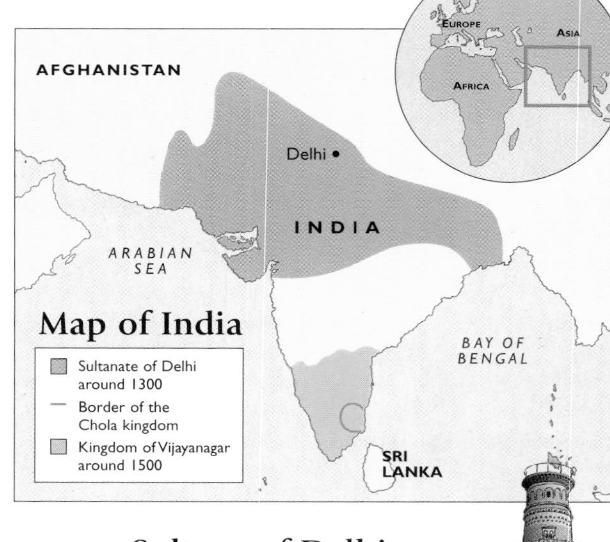

Map of India

Muslim invaders

Arab armies began invading northwest India in 711. The Arabs set up several peaceful Muslim kingdoms, but, around 1000, Mahmud of Ghazni led a series of savage raids on India from Afghanistan. Almost 200 years later, another Afghan, Muhammud of Ghur, conquered most of northern India. He killed hundreds of Indians and destroyed many Hindu temples.

Indian troops fighting Afghan invaders

Hindu temple

The Afghans surround the Indians.

The Afghans ride swift horses.

The Indian war elephants move very slowly.

Sultans of Delhi

In 1206, a Turkish soldier called Aibak took control of northern India and made himself Sultan (king) of Delhi. The sultans ruled for the next 300 years. They were great builders, but cruel rulers.

Sultan Aibak built this tower to celebrate his victories.

Mongol raiders

In 1398, the Mongol leader Tamerlane led a savage attack on the city of Delhi. The Mongols massacred most of the people of Delhi and left the sultans very weak.

500 600 700 800 900

Kingdoms of Southern India

The Hindu kings of southern India lived in beautiful palaces surrounded by towering temples. Holy men, called brahmans, helped the kings to govern, and hundreds of servants worked in the palaces and temples.

This picture shows an Indian king and his court. ★

The Chola kingdom

One of the most successful southern kingdoms was Chola. Its kings built up a great empire and sent merchants to Arabia and China. Chola craftworkers were famous for their graceful bronze statues.

Chola statue of a Hindu god ★

Vijayanagar fights back

Around 1300, the Muslim sultans of Delhi began to attack southern India. They won land rapidly until 1336 when two brothers created the new Hindu kingdom of Vijayanagar. The new kingdom's army soon defeated the Muslims, and Vijayanagar became the most powerful kingdom in the south.

Important dates

711	Arabs start to invade northern India.
886-1267	The Chola kings control most of southern India.
1001-1026	Mahmud of Ghazni leads raids on northern India.
1193	Muhammud of Ghur conquers northern India.
1206-1526	The sultans of Delhi control most of northern India.
1336-1565	The kingdom of Vijayanagar is successful.
1398	The Mongols invade northern India.

Buddhist teachers

Although the kings of southern India were Hindus, they allowed Buddhist monks to set up universities and teach their religion. Buddhism spread from India all over Southeast Asia, and many Chinese Buddhists came to study in India.

Buddhist monks in Sri Lanka

1100 1200 1300 1400 1500

Kingdoms of Southeast Asia

Traders from India began arriving in Southeast Asia during the 2nd century. The local people learned about the Indian way of life, and set up small kingdoms like the ones in India. By the 800s, there were several powerful kingdoms on the mainland and islands of Southeast Asia.

Courtiers kneeling before a king of the Sukhothai kingdom

Map of Southeast Asia

CHINA
Mekong
SOUTH CHINA SEA
Angkor
ANDAMAN SEA
INDIAN OCEAN
ASIA
AUSTRALIA

- Pagan kingdom
- Sukhothai kingdom
- Khmer kingdom
- Champa kingdom
- Srivijaya kingdom
- Sailendra kingdom

Hindus

The Hindu religion spread from India throughout Southeast Asia, and the kings built magnificent temples where their people could worship Hindu gods. The people also prayed to their kings, who they thought of as gods.

Buddhists

Around the year 300, Buddhist monks from India brought their religion to Southeast Asia. Buddhism was popular, but it did not destroy the Hindu religion, and most of the kingdoms had temples for Hindus as well as for Buddhists.

Statue of the Buddha ★ from the Sukhothai kingdom

People bringing gifts to a Hindu temple

Warring kingdoms

The kings of Southeast Asia were often at war with each other. Sometimes, warriors sailed over seas or along rivers to make surprise attacks on another kingdom.

Warriors from the Champa kingdom rowing up a river

500 600 700 800 900

Internet link: *For a link to a Web site with a great collection of photographs of Angkor Wat, go to* **www.usborne-quicklinks.com**

The Khmer kingdom

The greatest kingdom in Southeast Asia was ruled by the Khmers. Their capital city, Angkor, housed half a million people and was built close to a lake. The people of Angkor dug reservoirs to hold floodwater from the lake, and their farmers used the water to grow rice all through the year.

This picture shows a procession in the city of Angkor.

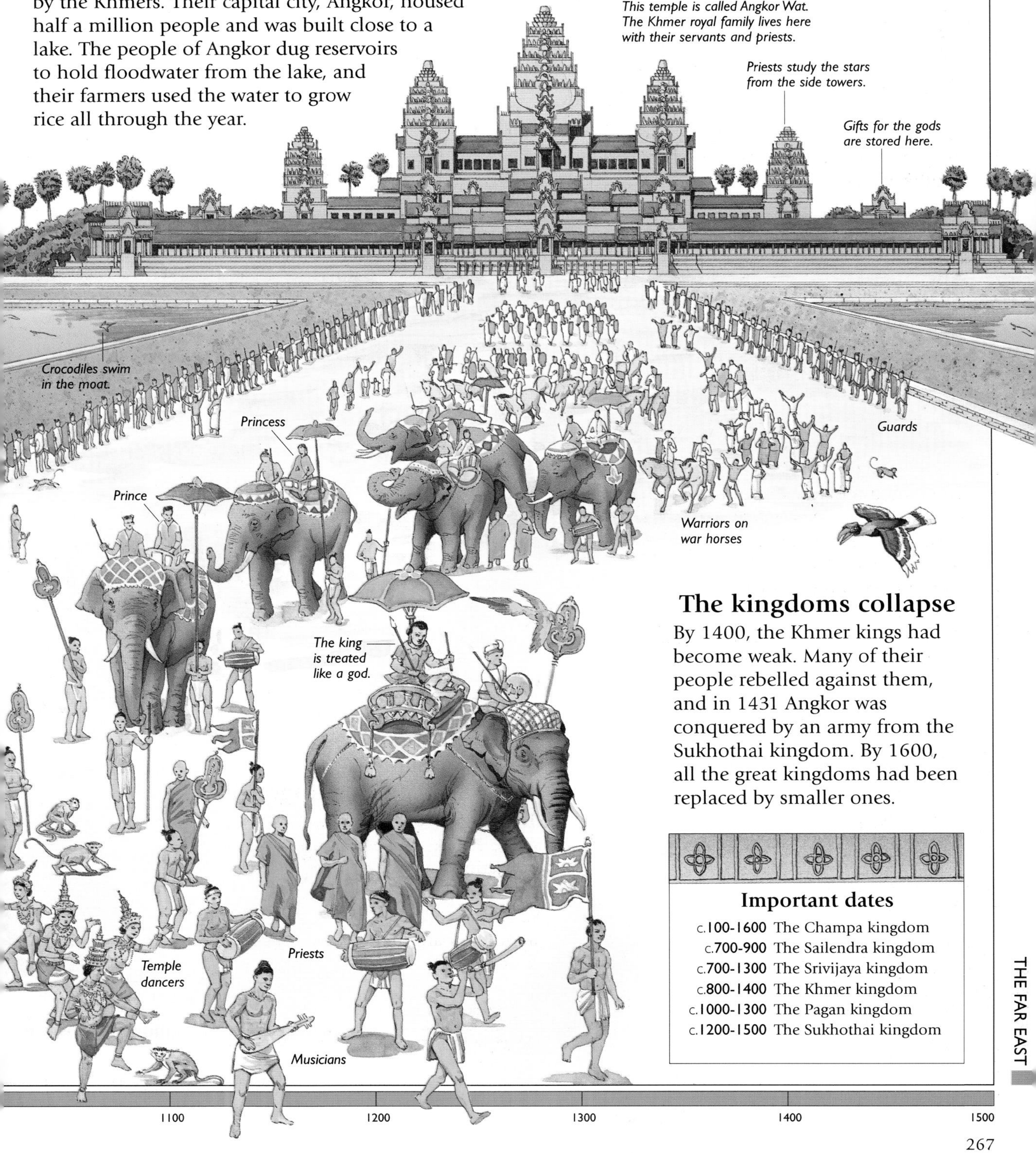

This temple is called Angkor Wat. The Khmer royal family lives here with their servants and priests.

Priests study the stars from the side towers.

Gifts for the gods are stored here.

Crocodiles swim in the moat.

Princess

Guards

Prince

Warriors on war horses

The king is treated like a god.

Temple dancers

Priests

Musicians

The kingdoms collapse

By 1400, the Khmer kings had become weak. Many of their people rebelled against them, and in 1431 Angkor was conquered by an army from the Sukhothai kingdom. By 1600, all the great kingdoms had been replaced by smaller ones.

Important dates

c.100-1600	The Champa kingdom
c.700-900	The Sailendra kingdom
c.700-1300	The Srivijaya kingdom
c.800-1400	The Khmer kingdom
c.1000-1300	The Pagan kingdom
c.1200-1500	The Sukhothai kingdom

1100 1200 1300 1400 1500

Dynasties of China

In 581, a ruling family (or dynasty) called the Sui took control of China. The Sui emperors built a network of canals, which made it much easier for merchants to travel around the country.

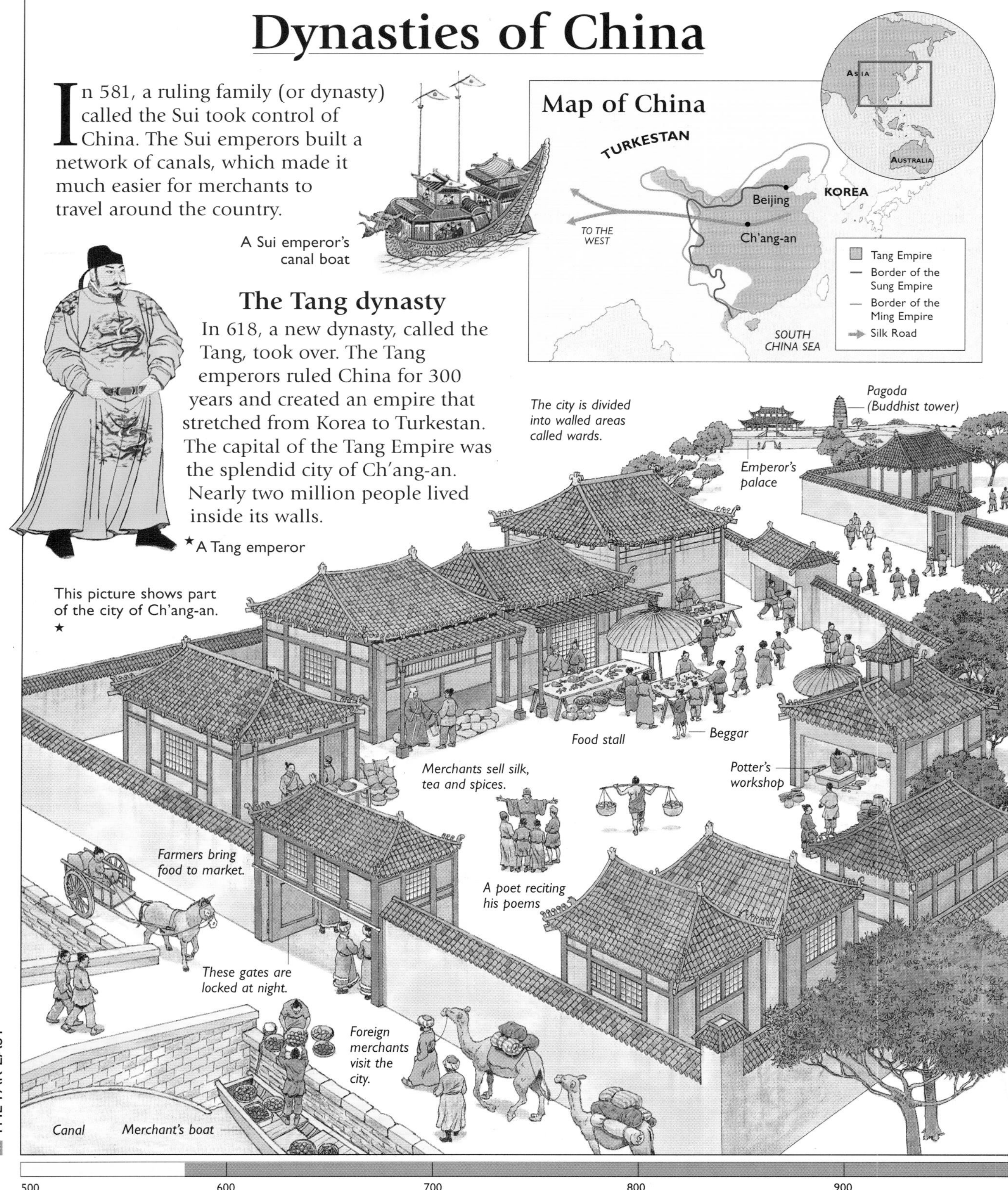

A Sui emperor's canal boat

The Tang dynasty

In 618, a new dynasty, called the Tang, took over. The Tang emperors ruled China for 300 years and created an empire that stretched from Korea to Turkestan. The capital of the Tang Empire was the splendid city of Ch'ang-an. Nearly two million people lived inside its walls.

★A Tang emperor

This picture shows part of the city of Ch'ang-an. ★

500 600 700 800 900

Tang inventions

During the Tang period, the Chinese discovered how to make gunpowder and a kind of fine pottery now called china. They also began to print on paper, using wooden stamps.

At first, gunpowder was only used for fireworks.

The Sung dynasty

By 900, the Tang emperors had beome very weak, and in 960 the Sung family took control of China. Under the Sung emperors, the Chinese had little contact with the outside world, but they continued to produce beautiful china and paintings.

Sung artists often painted scenes from daily life.

The Ming dynasty

In 1368, a Buddhist monk called Chu Yuan-chang led a rebellion against the Mongols and started the Ming dynasty. The Ming emperors built up a strong army and encouraged trade, exploration and art. They ruled from Beijing, which became one of the world's greatest cities.

★ Ming china is famous for its delicate patterns.

Adventurous traders

★ A Chinese trading ship, called a junk

Chinese merchants sailed as far away as Africa and also journeyed overland on a route known as the Silk Road. Traders on the Silk Road took silk, china and paper to the Middle East and Europe.

Mongol invaders

In 1211, tribes of Mongols began to invade China, and in 1279 the Mongol leader, Kublai Khan, became emperor (see page 251). Kublai Khan was visited by Marco Polo, a young merchant from Venice, who wrote about his travels in China.

Marco Polo at Kublai Khan's palace

Marco Polo brings gifts.

Guards

Chinese courtiers

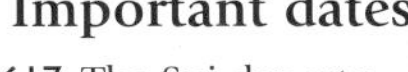

Important dates

581-617	The Sui dynasty
618-906	The Tang dynasty
960-1279	The Sung dynasty
1275-1292	Marco Polo visits China.
1280-1368	The Mongols rule China.
1368-1644	The Ming dynasty

Land of the Samurai

Chinese-style pagoda at Nara

By the year 500, a family of emperors called the Yamatos controlled most of Japan. They admired the way the Chinese emperors ruled China and they built their capital city, Nara, to look like the Chinese city of Ch'ang-an. (See pages 268 and 269 to find out more about China.)

The emperor's court

In 784, the emperor moved his court to Heian (modern Kyoto), where he lived a life of luxury, cut off from ordinary people. Many clever women lived at the court and one of these courtiers, Lady Murasaki Shikibu, wrote the world's first novel, called *The Tale of Genji*.

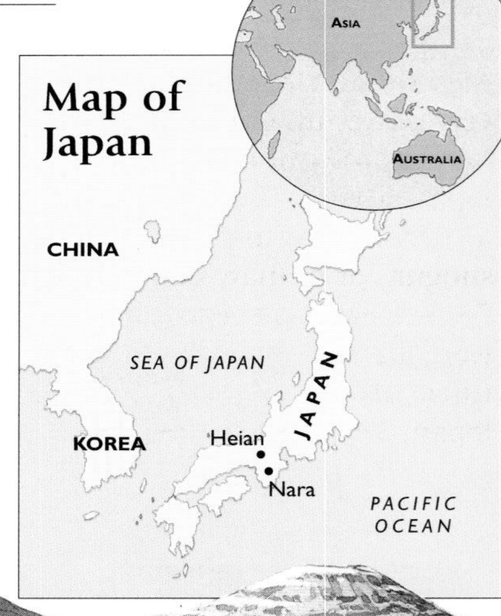

Shinto and Buddhism

Entrance to a Shinto shrine

Shinto was the local religion of Japan. Its followers believed in spirits that lived in rocks, trees and streams. Around 600, Buddhist monks from China and Korea brought their religion to Japan. Buddhism spread fast, but Shinto did not die out.

Japanese statue of the Buddha

The emperor and his courtiers at Heian

500 600 700 800 900

Nobles and shoguns

The emperors gradually gave away land to noble families. At first, the Fujiwara family were very powerful, but in 1192 the Minamatos gained control of Japan. The emperor made Minamato Yoritomo the first shogun, or military commander. For the next 700 years, shoguns were the real rulers of Japan.

Minamato Yoritomo, the first shogun

Noh plays

Actors performed dramas, called "Noh" plays, to entertain noble families. The actors were all men, and wore masks to show what sort of characters they played. A Noh play combined music, singing, dancing and poetry.

★ Noh masks

Jobs in Japan

Rice farmers working in flooded fields, known as paddy fields

Most Japanese people were rice farmers who worked on their lord's land. Others worked as fishermen, miners, paper-makers, silk-makers, sword-makers and carpenters. Farmers and craftworkers took their goods to sell in the towns.

Sword-makers sharpening blades

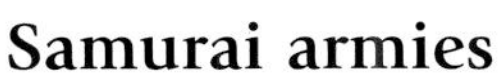

Samurai armies

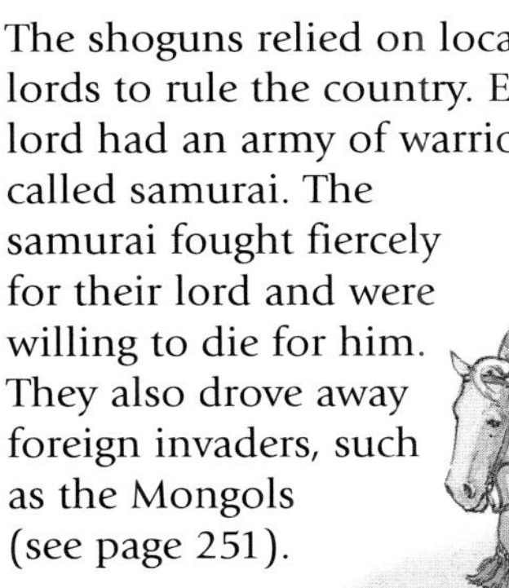

The shoguns relied on local lords to rule the country. Each lord had an army of warriors, called samurai. The samurai fought fiercely for their lord and were willing to die for him. They also drove away foreign invaders, such as the Mongols (see page 251).

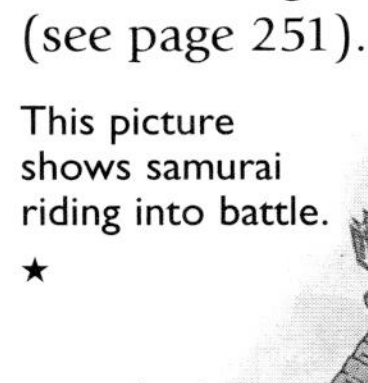

This picture shows samurai riding into battle. ★

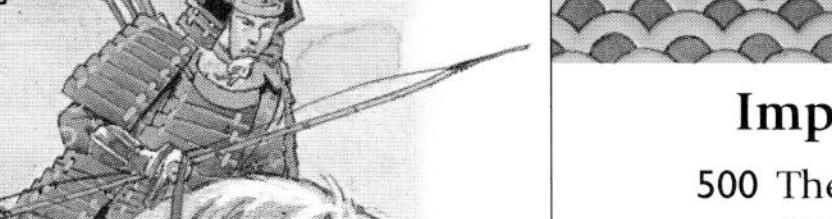

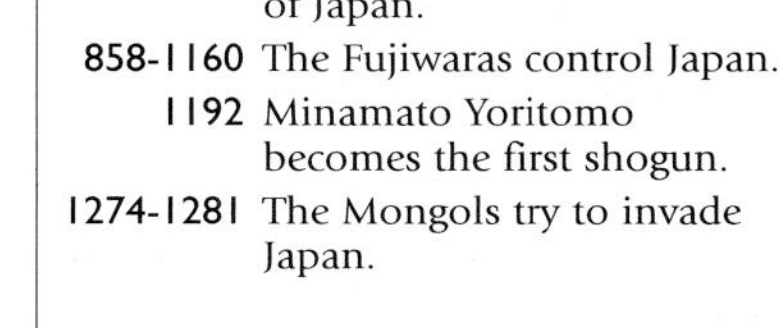

Important dates

500	The Yamato emperors control most of Japan.
710	Nara becomes the capital of Japan.
794	Heian becomes the capital of Japan.
858-1160	The Fujiwaras control Japan.
1192	Minamato Yoritomo becomes the first shogun.
1274-1281	The Mongols try to invade Japan.

1100 1200 1300 1400 1500

Explorers and Sailors

RUSSIA
Venice
Fez
Mecca
ARABIA
AFRICA
INDIA
CHINA
Beijing
Nanking
Ch'ang-an
PACIFIC OCEAN
INDIAN OCEAN
INDONESIA

Marco Polo brought back ginger from China.

Map of explorers' routes

- Hsuan-tsang's route
- Marco Polo's route
- Ibn Batuta's main journeys
- Cheng Ho's main voyages

Ibn Batuta sailed in a boat called a dhow.

Travel in the Middle Ages was very difficult and dangerous, but a few brave explorers set out on amazing jouneys. Although traders had reached Africa, India and China, these countries were almost completely unexplored.

Ibn Batuta's dream

Ibn Batuta was a wealthy Muslim from Fez in North Africa. When he was 21, he went on a pilgrimage (religious journey) to Mecca, in Arabia. On the way, he dreamed that a huge bird was carrying him over the Muslim world and beyond. This dream inspired him to spend his life exploring.

Ibn Batuta's dream

A lifetime of travel

An Indian sultan welcoming Ibn Batuta

Ibn Batuta's first journey took him to Arabia, southern Russia and India. Then, he sailed to China. On his second great expedition, he explored parts of Africa. Ibn Batuta covered over 120,000km (75,000 miles) during his 30 years of travel.

500 600 700 800 900

Hsuan-tsang goes west

In the 7th century, a Buddhist monk called Hsuan-tsang made the long and dangerous journey from Ch'ang-an in China to northern India. He spent 16 years visiting Indian monasteries and temples. Then, he returned to China with hundreds of manuscripts and statues.

Hsuan-tsang

Marco Polo goes east

Marco Polo left Venice for China when he was 17. He journeyed overland for three and a half years with his father and uncle. In Beijing, the Polos were welcomed by the Mongol emperor, Kublai Khan (see page 269). Marco Polo stayed in China for 17 years, before sailing back to Venice. He told many stories about the sights he had seen and the legends he had heard.

Marco Polo told a story about a man-monster with a single foot.

Cheng Ho's voyages

A Chinese explorer named Cheng Ho went on seven great voyages to Indonesia, Arabia and Africa. He sailed with over 300 ships (called junks), and brought back amazing treasures, such as gold, ivory and wild animals.

This picture shows Cheng Ho returning to China from Africa.

The Chinese emperor waits to welcome Cheng Ho.

Merchants, priests and translators all went on the voyage.

Cheng Ho

Important dates

c.628-645	Hsuan-tsang's travels
1271-1295	Marco Polo's travels
c.1325-1355	Ibn Batuta's travels
1405-1433	Cheng Ho's voyages

The People of the Pacific

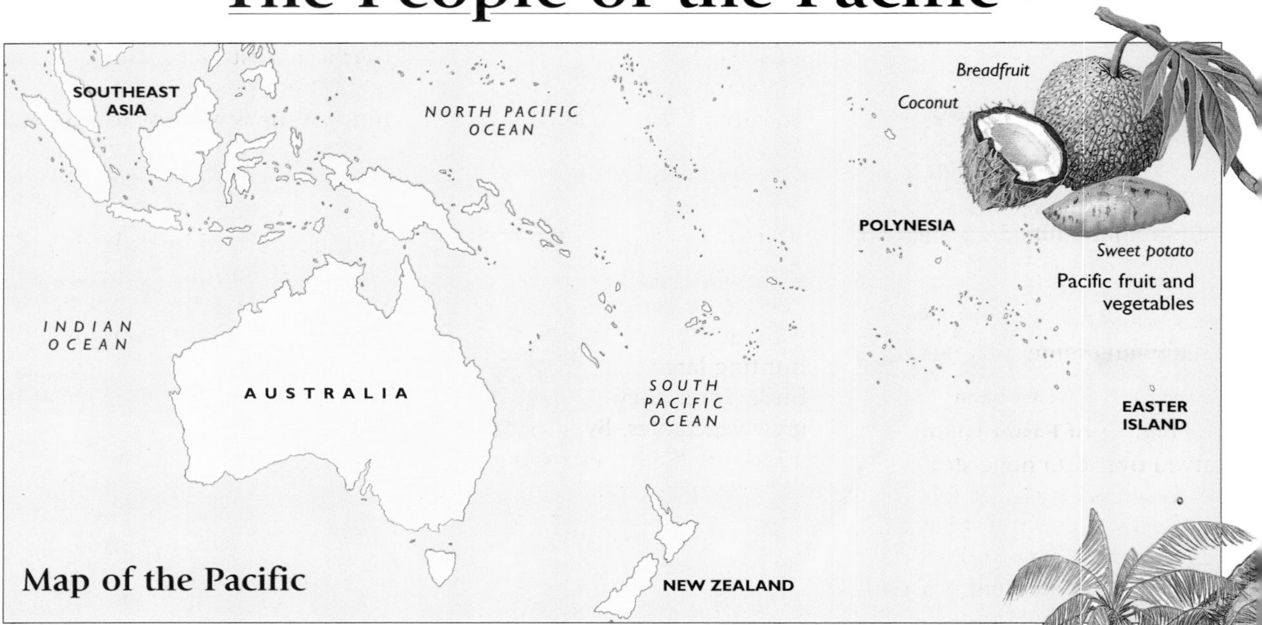

Map of the Pacific

Pacific fruit and vegetables

Around 6,000 years ago, settlers from Southeast Asia began arriving in the islands of the Pacific Ocean. They were skilled sailors who studied the winds, stars and ocean currents to help them find their way around. Very slowly, the settlers spread out. By around 400, they had reached as far east as Easter Island.

Island life

Most of the Pacific islanders lived in small tribes ruled by powerful chiefs. They went fishing, gathered fruit, grew vegetables, and kept pigs, dogs and chickens. The islanders prayed to many gods and offered them sacrifices.

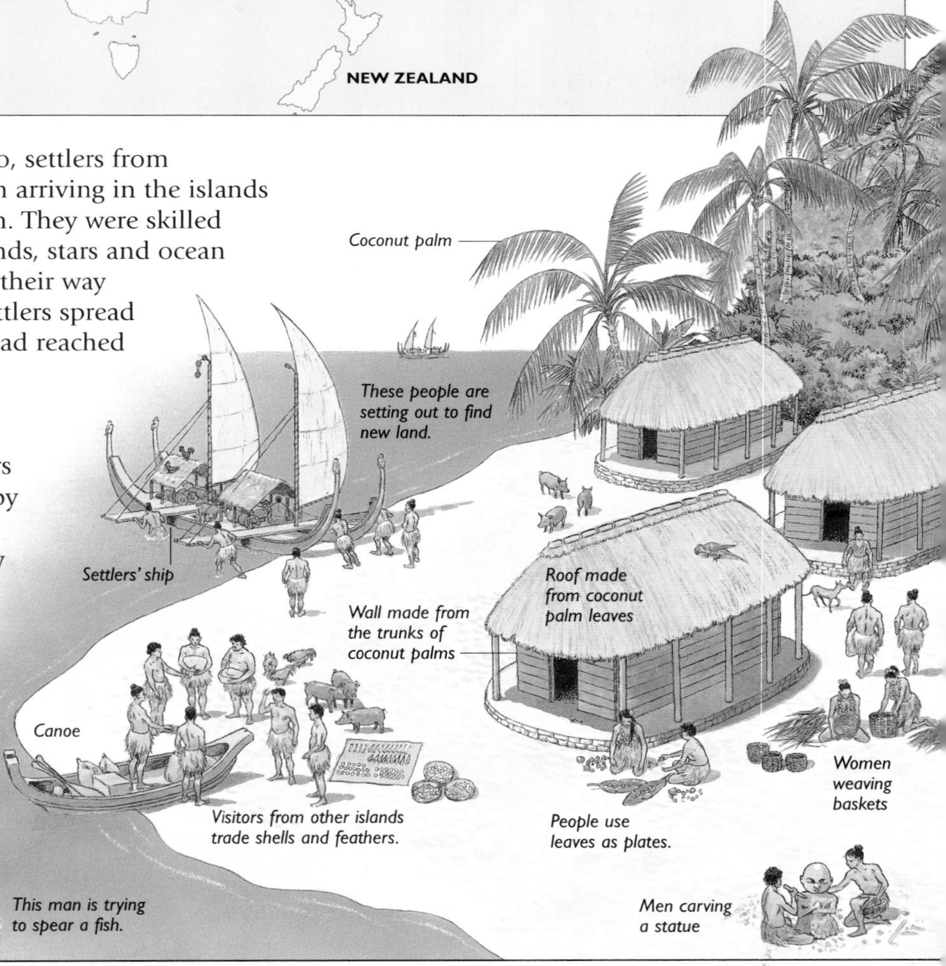

This picture shows a Pacific island village.

500 600 700 800 900

Big heads

Carved heads on Easter Island

The people of Easter Island carved over 600 huge stone heads and stood them on platforms all around the coast. These statues were probably meant to represent powerful chiefs. Some of them are over 12m (40ft) tall.

Banana plant

This man is planting sweet potatoes.

Tower built for a god

These people are bringing offerings to one of their gods.

Maori settlers

Around 750, a tribe called the Maoris set sail from the islands of Polynesia and reached New Zealand. At first, they survived by fishing, gathering fruit, and hunting large birds. Later, they grew vegetables. By 1500, the Maoris had become very warlike.

★ Maori chief

Spirits and taboos

The Maoris prayed to the spirits of their dead ancestors. They also believed that certain people and places were sacred. These sacred people and places were called "tapu", or taboo.

★ Good luck charm showing an ancestor

The first Australians

The Aboriginal people arrived in northern Australia around 40,000 years ago. They walked most of the way from Southeast Asia on land that is now under the sea. Slowly, they spread out all over Australia. The Aboriginals lived by gathering plants and hunting animals. Hunters used boomerangs to help them catch their prey.

Aboriginal hunters ★

Dream time spirits

Aboriginals believe that they were created by spirits who lived in a time called the dream time. Some of the spirits were humans, and some were animals and plants.

Painting of the Rainbow Serpent giving birth to the Aboriginal people

Important dates

c.400	Settlers reach Easter Island.
c.750	The Maoris reach New Zealand.
c.1000-1600	The Easter Islanders build huge stone heads.

1100 1200 1300 1400 1500

Native North Americans

Inuits

The people of North America had many different ways of life. In the frozen north, Inuits hunted seals and lived in igloos. In the forests, woodland people hunted deer, and gathered nuts and berries. The tribes of the northwest survived mainly by fishing, and the people around the Great Plains grew corn and hunted buffalo. Other ways of life began in the deserts of the southwest and around the Mississippi River.

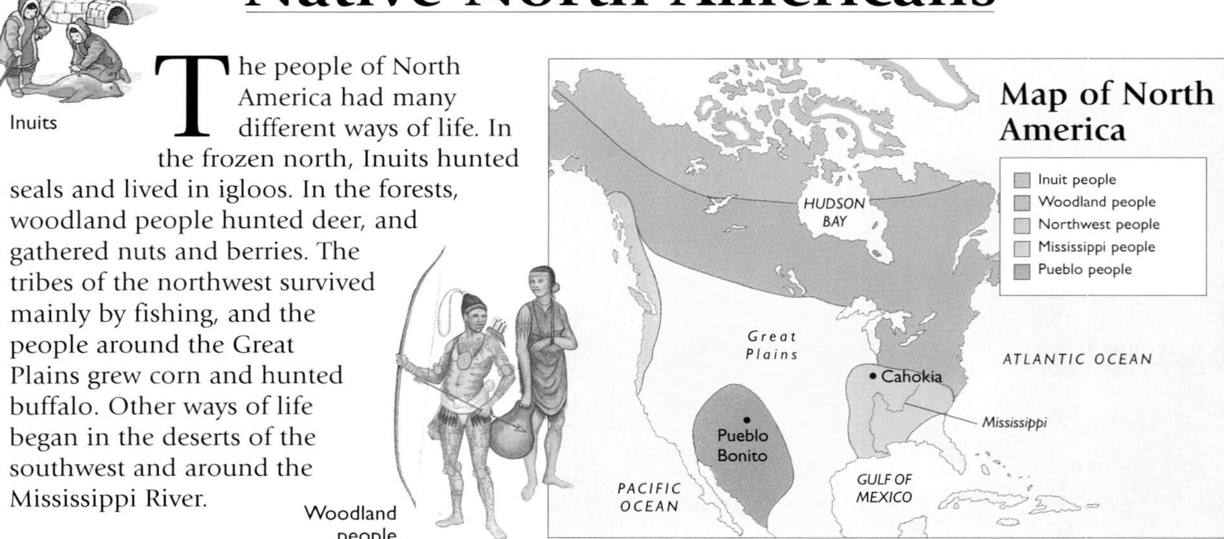

Woodland people

This picture shows a town in the Mississippi Valley. One house has been cut away so you can see inside. ★

Temple

Chief's house

Priests

Earth mound

Central square

Grain store

Hunters

The chief is carried by his servants.

Potter's house

Mississippi towns

Around 700, the farmers of the Mississippi Valley began to build towns. In the middle of the towns were groups of flat-topped mounds. The biggest town, Cahokia, had over a hundred mounds. Chiefs were buried under the mounds with pots, carvings and jewels.

★

Clay bottles made by Mississippi potters

500 600 700 800 900

Pueblo people

Around 750, some desert tribes in the southwest began to build villages with rooms stacked one above the other. Villages built like this were called pueblos, and the people who lived in them became known as the Pueblos.

In this picture of a pueblo, one house has been cut away to show what is happening inside. ★

This woman is repairing a wall.

People use ladders to reach their roofs.

The walls are made from dried mud, called adobe.

Weavers make cotton clothes and rugs.

Dried meat

Women grind corn.

Farmers grow corn, beans and cotton.

Potters make and decorate pots.

Clay pots are baked in ovens called kilns.

During the day, people work and eat on the roofs of their houses.

Trading towns

Towns grew up in places where the Pueblo people met to trade with each other and with people from other tribes.

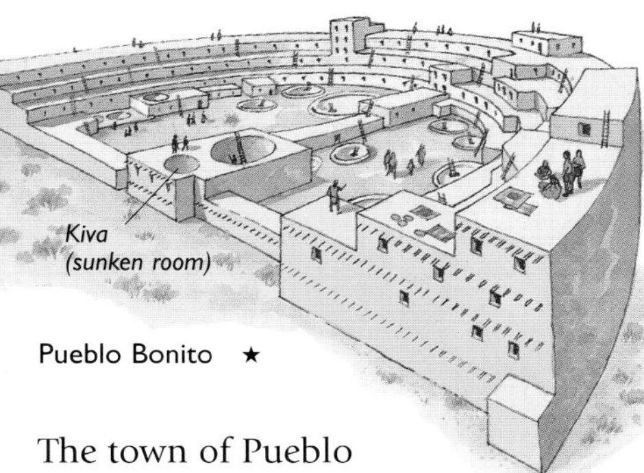

Pueblo Bonito ★

The town of Pueblo Bonito was built inside a deep valley and surrounded by a vast network of roads. It housed around 1200 people in 800 rooms. In the middle of the town were several sunken rooms, called kivas. These rooms were used for religious ceremonies and meetings.

Pueblo crafts

Carvers made ornaments from polished stone, weavers made clothes from brightly dyed cotton, and potters made jugs and pots that were covered with bold patterns.

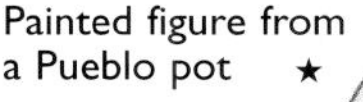

Painted figure from a Pueblo pot ★

Pueblo jug ★

Pierced pots

Special pots were placed in the graves of Pueblo chiefs. The pots were pierced to release the spirits of their painted figures.

Burial pot ★

Important dates

- c.700 The Mississippi people begin to build towns.
- c.750 The Pueblo people begin to build villages.
- c.1300 The Pueblo people abandon their towns and villages.
- c.1500 The Mississippi people abandon their towns.

1100 1200 1300 1400 1500

The Aztec Empire

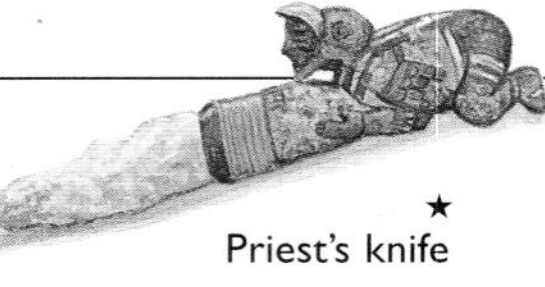

★ Priest's knife

North America
Europe
Africa
South America
Aztec Empire at its largest
GULF OF MEXICO
MEXICO
Tenochtitlán
Lake Texcoco

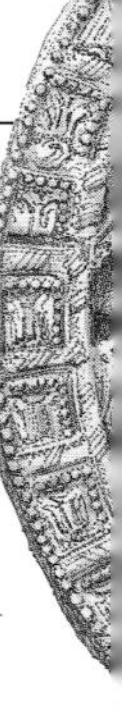

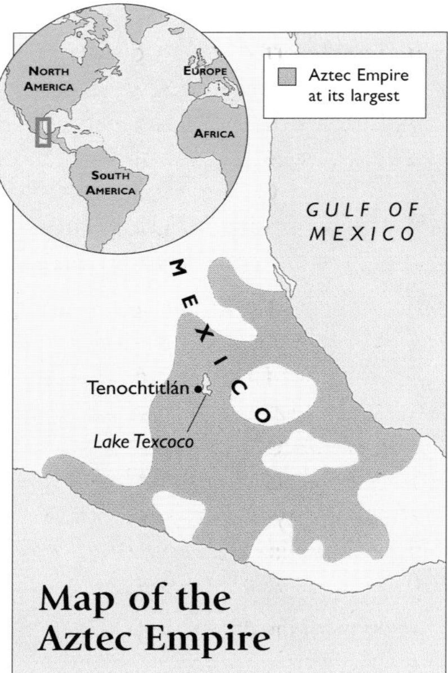

Map of the Aztec Empire

The Aztecs were wandering, warlike people who arrived in central Mexico around 1300. They settled on an island in Lake Texcoco and started to build the village of Tenochtitlán. Over the next 200 years, Tenochtitlán grew into a great city and the Aztecs built up an empire around it.

The city on a lake

Tenochtitlán spread over a group of islands at the edge of Lake Texcoco. In the middle of the city was a beautiful square, filled with temples where priests held ceremonies.

Sacrifices to the sun

The Aztecs believed that their sun god, Huitzilopochtli, might die unless they kept him strong. To keep him alive, they fed him human hearts. Priests cut out their victims' hearts, then hurled the bodies down the temple steps.

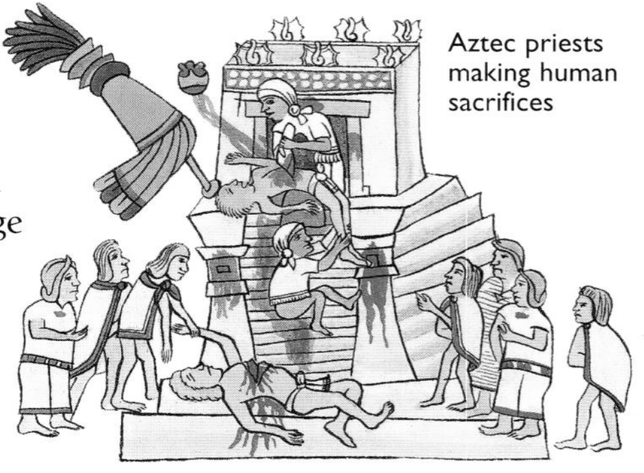

Aztec priests making human sacrifices

This picture shows part of the city of Tenochtitlán.

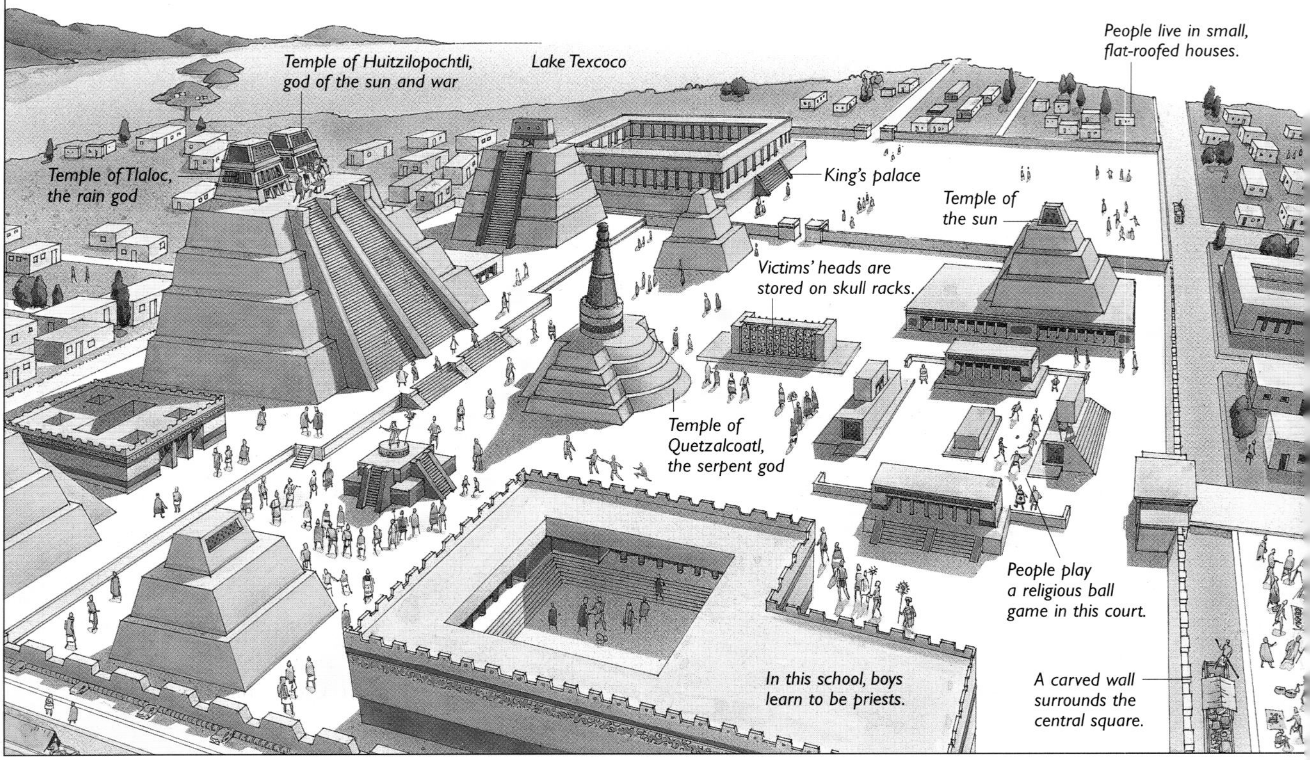

Temple of Huitzilopochtli, god of the sun and war
Lake Texcoco
People live in small, flat-roofed houses.
Temple of Tlaloc, the rain god
King's palace
Temple of the sun
Victims' heads are stored on skull racks.
Temple of Quetzalcoatl, the serpent god
People play a religious ball game in this court.
In this school, boys learn to be priests.
A carved wall surrounds the central square.

500 600 700 800 900

The Aztec year

It was important for the Aztecs to know when to hold their festivals. They divided the 365 days of the year into 18 months of 20 days each. The remaining 5 days were believed to be unlucky.

The outer rings of this calendar stone show the days of the year.

Aztec wars

The Aztec army fought constant wars against surrounding tribes. They forced the defeated tribes to give them food and treasure, and took thousands of prisoners to be sacrificed to their gods.

Aztec eagle knight ★

Floating fields

Farmers filled huge baskets with earth and floated them on lakes. In these floating fields, they grew corn, beans and chili peppers.

An Aztec god protecting a corn plant

Bird attacking the corn

Corn plant

God of planting and spring

Crafts

Many Aztecs worked as potters, weavers and carpenters. Sculptors carved huge statues, and craftworkers made beautiful objects from gold and feathers.

Gold pendant

Canoe

Bridges link plots of land.

Raised roads join the city to the mainland.

Merchants trade goods in the market.

Feathered costume

Shield made from feathers

★ Aztec warrior

The end of the Empire

In 1519, the Spanish soldier Hernando Cortés arrived in Mexico determined to conquer the Aztecs. The Aztecs were terrified by the Spanish guns and horses. Some thought that Quetzalcoatl, the serpent god, had come back to earth.

Mask of Quetzalcoatl

At first, Cortés did not attack the Aztecs, but in 1521 he invaded Tenochtitlán and conquered its people. After this defeat, many Aztecs died from European diseases and their way of life soon disappeared.

The defeat of the Aztecs

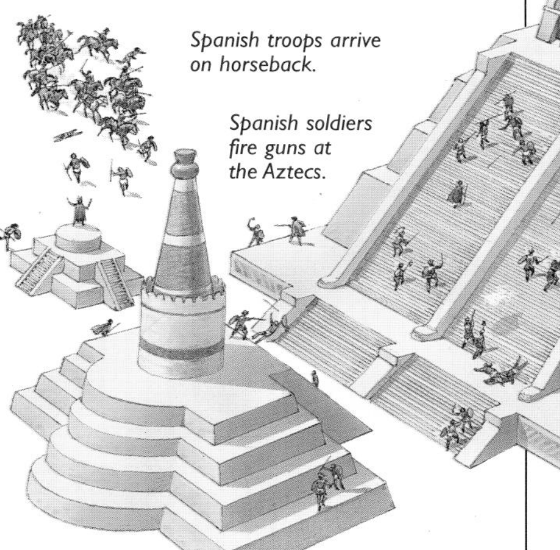

Important dates

c.1300	The Aztecs arrive in the Valley of Mexico.
c.1325	The Aztecs start to build Tenochtitlán.
1420s	The Aztecs begin to conquer the surrounding tribes.
c.1500	The Aztecs control the Valley of Mexico.
1521	Cortés conquers the Aztecs.

1100 1200 1300 1400 1500

The Maya and the Toltecs

The Maya people lived in small kingdoms in the rainforests and plains of Central America. They were ruled by powerful kings who were also priests and warriors.

A Mayan king with his servant

Gods and kings

The Maya prayed to many gods and gave them gifts of human blood. They also believed that their kings had godlike powers. Mayan kings were buried under temples and people prayed to them as if they were gods.

★

This jade mask was found in the tomb of a Mayan king.

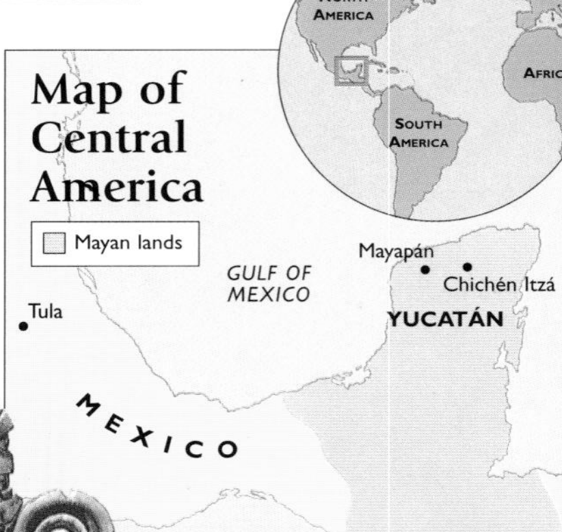

Cities of stone

Each Mayan kingdom had a splendid capital city built from stone. The king lived in the city with his nobles, warriors and priests. Farmers from the country brought food to the city and came to watch the spectacular ceremonies that were held there.

This picture shows a ceremony in a Mayan city.

★

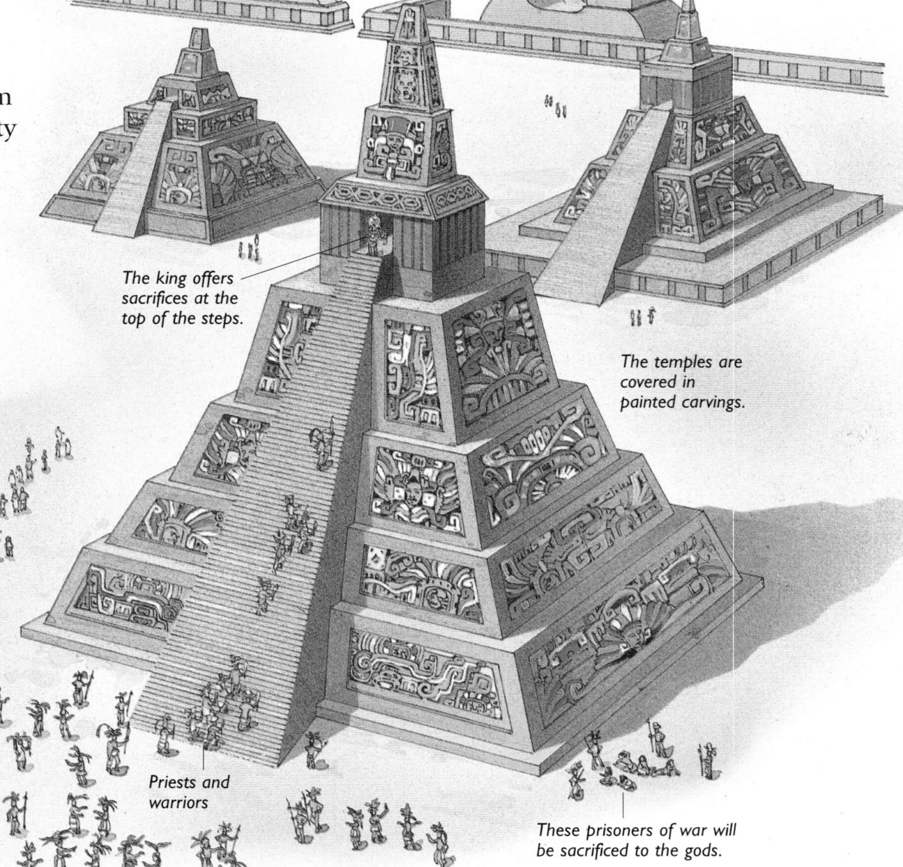

500 | 600 | 700 | 800 | 900

Game of life and death

Young warriors played a fast-moving ball game which was meant to symbolize the battle between life and death. At the end of the game, some players were put to death.

This picture shows a ball game. ★

Players hit a rubber ball with their arms, knees and hips.

Counting the days

Astronomer-priests studied the stars and invented two kinds of calendars. One was a very accurate 365-day calendar. The other was a religious guide which helped the priests to predict the future. They wrote out their calendars using special signs for words and numbers.

Part of a Mayan calendar

Dots, dashes and curved lines show dates.

Carving of a Toltec warrior

The rise of the Toltecs

Around 850, most of the Maya people moved north into an area known as the Yucatán. Meanwhile, in Mexico, the Toltecs were becoming powerful. The Toltecs controlled Mexico from their capital at Tula. They were warriors, traders and craftworkers.

The city of Chichén Itzá

In the 1100s, invading tribes drove the Toltecs out of Mexico and into the Yucatán. Many Toltecs settled in the Mayan city of Chichén Itzá. The city's Temple of the Warriors was probably built by the Maya and Toltec people working together.

Statue from the Temple of the Warriors

This bowl may have held human hearts which were offered to the gods.

The end of Chichén Itzá

Around 1160, fierce tribes from the north began invading Chichén Itzá. The Toltecs were scattered, and the Maya moved to new cities, such as Mayapán. By 1500, however, the Mayan kingdoms had shrunk to just a few small towns.

Important dates

c.600	The Maya are at their most successful.
c.850	The Maya abandon their cities in the south.
c.900-1000	The Toltecs are powerful in Mexico.
c.1100	The Toltecs arrive in Chichén Itzá.
c.1160	Chichén Itzá is invaded and the Toltecs are scattered.
c.1500	The Maya live in just a few small towns.

1100 1200 1300 1400 1500

Empires of the Andes

The strip of land between the Andes Mountains and the Pacific Ocean was home to several tribes, but one of the most powerful groups was the Chimú. Around 1100, the Chimú people began to conquer other tribes and started building up an empire.

★ Gold knife showing a Chimú noble

The rise of the Incas

The Incas lived in a small mountain kingdom around the city of Cuzco, but in 1438 their ruler, Pachacuti, set out to win more land. The Incas defeated the Chimú and won large areas of land in the south, creating an empire that stretched along most of the Pacific coast.

Inca warriors ★

Map of the Chimú and Inca Empires

The city of Chan Chan

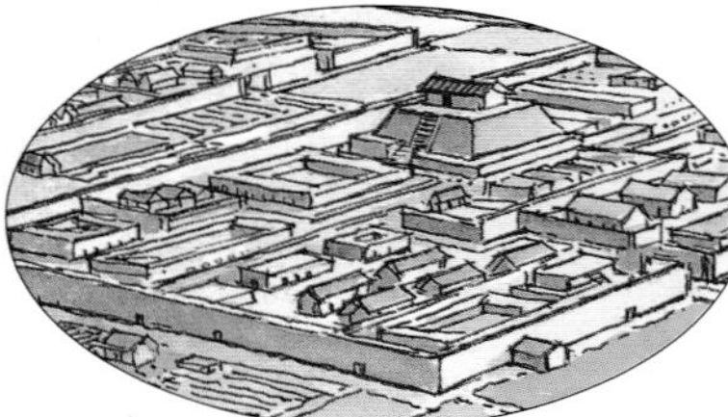

Part of the Chimú city of Chan Chan

By 1200, the Chimú ruler and his nobles controlled a large empire from their capital city at Chan Chan. Potters, weavers and goldsmiths all worked in the city, and farmers brought in food from the surrounding countryside.

Fish design

Chimú pottery jar

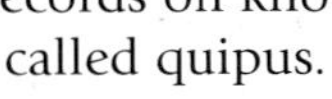

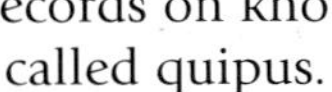

Chimú painting of a man with a serpent

Keeping count

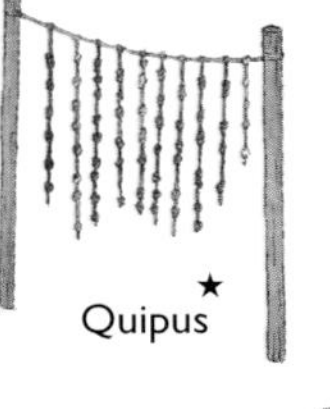

Quipus ★

The Inca Empire was very well organized and everyone had some kind of work to do. People were fed when food was short, and cared for when they were sick. To make sure the Empire ran smoothly, officials kept records on knotted cords, called quipus.

Cities of stone

Even though they had no wheeled vehicles or metal tools, the Incas built amazing cities from stone. The cities had temples, observatories and palaces, as well as ordinary homes.

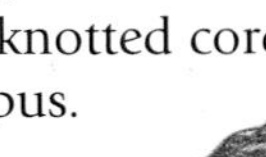

The mountain city of Machu Picchu ★

On the road

A network of roads linked all the parts of the Inca Empire. These roads were used by farmers, traders, messengers and soldiers. The emperor made frequent journeys through his lands to make sure that all his people stayed loyal to him.

This picture shows an Inca emperor on a journey through his empire.

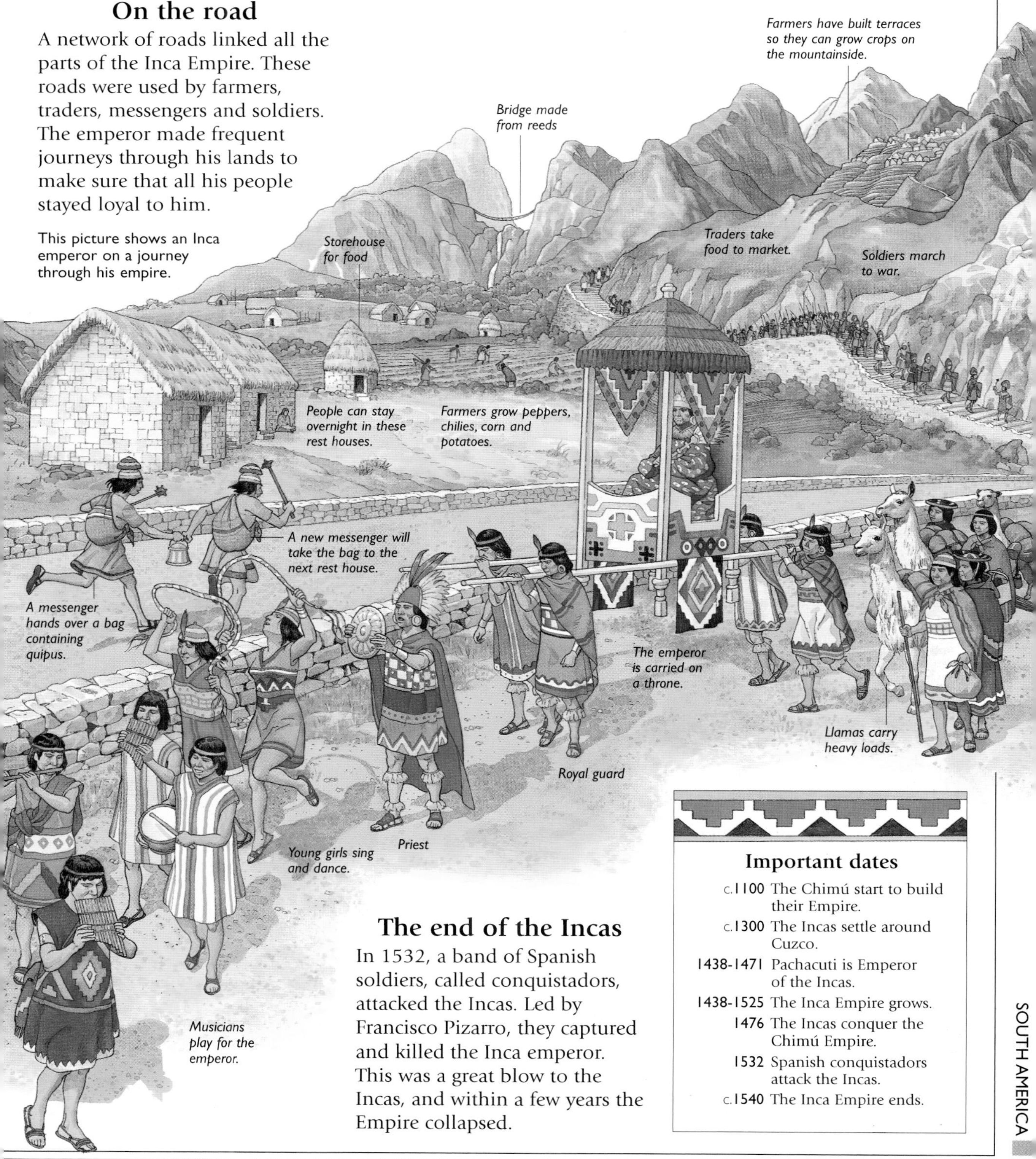

The end of the Incas

In 1532, a band of Spanish soldiers, called conquistadors, attacked the Incas. Led by Francisco Pizarro, they captured and killed the Inca emperor. This was a great blow to the Incas, and within a few years the Empire collapsed.

Important dates

c.1100	The Chimú start to build their Empire.
c.1300	The Incas settle around Cuzco.
1438-1471	Pachacuti is Emperor of the Incas.
1438-1525	The Inca Empire grows.
1476	The Incas conquer the Chimú Empire.
1532	Spanish conquistadors attack the Incas.
c.1540	The Inca Empire ends.

Artists of Italy

Around 1350, artists and thinkers in northern Italy became very interested in the art, architecture and learning of ancient Greece and Rome. They began to try out new ideas based on what they had learned. This movement is known as the Renaissance, which means "rebirth".

Patrons

Princes, popes and merchants paid money to artists, architects and writers and encouraged them to create works of art. Rich people who supported artists were known as patrons.

Medal showing Lorenzo de' Medici, a famous patron

★

Florence and the Medicis

The most powerful patrons of the Renaissance were the Medicis, a family of bankers from Florence. The Medicis encouraged artists and scholars to work in their city, and many new ideas were first tried out in Florence.

This picture shows the main square in Florence.

500 600 700 800 900

Architects

Architects designed buildings with pillars, rounded arches and domes. This style of building was created by the Greeks and Romans and is called classical architecture.

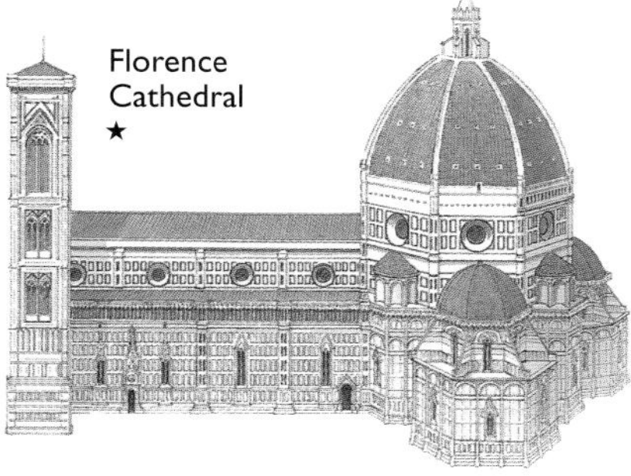

One of the first examples of the new classical style was the dome of Florence Cathedral, designed by the architect Brunelleschi.

This covered area is called a loggia. People hold meetings here.

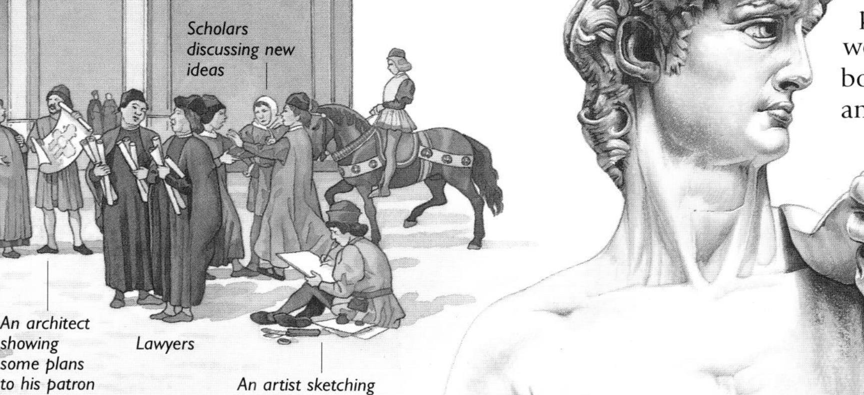

Painters

Primavera, by the painter Sandro Botticelli, shows a legend about the coming of Spring.

Inspired by Greek and Roman art, painters tried to make their pictures look as lifelike as possible. They discovered that things in the distance look smaller than things that are close up. They used this effect, called perspective, to give their pictures a feeling of depth.

Before the Renaissance, artists in Europe painted mainly religious pictures, but by 1400 the artists of Italy had become much more adventurous. As well as religious pictures, they painted portraits, landscapes, recent events, and scenes from Greek and Roman legends.

Sculptors

Sculptors copied Greek and Roman statues and used real people as models for their work. They even examined dead bodies to find out how bones and muscles worked. The statues of the Renaissance looked lifelike, strong and graceful.

Statue of David, a famous character in the Bible, by the sculptor and painter Michelangelo
★

1100 1200 1300 1400 1500

Ideas and Inventions

By the 1400s, many people were studying the works of the ancient Greeks and Romans. These works made them realize how much human beings could achieve, and started a new belief in human ability. This belief, called humanism, spread all over Europe, as artists, writers and scientists tried out new ideas.

Scientists and inventors

During the Renaissance, people started to ask new questions about the world. They carried out scientific experiments and studied plants, animals and humans. Inventors worked on new ideas for clocks, weapons, telescopes, water pumps and other machines.

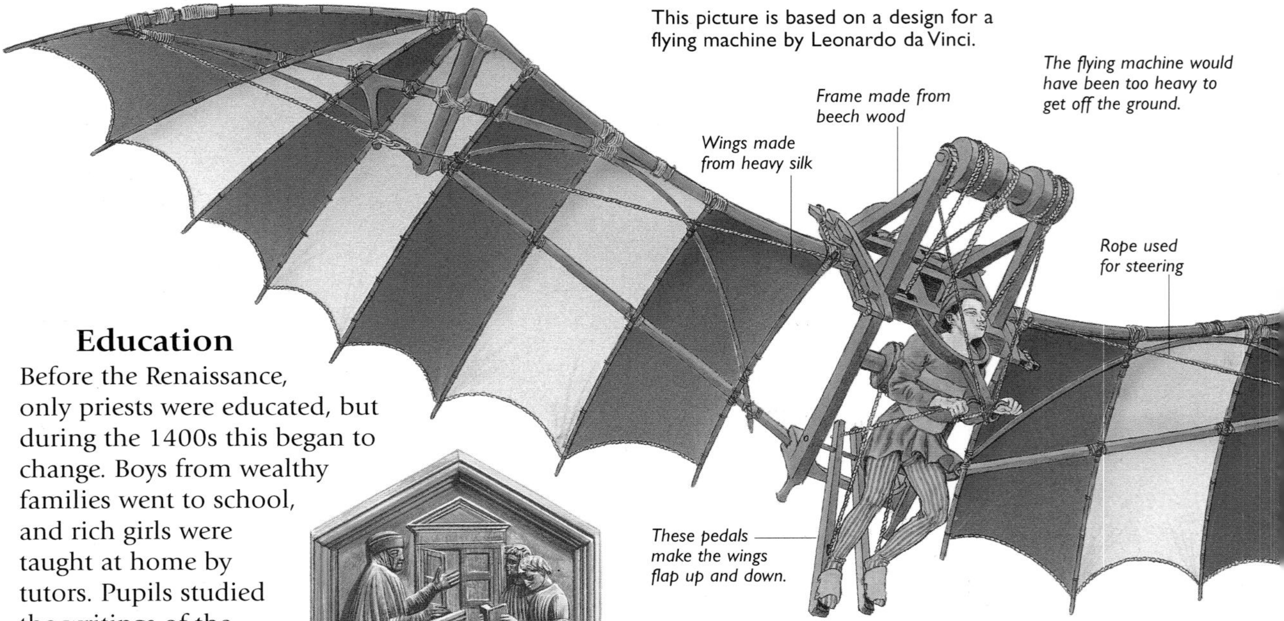

This picture is based on a design for a flying machine by Leonardo da Vinci.

The flying machine would have been too heavy to get off the ground.

Frame made from beech wood

Wings made from heavy silk

Rope used for steering

These pedals make the wings flap up and down.

Education

Before the Renaissance, only priests were educated, but during the 1400s this began to change. Boys from wealthy families went to school, and rich girls were taught at home by tutors. Pupils studied the writings of the Greeks and Romans, as well as music, art and foreign languages.

Boys at school

Leonardo da Vinci

Leonardo da Vinci was a perfect example of a well-educated Renaissance man. He was an artist, an inventor, an architect and a musician. He made detailed drawings of animals and people, and created designs for amazing machines.

Leonardo da Vinci

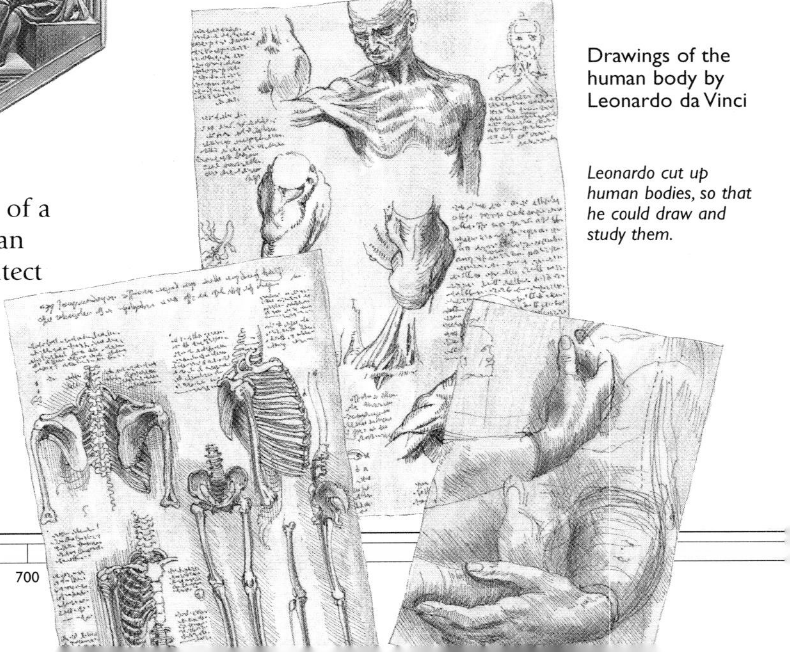

Drawings of the human body by Leonardo da Vinci

Leonardo cut up human bodies, so that he could draw and study them.

Alchemists

Many people in Renaissance Europe worked as alchemists. They tried to find a way to turn ordinary metal into gold, and some even thought that they could create a magic potion that would give people eternal life. Alchemists learned how to make chemicals and invented lots of scientific equipment.

Flasks of boiling chemicals

This man is using scales to weigh powder.

The alchemist follows instructions in a manuscript.

Hourglass used for timing experiments

This boy is grinding powder with a pestle and mortar.

An alchemist's laboratory

The birth of printing

In the 1450s, a German named Johann Gutenberg invented a machine called a printing press, which printed books a page at a time. Until then, all books in Europe had been copied by hand.

Wooden press

Paper

Metal letters arranged in a block and covered with ink

★ A printing press

Page from an early printed book

Soon, printing presses were set up all over Europe. Books were produced quickly and cheaply, and this helped to spread the new ideas of the Renaissance thinkers and scientists.

Writers and thinkers

Poets began to write about human feelings, and thinkers discussed how countries should be run. An Italian called Niccolò Machiavelli wrote a book called *The Prince*, which said that a ruler should always do what was best for his kingdom, even if it meant being cruel and ruthless.

Niccolò Machiavelli

Important dates

c.1350	The Renaissance begins in Italy.
1449-1492	Life of Lorenzo de' Medici
1452-1519	Life of Leonardo da Vinci
1455	Gutenberg produces the first printed book, a copy of the Bible.
1469-1527	Life of Niccolò Machiavelli

Voyages of Discovery

Map of voyages

- Bartholomeu Dias
- Vasco da Gama
- Christopher Columbus
- Amerigo Vespucci
- John Cabot

Columbus's ship, the Santa Maria

Compass used by sailors

Large areas of the world were completely unknown to the people of medieval Europe. Explorers and traders had reached North Africa, India and China, but no one had any idea that America existed.

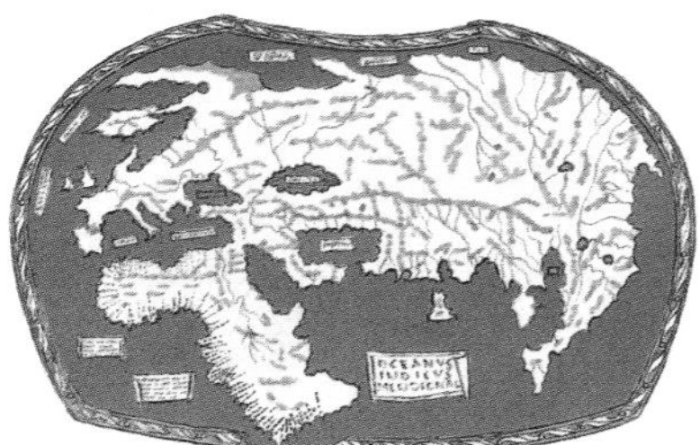

This map, made in 1489, shows how people saw the world at that time.

Finding a way east

By the 1450s, traders in Europe were desperate to find a way to the East by sea. Silks and spices from India and China were in great demand, but they had to be carried overland on long and dangerous journeys.

Henry the Navigator

Prince Henry of Portugal, known as Henry the Navigator, was convinced that ships could reach India by sailing south around Africa.

Henry the Navigator

He persuaded Portuguese explorers to sail south, even though they believed that the southern seas were boiling hot and filled with monsters. Henry paid for nearly 20 expeditions along the west coast of Africa.

Early artist's view of a sea monster ★

Sailing around Africa

In 1487, a storm blew the ship of a Portuguese explorer, Bartholomeu Dias, around the southern tip of Africa.

Part of a map showing a ship sailing around southern Africa

After this, other ships sailed around Africa, and in 1498 Vasco da Gama reached India by this route.

Christopher Columbus

Most people in the Middle Ages thought that the world was flat, but a few believed it was round. An Italian captain, named Christopher Columbus, was sure that he could reach China by heading west and sailing all the way around the world. He persuaded the King and Queen of Spain to pay for his voyage.

This picture shows Columbus leaving Spain. ★

Columbus finds land

After five weeks, Columbus arrived in the West Indies, a group of islands close to Central America. Columbus thought that he had reached the East, but people soon realized that he had discovered an exciting new land. They called this land the "New World".

Amerigo Vespucci

In 1499, another Italian, Amerigo Vespucci, reached the mainland of America. Vespucci sailed down the coast of South America as far as the Amazon River. America was named after him in 1507.

Amerigo Vespucci

John Cabot

In 1497, an expedition set out from England, led by an Italian captain called John Cabot. Cabot crossed the Atlantic Ocean in search of India, but instead he reached Newfoundland, off the coast of North America.

Columbus arriving in the West Indies

Important dates

- c.**1420-1460** Henry the Navigator encourages Portuguese expeditions.
- **1487** Bartholomeu Dias sails around Africa.
- **1492** Christopher Columbus discovers the West Indies.
- **1497** John Cabot reaches Newfoundland.
- **1498** Vasco da Gama sails to India.
- **1499** Amerigo Vespucci reaches South America.

1100 1200 1300 1400 1500

19th-century painting of workers shaping steel in a forge

THE LAST 500 YEARS

Looking at the Last 500 Years

Between the years 1500 and 2000, life changed dramatically in most parts of the world. At first, this transformation happened gradually, but by the 1800s people's lives were changing fast, and in the 20th century things really gathered speed.

Changing journeys

Moving from place to place in the 1500s was very slow and difficult, and journeys didn't get much easier for 300 years. Travel started to change in 1804, when the first steam train was built. Around 80 years later, the motor car was invented, and by the 1960s planes could cross the globe in hours, and spacecraft had taken astronauts to the Moon. By the end of the century, unmanned spacecraft had reached most of the planets in our solar system.

The American Henry Ford made motor cars that lots of people could afford. Here he is in one of his cars, around 1920.

World views

Most people in 1500 had no idea what the world looked like and many still believed that the Earth was flat. Gradually, over the next 500 years, scientists and explorers built up a picture of the globe. Today, satellites can take photographs of the Earth from space, and people can see television pictures of places all over the world.

Fighting for freedom

During the 16th century, a few powerful rulers governed large areas of the world, and ordinary people had very little say in how their countries were run. This began to change in the 1700s, when new ideas of rights for all spread through Europe and America. Rebels struggled to gain more freedom, and gradually more and more people won the right to vote for their country's leaders. Today, people are still fighting for freedom in many parts of the world.

This is a scene from the time of the French Revolution in 1789. It shows a man setting off to join the revolutionaries.

Science and technology

Daily life in the 1500s was extremely hard, but over the next 500 years new discoveries and inventions slowly changed people's lives. Advances in medicine meant that people lived much longer, while new machines made everyday tasks faster and easier. In the 20th century, cars, computers and television transformed the way that many people lived.

This is the Hubble Space Telescope. It allows scientists to see farther into space than they ever have before.

Internet link: For a link to a Web site where you can be a historian looking for clues to the past, go to ***www.usborne-quicklinks.com***

Where did it happen?

There are maps throughout the book to show you exactly where things happened. You can also check which area of the world you are reading about by looking at the bottom corner of each page. The different areas of the world are shown on the map below.

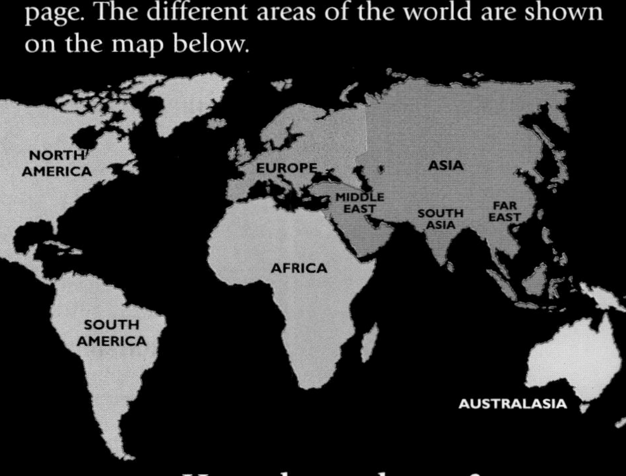
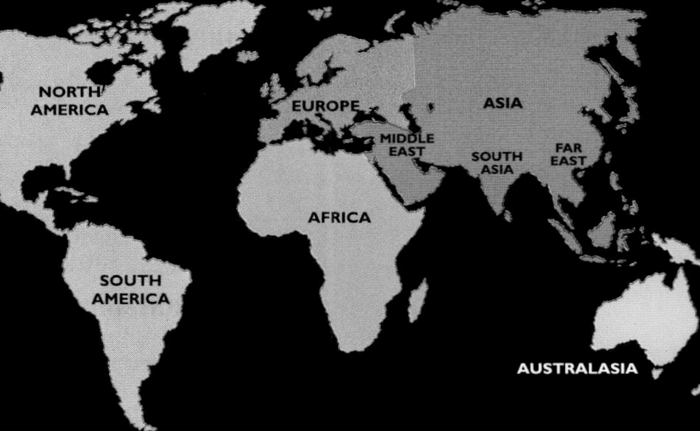

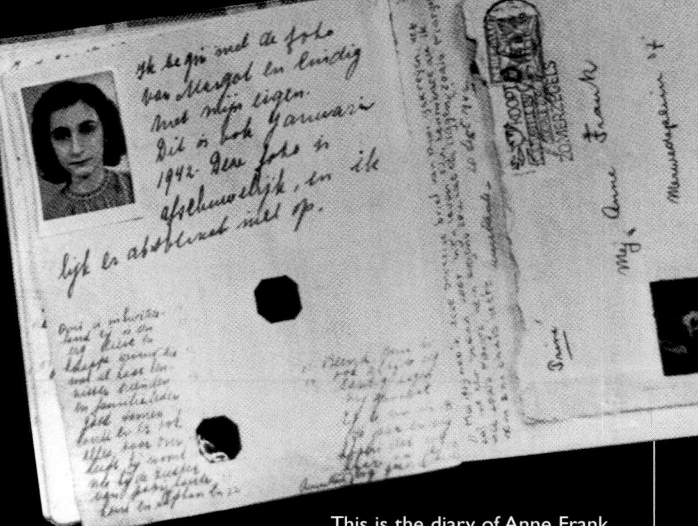

This is the diary of Anne Frank, a young Jewish girl who described her life in hiding during the Second World War.

How do we know?

Historians study history by collecting lots of different kinds of evidence. They piece this evidence together to create a picture of what happened in the past.

Letters and diaries give first-hand accounts of things that happened in the past, newspapers contain the news and views of the time, and government records provide many useful facts and figures. Maps give a clear idea of which parts of the world were known and explored, while scientific papers and notebooks describe experiments and discoveries.

Since the 1860s, photography has provided a vivid record of events all over the world. Historians who study the 20th century use film and sound recordings to help with their research, and also interview people about their memories and experiences.

Many buildings and objects have survived from the last 500 years, and these provide valuable clues about the way people lived and worked. Paintings, drawings and statues show famous people and events, and reveal fascinating details of daily life.

Many historians have studied film showing the murder of the US President John F. Kennedy in 1963. Here you can see the President and his wife minutes before he was shot.

The Last 500 Years Internet Links

This list gives a range of Web sites on the last 500 years of history.
To visit the sites, go to **www.usborne-quicklinks.com** and enter the keyword "history".

WEB SITE 1 An amazing site full of fascinating information, with sections on each of the last five centuries. Includes lots of video clips, timelines and interactive maps, as well as the chance to test your knowledge and have dinner with famous figures from history.

WEB SITE 2 Find out about the last hundred years of science and technology at this fantastic site. Go to the "You Try It" section and click on "Technology at Home" to see how daily life has changed, or click on "Doctor over Time" to visit a doctor in 1900. The "People and Discoveries" section has excellent files on the most important scientists, discoveries and inventions of the century.

WEB SITE 3 An enormous site from CNN that tells the complete story of the 20th century. In each of the 10 episodes you can read about the major news stories, culture and inventions of the time, or click on "More Profiles" for features on famous people. You can also test your knowledge with a series of fun quizzes.

WEB SITE 4 Watch video clips showing some of the most important news stories of the last 20 years of the 20th century at this CNN site. Most of the stories are from the USA.

WEB SITE 5 Listen to history being made at this site from the History Channel in the USA. You can hear dozens of famous speeches from throughout the 20th century, and read about why they were important. Choose a category for a selection of speeches, or click on "Speech Archive" to see a full list of the recordings.

WEB SITE 6 View a selection of clothes from around the world at this site from the Costume Institute of the Metropolitan Museum in New York. Fifty stunning highlights from the past five centuries are presented in chronological order. There's also a special exhibition showing how our ideas of fashion and beauty have changed over time.

WEB SITE 7 Choose "Dress the Men" or "Dress the Ladies" at this fun BBC site, and play an educational game about Tudor and Victorian fashions.

WEB SITE 8 Learn about the history of the USA at this great site from the American Library of Congress in Washington, DC. Click on "Jump Back in Time" for an interactive timeline, meet some amazing Americans or click on "Explore the States" for quick histories of each of the US states.

WEB SITE 9 The site of the National Civil Rights Museum in Memphis, USA. Click on "Interactive Tour" to learn about the struggles of African Americans, from the slave trade to Martin Luther King.

WEB SITE 10 A very moving BBC site about World War I. "The Soldier's Story" includes letters written by soldiers in the trenches, and "Voices from the Past" has sound and film recordings about the war (RealPlayer® needed).

WEB SITE 11 A large collection of online exhibitions about the two world wars from the Imperial War Museum in London. The site includes sound recordings and lots of photos. Click on "enigma" for the fascinating story of codes and code-breakers in World War II.

WEB SITE 12 An excellent site about World War II. See photos of British cities during the Blitz, hear the stories of children who were evacuated to the countryside, look at wartime newspapers and listen to radio broadcasts.

WEB SITE 13 A site about the Battle of Gettysburg, the biggest battle of the American Civil War. Look at animated maps, see paintings and photos of the battle, and listen to soldiers' stories (RealPlayer® needed).

WEB SITE 14 An exciting site about space travel and the first men on the Moon. "Launch Library" has video clips of space missions, while "Space Race" has an interactive timeline. Click on "Suit Up" to examine clickable photos of space suits, or choose "Virtual Apollo" for a virtual tour of a space rocket with panoramic movies.

WEB SITE 15 An excellent site about Africa created by the National Museum of Natural History in Washington, DC. Choose "History" for a clickable timeline of Africa's past with lots of vibrant pictures.

WEB SITE 16 A fascinating interactive tour of the Japanese city of Edo (present-day Tokyo) in the 18th century. Move your mouse over the pictures to reveal hidden facts, sounds and pictures.

WEB SITE 17 This is an enormous site on China. Go to the "Timelines" section and click on "This Century: Key Events in China and the World" for an interactive timeline that shows what happened in China and the rest of the world during the 20th century.

WEB SITE 18 Take a photo tour and see inside the Statue of Liberty, shown on this page. The statue was built in the 19th century to celebrate 100 years of American independence.

Exploring the World

The 16th century was a very exciting time for explorers. After Christopher Columbus arrived in America in 1492, people dreamed of finding treasure in the exotic New World. They also hoped they would find new routes to the rich trading countries of China and India.

Around the world

The Portuguese explorer Ferdinand Magellan discovered a route around South America into the Pacific Ocean. Magellan died during the voyage, but one of his captains, Sebastian del Cano, continued sailing west until he reached Europe. This was the first voyage around the world and it proved that the Earth was round.

Magellan's ship *Vittoria* as shown by an artist of the time

Spices and jewels from India

Exploring Canada

Jacques Cartier, a French explorer, sailed along the east coast of what is now Canada, searching for a new route to China. Later, he canoed up the Saint Lawrence River, and reached a small village which he named Montreal.

Sailing northwest

An English expedition led by Martin Frobisher tried to reach China by sailing around the top of Canada. Frobisher believed he had found a way around Canada, but in fact he had only sailed into a bay.

Sailing northeast

A Dutch sea captain named Willem Barents hoped to find a route to India by sailing northeast past Norway. His ship became trapped in ice in the Arctic Ocean, but he managed to build a shelter, and stayed there until the ice melted.

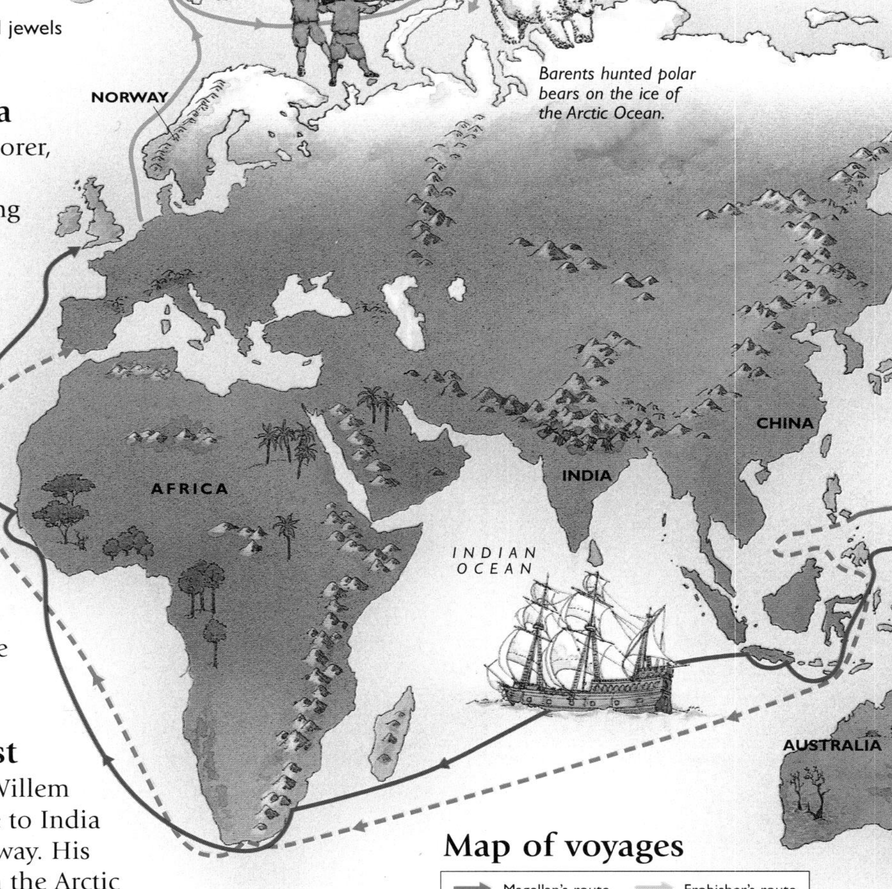

Spanish conquerors

Spanish soldiers, known as conquistadors, arrived in Central and South America, determined to win land and gold. They defeated the Aztec and Inca people who lived there, and destroyed their powerful empires.

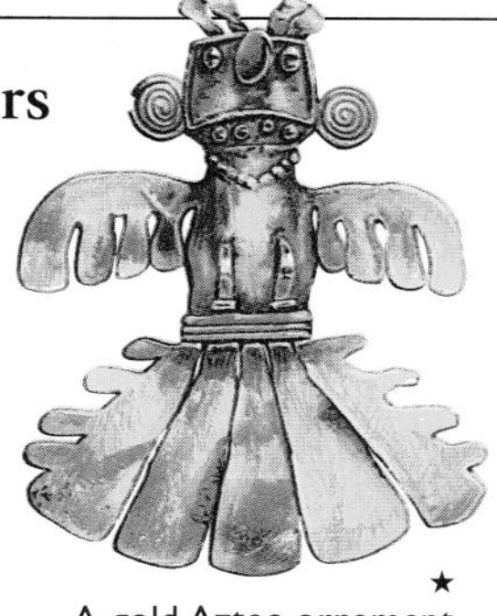

A gold Aztec ornament ★

Along the Amazon

A Spanish explorer, Francisco de Orellana, sailed along the entire length of the Amazon River in South America. His boat was often in danger from fast-flowing currents.

Sailing and stealing

Sir Francis Drake of England was a skilled sailor and a daring pirate. He sailed all the way around the world, stealing treasure from Spanish ships as he went.

A miniature portrait of Sir Francis Drake

CANADA

PACIFIC OCEAN

Cartier explored Canada with native North Americans as his guides.

Montreal

ATLANTIC OCEAN

CENTRAL AMERICA

Explorers brought back pineapples from Central and South America.

Amazon

SOUTH AMERICA

Important dates

1519-1521	Spanish conquistadors conquer the Aztecs.
1519-1522	Magellan's ship sails around the world.
1532-1534	Spanish conquistadors conquer the Incas.
1534-1536	Cartier explores eastern Canada.
1542	Orellana sails along the Amazon.
1576	Frobisher reaches northern Canada.
1577-1580	Drake sails around the world.
1596	Barents reaches the Arctic Ocean.

The Ottoman Empire

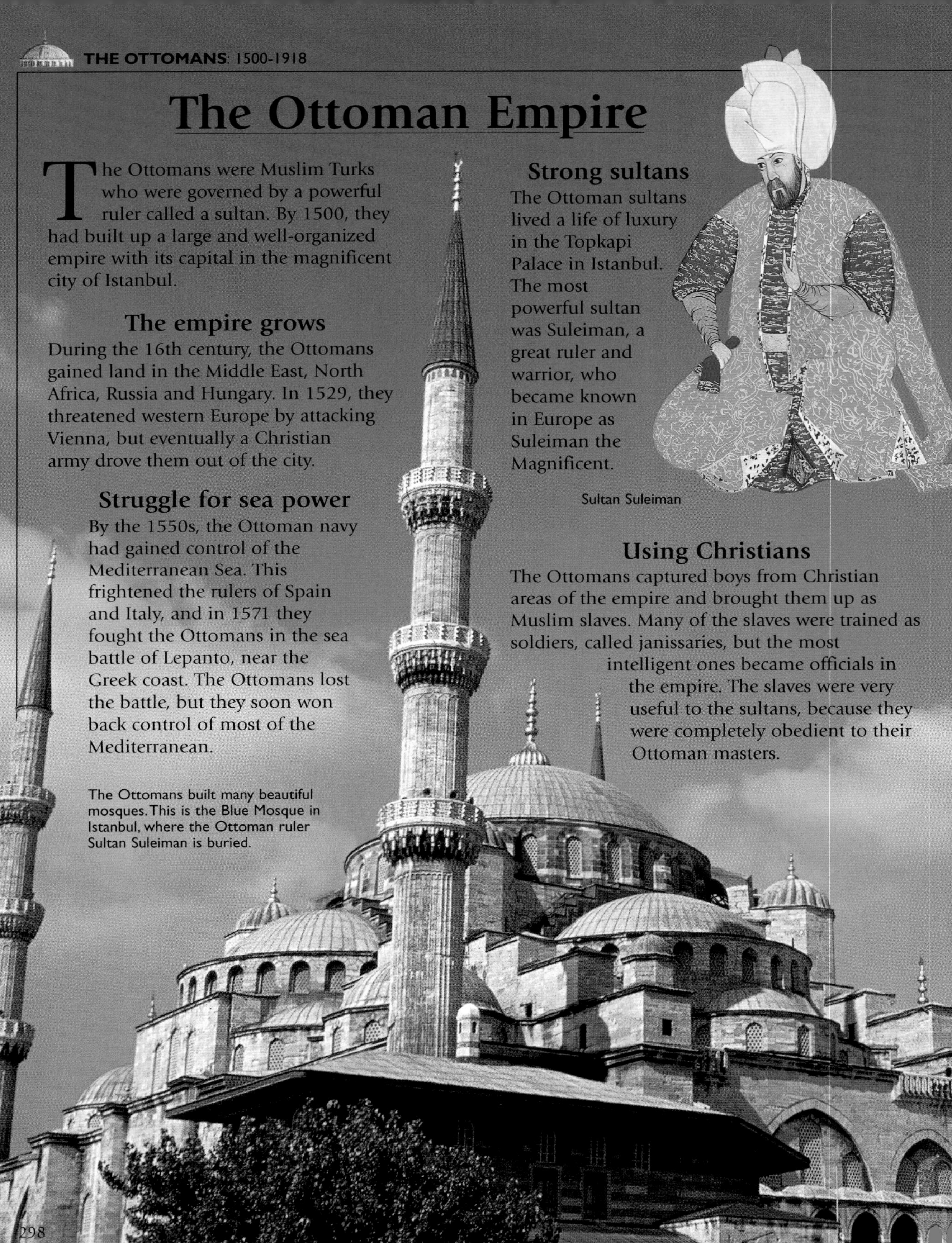

The Ottomans were Muslim Turks who were governed by a powerful ruler called a sultan. By 1500, they had built up a large and well-organized empire with its capital in the magnificent city of Istanbul.

The empire grows

During the 16th century, the Ottomans gained land in the Middle East, North Africa, Russia and Hungary. In 1529, they threatened western Europe by attacking Vienna, but eventually a Christian army drove them out of the city.

Struggle for sea power

By the 1550s, the Ottoman navy had gained control of the Mediterranean Sea. This frightened the rulers of Spain and Italy, and in 1571 they fought the Ottomans in the sea battle of Lepanto, near the Greek coast. The Ottomans lost the battle, but they soon won back control of most of the Mediterranean.

The Ottomans built many beautiful mosques. This is the Blue Mosque in Istanbul, where the Ottoman ruler Sultan Suleiman is buried.

Strong sultans

The Ottoman sultans lived a life of luxury in the Topkapi Palace in Istanbul. The most powerful sultan was Suleiman, a great ruler and warrior, who became known in Europe as Suleiman the Magnificent.

Sultan Suleiman

Using Christians

The Ottomans captured boys from Christian areas of the empire and brought them up as Muslim slaves. Many of the slaves were trained as soldiers, called janissaries, but the most intelligent ones became officials in the empire. The slaves were very useful to the sultans, because they were completely obedient to their Ottoman masters.

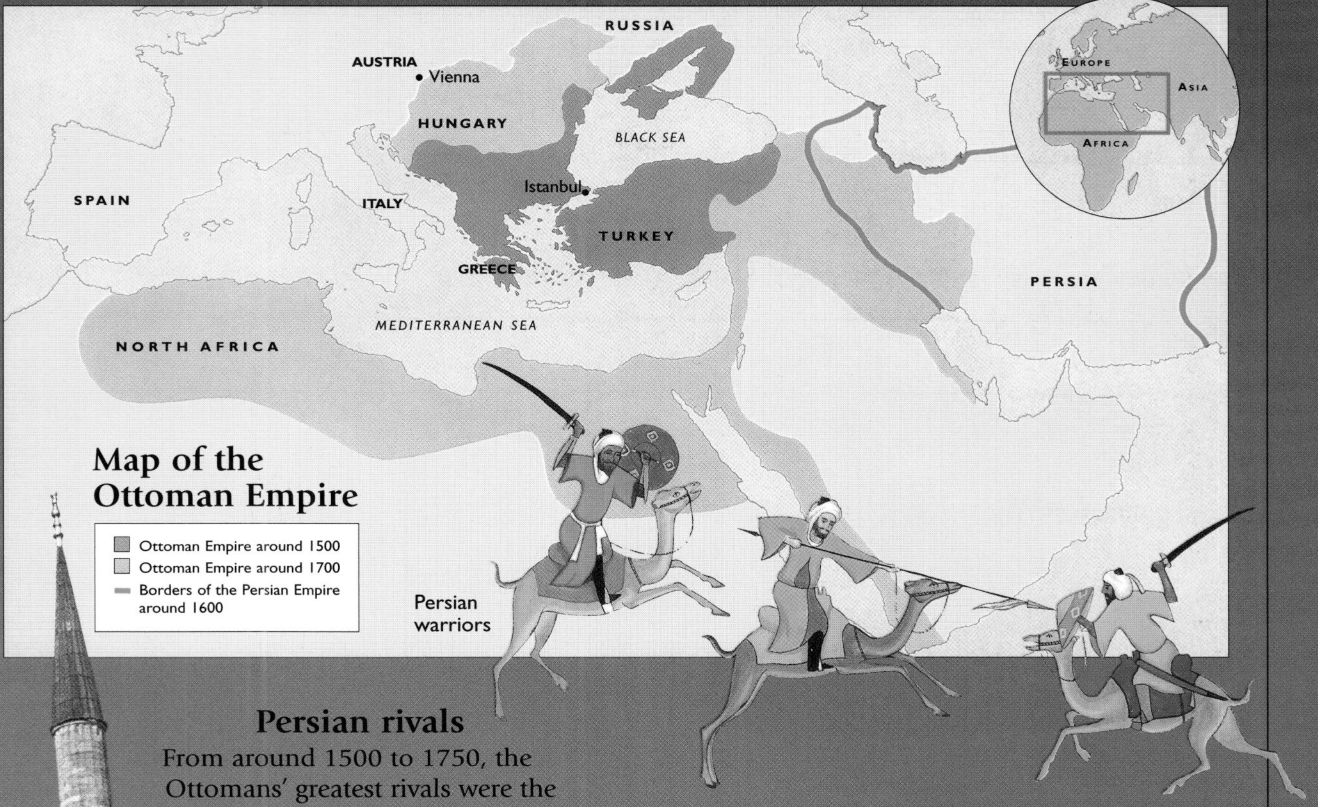

Map of the Ottoman Empire

Persian warriors

Persian rivals

From around 1500 to 1750, the Ottomans' greatest rivals were the Persians. Like the Ottomans, the Persians were Muslims, but they belonged to a group called the Shi'ites. Led by their rulers, the powerful Safavid family, the Persians fought the Ottomans for land. They also encouraged Shi'ite Muslims in the Ottoman Empire to rebel.

The empire weakens

After 1600, the Ottoman Empire continued to grow, but it was ruled by a series of weak sultans who couldn't control their people. At the same time, some of the sultans' enemies, such as Russia and Austria, grew stronger.

The end of the empire

In 1683, the Ottomans attacked Vienna again, but they were driven back. After this defeat, the empire gradually became smaller and weaker. It lasted until the 20th century, but by the end of World War I it had collapsed completely.

Important dates

1520-1566	Sultan Suleiman rules the Ottomans.
1529	The Ottomans attack Vienna.
1571	The Battle of Lepanto
1683	The Ottomans attack Vienna for the last time.
1918	The Ottoman Empire comes to an end.

The Mogul Empire

The Moguls were Muslims from the area now called Afghanistan. Like their ancestors, the Mongols, the Moguls were great warriors, but they also loved poetry and art, and created beautiful gardens.

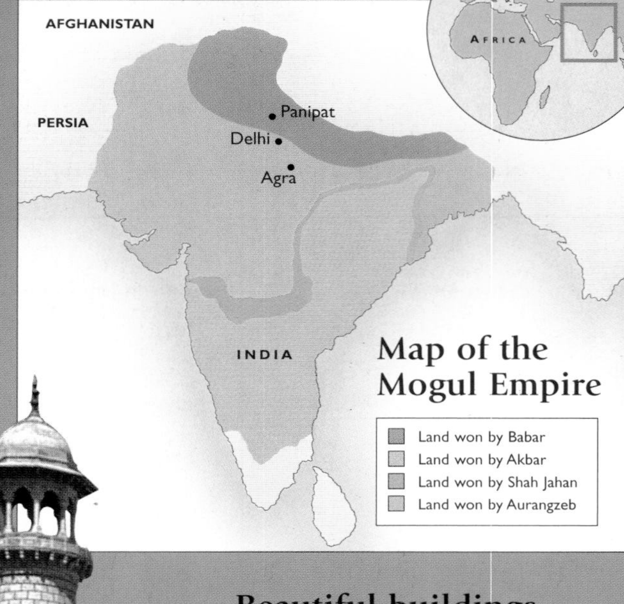

Map of the Mogul Empire

The first emperor

In 1526, a Mogul prince named Babar led his army into India. He defeated the Sultan (ruler) of Delhi at the Battle of Panipat and took control of northern India, becoming the first Mogul Emperor.

Akbar the Great

Babar's grandson, Akbar, won large areas of land from the Hindu princes who ruled most of India, but he still managed to keep the Hindus loyal to him. He did this by marrying a Hindu princess, and by allowing the Hindus to worship their own gods and goddesses. Akbar ruled for almost 40 years. He ran his empire very efficiently, and invited painters, poets and scholars to his splendid court at Agra.

Beautiful buildings

The Moguls built amazing mosques, forts and palaces, but their most famous building is the Taj Mahal, near Agra. It was built by Akbar's grandson, Shah Jahan.

Emperor Shah Jahan built the Taj Mahal as a tomb for his beloved wife, Mumtaz Mahal.

A Mogul painting showing the marriage of Emperor Akbar's brother

Internet link: *For a link to a Web site where you can visit Akbar's court and watch scholars discussing religion, go to* ***www.usborne-quicklinks.com***

A cruel emperor

The Mogul Empire reached its greatest size under Shah Jahan's son, Aurangzeb. But Aurangzeb was a cruel man and an unpopular ruler. In order to become emperor, he put his father in prison and murdered his two older brothers. Once he had gained power, Aurangzeb forced the Indian peasants to pay very high taxes. He also destroyed many Hindu temples and built mosques on top of their ruins.

Armies and traders

After Aurangzeb's death in 1707, there were no more strong emperors. A Persian army invaded northwest India, and the Hindu princes slowly won back land from the Moguls. Meanwhile, traders from Europe began to set up trading stations all over India.

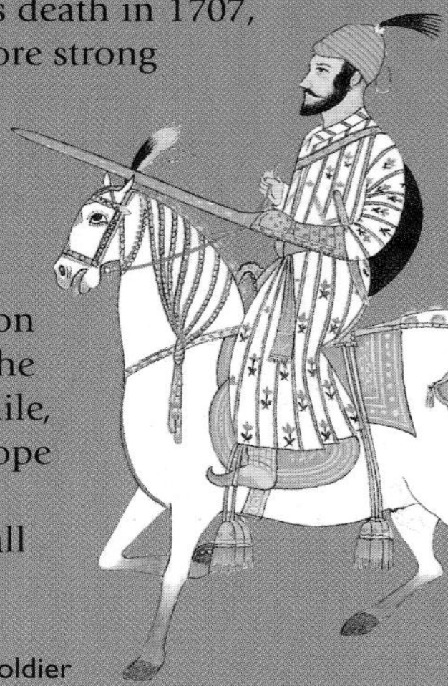

A Hindu soldier

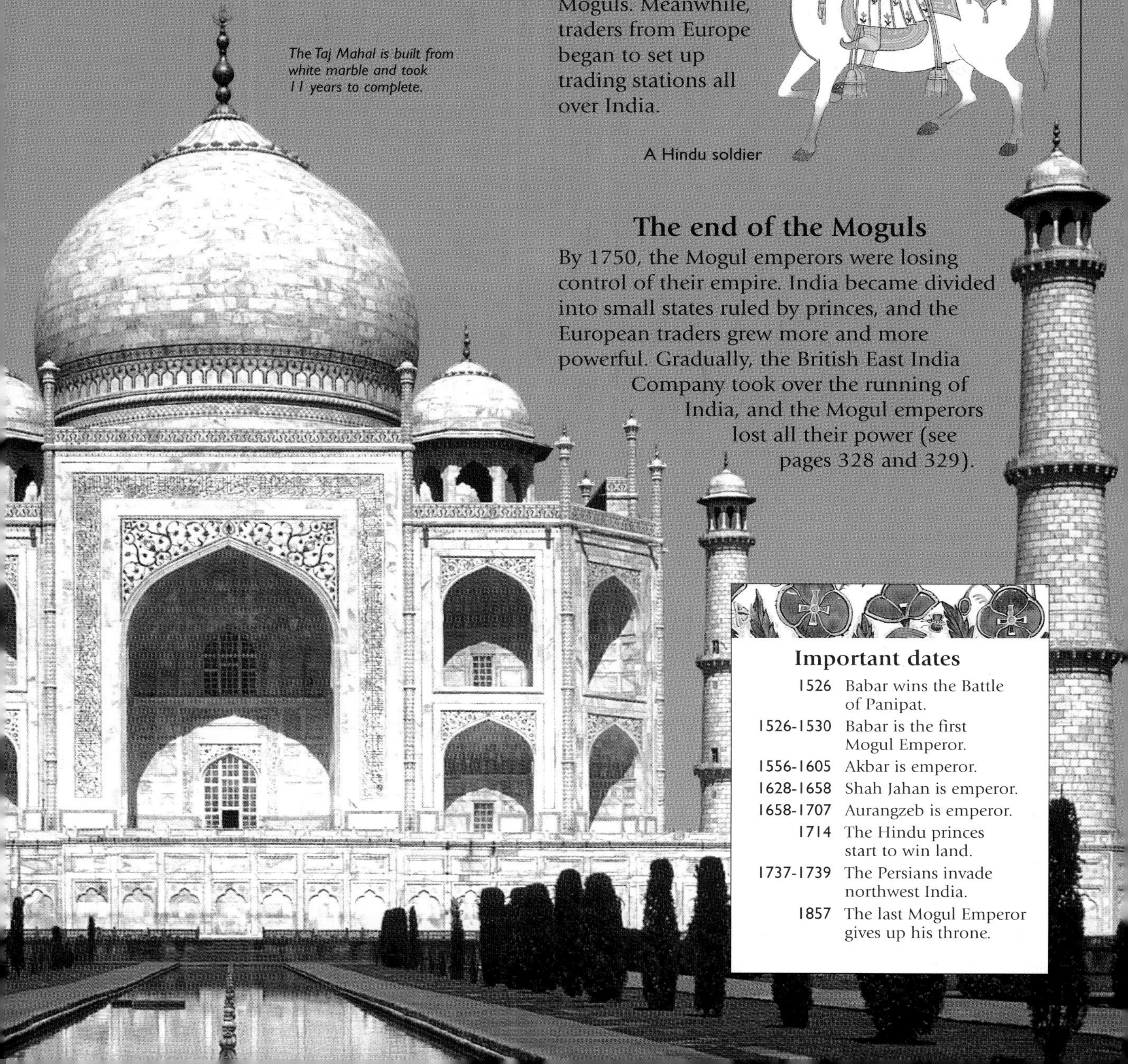

The Taj Mahal is built from white marble and took 11 years to complete.

The end of the Moguls

By 1750, the Mogul emperors were losing control of their empire. India became divided into small states ruled by princes, and the European traders grew more and more powerful. Gradually, the British East India Company took over the running of India, and the Mogul emperors lost all their power (see pages 328 and 329).

Important dates

1526	Babar wins the Battle of Panipat.
1526-1530	Babar is the first Mogul Emperor.
1556-1605	Akbar is emperor.
1628-1658	Shah Jahan is emperor.
1658-1707	Aurangzeb is emperor.
1714	The Hindu princes start to win land.
1737-1739	The Persians invade northwest India.
1857	The last Mogul Emperor gives up his throne.

Catholics and Protestants

By the 1500s, many people were unhappy with the Catholic Church. They thought that its leaders were only interested in wealth and power, and complained that many of its priests were badly educated and lazy.

A few determined people protested about the Church. At first, they tried to reform or improve it, but later they broke away completely. Their followers became known as Protestants, and the movement they started was called the Reformation.

Martin Luther, the leader of a growing protest against the Catholic Church

Luther's protest

In 1517, a German monk named Martin Luther wrote a list of 95 ways that the Catholic Church could be reformed. He nailed the list to the church door in Wittenberg, and his ideas soon spread. This made the Church leaders furious, and in 1520 the Pope issued a document that banished Luther from the Catholic Church for ever.

Luther burned his copy of the document expelling him from the Church.

Luther's changes

Luther went into hiding and worked on his ideas for how the Church should be run. He believed that church services should be kept simple, and that people should read the Bible for themselves, instead of learning everything from priests. Luther translated the Bible from Latin into German, and many copies of his Bible were printed.

By 1525, people all over Germany were holding simple services based on Luther's ideas, and the Lutheran Church was born.

John Calvin

In 1541, John Calvin, a French reformer, started the Calvinist Church in Geneva. Calvinism is a strict form of Protestantism, and it was very popular in Switzerland and Scotland. By 1560, large numbers of people in northern Europe had become either Lutherans or Calvinists (see map).

John Calvin, founder of the Calvinist Church

Henry's rebellion

King Henry VIII of England argued with the Pope because he refused to allow Henry to divorce his wife, Catherine of Aragon. In 1531, Henry decided to take the place of the Pope, and made himself head of the Church in England, which later became known as the Anglican Church.

Henry VIII thought many monks and nuns did not lead holy lives, so he closed down the abbeys where they lived. Most of these abbeys are now in ruins, like Rievaulx Abbey shown here.

Catholics fight back

The leaders of the Catholic Church tried hard to win people back to their Church. They made many changes, which together became known as the Counter-Reformation.

During the Counter-Reformation, sculptors carved beautiful statues for Catholic cathedrals and churches. This statue of St. Teresa and an angel is by the Italian sculptor Bernini.

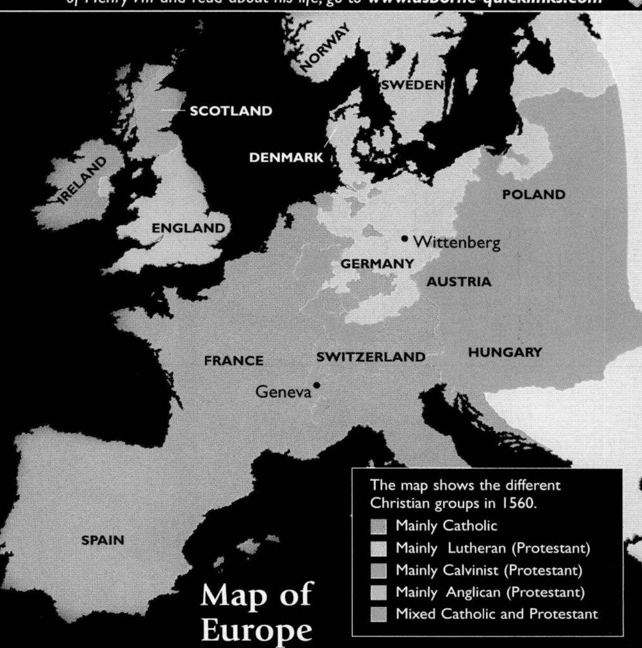

Map of Europe

Catholic leaders set up colleges for priests, built elaborate churches, and trained teacher-priests, called Jesuits. They attacked the Protestants in sermons and books, and also used the Inquisition, a system of courts run by monks, to find and punish Protestants.

Religious wars

During the 16th century, Protestants and Catholics fought each other all over Europe. One of the bloodiest struggles took place in France where French Protestants, known as Huguenots, fought the Catholic king and his supporters. The most horrific event in the French wars was the St. Bartholomew's Day Massacre, when thousands of Huguenots were slaughtered by Catholics. Eventually, after 30 years of war, the Huguenots were given the freedom to worship.

Important dates

- **1517** Luther writes his list of 95 suggested reforms.
- **1531** Henry VIII declares himself head of the English Church.
- **1541** Calvin starts his Church.
- **1545** The Counter-Reformation begins.
- **1562-1589** Religious wars in France
- **1572** St. Bartholomew's Day Massacre

Elizabethan England

Elizabeth I was the last and greatest of the Tudors, a line of kings and queens who had ruled England since 1485. She reigned for 45 years, making England a rich and powerful country that was respected throughout the world.

Great entertainment

Elizabethan England was famous for its writers and composers. The queen invited poets and musicians to entertain her at court, concerts were held in nobles' houses, and plays were performed in new London playhouses, such as the Globe Theatre.

Mr. WILLIAM SHAKESPEARES COMEDIES, HISTORIES, & TRAGEDIES. Publifhed according to the True Originall Copies.

This is the title page from a collection of plays by William Shakespeare, the most brilliant of all the Elizabethan writers.

Elizabeth's people

Although lots of merchants became rich in Elizabeth's reign, many of her people were still very poor, and some had to beg in order to survive. In 1563, the first Poor Law was passed. This allowed local officials to raise money to look after the poor.

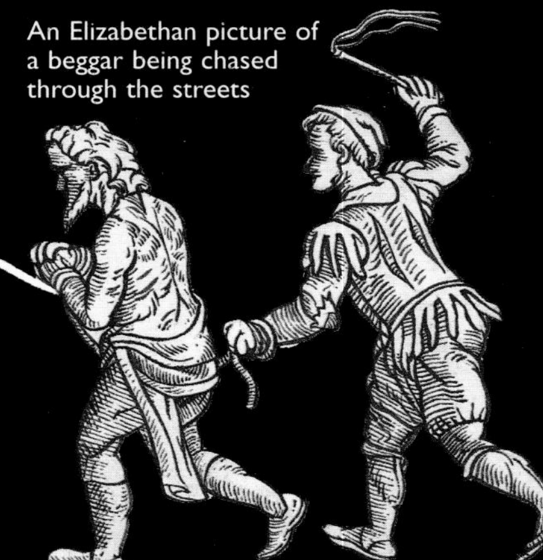
An Elizabethan picture of a beggar being chased through the streets

In this portrait, Elizabeth I wears thick, white face paint and a dress that is covered with jewels.

Catholic plots

Elizabeth was a Protestant, but some people wanted a Catholic ruler instead. A group of English Catholics tried to replace Elizabeth with her Catholic cousin Mary, Queen of Scots, but all their plots failed.

Explorers and raiders

During Elizabeth's reign, the great explorer Sir Francis Drake sailed around the world (see page 297), and Sir Walter Raleigh started a colony in North America. But English captains like Drake and Raleigh were raiders as well as explorers. They attacked Spanish ports and stole treasure from Spanish ships.

The Spanish Armada

King Philip II of Spain was furious that the English were raiding Spanish ships, and he decided to lead a Catholic attack on England. In 1588, he sent a large fleet of ships, called an armada, to invade England. The Spanish ships sailed to the Netherlands, where an army was waiting to join them, but on their way through the English Channel they were attacked by English warships.

Frightening fire ships

After four fierce sea battles, the Spanish fleet anchored close to Calais, on the northern coast of France. During the night, the English surprised the Spanish by sending eight fire ships (ships that had been deliberately set on fire) into the middle of the fleet. The Spanish panicked, and their ships scattered in all directions.

In this scene, English fire ships are approaching the Spanish Armada.

The fire ships are packed with rags, timber and oil.

The end of the Armada

The morning after the fire ships attacked, the English and the Spanish fought the sea battle of Gravelines. The battle lasted all day, and the Spanish were defeated.

After the battle, the Armada's ships were blown north. The Spanish were forced to sail around Scotland and Ireland, and most of their ships were wrecked in terrible storms.

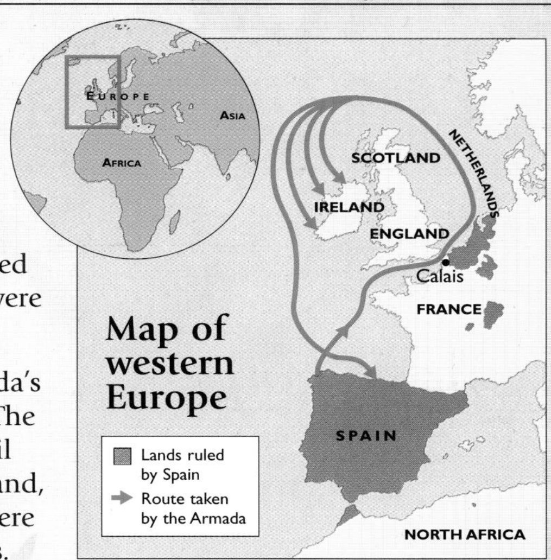

Map of western Europe

The fire ships are carried toward the Armada by the wind and the tide.

As the fire ships approach, the Spanish sailors panic and cut their anchor ropes.

The Spanish are terrified by fire because their ships are carrying gunpowder which might explode.

Heat from the flames makes the ships' guns fire.

Important dates

1558-1603	Elizabeth I is queen.
1563	The first Poor Law is passed.
1564-1616	Life of William Shakespeare
1577-1580	Sir Francis Drake sails around the world.
1588	The Spanish Armada is defeated.

Kings, Cavaliers and Roundheads

In 1603, James I became King of England and started a new line of Stuart rulers. James I and his son, Charles I, believed that God had chosen them to be supreme rulers and so they refused to accept any control from Parliament. This led to violent arguments.

The Civil War

In 1629, after several clashes with Parliament, King Charles I decided to rule without its help. Charles ruled alone for 11 years, but eventually he was forced to ask Parliament for money. Parliament refused to help, and in 1642 fighting broke out between the king's supporters and Parliament. This struggle is known as the English Civil War.

Followers of the king were called Royalists or Cavaliers, and supporters of Parliament were known as Parliamentarians or Roundheads. Some Cavaliers had flowing hair and fancy clothes, while most of the Roundheads were Puritans (very strict Protestants), who disapproved of fine clothes, acting and dancing.

The New Model Army

At first, the Cavaliers won most of the battles in the Civil War, but then a Puritan named Oliver Cromwell decided to reorganize the Roundheads' troops.

A 17th-century portrait of Oliver Cromwell

Cromwell's new fighting force was called the New Model Army. In 1645, it won the Battle of Naseby, and the following year the king was forced to surrender.

King Charles I, painted by the artist Van Dyck

Killing the king

For two years, there was no more fighting, but then war broke out again. Eventually, Parliament gave up any hope of agreeing with the king, and in 1649 Charles I had his head chopped off in front of a stunned crowd in London.

The dramatic death of Charles I, as shown by an artist of the time

Commonwealth and Cromwell

After Charles' death, Parliament ruled England for four years. This period of time was known as the Commonwealth. But Parliament did not govern well, and in 1653 Oliver Cromwell took control of the country, calling himself Lord Protector of England. Cromwell ruled efficiently but strictly. He closed down many ale-houses and declared that Christmas Day was no longer a holiday.

King Charles II

When Cromwell died, many people wanted to have a king again. The son of Charles I had escaped to France, and he was welcomed back and crowned King Charles II. The return of Charles II is called the Restoration.

Charles II, a popular king who loved music, dancing and beautiful women

Plague and fire

During Charles II's reign, a dreadful disease, known as the plague, killed thousands of people in London. The following year, a terrifying fire swept through the city. The fire destroyed hundreds of buildings, but it also killed the rats that spread the plague.

Rebuilding London

After the fire, large areas of London were rebuilt, using stone instead of wood. The architect Sir Christopher Wren designed over 50 churches for the city, and by the 1690s London had many elegant new buildings. People strolled through public gardens, and merchants met in coffee houses to make deals with each other.

This is St. Paul's Cathedral in London, Sir Christopher Wren's most famous building.

The Great Fire of London raged through the city for four days. In this scene, the flames have reached London Bridge.

A strong wind helps the fire to spread quickly.

London Bridge has many wooden houses on it and they burn very easily.

People try to cross the Thames to safety.

Important dates

1603-1625	James I is king.
1625-1649	Charles I is king.
1642-1648	The English Civil War
1649-1653	Parliament rules England (the Commonwealth).
1653-1658	Oliver Cromwell is Lord Protector of England.
1660-1685	Charles II is king.
1665	The Great Plague of London
1666	The Great Fire of London

The Power of the Habsburgs

The ambitious Habsburg family began ruling Austria in the late 13th century. By marrying into some of Europe's richest families, they gained vast areas of land, and soon became the most powerful rulers in Europe.

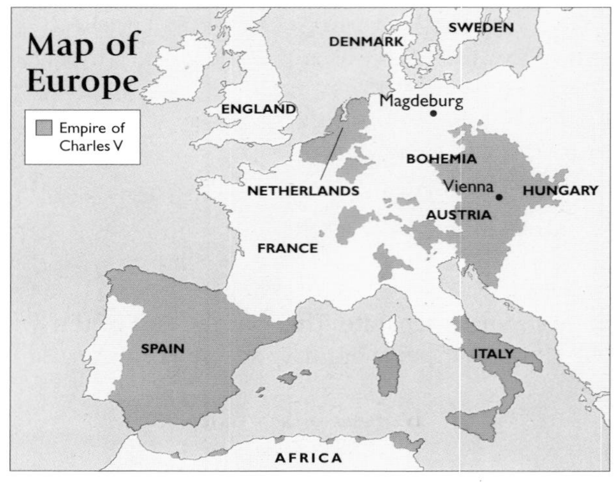

The empire of Charles V

In the first half of the 16th century, the Habsburg emperor Charles V governed large areas of Europe, as well as colonies in the Americas. Charles was a strong ruler who defended his empire well. He won wars against the French and drove an army of Ottoman Turks out of Vienna (see page 298).

The empire divides

In 1556, Charles V retired to a monastery, dividing his lands between his son, Philip II, and his brother, Ferdinand. Philip II became King of Spain, and also controlled Italy, the Netherlands and Spain's American colonies, while Ferdinand ruled from Austria and inherited the title of emperor.

This is King Philip II of Spain, who became fabulously wealthy when Spanish settlers in America started mining gold and silver.

The Thirty Years' War

The Thirty Years' War started as a religious struggle between Protestants and Catholics in central Europe. It began in Bohemia (now part of the Czech Republic), when a group of Protestant nobles threw some officials of the Catholic Habsburg emperor out of a window.

This 17th-century drawing shows the event which helped to start the Thirty Years' War.

Spain and the Catholic German states supported the Habsburg emperor, while Bohemia was joined by Denmark and the Protestant German states. Later, Sweden and France also fought against the Habsburgs. By the end of the Thirty Years' War, the Habsburgs had become much less powerful.

The War of the Spanish Succession

The last of the Spanish Habsburgs was Charles II, who died in 1700. Charles had no children, so he left his lands to his distant relative, Philip, the grandson of the French king. The English and the Dutch were afraid that France and Spain would unite, so in 1701 they formed a "Grand Alliance" to fight against France.

The war lasted for 13 years and many European countries joined in. Eventually, the Alliance allowed Philip to become King of Spain, on the understanding that France and Spain would always remain separate. This was the end of the Habsburgs in Spain, but they still ruled in Austria.

This portrait shows Maria Theresa, who ruled the Austrian Habsburg Empire for 40 years.

Maria Theresa

In 1740, the 23-year-old Maria Theresa became the new ruler of the Habsburg Empire. When she took over, the empire was poor and weak, but she managed to make it strong again. Maria Theresa welcomed many musicians and artists to her court in Vienna. One of these musicians was the brilliant composer Wolfgang Amadeus Mozart.

Here you can see the Schönbrunn Palace in Vienna, which was rebuilt by Maria Theresa.

★

The later Habsburgs

During the 18th and 19th centuries, the Habsburgs lost more and more land. But they managed to stay in power until 1918, when the last Habsburg emperor gave up his throne.

Important dates

1519-1556	Charles V rules a vast Habsburg Empire.
1556	The Habsburg Empire is divided in two.
1618-1648	The Thirty Years' War
1701-1714	The War of the Spanish Succession
1740-1780	Maria Theresa rules the Habsburg Empire.
1918	The last Habsburg emperor gives up his throne.

The Rise of the Dutch

By the 1550s, the low-lying lands that are now Holland, Belgium and Luxembourg were divided into 17 areas, called provinces. The people of the provinces had grown rich by weaving cloth and trading, but they weren't independent. Instead, they were ruled from Spain by the powerful Habsburg family (see page 308).

Catholics and Protestants

In 1556, King Philip II of Spain became the new Habsburg ruler of the provinces. Many people in the provinces were Protestants, but Philip was determined that they should all be Catholics. He sent the Duke of Alba to punish any rebels, and when two Protestant leaders were executed, war broke out between the provinces and Spain.

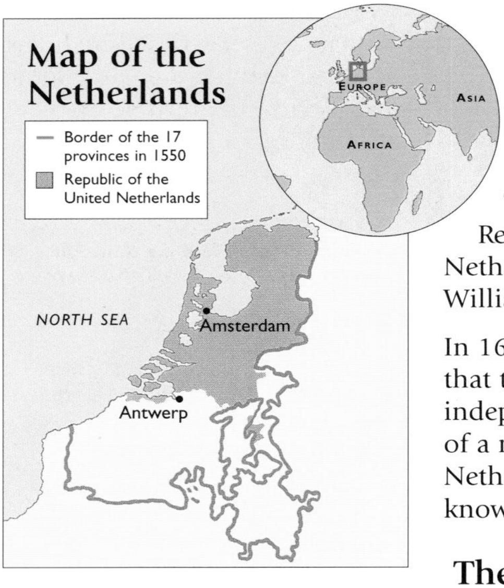

Map of the Netherlands

— Border of the 17 provinces in 1550

Republic of the United Netherlands

NORTH SEA

Amsterdam

Antwerp

EUROPE

ASIA

AFRICA

The Dutch Revolt

Led by a Dutch prince named William of Orange, the people of the provinces fought fiercely for their independence. This struggle is known as the Dutch Revolt, because the most determined fighters were the Dutch, who lived in the northern provinces.

A miniature painting of Prince William of Orange

Dutch independence

In 1581, the seven northern provinces declared that they were independent from Spain. They called themselves the Republic of the United Netherlands and chose Prince William of Orange as their ruler.

In 1648, Spain finally accepted that the Republic was independent. This was the start of a new country called the Netherlands, which is now also known as Holland.

The city of Amsterdam

During the Dutch Revolt, the wealthy port of Antwerp was destroyed by Spanish troops, and many of the provinces' merchants and bankers moved north to Amsterdam. The city of Amsterdam was rebuilt around a network of canals, and by the 1600s it was the busiest port in Europe.

This picture shows the bustling port of Amsterdam.

Merchant ships from all over Europe visit Amsterdam.

French trading ship

Art and science

This painting is by Jan Vermeer, who was famous for his scenes of everyday life.

During the 17th century, many great artists, thinkers and scientists lived and worked in the Netherlands. Inventors made microscopes, telescopes and clocks, and artists painted portraits and scenes of daily life.

The Dutch Empire

The Dutch built up an efficient navy and set up trading bases in Asia, South Africa, America, and even Japan. But their most valuable bases were in the East Indies (present-day Indonesia and Malaysia). From there, Dutch merchants sent shiploads of precious spices to Europe.

Using the land

The flat fields of Holland were often flooded by sea water, but Dutch engineers discovered new ways of draining the land. Some farmers made a fortune by growing exotic flowers from Turkey, known as tulips.

Dutch tulip-growers developed a wide range of flowers. Here are three kinds of tulips, painted by a 17th-century artist.

One tulip bulb could cost as much as a large country house.

William and Mary

In 1677, Prince William of Orange, great-grandson of the first Dutch leader, married the English princess Mary, and in 1689 they were crowned joint rulers of England. William ruled the Netherlands and England until his death in 1702, but the Dutch lost control of England when Mary's sister Anne became the next English queen.

Important dates

1568	The Dutch Revolt begins.
1581	The Republic of the United Netherlands is created.
1648	The Republic of the United Netherlands is recognized by Spain.
1689-1702	William of Orange is ruler of the Netherlands and King of England.

This Dutch merchant ship is bringing spices from the East Indies to the Netherlands.

France and the Sun King

King Louis XIV of France, known as the Sun King, was the most powerful ruler in 17th-century Europe. He controlled all of France for over 50 years, without ever consulting his nobles or the French parliament.

Louis XIV became known as the Sun King after he played the role of the Sun in a 12-hour ballet. This golden carving shows Louis as the Sun King. ★

Early lessons

Louis was only five when he became king, so his mother ruled for him. But after five years, the people of Paris rebelled, angry at the high taxes that they had to pay. Many nobles joined in the revolt, and Louis was forced to leave Paris.

In 1653, the rebellion collapsed, but Louis was still too young to rule on his own, so a powerful Church leader, Jules Mazarin, governed France on his behalf. Louis finally took control in 1661 when he was 22. He was determined that there would be no more revolts, so he kept all the power for himself, becoming what is known as an "absolute" ruler.

Running France

To help him run the country, Louis chose advisers who were talented, but loyal to him. His chief adviser, Jean Colbert, reorganized laws and taxes, set up new businesses in France and increased trade with other countries. Colbert also built new roads, canals and bridges all over France.

The Palace of Versailles

Louis gave orders for a magnificent palace to be built at Versailles, near Paris. Over 30,000 workers were needed to build the palace, which was filled with priceless statues, tapestries and paintings. In 1682, Louis moved to Versailles with his family and thousands of servants. He also forced many French nobles to live in the palace, so that he could keep an eye on them all the time.

Here you can see Louis XIV's palace at Versailles. Its extravagant Baroque style was copied all over Europe.

The palace gardens were laid out in a very formal design.

This is the glittering Hall of Mirrors in Louis's palace at Versailles.

A splendid court

Louis XIV's court at Versailles was famous for its drama, music and art. The playwright Molière wrote comedies to amuse the king, the musician Lully composed operas for the court, and artists painted flattering portraits of the king and his family.

This dramatic portrait of Louis XIV shows him as a dashing young horseman.

Wars in Europe

Louis wanted to conquer more land, and he fought many wars against other countries in Europe. The wars made France feared and respected, but they were very expensive and the French gained only small areas of new land.

Anger in France

In 1685, Louis took away the French Protestants' right to worship, and many of them fled abroad. Meanwhile, the French middle classes and peasants began to resent the taxes that they had to pay to keep the king and the nobles in luxury.

After the Sun King

The two French kings who ruled after Louis XIV were both very extravagant. Like the Sun King, they fought expensive wars and lived in incredible luxury.

Meanwhile, the French people continued to pay heavy taxes, and 70 years after the Sun King's death, the French Revolution began (see pages 332 and 333).

Important dates

1643-1715	Louis XIV is King of France.
1643-1651	Louis's mother rules for him.
1648-1653	Rebellion in Paris
1661	Louis XIV takes control of France.
1667-1713	France fights wars against other countries in Europe.

The Age of Ideas

Between 1600 and 1800, there was an explosion of new ideas in Europe. Scientists made dramatic discoveries, thinkers questioned the power of their rulers, and some daring writers challenged the teachings of the Church. Many people started to see the world in a new light, and the 18th century became known as the Age of Enlightenment.

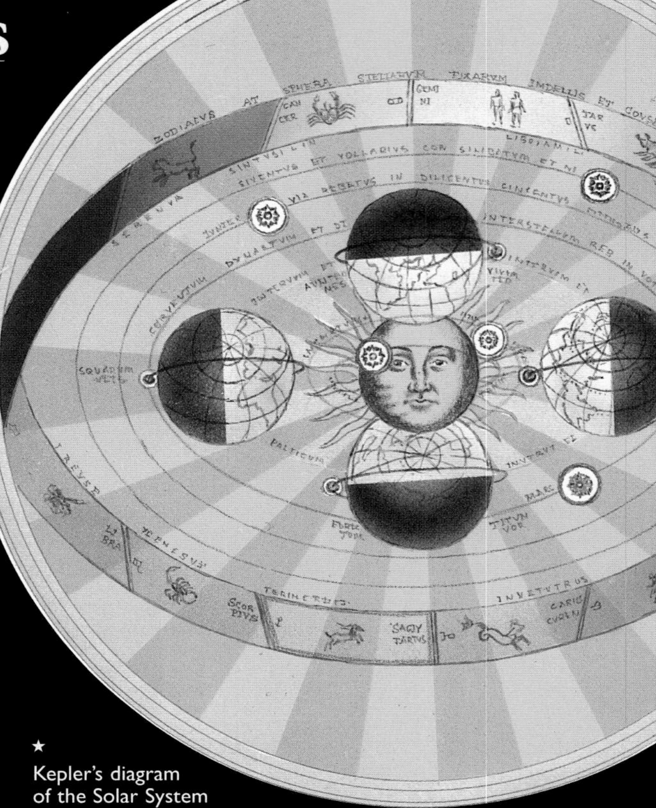

★ Kepler's diagram of the Solar System shows how the planets travel around the Sun.

Discoveries in science

By observing the world around them and doing experiments, scientists made amazing progress. Johannes Kepler studied the way planets move, and Galileo Galilei used the newly invented telescope to help him prove that the Earth circles the Sun. Robert Boyle experimented with chemicals and gases, and Isaac Newton discovered how gravity works.

The photograph on the left shows the surface of the Moon. Galileo studied the mountains of the Moon with the help of a telescope.

Advances in medicine

During the 17th and 18th centuries, doctors studied the human body, and surgeons performed difficult operations. Many doctors were forced to study secretly because the leaders of the Church wouldn't allow them to cut up dead bodies.

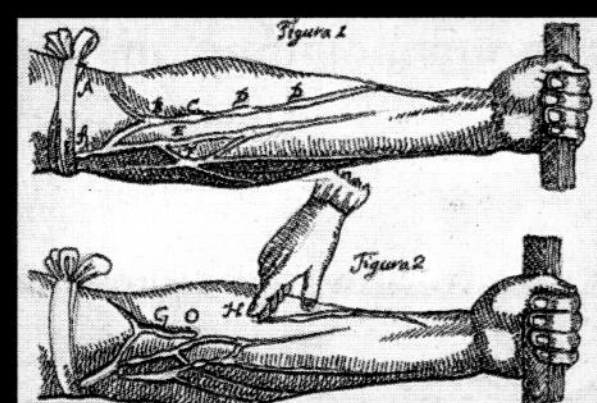

In 1628, William Harvey described the way blood moves around the human body. This is a diagram from Harvey's book.

This painting by the Dutch artist Rembrandt shows a group of 17th-century doctors examining the arm of a dead man.

Collecting knowledge

Many books were produced to record the new discoveries that were being made. Denis Diderot put together a 35-volume encyclopedia. Dr. Samuel Johnson wrote a vast English dictionary, and Carl Linnaeus published detailed studies of plants, dividing them into types, or species.

Linnaeus gave each plant a Latin name. The pansy shown here was named *Viola tricolor*.

Dangerous ideas

By the 1750s, thinkers in Europe had become very daring. In France, Jean Jacques Rousseau made the bold new claim that all people are equal, while Voltaire attacked the French king and the Church. Ideas like these got their writers into trouble, and Voltaire was sent to prison three times.

Like Voltaire and Rousseau, the writer Thomas Paine encouraged ordinary people to think about their rights. His most famous book, *The Rights of Man*, supports the ideas behind the French Revolution.

The writing in this 18th-century cartoon suggests that Thomas Paine's ideas were dangerous nonsense.

Spreading ideas

The new ideas spread fast among educated people. Discoveries were published in books, pamphlets and newspapers, and scientists formed societies where they shared their findings.

Rich people invited guests to their homes to discuss the latest discoveries, and people also met in coffee houses to read the newspapers and talk about ideas.

This golden ball represents the Sun.

These smaller balls represent the planets, which all move around the Sun.

Some planets have moons circling them.

Scientists often used models to help them explain their ideas. This is an 18th-century model of the Sun and the planets.

The model works when its handle is turned.

Rulers and ideas

Some European rulers encouraged the search for knowledge. King Louis XIV of France set up a society which paid scientists to carry out experiments, while Charles II of England started the Royal Society for scientists and thinkers. Charles also built an observatory, where astronomers could study the stars.

Important dates

1620s	Kepler studies the movement of the planets.
1630s	Galileo proves that the Earth travels around the Sun.
1660s	Newton discovers the laws of gravity.
1694-1778	Life of Voltaire
1712-1778	Life of Rousseau
1791-1792	Thomas Paine writes *The Rights of Man*.

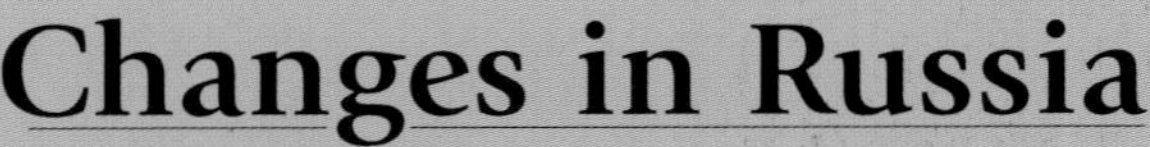

Changes in Russia

Russia in the 1500s was a fast-growing country ruled by a powerful tsar, or emperor. But Russia's position on the eastern edge of Europe made it isolated from the wealthy west. Large areas of Russia were too cold to grow food, and most Russians were peasants who were desperately poor.

This is a portrait of Ivan the Terrible, a powerful ruler who was often violent and cruel.

Ivan the Terrible

In 1547, Prince Ivan IV of Moscow became Tsar of Russia. He was a strong ruler who encouraged trade with western Europe, built up the Russian army, and won land in the valley of the Volga river.

At home in Russia, Ivan was ruthless and cruel, earning himself the title of Ivan the Terrible. He seized land from Russian nobles, called boyars, and gave it to his personal followers. He also made a law that took away all the peasants' rights, turning them into serfs who couldn't leave their master's land.

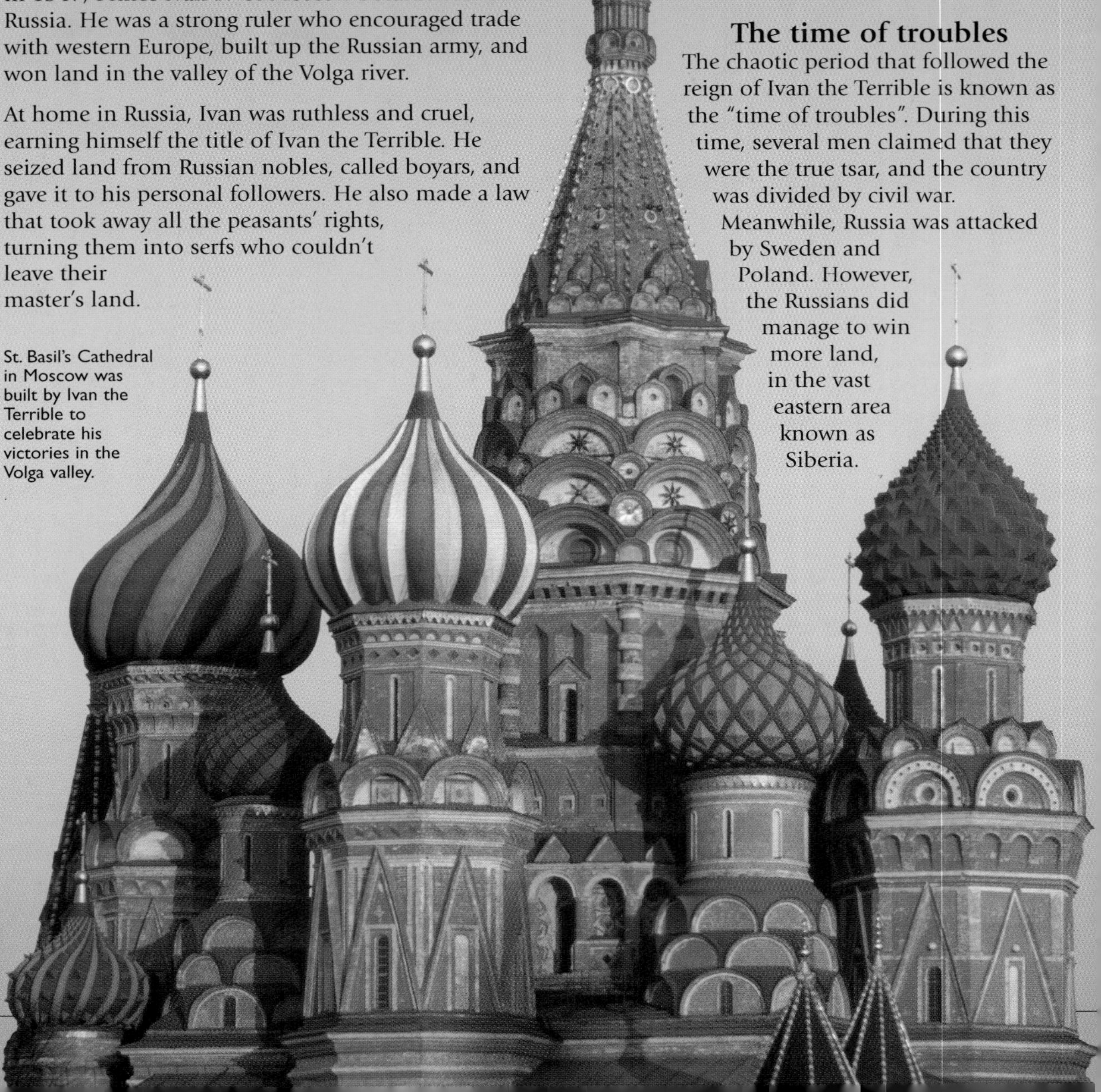

St. Basil's Cathedral in Moscow was built by Ivan the Terrible to celebrate his victories in the Volga valley.

The time of troubles

The chaotic period that followed the reign of Ivan the Terrible is known as the "time of troubles". During this time, several men claimed that they were the true tsar, and the country was divided by civil war. Meanwhile, Russia was attacked by Sweden and Poland. However, the Russians did manage to win more land, in the vast eastern area known as Siberia.

Internet link: *For a link to a Web site where you can watch a short video about Peter the Great, go to* ***www.usborne-quicklinks.com***

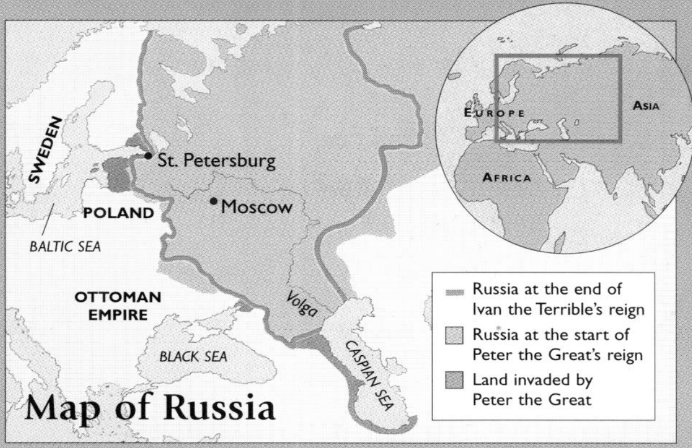

Map of Russia

Changing Russia

Back in Russia, Peter reorganized his country's government, and reduced the power of the boyars. Workers from Europe helped to build canals, ships and factories, and a new iron industry was set up in Russia.

Peter forced the boyars to cut off their beards, to show that they had given up their old powers. This cartoon shows him as a barber.

Peter the Great

In 1613, the Romanov family took control of Russia, starting a dynasty which would last for 300 years. The greatest of the Romanovs was Peter the Great, who became tsar in 1682. By the end of his reign, Russia was one of the strongest countries in Europe.

Learning from the west

Peter decided to modernize Russia by copying the way western countries were run. He spent 18 months in northern Europe, visiting factories, farms and hospitals, and he even worked in a shipyard.

Peter the Great was an energetic and inspiring leader, but he could also be frighteningly brutal.

Peter's wars

Peter strengthened the Russian army, created a navy, and won several victories against the Swedes and the Ottoman Turks. From Sweden, Russia gained a stretch of land beside the Baltic Sea. This meant that the Russians could at last build some ports which were close to western Europe and didn't freeze solid every winter.

A new capital city

Peter gave orders for an elegant new city to be built on the Baltic coast. He named it St. Petersburg and made it into Russia's new capital. The land around St. Petersburg was extremely swampy, and hundreds of serfs drowned while they were building the city.

Important dates

1480-1505	Prince Ivan III of Moscow is the first Tsar of Russia.
1547-1584	Ivan the Terrible is tsar.
1613	The Romanov dynasty begins.
1682-1725	Peter the Great is tsar.
1695-1706	Russia fights the Ottoman Empire.
1700-1721	Russia fights Sweden.
1712	St. Petersburg becomes the new Russian capital.

Russians and Prussians

During the 18th century, eastern Europe was dominated by two very powerful rulers. Catherine the Great of Russia and Frederick the Great of Prussia both insisted that they should have complete power, and both of them used their power to make their countries rich and successful.

Catherine the Great

Catherine the Great was an intelligent and determined ruler who demanded total obedience from her people.

Catherine II became Tsarina (empress) of Russia in 1762, and ruled for more than 30 years. She encouraged Russian trade, set up universities, and invited thinkers and writers to her splendid court at St. Petersburg. Later, she became known as Catherine the Great.

New lands

Catherine's army won new land around the Black Sea and the Baltic Sea, and the Russians built ports on both of these coasts. But Russia's most important gains came from the break-up of the weak kingdom of Poland. Poland was split between Russia, Austria and Prussia, and Catherine made sure that Russia had the largest share.

Life in Russia

While Catherine and her courtiers lived in luxury, the Russian peasants paid heavy taxes and had to fight in the army. At first, Catherine planned to make life better for her people, but most of her plans were never put into action. Peasant rebellions were brutally crushed, and when Catherine drove through Russia, her officials paid wealthy farmers to pretend to be peasants so that she wouldn't see how poor her people really were.

In this scene, Tsarina Catherine is driving through the Russian countryside in her sleigh.

Catherine's sleigh passes well-built houses like this, but most Russian peasants live in tumbledown shacks.

Wealthy farmers in warm clothes wave at the tsarina.

An official pushes the real peasants out of sight.

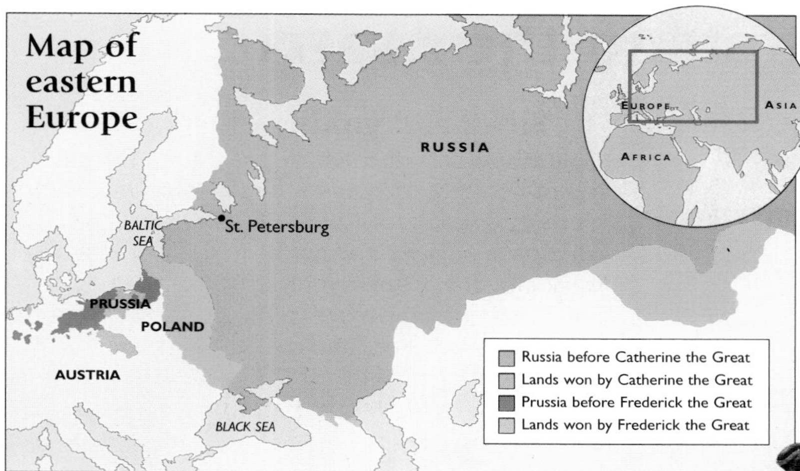

Frederick's wars

Frederick the Great was a brilliant soldier who used his well-trained army to conquer large areas of land. He won outstanding victories against France and Austria in the Seven Years' War, and by the end of his reign he had doubled the size of Prussia.

This 18th-century painting shows a violent battle in the Seven Years' War.

The rise of Prussia

In 1618, the weak state of Prussia was inherited by the ruler of the German state of Brandenburg. Prussia's new rulers built up a strong army and united all their lands under an efficient government. In 1701, the ruler of Brandenburg was crowned King of Prussia, and an ambitious new country was born.

Frederick the Great

Frederick II, known as Frederick the Great, became King of Prussia in 1740. He was a talented musician, a brave general and a stern ruler who believed that only a king with total power could make a real difference to the lives of his people.

Frederick improved education for middle-class boys, encouraged the study of science, and helped to build up farming and trade in Prussia. He also made it illegal to torture prisoners, and allowed both Catholics and Protestants to follow their own religion.

Important dates

1701-1713	Frederick I is the first King of Prussia.
1740-1786	Frederick the Great is King of Prussia.
1756-1763	Prussia and Britain fight France, Russia and Austria in the Seven Years' War.
1762-1796	Catherine the Great is Tsarina of Russia.

Early Settlers in the Americas

Soon after Christopher Columbus reached America in 1492, the first settlers from Europe began arriving in the New World. By 1550, there were thousands of Spanish and Portuguese settlers in the West Indies and South America. At the same time, settlers from France had begun to make their homes in the land that is now called Canada.

Soldiers and priests

Spanish soldiers conquered large areas of South America and set up colonies with Spanish rulers, called viceroys. Some soldiers and priests from Spain also settled in North America, building forts and churches in Florida and California.

This 19th-century painting shows a lakeside town in the Spanish colony of New Granada.

Silver and gold

Spanish settlers opened up mines in Mexico and Peru, and sent back shiploads of silver and gold to Spain. The Spanish forced the Native Americans to work in their mines, and many workers died of exhaustion or disease.

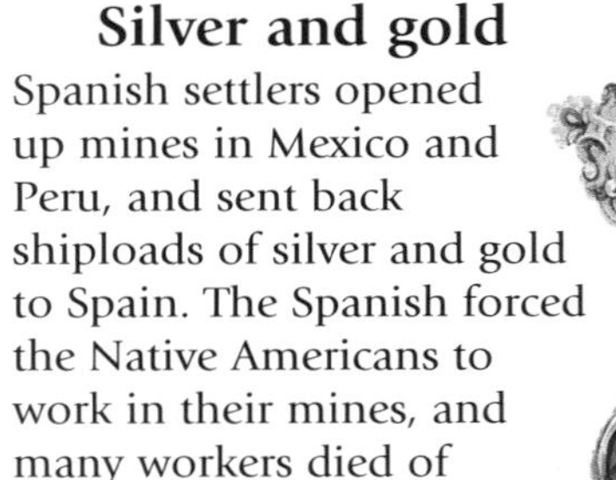

★ Spanish cross made from South American gold

Internet link**: For a link to a Web site where you can walk around a Spanish fort in Florida, go to **www.usborne-quicklinks.com

French settlers

The early French settlers in Canada built their homes close to rivers, and lived by trapping and hunting animals and catching fish. Slowly, the settlers spread out, and in 1699 they claimed all the land around the Mississippi River, naming the area Louisiana after the French king, Louis XIV.

Portuguese plantations

Portuguese settlers in Brazil grew sugar on vast farms called plantations, and brought slaves from Africa to work on their farms. (For more about slavery see pages 324 and 325.)

French losses

The French were not the only Europeans to settle in North America, and by 1700 the British also owned large areas of land. In 1754, the French and the British began fighting each other for land. At first, the French managed to fight off the British, but in 1759 British troops, led by General James Wolfe, captured the French city of Quebec. After this victory, the British won more land from France, and in 1763 the French signed the Peace of Paris, giving most of their land in Canada to Britain.

General James Wolfe

Map of the Americas

The map shows land owned by European countries in 1750.

- Spanish land
- Portuguese land
- French land
- British land
- Dutch land

Important dates

By 1600	The Spanish, Portuguese and French all have colonies in the Americas.
1699	The French create the colony of Louisiana.
1754	War breaks out in North America between the British and the French.
1759	The British capture Quebec.
1763	The Peace of Paris gives Britain control of Canada.

Settlers in North America

Near the end of the 16th century, groups of settlers from England tried to set up colonies on the east coast of North America. The first English settlers either died or returned home, but in 1607 a successful settlement was started in Jamestown, Virginia.

Pilgrim settlers

In August 1620, a group of English settlers set sail for Virginia in a ship called the *Mayflower*. The settlers belonged to a strict religious group who wanted to be free to worship God in their own way. Later, they became known as the Pilgrims, or the Pilgrim Fathers.

★ The *Mayflower* took three months to sail from England to America.

Land and freedom

By the 1650s, many settlers were sailing from Europe to North America. Groups of Puritans (strict Protestants) and Catholics settled in America so that they could be free to follow their own religion. But many other settlers left Europe in search of land and adventure.

New Amsterdam

In 1624, a group of Dutch settlers built a settlement on an island in the Hudson River and named it New Amsterdam. The Dutch controlled the island until 1664, when it was captured by the English, who renamed it New York.

The first Thanksgiving

The *Mayflower* was blown off course and landed in a place that the Pilgrims named Plymouth. The first winter was extremely hard, but, with the help of the local Native Americans, half of the settlers survived.

After their first harvest, the Pilgrims made a simple meal and held a service of thanksgiving. Every November, many Americans remember this event with a Thanksgiving meal.

This picture shows the Pilgrims preparing their first Thanksgiving meal.

Fish hung up to dry

These women are plucking wild turkeys.

House built from wooden planks, called clapboards

Some of the settlers are very weak and ill.

Map of the Thirteen Colonies

The Thirteen Colonies

By 1733, the British ruled 13 colonies on the east coast of America. The colonists grew tobacco, rice, and a blue dye called indigo. They sold these things to people in Europe in exchange for guns, clothes and tools.

Wars for land

At first, the settlers from Europe lived peacefully with the Native Americans, but as their colonies grew, battles for land began. By the 1720s, most of the native tribes on the east coast of America had been wiped out or had been driven west.

Native North Americans have taught the settlers how to fish, hunt and grow crops.

Fence to keep out wild animals

These Native Americans are bringing deer for the meal.

Chickens are kept for their eggs.

This woman is reading aloud from the Bible.

The settlers wear very plain clothes.

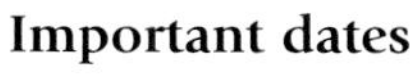

Important dates

1607	The English build a settlement in Jamestown, Virginia.
1620	The Pilgrims arrive in America.
1624	The Dutch settle in New Amsterdam.
By 1733	The British have 13 American colonies.

The Slave Trade

People had bought and sold slaves since ancient times, but in the 1580s this terrible trade increased dramatically. Millions of Africans were captured and sent across the ocean to the Americas. Those who survived the journey were sold as slaves, and most slaves had to work so hard they died within a few years.

Workers wanted

Since the 1500s, settlers from Europe had grown sugar and tobacco in the West Indies and South America. The settlers used native people to work on their vast farms, which were called plantations. However, by the 1550s, so many native people had died that the settlers were desperate for more workers.

Charlestown, July 24th, 1769.
TO BE SOLD,
On THURSDAY the third Day of AUGUST next,
A CARGO
OF
NINETY-FOUR
PRIME, HEALTHY
NEGROES,
CONSISTING OF
Thirty-nine MEN, Fifteen BOYS, Twenty-four WOMEN, and Sixteen GIRLS.
JUST ARRIVED,
In the Brigantine DEMBIA, *Francis Bare*, Master, from SIERRA-LEON, by
DAVID & JOHN DEAS.

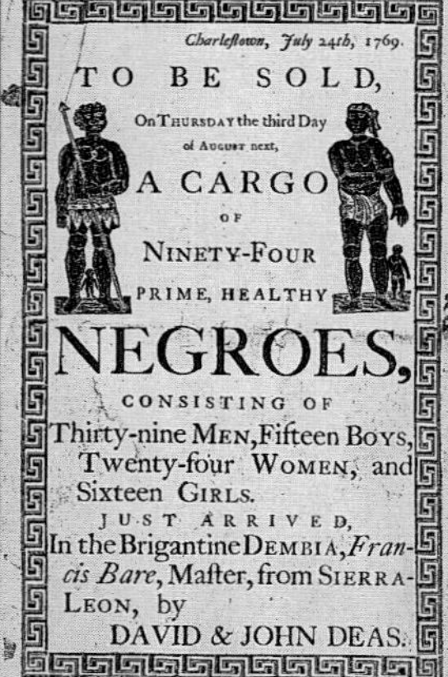

African slaves were sold to the buyer who offered the most money. Posters like this advertised the sales.

The slave trade begins

The Portuguese had colonies on the west coast of Africa and they began to buy Africans who had been captured by rival tribes. The captives were chained together and forced to march to the coast. Then they were packed onto ships and sent to the Americas to be sold as slaves.

A triangle of trade

By 1600, many European countries had joined in the slave trade. Their ships made a three-stage journey in the shape of a triangle (see map opposite). First, the slave ships sailed from Europe to Africa, carrying goods such as guns and cloth. In Africa, they exchanged their goods for slaves, and sailed on to the Americas. There, the slaves were sold in exchange for sugar, tobacco and cotton before the ships returned to Europe. This triangle of trade made the slave traders extremely rich.

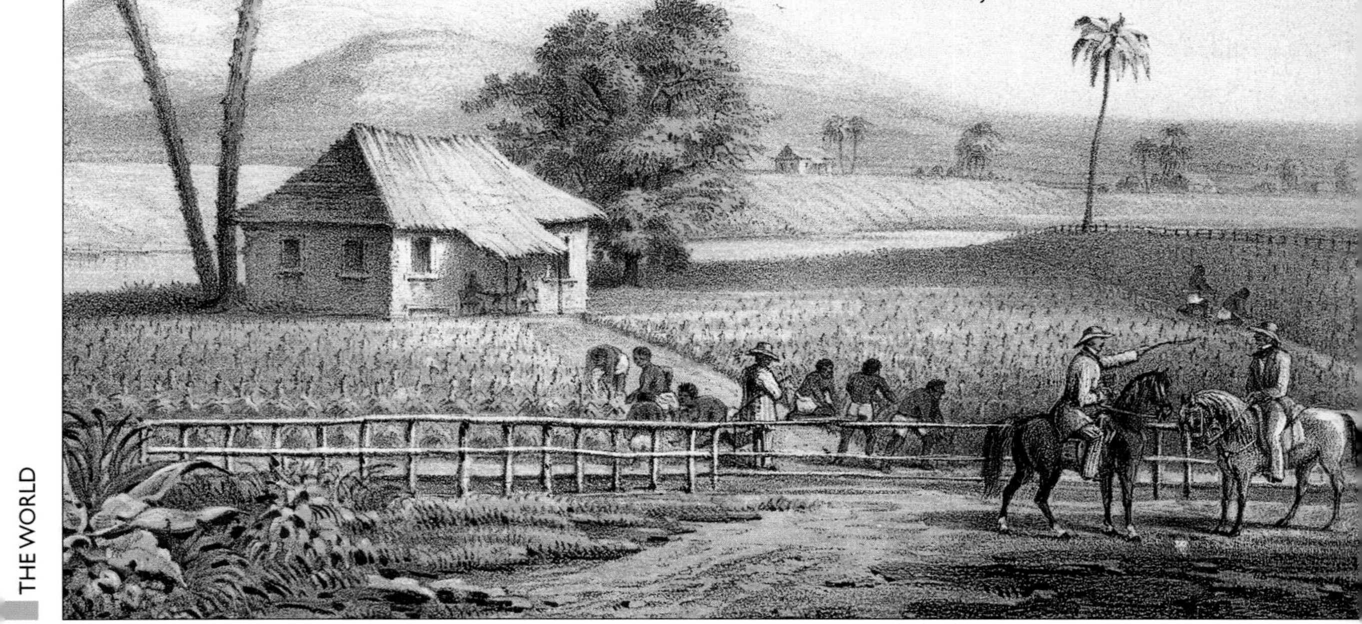

This 19th-century painting shows slaves from Africa working on a tobacco plantation in the West Indies.

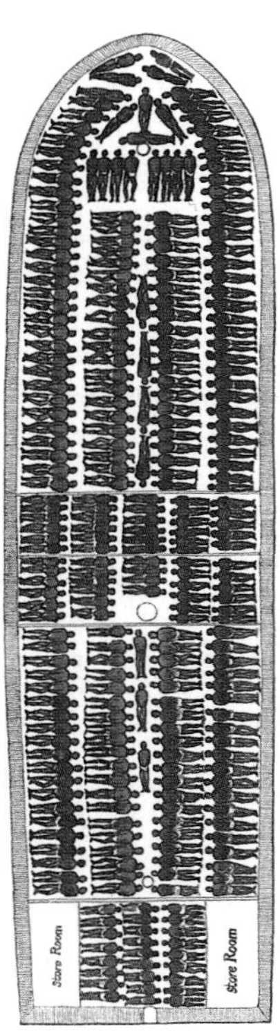

Slave ships

Conditions on board the slave ships were appalling. The slaves were packed tightly together and were kept chained up in the dark for all of their eight-week voyage. Diseases spread rapidly on the ships, and more than a third of the slaves died before they even reached the Americas.

This diagram of a slave ship shows how tightly the slaves were packed together.

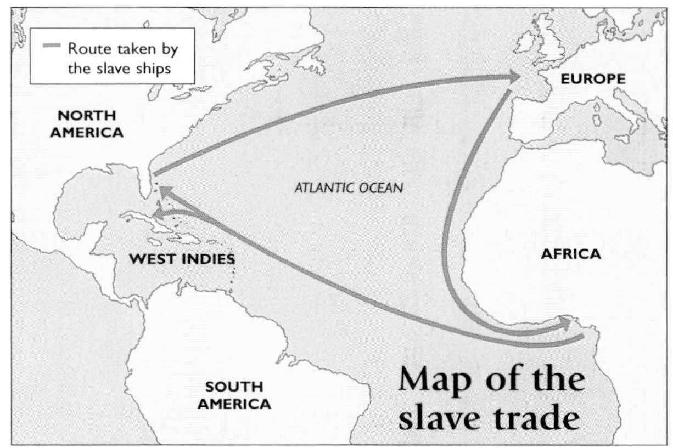

Map of the slave trade

Slaves at work

Most slaves worked in the plantations of the West Indies and South America, but some of them were sent to the USA to pick cotton and harvest tobacco. A few masters were kind to their slaves, but many slaves were treated cruelly and forced to work very long hours.

Slave rebellions

Some courageous slaves led rebellions against their masters, but most of these rebels were punished severely. In 1791, however, a successful revolt took place in Haiti in the West Indies, and the slaves' leader, Toussaint L'Ouverture, became ruler of Haiti.

Ending the slave trade

By the 1780s, many people in Europe had become unhappy about the slave trade. In 1792, Denmark became the first country to stop buying and selling slaves, and over the next 40 years the European slave trade slowly died out.

In 1804, slavery was banned in the northern states of the USA, but the people of the southern states continued to keep slaves for another 60 years. Gradually, slavery was made illegal all over the Americas, and the last slaves were set free in 1888.

Here is a family of slaves who worked in the cotton fields of the southern USA.

Important dates

1680-1780	The slave trade is at its peak.
1792	Denmark stops its slave trade.
1804	Slavery is made illegal in the northern states of the USA.
1865	Slavery is made illegal throughout the USA.
1888	Slavery ends throughout the Americas.

Exploring the South Seas

By the 1600s, European explorers had reached most parts of the world, but the South Pacific Ocean was still unknown. Sailors began to travel there, searching for new lands and riches.

Dutch explorers

In 1606, Dutch explorers reached the north coast of Australia, and in 1642 a Dutchman, Abel Tasman, sailed as far south as New Zealand. Tasman was also the first European to see the island of Tasmania, which was named after him.

Captain Cook

In 1768, Captain James Cook set out from Britain to explore the lands of the South Pacific. In some places, Cook's men were welcomed by the people who lived there. But when Cook's ship reached New Zealand, the native people, called Maoris, tried to frighten him away. Cook eventually made peace with the Maoris, and later drew detailed maps of New Zealand's coastline.

This picture shows Maori canoes approaching Captain Cook's ship, the *Endeavour*, as it arrives on the coast of New Zealand.

The ship is flying a British flag called the Red Ensign.

Scientists have come on the voyage to study wildlife in new lands.

Captain Cook

Cook's soldiers fire guns into the air, to drive the Maoris away.

The Maoris' canoes are covered with carvings.

Internet link: *For a link to a Web site where you can see a full-size replica of Captain Cook's ship, the* Endeavour, *inside and out, go to* **www.usborne-quicklinks.com**

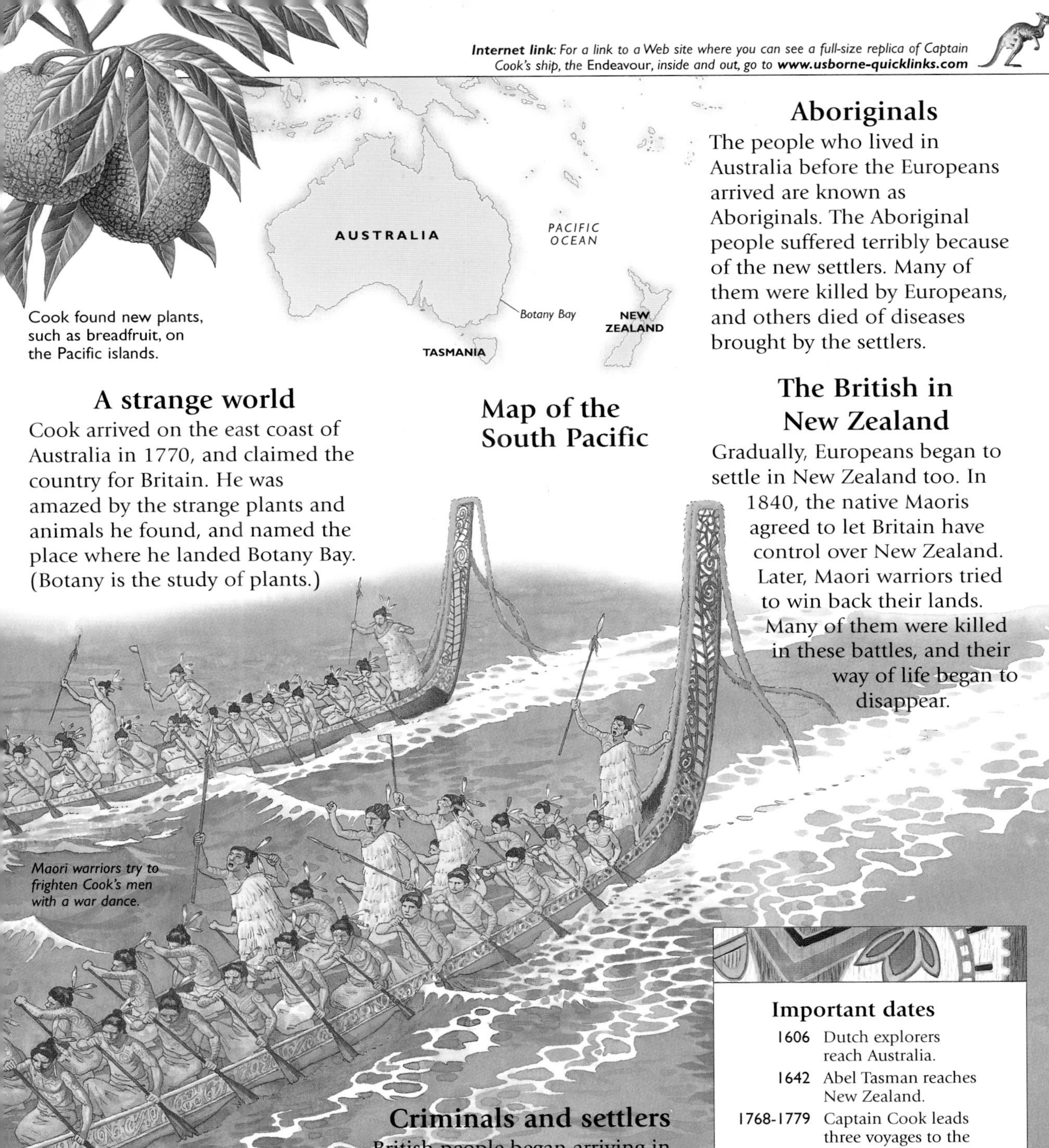

Cook found new plants, such as breadfruit, on the Pacific islands.

Map of the South Pacific

Maori warriors try to frighten Cook's men with a war dance.

Aboriginals

The people who lived in Australia before the Europeans arrived are known as Aboriginals. The Aboriginal people suffered terribly because of the new settlers. Many of them were killed by Europeans, and others died of diseases brought by the settlers.

A strange world

Cook arrived on the east coast of Australia in 1770, and claimed the country for Britain. He was amazed by the strange plants and animals he found, and named the place where he landed Botany Bay. (Botany is the study of plants.)

The British in New Zealand

Gradually, Europeans began to settle in New Zealand too. In 1840, the native Maoris agreed to let Britain have control over New Zealand. Later, Maori warriors tried to win back their lands. Many of them were killed in these battles, and their way of life began to disappear.

Criminals and settlers

British people began arriving in Australia in the 1780s. Many were criminals who were sent there to work by the British government, but others were farmers looking for land. By the 1830s, about 100,000 Europeans were living in Australia.

Important dates

1606	Dutch explorers reach Australia.
1642	Abel Tasman reaches New Zealand.
1768-1779	Captain Cook leads three voyages to the South Seas.
1770	Captain Cook reaches Australia and claims it for Britain.
1788	Britain begins sending convicts to Australia.
1840	The British take control of New Zealand.

The British in India

During the 16th century, many merchants from Europe arrived in India. They bought silk, cotton, tea and spices, and built up wealthy trading companies.

Indian crocuses, and a spice called saffron which comes from their flowers

By the 1700s, India was split into areas ruled by local princes. The princes often fought each other, and the Europeans sometimes took sides in their battles.

Clive of India

In 1756, the Prince of Bengal captured a British trading base and killed more than a hundred people. The following year, a British general named Robert Clive led an army that defeated the Prince. Clive forced everyone in Bengal to pay taxes to the British East India Company, which became very powerful.

Robert Clive, who became rich by seizing gold that belonged to the Prince of Bengal

The rise of the British

The East India Company gradually built up a big army. It was led by British soldiers, but many Indians joined as well. The army defeated more and more princes, and took control of large areas of India.

★ This mechanical toy belonged to an Indian prince. It shows a tiger eating a British soldier.

The Indian Mutiny

Many Indian soldiers in the British army became angry. They felt that the British didn't respect Indian religions and were changing the country too much. In 1857, some Indian soldiers in Bengal began a mutiny, or rebellion, against the British.

★ This scene is based on a 19th-century painting of a battle in the Indian Mutiny.

The fighting spread to many areas of northern India, but in 1858 the rebels were defeated. The British government took charge of the country, and India became an important part of the British Empire.

Princes and servants

After the mutiny, some Indian princes still lived in splendid palaces, but they no longer had any power. Most Indians remained poor, and many of them worked as servants for the British.

Making changes

The British built roads, railways and schools in India, and made the Indians learn English. Many British missionaries went to India and tried to persuade Indians to become Christians.

Life in the Raj

By the 1880s, lots of British families were living in India. They tried to keep to a British way of life, but they were also influenced by Indian culture. The British stayed in India until 1947, when the country became independent. The period of time when the British ruled India is known as the Raj.

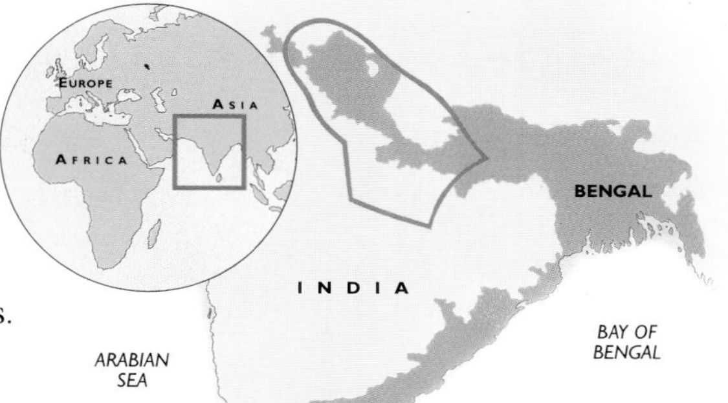

Map of India

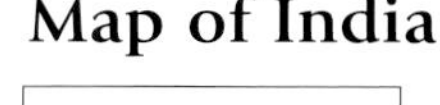

Areas controlled by the East India Company by 1805

Main area where the Indian Mutiny took place

★ British people were not used to the hot Indian weather, and women used parasols to protect themselves from the sun.

This photograph shows King George V of Great Britain hunting tigers during a visit to India in 1911.

Important dates

1600	The British East India Company is created.
1757	Robert Clive defeats the Prince of Bengal at the Battle of Plassey.
1757-1857	Britain conquers large areas of India.
1857-1858	The Indian Mutiny
1858	The British government takes control of India.

The American Revolution

By the 1700s, Britain had 13 colonies on the east coast of North America (see page 323). The British government ruled its colonies with strict laws, and made the colonists pay more taxes than people in Britain. Many colonists thought that this was unfair, and riots broke out.

Map of the Thirteen Colonies

British colonies

NORTH AMERICA

Boston

ATLANTIC OCEAN

Yorktown

Tea in the sea

One very unpopular tax made it extremely expensive to buy tea in America. In 1773, colonists climbed on board ships delivering tea to the port of Boston and threw all the tea into the sea. This famous protest is known as the Boston Tea Party.

Fighting begins

The British government punished the colonists with even stricter laws, and moved a large army into North America. Fighting soon broke out between the colonists and the British.

Breaking free

The colonists began to think of themselves as Americans and wanted to break free from Britain. In 1776, the leaders of all 13 colonies signed a statement called the Declaration of Independence.

This painting shows the leaders of the colonies signing the Declaration of Independence.

The Declaration said that the colonies were now an independent country. The colonists called their new country the United States of America (USA).

Early battles

The British didn't want to lose control of their North American land, and they fought hard against the new American army. Although the Americans had a strong leader, named George Washington, the British soldiers were better trained and more experienced. The British won several early battles and captured some important cities.

George Washington, a skilled soldier and an inspiring leader

French friends

In 1777, France decided to support the USA against Britain. By this time, the American army was stronger and, with the help of the French, the Americans began to win more battles. In 1781, the British surrendered after a long battle at Yorktown, and the war was over.

A new nation

Soon after the war, Britain signed a peace treaty and accepted the United States as an independent country. In 1787, a group of American lawyers and politicians wrote a set of laws for the new country. These laws are known as the American Constitution. In 1789, George Washington was elected the first President of the USA.

Here you can see the American army attacking a British fort during the Battle of Yorktown. The Americans have started their attack at night, in order to take the British by surprise.

The American flag has 13 stripes, one for each of the 13 colonies.

Americans from all 13 colonies fight alongside each other.

The American soldiers wear blue jackets.

The British have built a wall of soil and tree trunks to protect themselves.

American cannons have destroyed parts of the British wall.

This gun is called a musket.

Metal cannonballs

The British soldiers are known as "redcoats".

Important dates

1773	The Boston Tea Party
July 4, 1776	The 13 colonies declare independence.
1777	France joins the Americans in their war against Britain.
1781	Britain is defeated by the USA and France.
1787	The American Constitution is written.
1789	George Washington becomes the first President of the USA.

The French Revolution

By the 1780s, many French people were angry with their ruler, King Louis XVI, and the way he ran the country. Although the French government was running out of money, the king's nobles still led a luxurious life and paid no taxes. Meanwhile, the peasants and workers had to pay high taxes, and there wasn't enough work or food for them all.

Facing disaster

By 1789, the government had no money left at all, and France was in a desperate situation. In order to solve the country's problems, the king was forced to call a meeting of the Estates General, the French parliament, which had not met for almost 200 years.

Tax troubles

Some of those who came to the meeting of the Estates General were middle-class people, such as merchants and lawyers. Unlike the nobles, the middle classes had to pay taxes. They demanded that everyone should pay fair taxes, but the king refused. This made many French people furious.

Storming the Bastille

On July 14, 1789, a crowd of poor people, helped by some of the king's soldiers, attacked and captured an important prison in Paris, called the Bastille. This dramatic event is known as the storming of the Bastille.

In this scene, French rebels are attacking the Bastille. This was the start of the French Revolution.

A guard plummets from the battlements.

Cannonballs smash the prison walls.

The king's army has joined the rebels.

People shout and cheer.

The revolution spreads

The news that the Bastille had been captured encouraged many other people to rebel, and a revolution soon broke out all over France. The middle classes took control of the country, and in 1793 the king was executed.

Maximilien Robespierre, leader of the French people during the Reign of Terror

The Reign of Terror

The revolution quickly became very violent. The queen was executed, as well as thousands of nobles, and anyone else who was thought to be against the revolution. This frightening period became known as the Reign of Terror.

This is a guillotine, a machine used by the revolutionaries to execute their enemies. ★

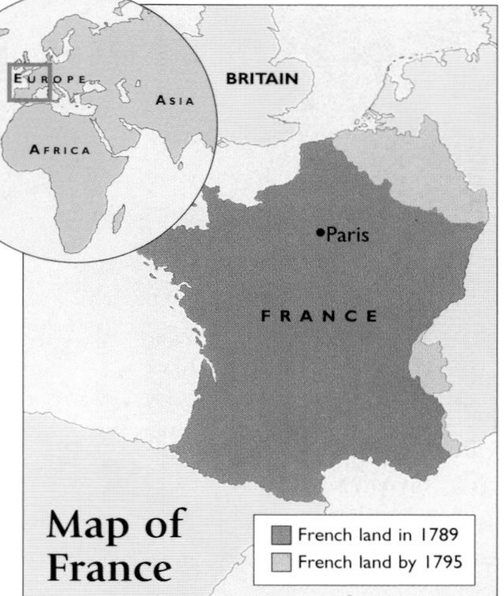

Map of France

War in Europe

The revolutionaries promised to help people in other nations to rebel against their rulers, and France began to invade nearby countries. Many European rulers were worried and wanted to stop the revolution. In 1793, several countries, such as Britain and Austria, attacked France, and war began. By 1795, the French had defeated most of their enemies and won new land in Europe.

Red, white and blue ribbons, like those worn by the French revolutionaries ★

Some buildings have been set on fire.

Rebels have broken through the prison gate.

Peasants use their farm tools as weapons.

Important dates

May 1789	Louis XVI calls a meeting of the Estates General.
July 14, 1789	The Bastille is captured by revolutionaries.
1793	Louis XVI is executed.
1793-1794	The Reign of Terror
1793-1795	France is at war with most of Europe.

The Empire of Napoleon

During the wars that followed the French Revolution, a brilliant young general named Napoleon Bonaparte won many battles for the French army. Napoleon became popular and powerful, and in 1799 he seized control of France.

New laws

Napoleon made many new laws, giving everyone in France the right to own land and to find a good job. However, he was also an extremely strict ruler who wanted as much power for himself as possible.

Napoleon the Emperor

In 1804, Napoleon made himself Emperor of France. His army won a series of spectacular victories, and by 1812 he had conquered most of western Europe. Napoleon ruled from Paris, and put his relatives in charge of parts of his empire.

Defeat at sea

One country that Napoleon failed to take over was Britain. Britain was hard to invade because it had a powerful navy. In 1805, British ships defeated the French navy just off Cape Trafalgar, in southern Spain. The British encouraged other countries to stand up to Napoleon.

Napoleon Bonaparte, painted in 1801 by the French artist Jacques Louis David

This 19th-century painting shows a scene from the Battle of Trafalgar.

The French and British ships have moved close together to fire at each other.

Disaster in Russia

In 1812, Napoleon invaded Russia. He won several battles, then marched his men into Moscow. But Russian soldiers had set fire to the city and taken away all the food.

Napoleon's army was forced to leave Moscow and march all the way back to France through the freezing winter snow. Thousands of men died, and Napoleon's attempt to conquer Russia ended in disaster.

Napoleon Bonaparte

Napoleon's army retreating from Moscow ★

Moscow
RUSSIA
BRITAIN
PRUSSIA
Waterloo
Paris
FRANCE
ITALY
SPAIN
Cape Trafalgar

Map of Napoleon's Empire

Land ruled by France in 1812

Enemies in Europe

When Napoleon's invasion of Russia failed, many European countries joined together against him. His army lost several big battles, and in 1814 he was captured and imprisoned.

Napoleon's downfall

A year after he was captured, Napoleon escaped and took control of France once more. However, after only a hundred days in charge, he was finally defeated by the British and the Prussians at the Battle of Waterloo. Napoleon was sent to live on the tiny island of St. Helena in the middle of the Atlantic Ocean. He died there in 1821.

Important dates

1799	Napoleon takes control of France.
1805	The Battle of Trafalgar
1805-1812	Napoleon conquers most of western Europe.
1812	Napoleon invades Russia, but is forced to turn back.
1814	Napoleon is defeated and captured.
1815	Napoleon returns to power, but is defeated at Waterloo.
1815-1821	Napoleon is imprisoned on the island of St. Helena.

Changes in Farming

Until the late 1600s, farming in Europe had hardly changed for hundreds of years. Most families grew their own food on small strips of land in big fields that belonged to wealthy landowners. There were no farm machines, and people had to manage with just a few simple tools.

By 1700, new ideas and machines were being tried out on farms in Britain and the Netherlands. The new ideas soon spread across Europe, and the changes that they brought became known as the Agricultural Revolution.

Rotating crops

Planting the same crop in a field year after year wears out the soil, so farmers regularly left a field unplanted to let the soil recover. But in the 18th century, some farmers discovered that they could stop the soil from wearing out by planting a different crop in each field every year. This new system was called crop rotation. It meant that farmers could use all their fields all the time, and grow more food.

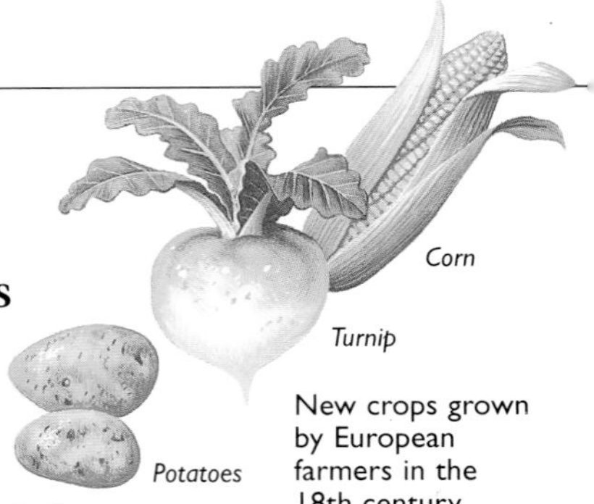

New crops grown by European farmers in the 18th century

This scene shows how a British farming village might have looked by the year 1800.

Planting seeds

One of the most important new machines was the seed drill, which was invented by an English farmer named Jethro Tull. Instead of scattering seeds onto the ground by hand, people could use the seed drill to drop seeds straight into the soil. This meant that far fewer seeds were blown away or eaten by birds.

Better breeding

Some farmers began using only their biggest, healthiest animals for breeding. These animals often had big babies, and over time farm animals became larger, so they could feed more people.

Wealthy farmers had pictures painted that made their animals, such as this sheep, look even bigger than they were.

Fields and fences

Some British landowners realized that it was more practical to grow crops in large fields than in lots of small strips. They took over the strips of land where families had grown their own food and put them together to make bigger fields for themselves.

The landowners built fences and planted hedges around their fields, and villagers were forbidden to use these fields. This meant that many people no longer had anywhere to grow their food, so they had to work for a landowner or find a job in a town.

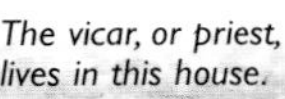

The vicar, or priest, lives in this house.

Church

This house belongs to the wealthy landowner who owns most of the land in the village.

The land has been divided into fields for the landowner.

Hedges have been planted around the fields.

Blacksmith's workshop

The landowner built these cottages for villagers who work for him.

This family is leaving to find work in a town.

Steam power

By the 1850s, some farmers were using new steam-powered machines (see page 338). The machines helped to harvest crops, dig the fields and pump water out of marshy land.

Here are some farm workers with a steam-powered machine for threshing crops. The machine separates the grain from the stalks.

The Industrial Revolution

In the 18th century, many changes began to take place in the way that people lived and worked in Britain. These changes later spread across the world, and together they became known as the Industrial Revolution.

Children working in a coal mine

Mining coal

Steam for the new engines came from boiling water, and huge amounts of coal were needed to heat the water. Deep coal mines were dug, and men, women and children worked in the mines. Working underground was very dangerous, and many people were killed or injured.

New machines

In 1700, most people in Britain lived in villages. Many villagers worked on farms, but others worked at home, spinning wool and cotton thread, then weaving the thread into cloth.

This way of life began to change in the 1700s, when British inventors first designed machines that could spin and weave cloth very quickly. The machines were too big and expensive for people to use at home, so wealthy businessmen built factories that could hold lots of machines.

This machine, called a Spinning Jenny, could spin 16 threads at once, instead of just one.

Steam power

At first, running water was used to turn the wheels that made the machines work, so all the factories had to be built near rivers. Then, in 1782, James Watt invented a powerful engine that was driven by steam. Hundreds of these new steam-engines were built to run machines in factories all over Britain.

Factories and towns

Busy towns soon grew up around the factories, as thousands of people moved out of their villages to work on the new machines. People had to work very long hours, and many workers were injured while using the machines.

During the Industrial Revolution, iron was used to make engines, boats, trains and bridges. This is the world's first iron bridge, built at Coalbrookdale in England in 1779.

Canals and trains

Roads were muddy and bumpy in the 18th century, and carts were often attacked by robbers, so factory owners had to find a different way to transport their goods. For many years, they used canals, but canal boats were slow. Then, early in the 19th century, British inventors discovered how to build steam-powered trains. This made it much easier to travel long distances.

The *Rocket*, a famous early steam train, designed by George Stephenson ★

The Rocket *could travel at up to 50km (30 miles) an hour.*

Britain booms

Here you can see inside the Crystal Palace, which was built to contain the Great Exhibition of 1851.

Britain had so many factories that it became known as "the workshop of the world", and by the 1800s it was an extremely rich and powerful country. In 1851, many British inventors displayed their machines at a huge event in London, known as the Great Exhibition. Millions of people came from around the world to admire the new inventions.

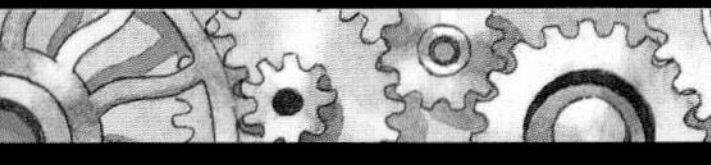

Important dates

1767	James Hargreaves invents the Spinning Jenny.
1782	James Watt invents a powerful steam engine.
1804	Richard Trevithick builds the first steam train to run along a track.
1811	The Luddites start smashing machines.
1825	Passenger trains start running in Britain.
1829	George Stephenson builds the *Rocket*.
1851	The Great Exhibition

The machine-smashers

The new machines worked so fast that people who made cloth at home couldn't earn a living. This made some people angry, and they tried to destroy the machines. The most famous machine-smashers were the Luddites, named after their leader Ned Ludd.

However, protesters like the Luddites could do nothing to stop the Industrial Revolution, and the number of factories continued to grow.

A Luddite

Life in the New Towns

By the 1850s, there were factories in many parts of Britain, and large, busy towns were growing up around them. Although the factory owners became rich and lived in grand houses, the workers were paid very little and were extremely poor. They lived in dirty, crowded parts of the town, known as slums.

This scene shows part of a British town around 1850.

Life in the slums

Factory workers lived in rows of tiny houses on narrow streets. Their houses had no inside toilets or running water, the air was full of smoke from the factories, and the streets were filthy, so diseases spread quickly. There was a lot of crime, because some poor people had to steal food or money to survive.

Workhouses

People who had no money or who couldn't work were sent to live in places called workhouses, which were almost like prisons. Once inside the workhouse, people had to work very long hours, and it was hard to get out again. Families were split up and hardly ever allowed to see each other.

The workers protest

Many workers, like these matchmakers, became ill because of the dangerous chemicals they had to handle.

Lots of factory workers felt they were being treated unfairly, so they started to form groups, called trade unions. The unions demanded better pay, shorter hours and safer places to work.

At first, trade unions were banned by the government, but in 1825 they became legal. When the members of a union wanted to protest about something, they all agreed to stop working and go on strike.

Making changes

Members of the trade unions and some wealthy people put pressure on the government to make life better for the poor. In the second half of the 19th century, factories became safer, and better houses were built. New drains and sewers made the streets cleaner, which helped to prevent diseases from spreading.

Going to school

In 1800, parents usually had to pay to send their children to school, so many children from poor families never learned to read or write. Over the next hundred years, laws were passed which allowed children to have a free education. By 1900, all children had to go to school until the age of 12. Schools were very strict, and pupils were often beaten by their teachers.

A group of children from the slums of London

The Year of Revolutions

By 1848, various groups of people in Europe had become unhappy with their rulers, and wanted more say in how their countries were run. In many places, there weren't enough jobs for everyone, and people were desperately short of food. They remembered the French Revolution of 1789, and thought they could solve their problems with more revolutions.

A year of chaos

In February 1848, a rebellion broke out in Paris and the rebels took control of France. When people in other countries heard about this, a wave of revolutions swept across Europe, and 1848 became known as the Year of Revolutions.

By the end of 1849, the revolutions had been crushed and most of the old rulers were back in power. However, rulers all over Europe realized that they would have to pay more attention to their people in the future.

New ideas

At the same time as the revolutions were spreading through Europe, some powerful new ideas were beginning to change the way people thought.

Karl Marx and the title page of *The Communist Manifesto*

In 1848, a British group called the Chartists demanded that men of all classes should have the right to vote. In the same year, a German thinker named Karl Marx wrote a book called *The Communist Manifesto*. This said that workers everywhere should unite to gain more power for themselves.

The rebels used whatever they could find to build barriers, or barricades, in the streets. This is part of a poster showing French rebels defending a barricade.

Internet link: *For a link to a Web site where you can see video clips from* Les Misérables, *a musical based partly on the 1848 revolution in France, go to* ***www.usborne-quicklinks.com***

New Nations

At the start of the 19th century, the countries now known as Greece, Italy and Germany did not exist. Germany and Italy were made up of lots of small states, and some of these states were ruled by foreign countries. Greece was part of the Turkish Ottoman Empire.

The nation of Greece

In 1827, the Greeks who lived in the Ottoman Empire decided to join together to fight against their Turkish rulers. The rebels defeated the Turks and formed the independent kingdom of Greece.

Greek soldiers fighting for independence ★

The prime minister of Prussia, Otto von Bismarck, was a strong leader. This cartoon from the 1800s shows him sweeping away German rebels.

Italy unites

By 1859, the Italian states of Piedmont and Sardinia, led by Count Camillo Cavour, had taken control of most of northern Italy. At the same time, a soldier named Giuseppe Garibaldi led an army of rebels that conquered large areas of southern Italy. In 1860, Count Cavour and Garibaldi agreed to join the north and south of the country together, and a year later the new nation of Italy was created.

Germany unites

In the 1860s, the most powerful German state was Prussia, governed by King Wilhelm I and his prime minister, Otto von Bismarck. Prussia already ruled Westphalia, and gradually took control of many other German states. Prussia also won impressive victories against Austria and France, and in 1871 the rest of the states decided to join the growing nation. Germany was united and Wilhelm became its first emperor, or kaiser.

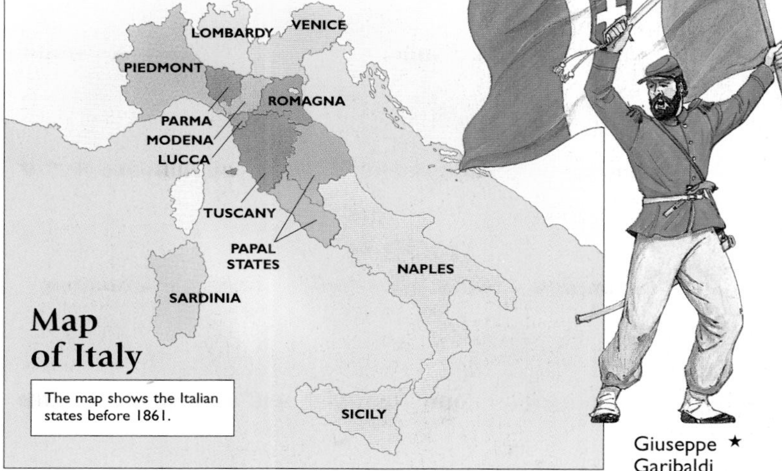

Giuseppe Garibaldi ★

Important dates

- 1827 Greece becomes an independent country.
- 1848 Revolutions in many parts of Europe
- 1861 The Italian states join together to form Italy.
- 1871 Germany is united under Wilhelm I.

Revolutions in South America

Since the 16th century, Spain and Portugal had owned vast colonies in South America. The colonies were ruled by a few rich landowners, but most South Americans were poor.

Fighting for freedom

By the 1800s, many South Americans wanted to break free from their foreign rulers and form their own nations. Portugal allowed Brazil to become a separate country in 1822, but the Spanish were determined to keep control of their land. This meant that all the Spanish colonies had to fight for their independence.

Bolivar the rebel

The most famous South American rebel leader was Simon Bolivar, from the northern colony of Venezuela. Bolivar became commander of Venezuela's rebel army in 1811, and fought the Spanish for three years, before being defeated.

Across the mountains

Bolivar realized he couldn't beat the huge Spanish army in Venezuela, so he planned a surprise attack on the nearby colony of New Granada. In 1819, he led his soldiers on a dangerous journey over the Andes mountains and into New Granada. There, he defeated the Spanish army and helped the colony to become an independent nation, known today as Colombia.

Flag of New Granada

People in New Granada celebrating independence with Bolivar's soldiers ★

These peaks in Venezuela are part of the Andes mountains. Simon Bolivar and his army crossed these huge mountains on their way to New Granada.

This is a portrait of Simon Bolivar. He was determined to free South America from Spanish rule.

Defeating the Spanish

Bolivar spent the next few years moving around South America, fighting the Spanish in different colonies. In 1821, he finally freed his home colony of Venezuela, and the next year he drove the Spanish out of Ecuador.

San Martín strikes

Another great rebel leader was José de San Martín. He led Argentina to independence and helped to free Chile.

A 19th-century painting of José de San Martín

Peru and Bolivia

In 1824, Simon Bolivar drove the Spanish from the rest of Peru. He then made part of Peru into a new nation, which was named Bolivia after him.

Freedom and war

By 1830, all of the South American colonies had become independent. However, in the years that followed, many wars broke out between the new nations, and life remained hard for the people of South America.

Map of South America

Important dates

1808	Some South American colonies start fighting against the Spanish.
1816-1824	Bolivar and San Martín help to win independence for many colonies.
1822	Portugal declares Brazil an independent country.
1825	Bolivar creates the country of Bolivia.
By 1830	All the South American colonies are independent.

The Scramble for Africa

For hundreds of years, the vast continent of Africa was divided into kingdoms led by powerful African rulers. In 1652, the Dutch conquered an area called Cape Colony in the south, and by the 1800s French, British and Portuguese traders had settled along the coast. However, most of Africa was still unknown to Europeans.

Things began to change in the 19th century, when European countries tried to win land for their empires. The Europeans also hoped to find gold and precious stones in Africa, and they competed fiercely against each other. This struggle became known as the Scramble for Africa.

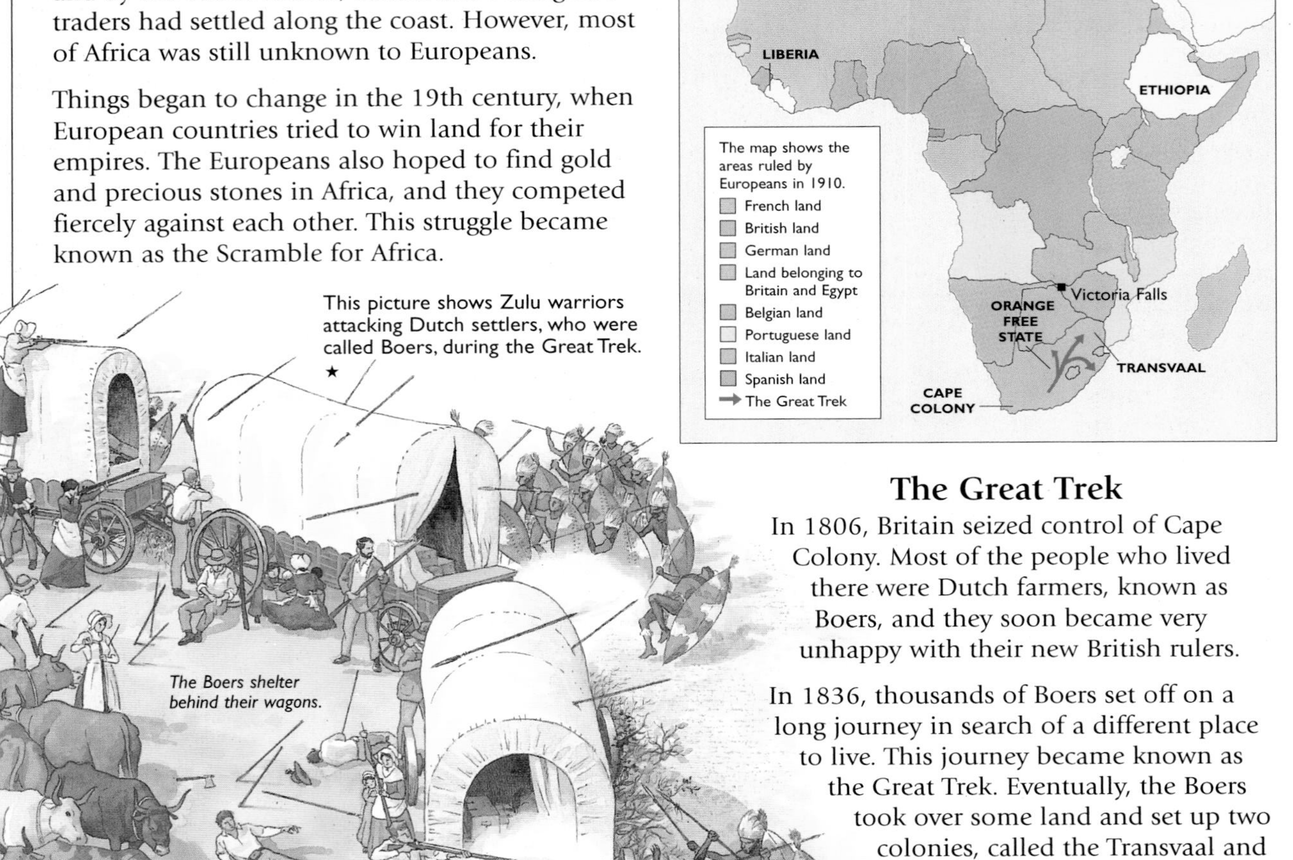

This picture shows Zulu warriors attacking Dutch settlers, who were called Boers, during the Great Trek. ★

The Great Trek

In 1806, Britain seized control of Cape Colony. Most of the people who lived there were Dutch farmers, known as Boers, and they soon became very unhappy with their new British rulers.

In 1836, thousands of Boers set off on a long journey in search of a different place to live. This journey became known as the Great Trek. Eventually, the Boers took over some land and set up two colonies, called the Transvaal and the Orange Free State.

The Zulu wars

The African people whose land the Boers seized were called the Zulus. For many years, Zulu warriors tried to win back their homeland by fighting bravely against the Boers. But the British helped the Boers, and the Zulus were defeated in 1879.

Exploring Africa

Although Europeans had settled on the African coast, many of them were scared of the deadly diseases and wild animals that they thought they would find inland. However, a few brave explorers went on dangerous expeditions. The most famous was the Christian missionary David Livingstone, who explored large parts of Africa and made maps of the land.

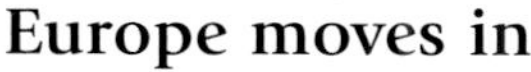

Europe moves in

By the 1880s, many European countries had begun to win land in Africa. The new nations of Italy and Germany were especially eager to build up empires for themselves, and soon the Europeans had conquered huge areas of the continent. Any Africans who tried to fight back were killed.

Europe takes over

In 1884, European leaders met in Berlin and decided to divide up Africa between them. Each country took over a different part of the continent, until eventually only Ethiopia and Liberia were still ruled by Africans (see map). Many Africans were treated very badly by their new rulers, and they often rebelled against the Europeans.

The Boer War

P.J. LEMMER J.D.L. BOTHA C.J. PRETORIUS

Here are some Boer soldiers. Most of the soldiers were not very well trained, but they fought hard to defend their land.

Despite the Europeans' agreement in Berlin, they continued fighting over land. In 1899, Britain tried to take over the Dutch colonies, and war broke out between the British and the Boers. The British imprisoned many Boers and destroyed their farms, and the Boers were forced to surrender. In 1902, the Boers' land became part of the British Empire.

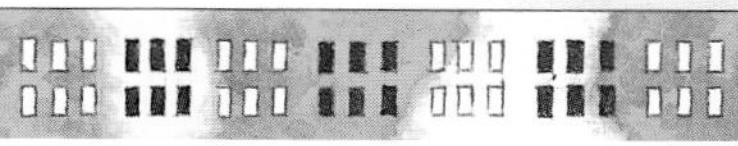

Important dates

1806	Britain takes control of Cape Colony.
1836-1845	The Great Trek
1841	David Livingstone starts to explore Africa.
1879	The Zulus are defeated.
1884	European leaders divide Africa between them.
1902	The British defeat the Boers. Transvaal and the Orange Free State become part of the British Empire.

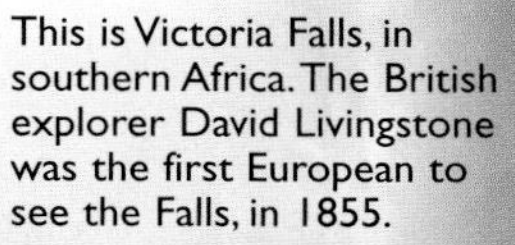

This is Victoria Falls, in southern Africa. The British explorer David Livingstone was the first European to see the Falls, in 1855.

The American Civil War

In the middle of the 19th century, the north and south of the United States seemed like two different countries. In the north, there were lots of big cities and factories, while most of the south was farmland.

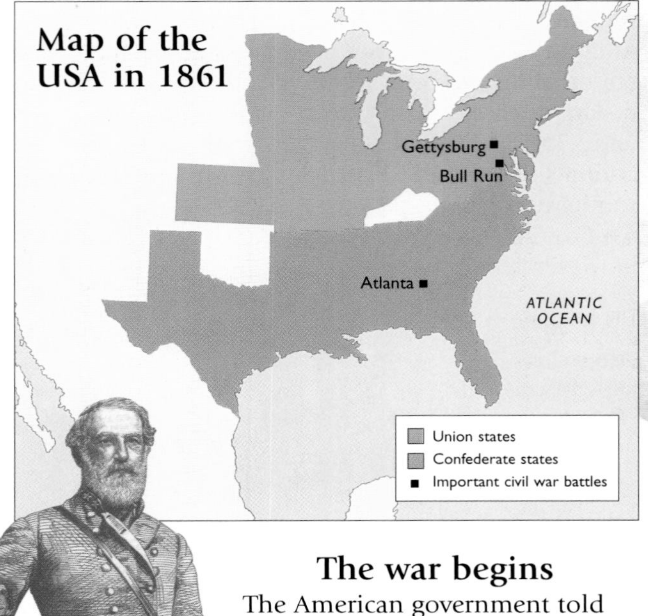

Slavery in the south

In the southern states, the two most important crops were cotton and tobacco, which were grown on vast farms, called plantations. Thousands of people had been brought from Africa to work as slaves on these plantations. But slavery was banned in the north, and this led to bitter arguments with the people of the south.

The USA splits

In 1860, Abraham Lincoln was elected President of the United States. Lincoln was against slavery, and this made many people in the south angry. A group of southern states decided to break away and form their own independent country.

The war begins

The American government told the southern states that they had no right to become a separate country, and in 1861 civil war broke out. For four years, the south, known as the Confederacy, struggled against the north, called the Union.

The Union had more soldiers and better weapons, but the Confederacy had brilliant generals, and the southern troops fought fiercely for their independence. The south won many battles in the early part of the war.

Robert E. Lee, an outstanding Confederate general

This is Abraham Lincoln. He was a strong leader who was determined to keep the United States together.

The Union advances

In 1863, Union troops won an important battle at Gettysburg, in the state of Pennsylvania. After this victory, Union armies began to advance into the south, burning and destroying all the farms and towns they found. Union ships surrounded the southern ports and prevented the Confederacy from bringing in more food and weapons.

The end of the war

Soon, the Confederate troops became weak and hungry. By 1865, large areas of the south had been destroyed, and the Confederacy surrendered. The war was over, but it had cost the lives of hundreds of thousands of soldiers on both sides.

A difficult peace

After the civil war, the United States became a single nation once again. Slavery was made illegal, and thousands of black slaves were freed. However, there were still problems between the north and south. Five days after the war ended, Abraham Lincoln was assassinated by an angry Confederate supporter, and black people continued to be treated appallingly in many parts of the south.

This scene shows Union soldiers destroying a southern town.

Confederate flag

Important buildings, such as factories and banks, have been set on fire.

This soldier is waving the Union flag.

Union soldiers smash the railway line to stop the Confederacy from transporting supplies.

Important dates

1860	Abraham Lincoln becomes President of the United States.
April 1861	Civil war breaks out.
1863	The Battle of Gettysburg
1863-1865	Union armies destroy many southern towns.
April 1865	The civil war ends. Lincoln is murdered.

The Growth of the USA

By the start of the 1800s, the United States of America was a large and growing nation. Over the next hundred years, the USA won huge areas of land, and millions of people came to settle in this exciting new country.

Buying land

Since 1700, France had owned the enormous colony of Louisiana in the middle of the North American continent, but in 1803 the US government bought it from the French. This dramatic deal is known as the Louisiana Purchase, and it doubled the size of the USA.

Americans began to settle on this new land and set up new states there.

War with Mexico

Many people from the USA settled in a southern area called Texas, which was owned by the country of Mexico. In 1835, the Texans declared that they were independent from Mexico. The Mexicans fought to keep Texas, but after two years they were defeated. In 1845, Texas joined the USA.

This is Davy Crockett, who fought for Texas against the Mexicans. He was killed in the Battle of the Alamo at the town of San Antonio, in Texas.

Moving west

Gradually, people moved farther and farther west, and the government encouraged settlers, known as pioneers, to make their homes there. When gold was discovered in California in 1848, many people rushed to live in the area, hoping to make a fortune.

Pioneers heading for California during the Gold Rush

Lots of families travel together in groups of wagons, called wagon trains.

This photograph shows a rocky valley in the state of Utah, one of the places the pioneers passed through on their difficult journey to the West.

Internet link: *For a link to a Web site where you can travel across the American West in the year 1804, go to* **www.usborne-quicklinks.com**

This poster from the 1870s offers a huge reward to anyone who captures the famous bandit Billy the Kid.

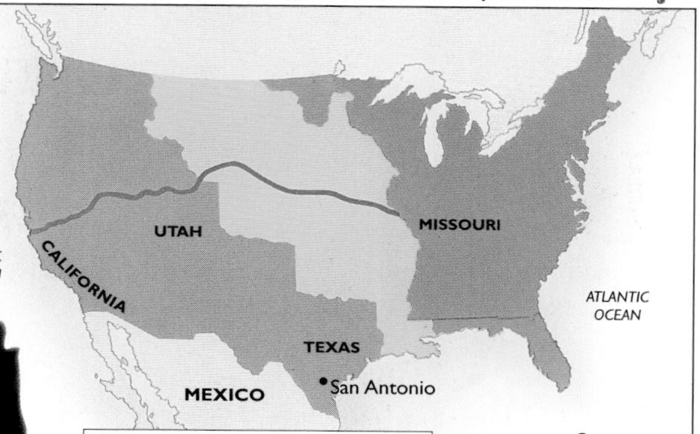

The Wild West

For many years, the American West was a wild and dangerous place, full of crooks and bandits.

Cattle herders, or cowboys, drove cattle over the plains to be loaded onto trains and sold in the east. There were many clashes between the cowboys and the Native Americans who lived on the plains.

Taking land

As the USA grew bigger, settlers moved into many areas where Native Americans lived. At first, the government promised to leave the Native Americans alone, but most of their land was gradually taken away.

Struggling to survive

Some tribes of Native Americans refused to leave their land, and they fought hard against the settlers and the US army. The Native Americans won some battles, but many tribes were completely wiped out. US troops and settlers also killed most of the buffalo that roamed the plains, leaving the remaining tribes with very little to eat. By 1890, many Native Americans had been captured and were forced to live in camps guarded by US soldiers.

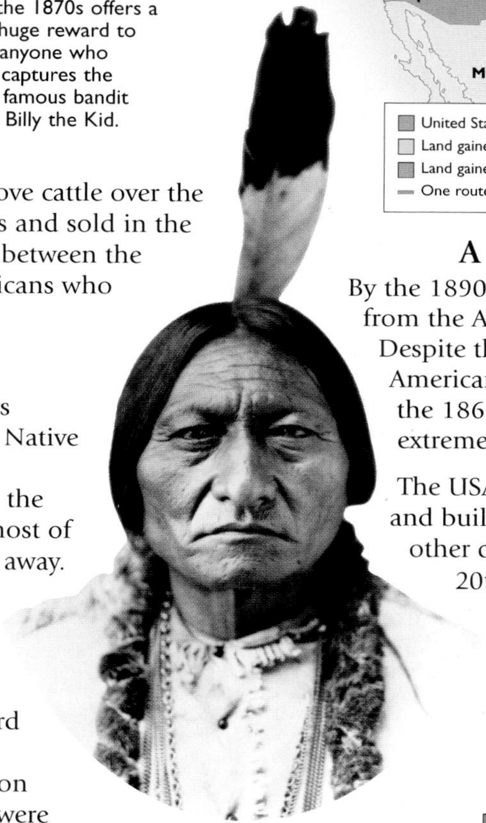

Sitting Bull, a Native American chief who fought the US army

Map of the USA

A new world power

By the 1890s, the USA stretched all the way from the Atlantic Ocean to the Pacific. Despite the wars against the Native Americans, and the terrible civil war in the 1860s, the country became extremely successful.

The USA was soon growing more crops and building more machines than any other country. By the beginning of the 20th century, it was one of the biggest, richest and most powerful nations in the world.

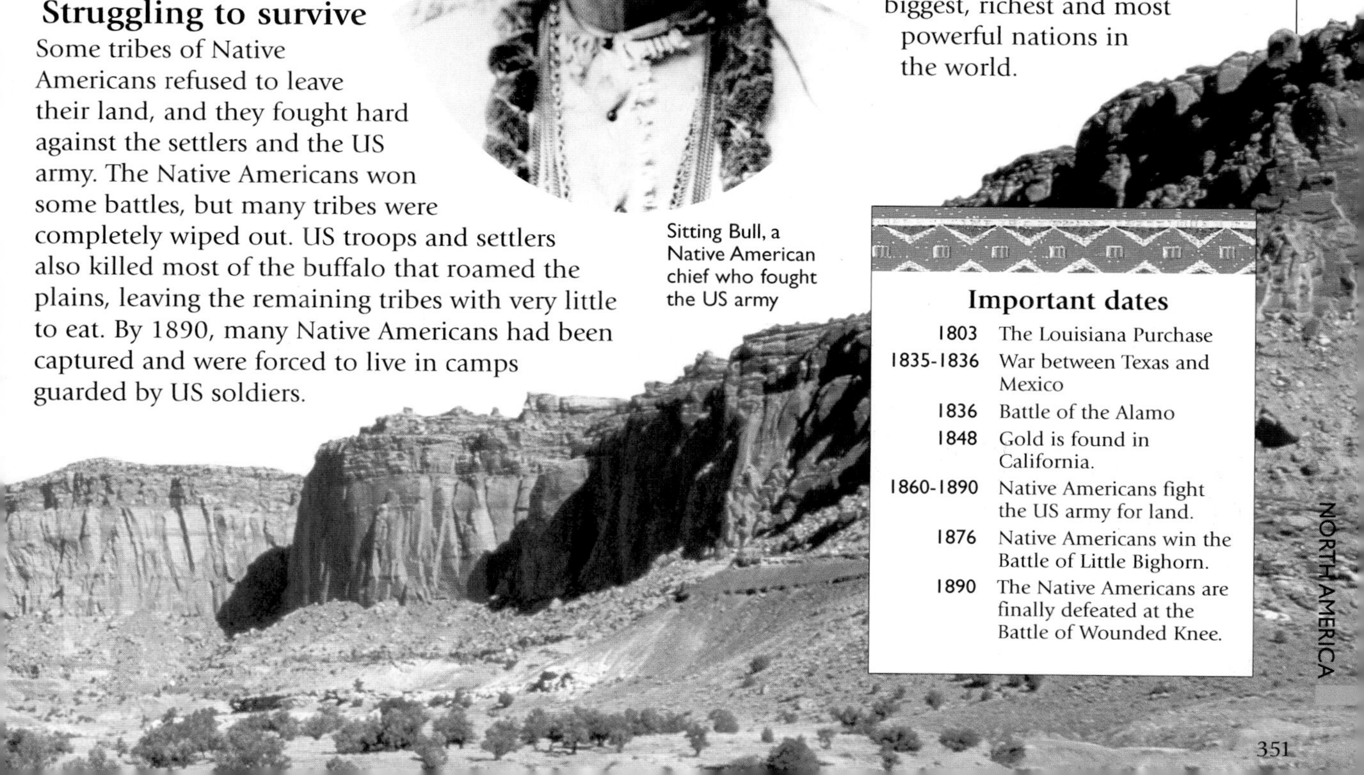

Important dates

1803	The Louisiana Purchase
1835-1836	War between Texas and Mexico
1836	Battle of the Alamo
1848	Gold is found in California.
1860-1890	Native Americans fight the US army for land.
1876	Native Americans win the Battle of Little Bighorn.
1890	The Native Americans are finally defeated at the Battle of Wounded Knee.

The Ming and the Ch'ing

The vast empire of China was ruled by powerful emperors for thousands of years. In the 14th century, a new family, or dynasty, took control of China. They were called the Ming dynasty, and their emperors ruled for the next 280 years.

The Forbidden City

The Ming emperors governed from the northern city of Beijing, where they lived in a fabulous walled palace, called the Forbidden City. Only the emperor's family and advisers were allowed to enter the palace.

Art and medicine

During the Ming period, the Chinese made exquisite vases and elegant wooden furniture. They also designed amazing gardens and made beautifully illustrated books. Doctors treated their patients by sticking lots of needles into their skin. This treatment is called acupuncture and it is still used today.

A decorated jar from the Ming period ★

This photograph shows the Hall of Supreme Harmony in the middle of the Forbidden City.

China and the world

By 1500, China was almost completely cut off from the rest of the world. The Ming emperors thought all foreigners were savages, and wanted to keep them out of China. Foreign merchants were only allowed to trade at a few Chinese ports.

Problems for the Ming

For a long time, China was peaceful, but problems began in the 16th century. The south coast was plagued by Japanese pirates and smugglers, and tribes from Mongolia often attacked northern China. To defend themselves against these attacks, the Ming emperors strengthened the Great Wall of China, which had been built in ancient times, and used thousands of soldiers to guard it.

Chinese rebels

By the 1630s, many Chinese people were angry with the government, because there wasn't enough food for everyone and people were forced to pay heavy taxes. Rebellions broke out in many areas, and the country was thrown into chaos.

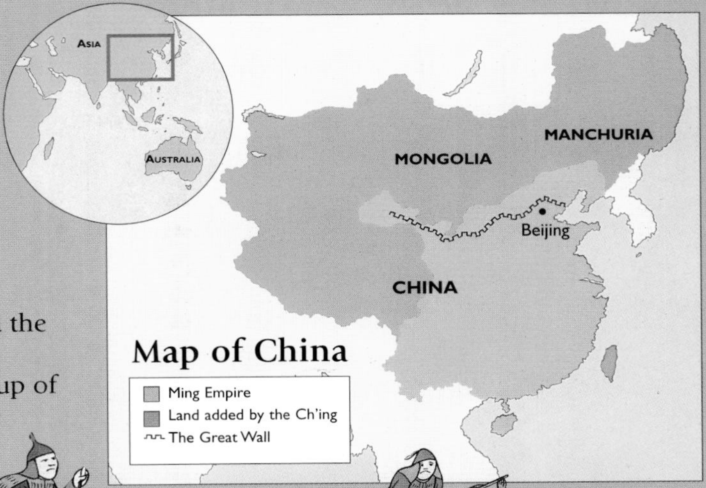

Attack of the Manchus

In 1644, rebels seized the city of Beijing, and the last Ming emperor committed suicide. The emperor's advisers asked the Manchus, a group of people from the north, to help them crush the rebellion. But the Manchus took advantage of the Ming's problems and took over Beijing. The Manchus gradually won more land, and by 1681 they had conquered all of China.

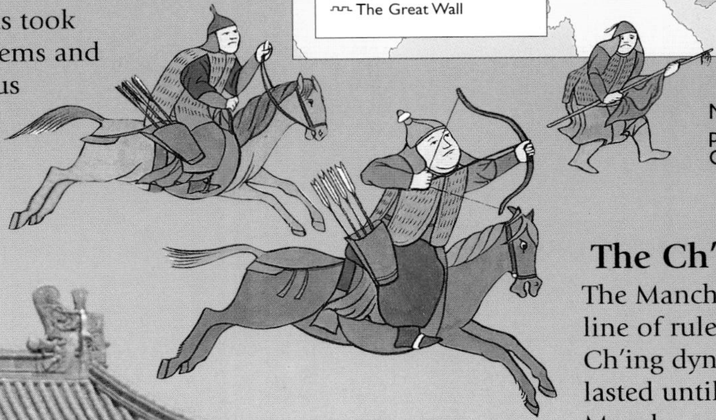

Map of China

Manchu warriors, painted by a Chinese artist

The Ch'ing dynasty

The Manchus started a new line of rulers, known as the Ch'ing dynasty, which lasted until 1912. The Manchu emperors won vast areas of new land to the north and west. They also made sure that China stayed independent from the rest of the world.

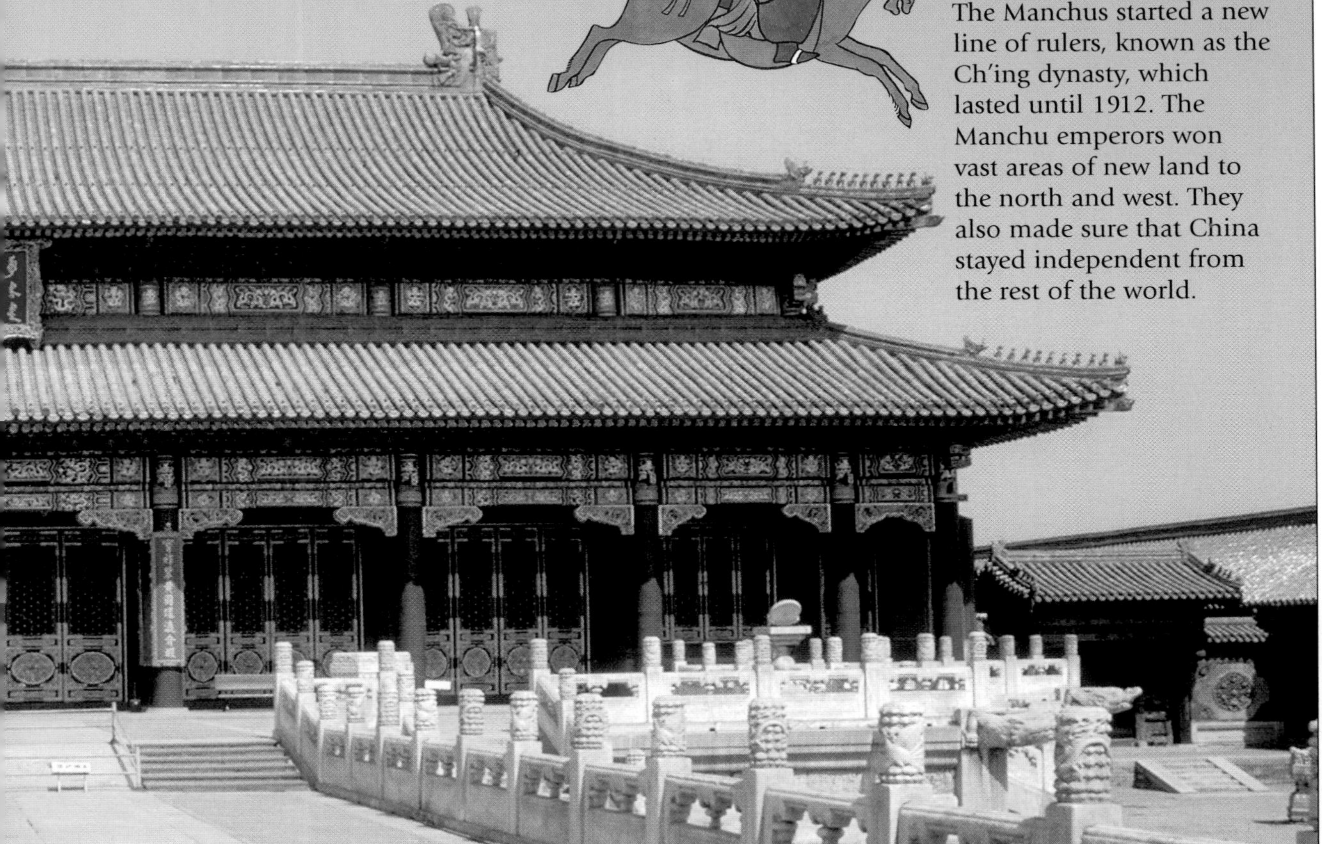

Changes in China

In the 18th century, European merchants were eager to buy Chinese goods, such as silk and tea. But China's Manchu emperors wanted to keep foreigners out of their country, so Europeans were only allowed to trade at the port of Canton.

K'ang Hsi, a powerful Manchu emperor

The Opium War

In 1839, a government official burned thousands of chests of opium, and the emperor banned all trade with Britain. This made the British furious, and they attacked China. The British had much better ships and weapons, and they easily defeated the Chinese navy. After losing the war, China was forced to allow British merchants to trade at lots of Chinese ports.

Silver and opium

The Manchu emperors made European traders pay Chinese merchants with silver, which was very costly for the Europeans. But in the 1720s, the British began paying the Chinese with a drug called opium instead.

Many Chinese people smoked opium, but the emperors disapproved of this, and in 1813 smoking opium was banned. However, the British continued selling opium to Chinese merchants, and this made the Manchu government angry.

This 19th-century British painting shows Chinese ships being destroyed by the British during the Opium War.

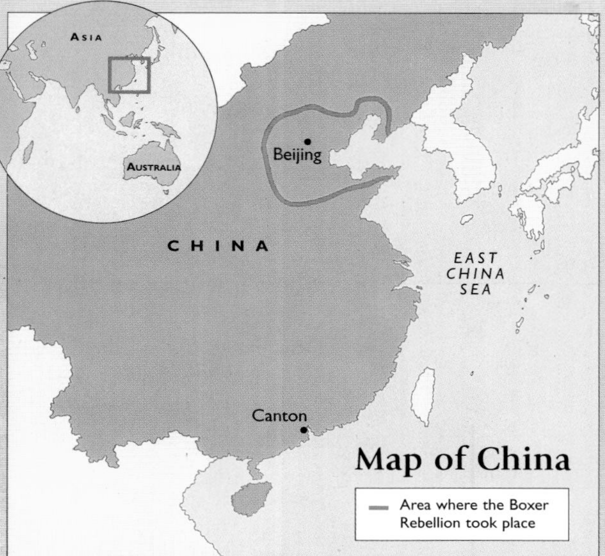

Map of China

Area where the Boxer Rebellion took place

The Taiping Rebellion

The Manchu emperors also faced other problems during the 19th century. Their government had become weak, and in the 1850s a violent revolution, known as the Taiping Rebellion, broke out. For more than ten years, peasants all over China attacked their rulers and destroyed cities. By the time the Manchu emperor regained control in 1864, up to 20 million people had been killed.

Trying to change

Some Chinese people thought China could only overcome its problems by becoming more like a modern European country. They encouraged the government to build lots of factories and trains, but change was slow.

The Boxer Rebellion

Many people in China hated the way that Europeans had changed their country. In 1900, a secret society of warriors, known as the Boxers, started attacking Europeans and Chinese Christians.

The Manchu government supported the Boxers, hoping that they would get rid of the foreigners, but the rebellion was crushed by European soldiers. The government became even weaker, and in 1912 there was a revolution in China (see page 364).

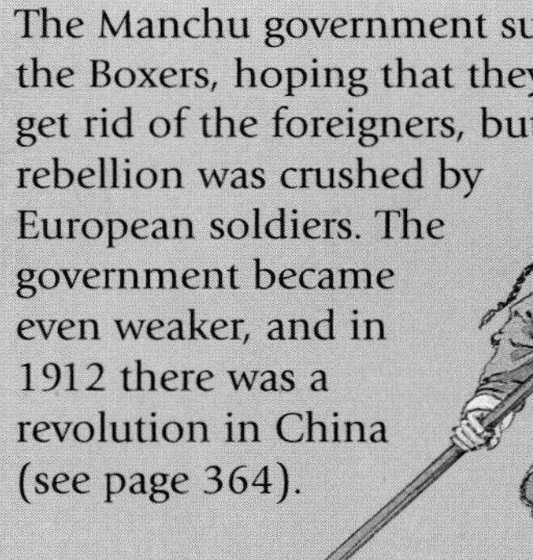

★ Boxer warriors like these thought they were protected by magic powers.

The Europeans advance

Soon, other European countries began forcing the Chinese to trade with them. They moved soldiers into China and took control of many ports. The Europeans wanted to persuade the Chinese to become Christians, so they began to send missionaries to China.

Important dates

1368-1644	The Ming dynasty
1644-1912	The Manchu dynasty
1839-1842	The Opium War
1850-1864	The Taiping Rebellion
1900	The Boxer Rebellion

Changes in Japan

At the start of the 16th century, Japan was in the middle of a long civil war. Fierce warlords, called samurai, fought each other for land, and the Japanese emperor had very little power.

Map of Japan

Strong samurai

The civil war ended in 1568 when the powerful samurai Oda Nobunaga took control of Japan. After him, another samurai, Toyotomi Hideyoshi, became chief minister of Japan. Hideyoshi set up an efficient tax system and worked hard to create a united country.

The first Tokugawa

After Hideyoshi's death, war broke out again. Ieyasu Tokugawa defeated his rivals at the Battle of Sekigahara, and in 1603 the emperor made him shogun (military commander) of Japan.

This is Osaka Castle, which was seized by Ieyasu Tokugawa from a rival samurai.

The Edo period

While the emperor stayed in his palace in Kyoto, Tokugawa set up his capital in Edo. This was the start of a long line of Tokugawa shoguns who ruled Japan on behalf of the emperor. The Tokugawas controlled Japan for over 250 years, and this period of time became known as the Edo period.

Japan's isolation

In the 1630s, the shogun Iemitsu Tokugawa became frightened that European merchants and priests in Japan had too much influence over his people. He banned Christianity and declared that only the Dutch and Chinese were allowed to trade with Japan. Foreigners could not set foot on Japanese soil, so the Dutch had to trade from an island in Nagasaki Bay.

Peace and wealth

Japan remained cut off from the world for over 200 years. During this time, the Tokugawas ruled very strictly and made sure that there were no more civil wars in their country. Japanese towns grew fast, and Edo became one of the largest cities in the world. As the towns grew, Japanese traders became wealthy, but the peasants and samurai didn't share in this wealth. By the 1800s, there were many rebellions against the Tokugawa family.

Contact with the west

In 1854, a group of American warships waited in Edo Bay while their commander, Commodore Perry, forced the shogun to sign a trading agreement with the USA. Other agreements followed, and by 1860 Japan had started to trade with several western countries.

The end of the Tokugawas

Most of the samurai hated the western traders and blamed the Tokugawas for allowing them in. Civil war broke out, and in 1867 a samurai army defeated the Tokugawas. In 1868, the victorious samurai helped the Japanese emperor to take control of Japan. This is known as the Meiji Restoration. The emperor moved from Kyoto to Edo, which he renamed Tokyo.

Even in the 1800s, the samurai still wore their traditional costumes. In this 19th-century Japanese print, two samurai warriors are fighting each other.

Modernization

The Japanese began building steam trains in the 1880s. Here are two engine drivers in front of their train.

In spite of the samurai's hopes, the emperors continued trading with the West and copied many western ideas. They set up a parliament, improved schools, and built factories, trains and ships. Meanwhile, the samurai lost most of their power, and most of them had to do ordinary jobs.

Japanese wars

In 1894, Japan tried to conquer Korea, and this led to war with China. The Japanese won an easy victory, but in 1904 they had to fight the Russians for control of Korea. Once again, the Japanese were victorious. In 1905, the Treaty of Portsmouth gave Japan control of Korea and some land in China. This made Japan the most powerful country in the Far East.

Important dates

1568-1582	Oda Nobunaga controls Japan.
1591-1598	Toyotomi Hideyoshi controls Japan.
1603-1867	The Tokugawa shoguns rule Japan (the Edo period).
1854	Japan signs a trading agreement with the USA.
1868	The emperor takes control of Japan (the Meiji Restoration).
1894-1895	Japan fights China.
1904-1905	Japan fights Russia.
1905	The Treaty of Portsmouth gives Japan control of Korea.

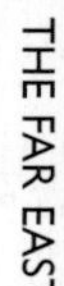

The First World War

World War I, also known as the Great War, involved more countries and killed more people than any other war that had ever been fought before. But how did it all start?

Friends and enemies

By 1914, the five strongest countries in Europe had split into two rival groups. Britain, France and Russia (called the Allies) were on one side, with Germany and Austria-Hungary (called the Central Powers) on the other. The situation became very tense. If a war were to start between any two rival countries, all the others would probably join in.

Murder in Sarajevo

The event that actually sparked off the war took place on June 28, 1914. Archduke Franz Ferdinand, the heir to the Austrian throne, was visiting the town of Sarajevo in Bosnia, when he was shot dead by a Serbian student.

On July 28, Austria, backed up by Germany, declared war on Serbia. Russia stepped in to help the Serbs, and soon the Allies and the Central Powers were at war.

The Western Front

German soldiers moved quickly into northern France, but they were soon stopped by the Allies. The two sides faced each other along a line known as the Western Front. Both sides dug deep ditches, or trenches, to defend themselves. After this, neither side was able to advance very far, and the war dragged on for four years.

Soldiers lived in the trenches for weeks at a time. During a battle, they climbed out of the trench and charged at the enemy across an area known as No Man's Land. Millions of men died in these terrible battles that sometimes lasted for months.

This scene shows British soldiers in a trench on the Western Front.

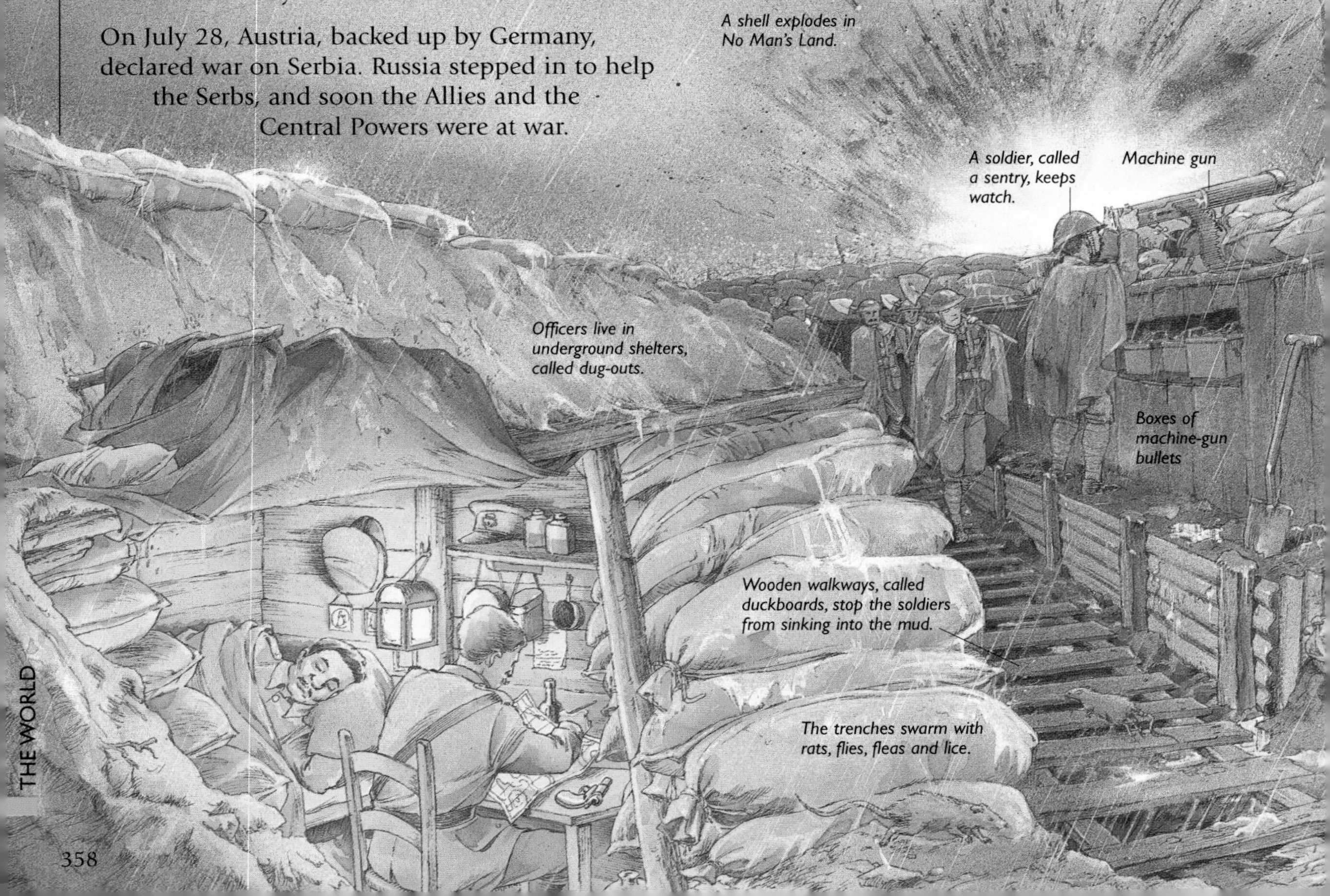

A shell explodes in No Man's Land.

A soldier, called a sentry, keeps watch.

Machine gun

Officers live in underground shelters, called dug-outs.

Boxes of machine-gun bullets

Wooden walkways, called duckboards, stop the soldiers from sinking into the mud.

The trenches swarm with rats, flies, fleas and lice.

★ Poppies that grew on the battlefields of the Western Front became a symbol for remembering the war.

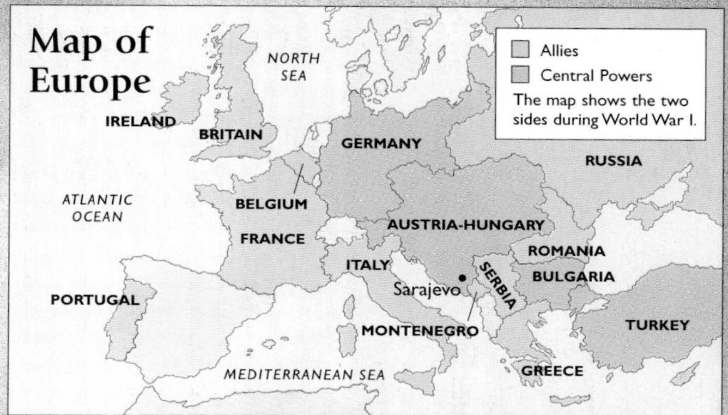

The war spreads

Other countries soon became involved in the war. Turkey and Bulgaria joined the Central Powers, while Italy, Greece and Portugal supported the Allies. The two sides also fought in Africa and the Far East, where Britain, Germany and other European countries had colonies.

Ships and submarines

Both sides tried to stop their enemies from getting food and raw materials to make weapons. German submarines, called U-boats, sank any ship going to a British port. Some of these ships were American, and this provoked the USA into joining the war, in April 1917, on the side of the Allies.

The war ends

By March 1918, the Russians were exhausted by the war, and they made peace with Germany. German soldiers made a series of final attacks on the Western Front, but they were forced back. Germany surrendered, and on November 11, 1918, the war finally came to an end.

Walls supported by wooden planks

Barbed wire

Sandbags

This man has been sent some extra food by his family.

The men rest in holes dug into the sides of the trench.

The soldiers' feet are always wet and often get infected.

Important dates

June 1914	Archduke Franz Ferdinand is murdered.
July 1914	Austria-Hungary declares war on Serbia.
Sep 1914	The Germans are stopped by the Allies at the Battle of the Marne.
July-Nov 1916	Over a million soldiers die at the Battle of the Somme, in France.
April 1917	The USA joins the war.
March 1918	Russia makes peace with Germany.
Nov 11, 1918	The war ends.

The Russian Revolution

At the start of the 20th century, Russia owned a vast empire that covered one sixth of the Earth's surface. Most of its people were peasants who lived in terrible poverty, but in the capital city of St. Petersburg, wealthy nobles lived a life of luxury.

Tsar Nicholas II of Russia with his wife and family, photographed around 1900

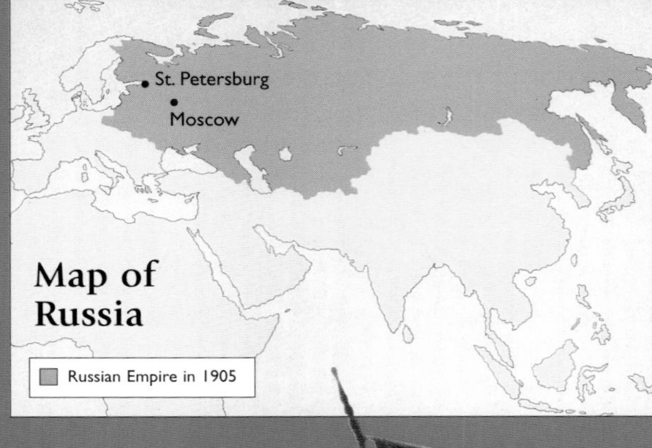

Russia was ruled by a powerful emperor, or tsar, who believed he had been chosen by God. The tsar was advised by officials from noble families, but most Russians had no say in how their country was run.

Time for change

Many Russians were unhappy that the tsar had so much power. Some wanted him to rule with the help of a parliament chosen by the people. Others wanted a revolution to get rid of the tsar altogether. One group of revolutionaries were the Bolsheviks, led by Vladimir Ilyich Ulyanov, better known as Lenin.

The Bolshevik leader Lenin

The 1905 Revolution

In January 1905, over 150,000 workers marched to the tsar's Winter Palace in St. Petersburg to protest about their dreadful working conditions. The army fired on the protesters, killing over a hundred people. Workers across Russia went on strike, and Tsar Nicholas was forced to set up a parliament. But he made sure it had very little power.

Russia at war

In 1914, Russia entered the First World War (see pages 358 and 359). The Russian army suffered terrible defeats, losing over a million men in the first six months. At home, the war caused shortages of food, and people began to starve. Many Russians blamed the tsar for all these problems.

Revolution!

By March 1917, St. Petersburg (which had been renamed Petrograd) was running out of bread. Riots broke out and workers went on strike. When the army joined in the riots, Tsar Nicholas realized he had lost control and gave up the throne.

A temporary government was set up, but it did nothing to solve Russia's problems and soon became unpopular. In November 1917, the Bolsheviks, led by Lenin, seized power and took control of the country.

A civil war poster urging people to join the Communist fighting force, known as the Red Army

Civil war

Lenin made peace with Germany and took Russia out of the First World War. He moved the capital to Moscow, gave land to the peasants and put workers in charge of the factories. Many wealthy Russians didn't like these changes, and this led to a bitter civil war between the Bolsheviks (now known as Communists) and their enemies. In 1918, Tsar Nicholas and his family were killed by a group of Communists.

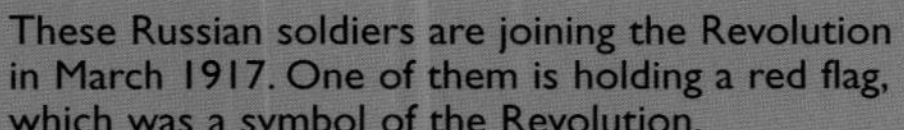

These Russian soldiers are joining the Revolution in March 1917. One of them is holding a red flag, which was a symbol of the Revolution.

Communist control

By 1921, the Communists had won the civil war, and Lenin was in complete control of Russia. He began the massive task of rebuilding the country, which was in chaos after years of fighting. In 1922, Russia was renamed the Union of Soviet Socialist Republics (USSR), also known as the Soviet Union.

Important dates

1894	Nicholas II becomes Tsar of Russia.
January 1905	Soldiers fire on protesters in St. Petersburg.
1914	The First World War begins.
March 1917	Riots break out in Petrograd. The tsar gives up his throne.
Nov 1917	The Bolsheviks seize power.
1918-1921	Civil war in Russia
May 1918	Tsar Nicholas II and his family are shot.
Dec 1922	Russia is renamed the USSR.

Stalin's Soviet Union

After the Russian Revolution, the Communist leader Lenin was seen as a hero by many Russians. But Lenin did not rule the new Soviet Union for long. From 1922, he was often unwell, and he died in 1924.

After Lenin's death, several leading Communists struggled for power. One of these men was Josef Stalin, the Secretary of the Communist Party. Stalin had many friends in the Party, and he used them to get rid of his rivals. By 1928, Stalin had complete control of the country.

Josef Stalin in military uniform

Factories and workers

Stalin launched a Five Year Plan to turn the Soviet Union into a modern, industrial country. He forced people to leave their villages and work in factories in the city. Factories were expected to produce much more than before, and workers who didn't work fast enough were punished like criminals.

A Soviet poster urging workers to carry out the Five Year Plan

Farms and peasants

To keep the factory workers well fed, Stalin needed to reorganize farming. Peasant farmers were told to give up their tiny strips of land, and these strips were then joined together to create vast farms, called collective farms. The peasants were paid to work on the farms, and the crops they grew were sold to the government at a low price.

This statue of a factory worker and a peasant woman makes the Soviet way of life look heroic.

The worker holds a hammer, while the peasant woman has a farm tool called a sickle.

Internet link: *For a link to a Web site with a fascinating collection of Soviet posters and paintings, go to* ***www.usborne-quicklinks.com***

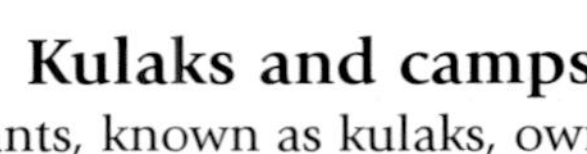

Kulaks and camps

Some peasants, known as kulaks, owned their own land, and when they refused to give it up Stalin used force. Millions of kulaks were arrested and sent to live in remote parts of the Soviet Union. There, they had to work in harsh prison camps, where many of them died of cold, hunger and exhaustion.

These Soviet farmers are carrying a banner which says that they will destroy the kulaks.

Many peasants destroyed their crops and killed their animals rather than hand them over to the collective farms. This meant that there was a terrible shortage of food, and millions of people died of hunger.

Removing enemies

By 1934, Stalin was worried that his enemies were plotting against him, so he decided to get rid of them. Anyone who criticized him was arrested by the secret police and executed, or sent to a prison camp. As many as 24 million people may have died in these brutal attacks, known as purges.

Counting the cost

Under Stalin, the Soviet Union became a strong, industrial country with factories, steel works, power stations and railways. Lots of new hospitals were built, and all children were given a free education. But Stalin was a ruthless leader. By the time he died, he had caused the deaths of as many as 40 million Soviet people.

War and after

In 1941, during the Second World War, the Soviet Union was invaded by Germany. After many fierce battles, the Soviet army drove the Germans back across eastern Europe. Stalin used this success to turn the Soviet Union into a great world power (see page 378).

The worker's hammer and the peasant's sickle became part of the symbol of the Soviet Union.

Important dates

1924	Lenin dies.
1928	Stalin begins a Five Year Plan to modernize industry and farming.
1929	Collective farms are set up.
1932-1933	Millions die in a terrible famine.
1934	The purges begin.
1941-45	The Soviet Union is at war with Germany.
1953	Stalin dies.

The People's Republic

Since 1644, China had been ruled by a family of powerful emperors called the Manchus. By 1900, the Manchus were very unpopular, but they refused to change the way the country was run.

In 1911, a revolution broke out. A group of nationalists, called the Kuomintang, seized power and set up a republic. The Kuomintang leaders found it hard to bring the country under control, but by 1928 they governed most of China.

Not everyone supported the Kuomintang. The Chinese Communist Party wanted China to be run by the workers and peasants, rather than by the rich. One group of Communists, led by Mao Zedong, set up their own government in Jiangxi (say "jang-shee"), in the south.

The Long March

In 1934, the Communists in Jiangxi were surrounded and attacked by the Kuomintang army. The Communists escaped and set off to find a safe place far away from the Kuomintang. This famous journey, which covered a distance of 8,000km (5,000 miles), is known as the Long March. Out of 100,000 people who set out on the march, 70,000 died on the way.

This picture shows Communists on the Long March. Most of the men have had to leave their wives and children behind.

The marchers are trudging down a rocky mountain path.

The men are wearing the uniform of the Communist Red Army.

During the Long March, the Communists had to cross 18 mountain ranges, including these mountains in Sichuan, in western China.

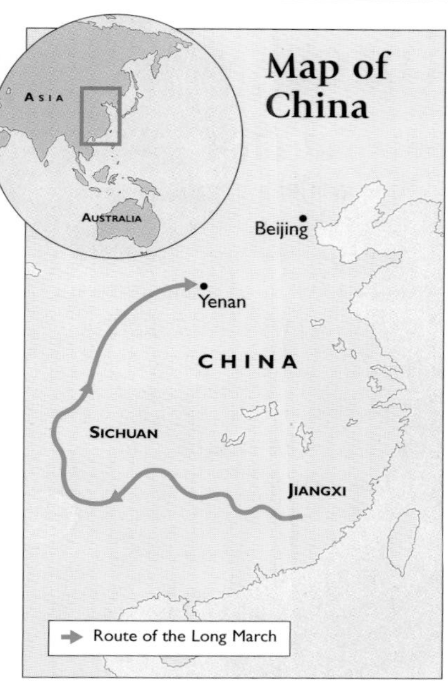

Communist China

Between 1937 and 1945, China was at war with Japan. After the war, the struggle between the Communist Party and the Kuomintang continued. In 1949, the Communists, led by Mao Zedong, defeated the Kuomintang. Mao set up the People's Republic of China and took control of the country.

The Great Leap Forward

In 1958, Mao started a campaign, known as the Great Leap Forward, to try to build up industry. Many peasants were taken away from farms to work in factories. This meant that not enough crops were planted, and millions of people died of hunger.

The Cultural Revolution

Mao became worried that China was moving away from true Communism. In 1966, he started a new campaign, called the Cultural Revolution. He encouraged young people to attack traditional ideas and to criticize their teachers, bosses and parents.

Schools and universities were closed, and educated people were forced to work on the land. Groups of teenagers, known as Red Guards, beat and tortured anyone they thought was against the Revolution.

★ A young Chinese Red Guard

After three years of chaos, the army was sent in to stop the violence. The Cultural Revolution finally came to an end when Mao died in 1976.

Mao Zedong, leader of the Chinese Communist Party from 1935 to 1976

Important dates

1911	The Kuomintang starts a revolution in China.
1912	The Kuomintang sets up a republic.
1934-1935	The Long March
1949	Mao Zedong sets up the People's Republic of China.
1958-1960	The Great Leap Forward
1966	Mao Zedong starts the Cultural Revolution.
1976	Mao Zedong dies.

Good Times, Bad Times

During the 1920s, the United States of America was the richest country in the world. Businesses boomed and factories produced lots of new goods, such as washing machines, vacuum cleaners and cars. Not everyone was rich, but most Americans thought life was getting better.

The Jazz Age

The 1920s are often known as the Jazz Age because of the new music and dances that were popular at that time. Some daring young women, known as flappers, cut their hair short and wore their skirts above the knee.

These two people are performing a popular 1920s jazz dance called the Charleston.

Banning alcohol

From 1920 to 1933, it was illegal to make or sell alcohol in the USA. This period of time is known as the Prohibition. Many people drank secretly in illegal bars, called speakeasies, and gangsters, such as Al Capone, grew rich by making, smuggling and selling alcohol.

This 1920s postcard encourages Americans to vote for the banning of alcohol.

The Wall Street Crash

The good times came to an end in 1929, when thousands of people were ruined in a financial disaster known as the Wall Street Crash.

During the 1920s, many Americans had bought shares in businesses, hoping to make money by selling them later at a higher price. But in October 1929 share prices began to fall. People panicked and started selling their shares. This made prices drop even lower, until the shares were almost worthless.

This disaster is known as the Wall Street Crash because Wall Street is the home of the New York Stock Exchange, where shares are bought and sold.

The Great Depression

After the Wall Street Crash, banks and businesses failed, and millions of people lost their jobs. Thousands of families lost their homes as well, because they couldn't afford to pay the rent. This period of terrible poverty is known as the Great Depression. It lasted for most of the 1930s and affected countries all over the world.

Some homeless families had to live in shacks like this that they built out of cardboard.

The Dust Bowl

The Great Depression also affected farmers. In the USA, the situation was made worse by the weather. In some central areas, fierce winds blew away the dusty soil, making it impossible to grow crops. These areas became known as the Dust Bowl. Many farming families left their homes to look for work in California, on the west coast.

Here you can see a farm in the Dust Bowl being battered by a violent dust storm.

The New Deal

In 1932, Franklin D. Roosevelt became President of the USA. He started up a series of projects, known as the New Deal, to help industry and farming, and create new jobs. This did not end the Depression, but it made life easier for many Americans.

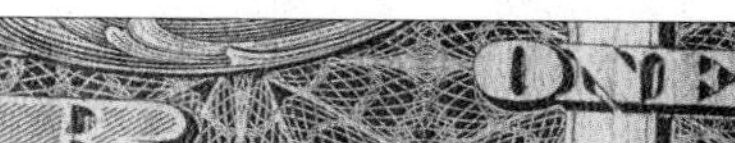

Important dates

1920-1933	The Prohibition
Oct 24, 1929	The Wall Street Crash
1932	Franklin D. Roosevelt becomes President.
1933	Roosevelt launches the New Deal.

The Rise of Fascism

After the First World War, many countries in Europe faced huge problems. Governments had very little money because they had spent so much on weapons for the war. Lots of people were out of work, and there wasn't enough food for everyone. People began to think that these problems needed drastic new solutions.

The first fascist

In Italy, the problems were particularly bad. Many people turned to Benito Mussolini, the leader of the Fascist Party. Mussolini became prime minister of Italy in 1922. Soon, he banned all other political parties and took complete control of the country. This way of ruling is known as fascism.

Mussolini salutes the crowd at a huge public meeting.

Germany defeated

After World War I, the winning countries decided that Germany should pay for the damage caused by the war. The Germans were forced to reduce the size of their army and navy, and were not allowed to have an air force. Germany also had to give up large areas of land. Many Germans felt angry and humiliated by all of this, and they blamed their government for agreeing to it.

The Depression

In 1929, Germany was hit by the Great Depression (see page 367). Millions of Germans lost their jobs, but the government did nothing to help. People became desperate, and some turned to the National Socialist Workers' Party (the Nazi Party), led by Adolf Hitler.

New hope

Hitler persuaded people that their problems were caused by foreigners, especially Jews. He believed that the Germans were superior to other races, and said he would make Germany powerful again. He promised strong leadership, jobs for everyone and an end to poverty.

Total power

The Nazis held huge meetings, or rallies, all over Germany to persuade people to vote for them. By 1932, they were the biggest party in the German Reichstag (parliament), and in 1933 Hitler became chancellor (head of the government). He then persuaded the Reichstag to give him complete control of the country.

This is the badge of the Nazi Party. The symbol in the middle is called a swastika.

Nazi Germany

Once Hitler was in power, he banned all political parties except the Nazi Party. He took control of all newspapers and radio, and forced schools and universities to teach Nazi ideas. Children had to join Nazi youth groups, and anyone who disagreed with the Nazis was arrested by the secret police, which was called the Gestapo.

In this photograph, the German leader Adolf Hitler (in the middle of the picture) is inspecting members of a Nazi organization called the SA.

Persecuting Jews

A Jewish boy and his family being driven out of their home by Nazi soldiers

The Nazis made life impossible for Jews. They weren't allowed to marry Germans, own land, do certain jobs, or even go out at night. Gangs of Nazi thugs attacked Jewish people, vandalized Jewish shops and burned synagogues.

Important dates

1919	Mussolini sets up the Fascist Party in Italy.
1922	Mussolini comes to power.
1929	The Great Depression begins.
1933	Hitler becomes chancellor of Germany.
1934	Hitler takes complete control as *Führer* (leader) of Germany.
Nov 9, 1938	On *Kristallnacht* (the Night of Broken Glass) Nazis attack thousands of Jewish homes, shops and synagogues.

Europe at War

By 1934, the Nazi leader Adolf Hitler had complete control of Germany (see pages 368 and 369). Hitler planned to create a powerful empire made up of all the German-speaking people in Europe. He began by taking over Austria in March 1938.

German troops with a machine gun

Hitler's next target was the German-speaking part of Czechoslovakia, known as the Sudetenland. Britain and France wanted to avoid another war with Germany, like the First World War, so they agreed to let Hitler have the Sudetenland. But he soon took over the rest of Czechoslovakia as well.

On September 1, 1939, Hitler invaded Poland. Britain and France had already agreed to help Poland if it was attacked, so two days later they declared war on Germany. Italy later joined the war on the German side. Together, Germany and Italy were known as the Axis Powers.

Europe under attack

Nothing much happened for the first six months of the war. Then, in April 1940, Hitler's troops began their attack. They used tanks and planes to advance at incredible speed. By June 1940, Hitler had taken over most of western Europe.

Escape by sea

As the Germans swept into northern France, many French and British soldiers were trapped near Dunkirk, on the north coast. The British organized a huge rescue, using small boats and yachts, as well as ships from their navy. In nine days, over 330,000 men were taken safely to Britain.

The Battle of Britain

Hitler planned to invade Britain, but he knew he needed to destroy the British Royal Air Force first. From August to October 1940, British and German planes fought a fierce battle in the skies over southern England. The British had fewer planes, but still managed to win. After this defeat, Hitler gave up the idea of invading Britain.

The British Prime Minister Winston Churchill, who inspired his country during the war

Internet link: *For a link to a Web site where you can hear air-raid sirens, bombs and famous radio broadcasts from World War II, go to* **www.usborne-quicklinks.com**

The Blitz

Hitler then tried to make the British surrender by bombing their cities. Night after night, German planes attacked, wrecking buildings and killing thousands of people. These attacks are known as the Blitz. The British fought back by bombing German cities, such as Dresden, where over 35,000 people were killed in one night.

This scene shows a typical London street ★ during the Blitz. The bombing continued for nine months.

The Eastern Front

At the start of the war, the Germans and the Russians had agreed not to fight each other. But in June 1941, Hitler broke this agreement and invaded the Soviet Union. By December, the Germans had almost reached Moscow. But they weren't prepared for the freezing winter weather, and the Russians managed to drive them back.

Powerful searchlights are used to spot German planes.

This building has been hit by a fire bomb.

Hundreds of families have lost their homes.

Anti-aircraft guns fire at the bombers.

This bus was thrown into the air by an exploding bomb.

Firefighters use water pumped from the river to fight the flames.

Rescue workers dig survivors out of the rubble.

The bombs have made huge holes, or craters, in the street.

Gas and water pipes have been shattered.

This unexploded bomb could blow up at any minute.

Thousands of British children were sent to live in the countryside, away from the bombing.

The World at War

At first, the war against Hitler was fought mainly in Europe. The USA supported Britain and the Soviet Union by sending them weapons and tanks, but the US government didn't want to get involved in the fighting.

All this changed on December 7, 1941, when ships from the US navy were bombed by Japanese planes, at Pearl Harbor in Hawaii. The next day, the USA declared war on Japan. Hitler had signed an agreement with the Japanese, so he then declared war on the USA.

US battleships on fire after the Japanese attack on Pearl Harbor

War in the Pacific

The Japanese already controlled parts of China, which they had invaded in 1937. Determined to build up a new Japanese empire, they now advanced with frightening speed. By June 1942, Japan had taken over most of Southeast Asia and many of the islands in the Pacific Ocean (see map).

The Allies advance

The countries that fought against Japan and Germany were known as the Allies. From June 1942, the Allies began to push the Japanese back across the Pacific. They also won important battles in other parts of the world, such as El Alamein in North Africa and Stalingrad in the Soviet Union.

D-Day

On June 6, 1944, known as D-Day, the Allies made a surprise attack on the Germans in northern France. Thousands of Allied soldiers crossed the English Channel and landed on the beaches of Normandy. Slowly, they fought their way across France, reaching Germany in September 1944.

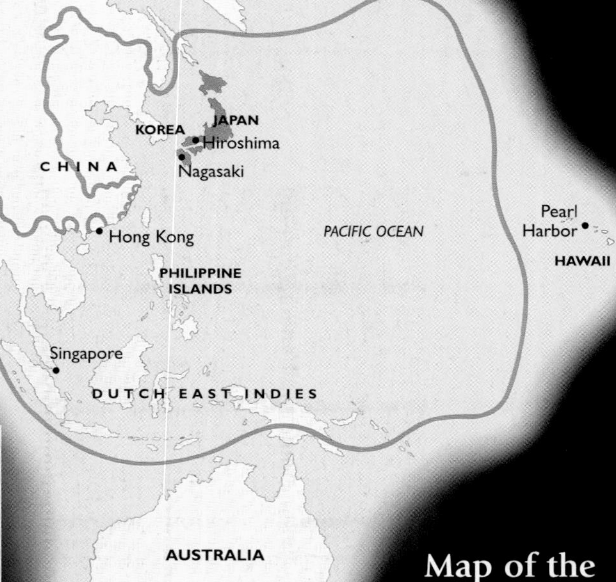

Map of the Pacific

Japan
Area controlled by Japan by 1942

This photograph, taken on D-Day, shows US soldiers wading from their landing craft onto one of the Normandy beaches.

Victory in Europe

Meanwhile, Russian troops were advancing into Germany from the east. In April 1945, they reached the capital, Berlin. Hitler realized he was defeated and killed himself on April 30. The Germans finally surrendered on May 8, known as V-E Day. (V-E stands for "Victory in Europe".)

The Holocaust

As the Allies advanced across Europe, they found prisons, or concentration camps, where the Nazis had sent Jews, gypsies and the mentally ill. Many of these people had been murdered by the Nazis. As many as 15 million people may have died in this way. This terrible event is known as the Holocaust.

The war ends

Although the war in Europe was over, fighting continued in the Pacific. On August 6, 1945, the USA dropped the first ever atomic bomb on the Japanese city of Hiroshima. About 80,000 people died in the explosion. Three days later, another bomb destroyed the city of Nagasaki, and the Japanese surrendered.

Atomic bombs, like the ones that destroyed Hiroshima and Nagasaki, form a huge, mushroom-shaped cloud when they explode.

Important dates

Sep 3, 1939	Britain and France declare war on Germany.
April-June 1940	Hitler occupies most of western Europe.
Aug-Oct 1940	The Battle of Britain
June 22, 1941	Hitler invades the Soviet Union.
Dec 7, 1941	Japan attacks US ships at Pearl Harbor.
June 6, 1944	The Allies land in France (D-Day).
April 30, 1945	Hitler kills himself.
May 8, 1945	Germany surrenders.
Aug 6, 1945	Hiroshima is destroyed by an atomic bomb.
Aug 14, 1945	The war ends.

From Colonies to Countries

Since the 19th century, all of India and most of Africa had been ruled by Europeans. But by 1945, Europe had been weakened by the Second World War. The people of India and Africa at last saw their chance to break free and govern themselves. At the same time, some Europeans began to think it was time for the countries of Europe to give up their colonies.

Gandhi and India

A group called the Indian National Congress had fought against British rule in India since the 1880s. This group became much stronger in 1920, when a Hindu lawyer named Mohandas Gandhi took over as leader. Gandhi led many protests against the British, and although he protested peacefully he was often thrown into prison.

Gandhi was an inspiring leader and he became known as Mahatma, which means "Great Soul".

Map of India and Pakistan

- India before 1947
- New borders created at Partition

Two countries

On August 15, 1947, India became independent, but the day before this happened, it was divided into two separate countries. The mainly Hindu areas became present-day India, and the mainly Muslim areas became Pakistan. This division into two countries was called Partition.

Partition happened very fast, and riots broke out when people found themselves trapped in the "wrong" country. In 1999, arguments were still going on between India and Pakistan over areas of land such as Kashmir.

The British give in

During the Second World War, thousands of Indians fought on the British side and this helped to change Britain's attitude to India. In 1942, Britain promised that it would grant India its freedom after the war, provided that the Indians continued to help the British.

Two religions

Although most Indians wanted independence, fierce arguments broke out between Hindus and Muslims. They clashed because the Muslims did not want to be ruled by Hindus after India had become independent.

This photograph, taken in 1999, shows Indian soldiers celebrating a victory over Pakistani troops in Kashmir. The soldiers are holding up the Indian flag.

African independence

Until the 1950s, most of Africa was divided into colonies ruled by European countries (see page 346). This began to change in 1951 when Libya became the first African country to win its independence.

This is Jomo Kenyatta, a leading fighter for independence in Kenya and first president of his country.

Over the next 30 years, more than 40 African countries became independent. In some countries, such as Kenya and Mozambique, rebel soldiers known as guerrillas fought savage wars against their European rulers. These struggles for independence often lasted many years, but most of them were successful in the end.

White rebels

In parts of southern Africa, power was seized by white Europeans who had settled there. The Prime Minister of Rhodesia, Ian Smith, declared his country's independence from Britain in 1965. Britain did not support Smith, and eventually the Africans took control. In 1980, Rhodesia became an independent African country and was renamed Zimbabwe.

Civil wars

After breaking free from European rule, many African countries still faced huge problems. Civil wars broke out in countries such as Nigeria, Angola, Chad and Somalia when people from different tribes or religions fought each other for power. Today, wars are still being fought in many parts of Africa.

Civil wars in Africa often force people to escape to nearby countries as refugees. These people are refugees from the civil war in Rwanda in 1995.

Important dates

1869-1948	Life of Mahatma Gandhi
Aug 14, 1947	India is divided into Pakistan and India (Partition).
Aug 15, 1947	India becomes independent.
1951	Libya becomes independent.
1960-1980	Most African states gain independence.
1965	Rhodesia becomes independent.
1971	East Pakistan breaks away from West Pakistan and is renamed Bangladesh.
1980	Rhodesia becomes the African country of Zimbabwe.

War in the Middle East

The Middle East is the area around the Red Sea and the Persian Gulf. Since 1945, there have been many changes, invasions and wars in this troubled part of the world.

A Jewish homeland

In 1945, the country that is now Israel was called Palestine. It was controlled by British troops, but most of the people living there were Muslim Arabs, called Palestinians. However, Jews all over the world saw Palestine as their home, because the Jewish people had originally come from there.

Israel is born

During the Second World War, Jews in Europe were brutally persecuted by the Nazis, but some of them managed to escape to Palestine. After the war, an organization called the United Nations was set up to encourage peace and understanding between nations. The United Nations decided that the Jews should have a country of their own, and on May 14, 1948, the Jewish state of Israel was created in Palestine.

The Arabs attack

The creation of the new Jewish state infuriated the Palestinians, who were supported by other Arab countries, such as Egypt, Jordan and Syria. In May 1948, the Arab countries attacked Israel, but the Israelis fought back. By January 1949, Israel had won the war and thousands of Palestinians had fled from Israel. Those who stayed behind were not given the same rights as the Israelis.

The fighting continues

Over the next 20 years, the Arabs often attacked Israel's borders. These attacks increased after 1964 when the Palestine Liberation Organization (PLO) was formed to fight for the right of all Palestinians to live in Israel.

During the 1960s, many Palestinians, like these, were forced to leave their homes to escape the fierce fighting.

In 1967, Israeli troops seized large areas of Arab land in the dramatic Six-Day War, and in 1973 Egypt and Syria led a surprise attack on Israel in the Yom Kippur War. This period of fighting ended in 1979 when the Egyptian and Israeli leaders signed an agreement at Camp David in the USA.

Peace plans

During the 1990s, there were several attempts to make peace over Israel, and in 1993 Israel and the PLO agreed that some groups of Palestinians could have their own governments within Israel. However, in the last years of the 20th century, there were frequent clashes between the Israelis and the Palestinians who were living in Israel.

Israeli leader Yitzhak Rabin (on the left) and PLO leader Yasser Arafat shake hands during the 1993 Middle East peace talks, while US President Bill Clinton looks on.

Revolution in Iran

For most of the 20th century, Iran was ruled by a series of kings, or shahs. The last shah tried to modernize his country, but he was opposed by strict Muslims who wanted to keep the old traditions. In 1979, the Shah was overthrown and Ayatollah Khomeini, a Muslim leader, took control of Iran. The Ayatollah ruled Iran very strictly and ordered all Iranian women to wear traditional dress.

Here, a young Iranian woman in traditional dress is walking past a gigantic portrait of Ayatollah Khomeini.

Map of the Middle East

IRAN
EUROPE
ASIA
AFRICA
SYRIA
LEBANON
IRAQ
ISRAEL
KUWAIT
JORDAN
EGYPT
PERSIAN GULF
SAUDI ARABIA
RED SEA

Areas claimed by Israel but occupied by Palestinians

The Gulf War

In 1990, Iraq invaded nearby Kuwait, hoping to gain control of Kuwait's oil wells. This led to the Gulf War, which started in 1991. A group of countries led by the USA and Saudi Arabia attacked Iraq to force it to free Kuwait. After just two months, Iraq lost the war, but both Iraq and Kuwait had been badly damaged.

The Iran-Iraq War

War broke out in 1980 between Iran and nearby Iraq. The war was really based on ancient differences between the two countries, but it began when Iraq invaded an area on Iran's border. The Iraqi leader, Saddam Hussein, thought Iran would be easy to beat, as it was in chaos after the revolution in 1979. In fact, the war dragged on for eight years and neither side won. By the time Iran and Iraq made peace in 1988, over a million soldiers had been killed.

Oil wells like this were set on fire by Iraqi troops as they retreated from Kuwait at the end of the Gulf War.

Important dates

1948	Israel is created.
1964	Palestinians form the Palestine Liberation Organization (PLO).
1967	Six-Day War
1973	Yom Kippur War
1979	Revolution in Iran
1980-1988	Iran-Iraq War
1990	Iraq invades Kuwait.
1991	Gulf War
1993	Middle East Peace Accord between Israel and the PLO

The Cold War

During the Second World War, the USA and the Communist Soviet Union fought on the same side. But soon after the war, they became suspicious of each other. For the next 40 years, they fought a war of words and threats that became known as the Cold War.

Communism spreads

By the end of World War II, the Soviet Army had advanced across eastern Europe and into Germany. After the war, Soviet soldiers remained in eastern Europe, and the Soviet leader, Stalin, helped to set up Communist rulers there.

Taking sides

Western countries, such as the USA and Britain, grew worried that the Soviets wanted to control all of Europe. So, in 1949, these countries formed an organization called NATO (the North Atlantic Treaty Organization). All the members of NATO agreed to defend each other if the Soviets attacked.

In 1955, the Soviet Union and the Communist countries of eastern Europe made a similar agreement among themselves, called the Warsaw Pact.

Germany divided

At the end of World War II, Germany was divided into four zones. The eastern zone was controlled by the Soviet Union, while the three western zones were run by the USA, Britain and France. In 1949, the Soviet zone became the Communist country of East Germany. The rest became West Germany.

The Berlin Wall

Berlin, the old capital city, now lay inside East Germany, and it too was divided into East and West. Life was much harder for people in East Berlin, and many of them tried to move to West Berlin. To stop this from happening, the Soviets built a huge wall between the two parts of the city. Any East Germans who tried to escape over the wall were shot.

This is part of the Berlin Wall, which became a symbol of the "Iron Curtain" that separated eastern Europe from the West.

East German flag

This is the Brandenburg Gate in East Berlin. It was built between 1788 and 1791 as a gateway into the city of Berlin.

West German police

Crisis in Cuba

During the Cold War, both sides built up huge supplies of weapons. In 1962, the USA discovered that the Soviet government was planning to use the island of Cuba, near the American coast, as a base for its nuclear missiles. The situation became very tense, as neither side wanted a nuclear war. After six days, the Soviet government was persuaded to back down.

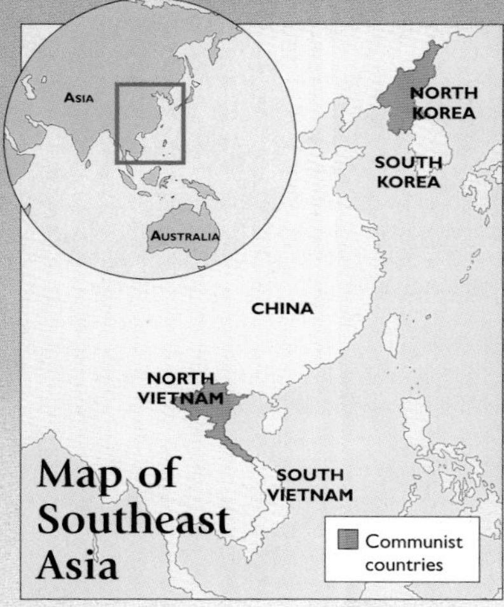

Map of Southeast Asia

Wounded American soldiers being rescued by helicopter during the Vietnam War

Korea and Vietnam

The USA and the Soviet Union never actually fought each other during the Cold War. But both sides sent weapons and troops to support Communists and anti-Communists who were fighting each other in different parts of the world. The main places where this happened were Korea and Vietnam.

Changing times

During the 1970s, the USA and the Soviet Union became more friendly. This changed when the Soviets invaded nearby Afghanistan in 1979, and the USA began planning powerful new weapons. In 1991, the Soviet Union split up, and the Cold War finally came to an end (see pages 382 and 383).

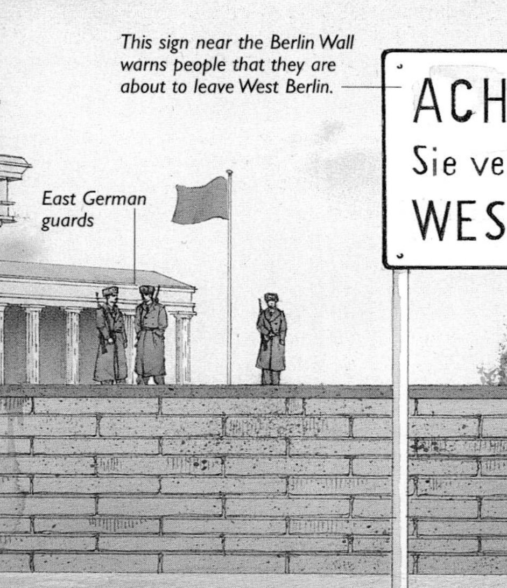

This sign near the Berlin Wall warns people that they are about to leave West Berlin.

East German guards

Important dates

1945	World War II ends.
1949	NATO is formed. Germany becomes two separate countries.
1950-1953	The Korean War
1954-1973	The Vietnam War
1955	The Warsaw Pact is signed.
1961	The Berlin Wall is built.
1962	The Cuban Missile Crisis
1979	The Soviet Union invades Afghanistan.
1991	The Cold War ends.

The Space Race

For hundreds of years, people dreamed of exploring space, but space travel only became possible when the rocket was invented in the 1930s. The first rockets were used during World War II to carry German bombs. After the war, scientists set about building a rocket powerful enough to travel into space.

Once the Cold War began in the 1950s, the USA and the Soviet Union competed fiercely to be the first country to send a rocket into space.

Yuri Gagarin, photographed on the way to his spacecraft *Vostok 1*

People in space

The Soviets scored another first in April 1961, when Yuri Gagarin became the first person to travel into space. During a flight that lasted 108 minutes, Gagarin made one complete orbit of the Earth. When he returned to the Soviet Union, he was treated as a hero

Flying to the Moon

In the early 1960s, the Soviets were winning the space race and the Americans were desperate to change this. The US president, John F. Kennedy, announced a daring plan to put American astronauts on the Moon.

Satellites in space

In October 1957, the Soviets launched *Sputnik 1*. This was the first man-made object to go into space, and circle, or orbit, the Earth. Today, objects like this, called satellites, are used to take detailed photographs of the Earth and to send television pictures all around the world.

The photograph above was taken by a modern satellite orbiting the Earth. It shows the Sacramento River and the city of Sacramento, in California.

This is one of the giant *Saturn 5* rockets that were used to send American astronauts to the Moon.

In December 1968, an American spacecraft, *Apollo 8*, flew around the Moon for the first time. Six months later, US astronauts Neil Armstrong and Buzz Aldrin became the first people to set foot on the Moon.

Buzz Aldrin on the surface of the Moon on July 20, 1969

The space shuttle

The early manned spacecraft of the 1960s and 1970s could only be used once. Their crews returned to Earth by dropping out of the sky in a tiny capsule that had parachutes attached to it to help break its fall.

All this changed in 1981 when the American space shuttle flew for the first time. The shuttle takes off like a rocket, but lands on a runway, like a plane, so it can be used many times.

The space shuttle *Endeavour* blasting off from Cape Canaveral in the USA

Two rocket boosters help the shuttle reach a speed of 84km (54 miles) per minute.

These wings help the shuttle glide back down to Earth.

At a height of 43km (27 miles), the boosters fall away. They drop into the sea and can be used again.

Space stations

During the 1970s, both the USA and the Soviet Union launched space stations, where scientists could live for weeks at a time and carry out experiments. When the Cold War ended, the two countries began to work together. From 1995 to 1998, American scientists worked on the Russian space station *Mir*.

The space station *Mir*

At the end of the 20th century, engineers around the world started work on an exciting new project, called the International Space Station. The first two parts were built in Russia and in the USA. They were launched separately and were joined together in space, in December 1998.

Important dates

1957	*Sputnik 1*, the first satellite, is launched.
1961	Yuri Gagarin is the first person in space.
July 20, 1969	*Apollo 11* reaches the Moon. Neil Armstrong and Buzz Aldrin make the first Moon landing.
1971	The Soviets launch the world's first space station, *Salyut 1*.
1981	The space shuttle makes its first flight.
1986	The space shuttle *Challenger* explodes after lift-off, killing seven astronauts.
Dec 1998	The first two parts of the International Space Station link up.

The Fall of Communism

By the 1980s, the Communist countries of Eastern Europe were facing serious problems. People there were much poorer than in the West, and in some of the countries there wasn't enough food for everyone. The Communist rulers were very unpopular, and they relied on the support of the Soviet Union and its army to keep them in power.

A new leader

In 1985, Mikhail Gorbachev became leader of the Soviet Union and began modernizing the country.

Mikhail Gorbachev, Soviet leader from 1985 to 1991

Gorbachev allowed people to set up their own businesses and to vote freely in elections for the first time. He also made it clear that the Soviet Union would no longer help the Communist leaders of Eastern Europe to stay in power.

Map of former Communist countries

Countries that were part of the Soviet Union

Eastern European countries

EUROPE
ASIA
AFRICA
ESTONIA
LATVIA
LITHUANIA
RUSSIA
Berlin
GERMANY
POLAND
BELARUS
KAZAKHSTAN
CZECH REPUBLIC
UKRAINE
SLOVAKIA
AUSTRIA
MOLDOVA
HUNGARY
ROMANIA
GEORGIA
BOSNIA-HERZEGOVINA
CASPIAN SEA
BLACK SEA
BULGARIA
YUGOSLAVIA
ARMENIA
ALBANIA
MACEDONIA
AZERBAIJAN

People power

In 1988, thousands of workers in Poland went on strike to protest against the government. The Polish Communist leaders were forced to allow elections, and the workers' trade union, known as Solidarity, won a huge victory. In August 1989, a non-Communist prime minister was elected, and a year later the Solidarity leader, Lech Walesa, became President of Poland.

SOLIDARNOŚĆ

The Solidarity logo, which includes the red and white flag of Poland

Opening borders

East Germany was one of the strictest Communist countries, and people there were forbidden to travel to the West. In September 1989, Hungary opened its border with Austria. Thousands of East Germans began escaping through Hungary into Austria and West Germany. Meanwhile, inside East Germany, there were massive protests against the Communist government.

The Wall falls

On November 9, the East German government agreed to let people travel freely to the West. In Berlin, people climbed onto the wall that divided the two parts of the city. The gates were opened for the first time in over 25 years, and thousands of East Germans crossed into West Berlin.

In March 1990, East Germany voted to join West Germany and, on October 23, the two countries became one again. Berlin later became the capital of the new, united Germany.

Here you can see people from East and West Germany celebrating together at the Berlin Wall, just after the Wall was opened up in November 1989.

A violent end

By the end of 1989, all the old Communist leaders of Eastern Europe had been replaced. In most countries, this happened peacefully, but in Romania the brutal Communist ruler, Nicolae Ceausescu, was taken prisoner and executed.

The break-up of the Soviet Union

Meanwhile, in the Soviet Union, the republics of Latvia, Estonia and Lithuania decided to break away and form countries of their own. Other regions tried to do the same, and fighting broke out in some places.

Boris Yeltsin, President of Russia from 1991 to 1999

President Gorbachev resigned, and on December 31, 1991, the Soviet Union split up into 15 independent countries. The largest of these was the republic of Russia, led by the non-Communist Boris Yeltsin. With the fall of Communism, the Cold War between the West and the Soviet Union was finally over.

Important dates

1980	The Polish trade union Solidarity is set up.
1985	Mikhail Gorbachev becomes leader of the Soviet Union.
August 1989	A non-Communist becomes prime minister of Poland.
Sep 1989	Hungary opens its border with Austria.
Nov 9, 1989	East Germans cross the Berlin Wall.
Oct 23, 1990	East and West Germany become one country.
Dec 31, 1991	The Soviet Union splits up.

Rights for All

Human rights are based on the idea that all people should be treated fairly and equally, whatever their race, religion or sex. They should be able to live in freedom, express their opinions, have a fair trial and vote in elections. Today, these basic rights are often taken for granted, but a hundred years ago things were very different.

Votes for women

In 1900, most countries in the world did not allow women to vote in elections. New Zealand had given women the vote in 1893, but other countries were slow to follow. In Britain and the USA, women known as suffragettes campaigned fiercely for the right to vote. Britain finally gave women the vote in 1918, and the USA did the same two years later.

Many suffragettes, like this woman, were arrested and sent to prison.

Black rights

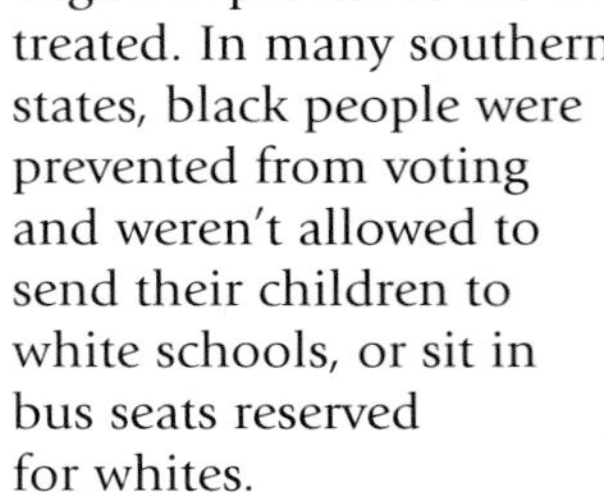

In the USA, during the 1950s, African-Americans began to protest at the way they were being treated. In many southern states, black people were prevented from voting and weren't allowed to send their children to white schools, or sit in bus seats reserved for whites.

This is Martin Luther King, a Baptist minister who led many black protests in the USA.

The largest protest took place in August 1963, when 200,000 people marched through the streets of Washington, DC. The next year, the US government passed new laws, making it illegal to treat people differently because of their race. In spite of this, even today, many black Americans do not have the same advantages as whites.

In some countries, such as China, people are not allowed to protest against the government. Here you can see Chinese students protesting in Beijing, in May 1989. Hundreds of them were killed when the army was sent in to stop the protests.

South Africa

Meanwhile, in South Africa, black Africans were treated appallingly by the whites who ruled the country. They weren't allowed to vote, and laws were passed to keep them out of white areas. This system of keeping blacks and whites apart was known as apartheid, and thousands of black Africans were jailed, beaten or killed for protesting against it.

In 1989, a new president, F. W. de Klerk, came to power and began changing the system. The following year, he released the black leader Nelson Mandela from prison. In 1994, black Africans were allowed to vote for the first time, and Nelson Mandela was chosen as South Africa's first black president.

Nelson Mandela surrounded by supporters during the election campaign of 1994

The right to land

Many native people around the world have been treated unfairly by white settlers. In Australia, the native Aboriginals lost their land and their way of life when Europeans arrived in the 18th century. Since the 1930s, the Aboriginal people have been campaigning to win back their land, but so far they have only been given a tiny fraction of what they lost.

Protecting rights

Today, there are still many parts of the world where people's rights are not respected. In many countries, women are still seen as second-class citizens, and people are treated unjustly because of their race.

International organizations, such as the United Nations, try to persuade governments to make fairer laws, while groups such as Amnesty International speak out on behalf of people whose rights are being ignored.

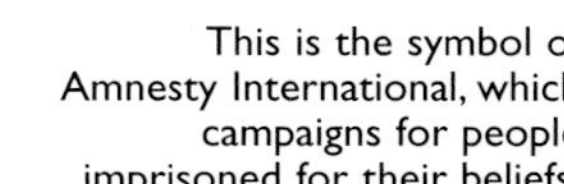

This is the symbol of Amnesty International, which campaigns for people imprisoned for their beliefs.

Important dates

1893	Women in New Zealand are given the right to vote.
1945	The United Nations is set up to encourage peace and to protect human rights.
1949	Apartheid is introduced in South Africa.
1964-1965	Civil rights laws are passed in the USA.
1989	Hundreds of protesters are killed in Tiananmen Square in Beijing, China.
1990	Apartheid ends in South Africa.

Sound and Pictures

In 1900, radios and moving pictures, or movies, had only just been invented, and television did not exist at all. Over the next hundred years, these new inventions created a whole new area of entertainment and completely changed our view of the world.

The birth of cinema

In 1895, two brothers, named Louis and Auguste Lumière, invented a machine called a Cinématographe, which could project moving images onto a screen. The brothers gave their first movie show in Paris in December 1895, and cinema was born.

Moving pictures quickly became very popular, and the craze soon spread to the United States. By the 1920s, Hollywood, on the west coast of the USA, was the movie capital of the world.

The comic actor Charlie Chaplin was the most famous movie star of the 1920s.

Mickey and Minnie Mouse were two very popular characters in early cartoon films.

The first talkie

Early moving pictures had no sound, but were accompanied by music from an orchestra or piano. The first major talking picture, or talkie, was *The Jazz Singer*, which was made in 1927.

Radio days

During the 1920s, radio also became popular. The first radio stations were set up in the United States in 1920, and by 1930 there were 12 million radio sets in the USA. Politicians soon realized that they could use radio to speak directly to people in their homes. During the Second World War, governments on both sides made radio broadcasts to encourage their own side and show the enemy in a bad light.

The start of television

The first public demonstration of a mechanical television was given by the British inventor John Logie Baird in 1926. The TV system we use today was developed in the 1930s, and in 1936 the BBC began regular TV broadcasts from London. At first, very few people had a TV set, as each one cost about the same as a small car. But by the 1950s, television was the most popular form of entertainment.

Satellite service

In 1962, for the first time, live TV pictures were sent across the Atlantic Ocean by a satellite orbiting the Earth. This meant that images filmed in the United States could be shown at the same time in Europe. Today, people can watch the news all over the globe as it happens, and our world seems a much smaller place.

This scene from *Lost in Space* shows a robot inside a space ship. The movie used a vast number of special effects to create a fantasy world in space.

Too much television?

By 1990, in the USA, the average teenager was spending 23 hours a week watching television. Some experts think that too much television makes people too lazy to think for themselves. Others worry that watching a lot of violence on television could make people behave in a violent way.

Movie magic

In order to compete with television, movie-makers had to create more spectacular effects. In the 1950s, new techniques were invented to improve sound and produce bigger, widescreen pictures. By the 1990s, movie companies were spending vast amounts of money on truly amazing special effects.

Important dates

1895 The Lumière brothers project moving images onto a screen.

1920 The first radio stations are set up in the USA.

1926 John Logie Baird demonstrates his television.

1927 *The Jazz Singer* is the first major movie with sound.

1936 The BBC begins regular television broadcasts.

1962 The satellite Telstar sends a TV image across the Atlantic.

Our Polluted Planet

During the 20th century, daily life changed dramatically. We now have cars to take us from place to place, gas and electricity for cooking and heating, and a vast number of gadgets and machines to make life easier. But as early as the 1960s, scientists began to realize that our way of life was gradually destroying the world around us.

Global warming

Most of the world's electricity is produced in power stations that burn coal, oil or gas. When these fuels burn, they release a gas called carbon dioxide into the air. Exhaust fumes from cars and buses also contain carbon dioxide. Scientists now believe that this gas may be making the Earth warmer. This is known as global warming.

Trees use up some of the carbon dioxide in the air, helping to reduce global warming. But all over the world, forests like this are being burned to make room for farmland.

The greenhouse effect

As carbon dioxide rises high into the air, it forms a blanket around the Earth, trapping heat underneath. This is known as the greenhouse effect and it is what causes global warming. As the Earth warms up, the weather all over the world could change dramatically. Sea levels might also rise, flooding large areas of low-lying land.

Poisoning the air

Cars, factories and power stations continuously pump out fumes which dirty, or pollute, the air. In cities, these fumes sometimes form a smoky fog, called smog, which makes it hard for people to breathe. The fumes also mix with clouds to form acid rain which kills plants.

The ozone hole

The Earth is surrounded by a layer of gas called ozone, which blocks out harmful ultraviolet light from the Sun. In 1985, scientists showed that there was a hole in the ozone layer above Antarctica. We now know that the ozone layer is getting thinner in other parts of the world too.

The ozone is being destroyed by man-made gases called chlorofluorocarbons, or CFCs, which are found in some aerosols and refrigerators. As the ozone layer gets thinner, more ultraviolet light gets through, and this can damage our eyes and skin.

Internet link: *For a Web site where you can find out more about how people are damaging the natural world, go to* ***www.usborne-quicklinks.com***

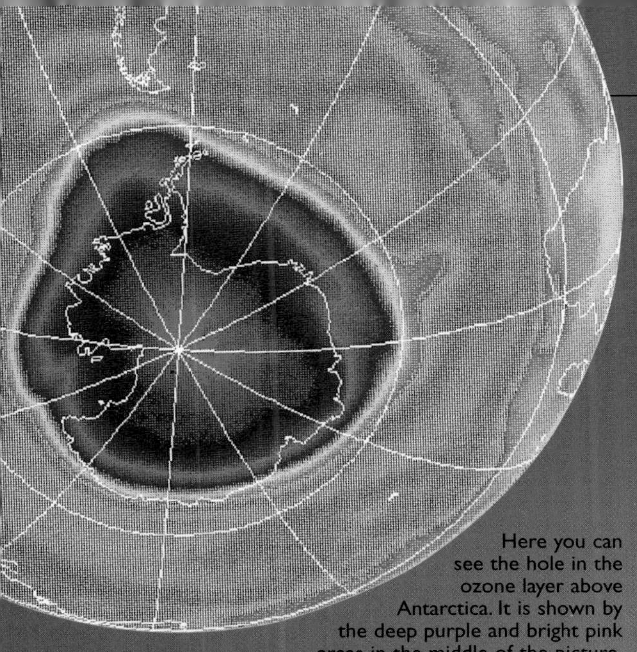

Here you can see the hole in the ozone layer above Antarctica. It is shown by the deep purple and bright pink areas in the middle of the picture.

Plastic pollution

Plastic is one of the most common materials around today. Because it is cheap, it is often used to make bags, bottles and wrappers which people throw away. Plastic doesn't rot, so it's very hard to get rid of. Lots of it ends up in the sea, where it kills millions of fish, birds and animals every year.

Turtles can die from eating plastic bags, which look like jellyfish in the water.

Saving the planet

Protest groups, such as Greenpeace, try to persuade governments to do something about pollution, and most world leaders now accept that there is a real problem. In 1992, politicians from over 150 countries met at the Earth Summit in Brazil to talk about the future of the planet.

In order to protect the ozone layer, a total of 140 countries have now agreed to stop making CFCs, and some countries have also agreed to cut the amount of carbon dioxide they produce. Scientists hope that this will help to slow down global warming.

Polluting the water

The world's seas and rivers are being polluted by sewage (waste from drains and toilets) and poisonous chemicals dumped from factories. Our seas and rivers are also being poisoned by fertilizers that are washed off farmland. All around the world, beaches are ruined and seabirds are killed when oil leaks out of tankers that have run aground.

One way to reduce global warming is to find cleaner ways of making electricity. These are wind turbines, which can produce electricity without releasing carbon dioxide into the air.

Important dates

- **1967** Scientists first become aware of the greenhouse effect.
- **1971** Greenpeace is set up.
- **1985** Scientists measure the hole in the ozone layer.
- **1992** The Earth Summit is held in Rio de Janeiro, in Brazil.

The Computer Revolution

Computers allow us to do things that people used to think were impossible. We can test cars and planes before they are even built, explore imaginary worlds using virtual reality, and send information around the world in seconds on the Internet. Today, computer technology is changing incredibly fast, but progress was slow at first.

The first computers

The very first computers were invented in the 19th century. They made calculations mechanically, using lots of connected cogs and wheels. The first electronic computers did not appear until the 1940s, over a hundred years later. These early computers were immense. ENIAC, completed in 1946, filled a whole room and weighed as much as 500 people.

From valves to chips

Computers use electrical signals to process, or work on, information. Early computers, such as ENIAC, had thousands of large valves which switched on and off to produce these signals. Then, in 1947, a much smaller switch, called a transistor, was invented. Computers no longer needed to be quite so huge.

In 1958, an American scientist named Jack Kilby invented the microchip, which contained more than one transistor. By using microchips, it was possible to build computers that were much smaller and more powerful than before.

Today, microchips, like the one shown above, can contain millions of tiny transistors.

Personal computers

The first small home computer, the Altair, was sold in 1975. It was named after a planet in the TV series *Star Trek*. The Altair had to be bought as a kit and then built at home. Most modern computers are based on a type of computer called a PC that was first made in 1981.

The Internet

The Internet is a huge network that links together millions of computers all around the world. It grew out of a network called ARPANET, which was set up in 1969 by the US armed forces. At first, computers had to be connected to the Internet by special cables. It wasn't until the 1990s that people could link up by using their own phone line.

Here are some pages from the part of the Internet known as the World Wide Web.

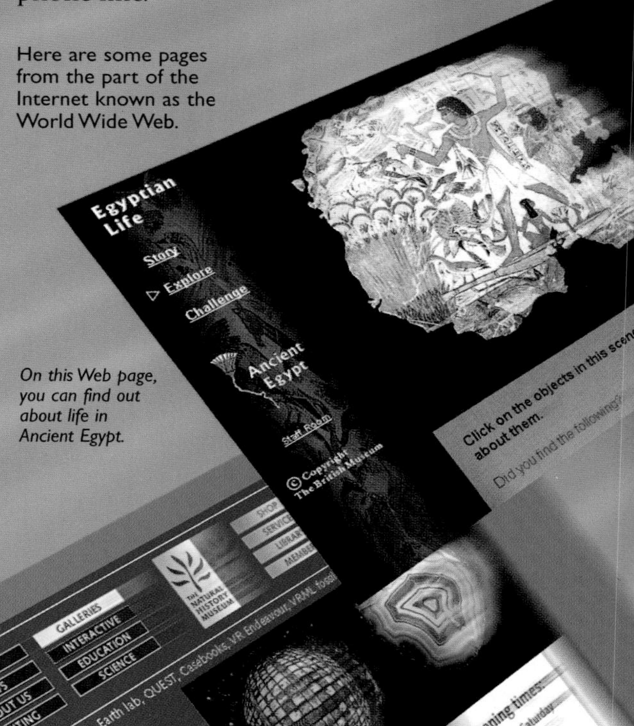

On this Web page, you can find out about life in Ancient Egypt.

Starting at this Web page, you can go on a tour around a museum.

The World Wide Web

Using the Internet, we can send electronic messages, or e-mail, around the world in seconds and find information on any topic we want, by searching the pages of the World Wide Web. Lots of people now shop on the Internet, buying anything from groceries to plane tickets.

Living with computers

Computers have had a huge effect on the way we live. Today, many people work from home, using a computer to connect to their workplace. Other jobs, such as assembling cars, can be done by computers instead of people. Many of the gadgets in our homes, such as washing machines and CD players, rely on tiny computers to make them work.

This page lets you see inside the human body.

This page gives you an up-to-date weather forecast.

Using this Web page, you can create your own puppet show.

Just for fun

The first popular electronic game, a simple tennis game called Pong, appeared in 1972. Today's computer games are much more complicated, with realistic images and dramatic sound effects. Computers are also used to create the amazing special effects you see at the movies. These techniques are now so good that it's impossible to tell what's real and what isn't.

This is a character from the 1995 movie *Toy Story*, which was the first full-length movie to be made entirely on computer.

Important dates

1834-1871	Charles Babbage designs the first mechanical computer.
1946	The ENIAC computer is completed.
1947	The transistor is invented.
1958	Jack Kilby makes the first microchip.
1969	The computer network ARPANET is set up.
1975	The first small home computer is sold.
1981	The first PC is made by the American firm IBM.
1989	British scientist Tim Berners-Lee invents the World Wide Web.

The End of the Century

The end of the 20th century was an exciting time, as new discoveries and inventions changed people's lives faster than ever before. At the same time, several parts of the world were devastated by terrible wars.

Yugoslavia breaks up

At the start of the 1990s, the country of Yugoslavia, in eastern Europe, split into separate republics. The largest of these republics, Serbia, wanted Yugoslavia to remain a single country, and war soon broke out between Serbia and the other republics. Fighting was especially violent in the republic of Bosnia-Herzegovina and in Kosovo, in southern Serbia.

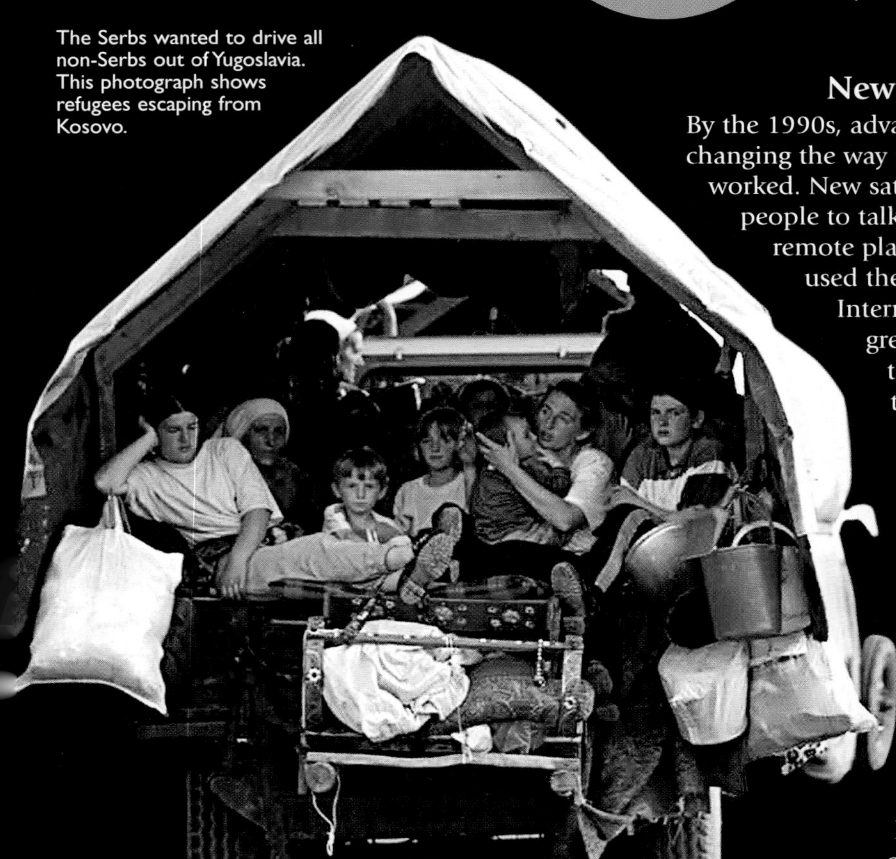

The Serbs wanted to drive all non-Serbs out of Yugoslavia. This photograph shows refugees escaping from Kosovo.

East Timor breaks free

In August 1999, violence broke out in East Timor, in Southeast Asia. For more than 20 years, East Timor had been ruled by Indonesia, and when the East Timorese voted to become independent, Indonesian soldiers began attacking them. The United Nations (UN) sent troops to protect the people of East Timor, and Indonesia soon agreed to let East Timor govern itself. UN soldiers stayed there to make sure the area remained peaceful.

The symbol of the UN

New technology

By the 1990s, advances in technology were changing the way many people lived and worked. New satellite phones allowed people to talk to each other from very remote places. More and more people used their computers to connect to the Internet, and a whole new industry grew up, as companies began using the Internet to sell things directly to people in their homes.

Understanding genes

By the end of the century, scientists had built up a vast amount of knowledge about human genes, the coded chemical messages that are passed on from parents to children. In 1990, a project was set up to discover how each gene in the body works. This is known as the Human Genome Project, and scientists hope that it will help them find cures for many diseases.

Internet link: *For a link to a Web site where you can see how people celebrated the millennium in different countries around the world, go to* ***www.usborne-quicklinks.com***

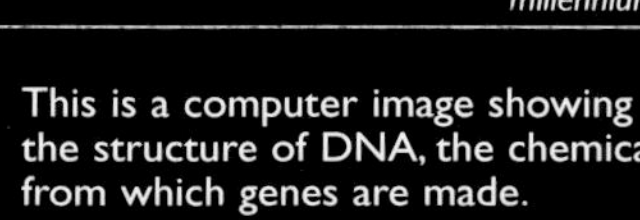
This is a computer image showing the structure of DNA, the chemical from which genes are made.

GM food

In the 1990s, scientists discovered how to transfer genes from one type of plant or animal to another. They used this knowledge to create crops that were protected against insects and diseases. Food from these crops is known as genetically modified, or GM, food. Although GM crops could help to provide enough food for everyone in the world, many people are afraid that they could also damage the environment.

The year 2000

The century ended with a bang as many countries held spectacular firework displays to celebrate the start of the year 2000. For the first time ever, television made it possible to watch people celebrating the dawn of a new century in different places all over the world.

Fireworks exploding in Paris at midnight on December 31, 1999

Ancient World Time Chart

This chart shows what was happening at the same time in different parts of the ancient world.

DATE	THE AMERICAS	EUROPE	AFRICA
BEFORE 10,000BC	By c.13,000BC People arrive in North America.		
10,000BC	c.6000BC Farming begins in Central America.	c.6000BC Farming begins in Greece and spreads across Europe.	c.6000BC People in the Sahara tame cattle.
5000BC	 c.1200BC The Olmecs build temples. The Chavín way of life begins.	c.3000-1500BC Stonehenge is built in Britain.  c.1900-1450BC The Minoans build palaces on Crete. c.1600BC The Mycenaeans become powerful in Greece. c.1450BC The Mycenaeans invade Crete. c.1100BC The Greek Dark Ages begin.	c.5000BC Farming begins in the Nile Valley. c.3100BC King Menes unites Upper and Lower Egypt. c.2686BC The Old Kingdom begins in Egypt. c.2530BC The Egyptians start building the Great Pyramid at Giza. c.2040BC The Middle Kingdom begins. c.1720BC The Hyksos invade Egypt. The Middle Kingdom ends. c.1570BC The New Kingdom begins. c.1450BC The Egyptian Empire is at its largest under King Tuthmosis III.
1000BC	c.1000BC The Adena build earth mounds. 	c.800BC The Celtic way of life spreads across western Europe. c.776BC The first Olympic Games. 753BC The city of Rome is set up, according to legend. c.509BC Rome becomes a republic.	c.814BC The city of Carthage is built by the Phoenicians. 
500BC	c.300BC The Hopewell take over from the Adena. c.200BC The Nazca start to draw lines in the desert.	c.500-350BC The Greeks are at their most successful. 431-404BC The Peloponnesian War. 356BC Alexander the Great is born. 44BC Julius Caesar is murdered. 27BC Augustus becomes the first Emperor of Rome.	c.500BC The Nok way of life begins. 332BC Alexander the Great conquers Egypt. 146BC The Romans destroy Carthage. 30BC The Romans conquer Egypt.
AD1	c.AD1-700 The Moche are ruled by warrior-priests. c.AD250-900 The Maya are at their most successful. c.AD500 Teotihuacán is the sixth largest city in the world.	AD117 The Roman Empire is at its largest under the Emperor Trajan. AD395 The Roman Empire splits permanently in two. AD476 The Western Roman Empire collapses.	c.AD100 The kingdom of Axum becomes powerful. c.AD500 The Bantu people reach southern Africa.

Saharan rock painting

Olmec ball-players

Mycenaean woman

The Great Serpent Mound

Nok sculpture

ASIA			AUSTRALASIA
THE MIDDLE EAST	**SOUTH ASIA**	**THE FAR EAST**	c.40,000BC People known as Aboriginals arrive in Australia.
c.10,000BC Farming begins in the Fertile Crescent. 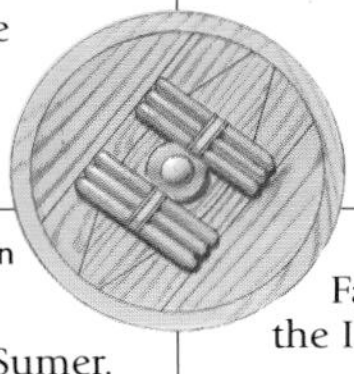		c.9000BC The Jomon people of Japan hunt and fish for food.	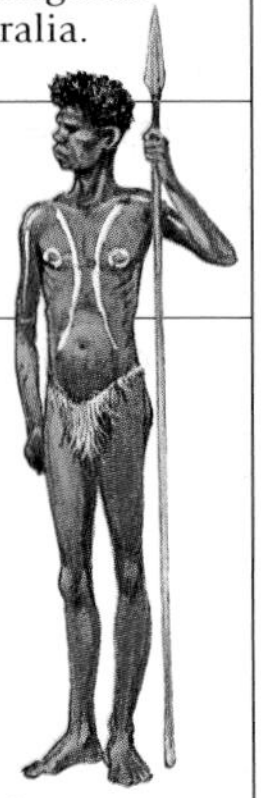 Australian Aboriginal
c.3500BC The wheel is invented in Sumer. Sumerian wheel c.3300BC Writing is invented in Sumer. c.2350BC Sargon of Akkad creates the world's first empire. c.2000BC The Hittites settle in Anatolia. c.1792-1750BC King Hammurabi rules Babylon. c.1400BC The first alphabet is invented in Canaan. c.1250BC The Hebrews arrive in Canaan. c.1200BC The Phoenicians become successful sailors and traders.	c.3500BC Farmers settle in the Indus Valley. c.2500-1800BC The Indus Valley people are at their most successful. c.1500BC The Aryans arrive in the Indus Valley.	c.5000BC Farming begins in China. c.2700BC Silk is first made. 1766-1027BC The Shang kings rule China. c.1400BC People in China write on oracle bones.	c.1500BC People begin settling on islands in the Pacific Ocean.
c.1000-663BC The Assyrians build up a strong empire. c.965-928BC King Solomon rules Israel. 605-562BC King Nebuchadnezzar II rules the Babylonian Empire. 559-530BC King Cyrus II rules Persia and builds up an empire.	c.560BC Siddhartha Gautama (the Buddha) is born.	1027BC The Zhou kings take control of China. Confucius 551BC Confucius is born.	
490-479BC Wars between the Persians and the Greeks. 331BC Alexander the Great defeats the Persians.  Alexander the Great 64BC The Romans conquer parts of the Middle East.	272-231BC Asoka rules the Mauryan Empire.	c.500BC Farming begins in Japan. 481-221BC The Warring States Period in China. 221BC Qin Shi Huangdi becomes China's first emperor. 202BC The Han Dynasty begins.	
c.AD29 Jesus Christ is crucified.  Jesus on the cross	AD320-535 The Gupta Empire in India.	c.AD100 Paper is invented in China. Yamato warrior c.AD300 The Yamato tribe rules in Japan.	

Medieval World Time Chart

This chart shows what was happening at the same time in different parts of the medieval world.

DATE	THE AMERICAS	EUROPE	AFRICA
Before 500		c.450 The Angles, Saxons and Jutes begin to rule Britain.	429 The Vandals invade North Africa.
500	c.600 The Maya are at their most successful. Mayan mask	481-511 Clovis creates the kingdom of the Franks. 507 The Visigoths invade Spain. 527-565 Justinian rules the Byzantine Empire. Coin showing Justinian	533 The Byzantines conquer North Africa. 697 The Arabs conquer North Africa.
700	c.700 The Mississippi people start to build towns. c.850 Many Mayan towns are abandoned.	711 The Moors invade Spain. c.790 The Vikings begin raiding Europe. 800-814 Charlemagne rules his Empire. c.862 Rurik creates a kingdom in Russia.	c.700 The kingdom of Ghana is at its most successful.
900	c.900 The Pueblo people start to build towns. c.900-1200 The Toltecs are powerful. c.1000 Leif Ericson reaches North America.	962-973 Otto I is the first Holy Roman Emperor. Emperor Otto's crown 1037-1492 The Christians win back Spain from the Moors. 1054 The Church in eastern Europe splits from the Church in western Europe. 1066 The Normans conquer England.	969-1171 The Fatimids rule Egypt. c.1000 The kingdoms of Benin and Ife are created.
1100	c.1100 The Chimú start to build their Empire.	c.1100 The Viking raids end. 1215 King John of England signs Magna Carta. King John c.1250-1480 The Mongols rule southern Russia.	c.1200 The kingdom of Mali is created. 1250-1517 The Mamelukes rule Egypt.
1300	c.1300 The Pueblo people abandon their towns. c.1345 The Aztecs start to build their Empire. Aztec warrior 1438 The Incas start to build their Empire.	c.1300 The city of Moscow starts to beome powerful. 1337-1453 The French and the English fight the Hundred Years' War. 1347-1353 The Black Death spreads through Europe. c.1350 The Renaissance begins in Italy. 1378-1417 Rival popes rule in Avignon and Rome. Florence Cathedral	c.1350 The city of Great Zimbabwe is at its largest.
1450	1492 Columbus discovers the West Indies.	1453 The Ottoman Turks capture Constantinople and the Byzantine Empire collapses.	c.1450 The Portuguese start trading in West Africa.

ASIA			AUSTRALASIA
THE MIDDLE EAST	**SOUTH ASIA**	**THE FAR EAST**	c.400 Settlers reach Easter Island.
c.570-632 The life of Mohammed. 632 Arab caliphs (rulers) start to build the Islamic Empire.	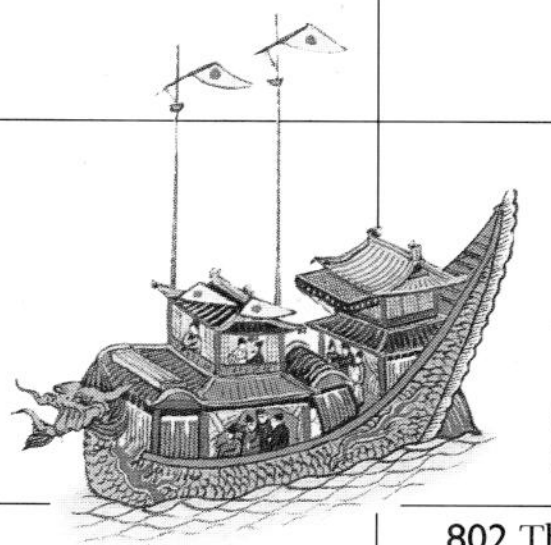	Sui Emperor's boat 581 The Sui dynasty begins in China. 618 The Tang dynasty begins in China.	
750 The Abbasid Caliphs start to rule the Islamic Empire from Baghdad.	711 The Arabs invade northern India. 886 The Chola kingdom is created in southern India.	802 The Khmer kingdom is created in Cambodia. 858 The Fujiwara family take control in Japan. 868 The earliest printed book is produced in China.	c.750 The Maoris reach New Zealand.  Maori good luck charm
1055 The Seljuk Turks capture Baghdad and control the Islamic Empire. 1071 The Seljuk Turks beat the Byzantines at the Battle of Manzikert. 1096 The Crusades begin. 1099 The Crusaders capture parts of Palestine.		960 The Sung dynasty begins in China. Painting by a Sung artist	c.1000 The Easter Islanders start to build stone heads.
 1258 The Mongols capture Baghdad. 1290 Osman I starts to build the Ottoman Empire. Osman I 1291 The Crusades end.	1206 The Sultans of Delhi start to rule northern India.	1192 Shoguns start to take control in Japan. c.1230 The Sukhothai kingdom is created in Thailand. Statue from the Sukhothai kingdom 1206-1226 Genghis Khan builds the Mongol Empire. 1279-1368 The Mongols rule China.	
1360-1405 Tamerlane builds a new Mongol Empire.  Tamerlane	1336 The kingdom of Vijayanagar is created in southern India. 1398 Tamerlane invades northern India.	1368 The Ming dynasty begins in China.	

World Time Chart for the Last 500 Years

This chart shows what was happening at the same time in different parts of the world.

DATE	THE AMERICAS	EUROPE	AFRICA
1500	**1500s** Portuguese settlers arrive in Brazil. **1519-1521** Spanish conquistadors conquer the Aztecs. **1532-1534** Spanish conquistadors conquer the Incas.  Inca priest **1580s** The Slave Trade begins.	**1520s** The Reformation begins. **1545** The Counter-Reformation begins. **1547-1584** Ivan the Terrible is Tsar of Russia. **1556** Charles V divides the Habsburg Empire in two.  Flag of the Habsburg Empire **1558-1603** Elizabeth I is Queen of England. **1581** The Republic of the United Netherlands is created.	**1505** The Portuguese establish ports on the coast of East Africa. **1516-1560** The Ottoman Turks conquer large areas of North Africa.
1600	**1603** French settlers start to set up colonies in Canada. **1620** The *Mayflower* arrives in North America carrying English pilgrims. **1699** The French create the colony of Louisiana.	**1618-1648** The Thirty Years' War. **1630s** Galileo proves that the Earth travels around the Sun. **1642-1646** The English Civil War. **1643-1715** Louis XIV is King of France. **1660s** Isaac Newton discovers the laws of gravity. **1689-1725** Peter the Great is Tsar of Russia.	**1616** Dutch and French traders set up trading posts in West Africa. **1652** Dutch settlers conquer Cape Colony.
1700	**1759** British troops capture Quebec from the French. **1776** American colonists sign the Declaration of Independence. **1789** George Washington becomes the first President of the USA.	**1740-1780** Maria Theresa rules the Habsburg Empire. **1740-1786** Frederick the Great is King of Prussia. **1750s** The Industrial Revolution begins in Britain. **1762-1796** Catherine the Great is Tsarina of Russia. **1789** The French Revolution begins. Ribbons worn by French Revolutionaries **1799-1815** Napoleon Bonaparte rules France.	**1700-1800** The African kingdoms of Benin, Oyo and Ashanti are flourishing.  Ashanti gold ornament
1800	**1816-1824** Simon Bolivar and José de San Martín win independence for colonies in South America. **1860** Abraham Lincoln becomes President of the USA. **1861-1865** The American Civil War. **1888** Slavery ends throughout the Americas. US President Abraham Lincoln	**1848** Revolutions in many parts of Europe. **1861** Italy is unified. **1871** Germany is unified. **1895** Karl Benz, a German engineer, builds the first motor car. Benz's first motor car ★ **1895** The Lumière brothers give the first ever movie show, in Paris.	**1806** Britain takes control of Cape Colony. **1836** The Boers set out on the Great Trek. **1841** David Livingstone starts to explore Africa. **1879** The Zulus are defeated by the British and the Boers. **1899** The Boer War begins.

ASIA			AUSTRALASIA
THE MIDDLE EAST	**SOUTH ASIA**	**THE FAR EAST**	
1502 The start of the Safavid dynasty in Persia. **1520-1566** Sultan Suleiman rules the Ottomans. Sultan Suleiman	**1526-1605** Babar is the first Mogul Emperor of India. **1556-1605** Akbar is the Mogul Emperor of India.	**1568-1582** Oda Nobunaga controls Japan. **1591-1598** Toyotomi Hideyoshi controls Japan. **1595** Dutch traders start to set up colonies in the East Indies.	Australian Aboriginal musical instruments, called clapsticks
1680s The Ottoman Empire begins to weaken.	**1600** The British East India Company is created. **1632** The Mogul Emperor Shah Jahan starts to build the Taj Mahal in India. **1690s** The Mogul Empire is at its largest.	**1603** The Tokugawa shoguns start to rule Japan. **1644** The Ming dynasty ends and the Manchu emperors take over China.	**1606** Dutch explorers reach Australia. **1642** Abel Tasman reaches New Zealand.
Persian Safavid warriors **1730** The Safavid dynasty in Persia ends.	**1714** Hindu princes start to win land in northern India. **1757** Robert Clive defeats the Prince of Bengal at the Battle of Plassey in India.	 Ming jar	Australian kangaroo **1770** Captain Cook reaches Australia. **1788** Britain begins sending convicts to Australia.
1854-1869 The Suez Canal is built in Egypt.	**1857-1858** The Indian Mutiny. **1858** The British government takes control of India. **1885** The Indian National Congress is set up to campaign for independence.  Symbol of the Indian National Congress	**1839-1842** The Opium War in China. **1850-1864** The Taiping Rebellion in China. **1868** The Emperor takes control of Japan. **1894-1895** War between Japan and China. **1898-1900** The Boxer Rebellion in China. Boxer warrior	 **1840** The British take control of New Zealand. **1860-1861** Explorers cross Australia. **1893** Women in New Zealand are given the right to vote.

DATE	THE AMERICAS	EUROPE	AFRICA
1900	**1914** Opening of the Panama Canal. **1917** The USA joins World War I. **1920** Prohibition begins in the USA. **1927** *The Jazz Singer* is the first major movie with sound. **1929** The Wall Street Crash. **1933** US President Roosevelt launches the New Deal. **1941** The USA joins World War II after Pearl Harbor is bombed.	**1914-1918** World War I. Poppies from the battlefields of World War I **1917** The Russian Revolution. **1922** Benito Mussolini takes control of Italy. **1928-1953** Josef Stalin controls the Soviet Union. Symbol of the Soviet Union **1933** Adolf Hitler becomes Chancellor of Germany. **1939-1945** World War II. **1948** Communists come to power in Czechoslovakia, Hungary, Romania, Bulgaria and Poland. **1949** Germany is divided into East and West.	**1902** The Boer War ends. **1942** The Allies defeat the Germans at El Alamein in North Africa. **1949** Apartheid is introduced in South Africa. 
1950	**1958** Jack Kilby invents the microchip. **1962** The Cuban Missile Crisis. **1963** US President Kennedy is assassinated. **1968** Martin Luther King is assassinated. **1969** US astronaut Neil Armstrong is the first man on the Moon. US astronaut Buzz Aldrin on the Moon, photographed by Neil Armstrong **1981** The US space shuttle makes its first flight. **1992** The Earth Summit is held in Rio de Janeiro, Brazil.	**1953** The structure of DNA is discovered in Britain by Francis Crick and James Watson. **1957** The Soviet Union launches *Sputnik I* into space. **1961** Yuri Gagarin of the Soviet Union is the first person in space. **1980** Solidarity is set up in Poland. **1985** Mikhail Gorbachev becomes leader of the Soviet Union. **1989** The Berlin Wall falls. **1989** Tim Berners-Lee invents the World Wide Web. **1991** The Soviet Union splits up. **1991-1995** War in Yugoslavia. **1998-1999** War in Kosovo.	**1951** Libya becomes independent. **1952-1955** Rebellion in Kenya against British rule. **1957** Ghana becmes independent. **1960-1980** Most African states become independent. **1967-1970** Civil war in Nigeria. 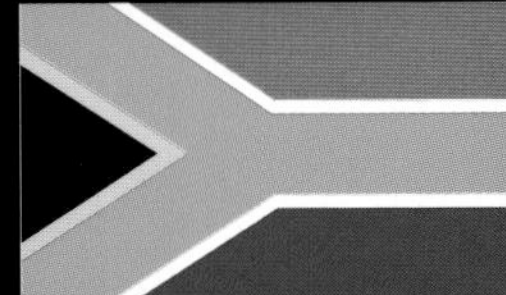 Flag of South Africa **1990** Apartheid ends in South Africa. **1994-1999** Nelson Mandela is President of South Africa.
2000			

ASIA

THE MIDDLE EAST

1918 The Turkish Ottoman Empire ends.

1922 The Republic of Turkey is formed.

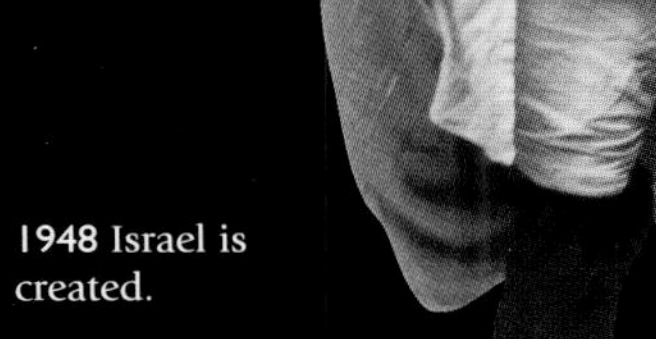

1948 Israel is created.

1948-1949 Arab-Israeli War.

1956 Second Arab-Israeli War.

1967 Six-Day War between Israel and the Arab states.

Israeli fighter plane

1973 Yom Kippur War between Israel and the Arab states.

1979 Ayatollah Khomeini takes control of Iran.

1980-1988 Iran-Iraq War.

1990 Iraq invades Kuwait.

1991 The Gulf War.

1993 Peace agreement between Israel and the Palestinians.

SOUTH ASIA

Mahatma Gandhi

1920 Mahatma Gandhi starts a non-violent campaign for Indian independence.

1947 India and Pakistan become independent.

1960 Mrs Bandaranaike of Ceylon is the first woman prime minister in the world.

1971 Bangladesh is formed.

THE FAR EAST

1904-1905 War between Japan and Russia.

1910 Japan gains control of Korea.

1911 The Kuomintang start a revolution in China.

1912 The last Manchu Emperor of China gives up his throne.

1934 Communists in China set out on the Long March.

1941-1945 Japan fights the Allies in World War II.

1945 The first ever atomic bomb is dropped, on Hiroshima in Japan.

1949 Mao Zedong sets up the People's Republic of China.

1950-1953 The Korean War.

1954 The Vietnam War starts.

1966 The Cultural Revolution in China.

A Chinese Red Guard from the time of the Cultural Revolution

1973 The Vietnam War ends.

1976 Death of Mao Zedong.

1989 Hundreds of Chinese protesters are killed in Tiananmen Square.

Symbol of the UN

1999 UN soldiers are sent to East Timor to help it become an independent nation.

AUSTRALASIA

1914-1918 Troops from Australia and New Zealand fight in World War I.

1939-1945 Troops from Australia and New Zealand fight in World War II.

1993 The Native Titles Bill gives some land rights to Aboriginals in Australia.

Word List

This list explains some of the words that are used in the book.

Aboriginals The native people who lived in Australia before the Europeans arrived.

allies People who fight on the same side in a war. During the two world wars, the countries that fought on the same side as Britain were known as "the Allies".

amphibian An animal that can live on land, but lays its eggs in water. Frogs are amphibians.

apartheid The South African system of keeping different races of people apart. Apartheid lasted from 1949 to 1990, and meant that non-whites were treated as second-class citizens.

archbishop An important Christian priest, in charge of the Church over a large area.

arthropod A creature with jointed legs and a hard, outer skeleton. Spiders and insects are arthropods.

assassinate To murder a leader or a politician.

Axis Powers The countries that fought on the same side as Germany in the Second World War.

barbarian A member of one of the warlike tribes that came from the lands outside the Roman Empire.

bishop An important Christian priest, who has the rank below an archbishop.

Bolshevik A Russian Communist who supported Lenin. The Bolsheviks led the revolution against the Tsar of Russia in 1917.

caliph An Arab ruler.

carnivore An animal that only eats meat.

Catholic A person who belongs to a branch of the Christian Church which is led by the Pope in Rome.

cells The tiny "building blocks" from which all living things are made.

Central Powers The countries that were on the same side as Germany in the First World War.

city-state A city and surrounding land, which has its own rulers.

civilization An advanced way of life, where people live in towns and have a system of laws and a way of writing.

civil war Fighting between different groups of people within the same country.

Cold War The struggle for power between the United States and the Soviet Union, which was at its height during the 1950s and 1960s.

colonists People who set up a colony, or their descendants who live there.

colony
1. A settlement created in a foreign land, by people who have moved away from their homeland.
2. A group made up of large numbers of one kind of plant or animal. All the members of a colony live or grow together.

Communism A form of government where the state owns all land and factories, and provides for people's needs. Today, China is the world's largest Communist country.

constitution A set of laws used to rule a country.

continent A large area of land on the surface of the Earth. Africa and North America are two of the Earth's continents.

convict A person who has been found guilty of a crime and put in prison.

crusade A war fought for a religious reason.

culture The shared ideas, beliefs and values of a group of people.

cuneiform writing An ancient form of writing made up of wedge-shaped symbols.

democracy A system of government where the people have a say in how their country is run.

dynasty A series of rulers from the same family.

ectothermic A word used to describe cold-blooded creatures that cannot produce their own body heat. Snakes and lizards are ectothermic.

election The selection, by voting, of a person or a party to a position of power.

empire A large group of lands that is ruled by one powerful person or government.

endothermic A word used to describe warm-blooded animals that can produce their own body heat. Mammals are endothermic.

evolve To change or develop gradually.

extinct A word used to describe a creature or plant that has died out. Dinosaurs are extinct.

famine A serious shortage of food which causes many people to die.

Fascism The military form of government in Italy from 1922 to 1943, led by Benito Mussolini, which banned all opposition. Fascism is also used to describe similar forms of government in other countries, such as Hitler's Germany.

fortress A group of buildings surrounded by a wall so that they can be easily defended.

fossil The remains of a prehistoric creature or plant. Fossils are often made of stone.

fossilize To turn into a fossil.

fresco A picture painted on a wall while the plaster is still damp.

general A person who leads an army.

gills The parts of an underwater creature that take in oxygen from the water. Fish have gills.

global warming The slow warming of the Earth's climate, which is caused by harmful gases from power stations, factories and car exhausts.

government The group of people who run a country.

Great Depression The period of worldwide unemployment and poverty, which began after the Wall Street Crash of 1929 and lasted until the late 1930s.

guild An organization for craftworkers or traders, with strict rules for all its members.

hadrosaur A plant-eating dinosaur with bird-like feet and a beak shaped like a duck's bill.

herald A person in medieval times who made announcements and carried messages.

herbivore An animal that only eats plants.

heretic A Christian whose ideas were different from the teachings of the Church.

Fossilized skull of a dinosaur called *Triceratops*

hieroglyphs Picture writing that was used in Ancient Egypt.

Hindu A person who follows the Hindu faith, the main religion of India. Hindus pray to many gods and goddesses.

Holocaust The murder of six million Jews by German Nazis between 1940 and 1945.

hominid An ape that has a large brain and walks upright. Humans are hominids.

ice age A period of time when large parts of the Earth were covered with ice.

ichthyosaur A sea reptile that was shaped like a dolphin.

icon A religious picture, usually painted on a wooden panel.

incense A sweet-smelling substance that was burned in ancient temples or in the presence of kings.

Internet The vast computer network that links millions of computers around the world.

Iron Curtain A phrase used to describe the boundary that existed until 1989 between Western Europe and the Communist countries of Eastern Europe.

Islam The religion based on the teachings of the Prophet Mohammed and on the holy book, the *Koran*.

Jew A person who belongs to the race of people who are descended from the ancient tribes of Israel. The Jewish religion is based on the teachings of the Old Testament of the Bible.

khan A Mongol ruler.

knight A man in the Middle Ages who was trained to fight on horseback for his lord.

lacquer A substance that can be painted onto wood, to make it shiny and waterproof.

lance A long pole with a pointed end, used as a weapon.

mammal An animal with hair on its body that feeds its babies with milk. Dogs and humans are mammals.

mammoth A large prehistoric elephant with long, curved tusks. Some mammoths had thick, woolly coats.

manuscript A handwritten book or document.

Maoris The native people who lived in New Zealand before the Europeans arrived.

marsupial A mammal whose babies stay in a pouch on their mother's stomach until they are large enough to survive on their own. Kangaroos are marsupials.

Middle Kingdom The second main period in Ancient Egyptian history (c.2040BC-c.1720BC).

missionary A person who travels to a foreign country and tries to persuade the people living there to follow a different religion.

mosaic A picture made from lots of small pieces of stone or glass.

mosque A building where Muslims pray.

Muslim A person whose religion is based on the teachings of the Prophet Mohammed and on the holy book, the *Koran*.

nationalism The shared feeling among people who live in the same region and who have the same culture, language or religion. Nationalism often leads people to form their own independent nation.

NATO The North Atlantic Treaty Organization, an international organization which was set up in 1949 to defend Western countries against the Soviet Union. The USA, Canada and Britain are members of NATO.

Nazi Party The German National Socialist Workers' Party, led by Adolf Hitler who ruled Germany between 1933 and 1945. The Nazis were extremely anti-Jewish, and used force against anyone who opposed them.

New Kingdom The third main period in Ancient Egyptian history (c.1570BC-c.1070BC).

noble A member of a family that belongs to the ruling class of a country.

nomads People who have no permanent home, but who move around from place to place.

observatory A building from which people study the stars.

Old Kingdom The first main period in Ancient Egyptian history (c.2686BC-c.2180BC).

ornithopod A plant-eating dinosaur with bird-like feet and a beak.

oxygen A gas that all living creatures need to breathe.

pagan A person who believes in many gods.

parliament A group of people who meet to make decisions and create laws for their country.

particle A tiny speck.

patron A rich person who pays artists, architects or writers to produce works of art.

peasant A person who works on the land.

pharaoh An Ancient Egyptian king.

photosynthesis The process that plants use to make food from water and sunlight.

pilgrimage A journey to a holy place.

pioneer A person who explores a new country or a new area of country. Pioneers usually settle in the place they have explored.

placental A mammal whose babies grow inside their mother's belly until they are large enough to survive in the outside world. Rabbits and humans are placentals.

plague A disease which spreads fast and kills many people.

planet A huge ball of rock, gas or metal that spins around a star.

plantation A large farm where crops such as cotton, coffee and tobacco are grown.

plesiosaur A sea reptile that had a long neck and big, paddle-shaped flippers.

predator An animal that hunts and eats other animals.

prey An animal that is hunted by another animal for food.

primate A mammal with hands and feet and a large brain. Apes and humans are primates.

prime minister The leader of a government that has been chosen by the people.

proteins Chemicals that form part of all living cells.

Protestant A person who belongs to a branch of the Christian Church that started in western Europe in the 1500s. The Protestant Church does not have the Pope as its leader.

province An area within an empire, such as the province of Britain in the Roman Empire.

pterosaur A prehistoric reptile that could fly.

pueblo A village or town built by the Pueblo people in the southwest of North America between 700 and 1300.

Puritan A person who belongs to a very strict Protestant branch of the Christian Church.

refugee A person who is forced to leave their homeland and live somewhere else. Refugees have usually escaped from wars or famines.

reptile An animal with scaly skin that lays its eggs on land. Lizards and snakes are reptiles.

republic A country without a king or queen, whose leaders rule on behalf of the people.

revolution A successful rebellion by the people against a leader or a government.

rodent A mammal with very strong teeth that gnaws on roots, bushes and tree trunks.

satellite An object which circles the Earth in space. Man-made satellites can take photographs of the Earth, and are also used to send phone calls and television pictures from one part of the world to another.

sauropod A large, plant-eating dinosaur that had a long neck and tail and walked mainly on four legs.

scavenger A creature that eats meat from dead animals that it finds.

scholar A person who studies, teaches, and writes books.

scribe A person in the ancient world whose job was to read and write for everyone else.

shrine A sacred building or place, where people worship or where something holy is kept.

Soviet Union The Communist country that was formed in 1922 after the Russian Revolution. It was also known as the USSR.

species A group of similar plants or animals that can breed together. Lions are one species and tigers are another.

standard-bearer A soldier who carries his leader's flag into battle.

state An area with its own laws. A state can be independent, or part of a larger country.

stegosaur A large, plant-eating dinosaur with a row of upright bony plates along its back.

stocks A heavy wooden frame with holes in it, used in the Middle Ages for locking up criminals.

strike A protest in which workers demand better pay or fairer working conditions by refusing to work.

suffragette A woman who campaigned for the right to vote at the end of the 19th and the beginning of the 20th century.

sultan A ruler of the Turkish Ottoman Empire or of other Muslim lands.

synagogue A building where Jews worship.

taxes Money collected from the people by a government or a ruler.

theropod A meat-eating dinosaur.

trade union An organization of workers who campaign together for better pay or fairer working conditions.

treaty An agreement between two or more countries.

tsar A Russian emperor.

tsarina A Russian empress.

UN The United Nations, an international organization which was set up in 1945 to encourage world peace.

vertebrate An animal with a backbone.

the West The western part of the world which includes Europe and America. During the Cold War, the non-Communist countries of Europe and America were known as "the West".

World Wide Web A vast network of linked pages which are stored on computers around the world, providing information on a huge variety of subjects.

yurt A circular tent made from felt or animal skins, used in central Asia.

Index

Pages where you can find out most about a subject are shown in **bold** type.
The Latin names of prehistoric plants and creatures are shown in *italic* type.

Photo Credits

Every effort has been made to trace the copyright holders of material in this book. If any rights have been omitted, the publishers offer their sincere apologies and will rectify this in any subsequent editions, following notification. The publishers are grateful to the following individuals and organizations for their permission to reproduce material on the following pages *(t = top, m = middle, b = bottom, l = left, r = right)*:

front cover ©Copyright The British Museum; **p1** ©Gianni Dagli Orti/CORBIS; **p2** ©Kevin R. Morris/CORBIS; **p4** ©Adam Woolfitt/CORBIS; **p7** ©Digital Vision; **p8** ©Hubert Stadler/CORBIS; **p10** ©Roger Ressmeyer/CORBIS; **p12** *(bl)* ©Digital Vision, *(br)* ©Digital Vision; **p18** FPG International; **p19** *(bl)* ©Digital Vision, *(m)* ©Digital Vision; **p23** ©Bill O'Connor/Still Pictures; **p24** *(tl)* Dr. Kari Lounatmaa/Science Photo Library, *(bl)* ©Digital Vision, *(r)* Sinclair Stammers/Science Photo Library; **p25** Sinclair Stammers/Science Photo Library; **p31** ©Peter Scoones/Planet Earth Pictures; **p38** ©Digital Vision; **p59** ©Digital Vision; **p67** ©Peter Weimann/Still Pictures; **p73** ©Bill Ivy/Tony Stone Images; **p75** ©Digital Vision; **p76** ©NOVOSTI (London); **p102** Egyptian Museum, Cairo/Dagli Orti/The Art Archive; **p105** *(main)* ©Roger Ressmeyer/CORBIS, *(tl)* The British Museum, London/Werner Forman Archive; **p106** ©Wolfgang Kaehler/CORBIS; **p122** Nicholas Shea; **p125** The Art Archive; **p136** The Stock Market; **p159** James Green/Robert Harding Picture Library; **p167** Julian Calder/Tony Stone Images; **p171** Jean-Louis Nou/AKG London; **p179** N. J. Saunders/Robert Harding Picture Library; **p181** Robert Frerck/Robert Harding Picture Library; **p189** J. E. Stevenson/Robert Harding Picture Library; **p196** The Art Archive; **p198** ©Archivo Iconografico, S. A./CORBIS; **p199** *(tl)* ©John Heseltine/CORBIS; *(br)* ©Michael T. Sedam/CORBIS; **p200** ©Adam Woolfitt/CORBIS; **p203** Ronald Sheridan/Ancient Art and Architecture; **p205** The Art Archive; **p207** Ronald Sheridan/Ancient Art and Architecture; **p220** Ronald Sheridan/Ancient Art and Architecture; **p239** National Gallery, London; **p246** National Gallery, London; **p249** Bridgeman Art Library; **p259** © Michael Holford; **p275** Clive Gifford; **p281** Sybil Sassoon/Robert Harding Picture Library; **p285** Bridgeman Art Library; **p290** Musée d'Orsay, Paris/Dagli Orti/The Art Archive; **p292** *(bl)* ©Bettmann/CORBIS, *(br)* Digital image ©1996 CORBIS/Original image courtesy of NASA/CORBIS; **p293** *(tr)* ©Bettmann/ CORBIS, *(br)* ©Bettmann/CORBIS; **p294** ©Gail Mooney/CORBIS; **p297** *(tr)* Sir Francis Drake, 1581 by Nicholas Hilliard/Kunsthistorisches Museum, Vienna, Austria/Bridgeman Art Library; **p298** ©Wolfgang Kaehler/CORBIS; **p300** *(bl)* The Art Archive, *(main)* ©Sheldan Collins/CORBIS; **p302** *(bl)* ©James L. Amos/CORBIS, *(t)* ©Bettmann/CORBIS, *(mr)* Mary Evans Picture Library; **p303** *(tl)* ©Gianni Dagli Orti/CORBIS, *(b)* ©Patrick Ward/CORBIS; **p304** ©Bettmann/CORBIS; **p306** *(tl)* ©Bettmann/CORBIS, *(b)* King Charles I of England out hunting, c.1635 by Sir Anthony van Dyck/Louvre, Paris, France/Giraudon/Bridgeman Art Library; **p307** ©WildCountry/CORBIS; **p308** *(bl)* ©Archivo Iconografico, S. A./CORBIS, *(r)* ©CORBIS; **p309** ©Archivo Iconografico, S. A./CORBIS; **p311** *(tl)* ©Francis G. Mayer/CORBIS, *(tr)* Wageningen UR Library; **p312** ©Macduff Everton/CORBIS; **p313** *(t)* ©photo RMN/J. Derenne, *(m)* ©Archivo Iconografico, S. A./CORBIS; **p314** *(ml)* ©Digital Vision, *(bl)* The Anatomy Lesson of Dr. Nicolaes Tulp, 1632 (oil on canvas) by Rembrandt Harmensz van Rijn/Mauritshuis, The Hague, The Netherlands/Bridgeman Art Library; **p315** Science Museum/Science and Society Picture Library; **p316** ©Galen Rowell/CORBIS; **p317** *(b)* ©Archivo Iconografico, S. A./CORBIS, *(tr)* NOVOSTI (London); **p318** ©Archivo Iconografico, S. A./CORBIS; **p319** The Art Archive; **p320** ©The Corcoran Gallery of Art/CORBIS; **p324** *(main)* ©Historical Picture Archive/CORBIS, *(t)* The Granger Collection, New York; **p325** US Library of Congress; **p328** National Trust Photographic Library/Erik Pelham; **p329** ©Hulton-Deutsch Collection/CORBIS; **p330** *(bl)* ©Philadelphia Museum of Art/CORBIS, *(tr)* Peter Newark's American Pictures; **p333** ©Archivo Iconografico, S. A./CORBIS; **p334** *(t)* ©Archivo Iconografico, S. A./CORBIS, *(b)* ©Archivo Iconografico, S. A./CORBIS; **p337** *(t)* The Art Archive, *(br)* National Museums & Galleries of Wales (Museum of Welsh Life); **p338** ©Robert Estall/CORBIS; **p339** ©Historical Picture Archive/CORBIS; **p341** *(m)* Hulton Getty, *(br)* Hulton Getty; **p342** *(mr)* ©Bettmann/CORBIS, *(b)* ©Gianni Dagli Orti/CORBIS; **p343** ©Gianni Dagli Orti/CORBIS; **p344** *(bl)* The Art Archive; **p345** *(tl)* The Art Archive, *(main)* ©Pablo Corral V/CORBIS; **p347** *(mt)* ©Hulton-Deutsch Collection/CORBIS, *(r)* ©Eric and David Hosking/CORBIS; **p348** *(bl)* Illustrated London News, *(m)* Illustrated London News; **p351** *(tl)* ©Bettmann/CORBIS, *(m)* ©Bettmann/CORBIS, *(b)* ©Dave G. Houser/CORBIS; **p352** ©Ric Ergenbright/CORBIS; **p354** The Art Archive; **p356** ©Michael S. Yamashita/CORBIS; **p357** *(t)* ©Underwood & Underwood/CORBIS, *(b)* ©Michael Holford; **p360** *(tl)* Illustrated London News, *(mb)* ©Brian Vikander/CORBIS; **p361** NOVOSTI (London); **p362** *(tl)* NOVOSTI (London), *(bl)* NOVOSTI (London), *(r)* ©Gregor Schmid/CORBIS; **p363** ©Bettmann/CORBIS; **p364** ©Tiziana and Gianni Baldizzone/CORBIS; **p365** AKG London; **p366** *(bl)* Archive Holdings, Inc./The Image Bank, *(tr)* Mary Evans Picture Library; **p367** *(tr)* ©CORBIS, *(br)* ©Digital Vision; **p368** *(main)* Hulton Getty, *(tr)* Hulton Getty; **p369** ©Hulton-Deutsch Collection/CORBIS; **p370** *(mt)* ©CORBIS, *(br)* Illustrated London News; **p371** ©Hulton-Deutsch Collection/ CORBIS; **p372** *(t)* ©Bettmann/CORBIS, *(br)* ©Bettmann/CORBIS; **p373** ©CORBIS; **p374** *(tl)* Illustrated London News, *(b)* ©AFP/CORBIS; **p375** *(t)* ©Bettmann/CORBIS, *(b)* ©Howard Davies/CORBIS; **p376** *(tr)* ©Tim Page/CORBIS, *(b)* ©David Ake/AFP-Popperfoto; **p377** *(tl)* ©AFP/ CORBIS, *(main)* Associated Press; **p379** ©Tim Page/CORBIS; **p380** *(l)* ©Digital Vision, *(t)* ©Bettmann/CORBIS, *(b)* ©Digital Vision, *(r)* ©Digital Vision; **p381** *(main)* ©Digital Vision, *(tr)* ©CORBIS, *(br)* ©Digital Vision; **p382** *(tl)* ©Bettmann/CORBIS, *(b)* Rex Features; **p383** *(tr)* ©Reuters Newmedia, Inc./CORBIS; **p384** *(l)* ©Hulton-Deutsch Collection/CORBIS, *(b)* ©Peter Turnley/CORBIS, *(tr)* ©Bettmann/CORBIS; **p385** *(mt)* ©Peter Turnley/CORBIS; **p386** *(bl)* ©Bettmann/CORBIS, *(mt)* ©Disney Enterprises, Inc./supplied by Vin Mag Archive Ltd.; **p387** Copyright ©1998, New Line Productions, Inc./The Moviestore Collection; **p388** *(main)* ©Digital Vision, *(l)* ©Digital Vision; **p389** *(tl)* NASA/ Science Photo Library, *(tr)* ©Digital Vision, *(br)* ©Digital Vision; **p390** *(bl)* Photo courtesy of STMicroelectronics, *(br)* **www.nhm.ac.uk/museum/ index.html** ©The Natural History Museum, London, *(mr)* **www.ancientegypt.co.uk/life/explore/main.html** ©Copyright The British Museum; **p391** *(ml)* **www.childrensmuseum.org/artsworkshop/puppetshow.html** Courtesy of The Children's Museum of Indianapolis, *(m)* "A Gutsy View" graphic image from Human Anatomy Online (**www.innerbody.com**) provided by INTELLIMED International Corporation, *(mr)* **weather.yahoo.com/graphics/temperature/Europe_Hi.html** Reproduced with permission of Yahoo! Inc. ©2000 by Yahoo! Inc. YAHOO! and the YAHOO! logo are trademarks of Yahoo! Inc./Map courtesy of Weathernews Inc., the world's largest commercial weather forecasting organization, *(tr)* ©Digital Vision, *(mb)* ©Disney Enterprises, Inc./Ronald Grant Archive, *(br)* ©Digital Vision; **p392** ©AFP/CORBIS; **p393** *(tl)* Alfred Pasieka/Science Photo Library, *(main)* ©Reuters Newmedia, Inc./CORBIS; **p398** Illustrated London News; **p400** ©Digital Vision; **p401** Illustrated London News.

Cover design:	Mary Cartwright & Zöe Wray
Digital imaging:	John Russell
Additional designs:	Robin Farrow, Matthew Hart & Susannah Owen
Additional consultants:	Stuart Atkinson, Chris Chandler, Dr. John Rostron & Dr. Margaret Rostron
Additional illustrations:	Susanna Addario, Stephen Conlin, Peter Dennis, Richard Draper, John Fox, Bob Hersey, Jason Lewis, Chris Lyon, Susie McCaffrey, Joseph McEwan, Malcolm McGregor, Cecco Mariniello, Peter Massey, Sean Milne, Louise Nixon, Andrew Robinson, Simon Roulstone, Claudia Saraceni, Chris Shields, Sue Stitt, Ross Watton & Gerald Wood
Picture researchers:	Ruth King & Sophy Tahta
Artwork co-ordinator:	Cathy Lowe
Additional contributions:	Anna Claybourne

First published in 2000 by Usborne Publishing Ltd, Usborne House, 83-85 Saffron Hill, London EC1N 8RT, England.
www.usborne.com